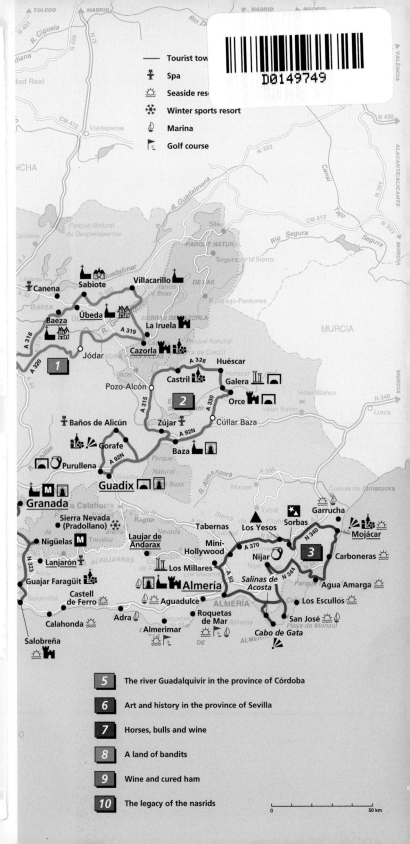

Legend:

— Tourist tow[...]

⚕ Spa

🌅 Seaside res[...]

❄ Winter sports resort

⚓ Marina

⛳ Golf course

TOLEDO — **MADRID** — **MADRID** — **MADRID** — **CUENCA**

R. Cigüela
R. 420
VALENCIA
Ciudad Real
N 430

RÍO ZÁ[...]
N 401

ALACANTE/ALICANTE

N 322

Canal

Río Segura

CM 412 Tajo

N 301

MURCIA

PARQUE NATURAL
Segura de la Sierra

R. Guadalmena

DE LAS

SIERRAS DE CAZORLA

Parque Natural
de Despeñaperros

Carolina

R. Guadalimar

⚕ Canena
Sabiote
Villacarillo
Santiago-Pontones

⚕ Baeza
Úbeda
La Iruela
A 319

A 316
Jódar
Cazorla

1
A 320
A 326
Huéscar
Castril
Galera
Pozo-Alcón
A 315
2
A 330
Orce
Vélez Blanco

Vélez Rubio
N 340
Lorca

⚕ Baños de Alicún
Zújar ⚕
Cúllar Baza
A 92N

Gorafe
Baza
A 92N

Purullena

Guadix

M Granada
a Calahorra

Sierra Nevada
(Pradollano) ❄
Tabernas
Los Yesos
Sorbas
Garrucha

Nigüelas **M**
Trevélez
Laujar de
Andarax
A 370
N 340
Mojácar

Lanjarón ⚕
Mini-
Hollywood
Nijar
3
Carboneras

Guajar Faragüit
Los Millares
Almería
Agua Amarga

Castell
de Ferro
Aguadulce
Salinas de
Acosta
Los Escullos

Calahonda
Adra
Almerimar
Roquetas
de Mar
San José
Cabo de Gata
Playa de Mónsul

Salobreña

5 The river Guadalquivir in the province of Córdoba

6 Art and history in the province of Sevilla

7 Horses, bulls and wine

8 A land of bandits

9 Wine and cured ham

10 The legacy of the nasrids

0 ————————— 50 km

D0149749

ANDALUCÍA

B. Kaufmann/MICHELIN

Editorial Director   Cynthia Clayton Ochterbeck

THE GREEN GUIDE ANDALUCÍA

Editor   Rachel Mills
Principal Writer   Paul Murphy
Production Manager   Natasha G. George
Cartography   Alain Baldet, Michelle Cana, Peter Wrenn
Photo Editor   Yoshimi Kanazawa
Proofreader   Jonathan P. Gilbert, Alison Coupe
Layout & Design   John Higginbottom, Natasha G. George
Cover Design   Laurent Muller, Ute Weber

Contact Us: The Green Guide
                                Michelin Maps and Guides
                                One Parkway South
                                Greenville, SC 29615
                                USA
                                www.michelintravel.com
                                michelin.guides@us.michelin.com

                                Michelin Maps and Guides
                                Hannay House
                                39 Clarendon Road
                                Watford, Herts WD17 1JA
                                UK
                                ☎ (01923) 205 240
                                www.ViaMichelin.com
                                travelpubsales@uk.michelin.com

Special Sales: For information regarding bulk sales,
                                customized editions and premium sales,
                                please contact our Customer Service
                                Departments:
                                USA   1-800-432-6277
                                UK   (01923) 205 240
                                Canada 1-800-361-8236

Note to the Reader

One Team…
A Commitment to Quality

There's just one reason our team is dedicated to producing quality travel publications—you, our reader.

Throughout our guides we offer **practical information**, **touring tips** and **suggestions** for finding the best places for a break.

Michelin driving tours help you hit the highlights and quickly absorb the best of the region. Our descriptive **walking tours** make you your own guide, armed with directions, maps and expert information.

We scout out the attractions, classify them with **star ratings**, and describe in detail what you will find when you visit them.

Michelin maps featured throughout the guide offer vibrant, detailed and easy-to-follow outlines of everything from close-up museum plans to international maps.

Places to stay and eat are always a big part of travel, so we research **hotels and restaurants** that we think convey the essence of the destination and arrange them by geographic area and price. We walk you through the best shopping districts and point you towards the host of entertainment and recreation possibilities available.

We **test**, **retest**, **check and recheck** to make sure that our guidebooks are truly just that: a personalized guide to help you make the most of your visit. And if you still want a speaking guide, we list local tour guides who will lead you on all the boat, bus, guided, historical, culinary, and other tours you shouldn't miss.

In short, we remove the guesswork involved with travel. After all, we want you to enjoy exploring with Michelin as much as we do.

The Michelin Green Guide Team

PLANNING YOUR TRIP

INTRODUCTION TO ANDALUCÍA

B. Kaufmann/MICHELIN

CONTENTS

DISCOVERING ANDALUCÍA

HOW TO USE THIS GUIDE

PLANNING YOUR TRIP

The blue-tabbed PLANNING YOUR TRIP section at the front of the guide gives you **ideas for your trip** and **practical information** to help you organise it. You'll find tours, a host of breaks in the great outdoors, a calendar of events, information on shopping, sightseeing, kids' activities and more.

INTRODUCTION

The orange-tabbed INTRODUCTION section explores **Nature** from landscape to flora and fauna. The **History** section spans the Phoenicians, to the Romans and the Reconquest, through to the Golden Age and today. **Art and Culture** covers architecture, art, literature, music and cinema, while **The Region Today** delves into modern Andalucía.

DISCOVERING

The green-tabbed DISCOVERING section features Andalucía's Principal Sights, arranged alphabetically, featuring the

Sidebars

Throughout the guide you will find peach-colored text boxes (like this one), with lively anecdotes, detailed history, and background information.

most interesting local **Sights**, **Walking Tours**, nearby **Excursions**, and detailed **DrivingTours**.

▯Contact information, ⊚admission charges, ◷hours of operation, and a host of other **visitor information** is given wherever possible. Admission prices shown are normally for a single adult.

STAR RATINGS★★★

Michelin has given star ratings for more than 100 years. If you're pressed for time, we recommend you visit the ★★★, or ★★ sights first:

★★★	Highly recommended
★★	Recommended
★	Interesting

Address Books - Where to Stay, Eat and more...

WHERE TO STAY

We've made a selection of hotels and arranged them by price category to fit all budgets (*◔see the Legend on the cover flap for an explanation of the price categories*). For the most part, we've selected accommodations based on their unique regional quality, their regional feel, as it were.

◔See the back of the guide for an index of where hotels featured throughout the guide can be found.

WHERE TO EAT

We thought you'd like to know the popular eating spots in Andalucía. So, we selected restaurants that capture the regional experience. We're not rating the quality of the food per se; as we did with the hotels, we selected restaurants for many towns and villages, categorised by price to appeal to all wallets.

◔See the back of the guide for an index of where restaurants featured through-out the guide can be found.

MAPS

- Ⓐ **Principal Sights map** and **Driving Tours Map** on the inside covers.
- Ⓐ Detailed maps for **major cities** and **villages**, including **Driving Tours maps** and larger-scale maps for **walking tours**.

All maps in this guide are oriented north, unless otherwise indicated by a directional arrow. The term "Local Map" refers to a map within the chapter or Tourism Region. A complete list of the maps found in the guide appears at the back of this book, along with a comprehensive index.

Ⓐ See the map Legend at the back of the guide for an explanation of map symbols.

> Ⓐ **A Bit of Advice** Ⓐ
>
> Green advice boxes found in this guide contain practical tips and handy information relevant to the sight in the DISCOVERING section.

ORIENT PANELS

Vital statistics are given for each principal sight in the DISCOVERING section:

- 🔲 **Information:** Tourist Office/Sight contact details.
- ▶ **Orient Yourself:** Geographic location of the sight with reference to surrounding boroughs, towns and roads.
- Ⓟ **Parking:** Where to park.
- Ⓐ **Don't Miss:** Unmissable things to do.
- Ⓢ **Organising Your Time:** Tips on organising your stay; what to see first, how long to spend there, crowd avoidance, market days and more.
- Kids **Especially for Kids:** Sights of particular interest to children.
- Ⓒ **Also See:** Nearby PRINCIPAL SIGHTS featured elsewhere in the guide.

SYMBOLS

Spa	**Spa Facilities**	🔾	**Tours**
Kids	**Interesting for Children**	Ⓟ	**On-site Parking**
Ⓒ	**Also See**	▶	**Directions**
🔲	**Tourist Information**	✕	**On-site eating Facilities**
Ⓢ	**Hours of Operation**	△	**Camping Facilities**
Ⓞ	**Periods of Closure**	≗	**Beaches**
⚊	**Closed to the Public**	☕	**Breakfast Included**
Ⓐ	**Entry Fees**	Ⓐ	**A Bit of Advice**
↗	**Credit Cards not Accepted**	Ⓐ	**Warning**
♿	**Wheelchair Accessible**		

Contact – Addresses, phone numbers, opening hours and prices published in this guide are accurate at the time of press. We welcome corrections and suggestions that may assist us in preparing the next edition. Please send your comments to:

UK
Michelin Maps and Guides
Hannay House
39 Clarendon Road
Watford, Herts WD17 1JA
travelpubsales@uk.michelin.com
www.michelin.co.uk

USA
Michelin Maps and Guides
Editorial Department
P.O. Box 19001
Greenville, SC 29602-9001
michelin.guides@us.michelin.com
www.michelintravel.com

El Rocio Pilgrimage
R. Mattès/MICHELIN

MICHELIN DRIVING TOURS

Local Driving Tours

Listed below are driving tours within the *Discovering Andalucía* section of the guide, which are not listed on the Driving Tours map.

LAS ALPUJARRAS–
The Granada Alpujarras*:*
From Lanjarón to Bayárcal
*(100km/62mi)***; The Amlería**
Alpujarras: From Bayárcal to
Alhama de Almería*; **The Almería***
Alpujarras *(73km/45mi)*

ANTEQUERA –
Valle Del Guadalhorce:
From Antequera to the
Cueva de Ardales
(70km/44mi)

PARQUE NATURAL DE LA
SIERRA DE ARACENA Y PICOS
DE AROCHE –
From Aracena to Aroche
(64km/40mi)

LA AXARQUÍA –
From Málaga to Nerja
(99km/62mi)

PARQUE NATURAL DE CABO
DE GATA-NÍJAR –
Around the Park *(90km/56mi)*

SIERRAS DE CAZORLA,
LAS VILLAS Y EL POZO –
From Cazorla to Tiscar
*(92km/57mi)***; From Cazorla to**
the Embalse del Tranco de Beas
(56km/35mi)

CÓRDOBA –
From Córdoba to Fuente
Obejuna
(49km/30.5mi).

COSTA DE ALMERIÁ –
From Adra to Almería
*(117km/73mi)***; From Almería to**
Mojácar *(132km/82.5mi).*

COSTA DE HUELVA –
Parque Nacional de Doñana to
Palos de la Frontera
(49km/30mi); **From Huelva to**
Ayamonte *(77km/48mi)*

COSTA DEL SOL –
From Torremolinos to
Sotogrande
(234km/146mi)

SIERRA DE LOS FILABRES –
The Land of Marble
(79km/49mi)

MARBELLA –
Excursion Inland
(51km/32mi)

PUEBLOS BLANCOS DE
ANDALUCÍA –
Found trip from
Arcos de la Frontera
(217km/135mi)

EL ROCÎO –
The Wine Route from
El Rocío to Niebla
(36km/22mi)

RONDA –
From Ronda to
San Pedro de Alcántara
(49km/30.5mi)

SIERRA NEVADA –
From Granada to El Dornajo
(39km/24mi).

PARQUE NATURAL DE LA SIERRA
NORTE DE SEVILLA –
From Lora del Río to
Guadalcanal
(90km/56mi)

TABERNAS –
From Tabernas to
Los Molinos del Río Aguas
(41km/25.5mi)

Regional Driving Tours

We've put together ten different itineraries for visitors who wish to spend a few days exploring Andalucía by car. *Refer to the Driving Tours map on the inside front cover of the guide in order to make the most of the following tours .* You may also wish to refer to the map of **Principal Sights** (*inside back cover*), which are described in the **Discovering Andalucía** section of this guide.

①THE LAND OF THE OLIVE TREE

Round trip of 225km/141mi from Jaén

This tour through the Jaén countryside is punctuated with dramatic mountain scenery, hills shaded by olive trees, and historic villages and towns embellished with some of the region's most important Renaissance buildings. After exploring the provincial capital, **Jaén**, famous for its Moorish fortress (Castillo de Santa Catalina), its awe-inspiring Renaissance cathedral and magnificent Arab baths, head east to **Baeza** and **Úbeda**. These delightful towns, just 9km/5.6mi apart, have two of the best preserved monumental centres in Andalucía. From Úbeda, continue to **Sabiote** to admire its splendid castle and wander narrow streets lined by elegant mansions. The itinerary then heads a short distance south to **Torreperojil**, its centre dominated by the Gothic-style Iglesia de la Asunción. After a brief stop in **Villacarrillo**, where the highlight is undoubtedly its Renaissance church, the route winds to picturesque **Cazorla**, a mountain village crowned by the craggy relief of its imposing castle, and the ideal departure point for the spectacular **Parque Natural de las Sierras de Cazorla, Segura y las Villas**. Return to Jaén through **Jódar**, where you will find the information centre for another of Andalucía's natural treasures, the **Parque Natural de Sierra Mágina**.

②TROGLODYTE LANDSCAPES

Round trip of 272km/170mi from Guadix

The Sierra Nevada and Sierras de Cazorla y Segura are separated by valleys and mountain chains rich in archaeological interest. An outstanding feature of local villages is the abundance of troglodyte dwellings built into the clay.

The journey starts in **Guadix**, a town overlooked by one of the finest areas of troglodyte houses. Nearby **Purullena** is an unusual village where cave dwellings" and pottery shops line both sides of the main road. The tour skirts the River Farbes as far as the spa of **Baños de Alicún** before heading southeast along the Gor Valley. **Gorafe**, halfway along the valley, is marked by some 200 dolmens dating from Neolithic times, and an impressive series of troglodyte dwellings. After a short section along the A 92 heading northeast, the tour veers into the mountains, to **Zújar**, at the foot of Monte Jabalcón, close to the Negratín Resevoir, whose waters have been renowned since Antiquity. Continuing north, the route borders the southern section of the **Parque Natural de las Sierras de Cazorla, Segura y las Villas** before reaching picturesque **Castril**, a village nestled beneath an imposing cliff; close by is the scenic the scenic **Parque Natural de la Sierra de Castril**. A short distance east iies **Huéscar** with its splendid main square (plaza Mayor).

Olive groves

As the road descends south, it is worth stopping in **Galera** to admire the remains of an Iberian necropolis, the vestiges of its Moorish quarter and a group of cave dwellings in the upper reaches of the town.

Some 8km/5mi southeast, nestled amid bucolic landscape, is **Orce**, which became famous in the 1980s when the remains of a child remains dating back one and half million years were discovered here.

The last stage of the tour before returning to Guadix is **Baza**, an important Iberian settlement dating from the 4C BC, where the famous Dama de Baza sculpture was discovered. Bordering the **Parque Natural de la Sierra de Baza**, the town features an interesting architectural heritage that includes Moorish baths dating from the caliphal period and an imposing fortress-like collegiate church, the Colegiata de Santa María de la Encarnación.

③THE DESERT AND BEACHES OF THE PROVINCE OF ALMERÍA

Round trip of 254km/159mi from Almería

This tour leads through stunning desert landscapes and dramatic isolated beaches, unexpectedly verdant orchards, lofty mountain vistas, summer coastal resorts and Almería's picturesque inland villages – all beneath the year-round bright-blue sky of southeastern Andalucía.

Almería, crowned by its magnificent Moorish fortress, is the starting-point. Head southeast to the **Parque Natural de Cabo de Gata**, with its strikingly beautiful beaches, dunes and reefs. After **Níjar**, a small whitewashed town built around a 15C parish church on the fold of a hill, return to the coast for splendid views of the Mediterranean along the road linking **Agua Amarga** and Mojácar, and the occasional view of an old watchtower. **Mojácar**, perched on a rocky promontory just 2km/1.2mi inland, is one of the most enchanting small towns in the province of Almería, with an old quarter that preserves an

unmistakable Moorish air. The tour then penetrates into the Almerían desert, characterised by a rugged, arid landscape of rocks and low-lying hills. Continuing west, the road passes on the right the impressive **Paraje Natural de Karst en Yesos**, a nature reserve made up of thousands of limestone caves formed by erosion, before reaching **Sorbas**, an attractive small town built on a clay escarpment on a meander of the River Aguas.

The road continues 30km/18.6mi further west to **Tabernas**, at the foot of a Moorish castle, and **Mini-Hollywood**, a reconstructed American Wild West town used as a set for "Spaghetti Westerns". Before returning to Almería, a short detour to **Los Millares**, the most important Copper Age settlement ever discovered in Europe, is well worth it.

④THE VILLAGES OF THE PARQUE NATURAL DE LA SIERRA SUBBÉTICAS

Round trip of 175km/109mi from Lucena

This route through the Sierra Subbética in the province of Córdoba is characterised by dramatic viewpoints, hillsides carpeted in olive groves, and attractive villages clinging to mountain slopes, some crowned by fortresses hewn out of rock.

After exploring the centre of **Lucena**, including its main church of interest, the Iglesia de San Mateo, head up to the **Santuario de la Virgen de Araceli** for the impressive view from its esplanade.

Pass through **Rute**, a village renowned for its anise-flavoured liqueur, and enjoy more superb views.

The picturesque village of **Iznájar** overlooks its man-made lake from atop a hill.

The next stop is the delightful town of **Priego de Córdoba**, capital of Córdoban Baroque. From here, head west to **Carcabuey**, which lies at the foot of a ruined castle, then Luque, before reaching **Zuheros**, a charming village straddling a rocky outcrop beneath the remains of a stone castle. A scenic road then winds it way to the **Cueva de los Murciélagos**, renowned for its chambers of impressive stalactites and stalagmites, as well as the remnants of Neolithic wall paintings and engravings. Return to Zuheros, before continuing to **Baena** – not only one of Spain's leading producers of olive oil, but also home to several churches of interest.

Heading southwest, the A 316 leads to **Cabra**, a tranquil town spread out in a swathe of white across the sierra of the same name. Before heading back to Lucena, be sure to visit the **Ermita de la Virgen de la Sierra**, a sanctuary which enjoys a superb setting with expansive views of the Subbética range and the Córdoban countryside.

⑤ FOLLOWING THE GUADALQUIVIR THROUGH CÓRDOBA PROVINCE

Round trip of 241km/151mi from Montoro

The Río Guadalquivir winds its way through the province of Córdoba, reflecting picturesque villages and castles and ruins that recall past glories.

This drive begins in **Montoro**, a charming and elegant whitewashed town huddled around a meander in the river. From here, head northwest away from the river to **Adamuz**, situated amid a vast expanse of olive groves, before following a minor road skirting the river west to **Córdoba**. A visit to the Mezquita (mosque), whose construction began in 784, and a stroll through the city's Jewish quarter are the high points of this magnificent city which teems with art and history; delightful small squares and charming flower-decked patios beckon at every turn.

Las Ermitas, a group of 13 hermitages set in a wild mountainous landscape on the northern outskirts of the city, afford memorable views and a bucolic contrast to the hustle and bustle of the provincial capital. The next stage of the tour encompasses **Medina Azahara**, and the remains of a sumptuous palace city built at the end of the 10C and destroyed early in the 11C; this caliphal complex is one of the finest examples of Hispano-Moorish architecture in Andalucía.

Some 20km/12mi southwest, on the banks of the river, is **Almodóvar del Río**, huddled at the foot of a hill crowned by a majestic castle. Continue west along the Guadalquivir to visit the attractive gardens in the village of **Moratalla**, before reaching the whitewashed town of **Palma del Río**, set on a plain between the Guadalquivir and Genil. Its sights include the vestiges of Almohad defensive walls and several noteworthy churches. After returning to the A 4, stop briefly at **El Carpio**, straddling a hill dominated by an imposing Mudéjar brick tower.

⑥ ART AND HISTORY IN THE PROVINCE OF SEVILLA

Round trip of 278km/174mi from Sevilla

This tour, centred on the area close to the A 4–E 5 and A 92 highways, includes some of the finest and most elegant towns and villages in the province. Impressive churches and magnificent civic buildings stand alongside historic palaces and vestiges from Roman and Moorish times.

The departure point is **Sevilla**, capital of Andalucía, famous for its folklore, myths and its myriad attractions.

Eastwards is the historic city of **Carmona**, lesser known than Seville, but still very attractive, with a fine

Casa de los Visires,
Medina Azahara, Córdoba

H. Champollion/MICHELIN

alcázar (fortress-palace) of its own and a Roman necropolis.

Next stop is elegant **Écija**, renowned for its churches and palaces. Numerous Baroque towers stand proudly above the rooftops.

A fine monumental centre is the highlight of historic **Osuna**, perched on a hill 34km/21mi further south. Seat of the House of Osuna, this ducal town has a rich architectural legacy, which includes a number of fine palaces, seigniorial mansions and Baroque churches.

Continue to **Estepa**, another hilltop town, where the highlights are the vestiges of the old Moorish walls and several impressive churches, convents and towers. From here, head directly west past Osuna and then north along the A 364 to **Marchena**, renowned for the outstanding works of art within the walls of the Iglesia de San Juan Baptista, including its museum devoted to Zurbarán.

Pass through **Paradas**, which owes its name to the caravans that passed through here in olden times, before reaching **El Arahal**, a charming village of Moorish origin subsequently embellished with an interesting mix of Baroque and neo-Classical buildings. Before heading back to Sevilla, it is well worth making a final stop in **Alcalá de Guadaira**, impressively sited at the foot of an imposing Almohad fortress.

7 HORSES, BULLS AND WINE

Round trip of 216km/135mi from Cádiz

This tour, through the western reaches of Cádiz province, takes in picturesque coastal and inland towns and villages, plus rural landscapes where the region's most emblematic traditions (including the *feria*, Andalusian horsemanship, bullfighting, guitar music and sherry-making) continue to influence daily life.

The first port of call on this fascinating tour is **Cádiz**. This ancient city, long famous for the quality of its light, juts into the Atlantic on a virtual island, featuring a fascinating mix of elegant Baroque and Neoclassical buildings, and picturesque narrow streets and squares. An air of neglect lends the city a certain shabby chic charm.

El Puerto de Santa María, the city's summer resort, just across the Bay of Cádiz, is a lively place dotted with well-preserved buildings from the 18C and 19C.

Some 23km/14mi northwest of here, at the mouth of the River Guadalquivir, stands the coastal town of **Sanlúcar de Barrameda**, famous as the home of the sherry-like drink, *manzanilla*. The upper town has an abundance of wine cellars and attractive monuments, while the riverfront, in the lower section of town, is teeming with restaurants specialising in fish and seafood.

Return inland across a fertile landscape to the refined town of **Jérez de la Frontera**, whose medieval heart, constructed after the Christian Reconquest, is embellished by several fine churches and impressive monuments such as the Baroque cathedral; the Renaissance-style old town hall; the Iglesia de San Miguel; a remarkable clock museum; the Royal Andalusian School of Equestrian Art; and – of course – the town's eponymous sherry *bodegas*.

From Jérez, head inland along the A 382 to **Arcos de la Frontera**, a delightful town characterised by steep, narrow streets lined by whitewashed houses adorned with wrought-iron grilles; the views from the spectacular natural setting on a ridge overlooking the valley of the River Guadalete will linger long in your memory. The road south winds its away through the rural heart of the province to **Medina Sidonia**, a small hilltop town offering expansive views of the surrounding countryside. The main features of interest here are the remains of the town's Roman underground galleries, its old quarter, including the Iglesia de Santa María la Mayor, and its *alcázar*.

Continuing south, the A 393 skirts the exquisite, impressively located whitewashed hilltop town of **Vejer de la Frontera** before continuing north to

Chiclana de la Frontera. This popular holiday base is bordered to the east by a network of saltpans; to the west is the Playa de la Barrosa, a magnificent 7km/4.3mi-long beach, and the tourist complexes of Sancti Petri and Novo Sancti Petri. The last stop before returning to Cádiz is **San Fernando**, a town that has had strong links with the Spanish Navy since the 18C.

⑧ A LAND OF BANDITS

Round trip of 256km/160mi from Algeciras

This itinerary penetrates deep into spectacular and isolated mountain landscapes and on to picturesque villages and territory made famous by Andalusian bandits of the past before returning to sea level and some of the Costa del Sol's most famous resorts. The starting-point of the tour provides an opportunity to enjoy a superb view of the Rock of Gibraltar from the busy port of **Algeciras**, before heading inland to **Castillo de Castellar**, a charming village-fortress of Moorish origin nestled amid the wooded landscapes of the Parque Natural de los Alcornocales and overlooking the Guadarranque Reservoir. The next stop is **Jimena de la Frontera**, whose whitewashed houses and narrow cobbled streets extend across a hill. Like Castillo de Castellar (and the many other settlements in this region with the "Frontera" suffix), Jimena was the scene of fierce fighting between Christians and Moors for control of the area in the 15C.

The route heads further into the Serranía de Ronda mountains, past pretty **Gaucín**, tucked against the hillside, then gains altitude, winding its way up to **Ronda**. This famous romantic mountain town was the cradle of modern Spanish bullfighting and the home of many bandits in the past. Ronda enjoys a formidable site, perched on the top of a steep rock, cut in two by a deep ravine with the River Guadalevín at its base. The steep, winding descent to the Mediterranean is even more spectacular, particularly beyond the Alájar Pass, leading to

San Pedro de Alcántara, a mature resort which also boasts a number of interesting archaeological remains. **Puerto Banús**, 6km/3.7mi to the east, is home to the most famous and most glitzy marina on the Costa del Sol, and is followed by **Marbella**, the cosmopolitan centre of tourism along this costa, famous for over 40 years as the preferred anchorage and playground of the international jet-set during the summer months.

To return to Algeciras, head west past San Pedro de Alcántara to **Estepona**, another lively cosmopolitan resort, and **La Duquesa**, with its modern marina. As **Gibraltar** comes into view once more, the road skirts to the north of **Sotogrande**, passing a series of luxury tourist developments built close to Valderrama, one of the world's most famous golf courses.

⑨ WINE AND CURED HAM

Round trip of 338km/210mi from Huelva

This driving tour through the province of Huelva starts off along the coast before heading inland to visit the area's major wine-producing area and then climbing towards the Sierra de Aracena, where the best-quality jamón (Spain's emblematic cured ham) is produced.

From **Huelva**, hemmed in to the west and east by the mouths of the Tinto and Odiel respectively, make the short journey south to the **Monasterio de la Rábida** and discover its famous links with Christopher Colombus. After visiting the monastery, continue along the coast road, skirting the long sandy y **Playa de Mazagón**, before arriving in **Matalascañas**, a lively and popular summer resort.

Then leave the coast behind you as you head 16km/10mi north to the small town of **El Rocío**, on the edge of the **Parque Nacional de Doñana**. Each Whitsun weekend (usually end of May) this is the destination for the largest and most popular religious pilgrimage in Spain.

Directly north of El Rocío, the tranquil and elegant wine-producing towns of

Almonte, **Bollullos del Condado** and **La Palma del Condado** are known for their white wines and particularly their sweet wines of the Condado de Huelva appellation.

The HV 5131 then heads north into the sierra, joining up with the N 435 to reach **Zalamea la Real**, renowned for its anise-flavoured liqueurs.

From here, a winding road to the east skirts mountainous terrain as far as **Minas de Riotinto**, (Rio Tinto Mines) whose unusual landscapes have been sculpted by mining activities dating back many centuries. The spectacular open-cast mining area and the "English" district of Bellavista are unusual but very worthwhile sights of interest in and around the town.

An attractive mountain road leads from Minas de Riotinto deep into the **Parque Natural de la Sierra de Aracena y Picos de Aroche** and as far as **Aracena**, a charming small town standing in the shadow of its castle. Not to be missed on the southern outskirts of the town is the spectacular **Gruta de las Maravillas** (Cave of Marvels), which lives up to its name. The tour continues through wooded landscapes within the park to villages such as **Jabugo**, famous for its cured hams, **Cortegana**, an important arts and crafts centre dominated by a medieval castle, and **Almonaster la Real**, which has preserved the remains of a 10C mosque.

As you retrace your steps to Huelva, make a brief stop in **Valverde del Camino**, known across Spain for its high-quality boots, and **Niebla**, a charming medieval fortified village.

⒑ THE LEGACY OF THE NASRIDS

Round trip of 330km/206mi from Granada

This driving tour explores the lands of the former Nasdrid kingdom of Granada, passing through a region of mountainous landscapes, attractive towns and villages and a significant stretch of the Mediterranean coastline in the provinces of Málaga and Granada.

Following your visit to the Alhambra, one of the world's most breathtaking monuments located in the capital of the former Nasrid kingdom, **Granada**, begin your journey west to **Santa Fé**, where the Catholic Monarchs and Christopher Columbus signed their historic agreement, before continuing to **Loja**, towering above the Genil Valley on a low promontory.

The next stage of the journey leads to **Archidona**, nestling at the foot of the Sierra de Gracia amid a landscape of verdant olive groves.

Antequera, 19km/11.8mi further west, is a town of whitewashed houses fronted by wrought-iron grilles. It boasts several fine monuments including its former Moorish castle, and is an ideal base from which to explore the area's stunning natural landscapes. The busy route to the coast climbs steeply before descending dramatically to **Málaga**. Although known as the capital of the Costa del Sol, it remains a very uncommercialised and Spanish city at heart. Its fascinating historical heritage, dating back to Roman times is complemented by its Picasso Museum. The tour heads east along the coast of the Axarquía area, home to several famous popular summer resorts (such as **Torremolinos** and **Benalmádena**), to the **Cueva del Tesoro**, close to Rincón de la Victoria, and the spectacular **Cueva de Nerja**. From **Nerja**, a lively tourist centre, it is well worth a detour inland to visit the picturesque whitewashed village of **Frigiliana**, with its well-preserved architecture bearing the undeniable mark of its Moorish past. Continuing east, the corniche road provides further fine views of the indented coastline along this stretch of the Mediterranean, before reaching **Almuñecar** and then **Salobreña**, a charming village on a hill dominated by the remains of its Nasrid castle. From here the tour veers directly north to return to Granada, briefly leaving the N 323 to discover the charming villages of **Guajar de Faragüit**, to the west, and **Nigüelas**, at the western edge of the Alpujarras mountain range.

WHEN AND WHERE TO GO

When to Go

CLIMATE

Spring and autumn are the best seasons for touring inland Andalucía, as temperatures can exceed 40°C/104°F in summer. Winters are generally mild, although temperatures can dip dramatically at higher altitudes. The coastal resorts of the Mediterranean enjoy mild temperatures and plentiful sunshine even in winter.

In general terms, the climate of Andalucía is Mediterranean in nature with dry summers and relatively mild winters, during which the region receives the majority of its somewhat scarce and irregular precipitation. The region's average annual temperature is 16.8°C/63°F. Because of the size of Andalucía and the presence of high mountain ranges skirting an extensive stretch of coastline along two huge bodies of water, closer analysis of the Andalusian climate shows significant differences between areas. As an example, although the Guadalquivir Valley has a climate that could be described as typically Mediterranean, neighbouring mountain areas are much colder and receive far greater precipitation. Along the coast, a marked contrast can also be seen between the beaches of the Mediterranean, with its calm, warm waters, and those of the more open Atlantic coast, characterised by colder waters and frequent strong winds, particularly around Tarifa on the Straits of Gibraltar, a paradise for windsurfers, where the average wind strength is 30.6kph/19mph.

Specific areas clearly demonstrate the region's climatic differences; this can be seen along a line stretching from Andújar to Córdoba to Sevilla, where temperatures in summer often exceed 40°C/104°F and where spring, considered to be the best time of the year, starts at the end of February. The most westerly parts of the Sierra Morena, such as the Sierra de Cádiz and the Sierra de Málaga, in the Cordilleras Béticas, are the wettest areas of Andalucía due to the influence of Atlantic winds, while the Sierra de Grazalema registers precipitation levels above 4 000l/1 057gal per year, the highest in Spain. The

	Jan	Feb	Mar	Apr	May	Jun	Jul	Aug	Sep	Oct	Nov	Dec
Almería	16	16	18	20	22	26	29	29	27	23	19	17
	8	*8*	*10*	*12*	*15*	*18*	*21*	*22*	*20*	*16*	*12*	*9*
Cádiz	15	16	18	21	23	27	29	30	27	23	19	16
	8	*9*	*11*	*12*	*14*	*18*	*20*	*20*	*19*	*16*	*12*	*9*
Córdoba	14	16	19	23	26	32	36	36	31	24	19	14
	4	*5*	*8*	*10*	*13*	*17*	*19*	*20*	*17*	*13*	*8*	*5*
Granada	12	14	18	20	24	30	34	34	29	22	17	12
	1	*2*	*5*	*7*	*9*	*14*	*17*	*17*	*14*	*9*	*5*	*2*
Huelva	16	18	20	22	25	29	32	32	29	25	21	17
	6	*7*	*9*	*11*	*13*	*16*	*18*	*18*	*17*	*14*	*10*	*7*
Jaén	12	14	17	20	24	30	34	34	29	22	16	12
	5	*5*	*8*	*10*	*13*	*17*	*21*	*21*	*18*	*13*	*9*	*5*
Málaga	16	17	19	21	24	28	30	30	28	24	20	17
	8	*8*	*10*	*11*	*14*	*17*	*20*	*20*	*18*	*15*	*12*	*9*
Sevilla	15	17	20	23	26	32	36	36	32	26	20	16
	6	*6*	*9*	*11*	*13*	*17*	*20*	*20*	*18*	*14*	*10*	*7*

Temperature chart (maximum temperatures in normal text; minimum temperatures in italics).

region's coldest temperatures have been recorded in the Sierra Nevada, where snow remains on the highest peaks all year round and where the ski slopes stay open until May. In complete contrast, the startling Campo de Níjar area in the province of Almería is arid, volcanic and desert-like, with temperatures to match.

For up-to-date information on **weather** in Andalucía log onto the Spanish Meteorological Office website at www.inm.es.

Where to Go

ROUTES IN AL-ANDALUS

The **Moorish Legacy** (El Legado andalusí) initiative has been developed by the Junta de Andalucía and the Spanish government to provide information for visitors on the Moorish presence in the Iberian peninsula. This includes a series of exhibitions, the creation of official tourist routes through al-Andalus (Andalucía, Murcia, Portugal and North Africa), the publication of works relating to this period, and the detailed cataloguing of all aspects of Moorish architecture. The designated tourist routes deliberately explore areas away from the well-trodden tourist centres.

They have been plotted out geographically based on references from both history and legend, researched and documented exhaustively by university lecturers, researchers and tourism experts. The routes offer an in-depth look at the historical and artistic heritage of one of the most brilliant civilisations in history.

ROUTES IN ANDALUCÍA

The following routes are all well signposted.

The Route of the Caliphate

This route links Córdoba and Granada, and is around 180km/112mi long (depending on whether you take the northern or southern route (see below). These were the two main cities of Moorish Spain and heirs to a vast cultural, political and social legacy from the civilisation of al-Andalus.

Starting in Córdoba, you have two options: the main road northwards along the N 432 in the direction of Baena, which follows the more popular and traditional route from the Guadalquivir valley towards Granada; the southern route which winds along the N 331. Both ways join up again at Alcalá la Real, from there through Moclín to Pinos Puente and across the plains of Granada, till the outskirts of the Nasrid capital are finally reached.

Towns and villages en route:
Fernán Núñez, Montemayor, Montilla, Aguilar de la Frontera, Lucena, Cabra, Carcabuey, Priego de Córdoba, Espejo, Castro del Río, Baena, Zuheros, Luque, Alcaudete, Castillo de Locubín, Alcalá la Real, Moclín, Pinos Puente, Colomera, Güevejar, Cogollos Vega, Alfacar, Viznar.

😊 **A Bit of Advice** 😊

Information for Tourist Routes in al-Andalus

El Legado Andalusí, Plaza Isabel La Católica 1, Granada, ☎958 22 59 95. http://legadoandalusi.andalucia.org.

Parque Natural Sierras Subbéticas

Near Zuheros is the Sierra Subbéticas Natural Park with its dramatic peaks, rugged scenery and a wealth of birdlife, especially birds of prey. Walkers, bird-watchers and children will love this area. Along with 16 other towns and villages, Cabra (where there is a visitor centre) also sits on the fringe of the park.

Accommodation: Camping facilities can be found in Carcabuey and Zuheros; there are also cottages for hire throughout the park and Luque has a youth hostel.

Visitor Centre Santa Rita: ☎957 33 40 34; Dirección del Centro de Visitantes Ctra. A 340 Km. 57. 14940 Cabra.

Cycling the Moorish Routes

If you are a very keen cyclist and have the time and energy to spare, you might like to note that specialised cycling guides have been produced for the Route of the Caliphate, of Washington Irving and of the Nasrids.

These can be downloaded from *http://legadoandalusi.andalucia.org*.
For more cycling tours of the area, see *www.otroscaminos.com/SITIO_INGLES/listados.jsp?tipo=No%20Guiado&modalidad=Bicicleta*.

The Washington Irving Route

This route follows closely the itinerary taken in 1829 by the American Romantic writer Washington Irving, who was fascinated by the exuberant and exotic nature of the Moorish monuments in Andalucía. Linking the towns of Sevilla and Granada, this historical route once served as an important communication channel between the Nasrid kingdom and the Christian authorities.

The route stretches for around 250km/156mi, largely on the A 92 dual carriageway. From Seville it passes through Alcalá de Guadaira, then Carmona, Marchena, Écija and returns to the A 92 once again. After passing Osuna, Estepa, La Roda de Andalucía, Fuente de Piedra, Humilladero and Mollina, the road reaches the plains of Antequera and Archidona, Loja and Huétor-Tájar. From Moraleda de Zafayona,the route leaves the main road to visit Alhama de Granada to the south. North of the A 92, the road goes to Montefrío and Íllora, returning by Fuente Vaqueros and Chauchina to the main route, ending in Santa Fe and Granada.

The Nasrid Route

Straddling the provinces of Jaén and Granada, this route is dedicated to the last chapter of the Moorish history in Spain. The itinerary starts in the hills of the Sierra Morena. It was in Las Navas de Tolosa, near Despeñaperros, that the famous battle took place (1212) which led to the Christian reconquest of Andalucía, finalised by the capture of Granada in 1492.

Towns and villages en route:

Las Navas de Tolosa, La Carolina, Baños de la Encina, Bailén, Mengíbar,

Salobreña

Andújar, Arjona, Porcuna, Torredonjimeno, Martos, Torredelcampo, Linares, Baeza, Úbeda, Mancha Real, Jódar, Jimena, Jaén, La Guardia de Jaén, Cambil, Huelma, Guadahortuna, Piñar, Iznalloz, Deifontes, Albolote, Maracena, Granada.

The Almoravid and Almohad Route

Work on preparing the interpretation and signposting of this route is currently underway.

The Almohad Route runs from Tarifa through the provinces of Cádiz and Málaga to Granada, crossing nature parks and the picturesque historocal Pueblos Blancos (White Villages) of Cádiz province.

Towns and villages en route:

Tarifa, Algeciras, Castellar de la Frontera, Jimena de la Frontera, Casares, Gaucín, Banalauría, Algatocín, Benadalid, Atajate, Alcalá de los Gazules, Medina Sidonia, Cádiz, Puerto de Santa María, Jerez de la Frontera, Arcos de la Frontera, Grazalema, Zahara de la Sierra, Algodonales, Olvera, Setenil, Ronda, Teba, Campillos,

Vélez Málaga, Alcaucín-Zafarraya, La Mala, Las Gabias, Granada.

The Route of Ibn al-Jatib

Ibn al-Jatib was the last great historian of Moslem Spain, born in Loja in 1313, died in Fes (Morocco) in 1374. Lorca, Vélez Rubio, Albox, Baza and Guadix are all towns along the route that are worthy of mention for their historical importance and for the Arab remains that can still be seen today.

The route passes from Granada to Murcia and provides some of Andalucía's most beautiful mountain scenery. The Sierra de María range, north of Vélez Rubio and Vélez Blanco, is today favoured by paragliders and hang-gliders. The mountain tops of the Sierra de Huétor Nature Park provide magnificent views of the Sierra Nevada.

The main towns en route:
Guadix, Baza, Huéscar, Vélez Blanco and Lorca before leaving Andalucía and heading east into Murcia province.

The Route of the Alpujarras

This Route links Almería and Granada, using a series of mountain passes. It stretches north to the peaks of Sierra Nevada and south to the Mediterranean.
One of this region's characteristics is its traditional isolation, to which it owes its ethnological and historical peculiarities. It was a centre of resistance against the advance of Islam and was the last redoubt of the Moriscos, the Christianised Spanish Moors. Numerous remains of the old mediaeval fortifications (watchtowers, castles, forts and towers) can be found, along with a valuable archaeological heritage from Moslem times.
Below the towering peaks of the Sierra Nevada Nature Park features, such as Mulhacén and Veleta, are walking tracks that wind through the Alpujarran foot-hills

Towns and villages en route:
Benahadux, Alhama de Almería, Laujar de Andarax, Ugíjar, Válor, Juviles, Trevélez, Pitres, Capileira, Pampaneira, Bubión, Cádiar, Torvizcón, Orgiva, Lanjarón, Dúrcal, Otura, Dílar, Gójar, La Zubia, Cájar and Huetor Vega.

The Route of Münzer

This route, linking Almería with Granada, is named after the Nüremburg physician, Hieronymus Münzer, who in 1494–5, at the relatively advanced age of 56, walked around much of Spain (and Italy) to avoid the plague afflicting his homeland.
The route is also known as the Royal Way, and was one of the oldest communications routes in al-Andalus between the lands of Granada and Almería. The route winds around mountain ranges until reaching the flatter lands of La Hoya de Guadix. Moorish remains include the citadel and old mosque in Almería and the fortresses of El Cenete and La Hoya de Guadix. The area also preserves baths of Moslem origin, including those of Aldeire, Dólar, Ferreira, Huéneja, Jeres and Lanteira. Of particular interest are the spa baths in Graena, which have been used since the 12C.

Settlements en route:
Gádor, Santa Fe de Mondújar, Alhabia, Alsodux, Santa Cruz, Alboloduy, Nacimiento-Doña María, Abla, Fiñana, Huéneja, Dólar, Ferreira, La Calahorra, Aldeire, Alquife, Lanteira, Jérez del Marquesado, Cogollos de Guadix, Alcudia de Guadix, Guadix, Cortes y Graena, La Peza, Quentar, Dúdar, Cenes de la Vega.

Iberian pigs

B. Kaufmann/MICHELIN

KNOW BEFORE YOU GO

Useful Websites

www.andalucia.org: The Andalusian Tourist Board provides reasonable, though not comprehensive, information on the region, including transport, sport and leisure and accommodation with real-time booking.

www.andalucia.com: Unofficial long-running site with a wealth of detail and much useful information.

www.visitacostadelsol.com. A good website covering the Costa del Sol and its inland villages.

www.spain.info: The official visitors' information site for tourism in Spain.

www.okspain.org: Spain's site for visitors from the United States.

www.fco.gov.uk: The UK's Foreign and Commonwealth Office provides information on global travel.

www.state.gov: American visitors should check the US State Department website for worldwide travel advice.

If the above sites do not come up with what you want, go to **www.andalucia.com**, click on *Destinations in Andalucía* and follow the simple links to finding information about your chosen destination.

International Tourist Offices

London:
22–23 Manchester Square, London W1U 3PX.
☎020 7486 8077

New York:
666 Fifth Avenue, New York, NY 1010.
☎212-265-8822. Appointment required to visit office.

Chicago:
Water Tower Place, Suite 915 East, 845 North Michigan Avenue, Chicago, IL 60611.
☎312-642-1992.

Los Angeles:
8383 Wilshire Blvd, Suite 956, Beverly Hills, CA 90211.
☎323-658-7188.

Miami:
1395 Brickell Avenue, Miami, FL 33131. ☎305-358-1992.

Toronto:
2 Bloor St West, 34th Floor, Toronto, Ontario M4W 3E2
☎416-961-3131.
www.tourspain.toronto.on.ca.

Local Tourist Offices

Local Tourist offices are indicated on maps and plans by the ⬛ symbol. Their addresses and telephone numbers are listed for each town and city in the *Discovering Andalucía* section.

Tourist information hotline for the Costa del Sol and Málaga province (in English): ☎952 126 279 (Skype: cdscc_op1 or cdscc_op2)

International Visitors

SPANISH EMBASSIES AND CONSULATES

Spanish Embassy:
39 Chesham Place, London SW1X 8SB. ☎0207 235 5555. http://spain.embassy homepage.com.

Spanish Consulate:
20 Draycott Place, London SW3 2RZ. ☎0207 589 8989; **consulates** also in Manchester and Edinburgh.

Embassy of Spain:

2375 Pennsylvania Avenue NW, Washington DC 20007; ☎202 452 0100. www.spainemb.org; **consulates** in Boston, Chicago, Houston, Los Angeles, Miami, New Orleans, New York and San Francisco.

FOREIGN EMBASSIES AND CONSULATES

American Embassy:

Serrano 75, 28006 Madrid, ☎91 587 2200. www.embusa.es.

Australian Embassy:

Plaza del Descubridor Diego de Ordás 3, 28003 Madrid. ☎91 353 6600. www.embaustralia.es.
Consulates: Sevilla. ☎95 422 09 71; .

British Embassy:

Calle Fernando el Santo 16, 28010 Madrid. ☎91 700 82 00. www.ukinspain.com.
Consulate: Málaga.☎952 35 23 00.

Canadian Embassy:

Calle Núñez de Balboa 35, 28001 Madrid. ☎91 423 32 50. www.canada-es.org.
Consulate: Málaga. ☎952 22 33 46.

Embassy of Ireland:

Ireland House, Paseo de la Castellana 46, 4°, 28046 Madrid. ☎91 436 4093. http://ireland.visahq.com.
Consulates: Málaga, ☎952 47 51 08; Sevilla, ☎954 21 63 61.

ENTRY REQUIREMENTS

Visitors must have a **passport** valid for their entire trip. British, Irish and US passport holders need no visa to stay for up to 90 days. Others, and those planning to stay longer than 90 days, should enquire at a Spanish consulate. =US citizens should see *Tips for Traveling Abroad* online (http://travel. state.gov/travel/tips/brochures/bro- chures_1225.html), which includes general information on visas, customs regulations, and more.

CUSTOMS REGULATIONS

HM Customs and Excise ☎0845 010 9000 (National Advice Helpline). www.hmrc.gov.uk.
For **US nationals** *Know Before You Go* is available as a downloadable pdf from www.cbp.gov/xp/cgov/ travel/vacation/kbyg or visit www.customs.gov.

HEALTH

British citizens should apply for the European Health Insurance Card, either online (www.ehic.org.uk) or at a post office, to obtain free or low-cost treatment in the EU. All visitors should also be insured for uncovered medical expenses, lost luggage, theft, etc. The standard of healthcare in Spain is generally very high and as good, if not better, than anywhere else in mainland northwest Europe. There are several private care organisations with links to US and UK private healthcare organisations.

Accessibility

Sights which are fully (or near fully) accessible by wheelchair in this guide are indicated by the ♿ symbol. As always make arrangements in advance if possible.

A good starting point for UK visitors is **Tourism for All.** ☎0845 124 9971. www.tourismforall.org.uk/ Overseas-travel.html .
US visitors should consult the website portal, www.access-able.com.

A useful local organisation might be the **Confederación Andaluza de Minusválidos Físicos** ☎954 33 10 24. www.canfcocemfe.org (Spanish only).

Also visit **www.fuertehoteles.com/ guia/tourism/useful_inform ation/handicaped-travellers. htm**, which has particularly useful information on transport and travel accessibility.
♿*See Reduced Rates for rail discounts.*

GETTING THERE

By Plane

As airport security and baggage regulations can change at short notice, it is always advisable to check the rules before you fly. Visit www.dft.gov.uk/transportforyou/airtravel/airportsecurity for more information on what you can and cannot carry. If you are flying from or into the USA visit www.tsa.gov.

A number of Spanish and international airlines operate direct scheduled services to airports in Andalucía. These include:

Iberia Airlines:
☎0870 609 0500; www.iberia.com. Direct flights from London Heathrow to Sevilla, connections elsewhere.
Reservations within the US and Canada: ☎800-772-4642

British Airways:
☎0844 493 07 87. www.ba.com. Direct flights to Málaga and Gibraltar.
Reservations within the US and Canada: ☎1-800-772 4642. 1-800-AIRWAYS

A number of low-cost airlines also offer inexpensive flights to Andalucía from the UK. Book online.

Bmibaby:
www.bmibaby.com

easyJet:
www.easyjet.com

Flybe.com:
www.flybe.com

Monarch Airlines:
http://flights.monarch.co.uk

Ryanair:
www.ryanair.com

Thomas Cook:
www.flythomascook.com

Hundreds of weekly charter package flights also operate to Andalusian cities, particularly Málaga and Almería, from all over the UK. Avro is the UK's leading charter flight-only company: www.avro.co.uk.

AIRPORT TRANSFERS

Malaga
The airport is 8km/5mi southwest of the city centre. Taxi ranks are located outside Terminal 1 Arrivals and Terminal 2 Departures. Radio Taxi (☎952 040 804) and Unitaxi (☎952 333 333) can be pre-booked. However, it is much cheaper to take bus no. 19 (www.emtmalaga.es), which connects the airport with central Málaga, while Portillo buses (www.ctsa-portillo.com) provides services to and from Marbella and other popular destinations.
You can also catch the suburban train (www.renfe.es) east to Málaga or west along the coast as far as Fuengirola. The station is opposite Terminal 2.

Seville
The airport is located 10km/6mi to the northwest of the city centre,
An airport bus service is operated by Tussam (www.tussam.es) runs to and from the centre of town and also to the Santa Justa Railway Station; both run every half hour daily.
Taxi ranks are located opposite the terminal. Radiotaxi Giralda (☎954 675 555), Radiotaxi (☎954 580 000) and Teletaxi (☎954 622 222) can be pre-booked.

Almería
The airport is 9 km/5.6mi east of the city centre. Radiotaxi (☎950 226 161) or Teletaxi (☎950 251 111) can be pre-booked. Bus no. 20 runs between the airport and the city centre (www.surbus.com).

For more information on airport facilities (throughout Spain) visit www.aena.es.

By Ship (and Car)

Brittany Ferries and P&O Ferries both operate services to northern Spain from the UK.

Brittany Ferries run a ferry service between Plymouth and Santander (leaving Plymouth on Sundays and Wednesdays, returning from Santander on Mondays and Thursdays; journey time: 24hr). Motorists need to allow a further two days to reach Andalucía from northern Spain. Their *Pont Aven* features live entertainment, casino, cinemas, swimming pool and leisure area. For reservations contact:

Brittany Ferries:
England. ☎08703 665 333; www.brittany-ferries.com. Spain. ☎942 36 06 11.

P&O Portsmouth offer a thrice-weekly crossing from Portsmouth to Bilbao (days change by month) all year round (journey time: 30hr). Their *Pride of Bilbao* features live entertainment, two onboard casinos, saunas, gym and beauty salon. For reservations contact:

P&O Portsmouth:
☎08716 645 645. www.poferries.com/tourist.

By Train

Eurostar
Eurostar ☎08705 186 186. www.eurostar.com) operates high-speed passenger trains from the new London terminal of St Pancras to Paris, from where

overnight **Trainhotel** services operate to Madrid, with connections to destinations across Andalucía. Services can be booked through the Spanish State Railway Network's (RENFE) UK agent, the **Spanish Rail Service**, ☎0207 725 7063. www.spanish-rail.co.uk Alternatively, visit www.renfe.es.

By Train (and Car)

From the UK the high-speed **Channel Tunnel** rail link ferries motorists and their cars beneath the channel in around 35min on specially designed double-decker carriages.
For information and bookings contact Eurotunnel, ☎08705 35 35 35. www.eurotunnel.com.
The Calais terminal is linked to the French motorway network (the distance to Madrid by road is about 1 600km/just under 1 000mi, from where it is a farther 550km/344mi to either Sevilla or Málaga).
Michelin is able to work out driving routes from 43 European countries to Spain on the website, www.ViaMichelin.com. Details listed include the total distance, journey time, and tourist sights of interest, as well as a selection of Michelin-recommended hotels, restaurants and campsites. Tolls for using motorways along the route are also indicated.

By Bus

Regular long-distance bus services operate from London to major towns and cities in Andalucía.
For information, contact **Eurolines**: ☎08717 81 81 81; www.eurolines.co.uk.

GETTING AROUND

By Plane

The principal airports are Almería, Córdoba, Granada, Jerez de la Frontera Málaga, and Sevilla. Customer Services ☏902 404 704. www.aena.es.

MAIN SPANISH AIRLINES:

Iberia: ☏0870 609 0500.
www.iberia.com.Reservations
within the US and Canada:
☏800-772-4642
Air Europa: ☏902 401 501
(information and reservations).
www.air-europa.com
Spanair: ☏902 13 14 15.
www.spanair.com

By Ship

Andalucía's main ports are Algeciras, Cádiz, Málaga and Almería.
Acciona Trasmediterránea is the largest ferry company in the country, with a weekly service from Cádiz to the Canary Islands and daily crossings to Ceuta and Melilla from Almería, Málaga and Algeciras. ☏902 45 46 45 (information and reservations).
www.trasmediterranea.es

By Train

The rail network is operated by **RENFE** (Spanish State Railways). Information is available 24hr a day; reservations can be made from 5.30am to 11.50pm; ☏902 24 02 02; www.renfe.es.
In general, prices are inexpensive and there are a number of discounts available to:
- Travellers between 12 and 26 years old holding a Spanish or foreign **youth card (carnet joven)** receive a discount of 20–25%.
- The **Eurailpass**, available to visitors from abroad, offers unlimited use of the rail network and is priced in line with the number

A Trasmediterránea fast ferry in the port of Algeciras

of days purchased (15, 25, 30, 60 or 90 days). The **Spain Rail Pass** provides unlimited travel for a set period. For information, contact www.raileurope.com or www.eurail.com

The **AVE** (*Alta Velocidad Española*) high-speed train links Madrid with Córdoba (1hr 45min) and Sevilla (2hr 15min). Speedy **Talgo** trains run from Madrid to Córdoba and Granada; the **Talgo 200**, running at speeds of 200km/125mi per hour, links Málaga and Córdoba with Madrid in a few hours. For information and reservations, call ☏902 24 02 02.

TOURIST TRAINS

Train and visit to Isla Mágica
This package includes a return train ticket from various stations around Andalucía to Santa Justa station in Sevilla, plus entry to the Isla Mágica theme park. Discounts are available for children and those over age 65. Information can be obtained from any RENFE station in Andalucía.

El Transcantabrico
A luxury tourist train runs from either Santiago de Compostela to León or from León to Santiago. This luxury hotel-on-a-train takes you through old Castile and León right through to the Bay of Biscay.
The train is kitted out with beautiful private suites containing a double bed, luggage space, safety deposit box, wardrobe, desk, mini bar and

telephone. After a dreamy afternoon gliding through 'Green Spain', admiring the countryside, enjoy fine cuisine before entering a world of relaxation in the suite's adjoining private bathroom. Here you can lie back in the hydro-sauna, allow the turbo massager to ease any backache before sinking into the steam bath – all the while listening to music – all before enjoying a restful night's sleep. Comforts such as television, films, magazines, newspapers and books are all available to the traveller.

León – Santiago de Compostela
The eight-day journey (partly by coach) takes you through and to the following places, where you will alight and explore ancient monuments, national parks, and dine at wonderful restaurants:
León, Cistierna, Olmeda's Roman Villa, Romanesque art of Palencia, Carrion de Los Condes, Villalcazar de Sirga and Fromista, Mataporquera, Mercadillo, Ebro dam, Las Merindades. Valley of Mena, Vizcaya, Bilbao, Santander (optional evening trip to the casino), Cabezon de la Sal, Santillana del Mar, Asturias, Picos de Europa, Llanes, Ribadesella, Cangas de Onis, Covadonga, Gijon, Oviedo, Luarca, Vivero, Ferrol, Santiago de Compostela

Santiago de Compostela – León
This journey is also eight days long and takes you through and to the following places:
Ferrol, Vivero, Rias Atlas, Ribadeo, Luarca, Oviedo, Gijon, Arriondas, Picos de Europa, Covadonga, Ribadesella, Llanes, Cabezon de la Sal, Santillana del Mar, Santander (optional evening trip to the casino), Bilbao, Mercadillo, Mataporquera, Villalcazar de Sirga, Carrion de los Condes, Fromista, Guardo, Cistierna, León.

Information
A double cabin costs €2 300 (a single is €3 300). The trips run between March and October only. For more information and for bookings, contact Spanish Rail: ☎44 (0) 20 7725 7063; www.spanish-rail.co.uk

Tren de la Biosfera
A one-day journey from Guijon Feve to San Vincente, then on to Parque Natural de Redes, and finally visiting a Roman bridge. The trip starts at 9.20am and returns to Guijon Feve station, arriving at 8.50pm. €39. ☎942 20 95 74. www.feve.es (Spanish only).

By Coach/Bus

Travelling by bus is an inexpensive way of getting around the region and, thanks to the large number of bus companies operate services within Andalucía, can be a relatively efficient method of travel too. Bus is the only form of transport between small villages. The contact details of bus stations and major bus companies are listed in the **Address Books** of major towns and cities in the *Discovering Andalucía* section of this guide.
Also see www.andalucia.com/travel/bus/companies.htm for contact details.

By Car

DRIVING IN ANDALUCÍA

Motorists usually need only a current driving licence from home and vehicle documentation and insurance to drive in Spain. In certain situations an International Driving Permit is required. Check with the AA or RAC (UK), the AAA (US) or CAA (Canada).
The Andalusian road network has improved considerably in recent years. Today the region has over 24 000km/15 000mi of motorways *(autopistas)*, dual carriageways *(autovías)* and other roads of varying categories.
The most important road in Andalucía is the A 92 dual carriageway which crosses southern Spain from east to west, connecting, either directly or via other *autovías*, every provincial capital in the region.
Roads in Andalucía are being re-numbered; some numbers may have changed by the time of your visit.

Due to the excellent condition of roads in the region and, with the exception of some of the roads along the Mediterranean during the summer months, the relatively low volume of traffic, private car is the best means of transport for those with time to spare.

ROAD REGULATIONS

Maximum speed limits in Spain are:
  120kph/75mph on motorways and dual carriageways;
  100kph/62mph on national roads;
  90kph/56mph on minor roads;
  50kph/31mph in built-up areas.

Documents – A driving licence, car document and insurance (your hire car company will automatically provide these) must be carried at all times.
Seat belts – These must be worn in front and back seats at all times. Children under 12 must sit in the back seat of a car.
Drink-drive limit – Do not drink any alcohol; the limit here can be exceeded after consuming just one glass of wine or beer.
Safety and accidents – Two warning triangles and reflective vests (your hire car company will automatically pro-vide these) must be in your vehicle at all times, and used in case of accident or car problems.
Drivers are required to aid accident victims if they are the first on the scene.
Mobile phones – You must have a hands-free device to use a mobile phone while driving.
Babies and children must use age/weight appropriate safety seats.
Motorcyles/mopeds – Helmets are required for mopeds and motorcycles. You are not allowed to warn other drivers that police checkpoints are ahead and radar detectors are prohibited.

⊛ A Bit of Advice ⊛
• Drive on the right
• Give way to the right,
• Priority is given to traffic already on a roundabout

⊛Traffic violations are punished with on-the-spot fines for non-residents.

ROAD INFORMATION

The National Traffic Agency (Dirección General de Tráfico) provides information in English on road conditions, latest accidents, driving itineraries, regulations etc. Visit the agency's website at http://infocar.dgt.es/etraffic.

MAPS AND PLANS

To help you plan your holiday and choose the most appropriate route, consult the ⊛**Maps and plans** section at the back of the guide.

ROADSIDE ASSISTANCE

RACE (Spanish Royal Automobile Club) ☎902 40 45 45 and 902 30 05 05 (roadside assistance). www.race.es

PETROL/GAS

There are four grades of petrol/gas: *normal* (92 octane), *super* (97 octane), *gasóleo* (diesel) and *sin plomo* (unleaded). If you have a hire car it will probably run on unleaded fuel.
⊛*Ask your car hire operator know-how to unlock the petrol cap before you drive off, and also note which side it is on!*

RENTAL CARS

Vehicles in Andalucía can be reserved through the offices of all major car hire companies around the world. Alter-natively, cars can be hired at major airports, train stations and large hotels around Andalucía:

▢ **Avis** ☎902 18 08 54; www.avis.es
▢ **Europcar** ☎913 43 45 12; www.europcar.es
▢ **Hertz** www.hertz.es (online only)

⊛*Most companies will only rent out vehicles to drivers over the age of 21. A valid driving licence is required.*

WHERE TO STAY AND EAT

Hotels and restaurants are described in the Address Books which you will find throughout the *Discovering Andalucía* section of the guide. Within these Address Books we have listed a selection of hotels, restaurants and useful addresses that will enhance your stay and enable you to make the most of your holiday. A conscious effort has been made to cover all budgets, although some parts of the region, in particular the resorts along the Mediterranean are more expensive than others. Beware, too, that coastal hotels may also be block-booked months ahead.

♨ *For coin ranges and for a description of the symbols used in the Address Books, see the Legend on the cover flap.*

✍*These are generally the most expensive published prices and special deals are often available.*

Where to Stay

Address Books present a selection of hotels, *hostales* and *pensiones* divided into categories based on the price (excluding VAT) of a double room in high season, generally without break-fast unless otherwise indicated. The difference in rates between high and low season can be significant, particularly on the coast and islands, so it is always advisable to ask for confirmation of prices in writing at the time of booking. These recommendations have been chosen for their location, comfort, excellent value for money and in some cases for their charm. Prices for a double room in high season are classified by the following price brackets:☺(under €80 in large cities and high demand areas; under €60 elsewhere); ☺☺(€80–€105 in large cities and high-demand areas; €60–€85 elsewhere); ☺☺☺(€105–€140 in large cities and high-demand areas; €85–€120 elsewhere); ☺☺☺☺(more than €140 in large cities and high-demand areas; more than €120 elsewhere).

HOTELS

The Spanish Tourist Board publishes an accommodation guide, with hotels rated from one-star to five-stars. Hotel prices vary according to location and time of year – higher towards the coast (though tourist honeypots such as Seville and Granada are also very expensive) and during the summer months. Many hotels can be booked online through www.andalucia.org.

Discounted rates

Many chains and hotels offer reduced rates at weekends. It is also possible to purchase vouchers for one or several nights at advantageous prices. For further information on special offers, contact the following:

NH Hoteles: ☎902 11 51 16. Free-phone number from UK 800 0115 0116; from USA 888 726 05 28; from Canada 866 299 70 96. www.nh-hotels.com. Weekend rates with activities from around €100 per night per person, *Sleep and Go* rates for under-30s for around €30 per person.

Bancotel: ☎915 09 61 22 and www.bancotel.com. Booklets of discounted vouchers (up to 65% off standard rates) redeemable at selected three-, four- and five-star hotels are on sale at travel agencies and on its website.

B. Kaufmann/Paradores

Parador, Castillo de Santa Catalina, Jaén

Halcón Viajes: www.halconviajes. com (online and Spanish only) Vouchers for discounted weekend hotel stays as well as Web specials.
Hoteles Meliá: ☎902 14 44 40 or 0808 234 1953 from the UK . www. solmelia.com Discounts and special weekend offers.

PARADORES

This state-run network of luxury hotels is most famous for its accommodation in restored historic monuments, such as castles (for example, the magnificent *parador* at Jaén), or palaces, or monasteries, etc. While not so very long ago the sense of history was matched by the lack of modern facilities, today you might have a four-poster bed used by ancient kings but you can still enjoy Wi-Fi connection in the same room.
Alternatively, many paradores are built in modern functional blocks (such as the one at Mojácar). If it is the latter, there is generally the compensation of being located in outstanding surroundings with often magnificent views. Although state-run paradores are not cheap – the average price for a double room is around €130–150 (plus VAT) – out of season the network introduces special offers for guests, which vary according to the location. In addition, with the *Tarjeta Amigos de Paradores* loyalty card, guests are able to accumulate points which can be exchanged for free stays.

For more information, contact Paradores de Turismo, calle Requena 3, 28013 Madrid ☎(00 34) 902 54 79 79; www.parador.es.
The official UK representative is Keytel International. ☎020 7616 0300. www.keytel.co.uk.
In the US the agent is Inns en Route. ☎250 412 7336. www.paradors.net.
Special weekend offers are often available, in addition to a five-night "go as you please" **accommodation card**. *Paradors are indicated on Michelin maps by the symbol* ⊵

RURAL ACCOMMODATION

The Andalusian Network of Rural Accommodation **(Red Andaluza de Alojamientos Rurales)** or RAAR, is a private owners' association offering a choice of over 450 addresses to those interested in a holiday in the heart of the Andalusian countryside. The RAAR publishes a practical guide listing details of every type of accommodation available, including rooms in private houses, hostels for groups, entire houses for rent and farm campsites. Reservations can be made directly with the individual owners, through travel agents or via the RAAR reservations centre: ☎902 44 22 33 (Mon–Fri 10am–2pm, 5pm–7pm); www.raar.es.

The Association of Rural Hotels in Andalucía **(Asociación de Hoteles Rurales de Andalucía)** or AHRA, is a group of over 100 small **rural hotels** dotted around the region. The association operates a system of rural vouchers *(bonos rurales)* that can be bought for around €35 each. Contact the AHRA reservations centre, ☎807 51 72 06. www.ahra.es.
Some rural hotels may also be booked through www.andalucia.org.

YOUTH HOSTELS (ALBERGUES JUVENILES)

The **Inturjoven** organisation, set up by the regional parliament (Junta de Andalucía), manages a large network of youth hostels and organises a wide range of sporting, cultural and tourist activities. The 20 youth hostels belonging to this association are located at strategic centres in cities, along the coast and in the mountains across Andalucía.
A hostelling card, obtainable from any hostel or from the Inturjoven reservations centre, is required to stay in any of the hostels within the network. Cards issued by members of the IYHF (International Youth Hostel Federation) are also accepted.
Inturjoven, Central de Reservas, Calle Miño, 24, 41011 Sevilla; ☎902 51 00 00; www.inturjoven.com.

CAMPING AND CARAVANNING

The Junta de Andalucía publishes a comprehensive camping and caravanning guide listing the facilities available at every accredited site in the region. Camping outside of authorised sites is permitted in some areas. For further information visit www.guia ruralandaluza.com.

MICHELIN GUIDE

The annually updated red-cover **Michelin Guide España & Portugal**, is an indispensable complement to this guide with hotel recommendations based on category, price, level of comfort, setting and facilities (such as swimming pool, tennis court, golf course, garden, etc.).

Where to Eat

The restaurants described in the Address Books have been chosen for their surroundings, ambience, typical dishes or unusual character. Prices specified correspond to the average cost of both an inexpensive and expensive meal, but are given as a guideline only. Restaurants are classified into four price brackets: ⊜(under €25 in large cities and high demand areas; under €20 elsewhere); ⊜⊜(€25–€35 in large cities and high-demand areas; €20–€30 elsewhere); ⊜⊜⊜(€35–€55 in large cities and high-demand areas; €30–€45 elsewhere); ⊜⊜⊜⊜ (more than €55 in large cities and high-demand areas; more than €45 elsewhere).

A TYPICAL MEAL

Traditionally, a Spanish meal comprises a first course (primero) or appetiser (entremeses), such as a salad, soup or selection of cured meats; a main course (segundo), consisting of meat (carne) or fish (pescado); followed by a dessert (postre), usually fruit (frutas), a pastry (pastel) or ice cream (helado).

Small local restaurants often offer an inexpensive menu de la casa, which normally includes reasonable quality house wine (vino de la casa).

DRINKS

In restaurants, tap water (agua del grifo) will be provided in a carafe (jarra) if required, although most people tend to drink bottled **mineral water** (agua mineral), either sparkling (con gas) or still (sin gas). The excellent selection of Spanish wine (vino) usually on offer will include white (blanco), red (tinto) or rosé (rosado), available in carafes (frasca) as well as bottles (botella). **Beer** (cerveza) is available either draught (caña) or bottled; the main brands are San Miguel, Mahou, Águila and Damm. **Sangría** is normally served as an aperitif, accompanied by a selection of tapas. Visitors are often surprised by the large measures used in cocktails such as the popular **Cuba libre**, a mix of rum (ron) and Coke, usually served in a tall glass with lots of ice.

TAPAS

Given the region's reputation for tapas, we have included in several of the Address Books in the Discovering Andalucía section a list of tapas bars where visitors can enjoy an aperitif or meal throughout the day and late into the evening. Beware, however, that while these are a tempting and often very tasty treat, they are no longer the inexpensive tradition that they used to be; the tapas bill can quickly and very easily mount up and soon outweigh the cost of a conventional meal, while providing less sustenance.

MICHELIN GUIDE

The **Michelin Guide España & Portugal** recommends a selection of restaurants that will allow you to discover and sample the best that Andalucía has to offer. Those restaurants recognised for the exceptional quality of their cuisine are highlighted by Michelin's renowned star ratings.

WHAT TO SEE AND DO

Outdoor Fun

Andalucía's diverse landscapes and excellent climate make it possible to enjoy outdoor sporting activities all year round.

GOLF

Golfers are attracted to Andalucía all year round by the superb golfing conditions and the high quality of the 100 or so courses scattered around the region, ranging from 9-hole courses for beginners to elite championship golf clubs . The majority are along the Costa del Sol –the most famous of which, Valderrama, hosted the 1997 Ryder Cup – although excellent courses can also be found close to the cities of Sevilla, Huelva, Cádiz, Granada Jaén, Córdoba and Almería. Details on the specific aspects of each course are listed in the *Golf* brochure published by the Andalusian Tourist Board. Or visit the website of the **Royal Golf Federation of Andalucía** (☎952 22 55 90. www.fga.org) and click onto their excellent www.flash caddy.com link to explore all the major courses hole-by-hole.

HIKING AND MOUNTAIN-BIKING

It is often said that if there's an abundance of anything in Andalucía, it is nature and sunshine. What is certain is that walkers and cyclists are spoilt for choice in one of Spain's best regions for these two pursuits. Details of over 200 walking itineraries and 120 cycling routes are listed in the following guides published by the Andalucía Tourist Board: *Bicycle; Rural Andalucía;* and *Hiking.*
Also try www.cycling-hotel-andalusia. com/associations.html.
Both cyclists and walkers should avoid the hottest parts of the day and the peak summer months.

Stunning scenery for a round of golf

Cyclists should be wary that although the sport is highly revered in Spain (as in many parts of continental Europe) accidents are relatively commonplace. Choose your itinerary carefully (first-timers should keep away from the mountains!) and make sure you are fully insured. If you want to take a cycling holiday, or just devote part of your trip to cycling contact **Andalucian Cycling Experience**, based in Montecorto, Málaga province (☎952 18 40 42, www.andalucian cyclingexperience.com) who specialise in organising, Mountain Bike Biking Holidays, Road Cycling Holidays, Leisure Cycling Holidays , Winter Training Camps , Family Cycling Holidays, and Pueblos Blancos White Village Tour.

Hiking in the Alpujarras

The main pitfall for casual walkers is the lack of signposting. Stick to the National Parks If you intend doing it yourself and seek out wardens' advice wherever possible. Alternatively there are many walking companies, offering full holidays or just day trips. One reptable company is Spanish Steps based in picturesque Cómpeta, in Málaga province (☎95 255 3270) and with an office in England (☎01604 77 00 12. www.spanish-steps.com).

HORSE RIDING

The horse has long been a part of Andalusian culture. This tradition continues today throughout the region, perhaps most visibly during the pilgrimage to El Rocío, at the "mares' auction" *(saca de las yeguas)* held on 26 June every year in the Parque Natural de Doñana, the rounding-up of the bulls contests in Villamanrique and Sevilla (April), and the horse races on the sands of Sanlúcar de Barrameda *(✆see SANLÚCAR DE BARRAMEDA).*
For those who prefer to take the weight off their feet while sightseeing, Andalucía offers excellent options, including cross-country **treks** lasting several days and stays on horse farms, in country houses and rural hotels; as well as courses on breaking in horses and equestrian techniques.
The *Horse* brochure, available from tourist officesprovides further information on horse riding in the region. Also visit www.andalucia.org for information on the many operators in Andalucía.

La Duquesa, Costa del Sol

If you are holidaying in the Tarifa area and would llike to fulfil a dream of riding on the sands, visit www.aventura ecuestre.com.

HUNTING

The hills and mountains of Andalucía offer rich pickings for hunters. Very few parts of Europe are home to such a variety of large game, including wild boar (Doñana), mountain goat (Cazorla, Sierra Nevada, Ronda), deer (Serranía de Cádiz) and mouflon, the latter raised in enclosures. Smaller game is also hunted, such as hare (traditionally on horseback accompanied by hunting dogs), quail and partridge. Further information is contained in the *Hunting* brochure.
Visit **www.andalucia.com/rural/ hunting.htm** for a comprehensive listing of organisations, though do be aware that these are geared to local hunters, not visitors, and you won't get far unless you are fluent in Spanish.
By contrast is the prestigious visitor-orientated **Marbella Gun and Country Club** at Monda (☎952 11 21 61 www.marbellagunandcountryclub. com) whose outdoor activities include clay pigeon shooting, crossbow, air pistol target shooting plus quad bikes and horse riding.

MARINAS

Andalucía's seafaring tradition spans centuries. Today, there are over 30 puertos deportivos, "sports ports", or leisure marinas along the region's 836km/522mi of Atlantic and Mediterranean coastline, in addition to two river ports in Sevilla.
Most marinas can offer a choice of sailing, scuba diving and windsurfing opportunities; some have water skiing, rowing, canoeing, marine wildlife watching and water-based amusements, such as inflatable rides.
Two guides published by the Junta de Andalucía – *Nautical Guide* and the *Pleasure Craft Harbours* brochure – list information on every port and marina in Andalucía, as well as the facilities

available. An online marina directory may be viewed at http://web.eppa.es/GContenidos/index.php.

PARAGLIDING

Paragliding (or *parapente* as it is called locally) is an exhilarating and skilled pastime which involves leaping off a cliff or hill in to thin air and soaring high in the sky suspended beneath a manoeuvrable crescent-shaped aerofoil canopy, designed to fly on wind and air currents.

Popular venues include the Atlantic beaches of Tarifa, inland Cádiz province (particularly Grazalema Natural Park) and the Sierra Nevada Mountains.

For more information on parapente in the Granada region visit www.flygranada.com. A recommended operator in these parts is Horizonte Vertical, based near Granada (☎ 958 30 82 91. www.horizonte-vertical.net)

RIVER FISHING

Jaén and Granada are the two most popular provinces for fishing in Andalucía. Rivers and lakes teem with trout and, in some areas, carp and crayfish. In general, the season starts on 15 March and ends on 15 August, although some areas are open all year. Fishing enthusiasts must be in possession of a relevant fishing licence.

SCUBA DIVING

In addition to the schools located at various marinas along the Andalusian coast, the region has a number of scuba diving clubs for more experienced divers.

It should be noted that the areas renowned for diving in the Atlantic and Mediterranean are very different. The waters of the Atlantic are relatively cold, visibility varies between 15m/50ft–20m/65ft and almost zero. Dangerous currents make it advisable to dive with a local instructor. By contrast, the Mediterranean is characterised by warmer temperatures, good visibility and more tranquil sea conditions.

SPECTATOR SPORTS

Football is Spain's number one spectator sport and the top team in the region is **Sevilla FC** (www.sevillafc.es). Also in Seville and also playing in the top division (La Liga) are Real Betis. Málaga CF (www.malagacf.es) also rejoined La Liga in 2008 and have a significant and vociferous support from around 2 000 ex-pat English football fans (www.malagafootballenglish.com).

Tickets for most matches at all stadiums are available to buy at the gate (do not pay the hyper-inflated prices that ticket agents ask!). Unlike in the UK, the days and times of matches are not confirmed until around 7–10 days beforehand and are usually Saturday or Sunday evenings See the club websites, local newspapers or ask at the tourist office for details.

Several major international **equestrian** competitions are held during the winter in various locations along the Costa del Sol, while the polo tournaments in Sotogrande, during July and August, draw a monied crowd. The annual Jerez Horse Fair *(Feria del Caballo de Jerez)* held in May, and the SICAB, an international show in Sevilla during the last week of November, are the two most important events in the Andalusian equine calendar.

WATER SPORTS

From sailing to scuba diving and water-skiing to windsurfing, Andalucía offers a whole range of sporting options for beginners and more experienced water sports enthusiasts alike. There are operators on most beaches and at marinas. Most are reputable but do try to establish their professional qualifications before you sign up for anything and note their attitude to safety.

Tarifa is the windsurfing capital of Spain though beginners and less experienced boardsailors should build up their confidence and ability elsewhere before tacking this windy part of the coast.

The best surfing in the region is also around this area, on the Costa de la Luz, between Tarifa and Cádiz.

WILDLIFE WATCHING

Whale and dolphin watching is very popular in the Straits of Gibraltar where "running" alongside a pod of leaping dolphins is an almost guaranteed thrill. This is by no means the only place for spotting cetaceans however and trips leave from the Costa de la Luz, Cádiz the Costa del Sol, Málaga, and even from ports in Huelva provincel.

WINTER SPORTS

The Sierra Nevada ski resort, one of the most popular in Spain, is easily accessible by car (just 30min from Granada along Europe's highest road), bus (local services and a daily Madrid-Sierra Nevada service), train (the nearest railway station is just 33km/21mi away) and plane (Granada, Málaga and Sevilla airports). Sierra Nevada has 84km/43.7mi of marked runs and all the facilities expected of a major ski resort. The season generally runs, snow permitting, from late November/early December to some time in April. (⊘avoid the last week in February when the resort is crowded out by families on school holidays). Information on skiing in the Sierra Nevada (plus other year-round activities) is available from the resort operator, **Cetursa,** Plaza de Andalucía, Sierra Nevada, Monachil. ☎902 70 80 90. www.cetursa.es.

Spas `Spa`

The region's spa resorts offer rest and relaxation, cultural activities and health treatments in beautiful natural surroundings.These are growing in number all the time and cover the whole province. In addition, five "Curhoteles" (four in Málaga province and one in Almería) offer a high level of comfort and provide guests with the very latest techniques in health treatment. For further details, contact the **Andalusian Spa Association** (Asociación de Balnearios de Andalucía). ☎958 69 40 22. www. balneariosdeandalucia.com. Additional information can be found in the *Guide to Spas and Spa Hotels* or online at www.andalucia.org or www.balnearios.org.

The following are a selection, there are many more to choose from:

Balneario San Nicolas, Alhama de Almería. ☎950 64 13 61, www. balneariosannicolas.com.

Balneario Sierra Alhamilla, Pechina, Almería province). ☎950 31 74 13. www.balneariosierralhamilla.com

Balneario Alicun de las Torres, Villanueva de las Torres (Granada province). ☎958 69 40 22. www. alicundelastorres.com.

Balneario Alhama de Granada, Alhama de Granada. ☎958 35 00 11, www.balnearioalhamadegranada.com.

Balneario Graena, Cortes y Graena (Granada province). ☎958 67 06 81. www.balneario-graena.com.

Balneario Lanjarón, Granada province), ☎958 77 01 37, www. balneariodelanjaron.com.

Balneario San Andrés de Canena, Canena (Jaén province). ☎953 77 00 62. www.balneariosanandres.com/

Balneario Carratraca, Carratraca, Malaga province), ☎952 48 95 42. www.thermasde carratraca.com.

Balneario de Tolox, near Tolox, Málaga province), ☎952 48 70 91. www.balneariodetolox.com.

Balneario Chiclana, Chiclana (Cádiz province), ☎956 40 05 20. www.balneariodechiclana.net.

Activities for Children `Kids`

Sights of particular interest to children are indicated in this guide with a `Kids` symbol. All attractions offer discounted fees for children. The Costa del Sol is one huge children's playground with all amenities and facilities (water parks, zoos, marine attractions, fun-fairs) geared towards family holidays.

Some of the most popular are:
Parque Acuático Vera
(*see COSTA DE ALMERÍA*).
Isla Mágica theme park, Sevilla
(*see SEVILLA*).
Oasys (Mini Hollywood) theme park,
near Almería
(*see TABERNAS*).
Selwo Aventura safari park, near
Estepona
(*see COSTA DEL SOL*).
Selwo Aventura
(*see COSTA
DEL SOL*).
Tivoli World amusement park,
Benalmádena
(*see COSTA DEL SOL*).

Calendar of Events

Practically every day something is
celebrated or commemorated some-
where in Andalucía.
The list below includes some of the
better-known events, although exact
dates should be checked with the
appropriate tourist offices.

JANUARY

Jan 2: **Fiesta de la Toma**. Commemo-
ration of the capture of Granada.
—Granada

FEBRUARY/MARCH

Feb 2: **Candlemass processions**—
Many towns and cities
Week prior to Ash Wednesday:
Carnival—Cádiz hosts
the biggest

HOLY WEEK (LAST WEEK BEFORE EASTER

Processions—Andalucía, particularly
in Sevilla, Málaga, Córdoba and
Granada

APRIL

Two weeks after Holy week (Semana
Santa): **Feria de abril de Sevilla.**
Seville Spring Fair.

Last Sunday in April: **Virgen de la
Cabeza pilgrimage**—Andújar
(Jaén)

MAY

Dates vary (late April to mid-May):
Horse Fair Jerez
19–24 May: **Manzanilla Fair**
Sanlúcar de Barrameda (Cádiz)
Throughout May (all in Córdoba) **May
Crosses; Patio Competition;
Annual Fair; National Flamenco
Contest** (held every three years,
next in 2010)
www.flamenco-world.com

WHITSUN (MAY OR JUNE)

El Rocío pilgrimage—Almonte
(Huelva). *www.rocio.com*

JUNE–JULY

Corpus Christi: **Processions**
c. 26 June–12 July: **International
Music and Dance Festival**
including the oldest flamenco\in
Spain—Granada.
www.granadafestival.org
16 July (Virgen del Carmen):
Seafaring processions—
Several towns and villages
along the Mediterranean,
particularly Almería
c. 22–26 July: **Nerja Cave Festival**—
Nerja (Málaga)
www.cuevadenerja.es

LAST WEEK OF JULY– FIRST WEEK OF AUGUST

Columbus Festival—Huelva

AUGUST

Horse races on the beach—
Sanlúcar de Barrameda
**International Music and Dance
Festival**—Priego de Córdoba
(Córdoba)
13–21 Aug: **August Fair**—Málaga
www.malagaturismo.com
22–31 Aug: **Virgin del Mar
Festival**—Almería

CARRERAS DE CABALLOS

H. Champollion/MICHELIN

Horse racing poster,
Sanlúcar de Barrameda

Penultimate Sun: **Moors and Christians Festival**—Bubión (Granada)

SEPTEMBER/OCTOBER

4–8 Sept: **Nuestra Señora de Regla Fair**—Chipiona (Cádiz)
First Sun in Sept: **Wine Harvest Festival**—Montilla (Córdoba)
8 Sept: **Virgen de Setefilla pilgrimage** Lora del Río (Sevilla)
First week in Sept: **Goya bullfights, Flamenco Singing Festival**—Ronda. www.turismoderonda.es.
Second fortnight in Sept and first fortnight in Oct: **Autumn Festivals (Wine Harvest and Horse Week)**—Jerez de la Frontera.

OCTOBER

St Luke's Fair—Jaén

DECEMBER

28 Dec: **Los Verdiales Festival**—Málaga

Sightseeing

OPENING TIMES AND FEES

Opening times (🕐) and entrance fees (👓) for monuments, museums, churches, etc. are listed in the **Discovering Andalucía** section of this guide. This information is given as a guideline only, as times and prices are liable to change without prior warning.

Except in cases where an attraction is geared to children, prices are listed for individual adult visitors only. As many monuments require frequent maintenance and restoration, it is always advisable to phone ahead to avoid disappointment.
Information for churches is only given if the interior contains a sight of particular interest, including specific opening times or if an entrance fee is payable. In general, religious buildings should not be visited during services, although some only open for mass, in which case visitors should show appropriate respect.

WORLD HERITAGE SITES

Andalucía holds several UNESCO World Heritage Sites including:
The **Historic Center of Córdoba**
The **Alhambra, Generalife** and **Albayzín** in Granada
The **Catedral**, **Alcázar** and **Archive of the Indies** in Sevilla
Parque Nacional de Doñana
The Renaissance cities of **Úbeda** and **Baeza**

BEACHES AND RESORTS

Andalucía has the geographical advantage of bordering both the Atlantic and the Mediterranean. This setting, coupled with the 25 protected areas along its two coasts, ensures a diversity of landscape and beaches unique to Spain.

Atlantic coast

This coastline, which is also known as the **Costa de la Luz** (Coast of Light), extends from the Portuguese border to the Straits of Gibraltar, a total length of 330km/206mi, in the provinces of Huelva and Cádiz. In general, its beaches are popular with Spanish visitors, particularly families. Days are hot, the evenings cooled by ocean breezes, and the sea temperature cooler than that of the Mediterranean. The 15 beaches in **Huelva** province are characterised by golden sand, clear water, surf, sand dunes and pine forests. A number of resorts, such as

Isla Canela, have excellent sporting and sailing facilities, while other wild and isolated stretches of coast are only accessible on foot from the larger resorts. Some of the Atlantic coast's best-known beaches include **Isla Cristina**, with a long fishing tradition; **La Antilla**, a 22km/14mi stretch close to Lepe; **El Rompido**, with its enormous dunes and pine forests offering superb views; **Punta Umbría**, famous for its marina; **Mazagón**, with its steep cliffs; and the renowned **Matalascañas**, bordering El Rocío and the Parque Nacional de Doñana.

The **Cádiz coast**, the most southerly in Spain, stretches 200km/125mi. Its beaches of fine, golden sand are lined by some of Spain's most historic towns and cities such as Sanlúcar de Barrameda, Rota, El Puerto de Santa María and Cádiz, so visitors can combine time on the beach with cultural visits to these fascinating places. To the south of the beach at **Bajo de Guía**, where horse races are held in summer, the resort of **Chipiona** has four beaches which have been popular for many years. El Puerto de Santa María, within the boundaries of which lies the glitzy **Puerto Sherry** marina, has some excellent beaches of its own, such as **La Puntilla** and **Valdelagrana**, while those close to Cádiz (**La Victoria**, **La Caleta** and **Cortadura**) are thronged during the summer months with inhabitants of the city. Also worthy of mention are the recently created tourist complex of **Sancti Petri**, and the series of delightful beaches near Conil (**Caños de Meca**, **Zahara de los Atunes** and **Bolonia**) which have thus far escaped the blight of mass tourism. The only drawback for sun-worshippers on this coast is the strong wind, a feature of the local climate that attracts thousands of windsurfers every year.

Mediterranean coast

This coastline includes areas with differing geographical characteristics, but all have a similar hot and dry climate. The waters of the Mediterranean are generally calm, warm and crystal clear.

Costa del Sol – The section of the Sun Coast in the province of Málaga is the leading tourist destination in Andalucía (*see COSTA DEL SOL*). The western section, from Gibraltar to the city of Málaga, contains over 50% of all hotel accommodation along the Andalusian coasts. Paradoxically, the majority of the beaches here are pebbly. The high-rise resorts along here have embraced mass tourism for better and for worse and have become world famous (some for the wrong reasons). Exclusive Marbella is at the top end of the spectrum, Torremolinos is at the bottom, though even here the Spanish Carihuela section of the resort has much to commend it. Both Marbella and Tirremolinos offer good long sandy stretches.

East of Málaga, as far as Nerja, in the area known as La Axarquía (*see LA AXARQUÍA*), tourist development is less pronounced and accommodation tends to be more apartment-based. Major resorts along this coastline, with its small beaches and numerous cliffs, are **El Rincón de la Victoria**, **Nerja** and **Torre del Mar**.

Costa Tropical – The shores of Granada province are known as the Tropical Coast; the sub-tropical climate results from the protection afforded by the Sierra Nevada. The beaches along this stretch range from coves protected by high cliffs to enormous beaches such as those in **Almuñécar**. Tourism is concentrated in Almuñécar; Salobreña, with its two large beaches; the more developed **Playa del Peñón** and the wilder **Playa de La Guardia**; in Motril (**Playa de Poniente** and **Playa de Granada**); and in Castell de Ferro and La Rábita.

Costa de Almería – The Almería Coast represents a quarter of the entire Andalusian coastline. Most development here is between Adra – including the immense sandy beaches of **Balanegra** and **Balerma** and the resort of **Almerimar** – and Aguadulce. The onward stretch from Aguadulce to Almería comprises an impressive series of steep cliffs. To the east of the provincial capital, the Mediterranean is bordered by the

San José, Cabo de Gata

Parque Natural de Cabo de Gata, with its superb beaches, such as **Morrón de los Genoveses**, and the attractive small resort of **San José**.

NATIONAL AND NATURAL PARKS

Over the past few decades, the regional government *(Junta de Andalucía)* has increased its efforts to protect the natural environment. Today, Andalucía has two national parks, 20 nature parks and a number of protected areas covering 18 percent of the region's area.
For further information visit www. spain.info/uk/TourSpain, go to its Site Map and choose "Its National Parks".

Souvenirs

HANDICRAFTS

Andalucía's handicrafts cover a wide range and, although many vary considerably from area to area – particularly pottery and ceramics – a lot of the region's traditions are common to most provinces. Over the past few years, strenuous efforts have been made to rediscover old techniques and decorative motifs that have been in danger of disappearing; sadly, however, some aspects of ornamental art, such as decorative work on silk – a common feature during Moorish times – have been lost forever.

Pottery and ceramics

Andalucía's pottery and ceramics industries produce an almost unlimited choice, ranging from items of everyday use (pitchers, jars and bowls) to those used for decorative purposes only, such as the high-quality Pickman-La Cartuja de Sevilla porcelain, with its delightful grey, pink and green decorative motifs.
The kilns used in the Almerían villages of Albox, Níjar and Sorbas are almost identical to those used in times past; the province of Granada retains many of its 19C wood-fuelled kilns; while the potters' wheels in Guadix remain as active as ever.
The numerous workshops in the Triana district of Sevilla still produce their traditional blue, yellow, orange and purple pottery and ceramics, while the village of Sanlúcar la Mayor to the west specialises in the reproduction of lustre ceramics with Hispano-Moorish designs.
Jaén is renowned for the blue and white ceramics of Andújar. Not to be outdone, the province of Córdoba has made its name with Caliphal ceramics decorated with geometric, plant and animal motifs.

Woodwork

The manufacture of furniture has become a feature of Andalusian industry, establishing itself alongside sculptural art with a tradition dating back several centuries and whose work is inspired by the creations of sculptors such as Martínez Montañés and Pedro Roldán.
In the 19C, following the arrival of a number of English wine and sherry producers, the coopers of Sanlúcar de Barrameda and San Fernando near the city of Cádiz, who had hitherto concentrated on barrelmaking, found it easy to develop their work to English tastes and create a range of high-quality mahogany furniture. Further to the east, the town of Ronda has made a name for the production of a more rustic style of furniture.
Granada is famous for its inlaid (marquetry with inlaid bone, mother-of-pearl, amber or marble) and gilded

work. Over the course of time, some villages within the province have also developed an excellent reputation for furniture produced in the Mudéjar (Capileira) and Renaissance styles (Baza).

So-called "Sevilla chairs", with their bright colours and flower motifs, are manufactured in several towns and villages in the province of Huelva, including Valverde, Galorza and Zalamea.

Leather goods

Because of the huge importance of horses to the region's economy, a large equestrian equipment industry has developed in Andalucía which produces saddles, riding breeches, leather pouches and other items used for horse riding and hunting.

The leading leather centres are found in Jerez de la Frontera, Alcalá de los Gazules and Villamartín (Cádiz); Almodóvar del Río (Córdoba) and various towns and villages in Huelva, particularly Almonte and Zalamea la Real.

Ubrique and Prado del Rey (Cádiz) have developed into capitals of leather fashion accessories. A number of workshops produce a range of bags, belts and gloves for leading companies around the world.

Shoes are also important to the local economy, as seen in Valverde del Camino (boots) and Montoro (hand-made shoes).

	Provinces	Ha/acres	☎ Information
National parks			
Doñana	Huelva-Sevilla-Cádiz	50 720/124 217	959 44 23 40
Sierra Nevada	Granada-Almería	86 208/213 020	950 51 35 48
Natural Parks			
Cabo de Gata-Níjar	Almería	33 663/83 181	950 38 97 42
Sierra María-Los Vélez	Almería	22 500/55 597	950 52 70 05
La Breña y Marismas de Barbate	Cádiz	3 797/9 382	956 59 09 71
Bahía de Cádiz	Cádiz	10 000/24 710	956 59 02 43
Los Alcornocales	Cádiz-Málaga	170 025/420 132	956 41 33 07
Sierra de Grazalema	Cádiz-Málaga	51 695/127 738	956 71 60 63
Sierra de Cardeña y Montoro	Córdoba	41 245/101 916	957 45 32 11
Sierra de Hornachuelos	Córdoba	67 202/166 056	957 45 32 11
Sierras Subbéticas	Córdoba	31 568/78 004	957 33 40 64
Sierra de Baza	Granada	52 337/129 324	958 86 10 13
Sierra de Castril	Granada	12 265/30 307	958 53 76 00
Sierra de Huétor	Granada	12 428/30 710	958 54 04 26
Sierra de Aracena et Picos de Aroche	Huelva	184 000/454 664	959 12 84 75
Despeñaperros	Jaén	6 000/14 826	953 12 50 18
Sierras de Andújar	Jaén	60 800/150 236	953 50 02 79
Sierras de Cazorla, Segura y Las Villas	Jaén	214 336/529 624	953 71 30 40
Sierra Mágina	Jaén	19 900/49 172	953 78 76 56
Montes de Málaga	Málaga	4 762/11 766	952 04 11 69
Sierra de las Nieves	Málaga	16 564/40 930	952 87 77 78
Sierras de Tejeda y Almijara	Málaga-Granada	40 600/100 323	952 04 11 48
Sierra Norte de Sevilla	Sevilla	164 840/407 320	955 95 20 49

Souvenir shop in Pampaneira

H. Champollion/MICHELIN

This list is not complete, however, without mentioning the magnificent Cordovans (famous for embossed leather) with their traditional and modern decoration produced, as the name would suggest, in the workshops of Córdoba.

IRON AND METALWORK

In many areas, iron is still worked by traditional methods, using the forge and anvil to produce grilles, fences and staircases. The towns of Arcos de la Frontera (Cádiz) and Torredonjimeno (Jáen) are both reputed for this type of metalwork.

Some smaller towns in the province of Málaga, such as Arroyo de la Miel, Cártama and Estepona all specialise in the production of artistic locks.

Also worthy of mention are imaginative tin and glass lamps from Úbeda, the unusual cowbells made in Cortegana (Huelva), and attractive carriages from Bollulos del Condado with their combination of iron and woodwork.

Books

HISTORY

- *A Concise History of the Spanish Civil War* by Paul Preston (1996)
- *Infidels: The Conflict between Christendon and Islam 638–2002* by Andrew Wheatcroft (2003)
- *Moorish Spain* by Richard Fletcher (1994)
- *The Inquisition* by Michael Baigent & Richard Leigh (1999)
- *The Spanish Labyrinth* by Gerald Brenan (1990). The social and political background to the Civil War through the eyes of the Anglo-Irish Brenan who lived for many years in Granada province

TRAVEL

- *Tales of the Alhambra* by Washington Irving (original 1832, latest edition 1995).
  Part Oriental-themed stories set in the Alhambra, part account of the American author's own residency here.
- *Driving Over Lemons: an Optimist in Andalucía* Chris Stewart (1999). Humorous account of former Genesis drummer's new life on a farm in the Alpujarras.
- *A Parrot in a Pepper Tree* by Chris Stewart (2002).
  More tales from the former rock musician, (*see above),* including a stint as a flamenco guitarist in Seville.
- *As i walked out one Midsummer Morning.* Laurie Lee. (1969).
  The sequel to *Cider with Rosie* deals with Laurie Lee's walk from Vigo in the north of Spain, to Málaga, just before the Civil War.
- *A Rose for Winter* by Laurie Lee. (1971). Lee's return to Andalucía 20 years on (*see above)*
- *Duende: A Journey into the heart of flamenco* Jason Webster (2003). Learning flamenco guitar, in Granada and other places.
- *The Face of Spain* by Gerald Brenan (1987). A 1920s travelogue with a

good part devoted to Andalucía where Brennan lived

- *South from Granada* by Gerald Brenan (1992).
  More from Brennan, including the visit of his Bloomsbury Set colleagues.
- *Spain* by Jan Morris (1986).
  Spain as it was in 1960.
- *The Houses and Palaces of Andalusia* by Monteros and Venturi (1998).
  The development of the distinctive regional style of architecture and decoration, and the stories of the families that built and lived in them.

FICTION

- *For Whom the Bell Tolls* by Ernest Hemingway (1940).
  The experiences of an American college professor who has volunteered to fight for the Loyalist cause in the Spanish Civil War in Andalucía.
- *Semana Santa* by David Hewson (1996).
  A murder story set against Holy Week in an Andalusian city

POETRY

- *Gypsy Ballads* by Federico García Lorca (1990)
- *Lorca: a Dream of Life* by Leslie Stainton (1999)
  Federico García Lorca was Andalucía's greatest playwright and poet writing in the turbulent pre-Civil War period about the region's gypsy traditions

Films

- *Bodas de Sangue (Blood Wedding)* Carlos Saura (1981).
  Based on the famous tragic play by Federico García Lorca (premiered in 1933), of two thwarted lovers.
- *Carmen* Francesco Rosi (1984).
  The first film version of Bizet's famous opera about the femme-fatale from the Seville cigar factory.to use spoken dialogue between the musical numbers.
- *Al sur de Granada (South From Granada)* (2003).
  The story of Gerald Brenan's love affair with Andalucía.

USEFUL WORDS & PHRASES

For vocabulary relating to hotels and restaurants, please refer to the **Michelin Guide España & Portugal**.

COMMON WORDS		TIME	
yes, no	**Sí, no**	when?	**¿cuándo?**
good morning	**Buenos dias**	at what time?	**¿a qué hora?**
good afternoon	**Buenas tardes**	today	**hoy**
goodbye	**Hasta luego, adiós**	yesterday	**ayer**
please	**Por favor**	tomorrow morning	**manãna por la manãna**
how are you?	**¿qué tal?**	tomorrow afternoon	**manãna por la tarde**

ON THE ROAD, IN TOWN			
car	**coche**	dangerous	**peligroso**
petrol, gasoline	**gasolina**	beware, take care	**cuidado**
on the right	**a la derecha**	to go round, tour	**dar la vuelta a...**
on the left	**a la izquierda**	after, beyond	**después de...**
road works	**obras**	to go round, to circle	**girar**

CORRESPONDENCE

post box, letter box	**buzón**	post office box	**apartado**
post office	**correos**		**(de correos)**
telephone	**telégrafos,**	stamp	**sello**
	teléfonos	telephone call	**conferencia,**
letter	**carta**		**llamada**
post card	**(tarjeta) postal**	tobacco shop	**estanco**

SHOPPING

thank you	**(muchas) gracias**	how much?	**¿cuánto (vale)?**
(very much)		(too) expensive	**(demasiado) caro**
excuse me	**Perdone**	a lot, little	**mucho, poco**
i don't understand	**No entiendo**	more, less	**más, menos**
sir/mr, you	**Señor, usted**	big, small	**grande, pequeño**
madam, mrs	**Señora**	credit card	**tarjeta de crédito**
miss	**Señorita**		

PLACES AND THINGS TO SEE

bodega	wine cellar/store	**puerta**	door, gate, entrance
calle	street	**puerto**	pass, harbour, port
campanario	belfry	**romano;**	Roman;
capilla	chapel	**románico**	Romanesque
carretera	main road	**talla**	carved wood
casa consistorial	town hall	**tapiz**	tapestry
castillo	castle	**techo**	ceiling
castro	Celtic village	**tesoro**	treasury, treasure
ciudad	town, city	**torre**	tower, belfry
collado, alto	pass, high pass	**torre del hom-**	keep
cruz	cross, Calvary	**enaje**	valley
cuadro	picture	**valle**	window (plain)
cueva, gruta	cave, grotto	**vidriera**	stained glass

PLACES AND THINGS TO SEE
(See also Architectural terms in the **Introduction** section)

where is?	**¿dónde está?**	**desfiladero**	defile, cleft
may one visit?	**¿se puede**	**embalse**	reservoir, dam
	visitar?	**ermita**	hermitage, chapel
key	**llave**	**excavaciones**	excavations
light	**luz**	**fuente**	fountain
sacristan	**sacristán**	**garganta**	gorge
guide	**guia**	**lago**	lake
porter, caretaker	**guarda, conserje**	**mezquita**	mosque
open, closed	**abierto, cerrado**	**monasterio**	monastery
not allowed, no entry	**prohibido**	**nacimiento**	source, birthplace
entrance, exit	**entrada, salida**	**palacio (real)**	(royal) palace
head toward	**dirigirse a**	**pantano**	marsh
wait	**esperar**	**paseo**	avenue, esplanade,
storey, stairs, steps	**piso, escalera**		promenade
		plaza	square
alcazaba	Muslim fortress	**plaza mayor**	main square
alcázar	Muslim palace	**plaza de toros**	bullring
ayuntamiento	town hall	**portada**	portal, west door
balneario	Spa	**presa**	dam
barranco	gully, ravine	**pueblo**	village, market town
barrio	quarter	**puente**	bridge

BASIC INFORMATION

Business Hours

Restaurants
As a general rule, restaurants serve lunch from 1.30pm to 3.30pm and dinner from 9pm to 11pm.

Shops
Traditional shops are open mornings to 2pm; after lunch and *siesta,* they are open 5pm–8pm or 8.30pm.
Larger stores and shops in tourist resorts may not close for lunch. Most shops close on Sundays, a few on Saturday afternoon.
Those in tourist resorts may well open longer hours and on Sunday.

Banks
Banks are generally open 8.30am-2pm, Monday to Saturday and close on Saturdays in summer.

Communications

Directory enquiries: ☎1003
International enquiries: ☎025
Public telephones accept coins or phonecards *(tarjetas telefónicas),* sold at tobacconists and post offices. For **calls within Spain**, dial the full 9-digit number; **from abroad**, dial the international access code (00), then 34 for Spain, then the full 9-digit number.

Mobile/cell phones
Your **mobile phone** should automatically pick up the nearest/strongest network by itself. **Beware**: "local" calls made from a mobile are treated

---

International Codes

For **international calls**, dial 00 plus the following country codes:
- 61 for Australia
- 44 for the UK
- 1 for Canada
- 1 for the USA
- 64 for New Zealand

---

as international calls (as your phone is registered abroad) and incoming calls incur a charge. If you intend making a reasonable number of calls while in Spain, it is worth changing your SIM card for a local one – though check that this is possible first with your home network – or buy a cheap pay-as-you-go phone in Spain, which already has a local SIM card in.

Electricity

220v/50Hz (110v/60Hz in some older establishments). Plugs are two-pin.

Emergencies

Emergency services:
✚ ☎112 or 902 50 50 61.

Mail/Post

Post offices are open Mon–Fri 8.30am–2.30pm, Sat 9.30am–2pm. Stamps *(sellos)* can also be purchased at tobacconists *(estancos).*

Media

English-language newspapers are widely available on publication day. Sky and Cable TV is widely available in hotels, offering BBC News, Sky News, CNN and all manner of TV channels.

Money

The currency in Spain is the **euro** (€). In September 2008, the exchange rate was €1.25 to the pound, €0.70 to the US dollar. There are no restrictions on taking currency into or out of Spain.
• **Rates of exchange and commission** vary. If you exchange traveller's cheques or cash at banks and exchange offices *(cambios)* you will usually get a good rate of exchange,

but may have to pay a transaction charge (so it is best to exchange one or two large sums, rather than keep returning).

- Much easier and probably just as cheap is to obtain euros from cash machines (ATMs) using credit or debit cards, but do check before you go as to what the charges will be, as they can vary dramatically.
- Never exchange money in shops (apart from large reputable depart ment stores, such as El Corte Inglés) or markets, as you will almost certainly be given a poor rate of exchange.
- Major **credit cards** are accepted in most shops, hotels and restaurants. In the event of a **lost or stolen credit card**, contact the issuer as soon as possible:

Visa/Mastercard: ☎91 362 62 00
American Express ☎91 572 03 03
Eurocard ☎91 519 60 00
Diners Club ☎91 701 59 00
Lost Traveller's Cheques –
Thomas Cook ☎900 994 403

Public Holidays

Towns and cities have their own festivals and feast days. The following are national public holidays:

- 1 January (New Year's Day)
- 6 January (Epiphany)
- Holy Thursday
- Good Friday
- 1 May (Labour Day)
- 15 August (Assumption of Our Lady)
- 12 October (Virgin of the Pillar: Hispanic Day)
- 1 November (All Saints)
- 6 December (Spanish Constitution Day)
- 8 December (Immaculate Conception)
- 25 December (Christmas Day).

Reduced Rates

FOR YOUNG PEOPLE

ISIC (International Student Identity Card) – www.isiccard.com or isic. com. This card entitles the student bearer to discounts on admission fees, shopping, food, accommodation and travel. €9.
IYTC (International Youth Identity Card) – www.isiccard.com or isic.com. This card offers similar discounts for youths aged 12–25. €9.
EURO<26 Card – www.euro26.org. This card is very similar, but runs up to age 26. €14.
For rail discounts, ✆*see By Rail.*

FOR SENIOR CITIZENS AND DISABLED TRAVELLERS

Those aged 60+ qualify for significant discounts on transport and entrance fees to sights, events and shows.
The Tarjeta Dorada (Golden Ticket) offers persons over 60 and people with a 65% or more disability a 40% reduction on rail travel. Those travelling with the disabled traveller also receive the discount. **www.renfe.es**

Smoking

In general it is forbidden to smoke in bars and restaurants in Spain. In practice the rule may be flouted. Premises of over 100sq m/1 076sq ft can opt to provide a zone for smokers or to be wholly non-smoking. However, the cost of providing a separate non-smoking zone has persuaded most to become complete non-smoking zones.

Time

Spain is one hour ahead of the UK, 6 hours ahead of Eastern Standard Time and 9 hours ahead of Pacific Standard Time.

Tipping

If service is not included, it is customary to leave a tip in restaurants and hotels of up to ten per cent, if you consider the service satisfactory. Passengers are also expected to leave a small tip for taxi-drivers.

CONVERSION TABLES

Weights and Measures

1 kilogram (kg) 6.35 kilograms 0.45 kilograms	**2.2 pounds (lb)** 14 pounds 16 ounces (oz)	**2.2 pounds** 1 stone (st) 16 ounces	*To convert* *kilograms* *to pounds,*
1 metric ton (tn)	**1.1 tons**	**1.1 tons**	*multiply by 2.2*
1 litre (l) 3.79 litres 4.55 litres	**2.11 pints (pt)** 1 gallon (gal) 1.20 gallon	**1.76 pints** 0.83 gallon 1 gallon	*To convert litres* *to gallons, multiply* *by 0.26 (US)* *or 0.22 (UK)*
1 hectare (ha) **1 sq. kilometre (km²)**	**2.47 acres** 0.38 sq. miles (sq.mi.)	**2.47 acres** 0.38 sq. miles	*To convert* *hectares to* *acres, multiply* *by 2.4*
1 centimetre (cm) **1 metre (m)**	**0.39 inches (in)** 3.28 feet (ft) or 39.37 inches or 1.09 yards (yd)	**0.39 inches**	*To convert metres* *to feet, multiply* *by 3.28; for*
1 kilometre (km)	**0.62 miles (mi)**	**0.62 miles**	*kilometres to miles,* *multiply by 0.6*

Clothing

Women					Men			
	35	4	2½			40	7½	7
	36	5	3½			41	8½	8
	37	6	4½			42	9½	9
Shoes	38	7	5½		**Shoes**	43	10½	10
	39	8	6½			44	11½	11
	40	9	7½			45	12½	12
	41	10	8½			46	13½	13
	36	6	8			46	36	36
	38	8	10			48	38	38
Dresses	40	10	12		**Suits**	50	40	40
& suits	42	12	14			52	42	42
	44	14	16			54	44	44
	46	16	18			56	46	48
	36	06	30			37	14½	14½
	38	08	32			38	15	15
Blouses &	40	10	34		**Shirts**	39	15½	15½
sweaters	42	12	36			40	15¾	15¾
	44	14	38			41	16	16
	46	16	40			42	16½	16½

Sizes often vary depending on the designer. These equivalents are given for guidance only.

Speed

KPH	10	30	50	70	80	90	100	110	120	130
MPH	6	19	31	43	50	56	62	68	75	81

Temperature

Celsius (°C)	0°	5°	10°	15°	20°	25°	30°	40°	60°	80°	100°
Fahrenheit (°F)	32°	41°	50°	59°	68°	77°	86°	104°	140°	176°	212°

To convert Celsius into Fahrenheit, multiply °C by 9, divide by 5, and add 32.
To convert Fahrenheit into Celsius, subtract 32 from °F, multiply by 5, and divide by 9.
NB: Conversion factors on this page are approximate.

Casares
B. Kaufmann/MICHELIN

NATURE

The lands of Andalucía, which for centuries were a source of fascination for successive waves of colonisers, extend southwards from the Sierra Morena – a range of mountains separating the region from the communities of Extremadura and Castilla La Mancha – to the Mediterranean coast; and eastwards from the River Guadiana – a natural border with Portugal – to the community of Murcia.

Spain's most southerly autonomous community *(comunidad autónoma)* **covers 87 300sq km/33 706sq mi and is similar in size to Portugal and Switzerland. This figure represents 17.3% of the country's total area. Over seven million people (18% of the Spanish population) live in this historic region, which acts as a bridge between Europe and Africa and between the East and West.**

Landscape

Andalucía is a land of sharp contrasts in terms of both its climate and its landscape. The fertile **Guadalquivir Valley**, which has always been considered the region's most representative area, is set between two high mountain ranges, the Sierra Morena to the north and the Cordilleras Béticas to the south, while **Andalucía's coastal areas**, lapped by the waters of the Atlantic and the Mediterranean, have their own varied landscapes.

SIERRA MORENA

The modern-day name of this mountain range remains something of an enigma. There are those who believe that the name evolves from the Sierra Mariana (from Marius, a praetor in Roman Hispania), while others are of the opinion that the name alludes to the dark colour

Geology

In geological terms, Andalucía is a young region covering the large sea once situated between the continental masses of Eurasia and Goswana. The Cordilleras Béticas, which rose up as a result of Alpine movements during the Tertiary Era, and the River Guadalquivir, slowly sedimenting, cut off the sea, leaving just a 14km/8mi-wide stretch of water, the Straits of Gibraltar, which, with the exception of the Suez Canal, is the only navigable gateway to the Mediterranean.

of its landscape, with its predominance of slate.

Despite its rugged, mountainous appearance, the Sierra Morena is not a true sierra or cordillera, but rather the southern extension of the Castilian Meseta, which descends sharply into the Guadalquivir depression. It begins to the north of Jaén, where it reaches its maximum altitude (Sierra Madrona – 1 323m/4 339ft) and extends west to form the Sierra de Hornachuelos in the province of Córdoba, the Sierra Norte in the province of Sevilla and the Sierra de Aracena in the province of Huelva.

Despeñaperros mountain pass

Through the ages, the approach to Andalucía from the Meseta has been via the a defile cut by the river of the same name in an area of astonishing geological formations covered with cork, holm and gall oaks. In addition to its significant game, especially deer and wild boar, the Sierra Morena is home to a wealth of protected fauna such as wolves, Iberian lynx, imperial eagles, and black and tawny vultures. *See PARQUE NATURAL DE DESPEÑ APERROS*

The Sierra Morena contains three nature parks: **Despeñaperros** and the **Sierras de Andújar** are in the province of Jaén. **Sierra de Aracena y Picos de Aroche** in northern Huelva province is one of the largest in Andalucía (184 000ha/454 664 acres), encompassing a varied vegetation and 28 small communities with a total population of 41 000. Each community prospers from harvesting

Castril

cork, raising black pigs (the best hams in Spain are produced in Jabugo, Cortegana and Cumbres Mayores) and, in recent years, from rural tourism (mainly from the province of Sevilla), which is increasing in importance throughout the region.

The Parque Natural de las Sierras de Andújar occupies the heart of the Sierra Morena and is an excellent example of a Mediterranean ecosystem with varied, abundant vegetation and large swathes of forest and Mediterranean scrub.

GUADALQUIVIR DEPRESSION

The spine of Andalucía, as it is known, runs from the Sierra Morena in the north to the Cordilleras Béticas in the south. This former area of Tartessian settlement forms a triangle of flat landscapes whose highest point is found to the east, in the province of Jaén, descending to the lowest part of the depression along the Gulf of Cádiz, where the Atlantic exerts its considerable influence.

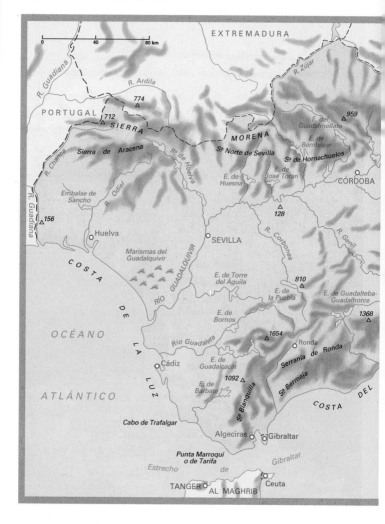

The whole valley, which covers 65% of Andalucía, is a densely populated, predominantly agricultural area owing to its deep, fertile black soil, which is irrigated to advantage by water from the tributaries of the Guadalquivir.

As a result, the valley is home to fruit and vegetable farms, with large areas devoted to cereal crops, olive groves and vineyards.

The Guadalquivir depression is also home to two of Spain's most historic cities, namely **Córdoba** and **Sevilla**, as well as one of Europe's most impressive national parks, the **Parque Nacional de Doñana** (&see National Parks), with its abundance of flora and fauna.

River Guadalquivir

The Romans called it Betis, while to the Moors it was known as the Great River (Guad-al-Quivir in Arabic); irrespective of its name, however, it has always been the soul of Andalucía, and is the only river (670km/419mi) to flow exclusively through the region. Due to the thrust of the powerful Cordilleras Béticas to the south, its path has gradually shifted northwards, to such an extent that it now flows at the very foot of the Sierra Morena (&see above).

The Guadalquivir rises in the **Sierra de Cazorla** (Jaén), at an altitude of 1 600m/5 248ft. After a brief journey through the mountains, it then enters

the Baetica depression, gently flowing from an altitude of 100m/328ft in the province of Córdoba to just 10m/32ft in Sevilla. With the additional waters of its tributary, the Genil, the river is navigable from the city of Sevilla to the Atlantic, where it forms a huge marshland area (Doñana), which the Romans named Lacus Ligustinus.

Although the Guadalquivir's tributaries flowing down from the Sierra Morena (the Viar, Bembézar and Guadiato) all follow a short course and are particularly erosive, those rising in the Cordilleras Béticas, the Guadiana Menor and Genil in particular, carry a far greater volume of water.

River Guadalquivir from Castillo de Almodóvar del Río

©Vera Bogaerts/iStockphoto.com

The rivers of Andalucía

In addition to the Guadalquivir basin, the region's hydrographic network consists of a variety of rivers, the volume of which can vary enormously from one season to the next. The reservoirs built during the second half of the 20C have enabled their flow to be regulated, thus increasing areas under cultivation.

Andalucía's major Atlantic rivers, such as the Guadiana, Tinto, Odiel and Guadalete, are all of significant length, carry relatively large volumes of water, and form estuaries and sand bars where they flow into the ocean.

The rivers descending to the Mediterranean coast (Guadiaro, Guadalhorce, Guadalfeo, Adra, Almería and Almanzora) rise in the Cordilleras Béticas, are shorter in length, and, in general, form deltas at their point of entry into the sea. During periods of low water in the provinces of Granada and Almería, the wide, deep gullies known as *ramblas*, which are in fact the beds of rivers, remain empty of water, to such an extent that during longer periods of drought, local people often use these ramblas for planting crops and even as building sites. Needless to say, during periods of heavy rain, the torrents of water cascading down these bare depressions destroy everything in their path, resulting in huge material losses and even loss of life.

Mention should also be made of Andalucía's large wetland areas, including the Ría del Tinto-Odiel, the Bay of Cádiz, Adra and Doñana National Park, as well as the region's salt marshes and lagoons, underground aquifers, and inland areas dotted with lakes, such as Fuente de Piedra (Málaga).

CORDILLERAS BÉTICAS

This chain is the steepest in Andalucía and acts as a natural barrier between the Guadalquivir and the coast. It occupies almost all of eastern Andalucía and is formed by two groups of Alpine-type ranges: the Cordillera Subbética to the north and the **Cordillera Penibética** to the south. An inner corridor, known as the **Depresión Penibética**, runs between the two.

This depression widens out to the east, forming the **Depresión de Granada**, irrigated by the Genil, continuing along to the **Guadix** and **Baza** basins, before skirting either side of the **Sierra de Filabres**, forming the Almanzora Valley and the Almería depressions.

The **Sistema Subbético**, which connects with the Sierra Morena to the east, is less well defined, however. The highest sections of this chain are the **Sierras de Cazorla**, **Segura and Las Villas** (600m/1 968ft–2 100m/6 888ft), which together have been designated a nature park. This particular area, dotted with oak, arbutus (strawberry tree) and rowan trees, is a haven for birds of prey, mountain goats and various types of game.

The Cordillera Penibética, which is higher than the Cazorla, Segura and Las Villas ranges, extends parallel to the coast from the Serranía de Ronda to the west, in the province of Málaga, as far as Murcia. The highest summits in Andalucía are found in the Sierra Nevada, near Granada, with a cluster of 14 peaks over 3 000m/9 840ft, including Monte Veleta (3 392m/11 125ft) and Mulhacén (3 481m/11 418ft), the highest peak on the Iberian Peninsula. On its southern flank is the historic Alpujarras region, renowned for its wilderness and difficult access. To the east, behind the Sierra de Los Filabres and the Sierra de Gádor in the province of Almería, lies a large volcanic region, the Cabo de Gata-Níjar, with its spectacular landscapes which provide a dramatic contrast with the deep blue sea.

THE COAST

Andalucía's 900km/562mi of coastline constitute one of Europe's most visited tourist areas. Its beaches, where many centuries ago merchants from the East and invaders from North Africa first set foot on European soil, are now the domain of visitors with more peaceful intentions from Spain and abroad, who wish to spend an enjoyable holiday in the sun or retire away from the colder climates of Northern Europe.

Costa de la Luz –The coastline extending from the Portuguese border to the Straits of Gibraltar is known as the Costa da Luz (Coast of Light) and enjoys the slightly cooler influence of the Atlantic. Until recently, these vast beaches of fine sand were deserted apart from a handful of small resorts such as La Antilla and Matalascañas in Huelva, which were popular with Spanish families, particularly from Sevilla. Over the past few years, a number of new large tourist complexes have begun to attract more foreign visitors, such as Zahara de los Atunes, Caños de Meca and Tarifa, a town popular with surfers from around the world. The beaches of the Mediterranean are neither as long nor as open as their Atlantic counterparts; they are, however, far better known, undoubtedly because visitors can be guaranteed fine weather almost all year round.

Costa del Sol – The beaches around Marbella, the capital of the famous Costa del Sol (Sun Coast), are not as attractive as those in Rincón de la Victoria, also in the province of Málaga; however the luxurious infrastructure

---

Ten Labour of Hercules

To commemorate his victory over Geryon, a winged monster with a huge herd of oxen, Hercules created two gigantic columns alongside the waters of the Ocean River. One of these, Abila, rose up on the present-day promontory of Ceuta; the other, Calpe, dominated the Rock of Gibraltar.

---

and sporting facilities of this glamorous resort more than make up for this.
See COSTA DEL SOL

Costa Tropical – The Tropical Coast to the south of Granada, is rocky with crystal-clear water perfect for snorkelling and scuba diving.

Costa de Almería – This coast, further east, attracts nature lovers with its quieter beaches, some of them protected, such as Los Genoveses and Cabo de Gata.
See COSTA DE ALMERÍA

Flora

Andalucía is home to a huge variety of plants and flowers. Perhaps the most representative landscapes of the region are the mountain ranges skirting the Mediterranean, with their small shrubs and bushes such as rockrose, lentisk (mastic tree) and juniper; aromatic plants (thyme, lavender and rosemary);

H. Champollion/MICHELIN

Cabo de Gata headland

Cork oak

Cork oak bark

and trees belonging to the Quercus family, including evergreen, gall and cork oak. Carobs, chestnuts, and wild olives, the latter occasionally attaining an impressive size, can often be seen in areas covered by forests of oak.

Pine trees are more prevalent at higher altitudes, as well as in coastal regions. Several species, including umbrella and maritime pines, are used to prevent sand dune erosion along the Atlantic coast. The resistant holm oak and larch are also found in this area. Many of these trees, along with the ubiquitous eucalyptus, are the result of reforestation schemes undertaken at a time when little thought was given to vegetation native to these areas. The **Spanish fir**, a tree considered a relic from the Tertiary Era, is also common to the region, although it is generally only found in the woods around Grazalema (Cádiz), and in the Sierra de las Nieves and Sierra Bermeja in the province of Málaga.

Forests of ash, willow and poplar all grow alongside rivers, streams and lakes, while wetland areas are the natural habitat for various species of reeds, salt cedars and coarse grasses – ideal nesting grounds for aquatic birds.

Andalucía's myriad protected habitats are also home to a breathtaking variety of vegetation (the oak forests of Sierra Quintana, near Andújar, and the cork oak groves in the province of Cádiz), much

of which is endemic to the region and has already disappeared from the rest of Europe.

Flowers

Andalucía is home to a rich variety of wild flowers in diverse habitats, some of which are endemic. These include Convoluulus (Pink and Dwarf Sea-Lavender, Crown Daisy, Purple Vipors Bugloss, Broom and Honeysuckle. The unmissable Bougainvillea decked around so many houses in the region, is a genus of flowering plants native to South America.

To the non-specialist visitor, Andalucía's best known flower is, of course, the **Sunflower** (Helianthus annuus L.). It is one of the few crop species that originated in North America and was probably first introduced to Europe through Spain. Growing between 2.5m and 3.5m (8ft to 12ft) tall, and in serried ranks across vast rolling fields, these bright yellow giants stand proud for between one and two months. They are a magnificent sight against the bright blue Andalusian sky and figure in the holiday snaps of all visitor who have been lucky enough to have been driving through the Andalusian countryside, particularly north of the Costa del Sol, at the right time of year. Rates of growth vary according to where they are planted, but in the relatively cooler, more temperate parts of

Andalucía (the best climate for them), a sunflower requires approximately 11 days from planting to emergence, 33 days from emergence to head, 27 days from head visible to first anther, and eight days from first to last anther. After another 30 days the heads are drooping, effectively dead, and ready for harvest.

In fact it is easy to forget that the sunflower is one of Andalucía's most important crops. The giant flower, or head, holds florets that mature into sunflower seeds; these are in fact the fruit of the plant. The seeds can be roasted and sold as a snack food, or bird food, or processed into a peanut butter alternative (popular in many parts of the world). In Germany, it is used in conjunction with rye flour to make Sonnenblumenkern-brot (sunflower whole seed bread), which is popular throughout German-speaking Europe.

The main by-product, however, is sunflower oil, extracted from the seeds. The oil is used for cooking, to produce margarine and, more recently, as a bio-fuel (an alternate fuel source in diesel engines). The "cake" which remains after the processing is used as livestock feed.

Another easily recognised and popular plant is **prickly pear** with a pretty red flower and a sweet fruit. Never attempt to pick it, however, unless you have special gloves on, as its hairlike spines will penetrate the skin and are fiendishly difficult to dislodge.

Moreover, the fruit, which is nothing like a conventional pear, must be processed before eating.

NATIONAL PARKS

Parque Nacional de Doñana

This famous wetland is one of Europe's great wilderness sites. Comprising 54 500ha/134 700 acres it is said to be the largest road-free area in Europe. The Park is made up of dunes, marshes, scrublands, beaches and fresh water, and is home to a large number of species. Most visitors come to watch its birds, with its myriad residents supplemented by winter visitors from north and central Europe and summer visitors from

Africa, the most colourful of which are pink **flamingoes** (*see Fauna*). Spring is a particularly good time to visit. Only a very lucky few have ever spotted the critically endangered **Iberian lynx** (Lynx pardina), endemic to the Iberian Peninsula, and an emblem of the Park, but sadly close to extinction (*see Fauna*). Access to the park is highly restricted to ranger-organised tours by road and by boat. *See PARQUE NACIONAL DE DOÑANA*

Parque Nacional de Sierra Nevada

Unlike in the Doñana National Park, access to the Sierra Nevada is unrestricted. This is Spain's most mountainous area and the highest in Europe after the Alps. It contains the two highest peaks in the Iberian Peninsula: Mulhacén at 3 482m/11 424ft, and Pico del Veleta, at 3 396m/11 141ft. In contrast to these harsh snow-covered peaks are the foothills of the Alpujarras, where gentle slopes are cultivated with terraces of almond trees and vegetables.

Parque Nacional de Despeñaperros

The Despeñaperros (*see Landscape: Sierra Morena*) was declared a National Park in 1989 and the main route through here is the A 4 motorway. *See PARQUE NATURAL DE DESPEÑAPERROS*

Fauna

The region has an equally rich and varied fauna, which includes a number of protected species, some of which are either extinct or dying out in the rest of the world.

BIRDS

Andalucía's birdlife includes 184 different species which nest in the region, in addition to the fifty or so others that spend their winters here. The area's numerous aquatic birds include the **pink flamingo**, which flourishes only in Fuente de Piedra (Málaga) and the French Camargue, and the eastern Glossy ibis, found only in Andalucía.

A profusion of plants and flowers

A lack of plants and flowers is not a criticism that can be levelled against Andalusian houses. Around the region, patios, balconies and terraces are bedecked in greenery, while streets and squares carry the scent of citrus blossom in spring and the enchanting aroma of jasmine in summer.

The patios of noble houses are resplendent with plants of every type, from leafy ferns to hyacinths, gladioli, tuberose and violets. In smaller abodes, the simplicity of the accommodation is often hidden behind whitewashed walls covered with myriad species of plants such as single, double, scented and ivy geraniums, carnations and jasmine.

The selection of the most suitable plants for different times of the year and their ground and wall arrangement is an art form which has been completely mastered by Andalusian women. Dark corners are ideal for aspidistras, while sun traps are perfect places for geraniums; carnations and other plants which are not particularly attractive when not in flower are left to grow on terraces and then brought onto patios when in bloom. As a general rule, plants are not purchased; instead, seeds and cuttings are passed on by friends and neighbours and then nurtured in pots of every description, from jam jars to magnificent ceramic flowerpots.

Birds of prey tend to nest in the more inaccessible parts of the region.

The imperial eagle, so majestic in flight, is to be found in the Parque Nacional de Doñana, while the increasingly rare black vulture is found mostly in the Sierra Morena at Paraje Natural Sierra Pelada y Rivera del Aserrador, south of Aroche in Huelva province. The Egyptian vulture may be found in the Sierra de Andújar, among other places.

Bird watching in Gibraltar and Tarifa

Gibraltar and Tarifa are two excellent places for bird watchers. Here you can find plenty of bird activity through the Straits of Gibraltar, especially in the form of raptors, storks and other migratory birds making their way to and from Africa and Europe.

An unforgettable sight is that of great flocks of storks, sometimes numbering up to three thousand strong, crossing the Straits.

In contrast to these white giants of the sky is the dazzling bright yellow golden oriole, which can be found in orchards and woodlands during the summer. Other flashes of colour are provided by the hoopoe, to be seen in open woodlands.

An extremely rare specimen is the **Mavasía**, a blue-billed duck, whose habitat is the lakes of the Sierra Subbética in the province of Córdoba.

Bee-eaters, woodpeckers, kestrels, owls and many other species are also to be seen around the area, and even those with little interest in ornithology cannot but admire the beauty of these birds.

ANIMALS

Andalucía's most spectacular mammal is the **lynx**. A smaller relative of the lion and tiger, with distinctive tufted ears, their population recently diminished to around 360. Lynx can be found mainly in the Coto de Doñana and the Sierra de Andújar. In an effort to avoid extinction within the decade, a breeding programme was set up in the Doñana park and this has had some success.

Another highly endangered species is the **wolf**, which inhabits the Sierra Morna – one of the few places it is still found in Andalucía. There are only around 75 left, though at least recent moves to compensate farmers for any animals that a wolf takes has eased pressure.

Many species of game such as wild boar, stag, deer, mountain goat and the Mouflon (particularly abundant in the Sierra de Cazorla and Sierra de Segura).

HISTORY

The mythical kingdom of Tartessus; a long period of splendour dominated by the civilisation of al-Andalus before its slow destruction by the Reconquest; and the golden age brought about by the discoveries of the New World. These are the key points in the history of a region which subsequently experienced a long and painful decline marked by poverty, occasionally violent conflict over land and nostalgia for its glorious past. That decline has now been checked by the advent of the post-industrial society and the region's evolution into an autonomous community which is quite distinct from the rest of Spain.

The Phoenicians

Towards the end of the second millennium BC, at the same time as the first Indo-European tribes were crossing the Pyrenees, navigators from the far east of the Mediterranean were landing on the southern coast of Spain.

The discovery of riches in the south of the peninsula (silver, gold, copper and tin) led the Phoenicians to found their first colonies here.

1100 BC — Foundation of Gadir (Cádiz), the largest Phoenician colony in the Western Mediterranean. Minerals extracted and exported from the Riotinto and Aznalcóllar mines.

8C–7C BC — The apogee of the kingdom of Tartessus, which traded with Phoenician and Greek colonies in the southern part of the peninsula.

The Carthaginians

BC

6C–4C — Various **Iberian tribes** continue to inhabit the peninsula. Andalucía remains the most homogenous region.

The Carthaginians gradually settle in southern Spain,

The Kingdom of Tartessus (c. 13C–6C BC)

This kingdom, which later came to be identified with the biblical Tarsis and whose legendary status is equal to that of Atlantis, reached its pinnacle in the 9C and 8C BC. It died out in the 6C BC, either a victim of the Carthaginian invasion or simply as a result of the major crisis which affected the Mediterranean after the conquest of the city of Tyre by Nebuchadnezzar (573 BC). The wealth of this kingdom dazzled the Greeks and Phoenicians and has amazed modern archaeologists, who have discovered numerous remains of this civilisation in Huelva, Sevilla and Córdoba.

Greek and Latin writers date the mythical foundation of Tartessus to around the year 1200 BC. Others believed that the Tartessian monarchy had two different dynasties. The first was founded by Geryon – a creature with three heads and three bodies – who was defeated by Hercules, and the second by Gargoris and his son Habis, the inventor of agriculture.

Modern researchers believe the Tartessian civilisation evolved from the Megalithic culture of southern Spain. The civilisation developed to such a degree that it had its own written laws, a well-organised society comprising seven social groups and an excellent knowledge of techniques for transforming metal. The dynasty's only historical king was Arganthonios, who ruled during the 7C BC and was praised by writers such as Herodotus, Anacreon and Pliny. Despite the many archaeological findings, the exact location of the civilisation's capital is still uncertain, although it is thought to have been situated close to Sanlúcar de Barrameda (Cádiz).

replacing the Phoenicians. Cádiz develops into a major port and a prosperous city, while the Mediterranean coast of Andalucía experiences increasing growth.

264–241 — First Punic War. Rome defeats Carthage and reduces its freedom of movement and its income in the Mediterranean significantly.

237 — The Carthaginian general, Hamilcar Barca, lands in Cádiz, makes a pact with the Iberians and establishes an operational base against the Romans in southern Spain. He is followed by Hasdrubal, who commandeers richer lands in the region and founds his capital at Nova Carthago (Cartagena, Murcia). The Carthaginians improve agricultural techniques in the Guadalquivir Valley, which they transform into an important grain-producing area. Carthaginian fishing boats ply the Andalusian coast and set up a flourishing salting industry.

218–201 — Second Punic War. Rome is victorious once more and the Carthaginians are forced to relinquish their Spanish territory.

Roman domination

197 — The Romans conquer Cádiz, the last Carthaginian stronghold in Spain.

83–45 — Hispania is the stage for the civil war between Sertorius and Sulla and for the Pompeyan wars, which are brought to an end by Caesar's victory in Munda (Montilla) in 45 BC.

40 — Caius Octavius **Augustus** is declared Roman Emperor. This heralds the integration of Hispania into the Roman sphere.

Romanisation

With the rise of Julius Caesar to power, Rome begins to establish a policy of determined colonisation, which involves the founding and regeneration of cities. Augustus divides the peninsula into three large provinces: Tarraconensis, Lusitania and Baetica (Andalucía). As a result of its greater degree of Romanisation, the latter comes to depend on the Senate even though the other provinces remain under the control of the Emperor. Perhaps in order to compensate for the bloodshed suffered in prior years, as well as to house veterans of the civil wars, many cities in Baetica receive special treatment, including Corduba (the capital), Gadir, Hispalis (Sevilla), and Itálica.

The region quickly adopts Roman habits and customs: Roman soldiers are granted land, become farmers and marry Iberian women. In order to facilitate the movement of troops and trade to the cities (metals, wine, oil and salted products) a number of roads are built; one of these is the Via Augusta, which runs parallel to the Mediterranean coast and crosses Baetica from east to west. Andalucía enjoys a period of peace spanning several centuries.

AD

14–37 — During the rule of Tiberius a number of Hispanic patricians obtain Roman citizenship and move to Rome. Inhabitants of Baetica who later became famous were among them, such as the philosopher Seneca, born in Córdoba in 4 BC, and his nephew Lucan (b. 39). On the orders of Nero, both men committed suicide in the imperial city in 65.

74 — Vespasian grants the right of citizenship to Hispanics in recognition of the part played by the peninsula during the crisis which followed Nero's assassination.

98–117 — Rule of Marcus Ulpius **Trajan**, born in Itálica in 53, the first Emperor to be neither Roman nor Italian.

The pantry of Europe

During their occupation of Hispania, the Romans exploited the mines of the Sierra Morena and Riotinto (Huelva), and the marble quarries at Macael (Almería), and encouraged the development of agriculture in Baetica.

Wines from Cádiz were exported to various parts of the Empire (especially to Italy and the south of France), olive oil was sold in the markets of Rome, Gaul, Germania and Britain, and there was growth in the raising of livestock in the north of Huelva and on the mud flats of the Guadalquivir. In addition, the fish-salting industry in Hispalis and Córdoba experienced great development as a result of the many marine species found along the Andalusian coast.

Despite its wealth, Baetica, along with the rest of the peninsula, tended to export the majority of its products and resources.

Roman mosaic, Casa del Planetario, Itálica

H. Champollion/MICHELIN

117–38 — Rule of **Hadrian**, also originally from Itálica. Baetica and the rest of Hispania reach their zenith.

3C — The arrival of Christianity, probably from North Africa. Rome moves its commercial axis to the East and the slow decline of Hispania begins.

300–14 — Council of the Hispanic bishops in Elvira (Granada).

395 — Death of **Theodosius**, the last great Roman Emperor, probably born in Itálica.

Visigothic domination

411–25 — The Vandals and Alans occupy Andalucía for a short period until the Visigoths, allied with Rome, and led by Athaulf, succeed in expelling them to North Africa.

441 — The Swabian king Rekhila conquers Sevilla.

484–507 — The Visigothic occupation of Andalucía is consolidated during the reign of **Alaric II**.

522 — The Byzantine Emperor **Justinian** establishes a Byzantine province in the southeast of the peninsula, which is later reconquered by the Visigoths.

568–86 — During the reign of Leovigild, Andalucía supports the revolt of **Hermenigild** against his father.

589 — Third Council of Toledo and the conversion of the Goths to Catholicism.

615 — **Sisebut** implements the first official attempt at eradicating Judaism from the Iberian Peninsula.

7C — During this period, under the influence of **St Leander** (d. 600) and **St Isidore** (d. 636), who dedicates his *Etymologies* to King Sisebut, Baetica is the only sizeable cultural region in Latin Christendom. Syrian and Greek merchants trade with the south of the peninsula. Jews begin to settle in Córdoba, Sevilla and Málaga. Roman Law is abandoned and the patricians are replaced by bishops and judges.

710 — Death of **King Witiza**. Faced with the claims to the throne of **Roderick**, Duke of Baetica, Witiza's followers turn abroad for assistance.

ATLANTIC OCEAN

Santiago de Compostela ○
Oviedo ○
Tolosa ○
Léon ○
Río
Pamplona ○
Oporto ○
Río   Duero
Ebro
(1118) Zaragoza ●
Barcelona ○
Madrid ●
Menorca (1286)
Río   Tajo
Lisboa ○   (1230) Trujillo (1232)
Mérida
Valencia (1238) ●
Ibiza (1235)
Mallorca (1229)
(1230) Badajoz ●   Guadiana
(1227) Baeza (1234) Ubeda
(1236) Córdoba
Sevilla (1248) ●   Guadalquivir
(1266) Murcia ●   Alicante (1304)
(1262) Niebla ●   (1246) Jaén ●   (1489) Baza
Cartagena (1243) ●
(1485) Ronda ●   Granada (1492)   Guadix (1489)
SEA
(1262) Cádiz ●   Almería (1489) ●
(1344) Algeciras   Málaga (1487)   MEDITERRANEAN
Gibraltar (1462)

Emirate of Córdoba (borders at the end of the Emirate in 929)
Almohad empire in 1212
Nasrid kingdom (Granada)
(1230)   Date of reconquest
Current borders of Andalucia

Muslim Andalucía or al-Andalus (8C–15C)

At the beginning of the 8C the Umayyad Caliphate from Damascus conquers the Berber lands of North Africa. This Caliphate had outgrown the lands of the Arabian Peninsula and the concept of 'holy war' enabled it to divert its aggression from Berber chiefs and towards an external enemy. The dominant tribes adhere to the Islamic faith and join together with the powerful Muslim forces.

711 — An army of 7 000 men under the command of the Berber **Tarik-ibn-Zeyad**, the governor of Tangiers, crosses the Straits and defeats King Roderick near the River Guadalete, or the La Janda lagoons.
They march north to conquer Toledo, the capital of the Visigothic kingdom, marking the beginning of Muslim domination in Spain.

712 — 18 000 soldiers land in Andalucía led by the governor Musa, Tariq's superior.
Damascus increases in size as a result of the Arab conquests. The Caliphs respect the local governments set up in the conquered territories. In 719 troops of the Caliphate attempt to conquer the south of France but are repulsed in Poitiers by Charles Martel. The Arabs settle in the Guadalquivir Valley and leave the Berbers the less productive lands of Castilla, León and Galicia.

740–50 — Confrontations between the various ethnic groups of Islamic faith occupying the peninsula.
In Arabia the Abbasid dynasty murders the Umayyads and seizes power from them.

Detail of the east door of the Mezquita, Córdoba

H. Belmenouar/MICHELIN

The Emirate of Córdoba (756–929)

The al-Andalus kingdom is created, eventually embracing almost the entire Iberian Peninsula. Although theoretically subject to the authority of the new Abbasid capital of Baghdad, the Andalusian Emirs are practically independent.

755 — Abd ar-Rahman, the only remaining member of the Umayyad family, lands in southern Spain and in a short period succeeds in uniting all Muslims. A year later he settles in Córdoba and proclaims himself emir ('prince'). **Abd ar-Rahman I** lays the foundation of the kingdom of al-Andalus.

784 — Construction of the Mezquita in Córdoba begins.

788–929 — On the death of Abd ar-Rahman I, the seemingly resolved tensions explode and conflict breaks out between ethnic groups (Arabs, Berbers, Jews and Christians converted to Islam. The Emirate is weakened and the Christian kingdoms of the north strike a number of major blows against the army of al-Andalus.

The Caliphate of Córdoba (929–1031)

The new Caliphate, which had finally broken all ties with Baghdad, becomes the most powerful kingdom in the West and its court the most cultured and refined. Spain regains its commercial impetus in the Mediterranean, which had practically been paralysed during Visigothic domination.

Muslims and Christians mount raids on each other's territory throughout the peninsula and a network of castles and watchtowers is built to keep an eye on the enemy.

San Tiago the Moorslayer

Tradition has it that St. James the Apostle was decapitated on Herod's orders in Palestine after seven years of preaching in Spain. Centuries later, in 834, the tomb of St James (San Tiago) was found in the diocese of Iria (Galicia). He was soon adopted as the patron saint of the troops of the Christian Reconquest and earned the sobriquet of Moorslayer (Matamoros) after he appeared on a white horse at the Battle of Clavijo (AD 844) to secure the Christian victory.

Some say this battle never took place. Nevertheless, "Santiago and strike for Spain" became the Christian battle cry.

929 — Beginning of the rule of **Abd ar-Rahman III** (912–61) who declares himself Caliph and Commander of the Believers, brings peace to his kingdom and reinforces the frontier provinces of Toledo, Badajoz and Zaragoza.

936 — Construction of the city of Medina Azahara begins.

978 — General **Almanzor** seizes power and establishes himself as Prime Minister. The Caliph becomes a figurehead.

1002 — The death of Almanzor in Calatañazor. The first skirmishes in a civil war destabilise the Caliphate.

1031 — End of the Umayyad dynasty. Rebellion of the Córdoban nobility and the destruction of Medina Azahara. The provinces and cities exert their independence and a number of autonomous kingdoms are created.

First Taifa kingdoms and Almoravid supremacy (1009–1110)

The taifa (group or faction in Arabic) kingdoms which appeared at the beginning of the 11C organise according to ethnic criteria. Berbers control the coast from the River Guadalquivir to Granada and the Arabs hold power in Córdoba and Sevilla.

At first the taifa kingdoms make alliances with their neighbours, although some also enter into pacts with the Christians where necessary, even to the extent of paying tribute in order to remain on their own land.

The Christian monarchs exploit their enemies' weaknesses and succeed in conquering a number of large towns.

1042 — Construction of the Alcázar begins in Sevilla.

1064 — Work begins on the Alcazaba in Málaga.

1085 — **Alfonso VI** of Castilla and León conquers Toledo. Lengthy Christian campaigns are waged against Sevilla and Badajoz.

Al-Mutamid, king of Sevilla, feels threatened and calls upon the Almoravids of North Africa for assistance.

Yusuf Ibn Tashunin responds to the plea, crosses the Straits of Gibraltar and in a short time manages to assume control of all the taifa kingdoms.

1118 — The expeditions of **Alfonso I** (El Batallador) in Andalucía expose the weakness of the Almoravids at a time when the Almohad movement is

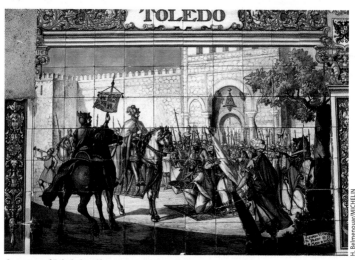

Conquest of Toledo by Alfonso VI on 25 May 1085

beginning to gain ground in Morocco.

Second Taifa kingdoms (1144–70) and Almohad supremacy

For a short period of time the taifa kingdoms reappear, taking advantage of the decline of the Almoravids, but they fall once again, this time as a result of the Almohad invasion led by Abd al-Mumin (the Miramamolin of Christian chronicles).

1147 — Almohad troops occupy Marrakech, Tarifa and Algeciras. Overcoming resistance by Christians and some Moorish kings in the eastern provinces, the Almohads manage to take control of southern Spain.

1163 — Sevilla becomes the capital of al-Andalus.

1184 — Work starts on the Great Mosque (Mezquita Mayor) in Sevilla, whose minaret is later known as the Giralda.

Almoravids and Almohads

The **Almoravid** religious movement developed at the beginning of the 11C when a Berber chieftain in Mauritania founded a monastery to prepare soldiers for holy war against the infidels.

This institution was the origin of an empire which extended along the Atlantic and North African coasts. After founding the city of Marrakech (1070), which they subsequently turned into their capital, the Almoravids occupied Fez and extended their power across the whole of what is now Morocco.

The **Almohad** empire was founded by Abd al-Mumin (1130–63), the follower of a Berber religious leader who instituted far-reaching legal and religious reforms based on the strict observance of the Qu'oran (Koran). By the middle of the 12C the Almohad dominions stretched from the Atlantic coast to Libya and from the River Tagus to the Sahara.

1195 — The Battle of Alarcos (Ciudad Real), in which Al-Mansur is victorious over the Castilian king Alfonso VIII, is the last great triumph of the Almohad army. The decline of the Muslim invaders is to follow.

1212 — **Battle of Las Navas de Tolosa**. The armies of Castilla, Aragón and Navarra inflict a decisive defeat on the Almohads.

The Nasrid kingdom (1232–1492)

During the last phase of declining Almohad power, Mohammed I, of the Banu Nasr or Nasrid dynasty, succeeds in uniting the territories of Granada, Málaga and Almería to create a kingdom that is to last for two and a half centuries, protected by sea and mountains.

In order to secure power, he willingly acts as vassal of the Castilian kings and even joins them in the conquest of Sevilla. However, he subsequently takes advantage of the expulsion of the Moors from Christian lands to build up a highly populated and productive kingdom.

The reigns of the 23 Nasrid kings were often beset with interminable internal strife, and the kingdom fell amid violent disputes between the Cegri and Abencerraje families.

1237 — Work starts on the Alcazaba, the oldest part of the Alhambra palace.

1248 — The **conquest of Sevilla** by Christian troops establishes a frontier which remains unchanged until the 15C.

1313 — Construction of the Generalife begins.

1410 — Don Fernando, the ruling Castilian prince, takes Antequera.

1462 — **Enrique IV** conquers Gibraltar and Archidona. The Nasrids appeal in vain for assistance from Muslim lands.

1464–82 — Reign of **Muley Hacén** (Abu I-Hasan in Arabic), who provokes the animosity of his people by introducing high taxes.

1482–92 — **Boabdil**, son of Muley Hacén, deposes his father and accedes to the throne. He decides to attack Lucena but is taken prisoner by the Catholic Monarchs, who release him in exchange for his continuing opposition to his father.

Muley Hacén dies and is succeeded by his brother, El Zagal.

The Nasrids suffer a series of defeats.

1492 — Boabdil surrenders and retires to the Alpujarras estate placed at his disposal by the victors. Shortly afterwards he moves to the Maghreb and settles in Fez.

The Reconquest (12C–15C)

The break-up of the Caliphate and the proclamation of the Kingdom of Taifas weakens Moorish power.

Muslim troops from the various kingdoms concentrate their efforts on fighting over territory rather than holding back the Christian advance.

1158–1214 — Reign of **Alfonso VIII**. Beginning of the Christian campaigns in Andalucía. Castilla seizes the Sierra Morena. The Almohads are defeated at Las Navas de Tolosa.

1217–52 — **Fernando III the Saint**, King of Castilla, takes a decisive step towards the reconquest of Andalucía by first seizing eastern Andalucía, culminating in his entry into Córdoba in 1236, and then western Andalucía (including Sevilla in 1248).

1252–84 — Fernando III's son, Alfonso X the Wise, conquers the kingdom of Niebla (Huelva), consolidates the Castilian dominions in Lower Andalucía, suppresses revolts in Cádiz and Jerez and expels large numbers of Muslims.

1284–1469 — The Reconquest advances slowly and is halted from the middle of the 14C to the beginning of the 15C. The 15C sees Christian victories during the reigns of Juan II and Enrique IV.

1469 — The marriage of **Isabel of Castilla** to **Fernando of Aragón**, to whom the Valencian pope Alexander VI grants the title of the Catholic Monarchs in 1496. Beginning of the unification of the Christian kingdoms.

1481 — The Inquisition holds the first auto-da-fé in Sevilla.

1482–92 — The Catholic Monarchs begin their major offensive against the Nasrid kingdom of Granada. Muslim cities fall to the Christians one after the other, Ronda in 1485, followed by Málaga (1487), Baza (1489), Almería and Guadix (1489).

2 January 1492 — **Boabdil** hands over the keys of the city of Granada to the **Catholic Monarchs**. The victorious Christian monarchs agree to respect the religion, laws and customs of those Muslims who wish to remain.

Consequences of the Reconquest

In the 13C the repopulation of Andalucía took place in two stages: the first during the reign of Fernando III and the second during that of Alfonso X; those Moors who resisted were forced to emigrate. It is thought that between 1240 and 1270 more than 300 000 Muslims fled their homes in order to settle, almost exclusively, in Granada. Immediately after the revolt of 1262 and the resulting expulsion of Muslims, the workforce was substantially reduced and the region saw an increase in the development of huge estates (latifundios).

The reconquest of the kingdom of Granada had very similar consequences. However, on this occasion the majority of inhabitants remained in their towns and villages as a result of the agreement signed by the Catholic Monarchs promising to respect their religion, laws and customs. The breaking of this promise by the Christians provoked two rebellions in the Alpujarras mountains, which were violently put down.

In 1570 the Moors were forced to disperse throughout Castilla. The final expulsion was ordered in 1609.

The Golden Age of Andalucía

Trade with **America** brought wealth to Sevilla and the surrounding region, including Córdoba and Málaga. Sevilla, which benefited from the monopoly, was transformed into a major Spanish city and a paradise for powerful merchants, adventurers and those on the margins of society. The situation in the rest of Andalucía was different. The arrival of new products from the Indies (cochineal, indigo) had an effect on the region's traditional textile industry, while Granada's silk industry, which produced satin, velvet and damask, suffered immeasurably from the austere clothing policy imposed on the Spanish

Empire by the Habsburgs. However, Córdoba began to specialise in the production of harnesses and cordovans made from American leather, while mercury from the mines of Almadén, used in the production of silver amalgams, became indispensable for exploiting the silver of Mexico and Peru. On the other hand, continuous increases in taxes and the relentless demand for agricultural produce helped to concentrate land in the hands of the most powerful.

1492 — **Christopher Columbus** sets sail from the port of Palos de la Frontera (Huelva) on 3 August. On 12 October he arrives at Guanahani Island (Bahamas).
Expulsion of the Jews who have not converted to Christianity. More than 150 000 people are forced to leave Sefarad (Spain). The majority settle in Mediterranean countries, where they form Sephardic communities in which some of the inhabitants continue to speak the Spanish of that period (ladino).
1499–1501 — **First Alpujarras rebellion**. The intransigence of

Christopher Columbus discovering America, 1492 (1590) by Theodor de Bry

Cardinal Cisneros provokes an uprising by Muslims from the Albaicín in Granada. It soon spreads to the Alpujarras region, the Sierra de los Filabres and the Serranía de Ronda.

1502 — Publication of a decree forcing the Muslim rebels to convert to Christianity or leave the country. The majority opt for baptism. Moors who convert become known as **Moriscos**.

1503 — The Casa de Contratación, which monopolises the colonial market, is founded in Sevilla.

1516 — **Carlos I**, later to become Emperor under the name Carlos V, inherits the Spanish throne on the death of his grandfather Fernando the Catholic.

1530 — Construction of Carlos V's palace begins in the Alhambra.

1556 — Carlos V abdicates in favour of his son **Felipe II**.

1568–71 — **Second Alpujarras rebellion**. Afraid that the Moors would ally themselves with the Turks and Berbers, Felipe II outlaws the use of Arabic and the observance of the Islamic religion. Revolts erupt throughout the region. The Moors from Granada disperse throughout Spain.

1599 — The painter **Diego Velázquez** is born in Sevilla, where he will work until 1622.

The crises of the 17C–18C

The first half of the 17C witnessed the beginning of Andalucía's decline. One of the causes was the drop in population, decimated by four major plagues (in 1649 the population of Sevilla was reduced by half) and by the final expulsion of the *moriscos*, whose labour was of fundamental importance to agriculture. In the next few years the situation in the Andalusian countryside continued to decline, with most of the land falling into the hands of large landowners.

More than 80 per cent of agricultural workers were day labourers and only seven per cent of land belonged to those who worked it. Gradually the wealthy created a powerful rural oligarchy closely connected to the municipal administration which completely controlled the life of the people. Industry in Sevilla, closely bound to maritime trade, collapsed after the silting up of the Guadalquivir at Sanlúcar, preventing large ships from navigating upstream.

1610 — **Decree of expulsion** of the morisco population.

1621 — **Felipe IV** ascends to the throne.

1641 — Riots in the region's main towns and cities are the result of the economic crisis.

1680 — Cádiz becomes an Atlantic trading port, taking over the role previously held by Sevilla.

1700 — **Carlos II**, the last monarch of the House of Austria, dies in Madrid.

The Spanish Inquisition

The Court of the Inquisition was set up in 1468 in order to punish converted Jews who continued to practice their religion in secret; although soon it was used to suppress any kind of moral or heretic deviation. Its extensive and complex organisation was made up of a council of the Supreme Inquisition and local, fiscal and domestic inquisitors. All methods were considered suitable for extracting a confession from the accused; however, once condemned, the offender was handed over to the secular branch of the organisation which carried out the sentence. During the four centuries of the Inquisition (it was abolished by the Cádiz courts in 1813) this highly effective tool of suppression was used by both the Church and the State, especially in the period up to the 18C.

1702 — Beginning of the **War of the Spanish Succession** between Felipe V and Carlos of Habsburg. In the course of the struggle, the British, who supported the Archduke Carlos, take **Gibraltar**. The Treaty of Utrecht (1713) ratifies English control of the Rock of Gibraltar.

1767 — **Carlos III** begins the repopulation of the Sierra Morena.

1788 — The colonial monopoly of Cádiz is abolished.

The social conflicts of the 19C

At the beginning of the century there was little industrial development in Andalucía. The mining of natural resources began towards the middle of the century, although in 1868 the mining industry was taken over by foreign monopolies, in particular the British.

At the same time, the shipbuilding industry experienced significant growth in Cádiz, agricultural produce began to be sold commercially and large sections of the railway network were built.

Continued trade with the colonies, which was to last until 1898, also enabled exchanges with a number of European countries. As a result of these contacts, groups of middle-class liberals began to develop in major towns and cities.

1808 — The French army enters Spain. Beginning of the **War of Independence** (Peninsular War). On 19 July General Dupont is defeated at **Bailén**, in the province of Jaén, by Spanish troops under the command of General Castaños.

1812 — During the French invasion the **Cortes de Cádiz** (Cádiz Parliament) is convened and the liberal Constitution of Cádiz is drawn up.

1814 — End of the War of Independence.

1820 — **Rafael del Riego** leads a liberal revolt in Andalucía and forces King Fernando VII to reinstate the 1812 constitution.

1835–37 — Minister Mendizábal orders the disentailment (*desamortización*) of the property of the Church and town councils.

1840 — Andalusian peasants, the victims of liberalism and disentailment, organise themselves in order to improve their living conditions.

1863 — Pérez del Álamo, a veterinary surgeon, starts a major Republican uprising which spreads to Málaga, Granada, Jaén and Almería.

1873 — Proclamation of the **First Republic**. Tentative efforts at land redistribution.

1875 — **Restoration** of the monarchy (Alfonso XII). Andalusian anarchism develops into terrorism. Labour strife and strikes increase.

The 20C

1900–31 — Strikes and social struggles continue unabated, led by the trade unions, particularly the CNT and FAI.

1931 — Proclamation of the **Second Republic** and minor attempts at agrarian reform, which do not satisfy Andalusian farm workers who are beset by hunger and unemployment.

January 1933 — The **Casas Viejas** incident in Cádiz. The revolutionary general strike, which started in Cádiz, comes to a tragic end when the Civil Guard and riot police set fire to the house in which the anarchist leaders had taken refuge.

This brings about the Socialists' defeat in the elections of the same year.

1936–39 — In the early days of the **Civil War**, most of Andalucía falls into the hands of military garrisons based in the region's cities (Cádiz, Granada, Córdoba and Sevilla), while the

AVE high-speed train, Santa Justa station, Sevilla

east of the region remains loyal to the Republic.

1960 — This decade sees an increase in **emigration** to the more industrialised regions of Spain (Basque Country and Catalunya) and to a number of European countries (West Germany, France and Switzerland).

1975 — Death of Francisco Franco. **Juan Carlos I** is declared king.

1977 — The Spanish Socialist Workers Party (PSOE) wins the elections in Andalucía.

1978 — The government of Adolfo Suárez approves the pre-autonomous status of the region and the Junta de Andalucía is established.

1980 — Andalusian autonomy is approved by referendum.

Cleaning up the Costas

Under the government of Zapatero, relations between the central government and Andalucía improved, no doubt helped by the fact that both tiers of government are of the same political party!

After decades of dodgy dealings on the Costas, particularly the Costa del Sol, where millions of euros had been flowing into a black economy, a crackdown on illegal construction and its associated crime and corruption was implemented.

1982 — The **Statute of Autonomy of Andalucía** comes into force.

First elections for the Andalusian Parliament. **Rafael Escuredo** becomes the first President of the Junta de Andalucía.

1984 — Presidency of Juan Rodríguez de la Borbolla.

1986 — Spain joins the European Union. Andalucía enjoys great benefits in infrastructure improvements and EU subsidies for agriculture.

1990 — Presidency of Manuel Chaves.

1992 — Universal Exposition (Expo) at Sevilla. Inauguration of the Madrid-Sevilla high-speed train (AVE).

1999 — World Track and Field Championships are held in Sevilla.

2002 — World Equestrian Championships are held in Jérez de la Frontera.

2004 — The PSOE (Spanish Socialist Workers' Party) led by José Luís Rodríguez Zapatero sweep into national office.

2005 — Mediterranean Games are held in Almería.

2006 — Andalucía experiences record high temperatures and tourist arrivals.

2008 — An end to E.U. subsidies for tobacco farmers means that 1 000 families on the Granada Vega can no longer make a living from the crop.

al-Andalus

For almost eight centuries, from 711 to 1492, Muslim Andalucía or al-Andalus was the backdrop for the cohabitation of two completely contrasting religious, architectural and cultural worlds: Islam and Christianity. The imprint left by those Muslims who inhabited this southern tip of Spain is immense.

THE POPULATION

The inhabitants of al-Andalus were of different origins and therefore had different physical characteristics. As the years passed the distinction between natives and foreigners lessened as the newcomers imposed their structures on the conquered territories. The natives were Hispano-Roman Visigoths, both Christian and Jewish, of Latin culture and organised according to a feudal system. The foreigners were Arabs and Berbers, of Muslim faith and Arab culture.

The process of "Islamisation" and "Arabisation" imposed by those in authority gave rise to a relatively uniform Moorish society, which was both Arabic and Muslim. Initially this society comprised two main social groups: the upper *(jassa)* and lower *(amma)* classes. These groups differed greatly, even in legal matters; a member of the nobility was not punished in the same way as a member of the lower class. A middle class, which continued to increase in size, came into existence around the 11C.

R. Corbel/MICHELIN

The poor *(miskin)* survived by taking on occasional work as labourers on farms and during harvests.

The clients or *maulas* were free servants who were bound to a master, from whom they could take their name. The largest number of slaves belonged to the siqlabi group *(esclavos)*, who were purchased on the international market or taken prisoner in times of war; these people usually worked for the most important nobles. Negro slaves *(abid)*, who worked mainly in the army, originated from the African slave market.

ORIGINS

Arabs

The Arabs arrived on the peninsula in two main waves – the first in the 8C and the second during the Almohad period in the 12C – and always occupied the most powerful positions. Their aim from the beginning was to Islamise the native population. In the later period, in order to be recognised as an Arab, it was enough to bear a suitable name, which could be acquired relatively easily by those with the right contacts.

Berbers

The first large contingent of this North-African ethnic group crossed the Straits of Gibraltar in the 8C, led by the generals Tarik and Musa.

In the second half of the 10C and beginning of the 11C, many of the same faith followed and eventually found themselves in control of some of the taifa kingdoms, including Granada.

Although many obtained positions of responsibility, the vast majority worked as agricultural labourers, cattle breeders and craftsmen.

Mozarabs

The Christians used this term to describe the arabised Christians who stayed on their land and remained true to their religion after the arrival of the Muslims. The Arabs referred to them as nazarenos *(naara)*.

Muladíes

These were Christians who converted to Islam and, in a number of cases, managed to obtain prominent positions. During the 11C they altered their family tree in order to create an ostensible Arab line that would allow them to retain their privileged position in society.

Jews

Badly treated by the Visigoths, they greeted the arrival of the Muslims with delight. They integrated into Islamic culture perfectly and experienced no major problems until the Almohad invasion.

DAILY LIFE

Towns

The Moors made profound changes to Hispano-Visigothic society which, having experienced a long period of decline, was extremely rural in character. This eminently urban Islamic civilisation founded a number of towns, some of which were quite sizeable; Córdoba, for example, became the largest and one of the most important cities in Europe at the time, both in terms of population and cultural activity. It should be noted that Andalusian cities of the period were equipped with sewerage systems, public lighting and various communal services. In fact, they were blessed with far more amenities than their contemporary Christian counterparts.

The Moorish **medina** (al-Madinat), the old walled centre of the city, followed an organised pattern within the chaos of its narrow streets and alleyways which developed as a result of a lack of building regulations. The districts (harat) were inhabited by craftsmen of the same guild or by families of the same religion (Jews and Mozarabs). The interior of the medina housed markets now known in Spanish as zocos (from the Arabic suq), public baths (hamam), mosques and restaurants, and even included a university or madrassa in larger towns and cities.

More modern districts or **arrabales** (al-Rabad) were situated around the medina and were soon walled. The **cemetery** (maqbara) was located outside the city walls, not far from the roads leading into the city, as was the sa'ría, a large esplanade that was occasionally used as a military training area (musalla), and sometimes as a meeting place for the faithful (musara) to celebrate the end of Ramadan; this often replaced the main mosque in smaller settlements. During the Christian period these esplanades were subsequently used to thresh grain and were known as eras (threshing floors).

The civil and military authorities, as well as the army and their families, lived in the **alcazaba** (al-Qasaba), an independent walled fortress equipped with its own services which was never a part of the main city.

Living quarters

In general only one Moorish family lived in each house. The wealthy could afford to have many wives, but for the rest of the population monogamous marriage was the norm. The surface area of those Moorish houses which have been excavated by archaeologists varies from 50 to 300sq m/538 to 3 229sq ft.

The most obvious feature of Moorish houses is the desire for privacy. Each individual built his house to meet his own needs, but nearly all houses were away from the road in order to avoid noise. Only the Jews built houses grouped together around a yard, with a joint entrance situated at the end of a cul-de-sac. Protected by a very plain façade, with few openings covered with shutters, Moorish houses were organised around a patio which was reached across a hallway. All houses had a privy, a kitchen and one or more rooms, as well as a barn. Water was stored in a cistern or drawn from a well in the patio. Fireplaces were not common as the houses

R. Corbel/MICHELIN

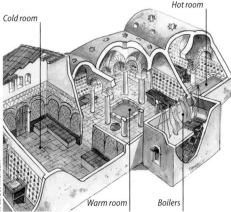

Cold room

Hot room

Warm room   Boilers

R. Corbel/MICHELIN

over 600), to meet the demands of a population with a great penchant for water and a desire to fulfil the Islamic obligations of spiritual and bodily cleanliness. As well as centres of hygiene with specialised staff, baths also acted as a place in which to meet and relax – in the mornings for men, and the afternoons for women and children.

The exteriors of the baths were topped with vaults with small skylights to enable the diffusion of a narrow, but pleasant, light. The interior, covered with azulejos, was divided into four main areas whose temperature progressively increased. In the first, visitors would undress once they had obtained towels and the obligatory wooden shoes. They would then enter a second section, a cold room, housing the latrines, where the bathing process would begin, before continuing to the remaining two rooms, one hot, the other warm. The purpose of the hot room was to open up the pores, while the warm room would have been used for massages. Men would take advantage of their visit to the baths to have their hair cut and beard trimmed, while women would apply a range of beauty products, such as depilatory creams, jasmine-scented perfume, henna to colour the hair and kohl to darken the area around the eyes.

were heated with braziers and the women cooked over fires contained in earthenware pots.

Household furnishings were simple: ceramic and earthenware utensils, chests and carpets, as well as tapestries and cushions which could be made from cotton, wool or silk depending on the financial standing of the family.

The market or souk

Although it also existed in rural areas, the souk or *zoco* was mainly an urban feature. Cities had specialised markets which sold and even manufactured products which came from the countryside. Articles of high quality and value were sold in special markets known as *alcaicerías*. These were also centres of export to much larger areas, such as the Mediterranean, Islamic countries, the Maghreb and other African markets. The market overseer, known as the *almotacén*, controlled commercial activity, which was regulated down to the smallest detail, in order to limit illegal practices and abuse.

Alhóndigas were used to store products and to house merchants. The Spanish word fonda, meaning inn, has evolved from the Arabic word for this particular building (funduq). The Corral del Carbón in Granada is a reconstructed old alhóndiga.

Baths

Every district in the towns and cities of al-Andalus would have had its own hamam (it is said that Córdoba had

The mosque

The mosque *(mezquita)* is a house of prayer to which Muslims over the age of 16 were called to midday prayer on Fridays. Towns would have small, local mosques, as well as larger ones, known as aljamas, as in Córdoba. In line with other parts of the Islamic world, mezquitas in al-Andalus were also used as large civic centres, similar to the Roman forum and the public squares of the Middle Ages. Here, documents of interest to the community could be read and flags would be blessed prior to the departure of a new military expedition. Initially, the mezquita would have also have been

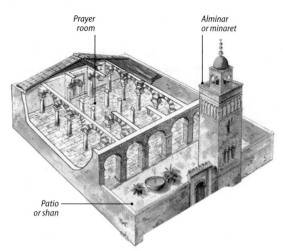

Prayer room

Alminar or minaret

Patio or shan

R. Corbel/MICHELIN

used as a teaching centre and the office of the town's treasury.

The layout of the mezquita was inspired by the house in Medina where the prophet Muhammad lived and imparted his teaching. As a result, in keeping with the design of a traditional house, it consisted of two clearly defined areas: the **covered area** or prayer room *(haram)*, with its floor covered in matting, and the **patio** *(shan)*, with a fountain or pool *(sabil)* for ritual ablutions. Other basic features included:

The **kiblah**, or main wall of the room, facing Mecca. Strangely, mezquitas in al-Andalus faced southwards rather than southeast, which would have been the direction towards Mecca from Andalucía. Some experts believe that this was due to Syrian influence, while others consider that the route to Mecca would first have involved a journey south.

The **mihrab**, an empty niche in the centre of the kiblah to remind the faithful of the place where Mohammed prayed.

The **maqsura**, an area surrounded by latticework screens located in front of the mihrab. It would appear that this area was reserved for the Caliph.

The **mimbar**, a type of wooden pulpit used by the imam to conduct Friday prayers *(jutba)*.

The **alminar** or minaret, the most symbolic feature of Islamic architecture, is a tower attached to one of the walls of the patio, the upper part of which is used by the muezzin to call the faithful to prayer. A typical Andalusian alminar would be crowned with three gilded spheres *(yamur)* of decreasing sizes and a fleur-de-lys.

THE COUNTRYSIDE

The outskirts of large cities were dotted with farms known as *almunias*. The beauty of these luxurious mansions with their own gardens, orchards, pools and fountains was said to rival that of some of the most sumptuous royal palaces. A fine example of this was the almunia of al-Rusafa, to the northeast of Córdoba. Although sovereigns and leading figures in Islamic life owned extensive land farmed by labourers, independent farmers and cattle breeders were also commonplace in al-Andalus. They lived within small communities known as **alquerías** which were generally protected by a castle. These hamlets included houses, outbuildings, farmland and barns. Larger ones were often surrounded by fortifications and had their own common amenities similar to those found in urban areas.

Agriculture

The introduction of sophisticated hydraulic techniques had a significant effect on the Mediterranean ecosystem of Andalucía. Although some of these techniques originated from the Roman period, such as the river water-wheel, it is undeniable that the Moors were superbly skilled at extracting water from below ground and channelling it to extensive areas of farmland. In fact, modern-day Spanish contains a number of agricultural terms which descend directly from Arabic.

In addition to terrace farming, the Moors introduced animal-powered wheels and an irrigation system of Oriental origin consisting of boring holes in the ground until a spring was discovered; the wells were used to control the pressure of the water, which was then channelled to those areas requiring irrigation.

Islamic law controlled the provision of water, which was considered an asset in common. The *zabacequia* would settle disputes and would establish an irrigation timetable which was scrupulously respected. If a farmer failed to make use of his slot, it would be channelled to other land; nobody, however, had the right to pass on water as a gift, sell it or exchange it.

Alongside the region's traditional crops (olives, cereals and vines), the Moors also grew other products imported from the East including rice, pomegranates, cotton and saffron, as well as what were considered to be luxury items, such as spices or mulberry trees to feed silkworms. The fertile, irrigated land *(huertas)* overflowed with high-quality products, many of which had been introduced by the Moors, such as the aubergine, artichoke, chicory and asparagus. Meanwhile, the magnificent gardens traditionally associated with Moorish culture were a feast of colour with violets, roses, honeysuckle and jasmine.

Animal breeding

The Moors were great breeders of animals, which were used for riding, as draft animals, and for the table. As an illustration of their importance, the **Andalusian horse**, whose origins can be traced back to the Moors, is now famous the world over. The leather industry was one of the most flourishing sectors of the region's economy. Documentary evidence has also shown that flocks of sheep were of enormous size during the period of Arab domination. It is also strange to note that although Muslims were prohibited from eating pork, old texts refer to the breeding of pigs and of payment to farmers for them. The main breeding areas were the marshlands of the lower Guadalquivir and the area to the east of Córdoba.

DEFENSIVE ARCHITECTURE

The Moors built numerous military installations both for defence and as bases from which to attack their Christian and fellow Muslim rivals. Many of these constructions were reused after the Reconquest and some are still standing today.

Besides the alcazaba, the most typical defensive buildings were the castles erected along the border with Christian-held territory. As a general rule, they were built with an east-west orientation and comprised two clearly defined sections: the alcázar or **fortress**, organised around a central patio, and a large esplanade in which the barracks for troops would have been located. On the outer limits of the central castle, and separate from it, there would have been a series of smaller fortresses in constant communication with a number of **watchtowers**.

The **walls** were strengthened by the construction of towers, used as garrisons and strategic points from which to harass the enemy, as well as pyramid-shaped merlons. Communication around the walls was via an inner circular path.

The 11C saw the construction of the first **barbicans** – defensive walls positioned in front of the main walls – and the first moats. Later on, during the period of Almohad domination, **turrets**, such as the Torre del Oro in Sevilla, began to appear. These defensive constructions were independent of the main fortified area, but connected to it via a wall with a narrow path **(coracha)**.

In the early days of Moorish rule, the gateways along the walls were strengthened using metal plates and leather. In the 11C, however, these gateways began to be built in the towers themselves, while later refinements saw the introduction of **machicolations** and platforms consisting of small raised structures erected on the external façade of the defensive wall.

Obviously, construction techniques evolved over the centuries. During the Caliphate of Córdoba, for example, ashlar stone was predominantly used, to be subsequently replaced by the more resistant clay mortar, a mixture of sand, lime and gravel made into moulds and then covered with brightly coloured plaster to physically dazzle the enemy.

A LAND OF SCHOLARS, POETS AND PHILOSOPHERS

For eight centuries al-Andalus was an important centre of artistic and scientific culture. While sovereigns elsewhere on the Iberian Peninsula were living in sombre castles, in which they were surrounded by men interested in nothing but warfare, Moorish emirs, caliphs and monarchs were inhabiting luxurious palaces and encouraging cultural development. Scientists, philosophers, poets and artists acted as the best possible ambassadors for the power and refinement of their Moorish rulers. Nor should it be forgotten that those at the vanguard of Andalusian culture were not isolated figures, for they carried out their work alongside a team of assist-

R. Corbel/MICHELIN

ants within the Court itself. This research would have taken place either in large libraries, such as the one created by Al-Hakam II, with over 300 000 volumes, or in the madrassas (religious academies) created for this very purpose.

From the 11C onwards, Arabic was the most widely used language across the entire peninsula, and although Christians and Jews preserved their own languages, they used Arabic in daily life and in their artistic and scientific work. Another feature of Moorish culture was the constant interchange with other areas, from the eastern boundaries of Islamic influence – on journeys to and from Mecca – to North Africa, particularly during the Almoravid and Almohad periods.

Much of the credit for the preservation of Muslim knowledge, which was highly valued by the Western world throughout the Renaissance and even beyond, is due to the efforts of Alfonso X. With the cooperation of Mozarabs and Jews alike, this Christian monarch had Arabic manuscripts copied and corrected following his conquests and those of his father, Fernando III.

The sciences

Moorish scientists took an interest in every conceivable aspect of science. Alchemists studied the behaviour of metallic substances and slowly discovered their basic processes; agronomists wrote agricultural papers including detailed information on the rearing of carrier pigeons, which at the time were the fastest and most efficient form of communication; **naturalists** created zoos housing unusual species; while **mathematicians**, such as Avempace, who was also a great astronomer, were noted for their work on trigonometry.

The field of **medicine** reached new heights through the work of specialists who published their scientific findings in encyclopaedia. Through these publications, it is known that they were able to perform somewhat complex surgery and were aware of illnesses such as haemophilia.

As well as the most famous physician of them all, **Averroës**, who was also a great philosopher, mention should also

R. Corbel/MICHELIN

be made of the five generations of the **Avenzoar** family. Medical science was strictly linked with **botany** – another field in which spectacular advances were made. An example of this can be seen in the work of Ibn al-Baytar, from Málaga, the author of a compendium in which he lists 1 400 plant- and mineral-based medicines which were of great importance during the Renaissance.

The extensive knowledge of Moorish scientists resulted in the development of **inventions** revolutionary in their time. These ranged from the construction of astrolabes and quadrants – fundamental to navigation – to refrigeration systems, lighting effects created via bowls of mercury, anaphoric clocks (moved by water) – very useful for fixing the hours of prayer – and even mechanical toys. The Moors also adopted Chinese paper-manufacturing techniques, resulting in the production of paper in Córdoba from the 10C onwards, and were responsible for introducing so-called **Arabic numerals**. It should also be noted that the Spanish words *guarismo* (a number or figure) and *algoritmo* (algorithm) derive from the name of the mathematician al-Khuwarizmi.

Literature

In Arabic literature, poetry was of greater importance than prose. Arab writers improvised; composing their poetry out loud, and on many occasions forced their slaves to learn poems by heart in order to sell them at a higher price.

Religions

Islam – The Umayyad rulers who invaded Spain in the 8C were noted for their tolerance towards other religions; however, this did not prevent them from attempting to Islamise the country's native inhabitants from the very outset, offering them incentives such as exemption from the payment of religious taxes. It would appear that in the 10C, fifty per cent of the region's inhabitants were Muslims, increasing to ninety per cent two centuries later. The al-Andalus kingdom of three religions only really existed during the first four hundred years of Moorish rule, after which non-Muslims were in the minority.

Christianity – Those who opted to retain their own religion were placed into the category of tributaries (dimmí). They had their own hierarchies but were subject to Muslim authority and had to pay a special tax (yizya).
The crisis enveloping Christianity in al-Andalus began with the arrival of the Almoravids. This period saw the initiation of compulsory conversions, emigration to Christian territories, and even deportations to various parts of the Maghreb.

Judaism – In line with Christians, Jews could continue to practise their religion after the arrival of the Moors, provided they paid tribute; as can be seen in the Jewish quarters of Andalucía today, they generally lived in enclaves in the heart of towns and cities. Following the decree implemented by the first Almohad king forcing Jews to convert to Islam or face expulsion, many settled in other Jewish communities across the Maghreb and in Egypt. Those who converted and remained in al-Andalus were forced to wear distinctive clothing or signs such as a yellow cap and a special belt.

Early divans (collections of poems) solely consisted of **qasidas**, classical, mono-rhymed love poems made up of three parts: the evocation of the beloved, the description of a journey, and an elegy of the poem's subject. At the end of the 9C, a poet from Cabra invented the moaxaja, with one part written in classical Arabic, the other in Romance vernacular (jarcha). The romantic couplets which appeared as **jarchas** in Arabic moaxajas are the oldest European lyrical poetry. The **zejel**, apparently invented by **Avempace**, was the other type of poem frequently used in al-Andalus; these were written in the vernacular and were generally narrative.

Al-Mutamid – King of Sevilla during the taifa period, this man was one of the finest Moorish writers, although the poet cited most by critics was the Córdoban **Ibn Zaydun**, lover of Wallada, an Umayyad princess, who herself was also a brilliant poet.

Abd al-Rabbini – In literary prose, during the Caliphal period the most significant written work was *El collar único* (The Single Necklace) by Abd al-Rabbini; he also wrote many epistles.

Ibn Hazm – The best-known writer of the period was the jurist and theologian, to whom we owe *The Dove's Necklace* on poetic diction and psychological truth. This book has been widely translated and in it he narrates amorous adventures set in the court of Córdoba, but always with exemplary, moral zeal.

Ibn Zamrak – The 14C saw the rise to prominence of this poet from al-Andalus; his verses are engraved on the walls of the Alhambra.

Averroës – It is highly probable that Greek philosophy, particularly that inspired by Aristotle, would not have reached us without **Averroës** (Ibn Rusd), the intellectual heir to Avicenna. This great Córdoban (1126–98), who was a magistrate in Sevilla and Córdoba and who even became physician to the court, relied on the texts of Greek thinkers to develop his own philosophy out of the pre-ordained ideas of Islamic religion. This physician, musician, astronomer, mathematician and poet was indisputably the most outstanding figure in Moorish culture.

ART AND CULTURE

Architecture

While the popular architecture of Andalucía is as varied as its landscape, many towns and villages have a number of features in common, such as narrow streets, whitewashed façades, niches with statues of saints or the Virgin Mary, and windows with wrought-iron grilles, as well as balconies, sun porches and drying galleries. Beyond the main door, access to the house is often via a hallway through to the patio; these two parts of the entrance area create an air circulation system which helps to temper the extreme heat of high summer. The kitchen and lounge are normally found on the ground floor; the bedrooms on the first floor.

The attic or *soberao* is used as a storeroom and an area for drying hams and sausages at the very top. Those with both the means and space may have two types of sleeping quarters: bedrooms on the ground floor for the summer and others on the upper floors for the winter months. Roofing varies from one province to the next; flat roofs (used as terraces), particularly in Almería, are as common as those with slopes.

In the countryside of Córdoba and Sevilla, where large estates or *latifundios* are the norm, *cortijos* (homesteads), haciendas and *lagares* (wine and olive estates) dot the landscape, and are now wrongly perceived as the archetypal "*casa andaluza*". These large rural units usually consist of a spacious patio surrounded by stables, storehouses and the accommodation provided for staff and some farm workers, and a smaller patio at the centre of the owner's house.

Up until the 19C, towns and cities were comprised of individual houses. However, emigration from the countryside and smaller towns resulted in the construction of new types of housing. It was from this time that the so-called "neighbourhood corrals" *(corrales de vecindad)* evolved, occasionally created in abandoned convents and monasteries. Today, following substantial

A familiar sight in the Spanish countryside

For the past three decades and more the lofty silhouette of this impressive metal bull has graced the tops of Spanish hillsides, establishing itself as one of the most characteristic features of the country's road network. Originally erected in 1956 as part of an advertising campaign for the Osborne sherry and brandy company, they were on the point of disappearing from the Spanish landscape altogether in 1988, when roadside advertising was banned outside of urban areas. Although the company subsequently

R. Mattes/MICHELIN

removed its name, leaving only the bulls in place, the controversy remained. Legal moves to have the bulls removed sparked a debate that received widespread media coverage, resulting in the signing of petitions and the formation of associations to preserve them. Their defenders were of the opinion that these black bulls had gone beyond their original marketing purpose and had become a decorative feature which was now an integral part of the Spanish landscape and a national symbol. The regional parliament (Junta de Andalucía) was moved to classify the bulls as official historical monuments, thus enabling them to fight another day!

H. Champollion/MICHELIN

Flower-decked patio, Córdoba

renovation, some of these corrals have been converted into expensive seigniorial residences popular with artists and high-earning professionals.

At the lower end of the economic scale, blocks of flats began to be built at the beginning of the 20C.

Andalucía also contains a number of unique types of housing such as caves in Granada, Almería and in particular Guadix; the humble homes of the Doñana National Park, built of wooden frames covered with rushes; the houses of the Alpujarras (Granada and Almería), the direct inheritors of Moorish architecture; the small houses tucked away down alleyways and under the arches of villages in the Axarquía region (Málaga); and the incomparable beauty of the pueblos blancos (white villages) of Cádiz and Málaga.

Architectural Terms

Alcazaba: fortified military settlement.

Alcázar: Moorish royal palace.

Alfiz: rectangular surround to a horseshoe-shaped arch in Muslim architecture.

Alicatado: technique of Persian origin consisting of cutting sheets of ceramic tiles *(azulejos)* in such a way as to form geometric patterns.

Altarpiece: retable. Decorative screen above and behind the altar.

Apse: far end of a church housing the high altar; can be semi-circular, polygonal or horseshoe-shaped.

Arabesque: a Romantic term used to express the ornamental effect of Islamic art.

Archivolt: each of the concentric ornamental mouldings on the outer edge of a splayed arch.

Artesonado: marquetry ceiling in which raised fillets outline honeycomb-like cells in the shape of stars.

Ataurique: stylised plant ornamentation inspired by the acanthus leaf, a feature of Moorish art.

Azulejo: glazed, patterned, ceramic tiles.

Cabecera: east (apsidal) end of a Christian church, housing the chancel.

Caliphal: architectural style developed in Córdoba under the Caliphate (8C–11C) of which the finest example is the Mezquita.

Camarín: small chapel on the first floor behind the altarpiece or retable. It is elaborately decorated and very often contains a lavishly costumed statue of the Virgin Mary.

Capilla Mayor: area of the high altar containing the Retablo Mayor or monumental altarpiece which often rises to the roof.

Churrigueresque: in the style of the Churrigueras, an 18C family of architects. Richly ornate Baroque decoration.

Coro: chancel in Spanish canonical churches often built in the middle of the nave. It contains the stalls (sillería) used by members of religious orders. When placed in a tribune or gallery it is known as the coro alto.

Crucero: transept. The part of a church at right angles to the nave which gives the church the shape of a cross. It consists of the transept crossing and arms.

Cuerda seca: glazed ceramic technique.

Estípite: pilaster in the shape of a truncated inverted pyramid.

Grotesque: typical Renaissance decoration combining vegetation, imaginary figures and animals.

Kiblah: sacred wall of a mosque from which the mihrab is hollowed, facing towards Mecca.

Kufic: Arabic script originating from the city of Kufa, characterised by large angled letters.

Lacerías: geometric decoration formed by intersecting straight lines making star-shaped and polygonal figures. Characteristic of Moorish architecture.

Lantern: an architectural feature in the highest part of a cupola admitting light to the area below.

Madrassa: a Moorish university or religious academy.

Mihrab: richly decorated prayer-niche in the sacred wall (kiblah) in a mosque.

Minaret: tower of the mosque (mezquita), from which the muezzin calls the faithful to prayer.

Mocárabes: decorative motifs of Muslim architecture formed by assembled prisms ending in concave surfaces. They resemble stalactites or pendants and adorn vaults and cornices.

Modillion: a bracket or console used to support a cornice, the springing of an arch, etc.

Mozarabic: the work of Christians living under Arab rule after the Moorish invasion of 711. On being persecuted in the 9C, they sought refuge in Christian areas bringing with them Moorish artistic traditions.

Mudéjar: the work of Muslims living in Christian territory following the Reconquest (13C–14C).

Plateresque: term derived from platero (silversmith), and used to describe the early style of the Renaissance characterised by finely carved decoration.

Predella: the lower part of an altarpiece.

Presbytery: the space in front of the main altar, separated from the nave by steps or a partition.

Sagrario: chapel containing the Holy Sacrament. May sometimes be a separate church.

Sebka: type of brick decoration developed under the Almohads consisting of an apparently endless series of small arches forming a network of diamond shapes.

Stucco: type of moulding mix consisting mainly of plaster, used for coating surfaces. It plays a fundamental role in the wall decoration of Hispano-Muslim architecture.

Trasaltar: back wall of the capilla mayor in front of which sculptures or tombs are often found.

Trascoro: the wall, often carved and decorated, which encloses the coro.

Triforium: arcade above the side aisles which opens onto the central nave of a church.

Tympanum: inner surface of a pediment. This often ornamented space is bounded by the archivolt and the lintel of the doors of churches.

Yesería: plasterwork used in sculptured decoration.

Pre-Muslim Art

Although the Moors embellished Andalucía with its most emblematic monuments, the land they conquered was far from being virgin territory. From the Palaeolithic period onwards civilisations succeeded each other on Andalusian soil, each leaving its indelible mark.

PREHISTORY AND ANTIQUITY

Palaeolithic Era – Of prime importance from the Palaeolithic Era (30 000–9 000 BC) are the **Pileta caves** at Benaoján (Málaga), with their miles of galleries decorated with paintings of animals and symbolic drawings, and the caves at Nerja (Málaga). The Ambrosio cave in Vélez Blanco (Almería), holds an unusual decorative engraved frieze.

Neolithic Era – This era saw the development of more schematic human and animal figures alongside drawings of the sun, idols and various symbols. Drawings in the caves at Tajo de las Figuras (Cádiz), La Graja (Jaén) and Los Letreros (Vélez Blanco, Almería) all date from this period.

The third millennium BC – This time saw the influx of civilisations from the Mediterranean, heralding early **Megalithic culture**, which reached its zenith in the second millennium; the most striking example of this period is at **Los Millares** (Gádor, Almería). This large complex of walls and collective sepulchres shows that its builders not only knew how to work metals, but also had significant knowledge of ceramics, basket-making and weaving. The collective Menga, Viera and El Romeral dolmens at Antequera, those at Castilleja de Guzmán and the 4C–3C BC Dolmen del Soto at Trigueros are the finest Megalithic constructions found anywhere in Spain, in terms both of size and level of development.

1C bronze statue, *Ephebus of Antequera*, Museo Municipal, Antequera

What about the Greeks?

Cádiz and Huelva contain the richest examples of Greek ceramics in Andalucía, despite the fact that neither province was home to Greek settlements of any importance. It is highly probable that many of these were in fact gifts that the Phoenicians bestowed upon the native inhabitants to win their friendship.

Oriental influences

The Phoenicians – Oriental art came to Andalucía via the Phoenicians who, having founded Gades (Cádiz), established outposts on either side of the Straits of Gibraltar in preparation for further advances along the Mediterranean coast. The oldest Phoenician remains discovered are from the settlement at Morro de Mezquitilla (Málaga), dating from the 9C BC. Other Phoenician vestiges have also been unearthed in the provinces of Cádiz, Málaga (the tombs at Trayamar) and Almería (Sexi necropolis).

B. Kaufmann/MICHELIN

The Tartessians

The kingdom of Tartessus (9C–4C BC), aligned with the Phoenicians, produced a variety of objects made from bronze and ceramic (jugs, water pitchers, amphorae), as well as delicate pieces of goldware (diadems, belts, pendants) decorated with distinctive motifs, undoubtedly linked to the worship of various divinities.

The Iberians

The earliest Iberian **sculpture** dates from the 5C BC and shows clear influences from Greek and Phoenician art, with rigid figures represented frontally. These artefacts were generally used to protect the dead, whose remains were cremated and deposited in urns or sarcophagi placed in large stone mausoleums, as can be seen at La Toya (Jaén), Baza (Granada) and Villaricos (Almería). The apogee of local sculptural art was from the 5C–4C BC, during which works with clear Hellenic influences were created, such as the magnificent **Dama de Baza**. Iberian **ceramics** also copied the red glaze used by the Phoenicians and Greek vases. Their varied designs evolved from primitive bands and circumferences to complex drawings of leaves and flowers interspersed with geometric motifs.

Roman art in Spain

In accordance with their custom, the Romans who came to Hispania in the 2C BC immediately introduced the official art from their imperial capital. Although, with the passing of time, many of these works were created entirely on the Iberian peninsula, it is not possible to talk of truly Hispano-Roman art, but of Roman art created in Hispania.

Baetica, the most advanced region on the Iberian peninsula during the Roman period, began to experience significant growth with the development of new settlements along the River Guadalquivir (Betis), planned according to the Roman grid system. Córdoba, the capital, could not match the splendour of **Itálica**, which attained maximum development under emperors Trajan and Hadrian, both of Andalusian extraction. The cities of **Hispalis** (Sevilla), **Carmona** and **Acinipo** (Ronda la Vieja) also contained opulent patrician mansions and large public buildings that used marble from Macael (Almería).

In Roman **sculpture**, representations of emperors (Trajan, Hadrian and Vespasian) and their families were common, as were sculptures of goddesses (Venus in Itálica, for example). The decoration of patrician mansions also imitated that of Rome. **Mosaics** and small bronze figures reproduced the work of slaves brought from Africa (standard-holders, candelabra). Tiny statues of household gods (lares) governed daily activities .

Lastly, the layout and design of **rural villas** would later provide inspiration for popular Andalusian architecture.

HISPANO-VISIGOTHIC ART (6C–8C)

The Visigoths who invaded Spain in the 5C were nomads without an architectural tradition. Consequently, palaeo-Christian forms, which had already absorbed Byzantine and Oriental influence, persisted throughout Roman Baetica until the end of the 6C.

The third Council of State in Toledo (589), which proclaimed the unity of the kingdom, marked the start of new architectural forms which consolidated to acquire undisputed uniformity.

In religious buildings, the classical basilican plan, slightly modified, as in Alcalá de los Gazules, developed into a cruciform shape. Aisles were separated by columns supporting **horseshoe arches**. Vaults were generally semicircular, while aisles often had a wooden framework. Decoration on walls, imposts and capitals showed a marked **Oriental influence** with mostly **geometric motifs** as opposed to vegetal and a few human figures. The exteriors were devoid of buttresses of any kind.

Given that almost every Visigothic temple was later modified, the original plan can now be recognised in just a few buildings, such as in San Pedro de Alcántara (Málaga), El Germo (Córdoba) and Gerena (Sevilla).

The most recognisable feature of Visigothic art is its **gold** and **silverwork**, which reached a level of perfection in the 7C. Craftsmen produced two types of work, namely liturgical items (processional crosses and votive objects such as their famous crowns) and articles of a personal nature (clasps, bracelets, necklaces and pendants). Some pieces now exhibited in museums, such as those from **Torredonjimeno** (Jaén), belong to treasure buried by the Visigoths in the face of the advancing Moors.

Hispano-Muslim Art (8C–15C)

The Moorish invasion, which may initially have appeared a tragedy, was in reality the beginning of a magnificent era of creativity and vitality as the inhabitants of Andalucía came into contact with the aesthetics of Islam.

However, through eight centuries of Moorish occupation, Andalusian art always retained basic artistic characteristics which clearly distinguished it from all other artistic trends of the period.

MOORISH ART

Arches

During the early days of Moorish rule, the **horseshoe arch**, with its Visigothic and Oriental influence and alternating red (brick) and white (plaster with lime) voussoirs, was the main feature of Moorish buildings. The arches had a dual purpose: as an element of support and as decoration, for example as a border for a blind arch. The development of intersecting arches gave rise to the pointed horseshoe-shaped arch, used extensively from the 12C onwards.

As time passed, the **foliated arch**, already in evidence in the Mezquita in Córdoba, evolved into the highly complex **multifoil arch**.

The **alfiz**, the rectangular moulding surrounding the arch, was another recurrent theme of Moorish art, and was to have a major influence on Mudéjar art in subsequent centuries.

Vaults, armatures and artesonado work

Hispano-Moorish vaults took their influence from Oriental Islamic art. Unlike those in Christian art (arris and fan vaults), their ribs do not cross at the centre. Perhaps one of the best examples is the enclosure of the mihrab in Córdoba's Mezquita.

Despite the uniqueness of Andalusian vaults, it is undoubtedly the widely used wooden armature which can be considered the architectural feature which best displays the Moor's technical and aesthetic expertise.

Wooden coverings evolved from simple paired and knuckle armatures to the most sophisticated of artesonado work decorated with stars to form attractive *lacería* ornamentation.

B. Kaufmann/MICHELIN

Arcades, Patio de los Loenes, Alhambra, Granada

Decoration:
materials and motifs

Behind austere outer walls, the interiors of Andalusian palaces were often of extraordinary splendour. Sometimes resplendent facing completely masked humble construction materials.

The refined aesthetic sense of the Hispano-Moors managed to successfully combine techniques as disparate as **azulejos** and **alicatados** (decorative sections of tiling), panels of stone or sculpted plasterwork, mosaics with Oriental influence, wood worked to form latticework, and exquisite *artesonado*, to create surprisingly sumptuous effects. The decorative motifs used can be classified into three main groups:

geometric designs, mainly used in the decoration of glazed ceramic friezes and in the ornamentation of wood (doors, latticework and artesonados), in which the lines are broken up by polygons and stars;

plant motifs, known as **atauriques**, used to decorate sculpted stone or plaster wall panels. Over time, these motifs (palm leaves, grapevines) were styled to create extremely complex designs. A common technique was the stylisation of the tree of life – vegetal decoration arranged around a vertical axis. Mocárabes, decorative motifs resembling stalactites, were used to decorate arches and cupolas;

epigraphs fulfilled the same informative function as images used by other architectural styles, with **Kufic script**, characterised by its large, angled lettering, and **Nesjí script**, with its more free-flowing characters, the most widely used.

Ataurique motifs, Medina Azahara, Córdoba

Applied arts

Andalusian decorative art produced a variety of elaborate objects which can be classified as household or luxury items. The latter were created to satisfy the demand of a more refined ruling class who afforded importance to interior decoration and who took great pleasure in bestowing unique and sumptuous gifts on foreign visitors.

In terms of **ceramics**, the following stand out: the earthenware known as **green and manganese**, the so-called **cuerda seca** ceramics (azulejos) used as wall decoration, and the gilded work known as **reflejo metálico** (lustre work). The latter, production of which began in Córdoba in the 9C, attained its full glory during the Nasrid period in the production centres in and around Málaga.

In addition to Córdoba, where Abd ar-Rahman II founded the Casa del Tiraz or

Other caliphal buildings

During the Caliphal period, other constructions included the minarets of San Juan and Santa Clara (Córdoba), El Salvador (Sevilla) and San José (Granada), in addition to the fortifications in Tarifa and the Pinos Bridge (Granada).

East façade, Mezquita, Córdoba

Royal Silk Factory, Almería specialised in the production of exquisite **fabrics**; during the 14C and 15C, the workshops of Granada also produced impressive silk fabrics entwined with gold thread. Intense colours predominated in these fabrics, which were decorated with inscriptions and architectural motifs.

Nasrid **gold** and **silversmiths** showed a special predilection for ceremonial swords, the hilts and guards of which were decorated with extraordinary combinations of marble, filigree and polychrome enamel.

To complete the full picture of Hispano-Moorish artistry, mention should also be made of the highly delicate marble carvings, which were popular decorative features used by the Caliphate, *taraceas* (wood inlaid with **marble** and woods of varying colours) used to decorate Nasrid furniture, and leatherwork (**cordovans** made from goatskin and embossed sheepskin **guadamecies**).

Many of these items were to remain in use by the Christians, who praised their quality and value. In fact, the sculpted marble boxes and chests in which Muslim women kept their jewels and perfume were subsequently used to preserve the relics of saints.

Córdoban caliphate (8C–10C)

The Mezquita in Córdoba and the Medina Azahara palace, the two great

Caliphal capital, Medina Azahara, Córdoba

monuments from this period, contain all the features associated with early Hispano-Moorish art, which developed during the three centuries in which Córdoba was the capital of al-Andalus.

In accordance with their custom of assimilating the culture of those they conquered, the Moors used techniques and features from both Visigothic and Roman art, skilfully combined with the traditions of the Arabian Peninsula.

The major imports from Caliphal art were the **foliated arch** and the **alfiz**, the rectangular surround of a horseshoe arch. In decoration, early geometric motifs containing squares and diamonds gradually evolved into designs encompassing floral motifs (vine leaves, bunches of grapes, acanthus leaves, palm trees and rosettes) inspired by the Umayyads; these were later replaced by heart-shaped floral drawings which took their inspiration from the Abbasids.

The Caliphate's economic prosperity was reflected in the materials used (ashlar stone and worked marble) and the opulence of the metallic lustre of Byzantine mosaics created by foreign craftsmen.

Taifa period (11C)

Despite the political dispersion which was a feature of the taifa (faction) kingdoms, Andalusian art of the period showed great unity, given that Andalucía had become isolated from the rest of Islam. Artists from the erstwhile Caliphate of Córdoba emigrated to the

10C bronze stag (cervatillo) from Medina Azahara, Museo Arqueológico Provincial, Córdoba

courts of various taifas where they continued the Córdoban tradition.

Economic decline resulted in the abandoning of noble materials such as ashlar stone on walls, and columns and pillars made from marble in favour of **brick**, **plaster** and **mortar**. To compensate for this, **decorative motifs** attained unexpected heights (epigraphic, geometric and plant designs) and combinations of **arches** (**foliated**, **mixtilinear**, semicircular, pointed, intercrossing, etc.) came into use to form arabesque features.

During this period, religious architecture was less important than both civil (numerous **public baths** such as the so-called Bañuelo de Granada) and military architecture (the alcazabas in Málaga, Granada and Almería).

Almoravid period (12C)

Following the arrival of the Almoravids, Andalusian art spread throughout the Maghreb. Marrakech and Sevilla developed into the capitals of a new kingdom on either side of the Straits of Gibraltar, gradually introducing new trends resulting from mutual influence between the peoples of the two continents.

Arches began to develop ever more complicated styles, as did **cupolas**, some of which contained openwork; others which were decorated with mocárabe motifs. This era heralded the appearance of geometric decoration in the form of networks of **sebka** or diamond-shaped designs; combinations of epigraphic and lacería motifs also increased in complexity.

Almost all buildings dating from this period have either disappeared or been swallowed up beneath additions introduced by the Almohads, although experts recognise features of the Almoravid style in the mihrab in one of

Torre del Oro, Sevilla

H. Belmenouar/MICHELIN

the mezquitas in Almería (the present-day Iglesia de San Juan).

Almohad period (13C)

The basic religious principles of the Almohads, which were based on **purity** and **austerity**, were reflected in the simplicity and monumental nature of their buildings, the majority of which were defensive in character, such as the Alcázar and the Torre del Oro in Sevilla. This type of fortified construction, with its delimiting gateways and defensive towers *(albarranas)* separated from the fortified buildings, would later be adopted by the Christians as a model for their own castles.

The new arrivals used the same construction materials as their predecessors, namely brick, mortar, plaster and wood, but opted for more sober decoration, with large empty spaces and geometric adornments replacing plant motifs. The traditional horseshoe arch was practically abandoned, except in exceptional circumstances, and replaced by **pointed horseshoe** and foiled arches.

Without doubt, the most representative monument from this period is the Giralda in Sevilla which, in its day, was the minaret for the main mezquita in the capital of the Almohad kingdom.

Inscriptions

Buildings in the kingdom of Granada contained three types of inscriptions: those of an informative nature relating to the origin of the building; religious inscriptions, taken from the Koran; and literary and poetic inscriptions.

The use of water in the architecture of al-Andalus

Throughout the kingdom of al-Andalus, that scarce commodity – water – played a fundamental role in architecture. Water had a triple function: practical, religious and aesthetic. Practical, because of its necessity for life (the irrigation of fields and the supply of drinking and bath water); religious, because the Koran states that a series of ablutions must be carried out prior to prayer; and aesthetic, because water stored in pools and basins reflected the elegant decoration of the walls and ceilings, while water running through channels, fountains and gutters produced a relaxing murmur and cooled the air. Water also enabled the creation of gardens that were so well integrated into the surrounding architecture that it is difficult to know where nature ends and where the works created by man begin.

Nasrid period (13C–15C)

In the eyes of many specialists, this represents the greatest period in Andalusian art. For many years, these experts highlighted the poverty of the materials used in Nasrid art, and their contrast with their abundance of decoration. Nowadays it is known that the function of the building determined the choice of materials. Consequently, in baths, as well as fortresses such as the Alcazaba in Granada, ashlar stone, bricks and mortar (of characteristic red colour) were used.

Palaces such as the Alhambra used **marble** on the floors and for its columns, **glazed ceramics** (azulejos) in areas exposed to friction, **elaborate plaster and stucco decoration**, wooden vaults and artesonados and **mocárabe vaults**.

Capitals were generally of two types: the first had a cylindrical base decorated with plain leaves which supported a parallelepiped adorned with additional foliage; the second type were mocárabe in style and derived from Asian art.

Although less spectacular nowadays due to weathering, **colour** was the other main feature of Nasrid buildings, the interiors of which, in their prime, must have looked like an Impressionist painting. In addition to the friezes of azulejos, the plaster and wood used to cover walls were painted in red, blue, green and gold tones, at a time when different-coloured marble was also used for capitals and columns. Given that the present-day appearance of the Alhambra continues to impress and amaze millions of visitors, we can only imagine how impressive it must have looked during its period of maximum splendour.

Azulejos, Alcázar, Sevilla

H. Champollion/MICHELIN

MEDIEVAL ANDALUSIAN ART

Mudéjar art (13C–16C)

Following the conquest of Córdoba and Sevilla in the first half of the 13C, Christian models were imposed on those buildings under the yoke of the kingdom of Castilla, although their construction was entrusted to skilled Muslim craftsmen. This resulted in the development of the typically Spanish Mudéjar art, the fusion of Islamic and Western artistic concepts.

Mudéjar architecture evolved over the centuries, adapting to the dominant features of each area, in such a way that the Mudéjar style in Andalucía is different from that of other Spanish regions. Despite these differences, in general it can be said that it remains loyal to Muslim traditions in terms of the materials used (plaster, brick and wood), its construction techniques (walls, horseshoe arches and wood ceilings) and decoration (fine artesonado work, the use of alfiz, and complicated plasterwork).

In the main, the churches of Sevilla (San Marcos, San Pablo and Santa Marina) are built using brick, with artesonados and traditional features of Almohad decoration. Major examples of civil architecture, in which roofs with two or four slopes predominate, include the Alcázar in Sevilla, which Pedro I rebuilt in 1366, the Torre de Don Fadrique (Sevilla), the Torre de El Carpio (Córdoba), the Castillo de San Romualdo (San Fernando, Cádiz) and the Casa de Pilatos (Sevilla).

Gothic art (13C–15C)

Early Andalusian Gothic art, which was inspired by the Cistercian model (large rose windows on the façades and a central nave with two side aisles of lower height with ogival vaults), produced works of great interest such as the so-called Fernandina churches of Córdoba (Santa Marina, San Miguel and San Lorenzo).

The construction of Sevilla Cathedral started in 1401. This is the largest Gothic building in Andalucía and one of the last Spanish Gothic churches to be built. The Flemish artists who worked on this ambitious project introduced a series of innovations, such as a rectan-

Iglesia de San Lorenzo, Córdoba

H. Champollion/MICHELIN

gular floor plan, a flat apsidal end with a small apse, slender fasciated pillars, complex star-shaped vaults and abundant decoration.

During the reign of Isabel the Catholic, the **Isabelline** style developed, halfway between Gothic and Renaissance, exuberantly combining Flamboyant and Mudéjar features. The Capilla Real in Granada, a work by Enrique Egas, is the best example of the Isabelline style.

Foreign artists who came to Sevilla in the 15C brought Flemish influence, with

Italian Ceramics in Andalucía

Glazed and painted ceramics from Italy, which co-existed with those created according to Mudéjar traditions, were brought to Andalucía at the beginning of the 16C by the Pisan, Francisco Niculoso, who was responsible for two interesting works in Sevilla, namely the portal of the church of the Convento de Santa Paula and the altarpiece in the oratory of the Alcázar. This type of decoration was inspired by the work of the Della Robbia family.

Andrés de Vandelvira

This brilliant architect (1509–75), a disciple of Diego de Siloé, enjoyed great prestige in his lifetime for the monumental aspect that he brought to Andalusian Renaissance architecture. Vandelvira's style blends in perfectly with the barrenness of Jaén's landscapes, where his ornamental features are reduced to a minimum of expression, yet at the same time embracing a taste for large, bare and luminous spaces.

its deep realism, to Andalusian sculpture. **Lorenzo Mercadante**, who was born in Brittany, is one of the best exponents of this Andalusian Gothic style. He worked mainly on the cathedral in Sevilla and introduced the technique of terra cotta, which was later used by numerous local artists. Spanish artists of the period worthy of mention include **Pedro Millán**, creator of the statue of the Virgin of the Pillar (Virgen del Pilar) in the same cathedral.

Renaissance and Baroque

The arrival on Spanish shores of seemingly limitless bounty from the Americas coincided with the introduction in the country of new artistic forms inspired by the Renaissance. This flowering of the arts, led by the appearance of leading artists of the time, saw Sevilla, Córdoba, Granada and many other towns and cities across the region establish themselves as centres of artistic creation. This expansion reached its zenith during the two centuries that followed – a period that saw the full expression and glory of Andalusian Baroque.

Palacio de Carlos V, Alhambra, Granada

THE RENAISSANCE (16C)

Architecture

The arrival of the Renaissance in Spain coincided with a new period of splendour in Andalucía. The monopoly on trade with the New World held by Sevilla resulted in the amassing of huge fortunes in the region's capital and other main towns and cities, which were soon embellished with myriad religious and secular monuments.

However, the magnificence of Late Gothic architecture and Mudéjar tradition initially prevented the total adoption of Renaissance ideas; in fact, the first three decades of the 16C saw the development of the **Plateresque style**, similar in style to Isabelline, and so called because of its lavish, refined decoration which was reminiscent of silverwork (plata: silver).

Although the masterpiece of this genre is undoubtedly the town hall (ayuntamiento) in Sevilla, a work by **Diego de Riaño**, a number of other fine examples of the style can be found across Andalucía: the gracious Lonja of the Chapel Royal and Diego de Siloé's doorway of the church at the Monasterio de San Jerónimo, both of which are found in Granada; a number of palaces in Baeza and Úbeda, in the province of Jaén; and the façade of the Iglesia de Santa María de la Asunción, by Alonso de Baena, in Arcos de la Frontera.

As the century evolved, greater importance was attributed to proportions than ornamentation, resulting in the total abandonment of Gothic ideas. Barrel, oval and oven vaulting became predominant features, along with the almost exclusive use of the semicircular arch; decorative motifs also increased in size at a time when the trend was for the concentration of decoration in specific

H. Champollion/MICHELIN

H. Champollion/MICHELIN

Tomb of Juana the Mad, Capilla Real, Granada

areas to allow for the development of vast open areas.

Three names stand out in Renaissance architecture in the region. Diego de Siloé (1495–1563) completed the work on Granada Cathedral, having modified the Gothic plans conceived by Enrique de Egas. The edifice, one of the most significant from this period, served as a model for the cathedrals in both Málaga and Guadix. De Siloé was also active elsewhere in the region, in particular Guadix, Montefrío (Iglesia de la Villa) and across the province of Jaén, where he worked in close collaboration with his disciple, Andrés de Vandelvira, who left his audacious mark on Jaén Cathedral and other buildings in the same province, particularly in Úbeda (Iglesia del Salvador) and Baeza.

Lastly, the architect and painter **Pedro Machuca** (d. 1550) always remained faithful to his Italian training, which he received alongside Michelangelo. Carlos V's palace in Granada's Alhambra, his most impressive work, is a work of extreme simplicity (a circle built within a square) and total innovation which was completely misunderstood at the time.

The most important figures of the Renaissance in Sevilla were **Martín Gaínza**, the architect for the chapel royal in the city's cathedral, and the Córdoban **Hernán Ruiz**, who was responsible for the modern-day appearance of the Giralda.

The last third of the 16C in Spain also saw the forceful imposition of the **Herreran** style created by **Juan de Herrera**, as seen at El Escorial. Sevilla is also home to a work by Felipe II's favourite architect: the Archivo de Indias which, with its sober, rectilinear façade, encompasses all the characteristic features of Counter Reformation art.

Sculpture

Realism and expression are the dominant sculptural themes from the Renaissance period, which was already providing a foretaste of Baroque imagery. Given that most projects were commissioned by the Church, religious figures predominate. It should also be remembered that the Counter Reformation was initiated in the last third of the century, on behalf of which Felipe II was determined to mount a strong defence. More often than not, these sculptures were carved in polychrome wood; marble, alabaster and stone were only used for rare secular figures, funereal and monumental art. As was the case during the Gothic period, the Renaissance in Andalucía saw an abundance of altars decorated with large-dimensioned retables.

Of the numerous Italian artists who worked in the region, the following stand out: **Domenico Fancelli** (1469–1518), the sculptor of the tombs of the Catholic Monarchs in the Chapel Royal in Granada Cathedral; **Jacobo Florentino** (1476–1526), who created the Burial of

Christ (Entierro de Cristo) exhibited in the Museo de Bellas Artes in the city; and **Pietro Torrigiano**, whose Penitent St Jerome (Museo de Bellas Artes, Sevilla) was to exert great influence on Sevilla's Baroque sculptors. The Burgundian **Felipe Vigarny** (d. 1543) worked mainly in Castilla in collaboration with Berruguete; however, he created one of his best works in Granada, namely the altarpiece for the city's Chapel Royal.

Although he died young, the most important Spanish sculptor of the period was **Bartolomé Ordóñez** (d. 1520), born in Burgos but trained in Italy, who died in Carrara after working on the tombs of Juana la Loca (Joan the Mad) and Felipe el Hermoso (Philip the Handsome) for the Capilla Real in Granada.

Painting

As with the sculpture of the period, religious rather than secular themes dominated Renaissance painting. It could be said that in the whole of Andalucía, the only city to stand apart was Sevilla, where several families with large fortunes decorated their mansions with secular, mythological and allegorical canvases (Casa de Pilatos). During the early decades of the century the Flemish influence, with its characteristic taste for concrete images, remained ever present. However, Tuscan mannerism and Raphael's classicism gradually paved the way for the arrival of Venetian painting.

The best exponent of the early Sevillian Renaissance was Alejo Fernández (c. 1475–1545), an artist of German extraction who adopted the Spanish surname of his wife.

In line with the themes popular with Flemish painters, he was first attracted by the effects of perspective and by the arrangement of space. During this period, when his studio was in Córdoba, he painted his famous Flagellation (Museo del Prado, Madrid) and Christ Tied to the Column (Museo de Bellas Artes, Córdoba). When he moved to Sevilla, his interest evolved to the human form, with works such as the Virgin of the Rose (Iglesia de Santa Ana) and the Virgin of the Navigators, his most famous painting of the period, on display in the Alcázar in Sevilla.

The Sevillian artist **Luis de Vargas** (1506–68), who trained in Italy with a disciple of Raphael, took his inspiration from the mannerism of Vasari and the delicate touch of Correggio. His most renowned work is the Generación temporal de Cristo in the city's cathedral, which was given the nickname of La Gamba due to the beauty of Adam's leg (gamba in Italian). In the eyes of many, **Luis de Morales** (c. 1520–86), an artist from Extremadura who had close ties with Andalucía, is the most interesting painter of his era; his highly personal works manifest both Flemish and Italian influence. The gentleness of his feminine characters and the expressiveness of his ailing Christs (Ecce Homo in the Academia de San Fernando, Madrid) made him the most admired artist of the time and subject to imitation by his peers.

During the 16C, Sevilla became popular with many Flemish artists who were attracted by the wealth and riches of the city and hope of commissions in America. These included Peter Kempeneer, known as **Pedro de Campaña** (1503–63), who painted the impressively large Descent from the Cross in the city's cathedral, and **Hernando Sturbio** (d. 1577), the creator of the Retable of the Evangelists in the same edifice.

BAROQUE (17C–18C)

Spanish Baroque shone forth in every aspect of art. During the first half of the 17C, the influence of the Herreran style remained: churches with a very simple rectangular plan, ornamental plaster motifs and occasionally façades decorated with panels of azulejos (Hospital de la Caridad, Sevilla). This austerity gradually softened, as buildings started to be covered with more ornate decoration, even though the structures themselves remained simple in design and many cupolas were deceptive in that they were often composed of a wooden arcature with a plaster facing instead of being made of stone.

It was during the course of this century that the architect, sculptor and painter **Alonso Cano** created the main façade of Granada Cathedral.

©Ken Sorrie/iStockphoto.com

Façade of Granada cathedral

However, it was not until after the rise to power of the Bourbons that Andalusian Baroque entered its most sumptuous phase, with the development of trade with the Americas (due to the silting up of the River Guadalquivir, Cádiz replaced Sevilla as the main trading port with the Americas in 1717) resulting in a period of frenetic construction across the entire region. Numerous small towns were soon embellished with seigniorial mansions and Baroque churches, such as Osuna (bell tower of the Iglesia de la Merced and Palacio de los Marqueses de la Gomera), Écija (Palacio de Benamejí, Palacio de Peñaflor and the bell tower of the Iglesia de San Juan), Lucena (Capilla del Sagrario), Priego de Córdoba, Alcalá la Real, Guadix (bell tower and façade of the cathedral), Carmona (Convento de las Descalzas) and Estepa (doorway of the Iglesia del Carmen).

The overflowing imagination of artists knew no bounds. Concave and convex structures gave undulating movement to façades, while decorative motifs such as volutes, floral bands and Solomonic columns adorned every surface. Beneath the common denominator of exuberance, architects felt free to interpret Baroque according to their own personal preferences. Moorish influence and a fantasy of colour were the prime influences behind the ostentatious Sagrario in the Carthusian monastery (Cartuja) in Granada, designed by **Francisco Hurtado** (1669–1725); in

the same city, the extraordinary decor of the Iglesia de San Juan de Dios stands out for the rich ornamentation of its façade. Meanwhile, **Vicente Acero**, the architect of the Real Fábrica de Tabacos (Royal Tobacco Factory), was inspired by Siloé's Renaissance cathedral in Granada, when he embarked upon

Alonso Cano, The Complete Artist

This Granada-born architect, sculptor, designer and creator of numerous altarpieces and canvases is now recognised as one of the key figures of the Spanish Golden Age. His irascible character, which sullied his reputation while he was alive, continued to blight him even after his death. Cano arrived in Sevilla at the age of 13, linking up with Velázquez, his fellow student in the workshop of Pacheco, before pursuing his training under Montañés. Financial worries (he even went to prison due to unpaid debts) saw him head north to Madrid in 1637, where he enjoyed the patronage of the Count-Duke of Olivares. His lifestyle remained largely unsettled, as borne out by his involvement in several duels and the accusation levelled against him of having ordered the murder of his wife. His return to Granada in 1651 saw the full flowering of his talents in the work carried out on the city's cathedral.

Cupola, Capilla del Sagrario, Priego de Córdoba

Spain's last great cathedral, in Cádiz, built between 1722 and 1729.

The Sevillian **Leonardo de Figueroa** (1650–1730), creator of a number of important civic buildings in his native city such as the Palacio de San Telmo (originally built as a school for future navigators and today the seat of the Andalusian parliament) and the Hospital de los Venerables, was also responsible for several fine churches, including the Iglesia del Salvador and the Iglesia de San Luis de los Franceses; the latter, with its central plan and Solomonic columns, demonstrates his great ability to combine brick, ceramics and coloured plaster.

Detail, Capilla del Sagrario, Priego de Córdoba

Sculpture

Although marble and bronze statues inspired by allegorical and mythological themes were popular in both Italy and France, in Andalucía – as in the rest of Spain – sculpture was used as a tool of the Counter Reformation, with realism as its dominant theme.

At the beginning of the 20C, the region became a fundamental focal point for religious sculpture – times were difficult and people were looking towards religion as a solution to their problems. Communities of monks and nuns developed, multiplying the need for sculpted images and groups of statues, both to be venerated at the altar and held aloft in street processions such as those during Holy Week. These increasingly realistic and expressive works continued to be carved from polychrome wood, although the colours became increasingly natural. In many cases fabric covered the whole body, so that only the face and hands were carved; it was also known for glass eyes and tears, added as a final touch of authenticity.

Juan Martínez Montañés – Known to his contemporaries as the "god of wood", Montañés was born in Alcalá la Real in 1568 and died in 1649. He was the true founder of Sevilla's sculptural school and the finest representative of the zenith of the art in Andalucía. More influenced by Renaissance ideas than his contemporaries, this masterful sculptor only evolved towards the Baroque style towards the end his career. The creator of numerous polychrome works (whose colours were often adopted by the artist Francisco Pacheco), he was able to confer great serenity upon the expressions depicted in his faces.

As well as numerous Mannerist-inspired retablos (Santos Juanes in the Iglesia de San Leandro), he also created countless images of Christ and saints (his best work is without doubt his Christ of Clemency in Sevilla Cathedral), including tiny marble figurines. From his Baroque period, particular attention should be paid to the extraordinary retable of the Battle of Angels (Iglesia de San Miguel, Jérez de la Frontera) and the magnificent, reflective Immaculate Conceptions in Sevilla Cathedral.

Not to be forgotten among the disciples of Montañés is one of his own sons, **Alonso Martínez** (d. 1668), who collaborated on a number of masterpieces by his master, the Córdoban **Juan de Mesa** (1583–1627), whose style was considered more dramatic; the latter was the creator of the venerated Jesús del Gran Poder (Jesus of Great Power), nowadays exhibited in the modern Templo de Nuestro Padre Jesús del Gran Poder, built in 1965.

Alonso Cano and the Sevilla School

The school was headed by the multifaceted **Alonso Cano** (1601–67), an architect, artist and sculptor born in Granada and who trained alongside Martínez Montañés. His simple, delicate figures would later be reinterpreted by his numerous pupils, such as **Pedro de Mena** (1628–93), the sculptor of the choir stalls in Málaga Cathedral, and José de Mora (1642–1724), whose psychological imbalance – he was to die insane – remain entrenched in his often striking works.

Italian influence

During the course of the **17C**, and particularly at the beginning of the 18C, Italian influence began to manifest itself, inspired by the style employed by Bernini. Agitation, movement and a sense of the dramatic in the scenes portrayed are the dominant features

La Roldana's Cribs

The tradition of cribs (nacimientos), which would appear to have been started by St Francis of Assisi, has always been very popular in Spain. During the Baroque period, many sculptors created, and inspired through their work, a huge variety of popular figures made from polychrome fired clay, which became part of the country's cultural heritage. La Roldana, the daughter of Pedro Roldán, was one of the finest exponents of this art form in the Andalusian School. One of her most notable works is the Virgen de las Angustias (Virgin of Anguish), in Cádiz.

of this style subsequently copied by Andalusian artists. Alongside **José de Arce** (d. 1666), who introduced this new trend, other artists who stand out include **Pedro Roldán** (1624–1700), who worked mainly in Sevilla (creating the Entombment in the Hospital de la Caridad), and **Pedro Duque Cornejo** (1677–1757), the creator of many works for Carthusian monasteries in and around Sevilla and the fine choir stalls in Córdoba Cathedral.

The long list of Baroque sculptors from the Granada School should also include **Torcuato Ruiz del Peral**, who carved highly expressive heads of saints and the choir stalls in Guadix Cathedral.

THE GOLDEN AGE OF ANDALUSIAN PAINTING

The 17C is without doubt the Golden Age of Andalusian painting, which started out loyal to the dominant Flemish tradition of the 16C before developing its own expression through opulence and light. From the middle of the century onwards, Sevilla and Madrid became the undisputed capitals of Spanish painting.

The renown of Sevillian artists in the early decades of the 17C, such as **Francisco Pacheco**, the father-in-law of Velázquez, has remained obscured by the brilliance of three undisputed masters: Velázquez, Zurbarán and Murillo.

Diego Velázquez

spent the majority of his professional life in Madrid as a portrait painter to the Court. However, neither fame nor the influence of Italian artists whom he admired greatly, in particular Titian, could bring him to forget his training in Sevilla. It was during this period (1617–23), before he left the city of his birth, that he painted works with predominantly religious themes and or in the costumbrismo genre (*Adoration of the Kings*, Museo del Prado, Madrid).

Francisco de Zurbarán

Living from 1598 to 1664 and coming from Extremadura, Zurbarán interpreted themes of monastic life, but also painted more popular themes, representing reality as accurately as possible, with an economy of means and a deliberately limited range of colour which emphasises the play of light and, in his portraits in particular, sees his characters burst forth from the canvas. His academy rapidly developed into one of the largest in Sevilla, exporting more works to the Americas than any other in the city.

Bartolomé Esteban Murillo

Murillo (1617–82), whose works of a religious nature (Virgin Mary, Infant Jesus) have been reproduced time and time again, was the most famous Spanish artist of the period. Through his academy, he also exported innumerable canvases destined for the churches of the New World. The delicate touch and warmth of these occasionally bland paintings cannot hide the qualities of an extraordinary painter who was a great master of both technique and colour, and highly skilled in the portrayal of genre scenes.

Juan Valdés Leal

In complete contrast to Murillo, Leal (1662–95) concentrated on expression and the macabre with a striking power and realism that at times touched on the morbid, as seen in the frescoes painted for Sevilla's Hospital de la Caridad.

In Granada, the aforementioned **Alonso Cano** (1661–67), a great friend of Velázquez, was the most classical of all Baroque painters. His most famous work is a series of canvases representing the Life of the Virgin (Granada Cathe-

©World Illustrated/Photoshot

St. Hugh in the Refectory (c. 1655) by Francisco de Zurbarán, Museo de Bellas Artes, Sevilla

dral), showing the major influence of the Venetian masters, whose work he became familiar with when he worked under the protection of the favourite of Felipe IV, the Count-Duke of Olivares.

19C–20C Art

After several centuries of artistic splendour, Andalusian creativity appeared to run out of steam as it entered the 19C. The severe economic crisis in the region was reflected in a dearth of commissions and the absence of prestigious projects. Despite this, a few Andalusian artists still managed to make their mark in Spain.

PAINTING

In Romantic painting, several Sevillian artists stand out. These include Antonio Martínez Esquivel, José Gutiérrez de la Vega and **Valeriano Domínguez Bécquer**; the latter, the brother of the poet Gustavo Adolfo Bécquer, was inspired by costumbrismo, with its joyful scenes so alien to his personal experiences of sadness. **Manuel Rodríguez de Guzmán** is worthy of special interest as a result of the huge excitement generated by his excellent sketches of Andalusian life. His warm portrayals of life in southern Spain, which were greatly admired by foreigners, helped to perpetuate the romantic image of Andalucía.

In the last quarter of the century, the realist **Julio Romero de Torres** (1880–1930) was born in Córdoba. This artist specialised in painting Andalusian women of great beauty and restrained sensuality *(Oranges and Lemons)*. Although his work was criticised in certain quarters, such was his popularity that shortly after his death a museum was created in the house in which he was born.

Very different from Romero de Torres, both in terms of his style and his life outside Spain, was the Málaga-born **Picasso** (1881–1973) who is undoubtedly the most famous figure of contemporary Spanish pictorial art. Although he lived in his native Andalucía for just eight years, he maintained close ties with his own region and kept alive his passion for bullfighting from afar.

Museo Julio Romero de Torres. Córdoue/ SCALA

Contradiction (1919) by
Julio Romero de Torres

Two artists who made their names in the early part of the 20C were **Daniel Vázquez Díaz** (1882–1969), who took his inspiration from Cubism to create works such as the frescoes in the Monasterio de la Rábida (Huelva), and **Rafael Zabaleta** (1907–60), an artist known for his stylised, rustic expressionism.

Other artists born towards the middle of the 20C include Luis Gordillo (1934) and Guillermo Pérez Villalta (1948), both involved in the renewed trend towards figurative representation, as well as Alfonso Fraile, Vicente Vela, Alfonso Albacete, Carmen Laffon, Chema Cobo and the Granada-born José Guerrero.

SCULPTURE

Mateo Inurria (1869–1924), the creator of the statue of El Gran Capitán in Córdoba, and **Jacinto Higueras** were the leading Andalusian sculptors from the first half of the 20C. **Miguel Berrocal** (1933), who in his early works manifested his keen interest in abstract forms, later moved on to more figurative subjects.

ARCHITECTURE

The widespread changes within the field of architecture were slow to take root in Andalucía. Modernismo merely produced a few strange examples of the genre within bourgeois society (the interiors

Puente de la Barqueta, Sevilla

F. Vidal/ MICHELIN

of houses and small shops), particularly in the province of Cádiz.

At the same time, and inspired by the Costurero de la Reina lodge (Sevilla, 1893), the historicist and revivalist movement was born, and came to the fore at the 1929 Ibero-American Exhibition, with its ornate pavilions. Other official buildings, such as the Palacio Provincial in Jaén and a number of cinemas and theatres, including the Teatro Falla in Cádiz and the Aliatar in Granada are further examples of this movement.

The architecture of recent decades, which has openly embraced these new trends, is a clear reflection of the positive development of the Andalusian economy. Since the sixties, during which the School of Architecture was created in Sevilla, a number of public buildings, tourist complexes and housing developments have been built, designed by the best architects from Andalucía and elsewhere in Spain (Saénz de Oiza, Moneo, de La-Hoz, García de Paredes, Cano Lasso, etc.).

The urban projects completed for the 1992 World Expo in Sevilla are further proof of the architectural renaissance which has taken place in the region.

Highwaymen of the Sierra Morena

Given the irregular profile of the Sierra Morena, it is easy to understand how, over the centuries, it became a refuge for those on the edge of the law.

Romantic writers, particularly English and French, were deeply attracted to the outlaws of the 18C and 19C, depicting them in many tales. Thus was born the archetype of the Andalusian highwayman, a seeker of justice and defender of the oppressed. Although it is true that on occasion peasants considered these *bandoleros* heroes, for the most part they protected them through fear.

In Spanish history, two influential characters personified the Spanish highwayman. The first was **Diego Corrientes** (1757–81), who specialised in the theft of horses from farms and homesteads, and who was executed in Sevilla. The second, and perhaps the most famous bandit of them all, was **José María el Tempranillo** (1805–35). Having killed a man to defend his honour, he joined the famous gang of the Niños de Écija (Children of Écija), devoting his life to extracting tribute from travellers passing through the Sierra Morena, as well as offering sporadic help to exiled liberals. Bowing to popular opinion, the king pardoned his crimes shortly before this young hero died from natural causes.

Literature

Andalucía has produced many figures of renown in the world of culture. From the Roman philosopher Seneca to Nobel Prize-winning authors such as Juan Ramón Jiménez and Vicente Aleixandre, and writers of the stature of Luis de Góngora, the list of national celebrities is long. And there are those from afar who have had a deep attraction for the soul of this complex region. We can mention just a few of those who have found inspiration in this magnificent land.

Notable figures of Andalusian literature from the second half of the 20C include **Félix Grande**, **José Caballero Bonald**, **Antonio Muñoz Molina** and, above all, **Antonio Gala**, the Córdoban writer.

Tirso de Molina (1579–1684), the probable author of *Don Juan*, set the conquests of the legendary rake Don Juan Tenorio on the banks of the Guadalquivir. Alongside Don Quixote and Faust, this great lover was to become one of the signature figures of world literature thanks to the playwright José Zorrilla. The latter, a prolific Romantic author, was a contemporary of a group of foreign writers who found their sought-after exoticism and mystery in Andalucía.

Among the first foreign tourists to travel to the south of Spain were British writers such as **Richard Ford**; **Théophile Gautier**, Victor Hugo and Latour from France; the American **Washington Irving**; and Italy's Edmundo d'Amicis. Between them they embellished and exported the myth of Andalucía – land of brigands, bullfighters, gypsies and carefree people – which had little in common with reality but met with great success abroad.

Poetry – The poetry of Andalucía reached its zenith early in the 20C, through the writing of members of the Generation of '27. **Antonio Machado** (1875–1939), author of *Cantares*, and forever nostalgic for his childhood in Sevilla, and his brother **Manuel Machado**, who wrote *Cante Jondo*, both reflected the true nature of the region. **Federico García Lorca** (1898–1936) lifted Anda-

Statue of Federico García Lorca, Madrid

©Picture Colour Library

lusian lyricism to its peak with the *Gypsy Ballads*, *Blood Wedding* and *The House of Bernarda Alba*. The poems of painter and poet **Rafael Alberti** (1902–99) were highly personal, gracious and popular in style, as well as typically Andalusian *(Marinero en tierra)*.

Music

Three great Spanish classical composers who drew their inspiration from popular music reflected the Andalusian soul perfectly. Strangely, just one of them was a native of the south; the other two were Catalan.

Manuel de Falla (1876–1946), born in Cádiz, is surely the most illustrious Spanish composer of the 20C. He took a studied approach to musical ethnography, and avoided being merely a conveyor of picturesque folklore.

The passion of gypsy song and the brilliance of flamenco are both present in his two most famous works, *El amor brujo* (Love, the Magician) and The Three-Cornered Hat.

Gerona-born **Isaac Albéniz** (1860–1909), a major exponent of the Spanish nationalist movement, dedicated some of his best works to Andalucía, such as *Caprichos andaluces* and a major part

The Cigarreras of Seville

Seville became the centre of the tobacco trade in the 17C after the Spaniards found the indigenous Americans smoking the plant. In 1614 King Philip III decreed that all tobacco grown in the Spanish New World should be shipped to Seville.

The world's biggest tobacco factory, the Royal Factory of Seville 9 (the setting of the first act of *Carmen*), was built in 1758 and continued to trade until the mid 20C. In 1953 it became home to the city's university.

In Bizet's day more than 3 000 female cigarreras would sit in a room hand-rolling cigarettes. "The cigarreras, many of whom are great beauties, form a class by themselves, and unhappily are not noted for their chastity", the 19C writer Howe Downes reported.

of his *Iberia*. Lastly, **Enrique Granados** (1867–1916) dedicated one of his three Spanish Danzas to Andalucía.

OPERA

Two great evergreen operas are set in Seville: Bizet's *Carmen* and Mozart's *Don Giovanni*.

Carmen

Carmen was born from the imagination of two Frenchmen: Prosper Mérimée, who wrote the novella; and composer and pianist Georges Bizet, who turned it into an opera. *Carmen* premiered in Paris in 1875. It was originally considered a failure, panned by critics as "immoral" and "superficial".

The story is set in Seville, around 1830. Carmen is a beautiful gypsy with a fiery temper who works at the tobacco factory. A naïve young soldier, Don José, falls in love with her. He rejects his former love, mutinies against his military superior and turns to a life of crime. Carmen then turns from him to a bullfighter (Escamillo) and, in a fit of jealousy, Don José murders her.

Don Giovanni

Don Giovanni is the Italianised version of Don Juan, the legendary Spanish libertine whose story is thought to be based upon *Don Juan Tenorio: Drama religioso-fantástico en dos partes (Don Juan Tenorio: Religious-Fantasy Drama in Two Parts)*, written in 1844 by José Zorrilla. The other contender for the originator of the legend is *El burlador de Sevilla y convidado de piedra (The Trickster of Seville and the Stone Guest)*,

by Tirso de Molina (*see LITERATURE)*, a play set in the 14C that was published in Spain around 1630. Both stories are set in Seville.

Cinema

Spanish cinema has often found inspiration in Andalusian themes. However, this trend, caricatured by Berlanga in *Bienvenido Mr Marshall* (1952), was to wane until Carlos Saura put Andalusian folklore back on the screen with works such as *Bodas de sangre/Blood Wedding* (1981), *Sevillanas* (1991), and *Flamenco* (1995).

In recent times, following his success with *Solas* (1995), critics pronounced **Benito Zambrano** the standard bearer of new Andalusian cinema.

For the very best in Spanish cinema each year look to the Málaga Film Festival (www.festcinemalaga.com) a major event in the world of cinema which every April brings stars and directors to the red carpet at the Teatro Cervantes in Málaga.

Orson Welles

Perhaps the greatest film director of all time, Welles fell in love with Andalucía while filming here. He became very friendly with the bullfighter Antonio Ordóñez (1932–1998), in Ronda, and is said to have remarked:

"I would love to have my ashes buried in your *pozo* (well) so my name will always be present in your garden".

On Welles' death in 1987, this is exactly what happened.

THE REGION TODAY

As an autonomous region within the Spanish state, Andalucía now possesses the political institutions necessary to ensure its own development. For years held back by the vagaries of history and by occasionally archaic social structures, the region is now blessed with a major asset in the form of tourism which, in its different forms, brings wealth to Andalucía without destroying its soul.

Economy

To express his admiration for the immense natural riches of Andalucía, the Greek geographer Strabo compared the region with the Elysian Fields. How is it possible, therefore, that in centuries to follow, peasants were plunged into starvation and then forced to emigrate? Agricultural decadence began with the expulsion of the Moors.

Land was abandoned while new settlers, fewer in number than those who had already left, showed greater enthusiasm for warfare and the colonisation of America than for agricultural labour. In years to come, large landowners (caciques) and the ruling classes did little to improve the situation. However, there are those who believe that the "traditional" underdevelopment of Andalucía is in reality a relatively new phenomenon which began in the second half of the 19C. In fact, at the beginning of the 19C, the distribution of wealth was reasonably uniform across the whole country.

The development of the Hispanic capitalist society had an extremely detrimental effect on the lands of southern Spain, to the extent that in 1935 per capita income in Andalucía was just 717 pesetas, against 1 307 pesetas in the rest of the country. The problems intensified in the post-war period, when the most impoverished felt obliged to emigrate to other Spanish regions (mainly Catalonia and the Basque Country) and to various

Palacio de San Telmo, the seat of the Andalusian Parliament in Sevilla

G. Bludzin/MICHELIN

Agricultural land near Jerez de la Frontera

H. Champollion/MICHELIN

European countries (particularly Germany, France and Switzerland). During the 1960s, over 900 000 Andalusians left their native region.

This situation slowly began to improve during the 1970s, although the endemic problems remained: the unequal distribution of land into large estates *(latifundios)*, low levels of industrial investment and poor professional training for workers. During the second half of the 1980s, the region enjoyed another economic revival, particularly in the provinces along the Mediterranean coast.

The year 1992 was to be key in Andalucía's economic development. The **World Expo** in Sevilla, which received 40 million visitors, brought tremendous economic benefits to the region's capital and coastal towns and cities, and had a positive effect on other provinces. This included the construction of the motorway linking Sevilla, Córdoba, Granada and Málaga, and the creation of the AVE high-speed rail link between Madrid and Sevilla via Córdoba.

Following the euphoria of 1992, a new industrial crisis hit the region, exacerbated by problems linked to drought, forest fires and unemployment.

In recent years, the growth rate in Andalucía has been similar to the national average, while the official unemployment rate, although the highest in Spain, has been significantly reduced to 13 per cent.

AGRICULTURE AND LIVESTOCK

Agriculture is the mainstay of the region's economy. Cereal production is concentrated in the province of Sevilla (which leads the country in production), Cádiz, Almería and Granada; fruits (particularly citrus fruits) and vegetables are mainly produced in the fertile lowlands of Granada; olives in Jaén and Granada; vines in Jerez, Montilla and Málaga; and cotton in Córdoba and Sevilla. Over the past few years, the provinces of Huelva and Almería have, controversially, become covered with a sea of plastic, used to protect early season produce and winter crops.

Livestock farming is concentrated on the pasturelands of the Sierra Morena, the Sierra de Cádiz and the Cordillera Subbética. In the main, these fenced lands have been stripped of their low bushes and scrub and, in places, of their natural vegetation of holm and cork oak. These areas constitute an agro-forestry system which is unique in Europe, where in addition to animal breeding, firewood, cork and honey are produced. Traditional livestock operations are extensive and take advantage of natural pasture to raise select and, in many cases, uniquely Andalusian, breeds, such as the Cartujana horse, Merino sheep, Iberian pig and the fighting bull.

The **food-processing** industry is also worthy of note given the widespread production and excellent quality of Andalusian wines (particularly around Jerez, Montilla and Málaga), and the reputation of the region's olive oil. Andalucía is also the country's second most important region for fish and seafood, in particular tuna, sardines, clams, cockles, shrimp and prawns.

INDUSTRY

Andalucía is a region with limited industry, with the exception of the province of Huelva and the area around La Rábida, where a number of chemical and petrochemical plants and factories have been established. Andalucía's traditional **mining** has declined dramatically and is now a mere shadow of its former self. Gone are the days when, at the end of the 19C, the English company which acquired the mines at Riotinto (Huelva) employed over 10 000 workers or when, in the time of the Phoenicians, the kingdom of Tartessus prospered from mineral and metal deposits.

Despite this decline, the extensive opencast pits at Ríotinto are still operational, lead is still mined in the provinces of Jaén, Almería and Córdoba, pyrite and manganese dioxide in Huelva, and iron in Granada, Sevilla and Almería.

TOURISM

In a surprising twist of fate, the tourist industry now brings wealth to regions and countries that were overlooked by the industrial revolution two centuries ago. Every year, more than 15 million tourists visit Andalucía, which is now the third most popular destination in Spain for foreign holidaymakers.

The region's many attractions appeal to a wide range of visitors. The mild climate and beaches of the Andalusian coast attract visitors in search of sea and sunshine, with the majority of tourists heading to the **coastline** between Málaga and Estepona on the Costa del Sol. This stretch caters to everyone, with package tours filling many of the hotels in Torremolinos and Benalmádena. The Spanish and international jet-set head for the more upmarket resorts of Marbella and Puerto Banús. Today, hotels, restaurants, nightclubs and marinas stand side by side along the seafront, changing forever the face of former fishing ports. Less crowded is the Atlantic coast of the provinces of Huelva and Cádiz, known as the Costa de la Luz (ⓒ see NATURE), whose long, sandy beaches are particularly popular with surfing enthusiasts. The indented, tropical coastline of the province of Granada has also retained much of its original charm, as has the Almería coast, especially around the protected areas of Cabo de Gata.

However, Andalucía has much more to offer than its coastline, as demonstrated by the increasing number of Spanish visitors attracted by the **outdoor activities** and **mountain tourism** on offer in inland areas.

Footpaths criss-cross the region, allowing visitors to discover its flora and fauna and to enjoy the relative cool of the mountains, whether they are exploring the Serranía de Ronda with its whitewashed villages; the Sierra de Cazorla, where the distant call of a stag can often be heard; the Sierra de Aracena, with its lakes and forests; the Sierra Morena or the Sierra Subbética. The scenery is varied and ever-changing, ranging from luxuriant vegetation to desert landscapes, from olive groves stretching as far as the eye can see to extensive sugar cane plantations, and from snowcapped mountain peaks to vast sun-scorched plains.

Finally, **cultural tourism** attracts visitors to the historical centres of Andalucía – not just the famous cities of Sevilla, Granada and Córdoba, but also to the lesser-known towns of Ronda, Carmona, Écija, Guadix, Úbeda and Baeza.

Government

AN AUTONOMOUS REGION

Once democracy was restored to Spain after the death of General Franco in 1975, Andalucía was the fourth *comunidad* to be recognised within the Spanish state, which is now made up of 17 autonomous communities.

The Statute of Autonomy, approved in 1981, was a response to the wishes of the

Andalusian coat of arms

R. Corbel/MICHELIN

Andalusian people as expressed in the referendum on 28 February 1980.

Political organisation

The **Junta de Andalucía** is the autonomous executive body that coordinates and manages the administration of the region. Its president works in collaboration with the *Consejo de Gobierno* (Cabinet), currently made up of 13 ministers, each responsible for a separate department.

Legislative functions are performed by the **Andalusian Parliament** *(Parlamento de Andalucía)*, the seat of which is in Sevilla. Its 109 members are elected by universal suffrage every four years.

Blas Infante (1885–1936)

During the Second Republic, this politician made his name as the leader of the Andalusian Movement. He participated in the drafting of the preliminary bill for the Statute of Andalucía (1933) and presided over the assembly formed to ensure the recognition of the Confederate Andalusian State.

The author of *El ideal Andaluz* (1915) among other works, he was shot shortly after the outbreak of the Spanish Civil War.

The region's highest court is the **Tribunal Superior de Justicia** in Granada. Centralised administration is the responsibility of the government's delegate for Andalucía *(Delegado del Gobierno)*, whose office is based in Sevilla, and beneath whom affairs are managed by a network of provincial subdelegates *(subdelegados)*.

THE SYMBOLS OF ANDALUCÍA

Although definitively approved by the Andalusian Parliament as part of the new democratic process, the three symbols of Andalucía are not new. In fact, the Statute of Andalucía (1982) clearly stated that the anthem, coat of arms and green and white **flag** would be those defined by the Assembly of Ronda in 1918 and by the Juntas Liberalistas de Andalucía in 1933.

The **coat of arms**, inspired by the escutcheon of the city of Cádiz, shows Hercules between two columns subduing two lions. Above him is the Latin inscription *Dominator Hercules Fundator* and at his feet the motto *Andalucía, por sí, para España y para la Humanidad* (Andalucía itself, for Spain and for Humanity). The **anthem**, the third symbol of Andalusian nationality, embraces the traditional claims of its people, reaffirming their love of peace and their desire for a future in which they regain the privileged position they occupied in the past.

Population

A GENTLE PACE OF LIFE

As you explore the delightful towns and villages of the region, it won't take long before you stumble upon a typical Andalusian scene: a small cobblestoned square surrounded by dazzling white-washed houses, an ornate fountain, the emblazoned façade of an aristocratic mansion, a Baroque church and a bar frequented in the early evening by locals of all ages, the women sitting in the shade playing with their fans. This indolent, seemingly timeless scene encompassing both the modern and the archaic is repeated throughout the region, providing a picture of Andalucía that is clichéd and yet authentic, full of the contrasts that make up this complex region.

Visitors soon adapt to the summer rhythm of life in Andalucía, with the impossibility of getting anything done during its long afternoon siestas, those late nights and late meal times and the constant noise of activity that reigns in the region's lively streets and public squares. Lottery ticket sellers calling "para hoooy", locals relaxing with the newspapers at outdoor cafés, seemingly oblivious to the *limpiabotas* shining their shoes, the sharp click of a fan expertly handled – all these vignettes of local life contribute to the gentle Andalusian way that slowly charms and delights visitors.

Behind the sunny facade however, there is a gloomier side. Andalucía has one of the highest unemployment levels in the European Union and is nicknamed "the workhouse of Spain" by the rest of the country. EU funding, particularly improvements in local infastructure, has greatly helped the situation but the region still lags behind.

In 2006 the GDP per capita of Andalusia was €17 401, the second lowest in Spain. At the same time, the economic growth rate for the 2000–2006 period was 3.72%, one of the highest in the country, so at least things are moving in the right direction.

A café terrace in an Alpujarran village

S. Ollivier/MICHELIN

Traditions and Customs

Andalusians are renowned for their fiestas, uniquely celebrated by entire villages, towns and cities. Through the course of the year over 3 000 festivals are held around the region, the majority of a religious nature (processions and *romerías*), although mention needs to be made of the famous fairs *(ferias)*, carnivals and Moorish and Christian fiestas.

HOLY WEEK (SEMANA SANTA)

Gold-embroidered capes glistening in candlelight, sumptuous statues lit by the moon borne reverently along streets lined by orange trees, the beating of drums, sacred flamenco *saetas* sung from a balcony as Virgin and Child pass below… such is the image of Semana Santa (Holy Week), the most important fiesta in the Andalusian calendar.

Towns, cities and villages across Andalucía all commemorate the Passion and the Death of Christ in their own way, carrying in procession works of art created by famous sculptors such as Alonso Cano, Martínez Montañés and Pedro de Mena (*see Art and Culture).* These images are transported on floats known as **pasos** in Sevilla and **tronos** in Málaga, all of which are decorated with richly sculpted wood, engraved silver and a multitude of flowers. Hidden by velvet gowns, the bearers or **costaleros** advance slowly with their load, weighing around three tonnes. Each carrier supports a weight of approximately 80kg/176lb.

To prepare for this arduous task, teams train for three months between Christmas and Semana Santa, during which younger members cover the route to be taken with a structure similar in weight and size to the one they will bear on the day of the procession.

Andalucía has close to a thousand Confraternities or Brotherhoods of the Passion, responsible for the creation and maintenance of these floats. Donations and raffles ensure that these pasos are impeccable and increasingly sumptuous. The statues of the Virgins themselves have an extensive wardrobe from which the *santera* (statue keeper) will choose as appropriate.

As the processions wind their way, onlookers take up strategic positions to admire the floats – illuminated as they negotiate a darkened lane – as well as the skill of the carriers beneath. Amid this endless shuffle, the outdoor terraces of bars are quickly swamped with people caught up in the sometimes surprising bustle that is so characteristic of religious expression in Andalucía.

"Al cielo con Ella!" (To heaven with Her!), rises the cry as the float is lifted and the procession advances.

RELIGIOUS PILGRIMAGES (ROMERÍAS)

Devotion to the Virgin is without doubt the most characteristic feature of Andalusian religious fervour, to the extent that it is said that "Andalucía is the land of the Blessed Mary". Countless sanctuaries advocate every possible veneration of the Virgin: de la Cabeza (the head), de la Bella (the beautiful) de la Regla (the rule), del Sol (the sun), de la Luna (the moon), de la Peña (cliff) and de la Sierra (the mountain), to name but a few.

Every *romería* (religious pilgrimage) has its idiosyncratic features, some particularly odd, but in general each consists of a pilgrimage to a church, often on decorated carts and horseback, and a religious ceremony with a procession, followed by dinner outdoors with dancing and singing until dawn, or beyond. The most famous *romería* is to the **Virgin of El Rocío**, an event attracting close to

El Rocío pilgrimage

R. Mattes/MICHELIN

one million pilgrims and visitors from around Spain as well as from other European countries (☝️ *see EL ROCÍO*).

MAY CROSSES (CRUCES DE MAYO)

The Festival of the Crosses *(cruces)*, held every year on 3 May, celebrates the Discovery of the Holy Cross. According to tradition, in the 4C the mother of the Emperor Constantine discovered the cross *(Lignum crucis)* on which Christ had died and distributed fragments throughout the Christian world.

The Cruces de Mayo are celebrated all over Andalucía, although veneration varies from province to province. In some areas, the crosses are fixed and venerated all year round, as in La Palma del Condado in the province of Huelva, while in others crosses are erected specifically for the celebration, as in Conil de la Frontera (Cádiz). In every case, the crosses are adorned with branches of rosemary and flowers. Religious ceremonies are followed by singing and dancing well into the night. In Córdoba, Cruces de Mayo erected around the city are particularly renowned for their imagination and stunning beauty.

CARNIVAL

In most Andalusian towns and cities, the *fiestas* during Carnival have a long tradition, initiated by Sevilla during its Golden Age and further developed by **Cádiz**, nowadays the site of the most spectacular celebrations. Carnival is a time of excess for the imagination and an opportunity for extravagant celebration. It is the culmination of months of hard practice and costume design.

The main participants are known as *comparsas* – groups dressed in similar costume who make their way through the streets singing ironic and humorous songs based on political and current affairs.

Carnival celebrations near the Meseta and the borders with Castilla tend to be more restrained in nature. More importance is attributed to the so-called "burial of the sardine", in reference to fish eaten during Lent.

THE FERIA

The Andalusian feria is a celebration encompassing all the colour, music, dance and exuberance of the region. Its origins lie in the spring and autumn cattle fairs, which were first held, as in the rest of Spain, during the Middle Ages. As these fairs developed over the centuries, they evolved into general celebrations where everyone would dress up in finery, bring out their finest horses and carriages, and above all, enjoy themselves to the full. Although every feria has its specific characteristics, they also have many features in common.

Illuminated casetas at the Sevilla Fair

R. Mattes/MICHELIN

Strangely, Sevilla's April Fair, the best-known of all Andalucía's festivals and one which was to serve as a model for other important modern ferias such as those held in Córdoba, Málaga and Jerez, is relatively recent, created in 1847.

The area used to host the feria is generally enclosed with access via a large entrance gateway decorated with myriad coloured lights. Inside, the fairground is separated into distinct zones: the so-called **calle del Infierno** (literally, the Street of Hell); the **Recreo** (entertainment area); **Los Cacharritos**, home to typical fairground attractions (Ferris wheel, roller coaster, shooting ranges, tombolas, etc.); the shopping area, or Rastro, (only generally found in small towns and villages); and the feria's **Real** area, with its succession of flimsy, ephemeral entertainment booths known as **casetas**. The booths are decorated with lamps, pictures and furniture designed for the simple pleasures of eating, drinking and dancing, day and night; some are private, with entrance strictly reserved for members or for those with tickets, while others are open to everyone.

Although it may not appear obvious to first-time visitors, there is a strict programme for the feria, as is the case with every traditional celebration in Andalucía. From noon until around four in the afternoon, everyone gathers in the Real dressed in traditional costume. As music starts up in the casetas, encouraging the more energetic early birds to dance a *sevillana* or two, others parade through the streets on magnificent horses with elaborately decorated harnesses and saddles or in elegant open carriages. The period after the siesta or the traditional bullfight is the time for children to make the most of the festivities. As darkness falls, more visitors return to the feria, in everyday dress, for more eating, drinking and dancing until the early hours of the morning. Such is the typical routine during feria week – a time for little sleep and significant reserves of energy.

BULLFIGHTING

The world of bullfighting, which excites the passions of its enthusiastic followers and staunch opponents alike, is indelibly associated with Andalusian life.

Whether the event is a full-fledged *corrida de toros* featuring leading matadors, a *novillada,* at which aspiring bullfighters take on three-year-old bulls, or a bullfight on horseback *(corrida de rejoneo)*, the bullfight is the highlight of the feria in every Andalusian town and city.

In general, a bullfight comprises the killing of six bulls by three matadors. Each combat is divided into three acts (or *tercios*): the mounted picador thrusts his lance into the bull's neck; the bandilleros plunge their decorative darts into the bull's back; and lastly, the matador himself performs his *faena* with his red cape *(muleta)* to demonstrate his art, technique and bravery, before finally putting the bull to the sword.

If the faena is performed successfully and the kill *(estocada)* is clean, swift and effective, aficicionados in the stands

Bullfight

will wave their white handkerchiefs to implore the presiding judge to award one ear, two ears or even the bull's tail to the matador in recognition of his skilful performance.

The expertise of the bullfighters and the knowledgable spectators in Andalucía makes the region the ideal centre in which to discover the world of the *corrida*. The magnificent *Plazas de Toros* in Sevilla and Ronda are a must. Good alternatives are the bullrings of Antequera, El Puerto de Santa María, or Sanlúcar de Barrameda, and attending the bullfights at the *ferias* held in Jerez, Córdoba, Granada, Almería and Jaén.

FLAMENCO

Flamenco was created towards the middle of the 19C from a combination of musical forms present in Andalucía, including Jewish, Byzantine, Moorish and even Hindu. Experts fail to agree on the scale of this influence, but what does seem clear is that it developed in Lower Andalucía (Jerez, Utrera, Lebrija, Cádiz) among families who passed the art from generation to generation. Though in no way of gypsy origin, it is generally acknowledged that the *gitanos* have incorporated their own personality and their considerable talents into flamenco.

For a long time considered to be an art form associated with "low lifes" – a view expressed at the turn of the century by writers such as Miguel de Unamuno – initiatives led by leading cultural figures such as Federico García Lorca and Manuel de Falla elevated flamenco to the status of the cultural expression of the Andalusian people.

Flamenco has seen the rise to fame of singers such as Antonio Mairena, Fosforito, la Niña de la Puebla and, in more recent times, **Camarón de la Isla**, renowned guitarists such as Paco de Lucía and dancers of the quality of Cristina Hoyos.

The new generations have demonstrated that flamenco remains a living art and that it is capable of evolving and assimilating new rhythms.

Purists do not agree, but groups such as Ketama and Navajita Plateá, guitarists such as Raimundo Amador and dancers of international renown such as Joaquín Cortés and Antonio Canales are ready to show that flamenco can explore new avenues.

Although to many observers and listeners the individual aspects of flamenco may be somewhat difficult to comprehend and interpret, it is impossible not to be moved by the passion of this truly Andalusian art form.

TRADITIONAL COSTUME

Each of Andalucía's provinces has its regional costume, which varies significantly from one area to the next. In Málaga, for example, part of the **verdiales** costume consists of a garish hat totally covered with flowers and a variety of coloured bands; this contrasts with the **piconera** costume in Cádiz, with its satin skirt, white blouse, black apron and hairnets of arbutus flowers; and the costume of the Alpujarras mountains (Granada), with its multicoloured striped skirt, long-sleeved blouse and flowery shawl.

However, what is considered to be the Andalusian costume par excellence is the one traditionally worn in Córdoba and Sevilla which saw various modifications during the second half of the 20C. In fact, the so-called Andalusian costume is perhaps the only one in the world with its own fashion, which varies from year to year in colour, number and length of pleated ruffles, the shape of the sleeves, etc.

Variations apart, the **traje de faralaes** or flamenco costume worn by women is characterised by bright colours and a tight fit, which highlights the figure. A wide neck and a skirt ruffled at the bottom complete the look.

The costume is sometimes accompanied by a shawl, earrings and bracelets to match, as well as real or artificial flowers in the hair. The country version, worn on horseback, consists of a riding skirt,

R. Mattes/MICHELIN

Traditional flamenco performance

a blouse with a lace apron, and a black jacket.

The men's costume, generally black, grey or dark brown in colour, includes a short jacket, white shirt without a tie, tight-fitting trousers and leather boots. The traditional headgear is either the wide-brimmed *sombrero cordobés* or the lower-crowned *sombrero sevillano*.

Food and Drink

The colourful cuisine of Andalucía is distinctly Mediterranean in character. Regional gastronomy is based on the wealth of local produce, with pride of place given to its olive oil, the key ingre-

Gazpacho

This chilled, refreshing and healthy soup is probably Andalucía's most famous dish. Its basic ingredients are tomatoes, cucumber, peppers, oil, vinegar, garlic and salt, the quantities of which vary from family to family and chef to chef; many people will also add croutons, raw onions and diced peppers. Variations on this chilled soup starter theme are *salmorejo* (bread mashed with tomatoes, garlic, oil, vinegar and salt), *ajo blanco* (similar to *salmorejo* but made with almonds instead of tomatoes and served with grapes or melon) and *porra antequerena*, similar to gazpacho with chopped, hard boiled eggs and jamón. serrano added

©Ramon Grosso Dolarea/Bigstockphoto.com

dient in many of the region's recipes. Another key component in Andalusian cuisine is wine, and in particular its world-famous sherries, which provide the perfect accompaniment to the typical dishes of southern Spain.

Eight centuries of Moorish presence have had a profound effect on Andalusian culture, including the region's cuisine. Moorish agricultural techniques, based on making the best use of water through irrigation networks, made it possible to grow crops on hitherto uncultivated land, thus enabling the region to produce fruits and vegetables throughout the year. The Moors also brought with them a whole range of new crops (rice, aubergines, artichokes and asparagus) as well as spices, which at the time were unknown in the Western world (such as pepper, cinnamon and cumin).

The Moors also introduced the modern-day order for the presentation of dishes which, until then, had been served at the same time. Yet, despite its deep influence on southern Spain, Arab cuisine failed to displace traditional Mediterranean cooking, centred on wine and olive oil, which remains very much alive today. Nowadays, the wines of Andalucía have a well-deserved worldwide reputation, while the region's olive oil, including two quality Denominación de Origen labels – Baena (Córdoba) and Sierra de Segura (Jaén) – currently enjoys great popularity.

The dominant features of Andalusian cuisine differ according to whether you are on the coast, where fish and seafood predominate, or inland, where the cooking is dominated by meat dishes, vegetables, hearty soups and stews.

Although fried fish (pescaíto frito) is a popular dish in bars along the coast, Andalusian cuisine is mainly based on its stews (guisos), which may also be known as cocido andaluz, olla or puchero. These can be found in every province, with variations according to local ingredients.

Dishes with either pork or chicken, vegetables and chickpeas and/or various type of beans (judías) are also popular across Andalucía. The local meat stew known as pringá is a popular tapa in the bars of Sevilla.

In the more mountainous parts of inland Andalucía, game stews are an important part of the local cuisine, providing energy and warmth on a cold winter's night. This contrasts with lighter fish dishes, prepared in every manner possible along the Mediterranean and Atlantic coasts; these may be boiled (cocido); grilled (a la plancha), particularly the shrimp and prawns from Sanlúcar de Barrameda; served in stews (guisados), such as the seafood stews (guisos marineros) from Cádiz; fried (frito), including anchovies, squid and cuttlefish; or barbecued (asado), an ideal way of grilling sardines caught off the Málaga coast.

Another important aspect of Andalusian gastronomy is the wide choice of cured hams and sausages (embutidos). Local products include morcón, a type of

Tapas

The tradition of eating tapas is synonymous with Spain, Andalucía and, more particularly, Sevilla, where they originated. Although tapas originally consisted of no more than just a thin slice of cured ham, a single prawn or a small piece of Spanish omelette to accompany a glass of wine, as time has passed, tapas have increased in size to such an extent that a selection of tapas or the larger raciones are often eaten instead of a full meal. The choice is seemingly endless, with a whole range of cured hams (including the famous jamon ibérico), cheeses, prawns either grilled (a la plancha) or with a garlic sauce (al ajillo), squid, tortillas (omelettes), fried fish (pescaítos fritos), etc. on offer. Locals will often be seen enjoying tapas standing at the bar or even out on the street at busy times, with refreshment taking the form of a chilled glass of draught beer or a glass of fino or manzanilla.

Visitors are often somewhat daunted by this hectic scene, but it's well worth fighting your way to the bar to order local specialities, which are usually posted on a board. If all else fails, point at what you want and hope for the best! Above all, make sure you enjoy the convivial atmosphere of this gastronomic art.

blood pudding; the cured legs of hams *(cañas)* from Jabugo (Huelva), one of Spain's main areas for the rearing of acorn-fed pigs for the famous *jamón ibérico*; *morcilla* (black pudding) from Ronda (Málaga) and the renowned sausages and hams from Trévelez, in the province of Granada.

BREAKFAST

In most bars and cafeterias you can try a typical Andalusian breakfast *(desayuno)* consisting of toasted bread with olive oil and manteca *colorá*, a reddish-coloured sort of dripping. If this traditional delicacy fails to whet your appetite, try deep-fried *churros*, long strips of doughnut, traditionally served with thick, hot chocolate.

Andalucía's cheeses are generally made from goats' or sheep's milk, although cows' milk is used on rare occasions. Although these predominantly strong-flavoured cheeses are little known outside the region, they are an ideal accompaniment to a glass of chilled fino, manzanilla or oloroso sherry, but (unlike in the French tradition) are never eaten after the main course. The main areas of cheese production are the mountains of Almería and Granada, the Serranía de Ronda (Málaga) and in the Sierra de Grazalema (Cádiz).

Moorish and Jewish influence is very evident in the tremendous variety of regional cakes and pastries. Some of the best- known, flavoured with cinnamon, almonds and anise, include the *polvorones* and *mantecados* from Estepa (Málaga), which are eaten throughout Spain at Christmas; the delicious *tocinos de cielo* (literally "bacon from heaven"), a custard pudding from Jerez de la Frontera; and flaky round cakes known as *roscos* in a variety of guises such as millefeuilles *(milhojas)* and honeyed fritters *(pestiños)*.

Nowadays, many of these cakes are produced by nuns according to traditional recipes dating back many centuries. Which is why so many of them have names such as *huesos de santo* (saint's bones), *cabello de ángel* (angel hair), *suspiro de monja* (nun's sigh) and the aforementioned "bacon from heaven".

LOCAL SPECIALITIES

Each province has its signature dishes. The specialities in the province of Granada include *habas con jamón* (broad beans with ham), *sopita de ajo* (garlic soup), a range of omelettes, including *tortilla del Sacromonte*, also known as *tortilla granaína* (with ham, brains and pig's kidneys), *rabo de toro* (oxtail), and the hearty *potaje de San Antón*, a soup made with broad beans, bacon, black pudding and pig's ears, which is traditionally eaten on 17 January.

Cod, potatoes and peppers are the main ingredients of *gurupina*, a speciality of the town of Baza, in the mountainous east of the province, where *testuz*, a dish comprising broad beans, white haricot beans, black pudding, bacon and pig's ears is also a local favourite.

Córdoba is known for its excellent grilled meats *(churrascos)*, in particular pork, and *alcachofas a la montillana* (artichokes from Montilla).

In the province of Jaén make sure you try the humble *Collejas* (bladder campion

H. Champollion/MICHELIN

Specialities of the region

The solera method

The solera blending process, which is applied to most Andalusian sherries, enables a constant quality to be maintained from one year to the next and is based on a system in which between four and eight levels of barrels are positioned one on top of the other. Once fermentation has taken place in accordance with normal wine-producing methods, and pure alcohol added, the new wine is pumped into the top barrel. The sherry to be bottled is taken from the solera (the barrel closest to the floor) and is immediately replaced by sherry from the barrel immediately above it *(criadera primavera)*; this process continues until every barrel in the chain has been refilled. By following this method, quality is maintained from one harvest to the next.

plant) in croquettes, asparagus *(espárragos)* coated in a variety of sauces, *empanadas del viernes*, literally "Friday pasties", and broad bean and aubergine soup *(potaje de habas con berenjenas)*.

The Sierra de Cazorla, in the same province, is known for its *talarines*, a type of tart stuffed with partridge or rabbit, its game dishes, marinated partridge, and the extraordinary bitter orange fish soup which is a speciality of Baena.

Arroz marinero, the Andalusian variant of paella, is more moist than its Valencian cousin, and can be found along both coasts.

WINE AND SHERRY

Andalucía has 86 000ha/212 500 acres of vineyards producing wines which have a superb reputation around the world. Almost all of this land is found within certified designations of origin *(denominación es de origen)*.

Denominaciones de Origen

Four *denominaciones de origen* (D.O.) currently govern the quality of Andalusian wines: Jerez, Montilla-Moriles, Condado de Huelva and Málaga. Each of these areas concentrates on the production of full-bodied wines, although recent diversification has seen their range expand towards young, light and fruity table wines.

D.O. Jerez

The sherries of the Jerez area, which include the famous *finos* and *manzanillas*, are Andalucía's best-known and most prestigious wines. Sherry, as the name suggests (the word sherry is the anglicised form of the town's name),

can only be produced in the designated area around Jerez, while *manzanillas* are the exclusive preserve of Sanlúcar de Barrameda. The Jerez appellation also produces sweet and dry *olorosos*, sweet wines *(vinos dulces)* such as Moscatel and Pedro Ximénez, and *amontillados*, which undergo a longer oxidisation in the barrel.

D.O. Montilla-Moriles

These excellent wines produced in the area south of Córdoba have a high alcohol content. Although they are classified according to the same criteria as those wines produced in Jerez, Montilla-Moriles wines are very different from those produced further west.

D.O. Málaga

Up until a century ago, sweet Málaga wines could be enjoyed on the finest tables in Europe. Despite their decline

Bodega, González Byass, Jerez de la Frontera

in fortune due to changing tastes, they are still the perfect accompaniment to many dessert dishes.

D.O. Condado

The pale and fruity Condado wines are produced from the Zalema grape. There are two types of Condado: Condado Pálido, reminiscent of the sherries of Jerez and manzanilla; and Condado Viejo, similar to an *oloroso*, which can attain an alcohol content of 23 per cent.

In addition to these leading regions, Andalucía also has other, smaller areas of vineyards producing wines rarely seen elsewhere in Spain or abroad. These include Aljarafe and Los Palacios (Sevilla); Villaviciosa de Córdoba (Córdoba); Bailén, Lopera and Torreperogil (Jaén); Costa-Albondón (Granada) and Laujar (Almería).

Serving suggestions

The sherries of Andalucía are produced according to a special solera blending process which guarantees uniform quality for years (&see box, opposite page). These wines are traditionally served in *catavinos* – narrow, tall glasses which enable the superb qualities of the wine to be enjoyed to the full.

Bottle of Montilla-Moriles

H. Champollion/MICHELIN

Each variety of sherry should be drunk at a different temperature:

- *finos* are generally chilled to between 8ºC and 10ºC. Once opened, a bottle should be drunk as quickly as possible;
- *amontillados* should ideally be served between 12ºC and 14ºC;
- *olorosos* are at their best at a temperature of 18ºC.

Brandies and liqueurs

Brandies and liqueurs are also an important feature of the Andalusian economy. Anise, brandy and rum produced in Andalucía are sold throughout Spain and are increasingly being exported.

The early **aniseed**-based liqueurs originated from Ojén (Málaga), next to Spain's very first blast furnace, at a time when it was thought that aniseed had a beneficial effect on respiratory tracts affected by the mining, iron and steel industries. Today, the main areas for anise are in Montilla (Córdoba), which produces liqueurs with a smooth aroma and high alcohol content; Cazalla and Constantina (Sevilla), famous for their strong *cazalla*; and Zalamea la Real and Alosno (Huelva), with its dry and potent aguardiente.

Most of the **brandy** served in bars around Spain comes from Jerez de la Frontera, Sanlúcar de Barrameda and Puerto de Santa María, all of which belong to a regulatory body for brandy quality, the Consejo Regulador del Brandy. However, it is also distilled in Rute and Montilla (Córdoba), Málaga and in La Palma del Condado (Huelva).

It should also be remembered that the distilling and production techniques for **rum**, which is now considered to be a typically Caribbean drink, and its main ingredient – sugar cane – were exported to Cuba from Spain. Centuries later, when Fidel Castro came to power on the island, some Cuban producers transferred their production plants to Andalucía, particularly to Málaga and Granada, the only parts of Europe where sugar cane is grown.

Patio de los Leones, Alhambra, Granada
B. Kaufmann/MICHELIN

AGUILAR DE LA FRONTERA ★

POPULATION: 13 397.

The historic, whitewashed border *(frontera)* town of Aguilar extends across a hill above green vineyards, with fine mansions and Baroque churches in its charming old quarter. During your visit, try the delicious *risaos* made with almonds, sugar, egg yolk and lemon, or the equally tasty coffee or strawberry meringues *(merengas)*.

- **Information:** Cuesta de Jesús, 2, 14920 Aguilar de la Frontera. ☎957 66 00 00.
- **Orient Yourself:** The town lies In southern Córdoba province, 51km/32mi south of the city of Córdoba via the A 45.
- **Parking:** Leave your car in the central llano de las Coronadas.
- **Don't Miss:** The 17C and 19C mansions in calle Arrabal (nos 5, 11 and 13).
- **Organising Your Time:** Allow a couple of hours.
- **Also See:** CABRA, LUCENA, MONTILLA, CÓRDOBA.

Walking Tour

> *Head towards placilla Vieja, then climb the cuesta de Jesús hill.*

Nuestra Señora del Soterraño ★

Open during services only.

The parish church, honouring Aguilar's patron saint, dates from the 16C.

Exterior

The Baroque left portal originates from an earlier church. It is similar to other doorways in Aguilar. The finely sculpted doorway to the right is Plateresque.

Interior

The chapel decoration is surprisingly rich. The main nave has a Mudéjar *artesonado* ceiling, while the high altar is crowned by a Gothic pointed vault. A large Baroque altarpiece in the presbytery honours the patron saint.

An 18C lectern and attractive walnut **choir stalls** are at the rear of the central aisle. Medallions on seat backs show primitive yet expressive saints and Apostles.

The **Capilla del Sagrario** ★ and the **Capilla de la Inmaculada** *(left and right of the Capilla Mayor)* hold notable 17C stuccowork. Note too the **high relief of the Last Supper** in the Capilla del Sagrario and the venerated statue of Jesus in the mid-18C **Capilla de Jesús Nazareno** ★. Stuccowork completely covers the cupola.

The ruins of a castle, the Castillo de Poley, lie on a small hill behind the church.

> *From llano de las Coronadas, follow calle Santa Brígida.*

Iglesia del Hospital de Santa Brígida

This 16C church was rebuilt in the 17C and 18C. Note the central tower flanked by simple Baroque doorways.

Unusually for the area, the 18C tower is neo-Classical.

> *Return to llano de las Coronadas and take calle Moralejo.*

Holy Week

As you wander through the streets of Puente Genil, you may notice the strange signs outside some of its houses such as *Imperio Romano*, *Cien Luces*, *Los Levitas* etc. These are the headquarters of the 65 brotherhoods that participate in the Holy Week festivities. The processions, which feature characters from the Old and New Testaments are a peculiarity of Aguilar's Semana Santa.

Monasterio de San José y San Roque

This Carmelite *convento* (convent) was built between 1668 and 1761.

The interior (🕐 *open during services only*) is Aguilar's Baroque masterpiece, with sumptuous retables, oil paintings, stucco foliage, volutes and angels.

Note the fine mansions on calle Moralejo and calle Carrera.

▷ *From calle Moralejo, take calle Granada or calle Mercaderes.*

Plaza de San José★

This unusual octagonal square, plain and harmonious, is dominated by the town hall *(ayuntamiento)*.

▷ *Leave plaza de San José via calle Don Teodoro.*

Torre del Reloj★

This 18C Baroque tower on the plaza de los Desamparados, built for civil use, became a model for contemporaneous belfries. Features include a cupola with *azulejo* decoration and a turret.

Calle del Carmen

Just off calle Desamparados, calle del Carmen affords views of surrounding vineyards.

In **placita del Carmen** stands a Christ of the Lanterns, similar in style to the one found in Córdoba.

▷ *Return to calle Moralejo and head along calle Vicente Núñez.*

At no 2, the **Casa Señorial del Caballo de Santiago**, is a mansion named after the horse of St James, depicted on the central balcony.

Excursions

Laguna de Zóñar

Follow the A 309 towards Puente Genil. At km 77 the **Centro de Visitantes Zoñar** (🕐☎*957 33 52 52*) has an interactive exhibition on the lagoon, which is home to the endangered and very rare **malvasia duck**.

Detail of Torre del Reloj

B. Kaufmann/MICHELIN

Puente Genil

18km/11mi along the A 309.

A pleasant walkway runs alongside the river of this village, named for its 16C bridge. This region is renowned for its quinces, which are used to produce a variety of local specialities.

In the centre are old mansion houses, particularly in calle Don Gonzalo, and the **Museo Arqueológico y Etnográfico** (🕐 *open Tue–Sun 10.30am–1.30pm;* ☎*957 60 29 34),* a small archaeological and ethnographical museum displaying local finds.

There are four notable churches: the 17C **Nuestra Señora de la Concepción**, with its tower-flanked portal and polychrome stucco main altarpiece; the **Iglesia de la Purificación**, with its attractive 19C bell tower and spire, and an Immaculate Conception by Pedro Duque Cornejo; the **Iglesia del Convento de San Francisco**, with its fine sculptures; and the **Iglesia de Jesús Nazareno**, decorated with paintings by local 19C artists, and housing a venerated image of Jesus of Nazareth, Puente Genil's patron saint.

ALCALÁ LA REAL★

POPULATION: 21 493

Hilltop Alcalá la Real is overlooked by the Fortaleza de la Mota, an imposing fortress offering magnificent views of the surrounding olive groves. The birthplace of poet Juan Ruiz, known as the **Arcipreste de Hita**, and medieval sculptors **Juan Martínez Montañés** and **Pablo de Rojas**, Alcalá today is an agricultural and commercial centre.

- **Information:** Paseo de los Álamos, Fortaleza de la Mota, 23680 Alcalá la Real. ☎953 58 22 17.
- ▶ **Orient Yourself:** Alcalá lies between Granada (52km/32mi southeast) and Jaén.
- **Don't Miss:** The Fortaleza de Mota for a sense of medieval Alcalá.
- **Organising Your Time:** Take two hours, or more if you enjoy old fortresses.
- **Especially for Kids:** La Mota is interesting for grown-ups and fun for kids.
- **Also See:** PRIEGO DE CÓRDOBA, MONTEFRÍO, GRANADA, JAÉN.

A Bit of History

The town's origins date back to prehistoric times; however, due to its strategic position on the border between Christian- and Muslim-held lands, it became synonymous with fierce battles between the two adversaries. During the period of Moorish domination, which lasted over 600 years, *Qalat*, (a fortified settlement in Arabic), as it was then known, reached the pinnacle of its splendour, until its reconquest by Alfonso XI in 1341.

Sights

Fortaleza de la Mota★★

Open year-round daily 10.30am–1.30pm, 5pm–8pm; Oct–May 3.30pm–6.30pm. ∞€1.50. ☎639 64 77 96.

This majestic fortress blends into the crags and rocks of La Mota hill. The Puerta de la Imagen is similar to the notable Puerta de la Justicia in the Alhambra.

The original Moorish *alcazaba* is a castle with three towers: the Torre de Mocha,

Fortaleza de la Mota, Alcalá la Real

R. Mattes/MICHELIN

Address Book

For coin ranges, see the cover flap.

WHERE TO STAY

Hospedería Zacatín – *Pradillo, 2.* ☎*953 58 05 68. www.hospederiazacatin. com. 15 rooms.* Basic, but with a certain charm thanks to the personal attention of the owner and its location. Attractive rustic dining (🍽) and a bar.

Hotel Torrepalma – *Conde de Torre palma, 2. www.hoteltorrepalma.com.* ☎*953 58 18 00. 38 rooms.* Comfortable and modern, on one of Alcalá's busiest and noisiest shopping streets. Ask for a room facing away from the street.

WHERE TO EAT

El Curro – *Ramón y Cajal, 6.* ☎*953 58 30 50. Closed Wed and Sept.* This is first and foremost a bar popular with locals. Although there is a somewhat nondescript dining room, regulars tend to eat in a more attractive room with a low ceiling and fireplace. Specialities here include grilled meats and ham.

LOCAL SPECIALITIES

A favourite local dish is *pollo a la secretaria*, chicken with peppers and peas in an onion and saffron sauce.

PASEO DE LOS ÁLAMOS

This delightful avenue is the ideal place to relax at the end of a long day and enjoy a chilled glass of the local wine on the outdoor terraces of its numerous tapas bars.

Torre de la Campana and Torre del Homenaje, built on the remains of the former mosque. Inside, the **Iglesia de Santo Domingo**★, a Gothic-Mudéjar church built by Alfonso XI, retains the tower of the former minaret – one of the most characteristic features of Alcalá – and holds a fine 15C retable. The **Iglesia de Santa María la Mayor**, on an esplanade of the fortress, was badly damaged in the War of Independence. Diego de Siloé is known to have worked on its attractive Renaissance **façade**, Plateresque in style. This monumental complex also houses the interesting **Museo Arqueológico**, inside the Torre del Homenaje, with its collection of archaeological exhibits from Alcalá region.

Nuestra Señora de las Angustias

This impressive octagonal 13C church built by Ventura Rodríguez holds exceptional medieval painted **tablets**★.

Ayuntamiento

The charming 18C Baroque town hall is on pleasant **plaza del Arcipreste de Hita**, flanked by two towers, opposite an artistic **sundial**★ by Fernando Tapia.

Palacio Abacial

The abbot's palace, in front of the attractive Los Álamos fountain at an end of the paseo of the same name, is soberly neo-Classical. The façade has a Renaissance-inspired balcony and an elegant doorway with reliefs and coats of arms.

Excursions

Castillo de Locubín

12km/8mi north.
The road winds to the Puerto del Castillo pass and this whitewashed settlement, with superb **views**★ of the River San Juan and Víboras Reservoir. Visit the remains of the **Moorish castle**, part of a system of border defences.

Alcaudete

26km/16mi northwest along the N 432.
Nestled amid olive groves on a promontory, Alcaudete was conquered by the Infante Don Fernando de Antequera in 1408, and became one of Granada's border bastions.
It is most famous today for its pastries: *hojaldrinas*, *empanadillas* and *roscos de vino* (the latter are doughnut-like cakes made by the nuns from the Convento de Santa Clara).

Castle ruins

The Moorish *alcazaba* was built on the site of a Roman fortress and has preserved several vestiges of its walls and keep.

Iglesia de Santa María

This Gothic church with its Plateresque side portal stands at the foot of the castle. Inside, note the fine *artesonado* ceiling, the Renaissance grilles in front of the high altar, and the doors of the sacristy.

Iglesia de San Pedro

This 16C Mudéjar-style church has a fine altarpiece.

Plaza Mayor

The main square is situated at the heart of a labyrinth of narrow streets with a number of shops and bars. The 18C town hall comes into view after passing through an archway known as the Arco de la Villa.

ALGECIRAS

POPULATION: 109 000.

Its strategic location, facing the Rock of **Gibraltar**, has exerted a major influence on Gibraltar since Moorish troops landed in the 8C. In modern times Algeciras bustles with commerce, links Europe and Africa, and is Spain's leading passenger port.

- **Information:** Juan de la Cierva, Algeciras, ☎956 78 41 31, otalgeciras@andalucia.org. Avda del Ejército/20 de abril, La Línea de la Concepción ☎956 78 41 35, otlinea@andalucia.org. Casemates Square, Gibraltar ☎9567 749 82. Cathedral Square (Duke of Kent House), ☎9567 749 50. www.gibraltar.gi./tourism. www.gibraltar.gov.uk.
- ▶ **Orient Yourself:** Algeciras and Gibraltar are magnificently sited at the southern tip of mainland Spain, in sight of North Africa, at opposite ends of a wide bay.
- **Don't Miss:** The views from the road to Tarifa, the views from the top of the Rock of Gibraltar.
- **Organising Your Time:** Allow a morning or afternoon for the main sights.
- **Especially for Kids:** Gibraltar's famous apes, the Tunnels and St Michael's Cave within the Rock, dolphin and whale watching in the Bay of Gibraltar.
- **Also See:** TARIFA, JIMENA DE LA FRONTERA, COSTA DEL SOL.

Visit

Museo Municipal

Open mid-Jun–late Sept Mon–Fri 10am–2pm; rest of year Mon–Sat 10am–2pm, 5pm–8pm. ☎956 57 06 72.

This large house in Parque de las Acacias displays Roman amphorae, which bear witness to the once-significant trade that took place in the Bay of Algeciras. Other exhibits relate to the Siege of Algeciras (1342–44), when Alfonso XI employed the first firearms in Spain, known as *truenos* (thunderclaps).

Market

This iron and concrete structure in the plaza Palma has an innovative roof supported at just four points.

Plaza Alta

Note the attractive 1930s Mudéjar-style azulejo-and-brick fountain surrounded by palms in the square. Nearby are the 18C Iglesia de Nuestra Señora de la

Paco de Lucía

Born Francisco Sánchez Gómez in Algeciras on 21 December 1947, **Paco de Lucía** is widely recognised as one of Spain's greatest ever flamenco guitarists, accompanying singers such as "Camarón de la Isla" and developing worldwide recognition for his improvisations in the company of renowned jazz musicians such as of John McLaughlin and Al Di Méola.

Address Book

For coin ranges, see the cover flap.

GETTING THERE

GIBRALTAR★
20km/12mi east of Algeciras.
Gibraltar is a British Crown Colony and requires a passport for entry. Visitors are advised to check the entry situation before arrival as long queues (1hr or more) occasionally develop for motorists entering and leaving Gibraltar. On these occasions, it is worth leaving your car on the Spanish side and walking across the border.

WHERE TO STAY

ALGECIRAS
◉◉**AC La Línea de la Concepción** – *Los Caireles, 2.* ☎*956 17 55 66. www. ac-hotels.com.* 80 rooms. Sleek, well-equipped rooms in this stylish chain hotel overlook the pool or Gibraltar.

GIBRALTAR
◉◉◉◉◉**The Rock** – *3 Europa Road.* ☎*350 730 00. www.rockhotelgibraltar. com.* Built in 1932 and retaining much of its colonial style and elegance this is easily Gibraltar's best hotel and restaurant with magnificent views across the Bay.

Palma, a mixture of Baroque and neo-Classical styles.

Merenid Baths (Baños Meriníes)
These 13C Moorish baths in Parque María Cristina were originally part of a Merenid dynasty residence. A Moorish wheel and well have been reconstructed.

Excursions

The road to Tarifa
This 21km/13mi stretch of the southernmost road in Europe offer stunning **views**★★★ of North Africa. Cars can stop at the Mirador del Estrecho, 13km/8mi along, though views are better near Algeciras. Note the wind turbines.

La Línea de la Concepción
17km/11mi west of Algeciras.
One of the youngest towns in Spain, this was built as part of a defensive line against the British. The town has little to offer tourists. The heavily built-up centre is laid out around calle Real and the Iglesia de la Inmaculada Concepción, built in 1879.

Gibraltar★

A little part of Britain, complete with warm dark beer and prices in Sterling (though Euros are widely accepted),

Gibraltar is synonymous with its Rock, a limestone promontory rising 423m/1 388ft above the sea, and visible from all around the bay.
The history of Gibraltar is all about its location. **Tarik-ibn-Ziyad**'s army of Moors landed here in 711. In antiquity, the Rock was know by its Latin name *Calpe*, or more colloquially one of the Pillars of Hercules.
Its present name derives from 'Tariq's Mountain' (in Arabic *Djebel Tarik*). Christians and Moors contested the Rock, until the Duke of Medina Sidonia took it in 1462. The British took permanent but disputed control during the 18C **War of the Spanish Succession**.

Gibraltar Museum
◷*Open Mon–Fri 10am–6pm. Sat, 10am –2pm.* ◉*£2.* ☎*350 74289. www.gib.gi/ museum/museum.htm.*
Housed in a simple colonial building above 14C **Moorish baths**★, exhibits cover the history of the Rock and rangie from the 1848 discovery of the **Gibraltar skull** (a Neanderthal woman), to Gibraltar's role in the Second World War. Don't miss the enormous **model**★ (1865) of the Rock.

Main Street and the Lower Rock
Gibraltar's main thoroughfare is lined by shops, banks and bars, many with a distinctly British feel. Worth seeing is **St Mary's Catholic Cathedral**, built above

Rock of Gibraltar

the former main mosque, and the **Convento**, the residence of Gibraltar's governor since 1728, where the changing of the guard occurs several times daily.
On Rosia Road is **Nelson's Anchorage** and the **100-tonne gun** (⏰*open daily year-round 9.30am–6.45pm.* ⮕*£1 (free with Upper Rock ticket).* Built in 1870 it has a barrel length of over 9.7m/32ft, and was capable of firing 13km/8mi.

Upper Rock★   `Kids`
The top of the rock is accessible via cable car, car or taxi. Follow Main Street and then signs to the Upper Rock:
⏰*Open daily year-round 9.30am–7.15pm (World War II Tunnels may close earlier Sat–Sun). Last cable car return 7.45pm.* ⮕*(all attractions) £8, child £4. World War II Tunnels additional charge £6, child £6.*
⮕*Access to Upper Rock: cable car £8, child £4.50; vehicle £1.50; pedestrian 50p.* ☎*350 74950 or 200 45957.*
The Upper Rock is home to Gibraltar's most interesting sights and also offers splendid panoramic views★.
The **Great Siege Tunnels** originated during the Great Siege of 1779–82 when Spain and France were besieging Gibraltar.
The attacking forces dug into trenches right beneath the Rock so that the British could not get an angle to fire on them. In order to do so they began to dig tunnels, by hand, to get to a higher projection of rock to allow their guns to fire onto the French and Spanish forces. The dust created by the tunnelling was so stifling that air vents were created out of the side of the Rock; only

then was it realised that these holes made excellent embrasures for guns. The **World War II Tunnels** were built in 1940 to house barracks, offices, and a fully equipped hospital complete with an operating theatre and X-ray equipment. From here Operation Torch, the Allied invasion of French North Africa in November 1942, was coordinated.
The spectacular natural caverns of **St Michael's Cave** with their giant stalactites and stalagmites, begin about 350m above sea level and descend into the Rock. The cavern forms a huge auditorium, home to a spectacular sound and light show, staged twice daily (weekdays only). Concerts and live shows are also performed here (visit www.philharmonic.gi for concert information).
The Upper Rock is also a designated Nature Reserve, home to the famous **Barbary apes**, brought here by British troops from North Africa at the end of the 18C.
They roam freely and are quite tame. However do not approach them directly nor should you feed them (they are fed twice a day). According to legend, if the Apes leave Gibraltar it will cease to be British.

Dolphin and Whale Trips   `Kids`
The Straits and Bay of Gibraltar are two of the best places in Europe for guaranteed sighting of dolphins and whales. There are three operators:
Dolphin Adventure (☎*350 200 50650;* ⮕*£20, child £10);* Dolphin Safari (☎*350 200 71914; www.dolphinsafari.gi;* ⮕*£25, child £12);* Dolphin World (☎*350 544 81000;* ⮕*£20, child £10).*

ALHAMA DE GRANADA★

POPULATION: 5 894.

With its whitewashed houses and narrow streets literally overhanging a gorge, Alhama de Granada inspires both poets and travellers. The Moors named it Al-Hamma ('hot spring'), and it became a Nasrid capital. During the Reconquest, Christians paid enormous sums to take the waters.

- **Information:** Calle Paseo Montes Jovellar. ☎958 36 06 86.
- **Orient Yourself:** Alhama lies 60km/37mi southwest of Granada along the A 338.
- **Don't Miss:** The Moorish Quarter, the Hotel Balneario's Moorish spa.
- **Organising Your Time:** Allow two hours, more to "take the waters".
- **Also See:** LOJA, ANTEQUERA, MÁLAGA, NERJA, ALMUÑÉCAR, GRANADA.

A Bit of History

A Valuable Prize – Alhama was captured from the Moors by Christian troops under the Castilian **Ponce de León** in 1482, signalling the start of the **War of Granada**, which ended with the capture of the Nasrid capital ten years later. Due to its magnificent, almost impregnable position, the fertile fields surrounding it and, above all, its springs of thermal water, the qualities of which have been known since Roman times, Alhama was considered one of the jewels in the Nasrid crown. As such, its capture by the Christians was a mighty blow.

Walking Tour

Moorish Quarter★

Alhama's interesting Moorish quarter is best explored on foot. Start with the **view**★ from behind the **Iglesia del Carmen** over the famous gorge of the River Alhama.

Walk around the church to the delightful Baroque **Capilla de Jesús Nazareno**, past an Arab fortress restored in the 19C. Head up calle Baja de la Iglesia to the imposing tower of the **Iglesia de la Encarnación**, rising above white-washed houses.

Moorish cistern, Hotel Balneario

B. Kaufmann/MICHELIN

Iglesia de la Encarnación★

Open Tue–Thu noon–2pm. €1. ☎958 36 06 86.
The church stands on a former mosque. The Baroque portal conceals an early Gothic façade of plant motifs and fantastic animals. The sober interior is topped by a complex pointed vault. In the sacristy museum are 16C vestments.

Upon leaving the church, admire the Isabelline **Casa de la Inquisición** (House of the Inquisition, *right*), rebuilt in the 1950s. The enchanting **Plaza de los Presos** is on the other side of the tower with, to the right, the former 17C **prison**, and opposite, the façade of the 16C **granary**. Calle Vendederas leads to the kingdom of Granada's first military field hospital, now the **tourist office**.

▶ *Walk around the tourist office and follow calle Caño Wamba.*

An unusual 16C fountain and the ruins of the **Iglesia de las Angustias** are farther along.

▶ *Head down calle de la Mina.*

The **Moorish dungeons** (*mazmorras árabes*), excavated out of the rock, were used as both a prison and grain silo.

Excursion

Hotel Balneario
see WHERE TO STAY.

ALMERÍA

POPULATION: 168 025.

The whitewashed town of Almería spreads out between the sea and the arid hill of its impressive fortress (*alcazaba*). Until relatively recently it was quite isolated with no inland or coastal links. Today it is a leader in Spanish agriculture and its hot dry climate has also led to a belated tourism boom.

- **Information:** Parque Nicolás Salmerón, 04002 Almería. ☎950 27 43 55. www.andalucia.org.
- **Orient Yourself:** Almería is 172km/107mi southeast of Granada via the A 92.
- **Don't Miss:** The Alcazaba.
- **Organising Your Time:** Allow a day.
- **Also See:** Parque Natural de CABO DE GATA-NÍJAR, COSTA DE ALMERÍA, TABERNA, GUADIX.

A Bit of History

Almería was founded in the 9C by Abd ar-Rahman II. His son built the *alcazaba* and walls in the 10C, creating the port. Later the capital of a Taifa kingdom and an important textile centre, it was attacked by Christian Aragón. Almería became part of Nasrid Granada, and fell to the Catholic Monarchs in 1489.

During the early 16C, the city suffered Berber attacks, the expulsion

Alcazaba and the town of Almería

of its *morisco* (converts from Islam) inhabitants and then in 1522 an earthquake destroyed the entire city. Almería recovered in the 19C, thanks to a growth in local mining, and the old city walls were demolished to allow expansion. Foreign mining companies withdrew after the First World War and the town slumped once more. In recent years, agriculture and tourism have brought prosperity.

Alcazaba★

Open Tue–Sun 9.30am–8.30pm (6.30pm Nov–Mar). €2; free for EU citizens. ☎950 27 16 17.
Abd ar-Rahman III had this superbly sited hilltop fortress built in the 10C. It was enlarged by Almotacín, and by the Catholic Monarchs.
The **first enclosure** (recinto) holds gardens and a cistern (aljibe). The bell tower once warned of pirate attacks. Walls connect the fortress with San Cristóbal hill.
The **second enclosure** housed the Caliphal residence, including the cistern room (now an exhibition hall), a Mudéjar hermitage, a pool and baths used by troops. The esplanade was a parade ground. The baths of the Caliph's wife are in one corner.
In the **third enclosure**, to the west, is the castle of the Catholic Monarchs.

The large parade ground is dominated by an imposing keep with a Gothic doorway.
The impressive **view**★ from the battlements takes in city and port, the working-class district of **La Chanca**, and a backdrop of arid hills and a shimmering azure sea.

City Centre Tour

Cathedral★
Open year-round daily. Guided tours available 10am–5pm. No visits during services. €2. ☎950 23 48 48.
This fortress-like cathedral was built on the site of a mosque in the 16C, when Barbary pirates were frequent unwelcome visitors. The large 17C tower is crowned by a small belfry. The Renaissance **main doorway**★ contrasts with the austere façade. The escutcheon of the founding bishop is on the door pediment, and that of Carlos I, with two-headed eagle, is on the upper floor. Before entering the cathedral, admire the unusual relief of the **Portocarrero sun**★ – an animated sunburst, the symbol of the city – at the east end.

Interior
Three Gothic aisles are topped with star vaults. The chancel, tabernacle, retable and ambulatory arches were remodelled in the 18C.

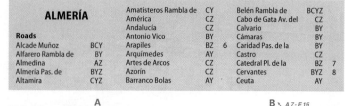

ALMERÍA		Amatisteros Rambla de	CY	Belén Rambla de	BCYZ
		América	CZ	Cabo de Gata Av. del	CZ
		Andalucía	CZ	Calvario	BY
Roads		Antonio Vico	BY	Cámaras	BY
Alcade Muñoz	BCY	Arapiles	BZ 6	Caridad Pas. de la	BY
Alfarero Rambla de	BY	Arquímedes	AY	Castro	CZ
Almedina	AZ	Artes de Arcos	CZ	Catedral Pl. de la	BZ 7
Almería Pas. de	BYZ	Azorín	CZ	Cervantes	BYZ 8
Altamira	CYZ	Barranco Bolas	AY	Ceuta	AY

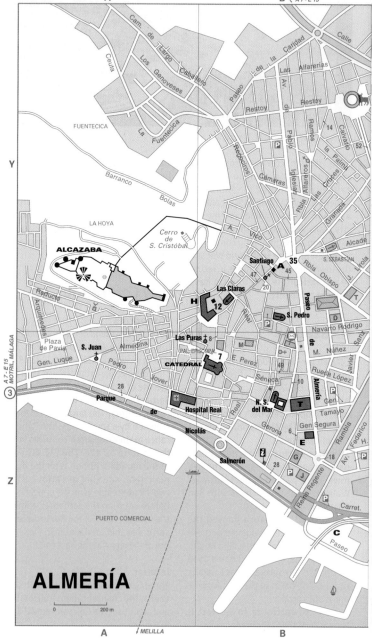

ALMERÍA

0   200 m

MELILLA

Detail, choir stalls

B. Kaufmann / MICHELIN

The Renaissance **choir stalls** have exceptional profile medallions in the upper stalls and full-bodied lifelike reliefs. Note too the neo-Classical back wall, in multi-hued marble, which was designed by Ventura Rodríguez. The transept door is Flamboyant Gothic.

The **ambulatory** has three chapels: the Gothic axial houses the venerated statue of Cristo de la Escucha, while St Indalecio, patron of Almería, can be seen in the right-hand Renaissance chapel, and various canvases by Alonso Cano are in the chapel to the left.

The late-19C Palacio Episcopal (Bishop's Palace) and the Iglesia de las Puras, part of an old convent founded in the 16C, front the **plaza de la Catedral**.

Iglesia de las Puras

The church and tower are both 17C. The escutcheon on the doorway is flanked by the heads of two lions and urns decorated with the sun and the moon. The Baroque altarpiece has an Immaculate Conception by Alonso Cano.

Plaza Vieja (Plaza de la Constitución)

The **town hall** dominates this lovely, arcaded 19C square, on the site of Moorish bazaars. A column commemorates the 1824 liberal revolt against Fernando VII.

Iglesia de las Claras

This small, 17C church, hidden behind a simple, yet elegant doorway, is noteworthy for its cupola above the transept decorated with stuccowork and escutcheons.

Iglesia de San Pedro

The present neo-Classical church was built in the 18C. The length of its central nave is accentuated by the balcony beneath the lunette-adorned barrel vault.

Iglesia de Santiago

This 16C church, one of the city's smallest, is in narrow calle de las Tiendas ("street of shops"). A **Renaissance portal**★, similar to the cathedral doorway, depicts St James the Moorslayer *(Santiago Matamoros)*. Scallop shells and crosses of St James decorate the space between the columns. The solid tower is pierced by arches in its lower section.

Ajibes de Jayrán

These 11C **Moorish cisterns**, in calle Tenor Iribarne, feature brick cannon vaults

Puerta de Purchena

This is the heart of Almerían life. Many of its seigniorial buildings date from the late 19C.

Paseo de Almería

The city's main avenue is fronted by a mixture of 20C buildings and modern tower blocks. The **Círculo Mercantil**, with 1920s ceilings, stuccowork and *azulejo* panelling, is one of its most attractive structures. Behind it, the landmark **Teatro Cervantes** opened in 1921. The nearby **Basílica de Nuestra Señora del Mar** houses the remains of Almería's venerated patron saint; its 18C cloister is now home to the city's **Arts and Crafts School**.

▶ *Return to paseo de Almería.*

The former casino (no 64), a 19C building with a central patio and seigniorial rooms, is the headquarters of the **Delegación del Gobierno de la Junta** (provincial government).

At the end of the street, by the plaza Emilio Pérez, is the **Casa Montoya**, built in a style associated with Santander in northern Spain.

Address Book

For coin ranges, see the Legend on the front cover flap.

WHERE TO STAY

The centrally situated placita de Flores isa good place to look for accommodation.

Hotel Costasol – *Paseo de Almería, 58.* ☎*950 23 40 11.www. hotelcostasol.com. 50 rooms.* Smart comfortable hotel on the busiest street in Almería. Rooms are large, some with balcony.

Torreluz II – *Plaza Flores, 6.* ☎*950 23 43 99. www.torreluz.com. 24 rooms.* A smart modern hotel, recently renovated with spacious rooms and a decent restaurant (). If you don't see what you want here try their two nearby sister hotels, Torreluz or Torreluz III.

Hotel AM Torreluz – *Plaza Flores, 5.* ☎*950 23 49 99. www. amhoteles.com. 105 rooms.* Not to be confused with the Torreluz chain (*see above*), this is a comfortable, recently renovated hotel in the heart of the city. Facilities include a private garage, piano-bar, swimming pool and fitness room. One restaurant specializes in grilled meats, the other in regional specialities.

WHERE TO EAT

Asador La Gruta – *5km/3mi west toward Aguadulce. Dinner only, closed Sun, two weeks in Feb and two weeks in Oct.* ☎*950 23 93 35. www.asadorlagruta. com.* The huge caves of this ex-quarry are a unique setting for a menu of prime grilled meats prepared in simple, time-honoured fashion.

Real – *calle Real, 15.* ☎*950 28 02 43. www.restaurantereal.es. Closed Sun.* This 19C mansion retains its original floor plan, with dining rooms decorated with locally sourced antiques. Seafood and modern regional dishes are the specialities *de la casa*.

TAPAS

Casa Puga – *calle Jovellanos, 7 (old town).* ☎*950 23 15 30. www. barcasapuga.es. Closed Sun and public hols (except Holy Week), and 1–21 Sept.* Almería is teeming with tapas bars, of which Casa Puga is the oldest. A huge choice of tapas, excellent wines and sausages.

El Quinto Toro – *calle Juan Leal, 6.* ☎*950 23 91 35. Closed Sat night and Sun.* Close by the central market, this is a tapas classic. Their speciality is *patatas a lo pobre*.

SPA

Lanjarón Spa – *Avdenida de la Constitución, Lanjarón.* ☎*958 77 01 37. www.balneariodelanjaron.coms. Closed Jan.* This excellent spa offers many types of treatments and therapies.

Parque de Nicolás Salmerón

This pleasant strip of greenery with its fountains and pools runs parallel to the port in a former warehouse district.

Hospital Real

Although the hospital was founded in the 16C, the façade and doorway of this large 18C building are distinctly neo-Classical in style.

Iglesia de San Juan

The church's exterior, with a sober portal of ringed columns, a pediment and coat of arms, has a distinctly civic air. The interior is something of a surprise, containing a 12C *mihrab* and *qibla* wall – vestiges of a 10C mosque.

Additional Sights

Museo de Almería

Open Tue 2.30pm–8.30pm, Wed–Sat 9am–8.30pm, Sun and hols 9am–2.30pm. €1.50; free to EU citizens. ☎*950 17 55 10.* This recently opened collection extends from prehistory through the Islamic era, with finds from El Argar and Los Millares.

Railway Station

The late-19C brick *estación* has attractive ceramic and wrought iron details.

Cable Inglés

The "English Cable" is an early 20C rail line from the terminus to the docks. It consists of a stone bridge and an iron mechanism which was used for loading.

Excursion

Los Millares★

19km/12mi north, to the west of Benahadux (reception hut at km 42).
Open year-round Wed–Sun 10am–2pm. ☎677 90 34 04 or 670 94 59 76.

Europe's most important Copper Age settlement was occupied from 2700 to 1800 BC.

It is thought that around 1 000 to 1 500 people lived a settled urban life at Los Millares.

Its inhabitants included arable and livestock farmers, as well as artisans of copper (available in the nearby Sierra de Gádor) and ceramic ritual objects.

The site had a wetter climate than today, with abundant game. The defensive wall is the longest known from this period. Dwellings were circular.

In the **necropolis** are a perfectly preserved tomb with atrium, a corridor with perforated slate tiles, and a chamber covered with a false cupola.

ALMUÑÉCAR

POPULATION: 20 997.

Hilltop Almuñécar began as a Phoenician colony named Sexi then became Hins-al-Monacar ("fortress city") under Arabic rule. Set at the mouth of the fertile **River Verde valley**, protected from cold by a mountain ridge and warmed by North African winds, Almuñécar is a year-round holiday destination. Fruits, vegetables and flowers proliferate all year.

▪ **Information:** Avenida de Europa, Palacete La Najarra. ☎958 63 11 25. www.almunecar.info.

▸ **Orient Yourself:** Almuñécar is at the southern tip of Granada province 47mi/75km east of Málaga along the coastal N 340-E 15.

🕐 **Organising Your Time:** Allow half a day to see Almuñécar, more to wander the coast and return to town.

👣 **Also See:** COSTA DEL SOL, La AXARQUÍA, MÁLAGA, ALMERÍA.

Visit

Palacete de la Najarra

Open (garden and foyer only) mid-Jun–mid-Sept 10am–2pm, 6pm–9pm; mid-Sept–mid-Mar 10am–2pm, 4pm–7pm; mid-Mar–mid-Jun 10am–2pm, 5pm–8pm. Closed 1 Jan and 25 Dec. ☎958 63 11 25.

This small, late-19C neo-Moorish palace houses the tourist office and is the ideal starting point for a tour of Almuñécar. Note the exotic garden inside the palace.

Castillo de San Miguel★

Open Apr–Oct Tue–Sat 10.30am–1.30pm, 5pm–7.30pm; Nov–Mar Tue–Sat 10.30am–1.30pm, 4pm–6.30pm (Sun and public hols 10.30am–2pm). Closed 1 Jan and 25 Dec. €2.10. ☎958 63 11 25.

This Roman (or perhaps Punic) castle lay in ruins from the war against the French in 1808 until recent times. A dungeon and house remain from service as a Nasrid palace. The entry towers were built under Charles V. The museum displays **models** of the Almuñécar area.

Parque Ornitológico Botánico Loro Sexi.

Open year-round daily 11am–2pm, 5pm–7pm. €4.

Located on the slopes of the hill below the San Miguel castle, these ornitho-

©Philip Lange/Bigstockphoto.com

Town of Salobreña with its castle

logical gardens are home to some 1500 birds, belonging to 200 different species, including peacocks, ostriches, parrots and Guacamayo cockatoos. In the highest part of the park, just below the castle walls is a cactus garden.

Cueva de los Siete Palacios (Museo Arqueológico)

🕑 *Open Tue–Sat mid-Jun–mid-Sept 10.30am–1.30pm, 6pm–9pm; Apr–mid-Jun 10.30am–1.30pm, 5pm–7.30pm; mid-Sept–Mar Tue–Sat 10.30am–1.30pm, 4pm–6.30pm; Sun and public hols all year 10.30am–2pm.* 🕑*Closed 1 Jan, 25 Dec.* ⊚€2.10. ☎958 63 11 25.

This archaeological museum is set in a Roman basement exhibits artefacts from Phoenician burials, including an outstanding Egyptian **funerary urn**★ of Apophis I, in grey marble, containing the oldest written document found in Spain. Also of note of note is an Egyptian glass sculptured in solid quartz.

It has hieroglyphic inscriptions that tell us that it belonged to the period under the reign of Pharaoh Apofis I, c. 1 500 BC.

Parque "El Majuelo"

This botanical garden contains 400 types of palm tree, among other species, as well as the ruins of a **Phoenician salting factory**.

Excursions

Costa Tropical

The Tropical Coast is the 100km/60mi stretch between La Herradura and La Rábita, characterised by mountains swoop down to the sea forming delightful coves.

La Herradura
8km/5mi west of Almuñécar.
This spectacular horseshoe beach lies between the watchtowers of **La Punta de la Mona** and **Cerro Gordo**. Rugged seaside mountains create an extraordi-

---

Three Princesses of Salobreña

In his *Tales of the Alhambra* **Washington Irving** wrote that the princesses Zaida, Zoraida and Zorahaida, daughters of King Mohammed IX of Granada, were confined to the sumptuous palace of Salobreña for many years by their father who, on the advice of his astrologers, decided to protect them from everyday temptation, not least that of meeting an undesirable suitor. The three princesses lived here surrounded by luxury, their every need attended to, until their father took them to his palace at the Alhambra. Destiny dictated that they encountered their predicted temptation on the journey to Granada, when the party fell upon three Christian prisoners who immediately fell in love with the young princesses.

Address Book

For coin ranges, see the cover flap.

WHERE TO STAY

ALMUÑÉCAR

Hotel Casablanca – Plaza San Cristóbal, 4. ☎958 63 55 75. www.almunecar.info/casablanca. *35 rooms*. With its pink façade and keyhole arches, the hotel's theme is resolutely Moorish. It is set between the town's two best beaches, facing the Ornithological Gardens and is 100 m from the El Majuelo Botanical Park.

COSTA TROPICAL

Best Western Salobreña – *On N 340, 3km/2mi toward Málaga*. ☎958 61 02 61. www.hotelsalobrena.com. *195 rooms*. This large tourist complex, with its gardens and swimming pool, comprises several modern buildings with rooms overlooking the sea or the rocky coastline. The views of the Mediterranean are superb and the complex is built away from the road so that the only sound here is of the waves breaking on the shore.

WHERE TO EAT

Vizcaya – *Paseo de las Flores (Playa de San Cristóbal)*. ☎958 63 57 12. Set on a pebbly beach, Vizcaya offers paellas, and grilled meats and fish in the style of the Biscay region, from which it takes its name. Atmospheric by day, romantic by night.

Mar de Plata – *Paseo San Cristóbal (Edificio Mar de Plata)*. ☎958 63 30 79. www.restaurantemardeplata.com. *Closed Tue and all May*. This beachside restaurant offers good value for money with paellas, seafood, and *pescado a la sal* (whole fish cooked in salt).

SCUBA DIVING

La Herradura has developed into an important centre for scuba diving. A number of dive companies operate here, offering courses for all levels.

Buceo La Herradura – *Puerto deportivo de Marina del Este*. ☎958 82 70 83. www.buceolaherradura.com.

---

nary setting. **Puerto Deportivo Marina del Este** is a marina at La Punta de la Mona. Stunning **views** abound towards Cerro Gordo.

Salobreña★

15km/9mi east of Almuñécar.

Hilltop Salobreña, a cluster of white-washed houses, is the most attractive town on this stretch of coast. Visit the imposing **castle**, the **Iglesia de la Virgen del Rosario**, and splendid beaches, such as **Playa de El Peñón**.

Salobreña Castle (open summer, 10.30am–2pm, 5pm–9.30pm; winter Tue–Sun 10.30am–2pm, 4pm–7pm; €2 (€2.55 including entry to museum); ☎958 61 27 33/03 14) best viewed from the Almuñécar road is a famous landmark. The original 10C castle was transformed into a luxurious residence (see 'Castle of Legends' box) – and royal prison – under the Nasrids. Access is via a corner doorway to the first enclosure. Continue to the *alcazaba* (fortress), with its two underground caverns, where prisoners were kept in total blackness, and keep.

Motril

21km/13mi east of Almuñécar and 6km/4mi east of Salobreña.

This community of 50 000 is the largest town along the Costa Tropical, a centre of sugar cultivation since the 18C, and before then, a backwater where the mother of the last king of Granada lived. Tourists flock to hotels along the **Playa de Poniente** (*4km/2.5mi SE*) which is the busiest of the town's two main beaches (the quieter being the Playa Granada). The **Parque Pueblos de América** situated below the Ntra. Sra. Virgen de la Cabeza Sanctuary, is home to a variety of exotic and sub-tropical plants, brought over from different countries of the American continent. From **Motril**, a coastal road passes through Torrenueva, **Carchuna**, **Calahonda** and Castell de Ferro. Beaches are long and wide. Medieval watchtowers – Torre de Carchuna, Torrenueva and La Rábita – are visible. From La Rábita, detour (5km/3mi) to **Albuñol**, a typical Andalucian "white village" (*pueblo blanco*) nestled in the Sierra de la Contraviesa.

LAS ALPUJARRAS ★

The Alpujarras (from the Arabic *al-bucharrat*, 'pastures') is a region of white-washed villages, rugged mountains and fertile valleys straddling Granada and Almería provinces. It was the final stronghold of the Nasrids. This magnificent range was rediscovered by 19C Romantic travellers, and today is one of Andalucía's most popular destinations.

- **Information:** Oficina de Información del Legado Andalusí, avenida de Madrid, Lanjarón. ☎958 77 02 82.
- ▶ **Orient Yourself:** This rugged and varied region extends across the southern slopes of the Sierra Nevada, inland from the Costa Tropical and Motril.
- **Don't Miss:** The views around Puerto de la Ragua.
- **Organising Your Time:** Allow two or three days.
- **Also See:** GRANADA, SIERRA NEVADA, GUADIX, Sierra de los FILABRES, ALMERÍA.

A Bit of History

Arab presence in the Alpujarras – The Berbers arrived with the Moors in 711 and began to grow olives and vines and breed silkworms. The Alpujarras prospered under the Nasrids between the 13C and 15C, when industry, especially textiles, flourished. After the fall of Granada, the Catholic Monarchs ceded this area to Boabdil. Intolerance led to revolts, the last in 1568 led by Don Fernando de Córdoba (known as **Abén Humeya**). The expulsion of the *moriscos* led to the decline of Alpujarras.

Driving Tours

1 Granada Alpujarras ★★

From Lanjarón to Bayárcal

▶ *100km/62mi (127km/79mi with an excursion to Puerto de la Ragua) – allow 2 days.*

Lanjarón
Lanjarón is the gateway to the Alpujarras from Granada. Famous for its medicinal waters, it attracts thousands of visitors every year. Its other attraction is a 16C **castle**, guarding the valley entrance. The A 348 road offers magnificent views of the arid and imposing Sierra de Lújar.

▶ *9km/5.5mi from Lanjarón, before Órgiva, take the A 7210, which crosses the northern slope of the Alpujarras. Be cautious on this narrow mountain road.*

Before Pampaneira, the road passes through three villages, **Cañar**, with its impressive views, Carataunas and Soportújar, none of which are on the main tourist track.

Narrow street in Pampaneira

B. Kaufmann / MICHELIN

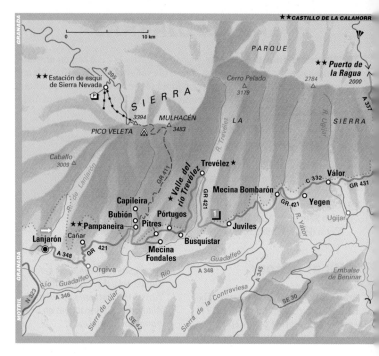

Pampaneira★★

Leave your car at the town entrance.
Pampaneira is in the **Poqueira Valley**★★ and preserves its traditional atmosphere. The main street, where shops offer only local products, leads to the **plaza de la Libertad**, dominated by the 17C Baroque Iglesia de la Santa Cruz. Stroll the narrow streets to appreciate the charms of Pampaneira, and stop at a traditional loom where Alpujarras rugs (*jarapas*) are made. The **NEVADENSIS Centre** (*see Address Book*), can organise excursions.

▶ *Continue along the A 7210. After 2km/1.2mi, turn towards Bubión and Capileira.*

Bubión

High in the hills, Bubión was a centre of the *morisco* rebellion. Its rugged white-washed walls and flat rooftops are reminiscent of North Africa.

Capileira

At 1 436m/4 710ft, Capileira is the highest village in the whole valley.
Its 16C parish church has an attractive Baroque retable.

A museum, the **Museo Alpujarreño de Artes y Costumbres Populares** (*open Tue–Fri 11.30am–2.30pm, Sat 4pm–7pm (8pm in summer); 958 76 30 51)* re-creates 19C Alpujarran traditions.

▶ *Return to the A 7210 junction.*

Mecina Fondales

Several excursions are possible from Mecina Fondales along the valley of the River Trevélez. A minor road leads to the village of Ferreirola. The name refers to the iron found throughout this region.

▶ *Continues through an area of outstanding beauty to the Trevélez Valley.*

Pitres

This is the largest of the seven settlements of the *taha* – the Moorish district – of Pitres, **Capilerilla**, Mecina, Mecinilla, Fondales, Ferreirola and Atalbéitar.

Pórtugos

The **Fuente Agria** is a spring of iron-rich water behind the hermitage of Nuestra Señora de las Angustias, at the exit to the village. Opposite, steps lead to **El**

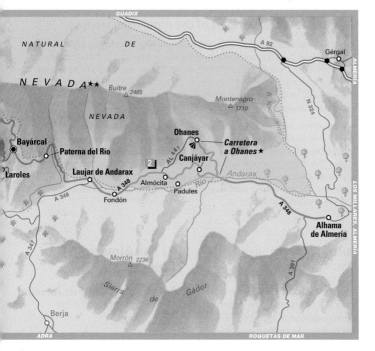

Chorreón, a waterfall reddened by minerals.

Busquístar

This quiet, Mozarabic village of gleaming white houses is the first in the spectacular **Trevélez Valley**★. The road ascends to Trevélez itself.

Trevélez★

Trevélez is the highest town in Spain (1 600m/5 250ft in the *barrio alto*). **Mulhacén**, towering above, is the highest peak on the Iberian Peninsula (3 482m/11 424ft).

▷ *Beyond Trevélez, the narrow A 7208 descends to Torvizcón and the A 348 which crosses the southern Alpujarras. Follow theGR 421 eastward to Juviles.*

Juviles

Green valleys yield to a wilder landscape. The 16C **Iglesia de Santa María de Gracia** is one of the prettiest churches in the Granada Alpujarras.

▷ *Upon leaving Bérchules, bear left onto the A 348.*

Mecina Bombarón

A drier Mediterranean vegetation dominates, particularly in the **Contraviesa** area to the south, famous for its wines. The village is divided by small ravines. Upon leaving, note the Roman bridge over the River Mecina.

Yegen

A plaque marks the house of **Gerald Brenan** who spent seven years here between 1923 and 1934. He was the author of *South from Granada*, a marvellous portrayal of the traditions and customs of the Alpujarras.

Trevélez cured ham

Ever since **Queen Isabel II** extolled the virtues of its **cured ham** (*jamón*) in the 19C, the name of Trevélez has been synonymous with this gastronomic treat. The secret of its drying sheds (*secaderos*) lies in their special climatic conditions (dry and cold) and the exclusive use of sea salt. White-coloured pigs are bred to produce these large hams (up to 10kg/22lb in weight), which are slightly rounded in shape.

Moorish Origins of the Alpujarran Houses

The local architecture is perhaps the best example of the region's Moorish past. Visitors who have set foot in North Africa will be surprised by the strong similarities, with the predominance of south-facing houses searching for the warmth of the sun and often following the relief of this mountainous landscape. The houses are usually built on different levels, forming spaced terraces and steep narrow streets acting as a conduit for rainwater.

Traditionally they comprise two floors, the walls of which are completely covered with lime. Their most typical feature is the flat roof, known as a *terrao*, made using large beams of chestnut and battens *(alfarjías)*, on top of which a layer of bluish-grey clay *(launa)* is added. Upon contact with water, this layer of clay solidifies to provide a waterproof covering. In the past, these flat roof terraces were used as meeting areas, although nowadays they are predominantly used for storage or for drying clothes, curing food etc.

Válor

Along with many other churches in this area, the 16C **Iglesia de San José** is, typically, in Mudéjar style. Note the late-18C fountain in the square. The leader of the *morisco* rebellion of 1568, Don Fernando de Córdoba (**Abén Humeya**, *see Box opposite*) came from Válor, the largest town in the area.

▸ *Follow the A 7208 for 11km/7mi.*

Laroles

Laroles stands at the foot of the Ragua Pass. Note the unusual tower of its parish church. The hamlets of Picena and Cherín are visible to the south.

▸ *2km/1.2mi beyond Laroles by an extremely narrow road is Bayárcal, the first village in the Almería Alpujarras. The road northwards to the Ragua Pass is the only link between the north and south slopes of the Sierra Nevada (closed in winter).*

Puerto de la Ragua★★

The road ascends gently to the summit (2 000m/6 559ft) amid a high mountain landscape, then narrows and descends abruptly to the Guadix Plateau, offering magnificent views of the **Castillo de la Calahorra** ★★ (*see GUADIX*).

▸ *Head back towards Bayárcal.*

② The Almería Alpujarras★

Bayárcal to Alhama de Almería
73km/45mi – allow half a day.

Bayárcal

The highest village in Almería (1 275m/4 182ft), Bayárcal includes one of the largest oak groves in the province. Explore on foot and enjoy superb views. Statues in the 16C Mudéjar-style **Iglesia de San Francisco Javier** include Saint Francis Xavier, an *Immaculate Conception* by Alonso Cano and an *Ecce Homo*.

Paterna del Río
7km/4.5mi east of Bayárcal.
The village is surrounded by chestnut, oak and poplar forests. The **Iglesia de San Juan Bautista** has an interesting Mudéjar *artesonado* ceiling.

Laujar de Andarax

The capital of the Almerían Alpujarras is by the source of the River Andarax, south of the sierra. Several 16C-17C mansions and fountains line the streets. Poet **Francisco Villaespesa** (1877–1936), admirer of symbolist Rubén Dario, was born here.

Its 16C brick **Iglesia Parroquial de la Encarnación** has a Baroque altarpiece with a statue of the Immaculate Conception attributed to Alonso Cano.

The façade of the 18C **ayuntamiento** (town hall) also of brick, is sober and harmonious. The **Pilar de los Cuatro**

Address Book

&For coin ranges, see the Legend
on the front cover flap.

WHERE TO STAY

Hotel La Fragua – *Barrio Medio,
San Antonio, 4. Trevélez.* ☎958 85 86 26.
www.hotellafragua.com. 24 rooms. Two
buildings, one traditional, the other
newer, all bedrooms with mountain
views. Private basic bathrooms. The
acclaimed bar-restaurant has views.

Hotel España – *Avenida de la Alpujarra, 42. Lanjarón.* ☎958 77 01 87. *www.
lanjaron.biz. 36 rooms*. This early-20C
hotel in the centre hosted García Lorca
and bullfighter Manolete. Rooms have
extremely high ceilings, some have
balconies.

Hotel Almirez – *Laujar de
Andarax, on A 348 towards Berja.* ☎950
513 514. *20 rooms. www.hotelalmirez.
com*. A good choice for spending a
night, but not a lot of money. Set In a
little hamlet, it offer simple rooms and
an attractive rustic restaurant.

Alquería de Morayma –
*between from Cádiar and Torvizcón.
www.alqueriamorayma.com.* ☎958 34
32 21. *13 rooms, 5 apartments*. Rustic
rooms in this country hotel look onto
mountains and the village of Cádiar.
Regional restaurant-bar.

Villa Turística Bubión – *Barrio
Alto, Bubión.* ☎958 76 39 09. *43 units*.
A village of regional-style cottages.
Units have kitchen and fireplace. The
restaurant, one of the best in the area,
specialises in kid, trout and sausages.

**Hotel Alcazaba de
Busquístar** – *4km/2.5mi S from Trevélez
towards Juviles.* ☎958 85 86 87. *www.
alcazabadebusquistar.com. 51 units*.
Regional materials predominate in this
beautiful hotel. Rooms are spacious;
terraces have superb views.

Cured hams, Trevélez

H. Champollion / MICHELIN

ACTIVITIES

**Centro de Interpretación del
Parque Nacional de Sierra Nevada
(NEVADENSIS)**, in **Pampaneira**, plaza
de la Libertad (☎958 76 31 27. *www.
nevadensis.com*). This visitor centre
organises hikes, climbing trips, and
horseback rides.

**Consorcio Estacion Recreativa
Puerto de La Ragua**. *Pl. de la Constitución, 3. Laroles*. (☎958 76 00 07).
Cross-country skiing and dog-sledding
can be arranged here. www.puerto
delaragua.com.

Rustic Blue, in **Bubión** (*Barrio la
Ermita,* ☎958 76 31 27, *www.rusticblue.
es*). This rural tourism operator books
accommodation and outdoor activities.

SHOPPING

Jarapas – Local rugs (*jarapas*), originally of joined brightly coloured sections,
are now woven whole. Two workshops
in Pampaneira are: **Hilacar** (*2 km N;*
☎956 76 32 26) and **La Rueca** (*Avenida
de la Alpujarra, 2;* ☎958 76 30 14).

LOCAL SPECIALITIES

Cured hams are best purchased in
Trevélez, where there are several
drying sheds.

A **rosé wine** is produced in Laujar
by private estates and one organic
producer, the Cortijo del Cura,
located on the outskirts of the town.

Abén Humeya

The leader of the 1568 *moriscos* revolt
in the Alpujarras, **Abén Humeya** was
assassinated in Laujar by his followers
on 20 October 1569. Once the revolt
had finally been quashed in 1571, the
moriscos were expelled from Spain.

H.Champollion / MICHELIN

Canjáyar

Caños, a public fountain, dates from the 17C. Follow the "Nacimento" signs (1.6km/1mi) to the source of the river Andrax- an attractive picnic spot.

▶ *Head east along the A 348.*

Laujar to Canjáyar

This road runs through the fertile Andarax Valley between terraces of orange trees, prickly pears and vineyards which grow the prized Almería grape. **Fondón** and **Almócita** are, *pueblos blancos* with attractive parish-churches.

The road offers a delightful view of **Padules** and its 16C church. Whitewashed **Canjáyar**, at the foot of the Ermita de San Blas, retains a Moorish air.

▶ *Continue along the A 348. After 3km/2mi turn-off to Ohanes.*

Road to Ohanes ★

The winding road up to Ohanes (958m/ 3 142ft) offers spectacular **views**★ with no trace of habitation.

The panorama encompasses the faraway Sierra de Gata.

Ohanes – Ohanes enjoys a magnificent **site**★ dominating the vine-planted Andarax Valley, a blanket of white against the verdant backdrop, punctuated by a stone church. Narrow, winding streets seem suspended against an intense blue sky.

▶ *Return to the A 348 and continue to Alhama.*

Alhama de Almería

Contrasts abound around Alhama: the desert-like Tabernas and the lush Andarax Valley lie to one side, the Sierra de Gádor to the other.

The village has its own source of mineral waters at around 46°C/115°F, several noble mansions and a café, the Tertulia, from the early 20C.

The Hotel Balneario San Nicolas (*http://balneariosannicolas.es*) spa, is located here.

Strange Devotion

In many places such as Laujar, Fondón, Ohanes and Canjáyar, small hermitages known as *ánimas* (souls) are visible as you come into or leave the village. These small chapels are adorned with an altar containing a picture representing the Virgen del Carmen extracting souls from flames with the help of angels. The entrance doorway often has a peephole to enable visitors to peer inside.

ANDÚJAR

POPULATION: 35 803.

Situated in the centre of Spain's olive-growing region are Andújar's narrow, winding streets, 15C and 16C churches and houses, and vestiges of monumental 9C Moorish walls. In the woods and streams of nearby **Parque Natural Sierra de Andújar** is the popular Santuario de la Virgen de la Cabeza (Shrine of the Virgin of the Head).

- **Information:** Plaza Santa Maria, Torre del Reloj. ☎953 50 49 59.
- ▶ **Orient Yourself:** Andújar sits in the depression of the Guadalquivir Valley, toward the west of the province of Jaén, 76km/47mi east of Córdoba along the A 4.
- **Don't Miss:** *Christ in the Garden of Olives* by El Greco, in the Iglesia de Santa Maria. The views while driving in the Parque Natural de la Sierra de Andújar.
- **Organising Your Time:** Take a few hours to see Andújar or a day or more if you linger at the Parque Natural de la Sierra de Andújar.
- **Also See:** MONTORO, CÓRDOBA, JAÉN, LINARES.

A Bit of History

Ancient Iberian Isturgis was conquered by Romans and Moors, then by Fernando III in 1225. Cosimo de' Medici and his entourage passed through, as did British traveller Joseph Townsend and French writer Prosper Merimée.

Sights

Iglesia de Santa María

This church, probably started in the 13C, was not completed until the 17C, hence its eclectic styles. The interior, a mixture of pointed, circular and groined vaults, holds an *Assumption of the Vir-*

Address Book

For coin ranges, see the cover flap

WHERE TO STAY

Hotel Del Val – *Hermanos del Val, 1.* ☎*953 50 09 50. www.hoteldelval.com. 79 rooms.* Right at the entry to town, the hotel has modest rooms, pool and gardens, and a fine restaurant with regional dishes.

Complejo La Mirada – *Santuario Virgen de la Cabeza. Approximately 30km/18mi N of Andújar on the A 1208.* ☎*953 54 91 11. 15 rooms.* In the heart of the Parque Natural de Andújar. Clean, modern, modest rooms. A good, reasonably priced hotel (though rates rise dramatically during the pilgrimage to the Virgen de la Cabeza, late April); cottages and camping also on site.

TAPAS

Mesón Ana Las Perolas – *Serpiente, 6.* ☎*953 50 67 26. www.lasperolas.com. Closed Mon and in Jul.* Ana Domínguez is a local character known for her cuisine. Specialities are pork, rabbit and beef stews *(guisos)* served in small pots *(perolas)*, as well as venison, boar, and other game. Friendly atmosphere.

Los Naranjos – *Guadalupe, 4.* ☎*953 51 03 90. Closed second half of Jul, Sundays in summer, Tuesdays rest of year.* This centrally located restaurant is known for value. The coffee shop and modest dining area have separate entrances.

SHOPPING

Andújar is famous for its ceramics, such as ashtrays, bowls, plates etc.

LOCAL SPECIALITIES

The region is renowned for such dishes as *ajo blanco* (a sauce made from garlic and breadcrumbs), *flamenquines* (fried veal and ham rolls), and asparagus *(espárragos)*.

Oak Groves

Although the landscapes of Jaén are dominated by the ubiquitous olive tree, the province is also home to a number of holm oak forests, most notably in the Sierra de Andújar. These noble trees adopt a different appearance depending on the light; this ability has undoubtedly spawned a famous local legend which says that the oak trees dance at night, but are then petrified by the first rays of sunshine early in the morning.

gin by Pacheco *(left-side apse chapel)*, an Immaculate Conception by Giuseppe Cesari, a manuscript signed by St John of the Cross.

its pride however is **Christ in the Garden of Olives**★★ by El Greco, in a chapel enclosed by a fine 16C **grille**★ by Maestro Bartolomé. This huge canvas depicts Christ in an elegant red tunic, illuminated from the sky, and the Apostles St Peter, St James and St John, who appear to be dozing at his feet.

Ayuntamiento

🕐*Open Mon–Fri, 8am–2.30pm.* 🕐*Closed Sat–Sun and public hols.* ☎*953 50 49 59.* The mid-17C **town hall** *(ayuntamiento)* retains its former Corral de Comedias, used for theatrical performances.

Iglesia de San Miguel

The imposing silhouette of this church dominates the plaza de España (aka plaza del Mercado). It holds unusual 17C and 18C murals, and an exceptional choir and a fine partition screen, both adorned with delicately carved reliefs.

Palacio de Los Niños de Don Gome

🕐*Open Tue–Sat Jul–mid-Sept 10.30am–1pm, mid-Sept–Jun 7pm–9pm.* ☎*953 51 31 78.* This fine 16–17C palace is topped with a sober tower with Indian-influenced decoration. Note the attractive patio portico and original stable.

Iglesia de San Bartolomé

The main attraction of this late-15C church is the façade. Its three stone

Gothic portals★ bear elegant and exquisitely carved ornamental features.

Torre del Reloj

The clock tower, along with part of the calle Silera and the Fuente Sorda and Tavira towers, was long thought to be part of the Moorish walls, but has been re-dated as being of 16C origin.

Excursions

Villanueva de la Reina

14km/9mi SE.
This tranquil town sits on the banks of the Guadalquivir between the Sierra Morena rising to the north and the horizontal plain. In the old quarter is the 18C **Iglesia de Nuestra Señora de la Natividad**.

Parque Natural de la Sierra de Andújar★

Leave Andújar to the north along A 1208. Park visitor centre: 🕐*open Jun–mid-Oct, Thu, Sat–Sun and public hols 10am–2pm, 4pm–6pm (Fri 4pm–6pm).* 🕐*Closed 1 and 6 Jan and 25 Dec.* ☎*953 54 90 30. www.e-andujar.com/turismoandujar/ parque/parque.htm.*
The access road winds up through an impressive landscape of holm oaks, cork oaks, wild olives and arbutus, offering magnificent **views**★★ of the surrounding area.

This protected park in the low foothills of the Sierra Morena above the Guadalquivir Valley spreads over 60 800ha/150 240 acres. It alternates from open pasture, grazed by fighting bulls, to dark ravines with dense vegetation ideal for deer, lynx and wild boar. The Jándula and Yeguas rivers are popular with sport fishermen, while the extensive network of marked paths criss-crossing forests and thickets carpeted in wild jasmine and mastic trees are a haven for hikers.

Santuario de la Virgen de la Cabeza

🕐*Museum open Sat noon–1.30pm, Sun and public hols, 10am–2pm, 4pm–6pm; Mon–Fri by arrangement.* ☎*953 54 90 15.*

The sanctuary is situated at the heart of the park near a hunting reserve, 32km/20mi from Andújar. According to tradition, the head (la Cabeza) of the Virgin Mary appeared to a local shepherd here and a chapel was built on the spot.

Later came a monastery which was destroyed in the Spanish Civil War. It is one of Andalucía's principal sites of pilgrimage to the Virgin, especially on the last Sunday in April.

Bailén

23km/14mi NE on the A 4.

Bailén was the scene of a Peninsular War **battle** in 1808. Spanish troops under General Castaños defeated the French, commanded by Dupont, turning the tide against French presence on Spanish soil.

The whitewashed houses and pleasant squares here are typically Andalusian. The **Iglesia de la Encarnación**, a 16C church with Gothic and Renaissance influences, holds the tomb of General Castaños.

ANTEQUERA★

POPULATION: 40 239.

Antequera (Roman *Anticaria*) is quintessential Andalusia: cobblestone streets, whitewashed houses with flower-decked balconies and wrought-iron grilles, monumental churches, and attractive avenues. The bell tower of the Iglesia de San Sebastián, with its fine Mudéjar brickwork, is emblematic of the town which extends below the Sierra del Torcal, opposite the imposing Peña de los Enamorados rock. Antequera was conquered by Fernando de Aragón in 1410. Its heritage buildings reflect its 16C–18C splendour.

- **Information:** Plaza de San Sebastián, 7, 29200 Antequera. ☎952 70 25 05. www.turismoantequera.com.
- ▶ **Orient Yourself:** Antequera is 55km/34mi south of Málaga, 7km/4.5mi from the A 92 linking Granada and Sevilla.
- **Don't Miss:** The strange limestone formations of Parque Natural de El Torcal. Flamingoes on the Laguna de la Fuente de Piedra. Views over the Garganta del Chorro gorge.
- **Organising Your Time:** Allow half a day in Antequera, longer to explore our suggested routes through the countryside.
- **Also See:** MÁLAGA, COSTA DEL SOL, OSUNA, LUCENA, CABRA, LOJA.

Town

Alcazaba

⚠️*Closed for restoration.*

The fortress is accessed via an avenue offering **views**★ of the Sierra del Torcal, the Antequera plain, painted roofs and graceful steeples. The first fortress in Moorish Granada to fall to the Christians (1410), it changed hands soon after. The 15C walls enclose a pleasant garden. The most interesting towers are the Torre de la Estrella, the Torre Blanca and, above all, the Torre del Homenaje (or Torre del Papabellotas), crowned by a small chapel housing the Antequera bell.

Town of Antequera

Peña de los Enamorados

The impressive "Lovers' Rock" rises up halfway along the road linking Antequera and Archidona. It has given rise to a romantic legend which tells of Tagzona, the daughter of the Moorish leader of the area, who had fallen hopelessly in love with Tello, a young Christian imprisoned near Antequera. They made the decision to elope but were discovered by the guards of Tagzona's father, who chased them to the very top of a rock on the outskirts of the town. Without any hope of escape, and with the arrows of Moorish marksmen bearing down on them, the two lovers launched themselves hand-in-hand into the void below, sealing their love for each other for eternity.

Colegiata de Santa María★

⏱Open Tue 10.30am–2pm, 4.30pm–6.30pm (9pm–11pm in summer); Sat–Sun and public hols 10.30am–2pm. ⏱Closed 1 and 6 Jan, Good Fri, 1 May, 23 Aug, 12 Sept, 24–25 and 31 Dec. ☎952 70 25 05 (tourist office).

This 16C collegiate church, at the foot of the castle gardens, is a fine example of early Renaissance style, mixed with earlier Gothic elements. Access is through the 16C **Arco de los Gigantes** (Giants' Arch), which incorporates Roman tablets and sculptures discovered around town. The monumental church has three aisles and Mudéjar vaults separated by semicircular arches on Ionic columns.

The splendid **façade**, inspired by Roman triumphal arches and adorned with slender pinnacles, is worthy of note, as is the rectangular chancel, with its Gothic-Mudéjar vault.

Iglesia del Carmen

⏱Open Jul–mid-Sept 10am–2pm, 5pm–8pm (10.30pm Wed–Fri); Sun and public hols, 10am–2pm. Otherwise 10am–2pm, 4pm–7pm (Sun and public hols 10am–2pm). ⏱€1.50. ☎952 70 25 05, or 609 53 97 10.

The church is all that remains of a Carmelite convent. Built in the 16C and 17C, it has a wide single nave and Mudéjar *artesonado* ceiling. The interior is profuse with paintings and polychrome stuccowork; note the fine 18C **retable** at the high altar by Antonio Primo, of wood without polychrome adornment.

Museo Municipal

⏱Open Tue–Fri 10am–1.30pm, 4pm–6pm. Sat 10am–1.30pm. Sun 11am–1.30pm. ⏱€3. ☎952 70 40 21.

The municipal museum is housed in the 17C **Palacio de Nájera** (interesting lookout tower) and holds many noteworthy artefacts. The highlight is the **Ephebus of Antequera**★, a 1C bronze Roman sculpture, which represents a naked boy whose hands held an object now lost. Note the lightness of the work, as well as the child's sublime expression.

Convento de las Carmelitas Descalzas

⏱Open Sept–Jul Tue–Fri 10am–12.30pm, 4.30pm–6.30pm (Sat 10am–12.30pm).

"May the sun come out in Antequera…"

At the beginning of the 15C, Antequera still found itself under Moorish domination, at a time when Christian troops continued their advance south to conquer further territory in al-Andalus. Unsure of what the best military strategy should be, the Infante, Don Fernando of Aragón, was confronted one night by an apparition of a beautiful young girl surrounded by lions who said to him: "Tomorrow, may the sun come out in Antequera and may whatever God ordains happen." The following day, 16 September 1410, Christian troops took the town of Antequera, which they dedicated to St Euphemia, the virgin and martyr from Chalcedon who so inspired Don Fernando. Since this time, the Spanish phrase *Salga el sol por Antequera* (May the sun come out in Antequera) has become a popular saying which serves as an inspiration for people to face up to whatever challenges present themselves in life.

Address Book

For coin ranges, see the Legend on the front cover flap.

WHERE TO STAY

Parador de Antequera – *García del Olmo.* ☎952 84 02 61. *www.parador.es. (in UK: 020 7616 0300, www.keytel.co.uk; in USA: various tel nos, visit www.eparadors.com). 55 rooms.* A modern, recently renovated *parador*, with gardens on the outskirts of Antequera.

WHERE TO EAT

El Escribano – *Plaza de los Escribanos, 11.* ☎950 70 65 33. *Closed evenings in winter and Mondays all year.* El Escribano is located by the Moorish castle. Enjoy regional plates such as partridge paté.

Lozano – *Avenida Principal, 2–2.5km/ 1.5mi E on old Málaga road.* ☎952 84 27 12. www.hotellozano.com. *Rooms* (☺☺). The industrial location is unattractive, but Lozano is one of the best restaurants in Antequera. Specialities are meat and fish dishes, served in a large dining room.

LOCAL SPECIALITIES

A rich culinary tradition includes *porra antequerana* (similar to *gazpacho*), pigs' trotters with chickpeas *(manos de cerdo con garbanzos)* and the almond-based *bienmesabe*, a Moorish-influenced dessert.

FESTIVALS

Renowned **Holy Week** celebrations peak on the night of Good Friday, with a moving "farewell" *(despedida)* in plaza de San Sebastián by the brotherhoods of Santa Cruz de Jerusalén (Holy Cross of Jerusalem) and Dulce Nombre de Jesús (Divine Name of Jesus), both founded in the 16C.

Guided tours (30min) in summer. €3 *(museum).* ☎952 84 19 77.

The façade of the convent, in the local Baroque style, is a highly original ensemble with a semicircular arch resting on *estípites* and figures which support a cornice with beautifully sculpted plant motifs and grotesque masks. Inside is an interesting collection of old paintings.

Convento de la Encarnación

This 16C convent, with its single aisle and lofty chancel, follows the pattern of Mudéjar churches in Granada. The pendentives of the arch on calle Encarnación depict the Angel and the Virgin Mary.

Iglesia de San Sebastián

The main portal of this 16C church is Plateresque. Its graceful 18C steeple, in four sections, is emblematic of Antequera. Works of art include a 15C sculpture *Virgin of Hope* and paintings by Mannerist, Antonio Mohedano.

Iglesia de San Agustín

Built by Diego de Vergara, who designed Málaga Cathedral, this 16C church has a single aisle, pointed Gothic vaulting and a fine 17C–18C tower. Niches in the Man-

nerist portal hold religious images. On the high altar, canvases by Mohedano narrate the story of St Augustine.

Palacio Municipal

The unusual neo-Baroque façade of this ex-Franciscan monastery was added as recently as 1953. The cloister has two elegant galleries: the lower on semicircular arches and arris vaulting, the upper level with large windows and broken pediments. The Baroque staircase has a stucco-adorned vault and polychrome marble decoration.

Convento de Nuestra Señora de los Remedios

This 17C church, dedicated to the patron saint of Antequera, has a Latin-cross plan with two side chapels. Sumptuous ornamentation is based on Franciscan themes and plant motifs. The fine gilded retable has a niche *(camarín)* decorated with delicate stuccowork, housing a 16C Virgin of the Remedies.

Real Convento de San Zoilo

Outstanding features in this 16C late-Gothic convent include rich polychrome stucco decoration highlighting plant and geometric motifs; a Mudéjar *artesonado* ceiling, an altarpiece comprising 16C Renaissance panels and the so-called Green Christ *(Cristo Verde)*, a Renaissance statue attributed to Pablo de Rojas.

Convento de Belén

The main nave of this richly decorated 18C convent has a barrel vault interspersed with lunettes. Semicircular arches separate the side aisles. On either side of the transept, topped by a semicircular cupola, stand two chapels; the one on the Epistle side contains a stucco-adorned niche *(camarín)* with a statue of Christ by José Mora. The nuns are renowned for their pastries which can be purchased by visitors.

Menga and Viera dolmens★

To the left on the way out of Antequera by the A 354, towards Granada.
◔*Open Tue–Sat 9am–6pm, Sun, 9.30am–2.30pm.* ◔*Closed 1 and 6 Jan, 28 Feb, 1 May, and 25 Dec.* ☏*952 70 25 05.*
These enormous Bronze Age burial chambers are at the foot of the Cerro de la Cruz, a small hill. The builders entered laterally to slide in stone slabs. The entry gallery of the **Menga dolmen** (2500 BC), 25m/82ft long and 2.70m/9ft high, holds 10 vertical and five horizontal monoliths. The spacious main oval chamber contains seven monoliths on each side and a large stone at its head. The third vertical monolith on the left side reveals human figures and solar

symbols. At the end of the **Viera dolmen** (2200 BC) is a cube-shaped burial chamber, with four monoliths and large stone slab.

Excursions

El Romeral dolmen★

4km/2.5mi northeast. Leave Antequera on the A 354. Turn left at signposted crossroads.
◔*Open summer Tue–Fri 9am–6pm (to 3pm Tue), Sun 9.30am–2.30pm. Rest of year 9am–5.30pm (to 3.30pm Tue), Sun 9.30am–2.30pm.* ◔*Closed 1 and 6 Jan, 9 Apr, 1 May, 16 and 20 Aug, 1 Nov, and 6, 24, 25 and 31 Dec.* ☏*952 70 25 05.*
The El Romeral dolmen, more complex than others in the area, dates from 1800 BC. It consists of projecting ashlar stone walls, two circular chambers and a gallery. The first chamber has a false ceiling and is enclosed by a large monolithic slab; a carved door leads to a second room with an altar-like structure.

Parque Natural de El Torcal★★

14km/9mi southeast. Take the C 3310 towards Villanueva de la Concepción, then bear right onto a signposted road. ⟳*The reception centre may be closed for renovation.* ☏*952 03 13 89.*
The park's 12ha/30 acres hold some of Spain's most unusual scenery, chasms, obelisks and other strange limestone formations created by erosion.
The native flora, including Spanish squill and Venus's navelwort, is particularly impressive in spring, when the colour and scent of wild flowers and plants are a botanist's delight.
Two signposted walks start at the reception centre. The shorter *(1hr there and back)* La Losa footpath leads to the Maceta corrie *(torca)*, passing the Ventanillas viewpoint *(mirador)*. **Views**★★ are quite exceptional. The longer walk *(3hr return)* traverses the Chamorro chasm *(sima)*, the Pizarro Rock *(peñón)* and the Los Topaderos trail *(vereda)*.

Archidona

19km/11mi northeast. Leave Antequera on the A 354. After the Peña de los Enamorados, follow the A 92 to exit 163.

Menga dolmen

B. Kaufmann / MICHELIN

Set in the Sierra de Gracia, at the foot of the Pico de Conjuro peak, Archidona recalls Moorish times.

Plaza Ochavada★

This unusual octagonal square, once used for bullfights, is the symbol of the town. Built in the 18C by architects Francisco Astorga and Antonio González, it melds French urban planning with traditional Andalusian architecture. The façades of the buildings fronting the square mix red-brick arches and pilasters and whitewashed masonry, embellished by flower-decked balconies.

Ermita de la Virgen de Gracia

Only a few walls, the keep, vestiges of a cistern and the restored Puerta del Sol (Sun Gateway) remain of this small 18C chapel in the old Moorish castle. There are three naves, a hemispherical dome and a stuccoed elliptical cap; ornamental features of the original mosque remain. The views of Archidona and its surroundings from here are delightful.

Iglesia de Santa Ana

Visit by prior arrangement.
☎952 71 40 82.
This predominantly Gothic construction includes several Baroque features, such as the fine 18C façade. The triangular-based tower is capped by a pyramidal pinnacle with glazed green and white roof tiles. The interior contains interesting works of art.

Convento de las Mínimas

The Baroque doorway of this former 18C convent is flanked by a polygonal red-brick tower with glazed ceramic decoration.

Iglesia de las Escuelas Pías

Visits by prior arrangement.
☎952 71 40 82.
This church houses a venerated statue of Jesus of Nazareth.

Laguna de la Fuente de Piedra★

22km/13mi northwest. Take the A 354, then the A 92 towards Sevilla. Turn right at the Km 132 exit and continue along A 6211 to Fuente de Piedra, then follow the signposts.

Parque Natural de El Torcal

This large lagoon is home to one of the largest colonies of flamingoes in Europe, plus storks, gulls, cranes and egrets. The spectacle of these birds in flight or massed on the water is quite remarkable, particularly in the late afternoon. The lagoon also supports a variety of flora (saltwort, *suaeda vera*, rushes etc).

Driving Tour

Valle del Guadalhorce★

From Antequera to the Cueva de Ardales

70km/44mi – Allow half a day.
The Guadalhorce River meanders through the Serranía de Ronda and the Montes de Málaga to the Guadalteba-Guadalhorce Reservoir *(embalse)*. It traverses a landscape of olive groves and fields between plain and mountains, hills dotted with whitewashed houses, vegetable plots and rocky walls, offering superb **views**.

▸ *Leave Antequera on avenida de la Legión. Turn right onto the A 343 towards Álora.*

The **road** winds its way through delightful landscapes, passing through the Abdalajís Valley, before heading south to Álora.

Álora★

The traditional home of the haunting fandango-style *malagueña* song, Álora perches on a hillside along the River Guadalhorce, at the foot of Monte Hacho. It is a maze of narrow streets lined by low, whitewashed houses, overlooked by a castle, with fine views.

▶ *On the way out of Álora, take the MA 404 towards El Chorro.*

Desfiladero de los Gaitanes★★

Given the dangerous nature of the gorge and to ensure your safety, we recommend that you go no farther than the metal bridge suspended high above the El Chorro defile.

The **winding road**★ crosses superb mountain scenery to the astonishing Garganta del Chorros gorge. Leave your car at the El Chorro campsite and continue on foot along a tarmac track *(30min there and back)* which climbs to a metal bridge offering magnificent **views**★★★ and the sensation of being suspended in mid-air far above the riverbed. A flimsy catwalk of wood and rope, the Camino del Rey, skirts the rockface to join a bridge in a worse state of repair.

▶ *Return to the road and continue towards Ardales. At a signposted junction, bear left onto a narrower track.*

This scenic winding **road**★★ crosses tranquil mountain landscapes before it reaches the Tajo de la Encantada Reservoir *(embalse)*.

▶ *Park your car and follow the marked path; allow 15min each way.*

Bobastro ruins

It was from Bobastro that General Omar Ben Hafsun, of noble Visigothic lineage, opposed the Umayyads. The rebellion against the Emirate of Córdoba lasted from 880 to 917. Today only the ruins of the *alcázar* walls remain, along with several caves and an unfinished 10C church, set in a sandstone outcrop. It exemplifies the synthesis of Hispano-Roman, Visigothic and Islamic art.

▶ *Return to the MA 444.*
  After 2km/1.2mi, turn right toward the Parque de Ardales information post (puntos de información) in front of the Conde de Guadalhorce reservoir.

Embalse del Guadelteba-Guadalhorce★

Park information centre: ⏰ *open 9am–10pm.* ☏ *952 11 24 01 or 607 39 21 41.*

This reservoir *(embalse)* is in the heart of the Parque de Ardales, an area of dark woods, light-coloured stone rocks and plentiful camping areas. Along with the neighbouring Gaitejo, Tajo de la Encantada and Conde de Guadalhorce reservoirs, it is a perfect escape to nature. Footpaths skirt the reservoir and criss-cross landscapes where not a soul can be seen. The silence, particularly in winter, the pure air and perfect climate are the main attractions. The views from the hills overlooking the reservoir are spectacular.

▶ *From the dam, take the MA 444 towards Ardales. Before reaching the village, follow the A 357 towards Málaga; the cave is located 3km/2mi farther on.*

Cueva de Ardales★

👁 *Visit by guided tour only (3hrs), must be booked in advance (up to 3 weeks). Jul–Aug Tue, Thu, Sat–Sun; rest of year, Sat–Sun.* ☏ *€5.* ☏ *952 45 80 46. www.cuevadeardales.com.*

The cave, running 1 600m/5 250ft, contains evidence of occupation from the Paleolithic period to the Bronze Age. It has exceptional wall paintings (54 representations of animals and 130 symbols), particularly a female deer, its legs and heart painted bright red.

ARACENA★

POPULATION: 6 500.

The whitewashed houses of Aracena rise in tiers on a hillside, overlooked by remains of a Templar castle. Its splendid caves mean a steady stream of day visitors while the **Museo al Aire Libre de Escultura Contemporánea**, an exhibition of modern art in streets and squares, adds a touch of modernity and culture.

- **Information:** Pozo de la Nieve. ☎959 12 82 06.
- ▶ **Orient Yourself:** Aracena is 93km/58mi north west of Seville, close to Extremadura in the northeast corner of Huelva province, at the heart of the Parque Natural de la Sierra de Aracena.
- **Don't Miss:** Gruta de las Maravillas.
- **Organising Your Time:** Allow several hours to a day for Aracena, depending on you (and any kids') taste for caves.
- **Especially for Kids:** Gruta de las Maravillas.
- **Also See:** Parque Natural de la Sierra de ARACENA Y PICOS DE AROCHE, Parque Natural de la SIERRA NORTE DE SEVILLA, MINAS DE RIOTINTO, SEVILLA, HUELVA.

Sights

Gruta de las Maravillas★★★

Open year-round daily by guided tours (50min) only 10am–1.30pm, 3pm–6pm. €7.70. ☎959 12 83 55 (advance booking advised). www.cuevasturisticas.com.
The aptly named Cave of Marvels descends over 100m/330ft deep) and underground lakes mirror the limestone ceilings to superb effect. Points of interest include the "organ chamber" *(salón de los órganos)*; the "cathedral chamber" *(sala de la catedral)* with a Virgin and Child formation; "Sultana's bath" *(baño de la sultana)*; and the stunning **"God's Crystal Chamber"**★★ *(salón de la Cristalería de Dios)*. The 70m/231ft high **salón del gran lago** (hall of the great lake) contains the largest subterranean lake where the *Sinfonía del Agua* by local musician Luis de Pablo and the

Gruta de las Maravillas

©Turespaña

Address Book

♨For coin ranges, see the Legend on the front cover flap.

WHERE TO STAY

☺☺**Hotel Los Castaños** – *Avenida de Huelva, 5.* ☎*959 12 63 00. www.loscastanoshotel.com. 33 rooms.* This attractive, centrally located, Andalusian-style hotel has modern, tasteful if simple rooms, some of which face onto a large inner patio, and a fine restaurant.

☺☺☺**Finca Valbono** – *Carboneras road (1.5km/1mi NE).* ☎*959 12 77 11. www.fincavalbono.com. 6 rooms, 20 apartments, restaurant.* This country hotel complex in a delightful setting has a choice of standard rooms, bungalows and private houses which sleep up to eight. Facilities include a swimming pool, horse-riding, handball court, a good restaurant (☺☺) and bicycles for hire.

WHERE TO EAT

☺☺☺**José Vicente** – *Avenida Andalucía, 53.* ☎*959 12 84 55 – Closed Tue and mid-Jun–mid-Jul.* One of the best restaurants in the province, serving only fresh produce. The menu in the small, tastefully decorated restaurant includes locally picked cep mushrooms and features pork dishes.

LOCAL SPECIALITIES

The many bars *(mesones)* dotted around Aracena offer ample opportunity to try local cuisine, particularly the renowned **serrano ham** *(jamón serrano)*.

Suite Gruta de las Maravillas by Don Primitivo Lázaro are played.

Film buffs might like to note that the caves were the setting for the Spanish 1973 film *Tarzan and the Mines of King Solomon.*

The **Museo Geológico Minero** (☾*open 10am–6.30pm)* geological and mining museum is part of the complex.

Castle

☾*Open by appointment.* ☎*959 12 82 06 (tourist office) or 959 12 88 25.*

This fortress dominates Aracena and the countryside. Groves of chestnut trees extend in the distance, pine groves surround the walls of the castle, built over a 9C Almohad fortress. The compound includes a Gothic church and a **Mudéjar-style tower** – once a minaret – with *sebka* panelling similar to that on the Giralda in Sevilla.

Iglesia de Nuestra Señora del Mayor Dolor

The Church of Our Lady of Great Suffering was built between the 13C and 14C on a site affording superb **views**★★.

It contains a sculpture of the Virgin Mary, the town's patron saint, as well as a recumbent statue by Pedro Vázquez.

Plaza Alta

This tranquil square, the hub of local life, borders several notable buildings, including the Iglesia de Nuestra Señora de la Asunción and the Cabildo Viejo.

The solemn Renaissance-style 16-17C **Iglesia de Nuestra Señora de la Asunción** has a well-preserved façade with fine decoration and large windows.

The 15C former municipal storehouse and town hall, **Cabildo Viejo**, houses the **Centro de Información del Parque Natural Sierra de Aracena y Picos de Aroche** (☾*open 9.30am–6.30pm;* ☎*959 128 825*), providing information on the park and area.

PARQUE NATURAL DE LA SIERRA DE ARACENA Y PICOS DE AROCHE★★

This superb nature park boasting mountain landscapes and picturesque villages is a sensory pleasure. Vast forests punctuated by slender peaks offer delightful views of the sierra, while the rush of flowing water blends with the wind whistling through the treetops.

- **Information:** Cabildo Viejo Visitor Centre, Plaza Alta, Aracena.
- **Orient Yourself:** Accessible from Huelva on the N 435 and Sevilla via the N 433 and A 66, the park extends across northern Huelva province, bordering Portugal to the west and Extremadura to the north.
- **Don't Miss:** The view from the Peña Arias Montano.
- **Organising Your Time:** Allow a day to drive from Aracena to Aroche.
- **Also See:** Parque Natural de la SIERRA NORTE DE SEVILLA, MINAS DE RIOTINTO, SEVILLA, HUELVA.

Driving Tour

Aracena to Aroche
64km/40mi.

Aracena★ – *see ARACENA*

▶ *Follow the A 470 west to Alájar.*

Alájar★
This whitewashed village, nestled at the foot of a church with a pointed belfry, is popular with walkers. The area around Alájar is a microcosm of the park: dark cork and holm oak forests, steep rugged rocks and stunning views.

Peña Arias Montano – This impressive rock *(peña)* several kilometres to the north of Alájar provides yet more superb **views**★★ of this extraordinary landscape. Its name recalls the learned **Benito Arias Montano**, tutor to Felipe II, diplomat and royal librarian. He retired to a contemplative existence in Alájar. The **Ermita de Nuestra Señora de los Ángeles**, a chapel, can be seen on a rocky outcrop.

▶ *Head north from Alájar to Fuenteheridos, then bear left onto the N 433.*

Jabugo
This isolated mountain village is world-famous for its prized **cured hams** *(jamones)* and **sausages** *(embutidos)*, which are available locally.

▶ *Follow the N 435 south, then bear left onto a minor road.*

View over the Sierra de Aracena

©Turespaña

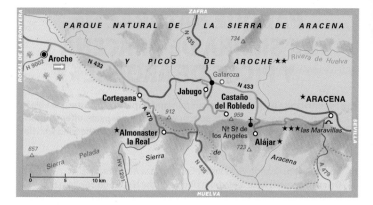

Castaño del Robledo

Hikers come to this village to walk trails through groves of chestnut trees, to scale peaks and to admire birds of prey gliding through the air.

▶ *Continue south along the N 435, then bear right onto the A 470, heading west.*

Almonaster La Real★

Almonaster is a pleasant surprise. Amid dense stands of chestnut, eucalyptus,

cork and holm oak this little town is a labyrinth of quiet streets and mansions where time has stood still. The local gastronomy is based on pork products. A major attraction is the *Cruces de Mayo* festival in May. A **park information point** is in the **town hall** (🕐open 9.30am–6.30pm; ☎959 14 32 06).

Mezquita★

🕐*Open Sat–Sun, pub hols 11am–7pm.* This 10C mosque is one of the few Caliphal structures left in the area. From its reddish walls are superb mountain views. An unusual bullring is visible to one side; the castle-fortress in the mosque enclosure offers **views** of the town below.

Iglesia de San Martín

This sober church is a mix of Gothic and Mudéjar styles.

▶ *Head northwest along the A 470 for 7km/4.5mi.*

Cortegana

The major activities in this pleasant town are processing meat and cork and making scales and pottery.

Historic buildings of note include the elegant 16C Gothic-Mudéjar **Iglesia del Salvador**, the Gothic-Renaissance **Iglesia de San Sebastián** and the medieval **castle** (🕐open Tue–Sun 10am–1pm (summer to 2pm) and 4.30pm–6.30pm. 💶€1.2; ☎959 13 16 56), which affords impressive **views**. It also includes an exhibition which traces the evolution of local defensive systems.

▶ *From Cortegana, follow the N 433 northwest for 14km/9mi.*

Aroche

Aroche is one of the oldest towns in the area, as evidenced by the **Piedras del Diablo** (Devil's Stones) dolmens in a delightful setting 3km/2mi to the southeast along the H 9002 (near the Ermita San Mamés). A maze of narrow, twisting alleyways, mansions, old buildings and small workshops specialising in saddles climb up to the **castle**★. Thissober 12C construction was once used as a refuge by King Sancho IV ("the Brave"). It houses a bullring, as well as a park information point dedicated to the black vulture, a species in danger of extinction. The park has one of the biggest black vulture breeding colonies in Spain.

A visit to the 13C **Iglesia de Nuestra Señora de la Asunción** and the **Convento de los Jerónimos**, a Hieronymite monastery, are also recommended.

> ### Medieval festivities
>
> On 9–12 August every year, the streets of Cortegana provide the backdrop for theatre performances, processions, medieval banquets, re-enactments of scenes of daily life in the Middle Ages and concerts of sacred Andalusian music, attracting thousands of visitors of all ages.

ARCOS DE LA FRONTERA★★

POPULATION: 27 897.

Arcos enjoys a remarkable clifftop **setting**★★ seemingly about to plunge into the deep valley of the River Guadalete. Its Renaissance and Baroque mansions and whitewashed houses are adorned with classic Andalucian wrought-iron grilles and balconies, trimmed with red geraniums.

The Roman colony on this site was Arx-Arcis, "fortress on high ground", though some have it that the town's name derives from Arcobrigán, the arch of Brigus, grandson of Noah. Arcos was capital of a taifa kingdom in the 11C. Following an initial incursion by Fernando III, it was finally conquered by Alfonso X in 1264

- ℹ **Information:** Plaza del Cabildo, 11630 Arcos de la Frontera, ☎956 70 22 64, turismo@ayuntamientoarcos.org. Plaza de San Sebastián, 7, 11630 Arcos de la Frontera, ☎952 70 25 05.
- ▶ **Orient Yourself:** Arcos de la Frontera is the western gateway to the White Villages (*Pueblos Blancos*), 40km/25mi northeast of Jerez de la Frontera. The best **views**★ are from the A 382, approaching from Jerez de la Frontera, and the A 372 linking Arcos with El Bosque and Grazalema.
- 🕐 **Organising Your Time:** Take at least half a day to absorb the charms of Arcos.
- 🅿 **Parking:** Park in the lower town (paseo de Boliches) to best appreciate Arcos on foot.
- ⚲ **Also See:** PUEBLOS BLANCOS DE ANDALUCÍA, JEREZ DE LA FRONTERA, El PUERTO DE SANTA MARÍA, CÁDIZ, MEDINA SIDONIA.

Walking Tour

Allow 2hrs.

Ascend the cuesta de Belén, a hill which connects the bustling 19C heart of Arcos with the upper town, the nucleus of the medieval city, with steeply sloping narrow alleyways and whitewashed houses.

Pass through the Puerta de Jerez, one of the gateways to the walled Moorish city. Beyond **callejón de Juan del Valle** note the 15C Gothic-Mudéjar **façade**★ of the **Palacio del Conde del Águila** to the right, fronted by a magnificent doorway with an *alfiz* surround decorated with finely worked tracery.

Arcos de la Frontera

▷ *Continue to the right on calle Nueva, which runs parallel to the castle wall.*

Plaza del Cabildo

The tower of the **Iglesia de Santa María** dominates the square, which is also lined by the town hall, the parador, housed in the former magistrate's house (Casa del Corregidor), and the castle, now privately owned. The terrace on the west side offers a magnificent **view**★ of the plains below and the Iglesia de San Pedro.

Iglesia de Santa María de la Asunción★

🕐 *Open summer Mon–Fri 4pm–7pm, Sat 10am–2pm.* ⊜ *€1.50.* ☎ *956 70 00 06.*

Holy Week

On **Good Friday**, a traditional procession winds its way through the streets of Arcos as part of the Semana Santa celebrations. Included in this religious ritual are the armaos – local men dressed in Roman costume who parade proudly through the town wearing helmets and armour and carrying standards and lances.

This splendid church was built around 1530 above an earlier 14C church, itself erected on the site of a mosque. Its **west façade**★, the work of Don Alonso de Baena, is an extraordinary example of Plateresque art. The interior, accessed via the neo-Classical south façade, has a basilical plan with three aisles separated by robust columns supporting star vaults with tiercerons. In the high altar, a 17C **retable** by Jerónimo Hernández and Juan Bautista Vázquez represents the Ascension of the Virgin. Hidden behind the high altar is the polygonal apse of the earlier Mudéjar church. The **frescoes**★ *(The Coronation of the Virgin)* which decorated the earlier high altar were transferred to the wall of the Evangelist nave *(to the left of the altar)* in the 1960s.

▷ *Continue along the west façade of the church into the evocative callejón de las Monjas.*

The flying buttresses were added in the 17C to counteract the movement of the walls. Pass the **Renaissance façade**★ of the Convento de la Encarnación, and continue along calle del Marqués de Torresoto. Note the 17C Classical-style patio of the **palace-residence of the Marquess of Torresoto** at no 4. The

Address Book

🪙 *For coin ranges, see the cover flap.*

WHERE TO STAY

🛏️🛏️**Marqués de Torresoto** –
Marqués de Torresoto, 4. ☎956 70 07 17.
15 rooms. This 17C palace has a central
location in the historical centre. It features a Baroque chapel and an attractive arcaded patio. Antique furniture
decorates the rooms.

🛏️🛏️**Hotel El Convento** –
Maldonado, 2. ☎956 70 23 33. *www.
webdearcos.com/elconvento. 11 rooms.
Closed 2 weeks in Jan.* As the name suggests, this hotel is housed in a former
17C convent, located in a narrow street
in the centre of Arcos. Rooms are quiet;
most have views of the valley.

WHERE TO EAT

🍽️🍽️**Restaurante El Convento** –
Marqués de Torresoto, 7. ☎956 70 32 22.
*www.webdearcos.com/elconvento.
Closed 7–22 Jan and first week of Jul.*
Opposite the Hotel Marqués de Torresoto (which owns it). Traditional decor and
a columned patio. Specialities include
local dishes and game in season.

TAPAS

Alcaraván – *Calle Nueva, 1.* Within the
walls of the castle and easily identified
by the numerous flowerpots outside.
Grilled meats, stuffed peppers and
lamb stew are just some of the dishes
on the menu, which diners can enjoy
the strains of flamenco music.

---

small square at the end of the street,
plazuela Boticas, is fronted by the **Convento de las Mercedarias Descalzas**,
where the nuns sell pastries, and the
unfinished 18C Jesuit house, now the
town market.

▶ *Calle Boticas and calle Nuñez
de Prado lead to the other main
section of the town.*

Close to the Iglesia de San Pedro stand
the **Capilla de la Misericordia**, a
chapel with a blind pointed arch, and
the **Palacio del Mayorazgo**, a palace
which houses a conservatory of music
and is adorned with an ornate Renaissance loggia.

Iglesia de San Pedro

🕐*Open Mon–Sat 10.30am–2pm, 4pm–
7pm (Sun and public hols 10am–1.30pm).*
💶*€1.* ☎956 70 11 07.
For many years this early 15C church
rivalled Santa María as the village's finest structure. The façade is crowned by
a large neo-Classical tower. The interior
consists of a single nave with a pointed
vault with tiercerons.
A ceramics shop is hidden behind the
Plateresque façade of no 7 calle San
Pedro.

▶ *Continue along calle Cadenas.*

The street has two interesting palaces.
To the left, in calle Juan de Cuenca, is
the palace-residence of the same name;
a little farther on, in plaza del Cananeo,
stands the former palace of the Marquess and Marchioness of Torresoto.

▶ *Continue along calle Bóvedas.*

On the corner with calle Boticas, note
the Casa de los Gamaza.

▶ *Continue along calle Boticas to the
plazuela de Boticas, then follow the
charming calle de los Escribanos
(delightful wrought-iron balconies)
back to plaza del Cabildo.*

Additional Sight

Convento de la Caridad★

The convent stands in plaza de la Caridad, outside the medieval walls in the
barrio bajo (lower town). It was built
in the middle of the 18C and exudes a
strong colonial influence. The entrance
to the church is preceded by an attractive atrium.

LA AXARQUÍA★

This area, blessed with a near perfect climate, offers both tranquil inland villages and lively coastal resorts. Until the 18C, marauding Barbary pirates forced the inhabitants into the mountains. Today the only invaders are northern Europeans in search of sun. Watchtowers still exist along the coast. Vineyards line mountain slopes, and orchards of fruit and subtropical crops, some in plastic greenhouses, cover valley floors.

- **Information:** Calle Puerta del Mar, 2. Nerja, ☎95 252 15 31. www.nerja.org.
- ▶ **Orient Yourself:** La Axarquía extends southwards along the slopes of the Sierra de Almijara, at the eastern extremity of Málaga province. The A 7-E 15 links the towns along this stretch of coastline, while minor roads run inland. Its best known and most popular resort is Nerja.
- **Don't Miss:** the Cave of Nerja, Frigiliana.
- **Organising Your Time:** Allow a day to drive to Nerja, with stops, then return.
- **Especially for Kids:** The Cave of Nerja, the area's excellent beaches.
- **Also See:** MÁLAGA, ALHAMA DE GRANADA, Las ALPUJARRAS, GRANADA.

National Park

Parque natural de las Sierras de Tejeda y Almijara

The Tejeda and Almijara mountain ranges form a line of rocky escarpments rising to an altitude of 2 068m/6 783ft (Pico Maroma), creating a natural barrier between the provinces of Málaga and Granada. Covering an area of 40 600ha/100 300 acres to the south of Alhama de Granada, the majority of the park is located in the area of La Axarquía.

The magnificent yet harsh landscape here is characterised by steep, pine-covered slopes inhabited by wild goats,

B. Kaufmann/MICHELIN

Rincón de la Victoria

sharp crests, deep ravines, winding streams and villages with a palpable *morisco* feel. In days gone by these provided shelter for the famous brigands who roamed the region. The towns of Frigiliana and Nerja are located on the southern boundary of the park.

Driving Tour

Málaga to Nerja

99km/62mi including excursions inland.

Málaga – *see MÁLAGA.*

▶ *Leave Málaga along the A 7–E 15 to the east. Take the Cueva del Tesoro after the first Rincón de la Victoria exit.*

Cueva del Tesoro (Cueva del Higuerón★)

Admission by guided tour only (every 45mins), mid-Jun–mid-Sept 10.45am–1pm, 4.45pm–7pm; mid-Sept–mid-Jun 10.45am–1pm, 3.45pm–5.15pm. €4.65. ☎952 40 61 62.

Tradition says that treasure *(tesoro)* was hidden here in Moorish times, though sadly none has ever been found. The cave, once under water, now dry, was created by erosion. Some of the shapes within its chambers could have inspired Antoni Gaudí in Barcelona.

Address Book

For coin ranges, see the Legend on the cover flap.

WHERE TO STAY

Hotel Rural Cortijo Amaya – *Torrox Costa. Take the N 340 for 1.5km/1mi, then go right 1km/0.6mi.* ☎952 53 02 45. www.cortijoamaya.com. *14 rooms*. An old farmhouse set into the hillside with views of the Mediterranean and the surrounding countryside. Simple, comfortable rooms, plus a well-maintained garden with a swimming pool and tennis courts.

Hostal Marissal – *Paseo Balcón de Europa, Nerja*. ☎952 52 01 99. www.hostalmarissal.com. *22 rooms*. This *hostal* has a prized location at the entry to Nerja's famed Balcón de Europa with fine views from its well-kept rooms. It includes a cafe and restaurant.

Nerja Princess Hotel – *Los Huertos Nerja.* ☎952 52 89 86. www.hotelnp.com. *20 rooms*. This small hotel with discreet façade is minutes from the Balcón de Europa. It features a marble entrance, attractive rooms and a pleasant pool. Good value.

Molino de Santillán – *near Macharaviaya (MA 106, Rincón de la Victoria.* ☎902 12 02 40. www.molinode santillan.es. *12 rooms*. This former mill, converted to a charming small luxury hotel which oozes local character, is located in a bucolic setting at the end of a country lane, 8 km inland. It includes a pool and tennis court.

WHERE TO EAT

Chiringuito de Ayo – *Paseo Antonio Mercero (Playa Burriana), Nerja*. ☎952 52 22 89. www.ayonerja.com. A longstanding favorite, this charming beach side "snack bar" was even the locale for a TV series. It specialises in paella and has a large terrace on Burriana beach.

Pepe Rico – *Almirante Ferrándiz, 28. Nerja*. ☎952 52 02 47. This Swedish-run restaurant on a pedestrianised street has a cosy dining room with fireplace (and oil paintings), as well as apartments for rent (). Specialities include Swiss suckling pig and duck in wine.

Rincón de la Victoria

The town is a popular seaside resort with a large number of tourist apartments and hotels, as well as a sandy beach over 3km/2mi long.

▶ *Return to the A 7–E 15 and continue east to exit 272.*

Torre del Mar

This large seaside resort with its extensive beach is the closest to Vélez-Málaga.

▶ *Head north along the A 335.*

Vélez-Málaga

The capital of La Axarquía, Vélez-Málaga is dominated by the keep of its former fortress, destroyed by Napoleon's troops. The **Barrio de la Villa**, a district of Moorish origin at the foot of the tower, offers superb views. It is a maze of steep, narrow streets, whitewashed houses and the 16C Mudéjar-style Iglesia de Santa María, with a fine bell tower. Access is from plaza de la Constitución, fronted by the Iglesia de San Juan Bautista, crowned by an attractive belfry, and containing a number of paintings and remnants of the old walls.

In the centre, the 17C Palacio de los Marqueses de Beniel, with a sober façade, now functions as the town hall *(ayuntamiento)*.

▶ *Return to the A 7–E 15. At exit 277, follow signs to Algarrobo.*

Algarrobo

Algarrobo's whitewashed houses rise on a cliff 190m/623ft above the sea. Typically Moorish narrow streets wind up to the Ermita de San Sebastián, a chapel with sea views.

▶ *Return to the A 7–E 15. Shortly before the junction with the coast*

Keeping the Currency Local

La Axarquía has steadfastly refused to succumb entirely to the Euro, creating its own currency, the *axarco*, which has been in circulation since 1988. While visitors and locals alike can still pay in euros, most shops also accept the local currency, which on one side bears the portrait of an Arab botanist who introduced citrus fruits to Andalucía in the 13C, and on the other that of Felipe II. The dangers of counterfeiting are eliminated by the fact that each note is signed in ballpoint pen by its creator, Antonio Gámez, a descendant of a family of *moriscos* who escaped the massacre ordered by Felipe II in the 16C. Subdivided into *axarquitos*, the *axarco*, which is worth around 60 cents, can be purchased in the region's town halls and, somewhat surprisingly, its banks.

road, go left toward the Necrópolis de Trayamar.

Necrópolis de Trayamar
The remains of this large necropolis includes Punic and Phoenician tombs, some from the 8C and 7C BC.

▶ *Continue along the coast. Two watchtowers come into view.*

Torrox
In the resort area of Torrox Costa, close to the lighthouse *(follow "faro" signs)*, excavations have revealed Roman basins used in the production of *garum (see TARIFA)*; some were used as burial urns. The beaches here are very pleasant.

Cueva de Nerja

H. Champollion/MICHELIN

▶ *Continue north, heading inland.*

From Torrox to Cómpeta
This winding road climbs along the spurs of the Sierra de la Almijara, dotted with whitewashed villages A bend in the road affords a delightful view of **Cómpeta**, a charming *pueblo blanco*.

▶ *Return to the A 4–E 15 via the same road, then continue for 8km/5mi.*

Nerja★
Nerja is an attractive whitewashed town of Moorish origin perched above the Mediterranean. The coast below the Sierra de Almijara is characterised by steep cliffs and delightful beaches. Numerous bars, outdoor cafés, restaurants and nightclubs have made Nerja one of the most popular summer resorts along the eastern Costa del Sol, though it is nowhere near as brash as its rivals to the west.

Balcón de Europa★ – This magnificent *mirador* (viewpoint) in old Nerja is on the site of the old castle. It is a landscaped square overlooking the sea. On a clear day you can see as far as Africa. The whitewashed 17C Iglesia del Salvador, with its impressive bell tower, stands alongside.

Cueva de Nerja (Cave of Nerja)★★   Kids
4.5km/3mi east towards Motril.
 Admission by guided tour only (45 mins) year-round daily 10am–2pm, 4pm–8pm; Sept–Jun 6.30pm. Closed 1 Jan and 15 May. €6, child €2.50. 952 52 95 20. www.cuevadenerja.es.

Frigiliana

Discovered in 1959, this enormous cave is set in the marble of the Sierra de Almijara. Pottery, ceramics, human remains and wall paintings, some exhibited in the first few rooms, indicate that the caves were inhabited during the Palaeolithic era.

The cave is hugely impressive in the scale of its chambers and its spectacular stalactites and stalagmites, one of which is the biggest in the world.

The **Sala de la Cascada** (Cascade Chamber), also known as the **Sala del Ballet** (Ballet Chamber), takes its name from the formations on the right-hand side. A **Festival of Music and Dance** is held here in the second or third week of July.

▶ *Head north from Nerja,*
following the MA 105 inland.

Frigiliana★

This charming *pueblo blanco* extends across the southern slopes of the Sierra de la Almijara. Its **Morisco-Mudéjar quarter**★★ is a superb ensemble of meticulously maintained whitewashed houses. Flowers add an extra dash of colour. Panels of *azulejos* on several walls recall battles here between Moors and Christians.

AYAMONTE★

POPULATION: 17 000.

Ayamonte marks the frontier with Portugal. The noise of the fleet unloading its catch and the hubbub of fish auctions blend in with the lively conversation in waterside cafés. Colonial-style houses were built by Spanish emigrants who returned from the Americas at the end of the 19C.

▪ **Information:** Puente Internacional (bridge to Portugal), 21400 Ayamonte. ☎959 50 21 21. turismo@ayto-ayamonte.es.
▶ **Orient Yourself:** Ayamonte is the southwestern most part of Spain, 60 km/37mi southwest of Huleva.
◷ **Organising Your Time:** Allow two hours, longer if you plan to sail up river or cross the river to visit Portugal's Algarve.
◔ **Also See:** HUELVA, COSTA DE HUELVA, La RÁBIDA, MOGUER.

Address Book

For coin ranges, see the cover flap.

WHERE TO EAT

Casa Barberi – *Plaza de la Coronación.* 959 47 02 89. Closed Tue.
The Casa Barberi on the main square has been run by the same family since 1917. Paellas are a specialty.

Acosta – *Plaza de las Flores, 13, Isla Cristina.* 959 33 14 2. A family-run restaurant on a pleasant square. Fish and seafood are good value.

Casa Rufino – *Avenida de la Playa, Isla Cristina.* 959 33 08 10. This fish and seafood restaurant is just a stone's throw from the sea. Ample desserts and wide selection of wines.

LOCAL SPECIALITIES

Among local specialities are *pestiños* (a type of honey fritter) and *coca ayamontina*, a flat biscuit-like cake.

FESTIVALS

Ayamonte and the surrounding area come to life at **Carnival**, with processions, masked balls and dances into the early hours.

Visit

Iglesia de las Angustias

Nestled between old houses, this 16C church with a colonial air has a spacious triple-nave interior, crowned by a tower which dominates Ayamonte.

Convento de San Francisco

A 16C Renaissance monastery with an elegant belfry, a Mudéjar polychrome wood ceiling, and columns decorated with old inscriptions.

Iglesia del Salvador

This 13C building with fine stucco work was erected on the site of an old mosque.

Muelle de Portugal

Boats depart from this dock *(muelle)* to cross the river to Portugal and go upriver to Sanlúcar de Guadiana (*see Box*)

Excursions

Isla Cristina

14km/9mi SE. Take the N 431 towards Lepe. Before El Empalme, go right on the A 4201.

Many houses in Isla Cristina's old quarter boast tiled *azulejo* decoration. You will find a marina, protected marshes and attractive beaches here.

Isla Canela

7km/4.5mi SE on the H 921.

A popular resort with a sandy beach and golf course.

Punta del Moral

9km/5.5mi southeast on the H 921.

This small resort has numerous beach bars and restaurants, and is favoured by fishing enthusiasts.

Across the Border

Ayamonte faces across the border to Vila Real de Santo António in Portugal. It's not the most interesting town in the Algarve but you might like to spend some time in its distinctive main square. With its black-and-white pavement markings and obelisk at the centre it resembles a sundial. It is fringed by orange trees, handsome late 18C buildings and outdoor cafes where you can order a *bica* (black coffee) or a *galao* (milky coffee) and a delicious typically Portuguese *pastel de nata* (custard tart). Just off the square is the Centro Cultural and the interesting, if small, Manuel Cabanas Museum, featuring the woodcut works of the eponymous local artist.

Further upstream the Guadiana is much more attractive and by the times it gets to Sanlúcar de Guadiana quite bucolic. Its possible to cross here too, to Alcoutim on the Portuguese side.

BAENA

The houses of Baena extend in a white swathe amid undulating groves famous for its virgin olive oil. The old *barrio alto* with its narrow streets is dominated by the tower of Santa María la Mayor; the lower Llano District is Baena's modern, commercial heart.

The drum *(tambor)*, emblem of Baena, plays a major part in celebrations, particularly during the lively Holy Week festivities.

- **Information:** Calle Virrey del Pino, 5. ☎957 671 757. www.baena.es.
- **Orient Yourself:** Baena is 65km/41mi southeast of Córdoba via the A 309.
- **Don't Miss:** An excursion to Zuherosa.
- **Organising Your Time:** Allow two hours.
- **Also See:** MONTILLA, AGUILAR DE LA FRONTERA, CABRA, LUCENA, PRIEGO DE CÓRDOBA, MARTOS, CÓRDOBA (62km/39mi NW).

Barrio Alto

In the Middle Ages, the upper town was the Moorish quarter.

Iglesia de Santa María la Mayor

The church, on the site of a mosque, dates from the 16C and has been repeatedly altered. The simple Plateresque portal (Portada del Ángel)has square decoration around the doorway.

The slightly leaning bell tower is the former minaret, and now comprises two Baroque sections crowned by a green and blue *azulejo* spire.

Iglesia del Convento Madre de Dios

🕐*Open for services only at 1pm (7pm Thu).* ☎957 67 09 10.

This convent was founded in the early 16C by Don Diego Fernández de Córdoba, fifth Lord of Baena. Renaissance influence is evident in the originally Gothic structure. The interesting **east end**★ is partly the work of Hernán Ruiz II, though the design is by Diego de Siloé. Note the sculpted decoration of Apostles and angels in the half-dome. The exterior is fronted by an attractive late-Gothic portal.

Llano District

Casa del Monte

This imposing three-storey building with its wide façade dates from 1774 and is home to the local history museum. It occupies one side of plaza de la Constitución (aka plaza Coso), which is dominated by the town hall.

Iglesia de Guadalupe

Beside plaza de España.

The chancel of the 16C church has a fine **Mudéjar artesonado**★ ceiling and 18C Baroque altarpiece. The **Capilla de la Virgen de Guadalupe**, a side chapel, has a Baroque altar covered with Mudéjar *artesonado* work.

Olive Oil

There's no escaping the distinctive smell of this golden liquid in Baena. The acclaim of Andalusian *aceite de olivo* dates to Roman times and the oil produced in Baena is among the best in southern Spain, certified by its *denominación de origen* label. It uses the *picuda* olive and is ideal for the table, for frying and as an ingredient in Andalusian stews.

Learn more about it at the **Museo del Olivar y el Aceite (Museum of the Olive and Oil)** on calle Cañada, 7 (🕐*Open Tue–Sat 11am–2pm & 5pm–7pm, Sun 11am–2pm,* ☎957 69 16 41, www.museoaceite.com).

Zuheros rising above a sea of olive groves

B. Kaufmann / MICHELIN

Antiguo Convento de San Francisco

On the outskirts towards Córdoba,
left after the petrol station.

◷Open Mon, Tue and Thu 10am–1pm,
5pm–7.30pm; Fri from 8am. ☎957 67 01 42.
The 18C **Baroque church**, (now a rest
home) with its Latin-cross ground plan,
is crowned with barrel vaults. Frescoes
cover the walls. A Baroque altarpiece has
pride of place in the east end.

Its 18C **Nazarene Christ** is said to have
been fired at during the Civil War without any damage.

Excursions

Zuheros★

17km/10.5mi S via the N 432,
A 318 and CV 241.
Picturesque Zuheros has a superb
setting★★, enhanced by fresh-look-
ing whitewashed houses on cobbled,
flower-decked streets.

Plaza de la Paz

This impressive viewpoint at 622m/
2 040ft provides stunning **views**★★ of
hills carpeted in olive groves, with Baena
in the distance.

Museo Arqueológico and Castle

♺◷*Visit by guided tour only (40min)*
10am–2pm, 4pm–6pm; Fri 5pm–7pm.
◷€1.80. Reservation advised. ☎957 69
47 75 – tourist office.

The town's archaeological museum dis-
plays artefacts from prehistory to the
Roman period, discovered at the nearby
Cueva de los Murciélagos.

The Romans founded a fortress on the
site of the **castle**. The tower and battlements are Moorish in origin, while the
remains opposite are from a 16C Renaissance palace.

Cueva de los Murciélagos

4km/2.5mi east of Zuheros.
♺◷*Visit by guided tours only (1hr) Sat–*
Sun and public hols at 11am, 12.30pm,
2pm, 5pm (4pm Oct–Mar) and 6.30pm
(5.30pm Oct–Mar). Advance booking
online highly recommended, though not
required. Also Mon–Fri 12.30pm–5.30pm
(4.30pm Oct–Mar), booking required.
◷€4.37 cave only; €5.50 cave, museum
and castle. ☎957 69 45 45. www.cueva
delosmurcielagos.com.

The road leading up to the cave offers
more delightful **views**★★.

The cave is a superb formation with
several chambers of impressive stalactites and stalagmites. It contains important archaeological remains from the
Neolithic period, including drawings,
engravings, a burial chamber tools,
ornaments and pieces of ceramic, dating
from between 4300 and 3980 BC.

Luque

5km/3mi northeast of Zuheros
along the CO 240. Leave your car in
the main square.
The village is crowned by a Moorish
fortress, restored and modified. The
Parroquia de la Asunción, a 16C Renaissance church attributed to Hernán
Ruiz II and Hernán Ruiz III has an elegant
tower and belfry adorned with columns
and a conical roof. The chancel houses
an 18C Baroque retable dominated by
an Assumption.

The remains of the **castle** are visible
on a rocky crag behind the town hall.
A staircase leading to the base of its
walls offers a panorama of Luque.

BAEZA ★★

POPULATION: 17 691.

Baeza extends across a low hill, surrounded by fields of cereal crops and olive groves stretching to the horizon, a setting immortalised by poet Antonio Machado: "Oh land of Baeza, I shall dream of you when I cannot see you." Churches, monuments and splendid mansions of golden stone recall the splendour of this peaceful provincial town during the 16C and 17C. The best time to visit Baeza is during the solemn processions of **Holy Week** or **Corpus Christi**.

- **Information:** Plaza del Pópulo, 23440 Baeza. ☎953 74 04 44. http://baezaturismo.es.
- **Orient Yourself:** Baeza is at the centre of the province of Jaén, 50km/31mi northeast of the city of Jaén.
- **Don't Miss:** The cathedral interior.
- **Organising Your Time:** Allow a full day.
- **Also See:** ÚBEDA (9km/5.5mi E), Parque Natural de las Sierras de CAZORLA, SEGURA Y LAS VILLAS (55km/34mi E), LINARES (27km/17mi NW) and JAÉN (48km/30mi SW).

A Bit of History

Originally a Bronze Age settlement, Baeza developed under the Romans into the town known as *Biatia*. Under the Visigoths in the 7C it was an episcopal see. Later it became the capital of a taifa kingdom. Following the reconquest by Fernando III (the Saint) in 1227, Baeza became a centre for the christianisation of al-Andalus. In the 16C and 17C, the town enjoyed its period of greatest splendour. Handsome buildings shaped the centre, and a university was established (unfortunately to be closed in the 19C). During these two centuries, intellectuals, architects and poets took up residence, including St John of the Cross, who completed his celebrated **Spiritual Canticle** here. Between 1912 and 1919, writer and poet Antonio Machado taught French at the new university.

Cathedral

Old Town★★★

Allow half a day – route marked on town plan.

Plaza del Pópulo★

In the centre of this small square is the **Fuente de los Leones** (Fountain of the Lions), built using stones from the ruins of nearby Cástulo. The central figure is said to be Imilce, the wife of Hannibal. The square is fronted by the former abattoir *(carnicería)* and the Casa del Pópulo, the former court. The **Arco de Villalar** (arch) commemorates the vic-

tory of Carlos I (Holy Roman Emperor Charles V) over the *comuneros* in 1521. Alongside, the **Puerta de Jaén** projects onto the Casa del Pópulo via an attractive quarter-circle balcony; this gateway marks the emperor's visit on his way to Sevilla to marry Isabel of Portugal.

Antigua carnicería – This elegant 16C Renaissance building, seat of the former Tribunal de Justicia, bears a large escutcheon of Charles V.

Casa del Pópulo – The former seat of the Caballeros Hijosdalgos de Baeza

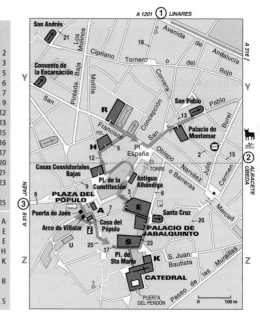

(Noble Knights of Baeza) and the Audiencia Civil (Civil Tribunal) houses the **tourist office**. The edifice has harmonious proportions and refined decoration. The façade, adorned by medallions and large windows, is fronted by six doors to clerks' chambers.

Plaza de Santa María

The **fountain**, decorated with caryatids and atlantes, is by Ginés Martínez. To one side stands the 17C **Seminario de San Felipe Neri**, whose sober façade bears the ancient inscriptions of students written in bull's blood to celebrate graduation. To the left is the **Casas Consistoriales Altas** or Casa Cabrera, emblazoned with the coats of arms of Juana the Mad and Philip the Fair between two attractive mullioned windows.

Cathedral★

Open Jun–Sept 10am–1.30pm, 5pm–7pm; Oct–May 10am–1.30pm, 4pm–6pm. ☎953 74 41 57.

Fernando III ordered the cathedral built over the destroyed mosque. In midafternoon, its silhouette casts a mysterious shadow over the narrow cobbled streets behind.

Exterior

The Renaissance-style façade contrasts with the west side's 13C Gothic-Mudéjar Puerta de la Luna (Moon Doorway), and 14C Gothic rose window. In the south wall is the 15C Puerta del Perdón (Pardon Doorway).

Interior★★

The severity of Castilian architecture combines harmoniously with graceful Andalusian features. Andrés de Vandelvira planned the 16C reconstruction, crowning the three aisles with oven vaults. The Capilla Dorada (Gold Chapel) has delicate Italianate relief; the Capilla de Santiago (St James's Chapel) on the left side has a fine antique setting; while the Capilla de San José is flanked by caryatids. The fine **Capilla del Sagrario** (Sacrarium Chapel) at the end of the north aisle holds a Baroque silver **monstrance**, carried in procession on Corpus Christi. Note the Plateresque door to the sacristy, with its delicate

Detail of the pulpit in the cathedral

B. Kaufmann/MICHELIN

reliefs, the polychrome metal **pulpit** (1580) in the transept, the Baroque retable, and the monumental iron **grille** by Maestro Bartolomé in the nave. Four Mudéjar chapels in the cloisters have decorative plant motifs *(atauriques)* and Arabic inscriptions.

There is a small **museum** (Open Jun–Sept 5pm–7pm, Oct–May, 10.30am–1.30pm).

Palacio de Jabalquinto★

Open Mon–Fri 9am–2pm. ☎953 74 27 75.

The Flamboyant Gothic former residence of Juan Alfonso de Benavides, the Capitán de Lorca, has an exceptional **façade★★**, attributed to Juan Guas and Enrique Egas. It is best seen in late afternoon when the shadows accentuate its details. Stylish features

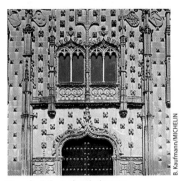

Façade, Palacio de Jabalquinto

B. Kaufmann/MICHELIN

Patios of Baeza

Baeza is a monument in itself, offering surprise after surprise in the form of elegant palaces, monumental churches, enchanting nooks and crannies and exquisite architectural detail.

The town's patios – havens of peace and quiet, hidden behind the attractive wrought-iron grilles of some of the town's most delightful buildings – are an essential part of any visit.

Every season highlights a different aspect: a blaze of colour in spring; an oasis of cool in summer; the brightness in which they are bathed in the clear light of autumn; and their dazzling architecture, best seen in winter.

of the day include projecting pinnacles, stone fleurons, elaborate escutcheons etc. Inside is a spacious Renaissance patio with marble Corinthian columns and a monumental Baroque staircase.

Iglesia de Santa Cruz

This small Romanesque church has a Gothic chapel, and murals in the apse.

Former university (Antigua universidad)

calle Beato Juna de Avila.
🕐*Open year-round daily 10am–2pm, 5pm–7pm (Oct–May 4pm–6.30pm).* ☎953 74 01 50.

To reach the university, pass through the Arco del Barbudo, which along with the Puerta de Jaén is the only vestige of the old walls. Founded in the 16C by Rodrigo López and Juan de Ávila, the university closed in 1875. Its most famous student was Antonio Machado who wrote his more melancholic poetry in the handsome Renaissance-style **patio**.

Plaza del Mercado Viejo or Plaza de la Constitución

This is the hub of town life, surrounded by the **Antigua Alhóndiga** (old corn exchange) and the 18C Baroque **Casas Consistoriales Bajas**, a former civic building. A number of traditional bars and cafés stand side-by-side beneath its arcades.

Ayuntamiento★

The town hall was formerly the law courts and prison. It is Plateresque in style, with two floors separated by a wide cornice. Armorial bearings can be seen on the façade.

Ruins of the Convento de San Francisco

Before the convent suffered disasters and pillage, it was considered one of Vandelvira's major works. The monumental transept and apse, fasciated columns and majestic altarpieces give an idea of how the beautiful 16C church once appeared. It is now an **auditorium**.

Palacio de Montemar (Palacio de los Condes de Garcíez)

This 16C palace has large Gothic windows and a Plateresque inner patio.

Iglesia de San Pablo

🕐*Open only for services.*
Set in the pretty street of calle San Pablo, this church has a Renaissance façade and three wide aisles supporting Gothic pillars. It has several painted panels and a statue of *Christ of the Expiration*.

Additional Sights

Iglesia de San Andrés

🕐*Open only for services, 7.30pm (also 11.30am Sun and public hols).* ☎953 74 06 78.

Following the Reconquest, Fernando III created in this church the Company of the Two Hundred Crossbowmen of St James. These were noblemen from Baeza who showed allegiance only to the king. The doorway is Plateresque. Note the **sacristy**, with its collection of nine **Gothic wood tablets**★, the colours of which bear witness to the technical expertise of Andalusian artists of the time.

Convento de la Encarnación

This convent, in transitional Renaissance-Baroque style, is still occupied by Carmelite nuns. It is where St John of the Cross completed his *Spiritual Canticle*.

BAZA

POPULATION: 20 113.

Native Iberians established Basti in the 4C BC. Excavations outside the present town unearthed the famous **Lady of Baza** (Dama de Baza) sculpture of a goddess (now in Madrid). With the expulsion of the *moriscos* at the end of the 16C, Baeza declined. The only remnants of the former Moorish city are the baths and the maze-like layout of several streets.

- **Information:** Plaza Mayor, 18800 Baza. ☎958 86 13 25. turismobaza@terra.es.
- ▶ **Orient Yourself:** Baza is 111km/69mi northeast of Granada via the A 92.
- ☺ **Don't Miss:** The Moorish Baths.
- ◷ **Organising Your Time:** Allow a couple of hours.
- ☧ **Also See:** GUADIX (48km/30mi N), GRANADA, Sierra de los FILABRES.

Walking Tour

Colegiata de Santa María de la Encarnación★

This fortress-like collegiate church, built over the destroyed mosque, stands behind an unusual wall of buttresses. There are three aisles of equal height and no transept.

The **Plaza Mayor** is fronted by the Renaissance former town hall, now the **Museo Municipal** (◷open year-round Mon–Fri 10am–2pm, 5pm–7pm; Oct–May 4pm–6.30pm; Sat–Sun 11am–2pm. ☜€1.20. ☎958 70 35 55) which displays a reproduction of the Dama de Baza.

▶ *Leave the plaza Mayor through the Arco de la Magdalena, beside the 18C bell tower. Follow calle Zapatería to the left to the old "morisco" quarter.*

The narrow alleyways are lined by several buildings of interest: the Mudéjar **Iglesia de San Juan Bautista**; the **Convento de la Merced**, housing the *Virgin of Piety*.

▶ *Return to the Arco de la Magdalena. Follow calle Zapatería. To the left, the former abattoirs (carnicerías), date from 1568. Continue to plaza de Santo Domingo.*

The **Convento de Santo Domingo** is in a state of poor repair. The better-preserved 17C cloister is concealed inside an early-20C building, once a theatre.

▶ *Follow calle Dolores.*

The façade of the 17C-18C **Iglesia de los Dolores** has an unusual Baroque portal framed between two sturdy Solomonic columns.

▶ *Continue on calle Dolores, then bear left onto calle del Agua as far as calle Caniles.*

Moorish baths (Baños árabes)★

In calle Caniles. If closed, go to calle Caniles, 19 and ask for Mateo or Manuela.
These simple baths, in the old Jewish quarter next to the Iglesia de Santiago,

B. Kaufmann/MICHELIN

Plaza Mayor

Fiesta de Cascamorras

This fiesta dates back to the 15C when, according to legend, an inhabitant of Guadix who was working in an Mozarabic chapel near Baza discovered a statue of the Virgin. However, the problem soon arose as to which town would keep the statue. The courts decided that the Virgin would remain in Baza, with the proviso that a fiesta in her honour would take place once a year in Guadix. Unfortunately, when the time came for the residents of Guadix – headed by a figure known as Cascamorras – to assert their rights and reclaim the Virgin Mary, they were chased out of Baza by locals brandishing sticks. Upon their return to Guadix, they were further punished by townspeople angry at their failure. Nowadays, on **6 September**, a resident of Guadix in multi-coloured attire plays the part of Cascamorras, and attempts to reach the **Iglesia de la Merced** to steal the image. During the course of his journey, he is jostled and provoked by the inhabitants of both towns.

date from the Caliphal period (10C) and are some of the oldest in Europe.

Excursion

Parque Natural de Sierra de Baza
15km/9.5mi towards Guadix along A 92, then 5km/3mi to the Visitor Centre in Narváez.

🕐*Open Jun–Sept Wed–Sun, 10am–2pm, 6pm–8pm; Oct–May Tue–Wed and Fri–Sun 10am–2pm, 4pm–6pm.* ✍*No charge.* ☎*958 00 20 05 or 670 94 28 89.*
Despite limited infrastructure, this park offers interesting walks.
Several peaks in the Sierra de Baza exceed 2 000m/6 560ft.

BELALCÁZAR
POPULATION: 3 879.

Formerly Gaete, Belalcázar, adapted its name in the 15C (from Bello Alcázar, a reference to its prominent fortress). Nobles of the most prominent family include Sebastián de Belalcázar, who founded Quito and conquered Nicaragua.

- ℹ **Information:** Plaza de la Constitución, 11 (town hall), 14280 Belalcázar. ☎957 14 60 04.
- ▶ **Orient Yourself:** Belalcázar lies 101km/63mi north of Córdoba, close to the River Zújar, the border with Extremadura.
- 🕐 **Organising Your Time:** Allow at least half a day.
- 👁 **Also See:** FUENTE OBEJUNA, CÓRDOBA.

Visit

Iglesia Parroquial de Santiago
🕐*Open Mon–Sat 6.30pm, 7.30pm (7.30pm, 9pm Jun–Sept); Sun 11am for Mass.*
The austere, granite parish church of St James dates from the 16C and 17C, An incomplete bell tower rises above its centre and sturdy buttresses support its walls.

Town Hall
This 19C granite building dominates Belalcázar's attractive main square. It features a clock in its central section.

▶ *Follow calle Sebastián de Belalcázar to the right of the church.*

The **Fuente del Pilar** (1570) was once a drinking trough. From here there is a superb view of the castle.

Castle★

Belalcázar's dominant structure rose in the late 15C where a Roman fortress might have stood. It is quadrangular with towers in the corners and the centre of its walls. Brackets run along the upper walls and towers.

The keep is notable for its imposing proportions. Lookout posts bear the chequered escutcheons of the Sotomayor family, lords of the castle.

Convento de Santa Clara

0.8km/0.5mi towards Hinojosa del Duque, along a road signposted to the left.
🕐*Open daily, 11am–1pm, 4pm–6pm.*
☎*957 14 61 24.*

The late-Gothic convent, one of the largest in the province, was founded as a monastery in 1476, and converted to a nunnery in 1483, forcing the monks to found the **Convento de San Francisco**, now in ruins. The east end, under a *Christ of the Column*, features a star vault with frescoes between the ribs. The three damaged sculptures in the doorway arch represent Christ, Mary Magdalene and St Clare.

Belalcázar also has several noble mansions such as the Casa Grande and the Casa de la Administración de los Osuna. A Roman bridge survives on the outskirts.

Excursion

Hinojosa del Duque

8.5km/5mi S.
The church in this small town is the most important monument in the north of the province.

▷ *Follow directions to the Catedral de la Sierra.*

Parroquia de San Juan Bautista★

🕐*Open daily 11.30am–noon.*
☎*957 14 18 31.*
Known as the *Catedral de la Sierra*, this church was built in the 15C and 16C by Córdoban architects Hernán Ruiz I, Hernán Ruiz II and Juan de Ochoa.The

impressive **northeast façade**★ has a fine Renaissance portal with Corinthian columns. The **sacristy** has magnificent **cresting** and windows decorated with armorial bearings, scallop shells etc. The **bell tower** (1590) is a nesting place for a family of storks.

The stone used **inside** to construct arches, pillars and vaulting contrasts with the whitewashed walls. The central nave is crowned by a fine *artesonado* ceiling.

In the main square, to the right of the church's façade, is the **Iglesia de la Virgen del Castillo**, now an exhibition hall.

Convento de las Madres Concepcionistas

This convent was built in the 16C. The sober **south façade**, a series of sturdy buttresses between arches, is crowned by a graceful belfry popular with storks.

PARQUE NATURAL DE CABO DE GATA-NÍJAR★★

Cabo de Gata–Níjar park includes cliffs, wild beaches, delightful coves and azure skies. The landscape is sprinkled with prickly pears, agave and species able to survive in this desert-like region registering the lowest rainfall in Spain.

- **Information:** Centro de Visitantes Amoladeras. ☎950 160 435. www.degata.com.
- ▶ **Orient Yourself:** The park is south of the volcanic Sierra del Cabo de Gata, running southwest–northeast parallel to the coast.
- **Don't miss:** The wild and secluded beaches on the edge of San José.
- **Organizing Your Time:** The driving tour takes a day.
- **Also See:** COSTA DE ALMERÍA, ALMERÍA.

Níjar

North of the park.
The whitewashed houses and cobbled alleyways of this old Moorish town are the essence of Andalucía. It sits on the southern slopes of the Sierra de Alhamilla, in view of the agricultural plain of **Campo de Níjar** below. Irrigation has transformed the surrounding landscape.

The town is known for its handicrafts: blue and green **pottery** produced from clay and marl is popular, as are *jarapas*, colourful cotton and wool rugs and blankets.

Iglesia Parroquial

The 15C parish church by the square bears Felipe II's coat of arms – the two-headed eagle – on its bell tower. The interior contains fine *artesanado* work.

Rugs on sale in Níjar

B. Kaufmann/MICHELIN

Watchtower (Torre-vigía)

Walk from the church to the market square *(plaza del Mercado)*, with its 19C ceramic fountain and hundred-year-old elm trees, then ascend a steep and stony path *(the last few metres are somewhat difficult)* to the hilltop watchtower for a commanding **view** of the Níjar plain, with Cabo de Gata and the Mediterranean in the distance.

Driving Tour

Park★★

90km/56mi – allow one day.

- ▶ *From Níjar, take the A 7-E 15 towards Almería and exit at km 467. Before reaching Retamar, follow a road heading southwest.*

Cross a desert-like terrain, with sea to the right and the sierra in the distance.

- ▶ *Upon reaching a junction, bear right.*

The seaside village of **San Miguel de Cabo de Gata** comes into view.

Saltpans

The Cabo de Gata saltpans *(salinas)* extend 4.5km/3mi southeast from Salinas, covering 300ha/740 acres. This protected area attracts thousands of migratory birds.

Address Book

🪙*For coin ranges, see the Legend on cover flap.*

WHERE TO STAY

🛏**Hostal Puerto Genovés** – *Balandro, San José.* ☎*950 38 03 20. www.puerto genoves.com. 18 rooms.* This small, family-run *pensión* just 200m from the sea has spotless modern rooms and a cafe.

🍴🍴🛏**Las Salinas de Cabo de Gata** *Almadraba de Monteleva. 4km/2.5mi SE of El Cabo de Gata.* ☎*950 37 01 03. www. lasalinascabodegata.com. 20 rooms.* In a peaceful setting within the Parque Natural del Cabo de Gata, its bedrooms overlooking the beach or saltpans, this is an ideal base from which to explore.

SCUBA-DIVING

Tranquil, crystal-clear waters, pleasant temperatures, a richness of species, fascinating caves and basalt columns and breathtaking underwater scenery have made Parque Natural de Cabo de Gata one of Europe's most important marine reserves and a paradise for scuba-divers. Underwater enthusiasts can choose from several sites: Cala San Pedro, Playazo de Rodalquivar, Cala del Embarcadero (in Los Escullos) etc. Underwater fishing is prohibited within the park. Authorisation is not required for scuba-diving; however, solo divers need a permit from the Consejería de Medio Ambiente of the Junta de Andalucía. Contact an area scuba-diving centre for further information.

Cabo de Gata

The road winds up to the lighthouse *(faro)* and volcanic formations called **The Finger** (El Dedo) and **Mermaids' Reef** (Arrecife de las Sirenas). A viewpoint (Mirador de las Sirenas) and an information point adjoin the lighthouse.

▶ *Return to the junction and take the road to the left.*

Centro de Visitantes Amoladeras

🕐*Open Jul–Sept and Holy Week 10am–3pm; Oct–Jun 10am–2pm, 5pm–9pm.* ☎*950 160 435. www.degata.com.*
The nearby visitor centre provides detailed park information and has a bookshop.
The inland road passes a number of fields under plastic, typical of the Almerían landscape. To the right is the **CEMA** (Michelin Tyre Experimentation Centre), where the company's new tyres are put to the test.

▶ *13km/8mi farther on, take the turn-off to Los Escullos.*

Los Escullos

This small fishing port nestles alongside a delightful long beach with an 18C watchtower known as Calahiguera. The road to Rodalquilar passes the **Isleta del Moro** cove and the viewpoint **Mirador de las Amatistast**.

Rodalquilar

This mining settlement was abandoned in the 1960s. The dirt track leading to the **Playa del Playazo** skirts a chain pump, the 16C Rodalquilar or Las Alumbreras tower, and the 18C coastal battery of San Román.

▶ *Return to the Los Escullos junction and follow signs to San José. At nearby Pozo de los Frailes is an information point.*

San José

The whitewashed houses of this small resort ascend from an attractive beach.

Blood Wedding

It was in 1928, at the Cortijo del Fraile, near Rodalquilar, that the tragic event occurred that was to inspire **Federico García Lorca** to write his famous play, *Blood Wedding.* The play recounts the tale of a young woman who fled with her cousin on the day of her wedding. This course of action was to end in the dramatic assassination of her lover.

Playa de los Genoveses

Note the half-domed cupolas which cool interiors. There is a small marina.

Beaches – Two superb beaches are on the edge of San José. **Playa de los Genoveses**★ lines a wide bay 2km/1.2mi from the centre to the left of a dirt track; the **Playa de Monsul**★, 2.5km/1.5mi from San José nestles between mountain spurs descending to the sea, a sand dune at one end, a rock in its centre, and a cove beyond.

CABRA

POPULATION: 20 057.

Cabra is a swathe of white across its sierra, amid rolling hills set with olive groves. Its imposing castle and the slender tower of the parish church rise on a hill above town.

- **Information:** Calle Santa Rosalía, 2, 14940 Cabra. ☎957 52 01 10.
- **Orient Yourself:** Cabra is in the southern part of Córdoba province, 114km/70mi due north of Málaga.
- **Don't Miss:** The views from the Ermita de la Virgen de la Sierra.
- **Organising Your Time:** Allow two hours.
- **Also See:** LUCENA, PRIEGO DE CÓRDOBA, BAENA, MONTILLA, AGUILAR DE LA FRONTERA.

Plaza Alta

From plaza Vieja, take the street up to an esplanade fronted by the parish church and the castle remains. On the way, note the stone benches with embedded fossils.

Parroquia de la Asunción y Ángeles

Cabra's main church, modified over the years, was once a mosque, hence the five aisles. The colourful brick tower and the marble Baroque side portal, adorned with *estípites* and Solomonic columns, stand out. The marble-like altarpieces, the stalls, and the cover of the baptismal font, a work by Benlliure, notable inside.

Torre del Homenaje

The castle of the Counts of Cabra was a Moorish fortress rebuilt after the Reconquest. Nowadays, the restored keep is part of a school, the Colegio de las Madres Escolapias. Walk into the patio of the school *(knock first at the gate)*. An octagonal room reveals neo-Mudéjar decoration.

Barrio de la Villa

This quarter *(barrio)* spreads out behind the church, within the town walls. Calle Villa extends as far as a lookout garden encircled by the battlements.

"El Cerro" Moorish quarter

On the Cuesta de San Juan.
Narrow lanes and whitewashed houses and arches, including the **Puerta del Sol** (Sun Gate), recall Cabra's Moorish past.

Iglesia de Santo Domingo

The church belongs to a convent founded in the 15C. The façade retains two 18C Baroque marble portals. The simple main doorway is adorned with balustered Solomonic columns.

Instituto Aguilar y Eslava

An image of the Immaculate Conception ornates the elegant 17C red marble doorway. The *Iglesia de la Virgen de la Soledad* dates from the 18C.

Seigniorial mansions

A number of fine noble houses stand in the centre of Cabra.

Museo Arqueológico

Calle Santa Rosalia 2.
Open Mon–Fri, 10am–2pm, 6pm–9pm (Sat–Sun and public hols 11am–2pm). ☎957 52 01 10.
Well-presented regional museum displaying local finds.

Parque Alcántara-Romero

The Paseo, as it's more commonly called, was laid out in the mid 19C.

Excursions

Ermita de la Virgen de la Sierra★

Take the road towards Priego de Córdoba. After 5km/3mi, bear left at a signposted junction.
The road climbs for 7km/4.5mi through an arid and rocky landscape, where wandering sheep are a road hazard. The sanctuary is in a delightful **setting**★, at the highest point of the Sierra de Cabra (1 223m/4 011ft), affording expansive **views**★★. The chapel dates to the Middle Ages and was rebuilt in the 16C. It features a *camarín* housing a sumptuously dressed Virgin of the Sierra.

Parque Natural de las Sierras Subbéticas

Centro de Acogida Santa Rita

Along A 340. www.subbetica.com.
Stop at the reception centre, at the Mojón Pass, for general information. The terrain can be divided into three areas: The Macizo de Cabra is a limestone massif which includes several naturally sculpted rocks – Lapiaz de Las Lanchas, Los Hoyones and La Nava (at the foot of the Ermita de la Virgen de la Sierra) – and the **Cueva de los Murciélagos** *(see BAENA)*. The Sierra de Rute and Sierra de la Horconera ranges contain the park's most spectacular scenery, culminating in the Pico de La Tiñosa (1 570m/5 150ft).

CÁDIZ

POPULATION: 143 129.

Touched by water on three sides, Cádiz is Spain's longest-established seafaring city, settled for over 3 000 years. It is also one of Andalucía's most delightful and engaging provincial capitals, with charming parks and squares, orderly if attractively dilapidated 19C streets, and a quietly confident air. Only February's exuberant Carnival, the best on the Peninsula, punctuates the usual tranquillity. Visitors will discover a friendly, cosmopolitan city, relatively poor in monuments, but rich in spirit.

- **Information:** Avda. José León de Carranza/Avda. de La Coruña ☎956 28 56 01. Paseo de Canalejas ☎956 24 10 01. www.cadiz.es/turism.cadiz.
- **Orient Yourself:** Cádiz is 138km/86mi northwest of Gibraltar and 35km/22mi southwest of Jerez de la Frontera.
- **Don't Miss:** The Cathedral, the Museo de Cádiz, Carnival.
- **Organising Your Time:** Allow at least two days.
- **Especially for Kids:** Playa de Barrosa at Chiclana de la Frontera.
- **Also See:** SANLÚCAR DE BARRAMEDA, El PUERTO DE SANTA MARÍA, VEJER DE LA FRONTERA, MEDINA SIDONIA, JEREZ DE LA FRONTERA, ARCOS DE LA FRONTERA.

A Bit of History

Cádiz might well be Europe's oldest city. It was colonised in 1100 BC by Phoenicians from Tyre who landed on an islet almost surrounded by water and founded Gadir ("fortress"). This first settlement extended from the castle of Santa Catalina to the island of Sancti Petri. The trading outpost was initially a dependency of Tyre and later of Carthage, it came under Roman rule in 206 BC, as Gades. Trade developed through Gades between Baetica and Rome, but apparently declined under the Visigoths and Moors. The city fell to Fernando III (the Saint) in 1240. His son, Alfonso X (the Wise), transformed Cádiz into a strategic port. The Pópulo district was developed and protected by walls. Three of the four original gateways remain: **Arco de los Blancos**, **Arco del Pópulo** and **Arco de la Rosa**. In the late 15C, Cádiz expanded into the present-day district of Santa María. The Earl of Essex sacked Cádiz in 1596. During the 17C, Cádiz underwent considerable growth, as testified by the numerous examples of Baroque architecture still visible today. Its zenith, however, followed the transfer of the Casa de Contratación (Exchange) from Sevilla to Cádiz in 1717, when it became the port of entry for all goods from America.

Walking Tour

The best way to discover the delightful squares, gardens and old streets of Cádiz is on foot. These two itineraries include the city's most characterful districts and its major sights (⌖see plan).

1 Around the Santa María and Pópulo Districts

This walk passes through two gypsy quarters where the traditions of flamenco, guitar and dance are part of everyday life. The Pópulo district is the early medieval section, while Santa María developed in the 15C beyond the Arco de los Blancos. Despite their attractiveness, they remain poor and rundown. Restoration projects have been undertaken in recent years on the houses, many dating from the 17C.

Plaza de San Juan de Dios

This 16C square, formerly plaza de la Corredera, is, along with plaza de San

©Turespaña

Cathedral viewed from Campo del Sur

Antonio, the oldest in the city. Its strategic position facing the port made it the hub of Cádiz life; for a long time the square was also the site of the city's market. On one side stands the neo-Classical façade of the **town hall** dating from 1799, a work by Torcuato Benjumeda; next to it is the Baroque tower of the **Iglesia de San Juan de Dios**.

▶ *Take calle Sopranis, to the left of the Iglesia de San Juan de Dios.*

Calle Sopranis

The street contains some of the best examples of Baroque civil architecture in Cádiz. The façades of nos 9–10 (known as the Houses of the Lilacs because of the doorway decoration) and the staircase in the patio of nos 17–19 are particularly noteworthy. At the intersection with Calle Plocia, to the left, is the old iron-and-brick **tobacco factory**, a superb example of 19C industrial architecture, now the city's conference centre (*Palacio de Congresos*). Opposite stands the **Convento de Santo Domingo**.

▶ *Follow calle Botica as far as calle Concepción Arenal.*

Cárcel Real★

The royal jail was the first neo-Classical building in the city. It was built in 1792 by local architect Torcuato Benjumeda. The centre of the single-section façade is an avant-corps, similar to a triumphal arch. Four Tuscan-style engaged columns and two lions flank the royal escutcheon. The interior, restored in 1990 for use as law courts, is set around one large central patio and two side ones.

▶ *Take calle Santa María to the church of the same name.*

Iglesia de Santa María

This 17C church was part of the old Convento de Santa María. Its façade can be seen at the end of the street of the same name. This Mannerist edifice is a work by Alonso de Vandelvira, the son of the famous Renaissance architect Andrés de Vandelvira, although the influence of Juan de Herrera can be detected. Its belfry is topped with an *azulejo*-adorned spire. Inside, note the dynamism of the Baroque altarpiece, as well as the

Plaza de San Juan de Dios

This square is popular with locals and visitors alike. Enjoy a break from sightseeing at two of the city's most popular cafés: the traditional-style Novelty Café, and La Caleta, with its boat-shaped counter.

Address Book

🪙*For coin ranges, see the cover flap.*

GETTING THERE AND GETTING AROUND

AIRPORT

The airport at Jerez de la Frontera is just 30min away on A 4. ☎902 404 704. www.aena.es.

TRAINS

The station is in plaza de Sevilla, near the centre and port. Trains operate to major cities. Provincial trains run every 30min or so. ☎956 25 43 01 (railway station) or 902 24 02 02 (RENFE).

INTER-CITY BUSES

Transportes Generales Comes *(Plaza de la Hispanidad, 1)* serves Cádiz province and Sevilla. ☎956 20 53 09 or 956 80 70 59. www.tgcomes.es.

Transportes Los Amarillos *(Avenida de Ramón de Carranza, 31)* serves the provinces of Sevilla and Málaga. ☎956 28 58 52.

Secorbus *(Plaza Elios, 1)* serves Sevilla and Madrid. ☎956 25 74 15. www.socibus.es.

LOCAL BUSES

The main stops are in plaza de España and close to the port. A single-journey ticket costs around €1, while a ten-trip ticket is on sale
for around €6.
☎956 21 31 47 or 956 28 38 04.

TAXIS

☎956 21 21 21/22/23.

HORSE-DRAWN CARRIAGES

In summer, carriages in plaza de San Juan de Dios may be hired for a one-hour trip. The cost is approximately €25–30.

WHERE TO STAY

🛏**Hostal Bahía** – *Plocia, 5.* ☎956 25 91 10. 21 rooms. Modern rooms in a small hotel in the old quarter.

🛏**Hostal Fantoni** – *Flamenco, 5.* ☎956 28 27 04. www.hostalfantoni.es. 12 rooms. Simple, modern rooms in a central locations.

🛏🛏**Hotel Francia y París** – *Plaza de San Francisco, 6.* ☎956 21 23 19. www. hotelfrancia.com. 57 rooms. An early 20C hotel on a charming square. Plain modern rooms.

🛏🛏🛏**Hospedería Las Cortes de Cádiz** – *San Francisco, 9.* ☎956 22 04 89. www.hotellascortes.com. 36 rooms. Characterful 19C house in the old quarter. Rooms around a patio are individually decorated on historical themes. Modern facilities include gym and jacuzzi. Good restaurant.

WHERE TO EAT

🍴**Terraza** – *Plaza de la Catedral, 3.* ☎956 26 53 91. Closed Sun in summer. Unpretentious and pleasant restaurant in a central location, specialises in fish and seafood.

🍴**La Marea** – *Paseo Marítimo, 1.* ☎956 28 03 47. Right on the beach in an area of bars, specializing in seafood and rice dishes.

🍴🍴 **El Faro** – *San Félix, 15.* ☎956 21 10 68 - www.elfarodecadiz.com. Modern, wooden decor, refined cuisine, regional emphasis, specialist in rice dishes.

TAPAS

Joselito – *San Francisco, 38.* ☎956 26 65 48. Closed Sun in summer. Central tapas bar with a pleasant sheltered terrace. Enjoy king prawns, rice dishes and stews.

Aurelio – *Zorrilla, 1.* ☎956 22 10 31. Closed Mon Oct–Jun. A small popular tapas bar next to the plaza de Mina where the emphasis is on fish and seafood.

El Cañón – *Rosario, 49.* ☎956 28 50 05. A small, traditional bar dating back to the 19C with a counter selling cured hams and local wines. **La Manzanilla**, on the opposite pavement, is the ideal place to try the wines of the area.

El Nuevo Almacén – *Barrié, 17 (by plaza El Palillero).* ☎956 22 10 33. Closed Sun. A fine tapas bar and Iberian delicatessen offering the best regional sausage, cheeses, chocolates and more.

Taberna Manteca – *Corralón de los Carros, 66.* ☎956 21 36 03. Closed Sun eve and Mon. The faded posters on the walls are a reminder that the owner of this traditional-style bar is a former bullfighter. The Manteca is renowned for its fine selection of chorizos, hams and sausages.

TAKING A BREAK

Café Parisien – *Plaza de San Francisco, 1.* ☎*956 22 36 77.* Terrace café on a quiet square popular with all ages.

Taberna La Manzanilla – *Feduchy, 19.* ☎*956 28 54 01. www.lamanzanilla decadiz.com.* This splendid little taverna has been serving manzanilla and all sorts of wines since 1900.

GOING OUT

During the winter, social life is concentrated around the **commercial centre**. The summer action is at the beach area of **Playa de la Victoria** and its **Paseo Marítimo**. The most popular bars are in **calle General Muñoz Arenillas**. The **Punta de San Vicente** at the other end of the city is another lively area.

El Café de Levante – *Rosario, 35 www. cafelevante.com.* This buzzing café with modern decor in the old quarter attracts a trendy mixed crowd.

La Cava – *Antonio López, 16.* ☎*956 21 18 66. www.flamencolacava.com. Daily Jul–Sept, Tue, Thu, Sat Oct–Jun.* Flamenco shows by local artists in an atmospheric bar.

La Mirilla – *Plaza Asdrúbal, 7–8.* ☎*956 25 17 12.* Have a drink or a coffee from the extensive list, while enjoying the ocean view.

O'Connell's. *Sagasta, near plaza de San Francisco.* Irish pub popular with locals and visitors.

Yunque– *Muñoz Arenillas, 5.* In the area usually frequented by youngsters, Yunque attracts a more mature crowd with danceable music for all tastes.

SHOWS

The **Gran Teatro Falla** *(plaza Falla)* organises theatre and concerts throughout the year, while **cultural centres** (El Palillero, El Bidón, La Viña and La Lechera) host exhibitions and workshops. Flamenco concerts are occasionally held at the **Baluarte de la Candelaria** *(alameda de Apodaca)*

SHOPPING

The most typical shopping area in Cádiz is the old part of the city. The long, narrow streets and squares, particularly **San Francisco**, **Columela**, **Compañía** and **Pelota**, in addition to **calle Ancha** and **plaza de San Antonio**, are crammed with traditional stores and more modern boutiques.

Shops in the old quarter sell traditional cakes and pastries. Try such local specialities such as *pan de Cádiz* at **Horno Compañía** *(calle Compañía, 7).*

Markets – Arts and crafts markets are regular events in the city. Head to the Sunday market near the **Arco de Pópulo**, or the market known as **El Piojito** (Little Flea)on avenida de la Bahía on Monday mornings, where you can buy virtually anything.

FESTIVALS

The **carnival** in Cádiz, generally held during February *(check dates and details of events by visiting www.carnavaldec-adiz.com)* is renowned throughout Spain and is said to be the third largest Carnival celebration in the world (after Rio de Janeiro and Trinidad). Even General Franco failed to suppress it and during his dictatorship it was the only Spanish Carnival that was still staged.

Delft ceramics covering the base of the Capilla del Nazareno.

The marble Casa Lasquetty in calle Santa María (no 11) is an example of early-18C civil architecture.

Cross calle Félix Soto to the 18C **Arco de los Blancos**, an arch formerly known as the Puerta de Tierra which leads into the working-class Pópulo district.

▸ *Pass through the arch and continue along calle Mesón Nuevo to plazuela de San Martín.*

Casa del Almirante

This fine Baroque palace was built by Admiral (almirante) Don Diego de Barrios at the end of the 17C. The most important feature is the double-section Genoa marble **doorway**★★, with its combination of Tuscan and Solomonic columns on the lower and upper storeys respectively.

▸ *Turn left along calle Obispo José María Rancés to the small plaza de Fray Félix.*

In the religious centre, the Iglesia de Santa Cruz stands on the site of the destroyed mosque. Note the Baroque Casa de Estopiñán on plaza de Fray Félix (no 1).

Iglesia de Santa Cruz (Catedral Vieja)★

This late-16C church was the city's second cathedral. The sober exterior is broken only by the glazed ceramics covering its umbrella cupolas. The finely proportioned interior consists of three aisles separated by robust Tuscan-style columns.

Teatro Romano

🕐 *Open year-round Wed–Mon 10am–2pm.* ☎956 21 22 81.
The Roman theatre, located immediately behind the Iglesia de Santa Cruz, preserves much of its seating area and several underground galleries.

▸ *From plaza de Fray Félix take the charming street of callejón de los Piratas to the Cathedral.*

Catedral★★

🕐 *Open Tue, Thu 4.30pm–7pm; Wed, Fri 4.30pm–6.15pm; Sun, 11am–1pm.* 💶 €4 *(including entrance to the museum).* ☎956 28 61 54.
Cadíz Cathedral's construction started in 1722, in pure Baroque style, but was only completed in 1883. The brightness and movement of its lines are particularly evident in the concave and convex features of its façade. Two

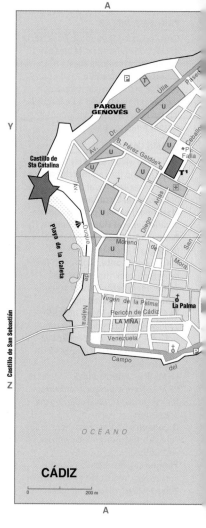

CÁDIZ

City of Towers

Cádiz is notable for its abundance of towers. Around 160 of these were built during the 17C and 18C by the merchants of Cádiz to watch over the arrival of their ships and, above all, to act as a symbol of their prosperity and prestige. They are differentiated by their final touches.

towers crowned by pavilions look like astronomical observatories. The large half-orange cupola, which appears to float high above the city when sea mist envelops Cádiz in winter, was completed in 1844. The interior, with its Latin cross ground plan and ambulatory, is surprisingly light and spacious.

▷ *The popular calle de la Pelota leads to plaza de San Juan de Dios.*

2 From Plaza de San Juan de Dios to the Cathedral

▷ *Follow calle Nueva, then turn left onto calle Cristóbal Colón.*

Casa de las Cadenas

The marble **doorway**★ of this late-17C Baroque mansion was made in Genoa. The building is similar to the Casa del Almirante, but for the pair of Solomonic columns framing the main entrance.

▷ *Continue along calle Cristóbal Colón, turn right onto calle Cobos then left along calle Nicaragua to plaza de la Candelaria.*

Plaza de la Candelaria

The major features around the square are the late-19C iron-and-glass-fronted building at no 6, and the small Isabelline-style palace at no 15. Note to one side of the square the birthplace of politician Emilio Castelar, whose bust adorns its centre.

▷ *From the square, continue along calle Santo Cristo as far as calle Nueva. Continue to plaza de San Agustín.*

Plaza de San Agustín

The Baroque church and an attractive neo-Classical **patio**, now part of a school, are all that remain of the Convento de San Agustín.

▷ *Take calle Rosario.*

Oratorio de la Santa Cueva★

🕐*Open Tue–Fri 10am–1pm, 5pm–8pm (4.30pm–7.30pm in winter), Sat–Sun 10am–1pm.* ✆€2. ☎956 22 22 62.

This small neo-Classical jewel is a feast of decoration. The upper, elliptical part consists of a cupola illuminated by lunettes, supported by Ionic columns. Three 1795 **canvases**★★ by Goya, recently restored, decorate this chapel.

Plaza de San Francisco

The 16C **Iglesia de San Francisco**, with its simple façade and separate 18C tower, stands to one side of this small square. The interior was restored in the 18C in Baroque style, with stucco and rocaille work. Below the pendentive-supported false ceiling, note the angels, attributed to Pedro Roldán.

On the corner of calle Sagasta and callejón del Tinte stands an **elegant building** with attractive windows. This Baroque edifice was modified in the 19C in Isabelline style. Continuing along callejón del Tinte, note the fine example of neo-Classical architecture at no 2, and the impressive, thousand-year-old dragon tree opposite.

Plaza de Mina★

The 19C saw the creation of several squares on land expropriated from religious orders. One was the plaza de Mina, created in 1838 on the vegetable garden of the nearby Convento de San Francisco.

Today, it is one of the city's most charming squares with a colonial feel, verdant appearance and fine examples of Isabelline-style architecture. In particular, note the houses at nos 11 and 16, as well as the neo-Classical palace housing the **Museo de Cádiz**★ (⌖*see Visit*).

Plaza de San Antonio

This spacious square is one of the oldest in Cádiz. Despite its lack of ornamentation, it was a popular place of residence for the local bourgeoisie in the 1600s; even in the 19C it was considered the city's main square. Over the centuries it has been used for events as diverse as bullfights and festivals. The Baroque façade of the **Iglesia de San Antonio** is to one side, while the rest of the square is fronted by elegant 19C buildings and, at no 15, the Casino de Cádiz, with its impressive neo-Mudéjar patio.

▸ *Continue along calle San José to plaza San Felipe Neri. Note the attractive example of Art Nouveau architecture at no 34 calle San José.*

Oratorio de San Felipe Neri

🕐*Open Mon–Sat 10am–1.30pm.*
👓€*1.20.* ☎*956 21 16 12.*

This Baroque oratory is one of the few churches in Andalucía with an elliptical ground plan. It was built between 1688 and 1719. The cupola was badly damaged in the Lisbon earthquake of 1755. Inside on the lower level are eight richly decorated chapels and a high altar with an altarpiece dominated by an unusual **Immaculate Conception** in which the Virgin Mary is dark-skinned – sadly the artist was killed in an accident while creating this work.

The Tuscan-ordered upper level, in the form of a bullfighting tribune, supports a lightweight cane-framed cupola. It was here that the Cortes gathered in 1812 to proclaim a liberal constitution following the invasion of San Fernando by French troops.

▸ *Follow calle Santa Inés to calle Sagasta.*

Iglesia de San Lorenzo

Blue and white *azulejos* decorate the polygonal tower of this sober church.

▸ *Return to calle del Hospital de Mujeres.*

Hospital de Mujeres★

🕐*Open Mon–Sat 10am–1pm.*
☎*956 22 36 47.*

The Hospital for Women is one of the major Baroque buildings in Cádiz. In order to overcome space limitations, the architect designed a narrow façade, behind which the building widens. It is laid out around two patios linked via an extraordinary Imperial-style **stairway**★★ with a cane-framed vault above it. The 18C *Vía Crucis* created from Triana *azulejos* in the patio is particularly attractive. The church *(ask at the porter's lodge for access)* contains a painting of **St Francis** by El Greco.

Torre Tavira★

🕐*Open daily: Jun–Sept 10am–8pm, Oct –May 10am–6pm; last admission 30min before closing.* 👓€*4.* ☎*956 21 29 10. www.torretavira.com.*

This tower, in the highest part of the city, was designated as the official watchtower in 1778, from which the entry and departure of ships was controlled by a complex system of semaphores. The very first **camera obscura** in Spain, an ingenious device capturing real-time images of the city's movements, was installed in the tower in 1995.

▸ *Head down to plaza del Mercado. The plaza de las Flores is located behind the brick Correos (main post office).*

Plaza de las Flores

This plaza is also known locally as the plaza Topete. The numerous flower and plant stalls, cafés and shops contribute to the delightful atmosphere in one of the city's liveliest squares. A number of important shopping streets, such as Calle Columela and Calle Compañía, branch off from here.

Visit

Casa de la Contaduría (Museo Catedralicio)★

🕐*Open year-round Tue–Fri 10am–1pm, 4.30pm–7pm; Sat 10.30am–1pm.* 👓€*4 (includes entrance to the cathedral).* ☎*956 25 98 12.*

Cádiz in 1777

In 1777 Carlos III commissioned a 1:250 scale **model**★ of the city of Cádiz. This apparent royal whim was to result in a magnificent 25m²/270sq ft maquette made from mahogany, ebony and marble.

Such was the precision of this superb work that even the smallest detail is represented on it.

The majority of buildings standing today can be made out on the model, which also provides an insight into the development of several open spaces within the city, such as the plaza de Mina and the plaza de la Catedral.

The model is on display at the **Museo de las Cortes de Cádiz** (calle Santa Inés, ☎956 221 788, same opening hours and website as Museo de Cádiz, & see below).

This complex of four buildings has been superbly restored to house the cathedral museum. The 16C **Mudéjar patio**★ is particularly fine. The museum displays a variety of liturgical objects, vestments and documents, including a letter bearing the signature of St Teresa of Jesus. Other objects of interest are the 16C **Custodia del Cogollo**★, a gold-plated silver monstrance attributed to Enrique Arfe, and the so-called 17C **Custodia del Millón**, named for its numerous precious stones.

Museo de Cádiz★

🕐Open Mon–Fri 9am–1pm, 5pm–7pm (Oct–May 4pm–7pm). Sat–Sun 9am–1pm. 🕐Closed ☎956 21 22 81. www.cadiz.es. The city museum is housed in a small neo-Classical palace with a sober façade built midway through the 19C. The clearly presented archaeological displays are worthy of special note, in particular the section dedicated to the Phoenicians. Two **anthropomorphous sarcophagi**★★ in white marble from the 5C BC imitate Egyptian models and were almost certainly carved by Greek craftsmen. In the fine arts section, the star exhibit is the collection of nine **pan-**

els★ painted by Zurbarán between 1638 and 1639 for the sacrarium in the Cartuja monastery in Jerez. Note the artist's mastery of light and shade.

Parque Genovés★

The park was formerly known as the paseo del Perejil. Nowadays, it is the city's main green area and delightful for a quiet stroll. The former barracks of Carlos III opposite have been converted into the main building for the University of Cádiz.

Castillo de Santa Catalina

🕐Open Mon–Fri 10am–2pm, 5pm–8pm; Sat–Sun 10am–2pm. ☎956 22 63 33.

The castle is situated at the far end of La Caleta beach. Built by Cristóbal de Rojas in 1598 following the sacking of Cádiz by the Earl of Essex, this fortification has an unusual star shape. It is currently under restoration.

Playa de la Caleta

Once the city's natural harbour, this is now the only beach in the old part of Cádiz. At one end, on a small island connected to the city by a small causeway, is the **Castillo de San Sebastián**, a castle built in the 18C and still used by the military. Legend has it that this was the site of the temple of Kronos. The handsome white **Balneario de la Palma** spa was built in 1925.

Barrio de la Viña

This working-class district (barrio), created in the early 18C away from the port area and shops in a part of the city exposed to the elements, is one of the most colourful quarters of Cádiz. Today, it is renowned as the setting for the **Cádiz carnival**★★, without doubt the liveliest in Spain, which takes place in February. If you intend visiting the city at this time reserve your accommodation several months ahead.

Summer is the season for tasty **mackerel**, which is sold on the streets of the Barrio de la Viña. A good place to try mackerel is the simple bar on the plaza del Tío de la Tiza.

Iglesia de la Palma – This circular Baroque-style church was built at the beginning of the 18C. A number of tapas bars nearby serve excellent fish.

Baluarte de la Candelaria
Built in the 17C, this bulwark (*baluarte*) formed part of the defensive wall which enclosed and protected Cádiz on three sides and was initially a platform for cannons. In the 19C, it underwent significant renovation, particularly its inner façade, resulting in its present-day neo-Classical appearance.

Iglesia del Carmen
This is the most Latin American of the city's churches and provides clear evidence of the reciprocal influences between Spain and her colonies. It was built in the mid-18C, with the main interest centred on its **Baroque façade**★.

Excursions

San Fernando
9km/5.5mi southeast along CA 33.
For centuries, San Fernando and Cádiz have always enjoyed close ties. San Fernando began to develop as a military and commercial outpost in the 18C, when Cádiz was enjoying its greatest splendour.
In 1766 Carlos III transferred the headquarters of the Navy here, since which time the town has been inextricably linked with the Spanish armed forces. Between 1810 and 1811, members of parliament convened here to promulgate the first Spanish constitution; in recognition of its resistance to the French during the Peninsular War, Fernando VII conferred the name of **San Fernando** upon the city.
On calle Real, the focal point of San Fernando, are the town hall *(ayuntamiento)*, the **Iglesia del Carmen** and the **Museo Histórico Municipal** (open Jun–Sept Mon–Fri 10am–2pm; Oct–May 10am–2pm, 6pm–9pm; ☎956 94 42 54). The neo-Classical **Iglesia Mayor**, dedicated to St Peter and St Paul, and the Teatro de las Cortes, where members of parliament sat in 1881, are in the nearby plaza de la Iglesia.

Belfry, Iglesia del Carmen, Cádiz

B. Kaufmann / MICHELIN

The city's most important civil building is the **Observatorio Astronómico de la Marina** (guided tours by appointment; ☎956 59 93 66 or 956 94 42 26, tourist office), a naval observatory built in neo-Classical style in 1753 by Jorge Juan. This observatory was the predecessor of the observatory in Madrid. A Roman bridge, the **Puente de Suazo**, is visible upon leaving San Fernando. Until recently, the bridge was the only link to the rest of Spain.

Chiclana de la Frontera
25km/15.5mi southeast along the C 33 and A 48.
Though surrounded by saltpans and countryside, Chiclana is a prime beach destination. The delightful **Playa de la Barrosa**★★, an 8km/5mi stretch of fine sand, is just 7km/4.5mi away. The beach has a number of hotels and excellent recreation facilities, particularly in **Sancti Petri** and **Novo Sancti Petri**. Chiclana's attractive main square *(plaza mayor)* is dominated by the imposing neo-Classical **Iglesia de San Juan Bautista**, a work by Torcuato Cayón.

CARMONA★★

POPULATION: 25 326.

Set on a plateau overlooking a fertile plain irrigated by the River Corbones, Carmona is one of Andalucía's oldest towns. It was founded by the Carthaginians, and played an active political role during Roman occupation and under both Moors and Christians. The past lives on in the old quarter's elegant palaces, seigniorial houses and solemn places of worship.

- ⓘ **Information:** Arco de la Puerta de Sevilla, ☎954 19 09 55. Plaza de las Descalzas, ☎954 14 22 00. www.turismo.carmona.org.
- ▶ **Orient Yourself:** Carmona, is 40km/25mi east of Sevilla via the A 4-E 5.
- ⓧ **Organising Your Time:** Allow half a day to visit Carmona's old quarter.
- ⓟ **Parking:** Leave your car in the lower part of town, near the Puerta de Sevilla.
- ⓒ **Also See:** ÉCIJA, MARCHENA, OSUNA, ESTEPA.

Walking Tour

Old Quarter★

Walls

The Moorish-arched **Puerta de Sevilla**★ in the lower fortress (alcázar de abajo), served as an entrance to the old quarter, where sections of Carthaginian walls remain. The **Puerta de Córdoba**★ has two superb octagonal Roman towers.

Iglesia de San Pedro★

ⓧ*Open Mon, Wed–Sat 11am–2pm; Mon, Thu, 4.30pm–6.30pm.* ⊚*€1.20.* ☎*954 14 12 70. www.sanpedrocarmona.es.*
The 15C Church of St Peter, on the paseo del Estatuto, has a fine **bell tower**★, similar to the Giralda in Sevilla, hence the nickname "Giraldilla". The **Capilla del Sagrario** (sacrarium) is richly decorated, and there is an extraordinary 16C green ceramic **baptismal font**. The church was heavily restored during the Baroque period.

Puerta de Sevilla

B. Kaufmann/MICHELIN

View of the town

Seigniorial mansions

A number of 17C and 18C noble residences are dotted around the town's squares. Of these, the most attractive are the Casa de los **Rueda**, Casa de los **Domínguez**, Casa del **Barón de Gracia Real**, Casa del **Marqués del Saltillo**, Casa de los **Lasso** and the Casa de las **Aguas**. These elegant mansions add a refined air to Carmona and provide an interesting contrast with the older buildings in the heart of the old quarter.

Convento de la Concepción

The convent contains charming **cloisters** and a Mudéjar-style church.

▸ *Walk through the Puerta de Sevilla.*

Iglesia de San Bartolomé

This Gothic church, rebuilt in the 17C and 18C, has a basilical plan and graceful neo-Classical tower. One chapel is covered with Renaissance *azulejos*.

Iglesia de San Felipe★

A fine 14C Mudéjar church with a handsome tower, *artesonado* work bearing the coat of arms of the Hurtado de Mendoza family, and chancel with 16C *azulejos*.

Plaza Mayor, or Plaza de San Fernando

This attractive square is fronted by Mudéjar and Renaissance mansions.

Ayuntamiento

🕐*Open Mon–Fri 8am–3pm.*
☎*954 14 00 11.*
The interesting Baroque town hall in the heart of the old quarter has an attractive Roman **mosaic** in its courtyard.

Iglesia del Salvador

🕐*Open Fri–Tue 10am–2pm, 4.30pm–6.30pm.* ✆€1.20.
This large Baroque building on plaza de Cristo Rey was built with a Latin-cross plan between the 17C and 19C. Note the impressive Churrigueresque **altarpiece** and the paintings, retables

and religious gold and silverware from the 17C and 18C.

Iglesia de Santa María la Mayor★

🕐*Open Mon–Fri 10am–2pm, 5pm–7pm.*
✆€3. ☎*954 19 14 82.*
This large 15C Gothic church replaced a mosque in calle San Ildefonso. Despite its restoration in Renaissance and Baroque style, it retains the Patio de los Naranjos (Orange Tree Patio) and beautiful horseshoe arches of the Moorish building. Note the 6C **Visigothic calendar** on one column. A monumental **Plateresque altarpiece★** exquisitely depicts sculpted scenes of the Passion. Side chapels hold magnificent retables such as the Christ of the Martyrs behind 16C **Plateresque grilles**.

Plaza de San Fernando

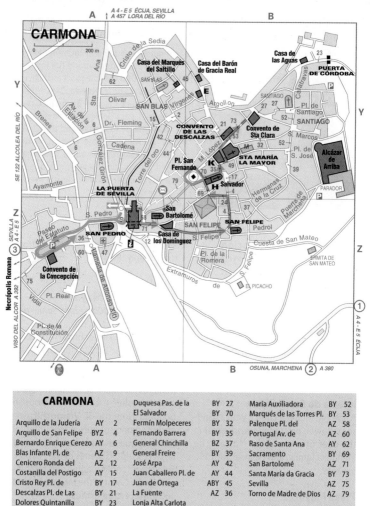

CARMONA

Convento de las Descalzas★

This magnificent example of 18C Sevillian Baroque has a Latin-cross ground plan, a tower with a double campanile and *azulejo* decoration.

Convento de Santa Clara

🕐 *Open by prior arrangement.*
☎954 14 21 02.
The 15C Convent of St Clare has two pleasant cloisters and a Mudéjar church with canvases by Valdés Leal, and a fine collection of female portraits in the style of Zurbarán.

Visit

Alcázar de Arriba

This old Roman fortress offers superb **views**★ of the countryside.
It was extended by the Almoravids, and later converted into the palace of Pedro I. Only fragments remain of the original structures but the magnificent **parador**, former residence of the Catholic Monarchs, (🔆 *see Address Book*) now stands in the parade ground and is open to the public for the price of a coffee.

Address Book

For coin ranges, see the Legend on cover flap.

WHERE TO STAY

◎ **Hostal Comercio** – *Torre del Oro, 56.* ☎*954 14 00 18. 14 rooms.* The same family has run this small *pensión,* dating from the 16C, for the past four generations. An attractive patio, and basic but clean rooms.

◎◎◎◎**Parador de Carmona** – *Alcázar.* ☎*954 14 10 10. www.parador. es. 63 rooms.* This magnificent *parador,* with superb views of the fertile Corbones plain, is the former residence of the Catholic Monarchs. Even if you don't stay here, do try their restaurant, one of the most attractive in the whole Spanish *parador* network. Specialties include Carmona spinach *(espinaca)* and partridge in season.

◎◎◎ **Casa de Carmona** – *Plaza de Lasso, 1.* ☎*454 19 10 00. www.casade carmona.com. 31 rooms, 1 suite.* The historic 16C palace of Lasso de la Vega (once Governor of Chile) in the old quarter. Grand salons, Moorish garden. Fine dining (◎◎◎).

WHERE TO EAT – TAPAS

◎◎ **La Almazara de Carmona** – *Santa Ana, 33.* ☎*954 19 00 76.* Housed in an old oil mill this bar features vaults and a wooden ceiling. Specialties are spinach dishes and suckling pig.

◎◎◎◎ **Parador de Carmona** (*see below*).

LOCAL SPECIALITIES

Pastries – Delicious pastries are baked in Carmona's convents. Local specialities include sponge-like *bizcochos marroquíes,* honeyed doughnuts known as *roscos almibarados,* a range of tarts *(tortas)* and *bollos de aceite,* literally "olive oil buns".

FESTIVALS

Carmona's **Carnival** is renowned throughout the province, as are its magnificent **Holy Week** processions through the narrow streets of the old quarter.

Roman necropolis★
At the end of calle Jorge Bonsor, on the road from Sevilla.
🕐 *Open mid–Jun–mid-Sept Tue–Fri, 8.30am–2pm, Sat, 10am–2pm; otherwise, Tue–Fri, 9am–6pm, Sat–Sun 9.30am–2.30pm.* ☎*954 14 08 11.*
This impressive site, in use around the 1st and 2nd centuries BC, holds over 300 tombs, mausoleums and cremation kilns. The **Tumba del Elefante** (named for an elephant statue) holds three dining rooms, while the **Tumba de Servilia** is the size of a villa.

Excursions

Viso del Alcor
12km/7mi southwest along the A 392.
This town of Celtic origin is at the highest point in the Sierra de los Alcores. The **Iglesia de Santa María del Alcor** is a Mudéjar church with Renaissance cupola in the presbytery and a collection of 17C paintings from the Venetian School. The 15C **Iglesia de la Merced** holds 17C and 18C altarpieces.

Mairena del Alcor
16km/10mi SW along A 392.
The remains of a Moorish fortress overlook Mairena del Alcor. The Mudéjar-style **Iglesia de la Asunción** has a handsome 17C–18C **main altarpiece**.

Alcolea del Río
17km/10.5mi north. Take the SE 122 towards Guadajoz then the SE 129.
Alcolea has two old water mills. The Iglesia del Cristo is an 18C Baroque building. The fine 15C Mudéjar **Iglesia de San Juan Bautista** holds an image of the Virgen del Consuelo (Virgin of Solace).

CAZORLA ★

POPULATION: 8 527

Cazorla lies in the heart of the **Parque Natural de las Sierras de Cazorla, Segura y Las Villas**★★★. The town's streets, lined by whitewashed houses with balconies replete with flowers, are perfect for a quiet stroll, for browsing and shopping, and as a backdrop for whiling away time over a drink on a *terraza*.

Information: Calle Juan Domingo, 2. ☎953 24 26 24. www.cazorla.es.

Orient Yourself: Cazorla is 46km/29mi southeast of Úbeda.

Also See: Parque Natural de las Sierras de CAZORLA, SEGURA y LAS VILLAS, ÚBEDA (46km/29mi NW), BAEZA (55km/34mi NW).

Visit

Castillo de la Yedra
Open Wed–Fri 9am–10pm, Tue 3pm–10pm, Sun and public hols 9am–3pm. ☎953 71 00 39.
The **views** from the keep of the Roman fortress above Cazorla are superb. A chapel contains a life-size Romanesque-Byzantine image of Christ, surrounded by 12 paintings of the Apostles.

Plaza de Santa María
In this pleasant square in the old quarter is the monumental **Fuente de las Cadenas**, a Renaissance-style fountain. The ruins of the Iglesia de Santa María are now used as an auditorium.

Ayuntamiento
Cazorla's town's hall is the impressive former Convento de la Merced (Convent of Mercy), with a large arcade on the ground floor and a graceful tower.

Iglesia de San Francisco
The church was part of a 17C Franciscan monastery. It contains a statue of the locally venerated Santísimo Cristo del Consuelo (Holy Christ of Solace).

Address Book

For coin ranges, see the Legend on cover flap.

WHERE TO STAY

Guadalquivir – *Calle Nueva, 6.* ☎953 72 02 68. www.hguadalquivir.com. *11 rooms.* Basic but cheerful rooms in a central location.

Villa Turística de Cazorla – *Ladera de San Isicio.* ☎953 71 01 00. www.villacazorla.com. *32 apartments.* Pictuesque village-like apartment-hotel complex set amid orchards with a pool and views of the castle.

Molino La Fárraga – *150m from Santa María ruins, calle de la Torre.* ☎953 72 12 49. www.molinolafarraga. com. This rustic hotel in an 18C mill has castle and mountain views, a pool, and a garden crossed by a stream.

WHERE TO EAT

La Sarga – *Plaza del Mercado.* ☎953 72 15 07. www.hotelescazorla.com/ sarga. *Closed Tue and in Sept.* This cosy restaurant in the centre serves regional specialties high-quality products. Friendly service, mountain views.

TAPAS

La Montería – *Corredera, 20.* ☎953 72 05 42. *Closed Jan–Mar.* A popular bar decorated with hunting trophies. The excellent tapas on offer include cured hams, cheeses and venison.

FESTIVALS

A major three-day blues music festival (est 1994) is held in late July, attracting international and Spanish acts.
For details visit *www.bluescazorla.com*.

PARQUE NATURAL DE LAS SIERRAS DE CAZORLA, SEGURA Y LAS VILLAS★★★

Covering over 214 000 hectares (529 500 acres), this is the largest park in Spain, designated as such in 1986; it features cliffs, gorges and a complex river network that includes the source of the River Guadalquivir. Altitude and humidity favour dense Mediterranean-type mountain vegetation. Many of the towns and villages in the park have managed to preserve their traditional cultures and crafts.

This is the largest protected area in all of Spain with luxuriant forests of pine groves. It was declared a Biosphere Reserve in 1983. The flora of the Park is one of the richest in Spain, with over 1 300 catalogued species. Of these, at least 24 are exclusive to this territory, among which are the Austrian pine, an indigenous species which can be found at heights above 1 200 metres. Unique flowers include the Cazorla violet, a daffodil which claims to be the smallest in the world, and a unique carnivorous plant. Rare fauna include the Valverde wall lizard, More common are mountain goat, deer, wild boar, and muflones The Guadalquivir rises here (in Cañada de las Fuentes, at a height of over 1 300m) as well as the river Segura. The reserve includes lands belonging to 23 townships.

- **Information:** Carretera del Tranco (Km 18), 23379 Torre del Vinagre. ☎953 71 30 40. www.cazorla.es.
- **Orient Yourself:** The reserve is situated to the Northeast of Jaén, covering the Cazorla, Segura and Las Villas ranges, at altitudes between 600m/1 950ft and 2 017m/6 616ft.
- **Don't Miss:** The views from and nearby La Iruela; the view from the castle of Segura de la Sierra.
- **Organising Your Time:** Allow a day for each suggested itinerary.
- **Also See:** ÚBEDA, BAEZA.

Driving Tours

See suggested route on the map.

Sierras de Cazorla, Las Villas y El Pozo

1 **Cazorla to Tíscar**
92km/57mi – allow one day.

Cazorla★ – *see CAZORLA.*

- *Head west along the A 319. At a crossroads, bear left onto the A 315 towards Quesada.*

Quesada
Set amid olive groves, Quesada was the birthplace of painter Rafael Zabaleta (1907–60). His work, shown in the Quesada **museum**, (open 11am–2pm,

La Iruela Castle and the Sierra de Cazorla

5pm–7pm (4pm–8pm in winter); €3; ☎953 73 30 25) captures the light of the region and the character of locals.

Flora and fauna

The park's high levels of precipitation have resulted in abundant vegetation. Flora here includes the beautiful Cazorla violet, an endemic species that appears in forests of black pine, holm and downy oak; hazel and holly. Native fauna includes wild boar, stags, mountain goats and deer; predators such as the genet, stone marten, wildcat and fox; aquatic fauna such as the otter; and numerous fish species, including trout, barbel, carp and black perch. The park is also home to a variety of birdlife (golden eagle, peregrine falcon, kite, osprey, etc.).

The **Cañada de las Fuentes**, a ravine 1 400m/4 592ft high, is the **source of the River Guadalquivir** *(access via a track off the A 315, to the north of Quesada).*
Wall paintings from the Palaeolithic era can be seen on Cerro Vitar (hill) and in the Cueva del Encajero, just a short distance from the town.

Tíscar★
20km/12mi southeast of Quesada on the C 323.
Below a statue of the Virgin in the **Santuario de Tíscar** is the impressive **Cueva del Agua**★ (Oopen for worship only Jun–Sept 11am–1pm, 5pm–7pm; Oct–May 11.30am–1pm, 4.30pm–6pm; ☎953 71 36 06), where a torrent emerges between rocks.

☑ Cazorla to the Embalse del Tranco de Beas
56km/35mi.

▶ *Leave Cazorla NW along the A 319.*

La Iruela
1.4km/0.8mi.
La Iruela was settled by Carthaginians in the 3C BC. The Iglesia de Santo Domingo, a Renaissance-style church designed by Vandelvira, stands at its centre. The remains of a Templar castle offering superb **views**★★ of the Guadalquivir Valley.

La Iruela to the Embalse del Tranco★
The first 17km/10.5mi of the winding A 319 afford **spectacular views**★★. The Parador de **El Adelantado** is reached via a branch road *(8km/5mi)* up through forests.

▶ *Continue along the A 319, travelling parallel to the river.*

Torre del Vinagre – The **Centro de Interpretación** (information centre) (Oopen 11am–2pm, 4pm–6pm (7pm in spring, 9.30pm in summer); ☎953 71 30 40) features a hunting museum and a botanical garden that displays native species. A game reserve, **Parque Cinegético de Collado del Almendral**, 15km/9.5mi farther along the A 319, has lookout points where wildlife (deer, mouflons, mountain goats etc) can be seen through binoculars early in the morning.
For further information, call☎953 71 01 25.

Embalse del Tranco de Beas – Several camping areas, hotels and watersport facilities are located near this reservoir on the River Guadalquivir.
The ruins of a Moorish castle stand on the **Isla de Bujaraiza**, an island opposite a viewpoint.

Sierra de Segura

☑ Santiago-Pontones to Siles
79.5km/49.5mi – allow a day.

This itinerary passes through white-washed towns with a distinct Moorish flavour.

Santiago-Pontones
A number of archaeological sites lie within this mountain municipality, such as the **Cueva del Nacimiento** and the **Cuevas de Engalbo**, caves with wall art.

Hornos
27km/17mi NW of Pontones along the A 317.
The remains of the fortress of Hornos rise above a cliff. From here there are

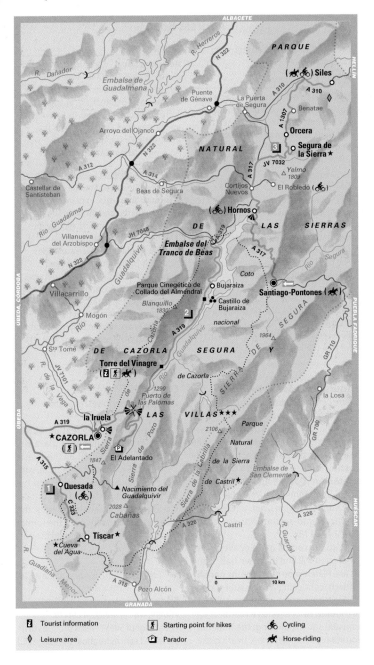

🛈 Tourist information	🚶 Starting point for hikes	🚲 Cycling
◊ Leisure area	🅿 Parador	🐎 Horse-riding

spectacular **views**★ of the Tranco Reservoir and Guadalquivir Valley. An arts and crafts market is held on the first Saturday of every month.

▶ *Follow the A 317 north for 23km, then bear right at a signposted junction onto the JV 7032.*

Address Book

For coin ranges, see the Legend on cover flap.

WHERE TO STAY

Sierra de Cazorla – *On the outskirts of La Iruela, heading towards the park.* ☎953 72 00 15. *www.hotelsierra decazorla.com. 59 rooms.* An outdoor pool and superb mountain views are the main attraction here.

Parador de Cazorla – *Lugar Sacejo, 26 km E of Cazorla.* ☎953 72 70 75. *www.parador.es. 34 rooms.* In the heart of the Parque de Cazorla, close to an old hunting reserve, this modern parador has been built in the style of a typical Andalusia mountain lodge. The facilities (including a pool) and location are ideal for nature-lovers.

WHERE TO EAT

El Mirador de Messia de Leiva - *Calle Postigo, 2.* ☎953 48 08 87. Traditional cooking and seven apartments for rent ( ).

SPORTS

Aventura Sport - *Rte de Huesa, 4, Quesada.* ☎953 71 42 18, *www.aven turasport.com.* Canoeing, canyoning, orienteering, paintballing, quad bikes, archery, mountain biking, 4x4 driving and horseriding are just some of the many activities on offer here. Accommodation also offered on site.

SIGHTSEEING

It is advisable to head to one of the **information points**, to plan a route that takes in the breathtaking landscapes. The largest information point is at the Torre del Vinagre; others are at **Cazorla**, Segura de la Sierra and Siles. Mountain-bikers, horse-riders and hikers can follow the extensive network of forest tracks and marked footpaths criss-crossing the park.

The itineraries described in this chapter are given as a guideline only; many others are possible depending on interests and on the direction of approach.

Segura de la Sierra★

24km/15mi northeast of Hornos.

The village of Segura de la Sierra straddles a hill at 1 240m/4 067ft. There is a sweeping **panorama**★★★ from the keep of its partially intact Mudéjar **castle**, home to the **Centro De Interpretación** (open Apr–Oct Tue–Sun 11am–2pm, 5pm–8pm, Nov–Mar Wed–Sun 11am–2pm, 4pm–7pm; €3; www. ayuntamiento-seguradelasierra.com. ☎902 43 04 18).

Explore the central maze of alleyways where you will find the **town hall**, with its fine Plateresque doorway; the **parish church**, containing an alabaster statue of the Virgin and a recumbent Christ attributed to Gregorio Hernández; an unusual square bullring: the imperial fountain *(fuente imperial)*, bearing the escutcheon of Charles V: and, most rewarding of all, at calle Baño Moro, the **Moorish baths** *(baños árabes)*, with horseshoe arches and star-shaped vault lights.

Orcera

7.5km/4.5mi northwest of Segura along the JV 7020.

The most interesting feature of this village is the pentagonal plaza del Ayuntamiento, fronted by the Iglesia de Nuestra Señora de la Asunción, with its sober Renaissance portal, and the Fuente de los Chorros, a 15C fountain. The three Santa Catalina towers, the only remaining vestiges of the former Moorish fortress, are visible on the outskirts of Orcera.

▶ *Take the A 1307, leading to the A 310.*

Siles

21km/13mi northeast of Orcera.

The village of Siles retains sections of its old walls. Learn more about the village and the area at its **Centro De Interpretación El Sequero** at Rte de Hellín 21 (open Apr –Oct Tue–Sun 11am–2pm, 6pm–9pm; Nov–Mar 9am–1pm, 7pm–9pm; ☎953 49 11 43). The nearby reserve of **Las Acebeas** is close to the source of the River Los Molinos. The ascent of Mount Acebeas (1 620m) offers splendid views.

CÓRDOBA ★★★

POPULATION: 310 388.

Magnificent Córdoba celebrates the very best of all four of Spain's major civilisations (Roman, Moorish, Jewish and Christian), most notably through its *Mezquita*, its mosque-cathedral masterpiece. The delightful Jewish quarter (*Judería*) overflows with charm with its romantic narrow streets and quaint small squares, embellished with wrought-iron grilles, flower-filled patios and shrines illuminated by beautiful lanterns.

- 🛈 **Information:** Calle Torrijos, 10, 14003 Córdoba. ☎957 47 12 35. www.turismodecordoba.org.
- ▶ **Orient Yourself:** Córdoba is 143km/89mi northeast of Seville.
- 🅿 **Parking:** You will find it difficult to get a space in the city centre, if possible, park and walk in. If you are staying in the historic quarter, it may be best to ask your hotel about parking before you arrive, as driving in this part of town is not recommended.
- ⊛ **Don't Miss:** The mihrab in the Mezquita, the Mezquita illuminated by night, La Judería, Palacio de Viana, the archaeological museum, Medina Azahara.
- 🕒 **Organising Your Time:** Allow at least three days.
- 🄺🄸🄳🅂 **Especially for Kids:** Take a trip around the city in a horse drawn cart.
- ⌀ **Also See:** MONTORO, ANDÚJAR, MONTILLA, AGUILAR DE LA FRONTERA, ÉCIJA.

A Bit of History

Roman Córdoba – Córdoba became a Roman colony in 152 BC and was the capital of Baetica until almost the end of the Empire. Leading intellectual figures included **Seneca the Rhetorician** (55 BC–AD 39); his son, **Seneca the Philosopher** (AD 4–65); and the poet **Lucan**, Seneca the Philosopher's nephew, companion to Nero in his student days. Christian Córdoba produced **Bishop Ossius** (257–359), counsellor to Emperor Constantine.

Muslim Córdoba – Emirs from Damascus established themselves as early as 719. Abd ar-Rahman I, sole survivor of the Umayyads, created an **independent emirate**. In the 9C, under Abd ar-Rahman II, the city underwent great cultural development, led by the Iraqi poet Ziryab.

The Caliphate – In 929, Abd ar-Rahman III proclaimed himself independent Caliph of Córdoba. Commerce, agriculture, and the city expanded, enhanced by an extensive network of roads. The 10C, a period characterised by peace and prosperity, brought with it unprecedented cultural splendour. Jewish, Christian and Muslim communities enriched the city and lived in peace. Córdoba became the capital of the entire Western world, with a population estimated to exceed 250 000 inhabitants, perhaps much more. The city had some 3 000 mosques, a multitude of markets and baths, and a complex sewage system. The university, the library (created by Al-Hakam II, the largest of the period) and Córdoba's many other sumptuous buildings amazed visitors and inspired artists.

A kingdom of taifas – The Caliphate dissolved amid power struggles early in the 11C and Al-Andalus fragmented into small warring kingdoms known as the **reinos de taifas**. However, artistic and cultural life continued unabated in the Caliphal tradition.

Until its reconquest in 1236, Córdoba was itself a taifa. Astronomy, mathematics, medicine and philosophy flourished. The writings of the **Averroës** (1126–98) on the works of Aristotle had a major impact, while the Jew **Maimónides** (1135–1204) stood out as a philosopher and physician. His *Guide of the Perplexed*, in which he establishes conciliation

Mezquita

between faith and reason, influenced Christian scholars, particularly St Thomas Aquinas.

Christian Córdoba – On 29 June 1236, **Fernando III the Saint** reconquered the city. The arrival of the Christians had a large impact on Córdoba's architecture with the construction of 14 parish churches.In 1486 **Columbus** presented

the plans for his expedition to the Indies to the Catholic Monarchs in Córdoba.

The Mezquita

Mezquita-Catedral★★★

Open Mon–Sat: Apr–Jun 10am–7pm; Jul–Oct 10am–6.30pm; Nov & Feb 10am–5.30pm; Dec–Jan 10am–5pm. 24–25 & 31 Dec–I Jan 1-am–2pm. Sun and hols all year 9am–10.15am & 2pm–7pm. €8. 957 47 05 12. www.artencordoba.com.

The Mezquita, a masterpiece of Islamic art, is one of the world's most extraordinary buildings. It was built between the 8C and 10C above the Visigothic basilica of San Vicente. Following the Reconquest, Christians erected a Gothic cathedral in the very heart of this Muslim place of worship, The result however is harmonious so that it incorporates religious and architectural features of the two faiths, in distinct, yet equally magnificent, parts.

The Mezquita follows the plan that draws its inspiration from the house of the Prophet Muhammad in Medina. A crenellated square perimeter encloses a patio for ritual ablution, the prayer hall

> ### Unique Structure of the Mezquita
>
> During the Moorish period, Córdoba had around 3 000 mosques. The one admired by visitors today was the main mosque, used for Friday prayers. Enlargements were carried out in line with the growth in the city's population.
>
> The Mezquita has a structure totally different to that found in Christian churches and as such could be extended without affecting the building's architectural style. Its simple structure, with parallel aisles, enabled further aisles to be built, while retaining the overall unity.

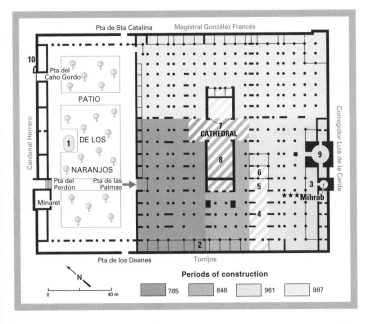

Periods of construction

785	848	961	987

and the minaret. The first Muslims in Córdoba shared the Visigothic church of St Vincent with Christians. Soon, however, Abd ar-Rahman I (758–88) razed the church and around 780 began the construction of a splendid mosque with 11 aisles, each opening onto the Patio de los Naranjos.

Marble pillars and stone came from Roman and Visigothic buildings. Innovations included the superimposition of tiers of arches to gain height and space. In 848 Abd ar-Rahman II had the mosque extended to the present-day Capilla de Villaviciosa (Villaviciosa Chapel); in 961 Al-Hakam II built the *mihrab* (prayer-niche); and in 987, Al-Mansur added eight aisles (recognisable by their red brick pavement).

Patio de los Naranjos

This spacious and enchanting patio, with porticoes on three sides, is named for the orange trees *(naranjos)* planted after the Reconquest. The ir allure and aroma are part of the Mezquita's charm.

Before prayer, Muslims would perform their ritual ablutions here. Several Mudéjar fountains remain, along with the 10C **Al-Mansur basin (1)**.

Interior

Entrance through the Puerta de Las Palmas. A spectacular forest of columns and arches greets the worshipper. Colour and shade play a fundamental role. Horseshoe-shaped arches are made up of alternate red (brick) and white (stone) blocks, while greys and pinks predominate in columns.

The doorway leads into the wide main aisle, leading to the *mihrab*. Aisles run perpendicular to the sacred walls of the *qiblah*, which unusually faces south, not toward Mecca.

After the Reconquest, chapels were built by the Christians in the west nave. These include the 17C marble-covered **Capilla de la Purísima Concepción (2)**.

In 833 **Abd ar-Rahman II** removed the wall of the *qiblah* to extended the 11 aisles.

The decoration was so striking that it was re-used in the extraordinary renovations carried out under **Al-Hakam II**. The aisles were further extended. All the columns and capitals were hand-carved for this part of the building. The rich ornamentation centred on the **mihrab**★★★ is the jewel in the Mezquita's crown. Its octagonal niche was decorated by Byzantine artists who

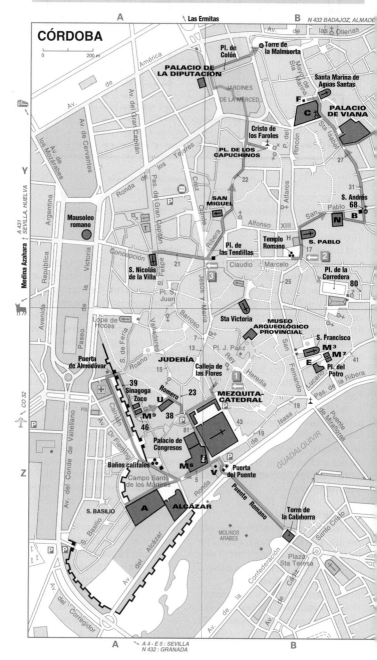

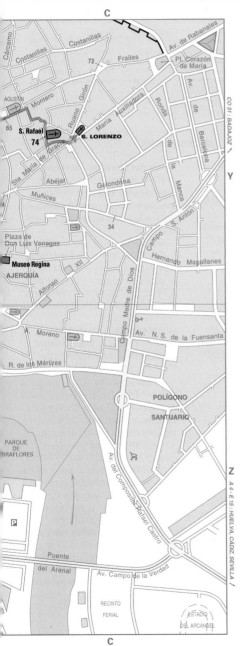

Address Book

💰*For coin ranges, see the Legend on cover flap.*

GETTING THERE AND AROUND

Airport – ☎957 21 41 00. www.aena.es/ Córdoba airport only serves domestic routes. The closest international connections are at Sevilla airport (☎954 44 90 00 www.aena.es), 140km/88mi south west.

Seville and Córdoba are connected by both **bus** (*domestic:* ☎901 33 31; *international:* 901 33 32 22) and **train** (*Plaza de las Tres Culturas.* ☎957 49 02 02). Córdoba is linked to Madrid by the high-speed AVE (*Alta Velocidad Española*) train (under two hours).

City buses – AUCORSA, Avenida Libia, 61. ☎957 76 46 76.

Inter-city buses – *Glorieta de las Tres Culturas.* ☎957 40 43 83.

Taxis – ☎957 76 44 44.

Horse-drawn carriages – Hire carriages are for hire next to the Mezquita (Calle Torrijos) and in campo Santo de los Mártires.

WHERE TO STAY

CÓRDOBA

⊖**Hostal La Milagrosa** – *Rey Heredia, 12.* ☎957 47 33 17. *8 rooms.* A good address in the old city near the Mezquita, with patio and airy rooms, all en suite.

⊖⊖**Albucasis** – *Buen Pastor, 11.* ☎957 47 86 25. www.hotelalbucasis.com. *15 rooms.* Basic hotel with large rooms in a typical house in the Judería.

⊖⊖**Hotel González** – *Manríquez, 3.* ☎957 47 98 19. www.hotel-gonzalez. com. *16 rooms.* Rooms off the patio in this 16C palace, between the Mezquita and the Judería, are spacious and well appointed.

⊖⊖**Hotel Maestre** – *Romero Barros, 4–6.* ☎957 47 24 10. www.hotelmaestre. com. *26 rooms.* One of Córdoba's better value accommodations, near the plaza del Potro, with spacious if plain rooms. The owners have another hotel and apartments nearby.

⊖⊖**Mezquita** – *Plaza de Santa Catalina, 1.* ☎957 47 55 85. *21 rooms.* Opposite the main entrance to the Mezquita. Spacious, attractive rooms.

⊖⊖**Hostal Séneca** – *Conde y Luque, 7.* ☎957 47 32 34. *12 rooms. Closed 2 weeks Aug and winter.* Close by the Mezquita, the Seneca offers comfortable characterful rooms in a traditional house.

⊖⊖⊜ **NH Amistad Córdoba** – *Plaza de Maimónides, 3.* ☎957 42 03 35. www.nh-hotels.com. *84 rooms.* A reliable chain hotel, with attractive large rooms set in two 18C mansions close to the city's Moorish walls. Spacious public areas and a large Mudéjar patio.

⊖⊖⊜ **Hotel Casa de los Azulejos** – *Fernando Colón, 5.* ☎957 47 00 00. www.casadelosazulejos.com. *8 rooms.* Charming hotel in a traditional house with plant-filled patio, large rooms, wrought-iron bedsteads, and designer baths. Good value.

FUENTE OBEJUNA

Hotel El Comendador – *Luis Rodríguez, 25, Fuente Obejuna.* ☎957 58 52 22. www.hotelcomendador fuenteobejuna.com. 13 rooms. Centrally located with large, comfortable rooms, some with valley views. Good restaurant.

WHERE TO EAT

Taberna los Faroles – *Velázquez Bosco, 1.* ☎957 48 56 29. Lanterns romantically illuminate the patio at night, hence the tavern's name. Specialities include *salmorejo* (like gazpacho) and *rabo de toro* (braised oxtail).

Almudaina – *Jardines Santos Mártires, 1.* ☎957 47 43 42. www. restaurantealmudaina.com. Closed Sun (Jun–Sept); Sun evenings the rest of the year. Attractive restaurant by the Alcázar with exquisite regional decor, serving specialities of Córdoba.

El Caballo Rojo – *Cardenal Herrera, 28.* ☎957 47 53 75. www.elca ballorojo.com. A Córdoba classic, alongside the Mezquita, with a small entrance patio and traditional decor.

Bodegas Campos – *Lineros, 32 (near plaza del Potro).* ☎957 49 75 00. www.bodegascampos.com. Closed Sun evening. The restaurant is set in venerable wine storehouses *(bodegas)* around several patios. The bar is decorated with photos of famous visitors.

El Churrasco – *Romero, 16.* ☎957 29 08 19. www.elchurrasco.com Closed Aug. A regional restaurant with pleasant patio and bar for an aperitif or a cheaper snack. Grilled meats are the house speciality. Several exquisite bedrooms are also available ().

TAPAS

Córdoba does full justice to Andalucía's great tapas tradition with bars offering a huge selection of tapas and the chance to try *salmorejo* (a type of local gazpacho), *rabo de toro* (braised oxtail), *embutidos* (local sausage) and many styles of wines and sherries.

Taberna San Miguel-Casa El Pisto – *plaza San Miguel, 1.* ☎957 47 01 66. Closed Sun and in Aug. Founded in 1886, plastered in bullfight posters, indispensable locale for tapas.

Taberna San Miguel-Casa El Pisto

B. Kaufmann/MICHELIN

Taberna Casa Pepe de la Judería – *Romero, 1 (between the Zoco and the Mezquita).* ☎957 20 07 44. This tavern opened in 1928 and retains all its character. Tapas rooms are arranged around a patio, upstairs is a restaurant.

Casa Gaudí – *Avenida Gran Capitán, 22.* ☎957 47 17 36. Modern cafe bar serving teas and coffees and tapas from 8am into the early hours.

Casa Salinas – *Puerta de Almodóvar, 2.* ☎957 29 08 46. Closed Wed and in Aug. This cosy, traditional bar has a small patio, tile decoration, celebrity photos and often stages impromtu flamenco shows.

La Bacalá – *Medina y Corella (near the Mezquita).* ☎630 37 56 82. Bar with a terrace on a little square, often with flamenco music. The speciality is cod.

Taberna Guzmán – *Judíos, 9 (opposite the synagogue).* ☎957 29 09 60. Closed Thu. A traditional bar with lots of character, *azulejo* decoration, bullfighting mementos and posters advertising the local *feria*. Good local sausages and cheeses.

Taberna Salinas – *Tundidores, 3 (plaza de la Corredera).* ☎957 48 01 35. www.tabernasalinas.com. Closed Sun and in Aug. Traditional 19C Córdoba tavern with covered patio. Specialities: eggs with prawns and ham, fried aubergine, *rabo de toro*.

GOING OUT

Most of Córdoba's bars and nightclubs are around the avenida del Gran Capitán in the centre and in the El Brillante residential area.

Cafetería Siena – *Plaza de las Tendillas.* ☎957 47 46 08. Closed Sun. A long-established café in Córdoba's main

Córdoban patio

square, with one of the city's most popular outdoor terraces.

Málaga Café – *Málaga, 3.* ☎*957 47 62 98.* A quiet, comfortable café near plaza de las Tendillas in the centre.

Sojo – *Benito Pérez Galdós, 3.* ☎*957 48 39 98.* Trendy Sojo serves from breakfast to the small hours and also stages art exhibitions and installations.

SHOWS

Córdoba is a provincial capital with a buzzing social and cultural life. During the winter, the **Gran Teatro** *(avenida Gran Capitán, 3;* ☎*957 48 02 37; www. teatrocordoba.com)* hosts a regular season of concerts and theatre.
In addition, the Filmoteca de Andalucía *(calle Medina y Corella, 5; www.filmo tecadeandalucia.com)* organises a varied programme of cinema.
See the official website, www.turismo decordoba.org and go to the What to Do (Qué Hacer) for listings.

SHOPPING

Córdoba's main shopping streets are concentrated around plaza de las Tendillas. These include pedestrians-only calle José Cruz Conde and Conde de Gondomar. The larger department stores along avenida Ronda de los Tejares include El Corte Inglés.
The Eroski shopping centre is next to the municipal stadium in the Arcángel district.
Traditional crafts in Córdoba include the famous *cordovans* (embossed leatherwork) and gold and silver filigree, on sale in shops throughout the city. La Purísima, a jeweller's located in the area behind the Alcázar, has an excellent reputation for its high-quality filigree products.
The municipal market or *Zoco Municipal* *(*☎*957 20 40 33)*, set around a small square and old lanes in the *Judería* includes ceramics, leather, pottery etc *(open Mon–Sat, 10am–8pm)*.
Neighborhood markets are held almost every day. The best is held Sunday mornings next to the municipal stadium.

CÓRDOBA CARD

The Córdoba Card comes, rather confusingly, in 6 different options, allowing visitors to save money by combining visits to the most popular attractions, as well as offering discounts at shops, restaurants and on transport. The card is available from tourist information offices and online at www.cordobacard. com.

FIESTAS AND EVENTS

Semana Santa – silent solemn processions take place against the stunning backdrop of the historic quarter, www.semanasanta-cordoba. com/www.guiasemanasanta.com/ cordoba/es.
Cruces de Mayo – (first days of the month), flower-decked crosses dot the city in this contest involving the city's guilds and civic groups.
Concurso de Patios – (early to mid-May), patios are transformed into breathtaking floral displays. www. patiosdecordoba.net, www.amigos delospatioscordobeses.es.
Córdoba Feria – (end May)
This annual fair is renowned for its *sevillanas*, and much feasting and drinking. http://www.ayuncordoba.es.
International Guitar Festival (first two weeks July)
Córdoba Guitar Festival. www.guitarracordoba.com.
Nights of Charm – During the nights of June, July and August, Córdoba hosts equestrian shows, flamenco nights in the historic centre, music, dance and theatre festivals, guided tours, artistic performances set in historic monuments, performances of classical, sephardic and jazz music and more… www.nochesdeembrujo.net.

Interior of the Mezquita

©Turespaña

also created the superb mosaics in the magnificent **cupola**★★ before it. The three ribbed domes of the **maksourah (3)** – the Caliph's enclosure – rest on unusual multifoil arches with interwoven ribs, oriental in origin. The ceiling of the Capilla Real (Royal Chapel) followed the same design.

Al-Mansur was responsible for the largest expansion of the mosque. With no more clearance on the river side, eight aisles were added to the east.

Christian features

With conversion of the Mezquita to a church, the aisles on the side of the Patio de los Naranjos were walled up, with the exception of the Puerta de las Palmas. In order to build the **first cathedral (4)**, columns were removed and a Gothic *artesonado* ceiling supported by pointed arches was erected in their place. Alfonso X was responsible for the chancel in the **Capilla de Villaviciosa** or **Lucernario (5)**, and built the **Capilla Real**★ **(6)**, decorated in the 13C with Mudéjar stucco, which retained harmony with the rest of the monument.

Cathedral

In the 16C, despite opposition from the cathedral chapter, Bishop Don Alonso Manrique received authorisation to build a cathedral in the middle of the mosque. And, in spite of the talent of the architects, Hernán Ruiz I, Hernán Ruiz II and Juan de Ochoa, and the beauty and richness of their creation, Emperor Carlos V could not hide his anger at the result: "You have destroyed something unique," he said, "to build something commonplace."

The styles of the 16C and 17C can be seen alongside each other in Hispano-

---

Decoration: Everything Except the Human Form

According to their religion, Muslims are forbidden to incorporate the human body in decorative features. Instead they maximised the use of plant and geometric motifs. Marble panels, sections of carved stucco and mosaics combine to produce unparalleled splendour. Given the sacred character of the Word, the other fundamental characteristic of Muslim art is the use of script, in the form of verses from the Koran. A superb example can be seen on the entrance arch to the *mihrab*, on which the rectangular surround (*alfiz*) bears inscriptions in Kufic (early Arabic) script.

Detail of the vaults in the cathedral

Flemish arches and vaults, a Renaissance dome, Baroque vaulting above the choir and a Baroque high altar. Major features include two **pulpits**★★ **(7)** in mahogany, marble and jasper by Michel de Verdiguier.

The **choir (8)** is spectacular, in particular the Baroque **choir stalls**★★ by Pedro Duque Cornejo (c. 1750). In exquisitely carved mahogany, they offer a complete iconographic programme, depicting saints, scenes from the lives of Christ and Mary, and the Old and New Testaments, in which the Ascension of Christ, in the centre, stands out. Note also the two impressive organs (17C and 18C).

Treasury
To the left of the mihrab.
The Baroque treasury *(tesoro)*, by Francisco Hurtado Izquierdo, is in the **Capilla del Cardenal** (Cardinal's Chapel) **(9)** and two adjoining rooms. A monumental 16C **monstrance**★ by Enrique Arfe and an exceptional Baroque figure of Christ in ivory stand out in this collection of liturgical objects.

Exterior
The **minaret** built under Abd ar-Rahman III is enveloped in a Baroque tower dating from the late 16C and early 17C. To the side, the 14C Mudéjar **Puerta del Perdón** (Pardon Doorway), a doorway faced with bronze, opens onto the street.

A small shrine to the much venerated **Virgin of the Lanterns (10)** is set into the north wall. Behind a metal grille and adorned with lanterns, it is a copy of a work by Julio Romero de Torres. Its illumination at night is particularly beautiful.

It is well worth walking around the exterior of the Mezquita to admire the elegant decoration on its **entrance gates**, most of which have now been permanently sealed. Particularly notable for their decoration are the two gates on calle Torrijos – the Puerta de San Esteban, created by Abd ar-Rahman I and one of the very first gates to the mosque subsequently modified by Abd ar-Rahman II – and the Puerta de Palacio.

Walking Tours

1 Mezquita Area★★

The suggested itinerary begins alongside the walls of the Mezquita, follows the Guadalquivir, then heads into the delightful whitewashed maze of the **Judería**.

Calleja de las Flores

This narrow street in the Judería is typically Córdoban with its arches and abundance of flowers *(flores)* and flowerpots. The street ends at a small square with a fountain, where you can enjoy one of the best views of the Mezquita's tower.

Palacio de Exposiciones y Congresos

The conference centre is set in the former Hospital de San Sebastián. It was once the city's orphanage and nowadays also houses the **tourist office**.

Its **doorway**★, with fine sculptures on the tympanum and jambs, dates from the early 16C. The wall is adorned with an ornamental border and fretwork, thistle leaves and stringcourses. The sober brick patio is entirely devoid of decorative features.

Museo Diocesano de Bellas Artes

○ *Open year-round Tue 2.30pm–8.30pm, Wed–Sat 9am–8.30pm, Sun 9am–2.30pm* ◉ *€1.50 (free to holders of Mezquita tickets and EU residents).* ☎ *957 35 55 50. www.artencordoba.com.*

The **Fine Arts Museum** is set in the 18C Bishops' Palace (Palacio Episcopal) built atop the former Moorish fortress. It has an interesting patio and a double Baroque black marble staircase topped by a fine cupola with stucco decoration.

The exhibition rooms, on the second floor, display sculptures, paintings, religious books and tapestries, some of which date back to the 13C. The highly restored Baroque chapel of Nuestra Señora del Pilar (Our Lady of the Pillar), can also be visited *(entrance from the patio, to the right of the staircase).*

Triunfo de San Rafael

This is the most impressive of all the city's monuments to St Raphael and dates from the second half of the 18C. The archangel can be seen on top of the monument, with sculptures of various allegorical figures at its base.

Minaret of the Mezquita

©Turespaña

Puerta del Puente

This imposing monument has the appearance of a triumphal arch, having lost its original function as an entrance gateway on the north bank of the river. It was built in the 16C to a classical design with large fluted Doric columns, entablature, frieze and a curved pediment with an escutcheon supported by two warriors. The decoration can be seen on the side facing the river.

Puente Romano

The Roman bridge rises above the waters of the Guadalquivir between the Puerta del Puente and the Torre de la Calahorra (which houses the Museo Vivo de al-Andalus, *see Visit)*. The bridge was built under Emperor Hadrian, and

Callejita del Pañuelo

This attractive alleyway *(callejita)*, accessed via the plaza de la Concha *(very close to the Mezquita, along Martínez Rücker)*, is one of Córdoba's most delightful sights. Although its official name is calle Pedro Jiménez, it is known as Pañuelo (handkerchief) because at its narrowest point it was said to have the width of a man's handkerchief placed diagonally. It comes to a dead end in a slightly wider, yet equally charming section with a small fountain, an attractive doorway and wrought-iron grilles.

St Raphael

Devotion to the archangel Raphael has been a deep-rooted feature of the city for many centuries. It is rare to find a family without at least one member named after him. Even the local football stadium is called El Arcángel. This devotion has its origins in the 16C, following an apparition of St Raphael *(San Rafael)*, who came forward as the protector of the city. Several original monuments, known as *triunfos* (literally "triumphs"), have been erected around the city to honour Córdoba's patron saint.

rebuilt on several occasions, most importantly under the Moors. The river's watermills, of Moorish origin, can be seen to the right.

A statue of **St Raphael** towards the middle of the bridge, on a low, altar-like wall, was erected in 1651, following a serious epidemic. It is usually adorned with candles and flowers, highlighting its importance as a place of devotion.

▶ *Cross the bridge, then follow calle Amador de los Ríos to the Campo Santo de los Mártires.*

Excavations at the Campo Santo de los Mártires have uncovered vestiges of **Caliphal baths**. The walls of the **Alcá-**

Waterwheel (noria) on the Guadalquivir

zar de los Reyes Cristianos★ (&see *below*) soon come into view on the left-hand side.

The **Caballerizas Reales**, royal stables, situated next to the Alcázar, were founded by Felipe II in the 16C. The present building dates from the 18C. Although it is closed to the public, it is well worth a look inside if the entrance happens to be open as you pass by.

At the end of the street, after the arch, enter the **San Basilio district**, famous for its charming patios. One of the most attractive is at no 50, calle San Basilio, seat of the Córdoba Patio Association.

▶ *Return to the Campo Santo de los Mártires, then head along calle Cairuán.*

City walls and Puerta de Almodóvar

The pedestrianised calle Cairuán runs parallel to the walls of the Judería, which were just a small part of the defence system protecting the city. This well-preserved section, built from ashlar stone, contrasts with the tapestry of greenery provided by the numerous cypress trees.

The Puerta de Almodóvar (Almodóvar Gate) provides access to the Jewish quarter. Its origins date back to Moorish times, although it was heavily restored in the early 19C, when an inner doorway was added. A statue of Seneca can be seen to the left of the gateway. The illumination of this area at night adds to the charms of this delightful quarter.

▶ *Walk through the Puerta de Almodóvar and head into the Jewish quarter.*

La Judería★★

Time seems to have stood still in the old Jewish quarter with its whitewashed alleyways, flower-filled patios, wrought-iron grilles and typical bars.

Calle Judíos

The Street of Jews, parallel to the walls, is one of the Judería's most famous thoroughfares. Look for the Bodega Guzmán, a charming bar at no 7 (&see

Exodus of Córdoba's Jews

The Jews arrived in Córdoba before the Moors and soon became influential, particularly in trade and the teaching of the sciences. Following the Moorish invasion, which was generally well received on their part, the city's Jewish population tended to concentrate in the area now referred to as the Judería *(Jewish quarter)*, mainly consisting of the streets close to the Puerta de Almodóvar, and built a fine synagogue in calle Judíos.

When Fernando III reconquered the city in 1236, the Jews maintained their influence, largely as a result of the prestige of their academies. However, as the Catholic church consolidated its power, their position in society became more complicated. In the middle of the 13C they were forced to destroy their synagogue and soon after were compelled to pay taxes for the upkeep of the Catholic Church. They were blamed for every epidemic and disaster, and in 1492 Isabel la Católica ordered their expulsion from Spain.

Address Book) and the **Casa Andalusí**, a 12C Moorish house at no 12, which exhibits Moorish paper-making tools.

Sinagoga

&♿️🕐*Open Tue–Sat 9.30am–2pm, 3.30pm –5.30pm; Sun and public hols 9.30am–1.30pm.* ◉€0.30 *(free to EU citizens).* ☎957 20 29 28.

This is one of only three medieval synagogues preserved in Spain (the others are in Toledo). Built in the early 14C, it consists of a small square room with a balcony on one side for women. The upper parts of the walls are covered with Mudéjar stucco and Hebrew inscriptions.

Zoco

25m/30yds further along.

Access to the former Moorish **souk** is under the brick arches of a narrow alleyway. Shops on the way to two delightful patios sell a range of Córdoban handicrafts.

A monument to **Maimónides**, the acclaimed Jewish philosopher and physician, stands in the tiny plaza Tiberiades, just a few metres farther along calle Judías.

Plazuela de Maimónides

This small square is fronted by the Casa de las Bulas, which contains the city's bullfighting museum, the **Museo Taurino** (🕐*see below*). Note the fine mansion opposite the museum, and the Hotel NH Amistad (🕐*see Address Book*) to the right.

▶ *Take calle Cardenal Salazar. This typical narrow alleyway climbs to the plazuela del Hospital del Cardenal.*

Facultad de Filosofía y Letras

The Faculty of Philosophy and Letters is housed in the former Hospital del Cardenal Salazar. Built in the early 18C, it has a Baroque stone façade bearing a cardinal's escutcheon.

From **calle Romero** *(to the rear of the square)*, the tower of the Mezquita is now visible. This street, along with **calle Deanes**, into which it runs, and the **Judería**, are part of the tourist area surrounding the Mezquita, with its myriad souvenir shops.

② San Andrés and Santa Marina Districts★

Templo Romano

Calle Capitulares, on the corner of calle Claudio Marcelo.

The imposing columns of this 1C AD Roman temple provide a reminder of the splendour of Córdoba under Roman rule. All are fluted and crowned with Corinthian capitals. The temple originally had a front portico raised on a podium and ten columns on each side, seven along the inner sanctuary *(cella)*.

Iglesia de San Pablo★

🕐*Open daily 9am–9.30am, 10.30am–1pm, 5.30pm–6.30pm, 8.30pm–9pm.* 🕐*No visits during religious services.* ☎957 47 12 00.

An oasis of greenery

The centre of Córdoba is a maze of narrow, winding streets, but, surprisingly, one of the its main thoroughfares has a wide stretch of greenery running through its centre. This little oasis links the avenida del Conde de Valledano, paseo de la Victoria and avenida de Cervantes.

The Church of St Paul is part of the former Convento de San Pablo, built to commemorate the reconquest of Córdoba on 29 June 1236, the feast day of St Paul.

The Baroque doorway on calle Capitulares was built in 1706. Solomonic columns flank the entrance arch which bears an image of St Paul. The doorway leads to the atrium, which opens onto the façade. The church has a carillon instead of a bell tower.

The well-proportioned interior has three wide aisles which have retained features of the transitional Romanesque-Gothic style despite subsequent restoration. The Mudéjar **artesonado ceiling**★ is worth particular note.

The chapel to the left of the presbytery contains the 18C image of **Nuestra Señora de las Angustias** (Our Lady of Anguish), by the great sculptor Juan de Mesa, who also carved the Christ of Great Power in Sevilla. The luxuriously dressed Virgin, her face awash with tears, holds the body of Christ in her arms.

Note also, in the Epistle nave, a 15C **Mudéjar chapel** with fine *artesonado* work, the walls of which are completely covered with stucco above a frieze of *azulejos*.

▷ *Head down calle de San Pablo and turn right into calle Villalones.*

Palacio de los Villalones

This impressive stone mansion has an interesting façade crowned by a gallery. The Plateresque-style decoration is concentrated around the bays. The palace is the setting for a sad legend from the 17C in which the beautiful daughter of a magistrate disappeared in the basement of the palace.

In spite of numerous searches and even excavations, her father was never able to find her. It is said that the young girl's ghost inhabits the house at night.

▷ *Exit onto the plaza de San Andrés.*

Plaza de San Andrés

Alongside this small square with orange trees and fountain is the **Casa de los Luna**, also known as the Casa de Fernán Pérez de Oliva. Built in the 16C, it has two unusual corner windows.

An escutcheon and a plain window can be seen above the door, which bears a Plateresque-style orle. Another Fernandine church, the 13C **Iglesia de San Andrés**, is to the left. It was rebuilt in the 18C.

▷ *Follow calle Hermanos López Dieguez, then head along calle Enrique Redel as far as the plaza de Don Gome.*

This square is dominated by the magnificent **Palacio de Viana**★★, accessible via a fine angled doorway (☏*see below*).

▷ *Take calle Santa Isabel to plaza de Santa Marina.*

Iglesia de Santa Marina de Aguas Santas

☏*Open daily 9am–12.45pm, 5pm–7.15pm.*

The 13C Church of St Marina of the Holy Waters was one of 14 built under Fernando III following the reconquest of the city. The austere **façade**★, divided by four heavy buttresses, shows the beauty and strength of the unadorned stone. The trumpet-shaped portal with its smooth, slightly pointed mouldings corresponds to the early ogival style.

Opposite the church, in plaza del Conde Priego, stands a **monument to Manolete** (born Córdoba 1917 – died Linares 1947), a bullfighting legend who spent his childhood here. The wall (left) is part of the **Convento de Santa Isabel**.

The nuns from the Convento de Santa Isabel are famous for their delicious **sweets** and **pastries,** which are generally crammed with almond (*almendrados*) and sultana (*sultanas*).

> *Turn around and head along calle Rejas de Don Gome.*

Note the imposing belfry on the Iglesia de San Agustín.

> *Continue calle Pozanco, and follow it to plaza de San Rafael.*

On the elongated **plaza de San Rafael** is the **Iglesia de San Rafael**, with its large neo-Classical façade.

> *Take the street to the right of the church as far as plaza de San Lorenzo.*

Iglesia de San Lorenzo★

🕐*Open daily 10am–1pm, 5.30pm–8.30pm.* ☎957 48 34 79.

This superb Fernandine church was begun in the late 13C and early 14C in early Gothic style. The original façade comprises a highly unusual portal which is rarely seen in this region, with three slightly pointed arches and a magnificent, finely worked **rose window**★.

The sober interior consists of three aisles with wooden ceilings and pointed arches on cruciform pillars. The chancel has Gothic vaulting. Illumination is provided by three high and narrow windows. Several 14C wall paintings remain at the apsidal end.

③ From Plaza de las Tendillas to Plaza de Colón

Plaza de las Tendillas

This spacious square is at the very heart of Córdoban life. The equestrian statue of Gonzalo Fernández de Córdoba, known as El Gran Capitán, is the work of Mateo Inurria. On hot days jets of water gush upwards, to the delight of children.

Iglesia de San Nicolás de la Villa

🕐*Open daily, 10.30am–11.30am.* ☎957 47 68 32.

This church was built after the Reconquest in the late 13C and early 14C. The peculiar 15C Mudéjar-style **tower**★ on the façade has a square base supporting a lofty octagonal structure with a ledge

along the top. A modern set of bells breaks its architectural harmony. Small reliefs depict people and the morals of patience and obedience. The simple portal was added in the 16C.

The nave is topped by a wooden ceiling, while the side aisles have more modern vaulting. The apsidal end has its original pointed vaulting. The richly decorated **Capilla del Bautismo** (Baptism Chapel), with baptism relief and oval cupola, is a mid-16C addition.

> *Return to plaza de las Tendillas and follow calle V. Ribera and calleja Barqueros.*

Iglesia de San Miguel★

🕐*Open for worship only at 7am, noon, 7pm.*

This 13C church is a popular gathering place. The lovely Romanesque ogival façade is set off by sober architectural features. Buttresses support the central section, which is embellished with a doorway of simple ogival archivolts and a large rose window.

The interior has three short naves, with a wooden ceiling above the central aisle; the chancel has pointed vaults with ribs set with jagged indentations. The 18C altarpiece is in red marble. Mudéjar features survive in the Capilla del Bautismo *(Epistle nave).*

Behind the church, look out for one of Córdoba's oldest bars, the Taberna San Miguel "El Pisto" (👜*see Address Book*).

> *Follow calle San Zoilo, behind the church, and then head along calle Conde de Torres.*

Plaza de los Capuchinos★

The impressive calvary of **Christ of the Lanterns** in this austere square was sculpted in the late 18C and was once part of a *vía crucis* (Stations of the Cross) processional way.

The Iglesia de los Capuchinos and the church of the former 18C Hospital de San Jacinto, containing a venerated, and luxuriously dressed Virgin of Pain, also front the square.

> *Exit the square via calle Cabrera and head to plaza de Colón.*

Entrance to the Palacio de Viana

B.Kaufmann/MICHELIN

Plaza de Colón

This pleasant square named for Columbus has a pretty fountain and gardens.

Palacio de la Diputación★ – The provincial Parliament building began life as the 18C Convento de la Merced (Convent of Mercy). It also served as a hospital for French troops in the Peninsular War. The attractive façades is painted to imitate marble.

The white marble doorway is decorated by two Solomonic columns, a pediment and two belfries. The patio *(entrance through the left-hand door)* is decorated in the same style as the main façade. Note the marble staircase, and the Baroque, stucco-adorned church *(access via the middle door)*.

Torre de la Malmuerta – This magnificent 15C octagonal tower was, according to legend built to imprison a knight who had killed his (apparently) unfaithful wife. In fact it is a turret which retains the arch connecting it to the defensive wall.

Visit

Palacio de Viana★★

🕓*Open mid-Jun–Sept Mon–Sat, 9am–2pm; Oct–May 10am–1pm, 4pm–6pm (Sat 10am–1pm).* 👓*Guided tours available (1hr).* 🕓*Closed first two weeks Jun.*

👓€6 (€3 patios only). ☎957 49 67 41. www.artencordoba.com.

This palace with its adjoining outbuildings is an outstanding example of 14C to 19C Córdoban civil architecture and has no less than 12 splendid patios. Enter from plaza de Don Gome, through an angled doorway. The interior is enhanced by its 16C Renaissance main staircase with magnificent Mudéjar *artesonado*. Several rooms also have fine *artesonados*.

Museo Arqueológico Provincial★★

🕓*Open Wed–Sat 9am–8.30pm, Tue 2.30pm–8.30pm; Sun and public hols, 9am–2.30pm.* 👓*€1.50 (no charge for EU citizens).* ☎957 35 55 17.

Andalucía's leading archaeological museum is set in the beautiful 16C Renaissance **Palacio de los Páez**. Its eroded **façade**★ depicts warriors and escutcheons.

The **ground floor** exhibits prehistoric and Iberian objects – such as zoomorphic sculptures – as well as Visigothic remains. The **Roman collection**★ around the patios includes toga-clad sculptures, reliefs, sarcophagi, mosaics, capitals and column tambours.

The **first floor galleries** display Hispano-Moorish ceramics, bronzes – note the 10C **stag**★ *(cervatillo)* from Medina Azahara entirely decorated with plant motifs – and a unique collection of Moorish and Mudéjar well copings. The unusual **capital of the musicians** is decorated with human figures with mutilated heads.

Ground floor:
◆ **Porcelain** of different provenances from the 17C to 20C.
◆ **Arquebuses**.

First floor:
◆ **Azulejos:** 236 pieces of ceramic from the 13C to 19C.
◆ **Córdoban leather:** the best collection of its kind, comprising articles of embossed leather and cordovans from the 15C to 19C.
◆ **Tapestries:** Flemish, French and Spanish, some based on Goya.
◆ **Flags**.

Alcázar de los Reyes Cristianos

♦ **The library** contains over 7 000 books from the 16C to 19C.

Alcázar de los Reyes Cristianos★

🕐*Open mid-Jun–Sept Mon–Fri 9am–2pm; Oct–May 10am–1pm, 4pm–6pm (Sat 10am–1pm).*🕐*Closed first two weeks Jun.* ⊛€4. ☎957 42 01 51. www.arten cordoba.com.

This fortress-residence was built by Alfonso XI in the 14C and served as the headquarters of the Inquisition until 1821.

On display are an exceptional 3C AD **Roman sarcophagus★**, with an outstanding treatment of facial features and fabric, and an interesting collection of **mosaics★**. The **baths** *(downstairs, to the right, at the end of the corridor)* are Moorish in design.

Cross the Mudéjar patio to visit the delightful Moorish-style **gardens★**.

Torre de la Calahorra: Museo Vivo de al-Andalus

🕐*Open May–Sept 10am–2pm, 4.30pm–8.30pm. Oct–Apr 10am–6pm.* ⊛€4.50. ☎957 29 39 29. www.artencordoba.com.

This Moorish fortress is at the southern end of the Puente Romano. Originally, its two towers were linked by a single arch; in the 14C, they were enlarged, and later modified again. The tower has been used variously as a prison for nobles, a barracks, and even a school.

Torre de la Calahorra

It now houses a museum dedicated to the history of the Córdoba Caliphate – a period of cultural, artistic, philosophical and scientific prosperity – and includes an impressive **model**★ of the Mezquita in the 13C. Enjoy fine **views** of the city from atop the tower.

Museo Municipal Taurino
Plazuela de Maimónides.
🕐*Open May–mid-Oct Tue–Sun 10am–2pm, 5.30pm–7.30pm; mid-Oct–Apr Tue–Sun 10am–2pm, 4.30pm–6.30pm; Sun all year 9.30am–2.30pm.* ✆€3 (free Fri). ☎957 20 10 56.

The **bullfighting museum** is housed in the 16C Casa de las Bulas. Access is via two attractive patios: the Mudéjar-influenced entrance patio, and the finely proportioned main patio. The collection includes engravings, posters, photographs and mementoes of Córdoba's most famous matadors, including Lagartijo, Guerrita, Machaquito and Manolete.

Plaza del Potro
The elongated plaza del Potro takes its name from the small statue of a colt (*potro*) crowning the fountain at one end. This fountain dates from the 16C; on the opposite side is a monument to San Rafael. The square was once the site of the city's lively horse and mule fair.

The **Posada del Potro** (🕐*open mid-Apr–Sept 10am–2.30pm, 5pm–8pm; Oct–mid-Apr 9.30am–2.30pm, 4.30pm–7pm;* ☎*957 48 50 01; www.artencordoba.com*) a charming inn described by Cervantes in *Don Quixote*, faces the square. It is now a cultural centre that mounts temporary exhibitions.

The entrance to both the Museo de Bellas Artes and the Museo Julio Romero de Torres is through a patio-garden opposite the fountain.

Museo de Julio Romero de Torres★
🕐*Open Tue–Sat: Jul–Aug 8.30am–2.30pm; May–Jun, Sept–mid-Oct 10am–2pm, 5.30pm–7.30pm (mid Oct–Apr 4.30pm–6.30pm). Sun and public hols all year, 9.30am–2.30pm. Last admission 20min before closing.* ✆€3 (no charge Fri). ☎957 49 19 09. www.artencordoba.com.

This mansion, the birthplace of Julio Romero de Torres (1880–1930), houses a collection of his paintings, many of beautiful, dark-skinned women.

The ground floor contains a number of posters advertising *ferias* of the past; the upper floor exhibits his attractive female portraits such as *La Chiquita Piconera* (The Charcoal Girl), which manifest a magnificent psychological treatment of the feminine world (note the gaze of his subjects).

Several canvases have religious themes, such as *The Virgin of the Lanterns*, a copy of which hangs in an altar outside the Mezquita.

Follow calle San Francisco as far as calle San Fernando. To the left, after an 18C arch, is the **Iglesia de San Francisco**. The church belongs to a convent of great historical importance, although only a part of a cloister, to the left, now remains.

Museo de Bellas Artes
🕐*Open Tue 2.30pm–8.30pm, Wed–Sat 9am–8.30pm. Sun and public hols 9am–2.30pm.* ✆€1.50 (free to EU citizens). ☎957 35 55 50. www.artencordoba.com.

The **Fine Arts Museum** displays works ranging from the 14C to the 20C, predominantly by local artists. It is housed in the former Hospital de la Caridad, founded in the 15C. The staircase, covered by a fine Mudéjar *artesonado* ceiling, has 16C and 17C murals.

Of particular interest are: *Immaculate Conception* by Juan Valdés Leal; the collection of modern Córdoban and Spanish art dating from the second half of the 19C and first half of the 20C (by the likes of Ramón Casas, José Gutiérrez Solana, Rusiñol and Zuloaga); and sculptures by the Córdoban artist Mateo Inurria.

Plaza de la Corredera
This large, porticoed, rectangular square, accessed via vaulted passageways, recalls the main squares found in Castille. For centuries it was an important meeting-place and the setting for *autos-da-fé*, fiestas, executions, markets and bullfights. The **calleja del Toril**, a narrow alleyway, was used as the bull enclosure.

On Saturdays, its usual tranquillity is broken by the hustle and bustle of a busy **market**.

Museo Regina de Joyería

🕐*Open daily May–Sept 9.30am–2pm, 5.30pm–9pm; Oct–Apr 10am–3pm, 5pm–8pm. ☎957 49 68 89. www.arten cordoba.com.*

This museum of jewellery documents a craft that is historically connected with the city. The permanent exhibition shows the fabrication processes. A hall for temporary exhibits occupies a 16C building.

Mausoleo Romano

This Roman mausoleum, discovered in 1993 during work in the Jardines de la Victoria, is a robust, circular monument from the 1C AD, the golden age of Roman Córdoba.

Iglesia del Colegio de Santa Victoria

The monumental columns decorating the façade of this church can be seen at the end of plaza de la Compañía. Part of the Santa Victoria school *(colegio)*, it is built in the neo-Classical style and dates from the middle of the 18C. Ventura Rodríguez was involved in its construction and designed the dome.

Excursions

Medina Azahara★★

Leave Córdoba by the A 431 west. After 8km/5mi bear right onto a signposted road.

Once on the road, the ochre mass of the 15C **Monasterio de San Jerónimo de Valparaíso** *(private residence; ⊶not open to the public)*, comes into view.

The palace-city of Medina Azahara was built at the behest of Abd ar-Rahman III in 936. Chronicles of the day contain many references to its amazing luxury and splendour.

However the city had only just been completed when it was razed to the ground by the Berbers in 1013 during the war with the Caliphate of Córdoba, and thereafter it served as a source of construction materials. Archaeological excavations began in 1911. Although little more than 10% of the original city remains, it is still possible to imagine what this sumptuous city must have been like.

Medina Azahara is built in terraces: the upper terrace contained the Alcázar, with the residences of the Caliph and other dignitaries, as well as administrative and military dependencies; gardens and the large reception room were in the middle

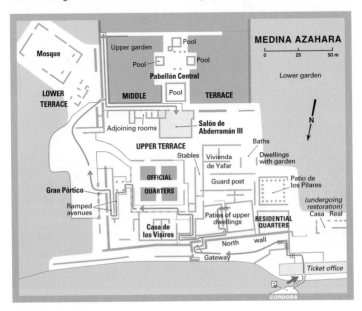

terrace, and a mosque (excavated) and other buildings were below.

Tour

Follow the signposted itinerary.

◷*Open May–mid-Sept Tue–Sat, 10am–8.30pm, Sun 10am–2pm. Mid-Sept–Apr Tue–Sat, 10am–6.30pm. Sun 10am–2pm.* ◷*Closed 1–6 Jan, 1 May, 24–25 & 31 Dec.* ⊚*€1.50 (free to EU citizens).* ☏*957 35 55 07. www.juntadeandalucia.es/cultura/museos/CAMA.*

The tour starts outside the north wall, marked by square towers. Access is via an angled doorway, typical of Islamic defensive architecture.

Upper terrace

The **residential quarters** are to the right. The rest of the upper dwellings were built around two large square patios. To the west, at the highest point of the Alcázar, is the **Casa Real** or Royal Quarters/*Dar al-Mulk* (o━ *currently under restoration, not open to the public*).

To the left of the entry door are the **official quarters**. The **Casa de los Visires** *(Dar al-Wuzara)* comprises a suite of rooms. A large basilica-like hall is surrounded by dependencies and patios.

The viziers held their civil audiences in the large hall. The garden in front is modern.

Several streets lead uphill to the impressive **portico**, the façade of a large parade ground. Only a few of the 15 magnificent arches remain; this was the monumental entrance to the Alcázar, through which ambassadors would enter.

Middle terrace

The remains of the **mosque**, which stood on the lower terrace, are to the left, along the path down. The five aisles are at right angles to the rectangular patio, as is the base of the minaret in the northwest wall of the patio.

The middle terrace, overlooking the gardens, is dominated by the jewel of this site: the restored **Abd ar-Rahman III Room** (Salón de Abderramán III), the decoration of which gives an idea of the city's splendour in the 10C. Only the finest materials were used. Beautiful horseshoe arches with alternating voussoirs are supported by grey and blue marble, contrasting with the large white marble flagstones used for the floor paving. Note the geometric and plant motif decoration on the magnifi-

Salón de Abderramán III, Medina Azahara

©Turespaña

Castillo de Almodóvar del Río

cent carved stone wall panels, including stylisations of the tree of life, a common theme in Hispano-Islamic art.

Opposite this room is the **Pabellón Central** or central pavilion, once used as a waiting room for those granted an audience with the Caliph. It is in the centre of the gardens and is surrounded by four small pools.

Castillo de Almodóvar del Río★★

25km/15mi west of Córdoba along the A 431. Follow the road skirting the town and continue to the fortress along a dirt track.

⊙*Open 11am–2.30p.m and 4pm–7pm (summer, 8pm); Sat–Sun and public hols, 11am–7pm (summer, 8pm).* ⊙*Closed 1 Jan and 25 Dec.* ☞€5. ☎957 63 40 55. *www.castillodealmodovar.com.*

The name Almodóvar originates from the Arabic *al-Mudawwar,* "the round one", a clear reference to the castle hill. In the 8C, under Moorish rule, a large fortress stood here. Almódovar was subsequently under the rule of various taifa kingdoms before its reconquest by Fernando III in 1240.

The present **castle** was erected in the 14C in Gothic style and is considered one of the most important in Andalucía because of its beauty and excellent state of repair. It was restored at the begin-

ning of the 20C when a neo-Gothic mansion was added. The town nestles below on the south bank of the River Guadalquivir.

From the castle the **views**★ of the river and the Córdoban countryside are quite magnificent. There are two walled enclosures – one in the form of a barbican – with eight towers of varying proportions. The largest, the *torre del homenaje* (keep), is in fact a turret.

Embalse de la Breña

5km/3mi northwest of Almodóvar. Head back towards the town and take a signposted turning to the left.

The road winds across hills carpeted in olive trees to the **Embalse de la Breña**, a reservoir used by the Córdoba sailing club. On the return journey look back to appreciate the magnificent silhouette of the Castillo de Almodóvar.

Princess Zaida

Every 28 March a woman dressed in white appears, wailing from one of the towers. It is said that this is the ghost of Princess Zaida, who was taken prisoner by the Almoravids, and died from grief in the castle's dungeon upon hearing of the death of her husband in battle.

View of Bélmez and the castle

Las Ermitas

13km/8mi northwest of Córdoba on the El Brillante road; 10km/6mi from Medina Azahara by A 431, then left at the first crossroads (follow signs to "Ermitas").

From either direction, the **views**★ of the sierra and the surrounding countryside are quite delightful.

These 13 hermitages (and a solitary church), set in a wild mountainous location, date from the 18C, although the hermit tradition in the area goes back centuries.

In the beautiful paseo de los Cipreses (Cypress Avenue), the skull and short poem on the **Cruz del Humilladero** serve as a reminder of the transitory nature of life. Past the cross, the **Ermita de la Magdalena** is to the left, along with the hermits' cemetery and the church in the distance. Entering the vestibule of the **church** *(on the right)*, note the skull once used as a cup and plate. The rich decoration of the church – the result of donations – contrasts with the hermits' austere existence. Behind the high altar, in the room used as a chapterhouse, note also the attractive frieze of lustre *azulejos*.

The rest of the hermitage spreads over the hillside. Back at the entrance, a path leads to the **Balcón del Mundo**. From this viewpoint, dominated by an enormous Sacred Heart (1929), enjoy a magnificent **panorama**★★ of Córdoba and its surrounding countryside. To the right, the view extends to the hilltop Castillo de Almodóvar del Río.

Driving Tour

Córdoba to Fuente Obejuna

131km/71mi.

▶ *Head north from Córdoba along the N 432. After 30km/18mi, turn left at a crossroads onto the CP 81 and continue for a further 17.5km/11mi.*

Obejo

The 13C **Iglesia Parroquial de San Antonio Abad** *(if closed, the person living opposite the church will show you around; ☎957 36 90 68)* is to the left, alongside the remains of a long-forgotten fortress. This small parish church is particularly charming. Note the last two columns on the left-hand aisle, topped by **capitals**★ with plant motifs of Moorish origin. Several of the bases are in fact inverted capitals. The church's most noteworthy external feature is its sober and rustic Mudéjar tower.

▶ *Rejoin the N 432.*

The **road**★ crosses mountain pastures populated by flocks of sheep, and oak forest where a deer might appear. Views of the River Guadalbarbo on this tortuous ascent are memorable.

▶ *At a crossroads, continue straight on for 2.5km/1.5mi.*

El Vacar

The ruins of an imposing rectangular fortress stand atop a hill to the right, looking down on the Puente Nuevo reservoir. Two dirt tracks heading off the main road, just before El Vacar, lead to an esplanade providing a better view of the sober walls of this 10C edifice.

▶ *Return to the N 432 and head northwest.*

Espiel

This picturesque village of cobbled streets and whitewashed houses features a town hall from 1792 which used to serve as a public granary. Espiel's 16C parish church, named after St Sebastian, is topped by a bell tower, a favourite nesting place for storks.

▶ *Continue for 21km/13mi along the N 432 to Bélmez.*

Bélmez

The town lies at the foot of a rocky outcrop crowned by a Moorish **castle** which was rebuilt after the Reconquest. Alongside the 19C town hall stands the **Museo Histórico de Bélmez y del Territorio Minero** (◷ *open Mon–Sat 10am–2pm, 6pm–9pm.* ☎957 58 00 12), housed in a former public granary. The museum retraces mining activities back to the 18C.

Castle – Although ruined, the keep and walls are largely intact. To reach the castle, follow the road from the square, opposite the 18C **parish church**. To the right, after 50m/55yd, note the **Ermita de la Virgen del Castillo** (Chapel of the Virgin of the Castle).

A ramp ascends to the foot of the castle walls *(5min)*. The more daring can continue up along a difficult path between the rocks to the first section of wall; note the cistern *(aljibe)* on the left-hand side. Steps lead from a patio to the terrace behind this first section. Beyond (⚠*only recommended for those with a good head for heights)*, the upper part of the castle offers magnificent **views** of Fuente Obejuna and its surroundings.

Fuente Obejuna

23km/14mi west along N 432.

A scenic drive through wooded landscapes leads to the small town of Fuente Obejuna, on a hill near the source of the River Guadiato. It is well worth strolling through this historic town to admire the Renaissance mansions which bear witness to past glories.

Plaza Mayor

In the upper section of the town is the impressive, irregular, largely granite square, fronted by the town hall and parish church.

Iglesia de Nuestra Señora del Castillo

◷ *Open summer Mon–Sat 8.30pm–9.30pm, Sun and public hols 8.30am–10am; otherwise Mon–Sat 7pm–8pm, Sun and public hols 8.30am–10am. If closed, call* ☎957 58 41 63.

This 15C church contains several interesting works of art within its frescoed walls. The presbytery houses a magnificent **Renaissance retable**★ with high-relief sculptures of scenes from the Life and Passion of Christ. It is dominated by the 14C statue of the Virgin of the Castle, which was discovered in a niche in the old castle walls.

The Sacrarium Chapel *(Capilla del Sagrario,* left of the chancel) is adorned with *azulejo* panelling. A 16C late-Gothic **retable** with seven tablets is dedicated to the Virgin Mary. A second, Baroque retable, dominated by the Virgin of the Rosary, is in the chapel to the right.

COSTA DE ALMERÍA★

This coast is characterised by extensive beaches, coves lapped by crystal-clear waters, fishing villages turned into resorts, and areas of outstanding, almost virgin, natural beauty. Add a hot climate with little rainfall and sunshine almost all year and the result is a location that is becoming one of the region's most popular tourist destinations.

- ▪ **Information:** Parque Nicolás Salmerón/Martínez Campos, Almería. ☏ 950 17 52 20. www.Almería-turismo.org.
- ▸ **Orient Yourself:** The Costa de Almería runs along the southeastern Iberian Peninsula from Adra to Mojácar, and includes the provincial capital, Almería. The A 7- E 15, just in from the coast, is the principal highway.
- ⊛ **Don't Miss:** The old town quarter of Mojácar.
- ◔ **Organising Your Time:** Allow a day or two to drive through picturesque villages, in addition to an extended beach stay.
- 🅺🅸🅳🆂 **Especially for Kids:** Beaches, Aquarium at Roquetas de Mar, Parque Acuático Vera water park.
- ◔ **Also See:** TABERNAS, Sierra de Los FILABRES, GUADIX (109km/68mi NW of Almería), Las ALPUJARRAS.

Driving Tours

1 Adra to Almería

117km/73mi – allow a day.

Adra

Set on a fertile plain, Adra has a fishing port, marina, beach and several 17C/18C mansions. It began life as a Phoenician and Roman outpost, and was the last coast town yielded by the Moors. The Iglesia de la Inmaculada Concepción contains a *Christ of the Expiration*, attributed to Alonso de Mena. The Torre de los Perdigones, a 45m/147ft-high tower once part of a 19C lead foundry, is the tourist office. The **Museum of Adra** is in the palatial Marques de Villacañas.

▸ *Head north along the A 347.*

Berja

The Roman Virgi (which evolved into *vergel*, meaning "orchard"), at the foot of the Sierra de Gádor, has a number

"Sea of Plastic" near Berja

B. Kaufmann/MICHELIN

of handsome noble Renaissance mansions and fountains, and the remains of a Roman amphitheatre.

▷ *Head back towards Adra, then follow the A 7–E 15 towards Almería.*

The road offers attractive **views** of the Sierra de la Contraviesa to the left, with the Cerrón peak (1 238m/4 060ft) in the foreground.

After a bend in the road, the plastic-covered fields of the **Campo de Dalías** come into view. Between Adra and Almería,the highway passes hundreds of plastic greenhouses which produce several crops a year, mostly for export to northern Europe. This "sea of plastic" is now emblematic of huge areas of Almería and although it has bought wealth to growers and distributors has become a very controversial addition to the landscape, not least among conservationists.

Almerimar

This modern tourist complex also has a golf course and marina.

▷ *Return to the N 340 – E 15 and turn off onto the A 391 at Km 429.*

Roquetas de Mar

This fishing village has been transformed into a lively resort. The remains of the old castle can be seen by the lighthouse *(faro)*. Roquetas has a fishing port and marina, golf course and a water park.

The **Urbanización Roquetas de Mar** *(3.5km/2mi)* has attractive beaches of fine sand and a long palm-lined promenade with views of the Gulf of Almería and Cabo de Gata. The avenida del Mediterráneo teems with shops and restaurants. Away from the beach its main visitor attraction is its **Aquarium** (☉*open year round daily 10am–9pm;* ☞*€10.95, child €8.95;* ☎*950 16 00 36, www.aquariumroquetas.com)* with its sharks, rays, tropical fish, freshwater tank and touch tank.

▷ *Head back along the A 391 and turn right at El Parador.*

Aguadulce

This large and popular Blue Flag beach resort is in an area of abundant vegetation just 11km/7mi from Almería. The nature reserve of Punta Entinas–Sabinar, an area of sand dunes and marshland, is to the southeast. Juniper bushes, bulrushes and canes predominate in this unusual landscape.

From Aguadulce to Almería

The road follows the coast, hugging cliff tops and tunneling through rock. The approach to Almería offers views of the city, the bay, the port and the fortress.

Almería – ⓒ*see ALMERÍA*

② Almería to Mojácar

132km/82.5mi – allow one day.

Níjar – ⓒ*see Parque Natural de CABO DE GATA-NÍJAR*

Parque Natural de Cabo de Gata-Níjar★★ –
ⓒ*see Parque Natural de CABO DE GATA-NÍJAR.*

Agua Amarga

The houses of this seaside village appear after a bend in the road. The resort's attractive and well-maintained beach is framed by two rocky promontories.

From Agua Amarga to Mojácar Playa
32km/20mi – allow 45min.

This stretch of road offers attractive views of the coast, including several watchtowers. After a short distance, a branch road to the right heads up to the Mesa Roldán lighthouse *(faro)* and fortified tower *(1.5km/1mi)*.

Back on the main road, pass a power station, the port of Endesa and a beach, the Playa de Marinicas. Opposite, the white-washed **Casa del Laberinto** or **Casa de André Block** – named after the Algerian designer and sculptor who built it in the 1960s – resembles a sandcastle made of icing sugar.

Address Book

For coin ranges, see the cover flap.

WHERE TO STAY

Hotel Hesperia Sabinal – *Avenida Las Gaviotas, Roquetas de Mar. 950 33 36 00. www.hesperia. com/hotels/Hesperia-Sabinal. 522 rooms.* In the heart of the beach area. A large hotel complex with spacious rooms overlooking the sea.

WHERE TO EAT

Náutico Almerimar – *in the Almerimar marina. 10 km/6mi S of El Ejido. 950 49 70 73. Closed Mon.* A famous fish and seafood restaurant, terrace with marina views.

Al-Baida – *Avenida Las Gaviotas, 94. Roquetas de Mar. 950 33 38 21. Closed Wed and in Mar.* A well-known local eatery serving fish and seafood. Simple decor, plus an aquarium containing live lobsters.

BOAT TRIPS

Excursions to Mojácar Bay, Carboneras and the Parque Natural de Cabo de Gata-Níjar are all available from Garrucha *(contact the tourist office for further information, 950 13 27 83).*

Carboneras

This fishing village developed around a 16C castle, the **Castillo de San Andrés**, built by the Marquess of Carpio. A small **market** is held Thursdays.

Between Carboneras and the Castillo de Macenas *(13km/8mi)*, the road traverses an arid mountain landscape with the occasional view of the Mediterranean, culminating in the **Torre-vigía del Rayo** watchtower.

Castillo de Macenas

This coastal watchtower dates from the 17C. Views extend to the south to the **Torre del Perulico** which, like so many other watchtowers, was built by the

Torre del Perulico

Moors in the 13C and 14C. A dirt track parallel to the coast runs south past the tower to several nudist beaches, including the Playa de Bordonares *(3km/2mi)*.

Mojácar Playa

The Mojácar municipality includes 17km/10.5mi of beaches and coves. Mojácar Playa is a modern resort of whitewashed tourist developments.

Mojácar★

This enchanting town, inhabited since antiquity, enjoys a superb **setting**★ on a promontory, with delightful views of the Mediterranean just to the east and the unusual rock formations of the surrounding plain. The old hillside quarter has a Moorish character, with narrow, cobbled streets lined by whitewashed houses adorned with floral arrangements. The town was only reconquered by the Christians in 1488.

A significant foreign community, particularly from northern Europe, gives Mojácar a cosmopolitan feel. The many small restaurants, cafés and craft shops attract tens of thousands of visitors every year, particularly in summer.

The town

Leave your car in the lower part of town. The beauty of Mojácar mainly resides in the charm of its well-maintained buildings and its superb vistas. It is ideal town for wandering with surprising discoveries at every turn.

The best starting point is the pleasant **plaza Nueva**, fronted by the 18C Ermita de Nuestra Señora de los Dolores, a former chapel and now a shop. The *mirador* on the square is the perfect viewpoint. Below are the remains of Mojácar la Vieja, the original town. Cuesta del Castillo, a street to the left of the square, heads up to the **castle mirador**; nothing remains of the castle but its views to the coast.

Calle de la Iglesia to the right of plaza Nueva leads to the **Iglesia de Santa María**, its ochre-coloured walls standing out against white houses. Built after the Reconquest, it has fortress-like walls, a bell tower to one side, and buttresses on the other. Several picturesque narrow streets surround the church.

Calle de Enmedio, parallel to calle de la Iglesia, is lined by small restaurants and bars. This street passes in front of plaza del Ayuntamiento, from where it is possible to walk down to the 15C **Puerta de la Ciudad** (Town Gate), once part of the defensive walls. Walk through to the charming **plaza de las Flores**.

▶ *Rejoin the coast road north.*

Garrucha
5.5km/3.5mi north.
This former fishing village with excellent beaches, marina and promenade, is a lively place in summer. An 18C fortified watchtower can still be seen along the coast to the south of the resort.

▶ *Head north from Garrucha along the C 3327.*

Vera
A popular **water park** Parque Acuático Vera (◔*open mid-May–Sept 11am–6pm, Jul–Aug 10.30am–7.30pm;* ▤€16, *child* €11; ☎*902 36 12 94 www.aquavera.com)* is located along the road between Vera and Garrucha, with the usual flumes and slides and children's areas.

The plaza Mayor is fronted by the fortress-like 16C **Iglesia de la Encarnación**, a church with four solid corner towers. To the left stands the 19C **town hall** with a sober stone doorway; note

the standard hanging in the council room, presented by the Catholic Monarchs. Next door the **Museo Histórico Municipal** (◔*open Mon–Fri 10am–2pm, 5pm–8pm; Sat 10am–2pm;* ☎*950 39 30 16)* has sections devoted to local archaeology, history and ethnography.

Along the coast is the Vera Natura nudist resort.

Cuevas de Almanzora
6km/4mi northwest via the A 8303 and then the A 7 – E 15.
The town of Cuevas de Almanzora is near a lake in an area rich in mineral deposits and archaeological remains. The town prospered in the 19C following the discovery of silver in the nearby Sierra de la Almagrera. Mansions in the old quarter, as well as the Capilla del Carmen in the Iglesia de Nuestra Señora de la Encarnación testify to the wealth of this period. There are cave dwellings close to the town.

Castle
(Museo Antonio Manuel Campoy and Museo de Arqueología)
◔*Open Jul–mid-Sept Tue–Sun 10am–1.30pm; mid-Sept–Jun Tue–Sat 10am–1.30pm, 5pm–8pm (Sun 10am–1.30pm).* ☎*950 45 80 63.*
The restored 16C castle is now home to two museums. Named for a local newspaper art critic, Campoy's private collection includes contemporary Spanish art (paintings, sketches and engravings), firearms and numerous personal mementoes.

The archaeological museum focuses on the El Argar (local Bronze Age) culture. Finds from nearby Antas and Fuente Álamo are on display.

When leaving the castle, note the cave dwellings to the left.

Huércal Overa
25km/15mi north along the N 340–E 15.
A Moorish fortress stands atop a hill on the outskirts of the village. The 18C **Iglesia de la Asunción** holds an interesting Baroque altarpiece and the sculptures (some by Salzillo) are carried in **Holy Week** processions, when three religious brotherhoods (*cofradías*) compete in pomp and ceremony.

COSTA DE HUELVA★

The Huelva coast, running southeast from Portugal, is a succession of sun-blessed beaches interrupted by deltas where the Guadiana, Guadalquivir and Tinto enter the Atlantic. Relatively undeveloped, it forms part of the Costa de la Luz (Coast of Light). Columbus departed from here on his epic voyage of discovery.

▶ **Orient Yourself:** The Costa de Huelva extends from Ayamonte, at the mouth of the River Guadiana, to the Parque Nacional de Doñana. The A 49-E 1 highway runs between Ayamonte and Huelva, while the N 442 and A 494 embrace the coast.

🕐 **Organising Your Time:** Allow two days.

🧒 **Especially for Kids:** The beaches.

⛪ **Also See:** LA RÁBIDA, El ROCÍO, SANLÚCAR DE BARRAMEDA.

Driving Tours

1 Parque Nacional de Doñana to Palos de la Frontera

49km/30mi – allow half a day.

Parque Nacional de Doñana★★★

⛪*See Parque Nacional de DOÑANA.*

▶ *Head south from the El Acebuche information centre along the A 483. Turn right in Torre de la Higuera towards the resort of Matalascañas.*

Statue of Martín Alonso Pinzón

The road to the resort crosses an attractive section of the Doñana National Park.

Matalascañas

Matalascañas is one of the busiest resorts in this part of the coast, with numerous apartment blocks, nightclubs, outdoor bars and a huge range of leisure facilities.

▶ *Return to Torre de la Higuera and head northwest along A 494.*

Mazagón

The fine sands of **Playa de Mazagón** extend 10km/6mi from the mouth of the River Tinto to the Torre del Loro. This quiet beach offers good-quality campsites and chalet complexes and a marina, but no high-rises.

The Parador de Mazagón (⛪*see Address Book*) commands delightful **views** of this part of the Atlantic coastline.

▶ *Continue northwest along the A 494.*

Palos de la Frontera★

Columbus sailed from this picturesque small town on his voyage of discovery in 1492.

It is also the birthplace of the Pinzón brothers, who accompanied Columbus. The charm of Palos lies in its whitewashed houses, narrow alleyways and lively atmosphere, best enjoyed in its charming squares.

Casa-Museo de Martín Alonso Pinzón

☛*Closed for restoration.*
☎959 35 01 99.

The home of the local navigator who accompanied Columbus to the New World. Alongside personal mementoes (signed letters, navigational equipment etc), is memorabilia relating to a rather more recent, though still very impressive transatlantic crossing; that of the seaplane *Plus Ultra*, which flew non-stop from Palos de la Frontera to Buenos Aires in 1926.

Iglesia de San Jorge

🕐*Open Apr–Sept Tue–Fri 10am–2pm, 5pm–9pm (Sat–Sun and public hols 11am –8pm); Oct–Mar Tue–Sun 10am–7pm.* ☞€3. ☎959 53 05 97.

This fine 15C Gothic-Mudéjar church fronts an attractive small square. Columbus prayed here on the morning of his departure (3 August) 1492. Behind the church, La Fontanilla, a fountain crowned by a small Mudéjar shrine, supplied the water for the three caravels, the *Niña*, the *Pinta* and the *Santa María*.

② From Huelva to Ayamonte

77km/48mi – allow one day.

Huelva★ – 👜*See HUELVA.*

▷ *Head west along the A 497 towards Punta Umbria.*

Punta Umbría

Punta Umbría can be reached in summer by ferry from Huelva.

This former rest centre for miners is in the salt marshes of the Paraje Natural de las Marismas del Odiel nature reserve. Nowadays it is a popular resort with a small marina and attractive beaches. The daily early-morning fish auction is worth seeing, as is the fishermen's procession to honour the Virgin Mary on 15 August every year.

The **Paraje Natural de Enebrales de Punta Umbría**, is a protected area of sand dunes in a landscape dominated by savin, juniper, mastic and hawthorn.

▷ *Head back along the same road. After 7km/4.5mi, leave the A 497 at El Portil.*

El Portil

This section of coast is one of the province's busiest resort areas. The nearby **Reserva Natural de la Laguna de El Portil**, a lagoon of outstanding beauty, is home to a variety of birds.

▷ *Continue northwest along A 4104.*

El Rompido

This small fishing port has a pleasant dune-lined beach popular with summer visitors. The **Paraje Natural Marismas del Río Piedras y Flecha de El Rompido★**, is a protected salt marsh *(marisma)* off the road towards La Antilla. This reserve is home to the black-headed gull, pintail, oystercatcher and common egret.

La Flecha de El Rompido

B. Kaufmann/MICHELIN

Address Book

For coin ranges, see the cover flap

WHERE TO STAY

Hotel Santa María – *Palos de la Frontera, near the Monasterio de Santa María de la Rábida.* ☎955 53 00 01. *18 rooms.* A small hotel with a large restaurant offering views of the Tinto estuary. Try to reserve the double room with river view.

Hotel La Pinta – *Rábida, 79, Palos de la Frontera.* ☎959 35 05 11. *30 rooms.* A delightful small hotel with decent rooms in the centre of town.

Hotel Carabela Santa María – *Avenida de Conquistadores, Mazagón.* ☎959 53 60 18. *www.hotelcarabela santamaria.com.* Comfortable modern hotel with swimming pool, bar and restaurant.

Hotel Pato Amarillo – *Urbanización Everluz, Punta Umbría.* ☎959 31 12 50 *www.hotelpatoamarillo. com.* 120 rooms. Several bedrooms have pleasant sea views. Garden, swimming pool, bar and restaurant.

Hotel Cortijo Golf – *Sector E, Parcela 15. Matalascañas.* ☎959 44 87 00. *126 rooms.* A large swimming pool, two restaurants, regional-style bar and comfortable rooms. Organised activities in summer.

Parador de Mazagón – *Playa de Mazagón, 7km/4mi SE along the A 494.* ☎959 53 63 00. *www.parador. es. 62 rooms.* This modern *parador* dominates Mazagón beach. Rooms with

terrace and panoramic views. Dining specialties include sea bass *(lubina)*, lobster *(langosta)*, crayfish *(langostinos)*, prawns *(gambas)* and loin of pork *(solomillo de cerdo)*.

WHERE TO EAT

Caribe II – *Calle Nao, El Rompido.* ☎959 39 90 27. The terrace of this smart portside restaurant is ideal for a leisurely lunch. Specialities include squid *(calamares)*, red mullet *(salmonete)*, crayfish *(langostinos)* and lobster *(bogavante)*.

El Remo – *Avenida de Conquistadores, 123. Mazagón (on the way to Matalascañas).* ☎959 53 61 38. *www. restauranteelremo.com.* One of the best restaurants in the area. A pleasant terrace with upholstered chairs and a bar overlooking the beach. The menu includes fish, seafood and grilled meats.

Miramar – *Miramar, 1. Punta Umbría.* ☎959 31 12 43. *www.restaurante miramarsl.com.* Recently remodelled with large, airy dining areas, the Miramar, on the beachfront, serves excellent fish and rice dishes.

The main square in **Matalascañas** is lined with restuarants. Two other recommended Andalusian-style restaurants in **Matalascañas** are : **Manolo León**, which specialises in meat dishes, and **Manolo Vázquez**, whose menu is dominated by fish and seafood. In **Punta Umbría**, the plaza del Mercado is a good place to find fresh seafood.

▶ *Head north along the A 4106.*

Cartaya

The **plaza Redonda** is a tranquil square adorned with orange trees and elegant wrought-iron street lamps. Around the square are the 16C Iglesia de San Pedro, with its *azulejo*-decorated campanile, the town hall and the Casa de Cultura.

▶ *Continue along N 431, heading southwest to Lepe.*

Lepe

The town is in an area that produces strawberries, figs and melons.

▶ *Head south.*

La Antilla

Crowds flock to La Antilla's delightful beaches, yet the quiet town of older houses remains sedate, in contrast to nearby Islantilla, a modern complex of apartment blocks and a luxurious golf course. At the mouth of the River Piedras is **El Terrón**, worth a visit to watch fishermen and to enjoy seafood.

▶ *Return to Lepe and follow the N 431 to the west.*

Ayamonte★ – *See AYAMONTE*

COSTA DEL SOL★★

The Sun Coast stretches along the Mediterranean from Tarifa on the Straits of Gibraltar to the Cabo de Gata, a headland east of Almería. Visitors are drawn to a wonderful climate, sandy beaches, whitewashed towns and villages and activities for every taste. Sadly, most of the charming fishing communities have been transformed beyond recognition since the tourist boom of the 1970s covered much of it in concrete and high rise hotels. By comparison with the often tawdry package hotels which are so prevalent here, over the past decade or so, many luxurious holiday complexes have sprung up, often very close to the dozens of golf courses that dot the coast, giving rise to a new nickname, the Costa del Golf.

- **Information:** ☎952 126 279. www.visitacostadelsol.com.
- ▶ **Orient Yourself:** The Málaga coast stretches from Sotogrande to Torremolinos, southwest of Málaga. The Serranía de Ronda mountain range protects the coast from weather inland. The A 7-N340 is the main coastal highway.
- **Don't Miss:** Marbella, Puerto Banús, old town Estepona, Casares.
- **Organising Your Time:** Allow at least a week.
- **Especially for Kids:** Sea Life Centre at Benalmádena, Fuengirola Zoo, Selwo Aventura park.
- **Also See:** ALGECIRAS, RONDA (50km/31mi N of San Pedro de Alcántara), MÁLAGA (9km/5.5mi NE of Torremolinos), ANTEQUERA (55km/34mi N of Málaga).

Torremolinos to Sotogrande

234km/146mi- allow two days.

Torremolinos

Torremolinos has experienced phenomenal growth since it first attracted artists in the 1950s. Traditional architecture has given way to high -rise hotels and tourist complexes for visitors attracted by the sunny climate, miles and miles of beaches, and endless choice of leisure activities. The **calle de San Miguel** is the commercial hub, but it's also here that you'll find the last of the windmills for which the town was named. The **paseo Marítimo**, an attractive tree-lined promenade along the beach, boasts dozens of restaurants. **Pueblo Andaluz** is a new district of old-looking bars and cafés.

Playa de la Carihuela, Torremolinos

Address Book

⏲For coin ranges, see the Legend on cover flap.

TOURIST OFFICES

Benalmádena – *Avenida Antonio Machado, 10, Benalmádena Costa.* ☎952 44 24 94. www.benalmadena. com/turismo.

Estepona – *Avenida San Lorenzo, 1.* ☎952 80 09 13. www.estepona.com.

Fuengirola – *Avenida Jesús Santos Rein, 6.* ☎952 46 76 25. www.fuengirola.org.

Marbella – *Plaza de los Naranjos.* ☎952 82 35 50. www.pgb.es/marbella.

Torremolinos – *Plaza Blas Infante, 1.* ☎952 37 95 12.

GETTING THERE AND AROUND

AIRPORT

The Costa del Sol is served by Málaga airport, 9km/6mi west of Málaga. ☎902 404 704. www.aena.es. Buses and the suburban train line *(tren de cercanías)* serve coastal resorts, connecting with points as far as Fuengirola. A hired car is also a good choice, given the coastal sprawl and excellent roads.

TRAINS

Long-distance trains depart only from the Málaga station *(Explanada de la Estación;* ☎952 36 05 60; *RENFE office in Málaga.* ☎902 24 02 02).

Local trains operate every 30 min to Fuengirola via the airport, La Colina, Torremolinos and Benalmádena.

Benalmádena – *Avenida de la Estación* ☎952 12 80 84.

Fuengirola – *Avenida Juan Gómez "Juanito".* ☎952 47 85 40.

Marbella – *Calle Strachan, 2* ☎952 21 31 22.

Torremolinos – *Avenida de la Estación* ☎952 12 80 85.

INTER-CITY BUSES

The **Portillo** company operates comfortable buses to major towns and many points between. Every town or city also has a station for buses to Spanish and foreign destinations.

Benalmádena – Portillo bus routes connect the three parts of Benalmádena with Torremolinos from 7am–10.30pm. Tickets can be purchased on board or at the booth in avenida Antonio Machado (near McDonald's).

Estepona – *Avenida de España* ☎952 80 29 54.

Fuengirola – *Matías Sáenz de Tejada at calle Alfonso XIII.* ☎952 47 50 66.

Marbella – Buses depart from avenida Ricardo Soriano, 21 (☎952 77 21 92) to destinations in Spain and abroad.

TAXIS

Benalmádena	☎952 44 15 45/ 11 00
Estepona	☎952 80 29 00/ 04
Fuengirola	☎952 47 10 00
Marbella	☎952 77 44 88/ 00 53
San Pedro de Alcántara	☎952 77 44 88
Torremolinos	☎952 38 06 00

LOCAL BUSES

Málaga bus information. ☎922 36 72 00.

Benalmádena – A regular bus service operates between Benalmádena Costa, Benalmádena Pueblo and Arroyo de la Miel, stopping frequently en route.

Torremolinos – Two bus lines (L1 and L2) cover Torremolinos.

Fuengirola, Marbella and Estepona – There is no local bus service in these three resorts.

MARINAS

Every major resort has a marina for pleasure craft. The main ones are:

Puerto Banús – *6km/3.6mi from central Marbella* – 915 moorings for boats ranging from 8m/26ft to 50m/164ft. Puerto Banús, home to some of the world's most luxurious sailing craft, is one of the resort's most popular attractions.

Puerto Marina – This newer marina in Benalmádena is one of the largest moorings for pleasure craft on the Costa del Sol with a capacity for 1 000 boats. Other marinas are in Estepona, Marbella and Fuengirola.

J. Malburet/MICHELIN

Puerto Banús

WHERE TO STAY

Hostal El Pilar – *Plaza de las Flores, 10. Estepona.* ☎*952 80 00 18. www. hostalelpilar.es. 20 rooms.* Time seems to have stood still in this pretty Andalusian house on Estepona's main square, with black and white family photos on the walls and an imposing staircase leading to the basic but pleasant bedrooms.

Hostal Guadalupe – *Calle Peligro, 15. Torremolinos* ☎*952 38 19 37. www. hostalguadalupe.com. 10 rooms.* A pensión in a narrow street just 50m/55yd from the beach. Basic, but spotless rooms. Rates rise to 🍽🍽 in August.

Mediterráneo Carihuela Hotel – *Calle Carmen, 43, Torremolinos.* ☎*952 38 14 52. www.usuarios.lycos. es/hotelmediterraneo. 33 rooms.* Modern hotel located in one of the liveliest and more attractive parts of Torremolinos right on the beach. Modest rooms, some with terraces overlooking the promenade.

Hotel Lima – *Avenida Antonio Belón, 2.* ☎*952 77 05 00. http://hotel limamarbella.com. 64 rooms.* Comfortable and smart hotel, just 60m from the beach and 100m from Marbella's old quarter. Good value.

Hotel La Fonda – *Calle Santo Domingo, 7. Benalmádena.* ☎*952 56 83 24. www.fondahotel.com. 26 rooms.* A charming traditionally-styled hotel (designed by the great Lanzarote artist and architect César Manrique) in the Sierra de Castillejos, overlooking the Mediterranean. Spacious rooms, indoor pool, patios and terraces with views of the hills and sea.

Hotel La Morada Más Hermosa – *Montenebros, 16 (old town), Marbella.* ☎*952 92 44 67. www.lamorada mashermosa.com. 6 rooms.* A delightful little boutique hotel personalized with arts and crafts on a lane bursting with plants. Charming rooms are individually decorated in country Andalusian style. Room no 2 has a pleasant terrace, room no 5 a wooden canopy.

Tropicana – *Calle Trópico, 6 – Torremolinos.* ☎*952 38 66 00. www. hotel-tropicana.net. 84 rooms.* A quality hotel in an excellent location on Carihuela Beach, with local architecture, private beach, swimming pool with garden and a good restaurant (Mango).

La Carihuela

Hotel El Fuerte – *Avenida El Fuerte, Marbella.* ☎*952 86 15 00. www. fuertehoteles.com. 233 rooms, 2 suites.* Luxury modern beachside hotel, renovated in 2007, with two pools in tropical gardens and many other leisure facilities, a few minutes stroll from Marbella's old quarter.

WHERE TO EAT

La Carihuela, the more Hispanic part of **Torremolinos**, has dozens of bars and restaurants, as well as shops and hotels. Outstanding restaurants include **Casa Juan** for seafood and **El Roqueo**, a classic with a sea-view terrace.

El Balcón de la Virgen – *Calle Remedios, 2 (old town), Marbella.* ☎*952 77 60 92 92. www.hosteleriamalaga.com/ elbalcondelavirgen. Open for dinner only. Closed Sun.* In an attractive street chock-a-block with places to eat, the image of the Virgin Mary beckons customers to this pretty, traditional restaurant serving good honest Andalusian cuisine.

Casa Eladio – *Virgen de los Dolores, 6 (old town). Marbella.* ☎*95 277 00 83. Closed Thu.* A longstanding family-run restaurant, serving real Spanish cooking at a reasonable price. Cool off with their *ajo blanco* (cold garlic and almond soup).

Los Rosales – *Damas, 12. Estepona.* ☎*952 79 29 45. www.infhos. com/losrosales. Closed Nov.* In an alley by the picturesque plaza de las Flores, this unpretentious seafood restaurant also has a good tapas bar.

TAPAS

Altamirano – *Plaza Altamirano, 3. Marbella.* ☎*952 82 49 32. Closed Wed.* This local restaurant on a small square in the

B. Kaufmann/MICHELIN

Plaza de los Naranjos, Marbella

old quarter specialises in fish and seafood. *Azulejo* decoration on the façade.

La Rada – *Avenida de España and calle Caridad, Neptuno bldg, Estepona.* ☎*952 79 10 36.* A pleasant atmosphere and delicious fish and seafood. Highly recommended.

La Venencia – *Avenida Miguel Cano, 15. Marbella.* ☎*952 85 79 13. www.bodegas lavenencia.com.* A small tapas chain with three branches in Marbella, this one is close to the sea with barrel tables on the pavement. Always busy.

GOING OUT

BENALMÁDENA

Nightlife centres on the Puerto Marina and nearby plaza Solymar. Bars in plaza de la Mezquita de Arroyo de la Miel are also popular, although the marina and port area are mainstays, attracting visitors 24 hours a day. Benalmádena has its own casino, the **Casino Torrequebrada** (☎*952 44 60 00, www. casinotorrequebrada.com*), as well as the **Tívoli World** amusement and show park in the Arroyo de la Miel district (⊙*open year round, Apr–Dec daily, see website for days and times.* ☞€*6.* ☎*952 57 70 16, www.tivolicostadelsol.com*) which in summer features concerts by major artists.

Maracas – *Puerto Marina.* ☎*649 88 11 32. www.maracas-bar.es.* This spacious, multi-functional bar with tropical decor in the port area is popular for a coffee on the terrace, a cocktail or for dancing until dawn.

Monet – *Puerto Marina.* A café by day and disco-pub by night. Views of the port and a large terrace with wicker chairs. A pleasant location for an early-evening drink. At night, drinks are served at the two bars, one outside, the other indoors, with dancing.

Tabú – *Puerto Marina.* Café, bar and disco set on the marina with Caribbean-inspired decoration and a huge choice of fruit juices and cocktails popular with young and old alike. Salsa classes.

Disco Kiu – *Plaza Solymar, Benalmá dena Costa. www.discotecakiu.com.* An enormous 80s-style nightclub with various rooms devoted to salsa, mainstream pop and house. Popular with a young international crowd.

ESTEPONA

Calle Real, in the town centre, and the **Puerto Deportivo** (marina) are the main centres of activity when the sun goes down. In the late afternoon and evening the port is pleasant for a quiet drink on one of the many terraces. Later, the action tends to move to the bars on calle Real, then on to harbourside bars in the early hours.

Pop and rock concerts are organised on the beach in summer.

Jazz Pub – *Puerto Deportivo (marina), Control Tower.* A quiet, welcoming bar with comfortable chairs and a pleasant terrace popular with an older crowd. An excellent cocktail list and intimate concerts on Friday and Sunday evenings.

Melody Cool – *Calle Real, 25.* This small bar with a spectacular, futuristic design attracts an eclectic young crowd. An excellent bar list, including a range of beers, coffees and cocktails.

Chico Diez – *Puerto Deportivo (marina), no. 27.* Attracts a more varied age group.

Ático – *Puerto Deportivo (marina), upper level.* Another place to be seen.

FUENGIROLA

Plaza de la Constitución is the heart of, the nightlife here. Nearby, calle Miguel de Cervantes, calle Emancipación and the Paseo Marítimo Rey de España are also popular areas.

Between July and September the town organises many activities, including art shows, concerts and theatre.

Café La Plaza – *Plaza de la Constitución, 9.* The La Plaza café is in a traditional house on the main square. Pleasant decor and a mixed clientele of all ages.

El Piso – *Avenida Conde de San Isidro, 24 (entrance on calle Estación)*. Cosy arm ambience and old-style decoration with Flamenco and Latin music nights.

Mahama – *On the ring road, in Mijas Costa*. Discoteca Mahama is laid out in Andalusian style out around a patio with greenery and fountains, quiet areas, an enormous dance floor, and an all-night grill. Locals of all ages drop in, getting younger as the night ages.

MARBELLA

The queen of the Costa del Sol, Marbella buzzes all year-round. Marbella's teenagers hang out near the **marina** *(puerto deportivo)*. Trendiest and most lively is **Puerto Banús**, which caters to all ages and tastes. Some of the best-known night-spots, however, are along the main coast road *(autovía)*.

Sinatra Bar – *Puerto Banús*. Long-established bar with a pleasant terrace and front-row marina views, popular with foreigners under 40. Good for yacht-watching over drinks.

La Abadía – *Calle Pantaleón (by plaza de los Naranjos)*. Tucked away in a small, attractive alleyway in the pedestrian-ised old part of town, but worth the effort to find. The 20–35 crowd starts the night between midnight and 2am.

Suite del Mar – *Hotel Puente Romano, on the Cádiz road*. DJs play R&B, soul and Latin house.

Olivia Valère – *On the Istán road – Marbella*. www.oliviavalere.com. The most exclusive and luxurious venue on the Costa del Sol, themed as a Moorish palace, with patios, terraces and gardens offering a variety of atmospheres for a quiet drink or dinner. *The* place to be seen with the rich and famous.

Oh! Marbella – *Hotel Don Carlos, on the Cádiz road*. Stupendous dance floor, terrace with Mediterranean views, very popular with visitors.

As well as attracting high rollers the **Casino de Marbella** *(Hotel Andalucía Plaza, www.casinomarbella.com)* stages glitzy shows. For more highbrow nightlife and the performing arts, the **Auditorio** in Parque de la Constitución is a venue for concerts and theatre.

TORREMOLINOS

The town hall organises shows and concerts all year; check with the town hall *(ayuntamiento)* or tourist office. Most bars and nightclubs are in calle San Miguel, plaza Costa del Sol and ave-nida Palma de Mallorca, although locals and tourists head to the nearby marina (Puerto Marina) in Benalmádena, for a greater variety and more sophistication. There is a thriving gay and transvestite scene aound 'Calle Nogalera'.

Palladium – *Avenida Palma de Mallorca*. www.myspace.com/discopalladium. One of the biggest discotecas on the Costa, with its own swimming pool.

SHOPPING

Benalmádena

Benalmádena Costa, which includes the marina, has thebest choice of shops in Benalmádena. Look for crafts stalls in the narrow streets and small squares behind the marina. Avenida de Antonio Machado is also busy. In Arroyo de la Miel, calle de las Flores has more traditional shops.

A typical **market** selling a vast array of products is held Friday mornings in the car park of Tívoli Park; on Sundays, there's a second-hand market in the same place.

In Benalmádena Pueblo, look at the Casa del Artesano, in plaza de España, particularly on Saturdays.

Estepona

The main shopping street here is pedes-trianised calle Real, between avenida Juan Carlos I and calle Terraza.

A Wednesday morning **market** is held on avenida Juan Carlos, while craftsmen sell their wares on Sunday mornings by the marina.

Fuengirola

Most shops are on or near plaza de la Constitución, avenida Matías Sáenz de Tejada and Ramón y Cajal.

On Tuesdays, the showground *(recinto ferial)* is the setting for the largest **mar-ket** on the Costa del Sol. A flea market selling second-hand goods is held here on Saturday mornings.

MARBELLA

This is one of the best, if not the cheap-est places for shopping on the Costa del Sol. All the top brands are represented. Most high-end stores are in Puerto Banús, and in the centre of Marbella, along avenidas Ricardo Soriano and

Ramón y Cajal. The best shopping centre on the Costa del Sol is found in Puerto Banús.

Markets are part of Marbella life. The Monday market next to the football stadium and the Saturday morning market next to the Nueva Andalucía bullring (*plaza de toros,* near Puerto Banús) are large and varied.

TORREMOLINOS

Boutiques of all kind line the busy noisy pedestrianised calle San Miguel. Howeve there are some **traditional stores nearby**, such as the *pastelería* at calle Isabel Manoja, 4, founded in 1908, where local cakes *(tortas)* are sold. The Cuesta del Tajo, a hill with impressive sea views, features stalls of more traditional wares and souvenirs.
A Thursday morning **market** is held in El Calvario.

▶ *Head southeast along the N 340.*

Benalmádena

Just before Benalmádena Costa are the highrises of **Arroyo de la Miel**.
Benalmádena is a summer destination at the foot of the Sierra de Mijas, though it is busy with expatriates all year round. There are excellent beaches, golf courses, a marina and myriad restaurants, nightclubs, bars and cafés.
The main family attraction in the marina is the **Sea Life Centre** (Kids ○*open year-round daily from 10am;* ∞€11.95, child €8.95; ☎952 56 01 50, www.sealife europe.com) with over 3 000 denizens of the deep and a shark tunnel.
The **old quarter** (*casco antiguo*), a few kilometres inland, preserves the Andalusian charms of whitewashed houses and flower-decked windows. The **Museo Arqueológico** (○*open summer Tue–Sun 9.30am–1.30pm, 5pm–8pm; otherwise 9.30am–1.30pm, 4pm–7pm; Sun and public hols 10am–2pm.* ○*Closed Good Fri, 1 May;* ☎952 44 85 93) displays pre-Columbian artefacts; the 16C Torremuelle, Torrequebrada and Torrebermeja **watchtowers** can be visited.

▶ *Take the A 368 west for 8km/5mi.*

Mijas★ – *see MIJAS*

▶ *Follow the A 387 northeast to Alhaurín el Grande.*

Alhaurín el Grande

This elegant town lies on a hill in the Sierra de Mijas, amid market gardens, lemon and orange orchards and olive groves. The old quarter is a maze of cobbled streets lined by whitewashed houses. The **Arco del Cobertizo** is a Moorish gateway, and the **Ermita de la Vera Cruz** is an unusual 20C chapel built in neo-Gothic style.

▶ *Follow the A 366 northwest.*

Coín

Coín is situated amid citrus groves. Its massive 16C **Iglesia de San Juan** contains a fine Baroque altarpiece and colourful *azulejos* on the spandrels and cornice. Other churches include the 15C **Iglesia de Santa María de la Encarnación**, incorporating a minaret; the **Iglesia de San Andrés**, with its rich *artesonado* work; and the Iglesia del Santo Cristo de la Veracruz.

▶ *Return to Alhaurín el Grande.*
   Take the A 387 and then the A 3108.

Fuengirola

Fuengirola is another of the Costa del Sol's major resorts, with 7km/4.5mi of beaches, packed with hotels, restaurants and leisure facilities attracting visitors all year round.
The 10C **Castillo de Sohail**, with its merloned towers and original walls dominates the town from on high. The **Santa Fe de los Boliches** district includes **archaeological remains** – some 1C AD baths and the vestiges of a Roman villa – and the **Museo Abierto**, an outdoor gallery with murals by well-known artists (Sempere, Rafael Peinado, Elena Asins etc).
Fuengirola Zoo (Kids ○*open year-round daily from 10am, see website for closing time;* ∞€14.90, child €10.20; ☎952 666

Alhaurín el Grande

301, www.zoofuengirola.com) is one of the most popular visitor attractions on this part of the coast. It has an excellent record inbreeding and conserving endangered species. During July and August the zoo opens until midnight (and stages African dancing) so that visitors can discover the nocturnal life of its inhabitants.

▶ *Head along the A 7 to Marbella.*

Marbella★★
see MARBELLA

Excursion inland to Tolox
See MARBELLA

▶ *Return to the A 7 and head west.*

Puerto Banús★★
see MARBELLA

San Pedro de Alcántara
This old town was once populated by labourers from the cotton and sugar cane plantations owned by the Marqués del Duero. Today, it is a large resort. Remains from the past include **Las Bóvedas** – unusual thermal baths with an octagonal floor plan and vaulted rooms – and the **Basílica de Vega del Mar**, a 6C palaeo-Christian temple containing tombs with valuable funerary objects. (*visit by guided tours only, 1hr 45min, Tue and Thu at noon, reservations recommended; ☎952 78 13 60).*

A winding **road**★★ links San Pedro de Alcántara with **Ronda**★★ (*see RONDA).*

▶ *Head north along the A 6205.*

Benahavís
This inland village is on the banks of the River Guadalmina, close to the impressive Las Angosturas Canyon *(cañón).* The remains of the Castillo de Montemayor, and several old watchtowers recall its Moorish origins. Benahavís has an extraordinary number of restaurants for a village its size, many of which are British-run.

▶ *Return to San Pedro de Alcántara and continue southwest along the A 7.*

Estepona
Estepona, at the foot of the Sierra Bermeja range, is one of the Costa del Sol's major resort areas. Its hotels and beaches stretch for 20km/12mi. The marina has a capacity of 900 boats, and there are a golf course, a scuba-diving centre, and the usual nightclubs and boutiques. There are watchtowers from the 15C and 16C are along the coast near town.

Old quarter★
Despite modern encroachments, this district preserves the charm of an Andalusian village; its narrow streets are lined by whitewashed houses adorned with wrought-iron balconies decked

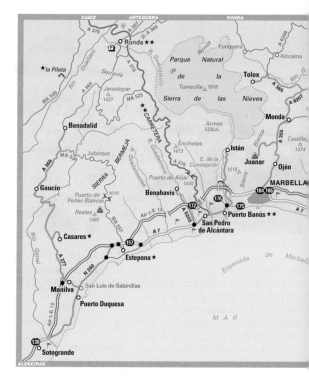

in flowers. The picturesque **plaza de las Flores**★ is one of Estepona's most famous sights.

Its **castle ruins** include two towers, the Torre del Reloj and El Vigía.

On Safari in Selwo

In **Selwo Aventura** park open-sided lorries takes visitors on safari into the hills above Estepona spotting rhinos, giraffes, zebras, lions, tigers and many other African and Asian creatures transported here to roam freely in very large enclosures.

Elsewhere in the park is a range of adventure sports to try out.

Autovía Costa del Sol, km 162,5 Las Lomas del Mont; ⏰ open mid-Feb–Oct daily from 10am, see website for Winter hours and all closing times; €23.15, child €16; ☎902 19 04 82, www.selwo.es.

Iglesia de Nuestra Señora de los Remedios

The 18C Church of Our Lady of Remedies highlights colonial influence. Part of an ex- Franciscan convent, it has three aisles separated by semicircular arches on pilasters. Its most outstanding feature is its Baroque **portal**★★, with unusual decoration representing the sun, the moon and the stars. The church is crowned by a tower in four sections, with a pyramidal ceramic spire.

Plaza de Toros

Estepona's bullring is unusual in as much as it is asymmetrical.

▷ *Take the N 340 to San Luis de Sabinillas, then bear left onto the A 377.*

Manilva

Hillside Manilva, surrounded by vineyards, is just a few kilometres from the Mediterranean. The 18C **Iglesia de Santa Ana**, has an unusual arch over the portal.

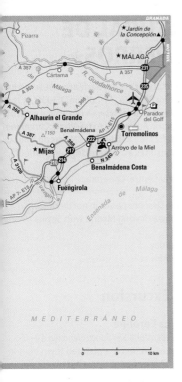

The main attractions of this area of natural beauty in the hills behind Estepona are the reddish rock formations and the Spanish fir – a tree only found in Andalucía. To get to the park, follow the MA 557 towards Jubrique.

ish fortress stand above the old quarter stand alongside the 16C Iglesia de la Encarnación, badly damaged during the Spanish Civil War.

▶ *Return to the A 377 and continue north.*

Gaucín
The whitewashed houses and narrow streets of pretty Gaucín, another of the region's classic *pueblo blancos,* lie on a rocky hill in the heart of the Serranía de Ronda. The **views**★ from the remains of the old castle are particularly spectacular. Gaucín is well known for its unfermented grape juice *(mosto)* and its *aguardiente,* a fiery brandy.

Benadalid
12km/8mi northeast along A 369.
This village in the shelter of a rocky outcrop is surrounded by olive and almond groves. *Azulejos* along the streets narrate anecdotes of local history. A Moorish fortress, in ruins, has its three flat cylindrical towers.

▶ *Return to San Luis de Sabinillas and rejoin the N 340.*

Puerto Duquesa
2km/1.2mi south. This lively marina teems with bars, restaurants and outdoor terraces. Nearby is the sober Castillo de Sabinillas (castle).

Sotogrande
These luxury housing complexes and elegant homes are next to the famous Real Club de Golf Sotogrande, often voted among the top ten golf courses in Europe, and which has hosted the prestigious Ryder Cup tournament.

Beaches to the south include Playa de la Paloma, Playa del Salto de la Mora and Playa Negra between San Luis de Sabinillas and **Puerto Duquesa**.

▶ *Continue north along the A 377, then bear right onto the MA 546.*

Casares★
The houses in this small settlement seem suspended above a promontory in the Sierra Crestenilla. The **approach**★★ to the village is stunning and this classic *pueblo blanco* vista is one of the most photographed sites in all Spain. Casares was one of the last mountain strongholds of the Moors in Málaga province. The birthplace of Andalusian nationalist **Blas Infante** (1855–1936), is at no 51, calle Carrera.
The old **Moorish quarter**★ retains its labyrinthine plan and low houses with reddish-coloured roofs. The 17C Iglesia de San Sebastián with an elegant Baroque tower stands by the plaza de España. The remains of a former Moor-

PARQUE NATURAL DE DESPEÑAPERROS★

This natural gateway to Andalucía is a spectacular gorge (desfiladero) carved by the River Despeñaperros through the Sierra Morena. At 1 000m/3 300ft, it is a superb belvedere from which to enjoy magnificent views★★★ of vertical walls of slate and the deep precipices that cut the park. According to tradition, Christians threw the defeated Moors into the ravine after the Battle of Las Navas de Tolosa, hence its unusual name (despeñaperros translates as "where dogs are hurled").

- **Information:** Puerta de Andalucía Visitor Centre. Carretera N-IV, km 257, Santa Elena, Jaén. ☎953 66 43 07.
- **Orient Yourself:** The Parque Natural de Despeñaperros in northern Jaén province is reached by the A 4 – E 5 highway linking Madrid with Sevilla and Córdoba.
- **Organising Your Time:** Allow at least a day.
- **Also See:** LINARES, ÚBEDA, ANDÚJAR, JAÉN.

Visit

The best way to enjoy the impressive natural beauty of the park is to follow planned **itineraries** by car or on foot, available from the Visitor Centre.
The 6 000ha/14 800 acre park includes oak (holm, cork and gall) forest and umbrella pine, rising above a dense arbutus, mastic and myrtle under-growth. This is an exceptional habitat for wolf, lynx, stone marten, genet, deer and wild boar, griffon vulture and the spectacular imperial eagle. The route from Arroyo del Rey passes through a landscape of vertical drops and strange formations created by erosion, such as "Los Órganos", where the rocks resemble gigantic organ pipes.

Santa Elena

This small town is the starting point for a number of excursions.
Local sights include the **Collado de los Jardines** (5km/3mi N towards Aldeaque-mada), an ancient Iberian holy sanctu-ary, and the **Cueva de los Muñecos** (3km/2mi W towards Miranda de Rey), a cave with impressive wall paintings of animals. The **Paraje Natural de la Cascada de Cimbarra**, 4km/2.5mi NW, is famous for its spectacular waterfalls (cascadas) and the canyons (gargantas) of the River Guarrizas.

Excursion

La Carolina
10km/6mi S of Santa Elena via A 4 – E 5.
La Carolina is a planned town built in 1767 by Carlos III in a bid to repopulate the Sierra Morena.

Iglesia de la Inmaculada Concepción
Open mid-Mar–Aug Mon–Sat from 8am, Sun and public hols from noon. ☎953 66 00 3.
The church is built above the vestiges of the Convento de La Peñuela, where St John of the Cross stayed. Its simple portal leads to an amply proportioned interior containing a fine 15C image of the Virgen de los Dolores (Virgin of Pain) and a Martyrdom of St Dominic, a work from the Ribera School.

Palacio del Intendente Olavide
This palace belonged to Don Pablo de Olavide, in charge of populating the area. The monumental neo-Classical façade bears the royal coat of arms.

Jail
The old jail (cárcel), a neo-Classical build-ing, is where General Rafael del Riego was held in 1820 before his execution in Madrid for leading a liberal revolt in Andalucía.

PARQUE NACIONAL DE DOÑANA★★★

Salt marshes, coastal dunes and dry, undulating scrub lands *(cotos)* combine in this exceptional park. A vast wetland, at its best in spring and autumn, it is a winter paradise for over 150 African and European birds. Apart from bird-watchers, Doñana attracts thousands to admire the contrasting landscapes of subtly moving sand dunes, marsh, and forests inhabited by lynx, deer, horses and wild boar.

- **Information:** ☎959 44 87 39, or ☎956 38 16 35. http://reddeparquesnacionales.mma.es/parques/donana. ♿ *see Visitor Centres below; the main one is El Acebuche.*
- ▶ **Orient Yourself:** The park encompasses the right bank of the River Guadalquivir between the provinces of Huelva and Sevilla.
- **Don't Forget:** Mosquito repellent.
- **Organising Your Time:** Allow at least a day.
- **Especially for Kids:** Spotting pink flamingoes.
- **Also See:** SANLÚCAR DE BARRAMEDA, JEREZ DE LA FRONTERA, El PUERTO DE SANTA MARÍA, El ROCÍO.

A Bit of History

Doñana is one of Europe's largest national parks, covering 73 000ha/180 400 acres. It is named for Doña Ana Gómez de Mendoza y Silva, wife of the seventh Duke of Medina Sidonia and the daughter of the famous Princess of Éboli, established a hunting reserve here in the 6C.

There are three **ecosystems**.

The 27 000ha/66 700 acres of **salt marshes** are the ideal habitat for wintering birds. Characteristics are a high salt content and unusual features such as **caños** (depressions formed by water), *lucios* (a permanent lagoon), *paciles* and *vetas* (mounds of land rising above water, favoured areas for saltwort).

The **sand dunes**, parallel to the Atlantic, are advancing at an alarming 6m/20ft per year. The land between dunes is known as a *corral*, while sand-levelled trees are *cruces* (crosses).

The **cotos**, originally hunting reserves, are dry, undulating areas covered with shrub sand aromatic plant such as

Aerial view of salt marshes in Parque Nacional de Doñana

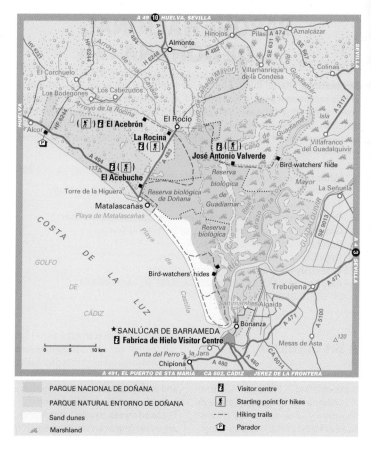

	PARQUE NACIONAL DE DOÑANA	🛈	Visitor centre
	PARQUE NATURAL ENTORNO DE DOÑANA	🚶	Starting point for hikes
	Sand dunes	---	Hiking trails
	Marshland	🅟	Parador

heather, rockrose, rosemary and thyme. Alongside these ecosystems is the **vera**, strips of land between woodlands and marshes.

Lagoons include Santa Olalla, a nesting place for ducks, geese and swans, and La Dulce, filled with crustaceans – tasty fayre for the park's pink flamingoes.

Parque Natural Entorno de Doñana – This nature reserve on the periphery of the national park covers 54 500ha/ 134 700 acres including the saltpans of Sanlúcar. Eucalyptus and pine predominate, though it does contain marshland and lagoons.

Visitor Centres

Entry to the park is rigorously controlled. Excursions into the park depart from *four visitor centres and last approximately 3hr 30min. It is advisable to book visits in advance.*

El Acebuche

🕐 *Open Jun–Sept daily 8am–9pm. Oct– Mar daily 8am–7pm.* ☎959 44 87 11. All reservations are handled here. There is an exhibition on the park's wetlands. Walks from this centre provide a closer look at the aquatic birds found in the lagoon.

La Rocina

🕐 *Open Jun–Sept daily 9am–9pm. Oct– May daily 9am–7pm.* ☎959 44 23 40. La Rocina is just a few kilometres from El Rocío, along the Almonte-Matalascañas road. It is the starting point of the popular **Charca de la Boca trail** *(14km/9mi)*, which leads to a various hides for birdwatching.

El Acebrón

Open Jun–Sept daily 9am–3pm, 4pm–9pm; Oct–May 9am–3pm, 4pm–7pm. ☎959 50 61 62.

This centre exhibits the "Man and Doñana" presentation on the evolution of the park and man's presence in it. The upper floor affords fine views. El Acebrón is the starting point of a 12km/8mi forest walk.

José Antonio Valverde

Open Jun–Sept daily 10.30am–7pm; Oct–May, 10.30am–6pm. ☎ 959 95 90 96.

This modern structure in the La Gallega section of Aznalcázar has large windows for bird observation.

Visit

On foot

Marked trails run from each information centre. Wardens will provide information on level of difficulty and duration.

By four-wheel drive

Book in advance. Two visits per day are organised, in the morning and mid-afternoon, with official park guides.

By horse

Horseback tours and horse-drawn carriages are available by arrangement, with optional picnic for groups.

By boat

From Sanlúcar de Barrameda (*see SANLÚCAR DE BARRAMEDA).*

ÉCIJA★

POPULATION: 37 113

The elegant Baroque churches, convents, palaces, mansions and soaring bell towers of Écija date from its economic peak in the 18C. Due to the fierce summer heat it endures, Écija bears the unwelcome nickname of "frying pan of Andalucía".

▪ **Information:** Plaza de España. ☎95 590 29 33. www.turismoecija.com.
▸ **Orient Yourself:** Écija lies on the River Genil, between Córdoba (53km/33mi NE) and Sevilla (85km/53mi W), on the A 4-E 5 highway.
◔ **Organising Your Time:** Take at least half a day to discover Écija on foot.
▣ **Parking:** Leave your car in the Plaza de España and visit on foot.
◔ **Also See:** OSUNA (34km/21mi S), ESTEPA (38km/24mi SE), MARCHENA (38.5km/21mi SW), CARMONA (53km/33mi W), SEVILLA, PALMA DEL RÍO (29km/18mi NW), CÓRDOBA.

Visit

▸ *Follow signs to the town centre (centro ciudad).*

Plaza de España

Called **El Salón** (The Drawing Room) by the locals, this is the hub of Écija. Do look into the **Iglesia de Santa Bárbara** to admire its impressive choir stalls); the **Convento de San Francisco**; and the town hall are also worth a visit.

Town Hall

The council chamber retains two **Roman mosaics★**. The 16C coffered wooden ceiling was transferred from the Convento de San Pablo y Santo Domingo.

Churches, Convents, Towers★

Torre de San Juan★

The beautiful Baroque 18C tower of the Church of St John is adorned with *azulejos.*

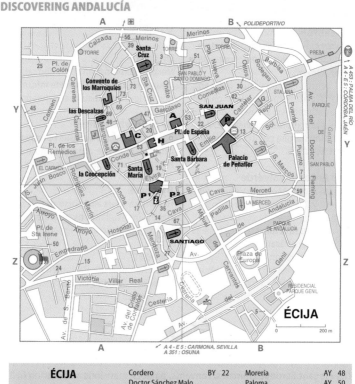

ÉCIJA

Iglesia de Santiago★

🕒*Open daily 10.30am–12.45pm (Sun 1pm) and 6pm–7.30pm.* ☎*954 83 05 88.*
The portal and tower of the Church of St James are Baroque; the remainder is Gothic-Mudéjar. Three harmoniously proportioned aisles have wooden ceilings, the apse has Gothic vaulting. The Gothic **retable**★ illustrates the Passion and Resurrection of Christ.

Iglesia de Santa María

🕒*Open Mon–Sat 10am–1pm, 6pm–9pm (Oct–Apr 5.30pm–7pm); Sun 10am–1pm only.* ☎ *954 83 04 30. www.iglesiade santamaria.org.*

This 18C church on plaza de Santa María has a handsome Baroque portal crowned by a large arch and a **tower** adorned with blue *azulejos*. Archaeological finds are displayed in the cloisters.

Convento de las Teresas

🕒*Open for mass only Mon–Sat 9am, Sun 9.30am.* ☎*954 83 02 95.*
This 14C–15C Mudéjar palace has a **portal** with *alfiz*, heraldic and rope decoration.

Iglesia de la Concepción

🕐 *Open by appointment Mon–Fri 10am–1pm.* ☎ *95 590 29 33.*

Simple, red-brick Renaissance doorway, fine Mudéjar-style *artesonado* work.

Iglesia de los Descalzos

⚷ *Closed for restoration.*

The sober exterior belies the exuberantly adorned **interior**★ of this church of this masterwork of Écija Baroque. Fine **stuccowork** adorns vaults and the cupola.

Convento de los Marroquíes

🕐 *Open for Mass only, daily 8.30am. Biscuits for sale 9am–1.30pm, 5pm–7pm.* ☎ *954 83 12 61.*

The convent is famous for its **belfry**★, and for *marroquíes,* biscuits baked and sold by the nuns.

Iglesia de Santa Cruz

🕐 *Open Mon–Sat 9am–1.30pm, 5pm–8pm (Oct–Apr 6pm–8pm); Sun 10am–1pm, 5pm–8pm (Oct–Apr 6pm–9pm).* ⊛€2 *(sacred art museum).* ☎ *954 83 06 13. www.museosantacruz.com.*

Note the remains of an earlier church, and **Renaissance tower**. The neo-Classical church holds a 13C image of the **Virgin of the Valley**, the patron saint of Écija, and a 5C **Christian sarcophagus**★. The museum exhibits 16–19C sacred art.

Palaces★

Palacio de Peñaflor

Calle Emilio Castelar.

⚷ *Closed for restoration.*

Now a cultural centre, the palace has a slightly curved **façade**★ with iron balcony and fresco decoration, and handsome pink marble doorway.

View of the town

©Turespaña

Palacio de Valdehermoso

Calle Caballeros.

⚷ *Closed to the general public.*

Note the column shafts on the lower section of the fine 16C **Plateresque façade**★. To the left, admire the view of the **Torre de San Juan**.

Palacio de Benamejí

Calle Cánovas del Castillo. 🕐 *Open Jun–Sept Tue–Sun 9am–2pm; Oct–May Tue–Fri 9.30am–1.30pm, 4.30pm–6.30pm (Sat–Sun 9am–2pm).* ⊛€1 *to go upstairs.* ☎ *955 90 29 19. http://museo.ecija.org.*

This elegant Baroque 18C brick-and-marble palace, now the **Museo Histórico Municipal**, comprises two storeys with curves throughout.

Palacio de los Marqueses de Santaella

Calle Ignacio de Soto (close to the Palacio de Benamejí). 🕐 *Private club; request permission for brief access to view entrance, stairs and dome.*

Past the entrance, above the staircase, is a magnificent **fresco-adorned cupola**★.

Festivals

September is the month for fiestas in Écija. On the 8th, there is a solemn procession in honour of the town's patron saint, the Virgen del Valle (Virgin of the Valley). The 21st is the Feria de San Mateo, celebrated with fiestas, bullfights, demonstrations of horsemanship etc. The Festival de Cante Jondo attracts leading flamenco performers.

ESTEPA
POPULATION:11 654

Lovely Estepa straddles the slopes of the Cerro de San Cristóbal (St Christopher's Hill) in Sevillian countryside, crowned by castle remains and Iglesia de Santa María de la Asunción; it was once the seat of the Knights of the Order of Santiago.

- ▤ **Information:** Calle Aguilar y Cano, 955 91 27 17.
- ▷ **Orient Yourself:** Estepa, on the slopes of the Sierra de Becerrero, is 116km/ 72mi east of Sevilla.
- ⊚ **Don't Miss:** The views from the Balcón de Andalucia.
- ◷ **Organising Your Time:** Allow half a day.
- ⚲ **Also See:** OSUNA, ÉCIJA, ANTEQUERA.

El Cerro★

Drive up to the Cerro de San Cristóbal.
The esplanade surrounded by pine trees is lined by several buildings of interest.

Walls
Moorish walls, rebuilt in the 13C by the Order of Santiago (St James), once circled the hill. Towers and sections remain.

Portal, Iglesia del Carmen
B. Kaufmann/MICHELIN

Keep
The massive square 14C *torre del homenaje* rises from the fortress ruins.

Iglesia de Santa María de la Asunción
Next to the castle ruins.
This 15–16C fortress church has wide buttresses and an unusual military-style tower. Nowadays, it is rarely used.

Balcón de Andalucía
The esplanade commands magnificent **views**★★ to the surrounding countryside and the town rising to the elegant Torre de la Victoria.

Convento de Santa Clara
This 16C brick-and-masonry convent, alongside the Iglesia de Santa María, houses an order of enclosed nuns. Note the heraldic decoration on the Baroque doorway.

The Town

Torre de la Victoria★
This handsome 18C tower is all that survives - its church and convent are now gone. Note the narrow charming, cobbled **calle Torralba**, its entrance, framed by an arch, heads off to the right of the tower.

Iglesia del Carmen★
Calle Mesones, next to plaza del Carmen.
This 18C church is a jewel of Andalusian Baroque, with an original stone- and-black-ceramic **portal**★ and fine belfry.

Casa-Palacio del Marqués de Cerverales

Calle Castillejos. Private residence.
Estepa's finest civil building was erected in the 18C. Solomonic and balustered columns, escutcheons and assorted figures adorn the doorway and main balcony. Bays are framed by pilasters, while the upper storey has a truncated pediment, decorated with a human face.
The **Iglesia de la Asunción**, to the right, holds some fine paintings.

Cakes and Pastries

Like many towns and villages in Andalucía, Estepa is renowned for its exquisite cakes with their traditional anise, sesame and almond flavourings, such as *polvorones*, *mantecados* and the yuletide treat, *dulces navideños*.

SIERRA DE LOS FILABRES ★

The Sierra de los Filabres range is renowned for its stark landscape, majestic natural formations, and some of Europe's clearest skies. The roads that wind among the quarries of Macael marble are accompanied by discarded blocks that imitate the mountains of this desolate landscape.

▶ **Orient Yourself:** The Sierra de los Filabres rises east of the Sierra Nevada and north of the Sierra Alhamilla.
◉ **Don't Miss:** The views from the road up to Calar Alto.
◷ **Organising Your Time:** Allow several hours for either of the drives.
◔ **Also See:** MOJÁCAR, SIERRA NEVADA, BAZA, GUADIX, GRANADA.

Driving Tours

The Land of Marble
79km/49mi – allow 3hr

Marble from these mountains was used to build the Alhambra in Granada, among other magnificent buildings. The town of **Macael** is the economic centre.

▶ *Head north from Macael along the AL 841 to Olula del Río. From here, follow the A 334 east, then turn right.*

Cantoria
A viewpoint at the entrance to this whitewashed village commands surrounding market gardens, orchards and olive groves. It's worth looking at the Casa del Marqués de la Romana, a noble mansion, and the Iglesia de Nuestra Señora del Carmen. The old railway station is unchanged since the last train chugged out in the 1980s.

In **Almanzora** (5.5km/3.4mi E) is the Palacio del Marqués de Almanzora, a noble residence arranged around a central patio.

▶ *Turn right towards Albánchez.*

Albánchez
11.5km/7.2mi S by the A 8200.
The whitewashed houses of this village climb the hillside amid a landscape of thyme, broom and anthyllis.
Beyond Albánchez, the road passes mountains and open-cast marble quarries to reach **Cóbdar**, popular with mountaineers who come to climb the marble rock known as Los Calares.
🚶 A pleasant 3km/1.8mi walk takes in an old mill and fortress *(follow a path parallel to the river at the exit to Cóbdar).*

▶ *From Cóbdar, head towards Alcudia de Monteagud, then turn right.*

Centro Astronómico Hispano Alemán

Calar Alto Astronomical Observatory

Chercos

This marble-quarrying village has an old quarter, known as El Soto.

Some 3km/1.8mi to the south is **Chercos Viejo**★ (P *leave your car at the entrance to the village*). Wander its cobbled lanes, under the remains of an old fortress *(alcazaba)*. Prehistoric carved stones have been discovered on the outskirts.

▷ *Head back along the road from Cóbdar to Alcudia de Monteagud.*

Alcudia de Monteagud retains 19C threshing floors and its old public washery.

Tahal

This well-kept whitewashed village dominated by the silhouette of its sturdy 15C Moorish castle is situated at the confluence of several ravines.

▷ *Return to Macael along A 349.*

The Blue Sky Road

Gérgal

Gérgal is situated on a fold of the Sierra de Los Filabres, some 50km/31mi to the north of Almería, and is crowned by a castle in a perfect state of repair.

To view the fortress from the outside (⊶ *private property – closed to visitors*), follow the road bearing right to Las Aneas upon exiting the village. The fortification comprises a square crenellated tower with smaller cylindrical turrets overlooking the whitewashed village at its feet.

The main feature of architectural interest in Gérgal is the **parish church**, with its Mudéjar *artesonado* ceiling in the main nave. The outlying area is particularly arid, in keeping with the rest of this part of the province.

The road up to Calar Alto★

Allow 1hr 30min excluding a visit to the Astronomical Observatory.
Follow the A 92 for 5km/3mi, then bear right onto the AL 871 for a further 26km/16mi to Calar Alto.

The road winds up through the Sierra de los Filabres to an altitude of 2 168m/7 111ft. Past Aulago, to the right of the road, no further villages are encountered. The arid landscape gradually gives way to an extensive planted pine woodland.

The superb **views**★ on both sides of the road encompass the city of Almería and Cabo de Gata to the south, the Sierra Alhamilla to the southeast, the Almanzora Valley to the north and the lofty peaks of the Sierra Nevada to the west.

On the summit of Calar Alto, the characteristic domes of an **astronomical observatory** can be seen (*open only to accredited astronomers by prior booking, www.caha.es*). The centre is the ideal location from which to observe the night skies as it claims to have the best visibility in Europe with over 200 cloud-free nights per year.

GRANADA★★★

POPULATION: 241 471

"Give him alms, woman, for there is no greater grief than to be blind in Granada."
This saying, inscribed in the Alhambra, evokes the beauty of this city, its delightful setting★★★ and its monuments, the jewel of which is the Alhambra itself, one of the most magnificent artistic creations of humankind.

Set in the garden plain watered by the rivers Genil and Darro, Granada rises onto the hills of the Albaicín, Sacromonte and Alhambra, Christian and modern below, Moorish above, in a perfect symbiosis of art and history, all beneath the snow-capped ridge of the Sierra Nevada.

- **Information:** Avenida del Generalife. ☎958 22 95 75. www.andalucia.org. www.turgranada.es.
- ▶ **Orient Yourself:** Granada is 139km/86mi northeast of Málaga.
- **Parking:** Driving is not recommended in Granada.
- **Don't Miss:** The Alhambra and the Generalife gardens; nighttime views of the illuminated Alhambra from the paseo de los Tristes; daytime views from the Mirador de San Nicolás; the mausoleums of the Catholic Monarchs in the Chapel Royal.
- ① **Organising Your Time:** Allow three days.
- **Especially for Kids:** Parque de las Ciencias.
- **Also See:** MONTEFRÍO, ALCALÁ LA REAL, SIERRA NEVADA, LAS ALPUJARRAS, GUADIX, ALMUÑÉCAR, JAÉN.

A Bit of History

Following early Iberian settlement, Romans founded Illiberis on the Albaicín hill. But the city was of little importance until the arrival of the Moors in the early 8C.

Moorish Granada – In 713, Tarik's troops conquered the city, which extended across the Alhambra and Albaicín hills. Granada became part of the Córdoban Caliphate, then, In 1013, it became the capital of a kingdom (taifa). The **Zirite dynasty** strengthened defences and built the El Bañuelo baths and a bridge, the Puente de Cadí.

In 1090, Granada fell to the **Almoravids**, then in the mid 12C to the **Almohads**. Despite frequent conflicts, the city underwent considerable development. Drainage and sewerage systems were built, and fortifications strengthened.

Nasrid kingdom – The ascendancy of the Nasrids in 1238 heralded the city's Golden Age. Mohammed ibn Nasar, the dynasty's founder, acknowledged his position as the vassal of Christian monarch Fernando II, ensuring stability and calm.

The kingdom at this time encompassed Almería and Málaga, and part of Cádiz, Sevilla, Córdoba and Jaén. Granada, prospered, expanded, and embellished itself. Yusuf I (1333–53) and Mohammed V (1353–91), under whose rule the Alhambra's Nasrid palaces were built, transformed Granada into one of the leading cities of the period.

The tears of Boabdil

Having handed over the keys to Granada, Boabdil, the last Nasrid king, began his journey into exile. At the place that has gone down in history with the name of The Moor's Sigh *(Suspiro del Moro)*, he stopped to cast a final glance at his beloved city, but was unable to hold back his tears. His mother is said to have turned on him: "You weep like a woman for what you could not hold as a man."

View of Albaicin district in Granada from Alhambra

The **15C** was marked by in-fighting. Territory was gradually yielded to the Christians. Following a long siege, the Catholic Monarchs took Granada on 2 January 1492, bringing to a close eight centuries of Moorish domination on the Iberian Peninsula.

Christian Granada – Under the Christians, the city's *morisco* population was concentrated on the Albaicín. By the end of the 15C the first conflict had broken out following the decree to force baptism upon Muslims. In 1568 rebel leader Abén Humeya, fled to the Alpujarras mountains, where he was subdued by Don Juan of Austria, on the orders of Felipe II. Following this episode, all *moriscos* were expelled from Granada. During the **16C** and **17C**, the city was transformed. The maze of Moorish lanes gave way to wider streets and spacious squares. The cathedral, Chapel Royal, Charles V's palace, Exchange, Royal Hospital, chancery and Carthusian monastery were built.

In the **18C**, and particularly the **19C**, Granada bewitched numerous visitors. Romanticism forged a new myth for a city long accustomed to praise. Its beauty, mysticism and exoticism became a literary theme for Victor Hugo, Alexandre Dumas and Washington Irving, who penned *Tales of the Alhambra*.

In the 19C Granada received unwelcome visitors.

The French sacked the city and even tried to raze the Alhambra, but only succeeded in destroying some towers and wall sections.

Granada today – The city is the capital of an agricultural and ranching province, busy all year round, with a lively atmosphere generated by the students of its respected university, and thousands of visitors. *Granadinos* believe that their city has the perfect location: on the doorstep of the Sierra Nevada with its sun-blessed ski slopes, just an hour's drive from the Mediterranean, offering the perfect escape in summer.

Fiestas and Festivals

Toma de Granada – The first important festival in the busy Granada calendar, on 2 January, commemorates Boabdil's surrender to the Catholic Monarchs. A procession climbs to the Alhambra, where the bell in the Torre de la Vela is rung. Tradition has it that young women who take part will be wed within the year.

San Cecilio – The day of St. Cecil (1 February), the city's patron, is celebrated by a pilgrimage *(romería)* to the Sacramonte district. Wine and broad beans *(habas)* are given out. It's also a time to sing, and dance traditional *sevillanas*.

Semana Santa – Granada's Holy Week is a time of restraint. Processions file along the steep, cobbled route. Valuable Baroque statues by masters such as Diego de Siloé and Pedro de Mena test the capacities of the *costaleros* (carriers), who kneel to squeeze floats into the cathedral.

Las Cruces de Mayo – Flower-decked crosses adorn streets in May.

Corpus Christi – Granada's annual *feria* is the biggest Corpus Christi celebration in Andalucia, with bullfights and amusements. Alongside it are the solemn Corpus Christi procession through streets carpeted in flowers.

Festivals – The calendar includes the International Theatre Festival (*May, Teatro Manuel de Falla*), the International Music and Dance Festival (*Jun–Jul, Alhambra; www.granadafestival.org*), and the International Jazz Festival (*Oct–Nov*).

Alhambra and Generalife★★★

Allow half a day.

⏍*There are only a limited number of tickets allocated per day. Purchase tickets in advance to avoid the possibility of not getting in, and the certainty of long lines, from any Caixa bank branch or online at www.alhambratickets.es. Or buy a Bono turístico pass (⏍see Address Book).*

🕐*Open Mar–Oct 8.30am–8pm (and 10–11.30pm Tue–Sat); Nov–Feb 8.30am–6pm (8am–9.30pm Fri–Sat). ⏍€12, garden only €6; ticket sale stops 1hr before last entry. Ticket for Alhambra and Generalife gardens specifies entry time to the Nasrid palaces. ☎958 22 09 12 or 902 44 12 21.* Access on foot is along cuesta de Gomérez, from plaza Nueva. Enter by the Puerta de Granadas (Pomegranate Gate, built by Machuca under Charles V), to reach the **shrubbery**★. If you are arriving by car, branch off from the Sierra Nevada road where signposted.

Alhambra★★★
The Calat Alhambra (Red Castle) is one of the most remarkable fortresses ever built and the finest Moorish palace still standing. It sits atop the highest hill in

©Turespaña

Alhambra

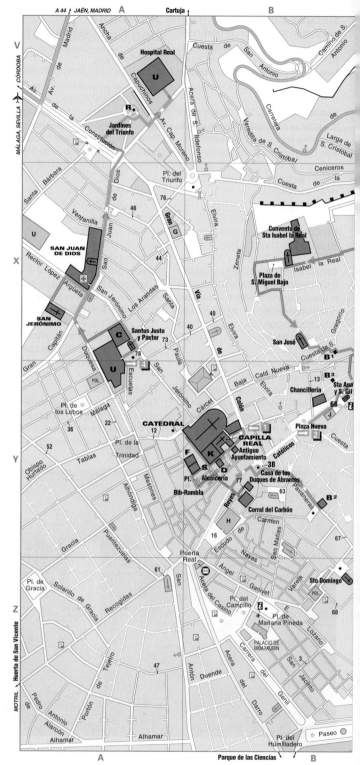

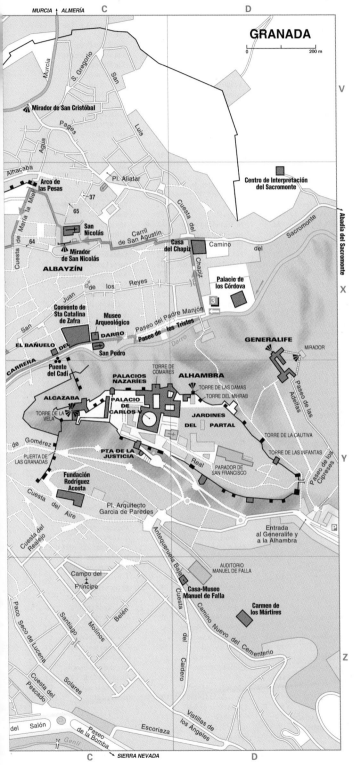

GRANADA

MURCIA ← ALMERÍA

0 — 200 m

Mirador de San Cristóbal

Centro de Interpretación del Sacromonte

Arco de las Pesas

San Nicolás

Mirador de San Nicolás

Casa del Chapiz

ALBAYZÍN

Palacio de los Córdova

Convento de Sta Catalina de Zafra

Museo Arqueológico

DARRO

GENERALIFE

MIRADOR

EL BAÑUELO

San Pedro

Puente del Cadí

PALACIOS NAZARÍES

TORRE DE COMARES

ALHAMBRA

TORRE DE LAS DAMAS

TORRE DEL MIHRAB

ALCAZABA

PALACIO DE CARLOS V

JARDINES DEL PARTAL

TORRE DE LA VELA

TORRE DE LA CAUTIVA

PTA DE LA JUSTICIA

TORRE DE LAS INFANTAS

PUERTA DE LAS GRANADAS

Real

PARADOR DE SAN FRANCISCO

Fundación Rodríguez Acosta

Pl. Arquitecto García de Paredes

Entrada al Generalife y a la Alhambra

Campo del Príncipe

AUDITORIO MANUEL DE FALLA

Casa-Museo Manuel de Falla

Carmen de los Mártires

del Salón

← SIERRA NEVADA

GRANADA

Address Book

♨ *For coin ranges, see the Legend on cover flap.*

GETTING THERE AND AROUND

Airport – The nearest international airport is Málaga. The airport bus Granada terminus is the convention centre (Palacio de Congresos, ☎958 27 86 77/ 958 13 13 09).

Trains – The station is on avenida de Andalucía (☎958 27 12 72). Service to the province and major Spanish cities.

RENFE (Spanish Rail) – *Calle Reyes*

Cars – Getting around by car is difficult, especially for those unfamiliar with local restrictions. Use public transport or taxis, or walk.

City buses – Buses serve all major monuments and suburbs. ☎900 71 09 00.

Bus station – *Carretera de Jaén* – ☎958 18 54 801. Service to Andalucía, Spanish cities and some European capitals.

The Sierra Nevada bus leaves from the Ventorrillo bar, paseo de Violón, by the la Virgen bridge (☎958 27 31 00).

Taxis. ☎958 15 14 61, 958 28 06 54.

Horse-drawn carriages – These can be hired near the Puerta Real.

WHERE TO STAY

◖◗🍺**Hotel Los Jerónimos** – *Calle Gran Capitán, 1.* ☎958 29 44 61. www.hotel osjeronimos.com. 30 rooms. Modern, minimalist, recently refurbished, good value, particularly in low season.

◖◗🍺 **Hotel Los Tilos** – *Plaza Bib-Rambla, 4.* ☎958 26 67 12. www.hotelos jeronimos.com. 30 rooms. Charmingly renovated hotel, clean lines, fresh bright colours and rustic touches. Terrace and views.

◖◗🍺**Hotel Maciá Plaza** – *Plaza Nueva, 4.* ☎958 22 75 36. www.macia hoteles.com. 44 rooms. Situated in a four-storey building on a central square at the foot of the Alhambra. Standard-quality rooms with wicker furniture.

◖◗🍺**Hotel América** – *Calle Real de la Alhambra, 53.* ☎958 22 74 71. www. hotelamericagranada.com. 17 rooms. Charming small family hotel superbly located within the Alhambra. Cosy and welcoming and characterful.

◖◗🍺**Hotel Palacio de Santa Inés** – *Cuesta de Santa Inés, 9.* ☎958 22 23 62. www.palaciosantaines.com. 35 rooms. 16C Mudéjar-style building in the Albaicín district, some rooms with Alhambra views, charming patio.

◖◗🍺**Carmen de Santa Inés** – *Placeta de Porras, 7.* ☎958 22 63 80. www.carmensantaines.com. 9 rooms. Albaicín Moorish villa. Elegant rooms, Alhambra views from the breakfast pergola.

◖◗🍺 **Parador de Granada** – *Alhambra.* ☎958 22 14 40. www.parador. es. 36 rooms. A magnificent example of an old parador, converted from the 15C Convento de San Francisco within the Alhambra grounds. Fine views of the Generalife gardens and Sierra Nevada.

WHERE TO EAT

◖◗🍺**Mariquilla** – *Calle Lope de Vega, 2.* ☎958 52 16 32. Closed Sun evening, Mon and mid-Jul–Aug. The Mariquilla is one of the best restaurants in the city, serving adventurous "market" cuisine. Cosy, with paintings of Granada.

◖◗🍺**Chikito** – *Plaza del Campillo, 9.* ☎958 22 36 64. www.restaurantechikito. com. Closed Wed. Reservations recommended. Hugely popular restaurant-bar. Artists and intellectuals such as García Lorca met here in the 1930s. Renowned for local specialities and its superb cured hams.

◖◗🍺**La Ermita en la Plaza de Toros** *Avenida Doctor Olóriz, 25 (at the bull-ring).* ☎958 29 02 57. www.ermitaplaza detoros.com. Unusual but very attractive and atmospheric setting within the bowels of the bullring: exposed brick, wooden tables, rustic chairs, bullfighting memorabilia… Restaurant upstairs, tapas bar on the ground floor, both serving typical Andalusian cuisine.

◖◗🍺 **Mirador de Morayma** – *Calle Pianista García Carrillo, 2.* ☎958 22 82 90 www.alqueriamorayma.com. Closed Sun Jul–Aug, Sun evening rest of year. One of the region's most romantic restaurants, with planted terrace, Alhambra views and rustic decor. Local specialities are broad beans with ham *(habas con* *jamón)* and lamb chops *(chuletas de cordero).*

🍽🍽🍽🍽 **Ruta del Veleta**, *Cenes de la Vega, Sierra Nevada, 8km/5mi from Granada.* ☎958 48 61 34. *www. rutadelveleta.com.* Elegant and popular, worth the trip, serving, fish, shellfish, game, according to the season. Don't miss the frozen rice pudding and warm chocolate sauce!

TAPAS

Bodegas Castañeda – *Almireceros, 1–3 (just off plaza Nueva).* ☎958 21 54 64. Patrons crowd into this typical *bodega* for a wide selection of delicious hot and cold tapas.

La Trastienda – *Placeta de Cuchilleros, 11.* ☎958 22 69 95. Descend a couple of steps to this 1836 grocery with tapas counter.

Casa Enrique – *Acera del Darro, 8.* ☎958 25 50 08. *Closed Sun.* This small 1870 tavern is a landmark meeting point in Granada. Fine wine cellar, delicious cheeses and cured hams.

TAKING A BREAK

El Tren – *Carril del Picón, 22.* This unusual café—a model train runs on suspended tracks here—is warm and friendly. Extensive choice of teas, coffees and cakes, varied clientele.

Café Central – *Elvira, 3 (plaza Nueva).* ☎958 22 48 98 – A classic Granada café on two levels, good for breakfast or a break, assorted coffees and teas.

La Fontana – *Carrera del Darro, 19.* Antique-adorned heritage house below the Alhambra, inviting, ideal for a quiet drink, coffee, or tea from an extensive menu.

Patio in Parador de Granada

Tea Houses – *Calderería Nueva* – Calle Calderería Nueva, between downtown and the Albaicín, transports you to an Arab souk full of *teterías* (Moorish tea houses). **Pervane**, for example, offers sweets, teas, coffees and shakes, while **Kasbah** has carpets and cushioned seating, befitting a Moorish guest. Find your own favourite…

GOING OUT

Granada has a good nightlife. Calle Pedro Antonio de Alarcón (popular with university students), and the carrera del Darro, close to the Alhambra and Albaicín district, attract a younger crowd.

Bohemia Jazz Café – *Calle Santa Teresa, 17.* ☎958 25 12 35 *www.andalucia jazz.com/bohemiajazzcafe.htm.* Perfect for a drink and chat to a jazz backdrop (the pianos are collectors' items) and live bands of course.

El Camborio – *Sacromonte, 47 (on Sacromonte hill).* For 30 years a leading nighttime haunt, four connecting cellars with danceable music for finishing the night. In a borderline neighbourhood, so best take a taxi.

Sala Príncipe – *Campo del Príncipe, 7.* ☎958 22 80 88. *www.salaprincipe.com.* This large fashionable venue hosts leading Spanish acts.

SHOWS

Granada's cultural traditions run deep. Events are programmed all year. Look out for first-class quality concerts at the Auditorio Manuel de Falla (www. manueldefalla.org). Shows and exhibitions are listed in the city's cultural guide available at tourist offices.

Flamenco: (👁*see the INTRODUCTION and the box at the end of GRANADA).*

SHOPPING

Granada's principal shopping area is along the main avenues in the city centre and in nearby pedestrian streets. Gran Vía de Colón, calle Reyes Católicos and calle Recogidas have a mix of traditional shops, modern boutiques and the occasional shopping centre, such as the Neptuno in calle Recogidas.

The former Moorish silk market, the Alcaicería, is a maze of alleyways in the same area, by the cathedral. Here you'll find souvenir and craft shops, in a Moorish atmosphere. Also in this part of the city, flower stalls add a delightful splash of colour to plaza de Bib-Rambla. Typical crafts of Granada include inlaid wood, particularly on small objects such as boxes and jewellery cases, and pottery. Examples of these can be found in the Alcaicería.

Every Sunday a **market** selling wares of every description is held at the Campo de la Feria on the carretera de Jaén.

Shopping in the Alcaicería

B. Kaufmann/MICHELIN

LOCAL SPECIALITIES

The Alcaicería has a number of pastry shops *(pastelerías)* selling *piononos*, the traditional delicacy of Granada. Pastelería Flor y Nata, in calle Reyes Católicos, is one of the very best.

SIGHTSEEING

Bonoturístico – This pass, valid for 5 days, includes the major sights, 9 trips on any municipal buses and minibuses and 1 day on the City Sightseeing tourist bus. It costs either €30 if you buy it on the same day from the Science Park, or the Audioguide kiosk in the city; "La Sabika (as the hill was called) is the crown on Granada's head... and the Alhambra is the ruby on the crown" wrote the poet Ibn Zamrak (1333–93). Visitors are spellbound by the splendour of its architecture which incorporates delightful gardens and running water into the overall plan, thus exemplifying a Koranic Eden like no other building. But its beauty is full of contradictions. Sumptuous appearances belie the poverty of the materials. It is also curious that not only should a power in decline build such a masterpiece but that the Alhambra would be so respected by its usurpers.

Plaza Nueva, or €32.50 if you buy it in advance online, by phone (902 100 095), or from either of the above places. You can either collect it from the Caja Granada in Plaza Isabel la Católica, from the Audioguide kiosk in Plaza Nueva, or from the Alhambra, but beware you might have to queue for some time if you pick it up from the Alhambra. When you buy your tickets, you also have to specify a time when you want to visit the Alhambra and Nazrid palaces. For more information, visit http://granadamap.com/bono.

Nasrid Palaces (Palacios Nazaríes)★★★

These palaces are the nucleus of the Alhambra. Nothing on their exterior presages their rich and original *mocárabe* vaults, domes, friezes and stuccowork.

The buildings are around three courtyards: the Patio del Cuarto Dorado (Courtyard of the Golden Room), the Patio de los Arrayanes (Myrtle Courtyard) and the Patio de los Leones (Lion Courtyard). The use of small interconnected passageways heightens the impact as one passes from one architectural masterpiece to the next.

The Mexuar

The tour begins in the rectangular **Mexuar**. Four columns support a stucco-adorned entablature. A frieze of *azulejos* and a calligraphic border cover the walls decorated with coats of arms. This room probably was a council chamber. Note

Key Dates

The most accepted chronology for the construction of the Alhambra and Generalife is as follows:
- late 12C: external walls;
- 14C: the Generalife, then the Nasrid palaces, built during the reigns of Yusuf I (1333–54) and Mohammed V (1354–59 and 1362–91).

Mirador de Lindaraja, Alhambra

B. Kaufmann/MICHELIN

the small oratory leading off the room to the rear.

Patio del Cuarto Dorado (1)
The magnificent south wall is a compendium of Nasrid art. This outstanding wall-façade comprises *azulejos* with geometric decoration, panels with vegetal features, calligraphic borders, a *mocárabe* frieze, a carved wood cornice and a large eave, all arranged around two doors and five windows.
Opposite is the Cuarto Dorado, with tiled panelling, fine stuccowork and a beautiful wooden ceiling. The **view**★ of the Albaicín from its windows is quite magnificent.

Patio de los Arrayanes
The entry to the Myrtle Courtyard is to the left of the south wall. This delightful patio has a long, narrow pool. A myrtle border reflects the mass of the **Torre de Comares**; the latter contrasts slender porticoes that give onto the **Sala de la Barca**, under a magnificent wooden vault with a quarter sphere at each end. Walls are adorned with the coats of arms of the Nasrids and calligraphy. This room leads to the **Salón de Embajadores** (Hall of Ambassadors), an audience chamber. The decoration

is exquisite: magnificent lustre *azulejo* panelling, delicate stucco with plant and geometric motifs, and calligraphic strips with religious and poetic inscriptions. The remarkable **dome**, above lattice-work windows, comprising over 8 000 pieces of multi-coloured wood, represents the seven heavens of the Koran. Lattice-covered niches on three sides allowing light to filter through.

Patio de los Leones
The justly famous Lion Courtyard dates from the reign of Mohammed V. The 11C fountain at its centre, supported by 12 rough stone lions, is surrounded by arcades of slender columns which lead to sumptuous state apartments. Two elegant pavilions on columns project over the sides of the courtyard.
The **Sala de los Abencerrajes** to the south is where the Abencerrajes were slaughtered and their heads piled in the fountain. The room has a stalactite ceiling and a splendid star-shaped lantern cupola illuminated by 16 windows.
The **Sala de los Reyes**, or Kings' Chamber, on the east side, comprises three square sections covered with *mocárabe* cupolas. The vaulting in the alcoves depicts pastimes of Moorish and Christian princes. It probably dates from the late 14C.
The **Sala de Dos Hermanas** (Hall of Two Sisters), is famed for a honeycomb cupola, and fine *azulejos* and stuccowork. A legend attributes its name to two sisters imprisoned within its walls. Beyond are the **Sala de los Ajimeces** and the **Mirador de Lindaraja**, both resplendent with stuccowork and honeycomb decoration. It looks onto the 16C Patio de Lindaraja.
A corridor passes the cupolas of the **Royal Baths** (*Baños Reales* to the left, only open certain days for conservation reasons, enquire at the tourist office). Continue to an open gallery with delightful **views**★ of the Albaicín; descend the stairs to the Patio de la Reja (2) and the Patio de Lindaraja.

▸ *Cross the Patio de Lindaraja to enter the Jardines del Partal.*

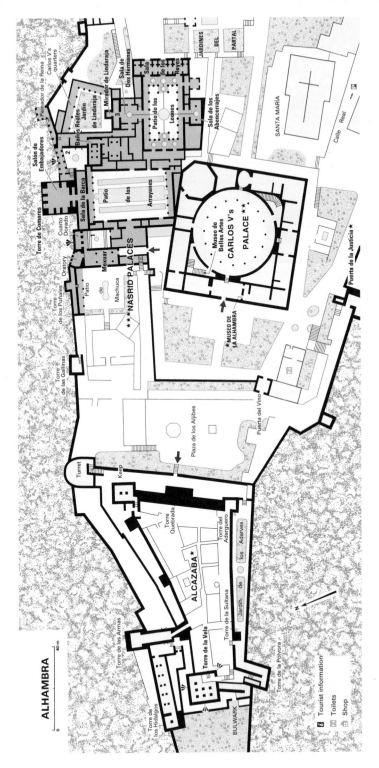

ALHAMBRA

0 — 40 m

Torre de los Hidalgos

Torre de las Armas

Torre de la Vela

BULWARK

Torre de la Pólvora

Torre de la Sultana

ALCAZABA ★

Jardín de los Adarves

Torre del Adarguero

Torre del Quebrada

Keep

Turret

Plaza de los Aljibes

Puerta del Vino

Peinador de la Reina

Carlos V's quarters

Mirador de Lindaraja

Sala de Dos Hermanas

Sala de los Reyes

Jardín de Lindaraja

Baños Reales

Patio de los Leones

Sala de los Abencerrajes

Salón de Embajadores

Sala de la Barca

Patio de los Arrayanes

Mexuar

Cuarto Dorado

Oratory

★ Torre de los Puñales

★★ NASRID PALACES

Torre de Comares

Torre de las Gallinas

Patio de Machuca

CARLOS V's PALACE ★★

Museo de Bellas Artes

★ MUSEO DE LA ALHAMBRA

SANTA MARÍA

JARDINES DEL PARTAL

Calle Real

Puerta de la Justicia ★

i Tourist information

🚻 Toilets

🏛 Shop

Torre de las Damas

Gardens and perimeter towers★★

To the east are the **Jardines del Partal**, terraced gardens which descend to towers punctuating the walls. The first is the **Torre de las Damas** (Ladies' Tower), built by Yusuf I at the beginning of the 14C, preceded by a graceful *artesonado* portico. The Torre del Mihrab and the former Nasrid mosque *(mezquita)* are to the right. The Torre de la Cautiva (Captive's Tower), also dating from the reign of Yusuf I, and the later Torre de las Infantas (Infantas' Tower), have sumptuous internal decoration.

Circular patio, Palacio de Carlos V

▶ *Enter the Palacio de Carlos V from the Jardines del Partal.*

Charles V's palace (Palacio de Carlos V)★★

Emperor Charles V commissioned **Pedro Machuca**, who had studied under Michelangelo to build this palace in 1526. The simplicity of its Classical plan – a circle in a square – and the harmony of its lines confer a majestic beauty.

On the main doorway of the lower level of dressed stone, note the medallions and superb bas-reliefs representing the triumph of peace (at the centre) and battles (to the side). The upper storey bears the escutcheon of Spain.

The outstanding feature is the **circular patio** (31m/102ft in diameter), fronted by Doric and Ionic (upper tier) columns. The patio's simplicity and its beautiful proportions combine to create a masterpiece of the Spanish Renaissance.

The palace contains two museums:

Museo de la Alhambra★

Entrance to the right of the vestibule.
This pleasant museum exhibits ceramics, wood carvings, panels of *azulejos* and *alicatados*, stuccowork, bronzes, fabric etc. Outstanding objects include a 10C ablutions basin, known as the Pila de Almanzor, decorated with lions and stags, the famous **blue** or **gazelle**

amphora★, a delicate 14C masterpiece, unusual ceramics representing animals, and replicas of household objects.

Museo de Bellas Artes
(Fine Arts Museum)

Entrance on the upper storey.

Paintings from the 15C and 16C include religious works by renowned artists such as Sánchez Cotán, Siloé, Alonso Cano and Pedro de Mena, and a magnificent still-life, *Thistle and Carrots★★*, by Sánchez Cotán, the equal of Zurbarán. 19C and 20C galleries contain works by Rodríguez Acosta, Muñoz Degrain, López Mezquita and Manuel Ángeles Ortiz, including more avant-garde exhibits.

Puerta del Vino

The Wine Gateway, built by Mohammed V, is purely monumental.

▷ *Pass through the gateway to reach the Alcazaba.*

Alcazaba★

To the left of the Plaza de los Aljibes (Cistern Court) stands the Alcazaba, the oldest part of the Alhambra, with its defensive walls. Three towers overlook the courtyard: the Torre del Adarguero, the Torre Quebrada and the Torre del Homenaje (keep). View the Alhambra wood from the Jardín de los Adarves on the south side. At the remains of the **Torre de la Vela** (Watchtower) the Catholic Monarchs first hoisted their flags. The tower provides a magnificent **panorama★★** of the palace, Granada and the Sierra Nevada. To the west are the **Torres Bermejas** (Red Towers). These were built in the late 8C and early 9C, and subsequently modified.

Love and Death

According to legend, it was by the Sultana's cypress tree that the wife of the sultan Boabdil and a leader from the rival Abencerraje family would meet. Upon hearing of these secret liaisons, the sultan ordered a massacre of the members of the Abencerraje family in the room of the palace that now bears their name.

Generalife gardens

B. Kaufmann/MICHELIN

Puerta de la Justicia★

Built by Yusuf I, the massive Justice Gateway is set in a tower in the outer walls. It comprises a large horseshoe arch and a wide strip of delightful *azulejos* with an image of the Virgin and Child from the 16C.

Generalife★★

The name Generalife name derives from *Yannat al-Arif*, possibly "most noble of gardens". Terraced **gardens** in which running water plays a predominant role surround a palace. An avenue of cypress trees leads to the new gardens and an auditorium – the setting for Granada's annual Festival of Music and Dance.

The central **Patio de la Acequia**, a long pool *(acequia)* lined with water jets, has a pavilion at either end. A *mirador* alongside affords superb views of the Alhambra. The Sala Regia in the rear pavilion (reached through a portico) has fine stuccowork.

The Patio de la Sultana, enclosed on one side by a 16C gallery, owes its names to the so-called **"Sultana's cypress tree"** (⌖ *see Box left*).

In the gardens above is the famous **escalera del agua**, or water staircase.

Exit the gardens by Paseo de las Adelfas (Oleander Avenue) and paseo de los Cipreses.

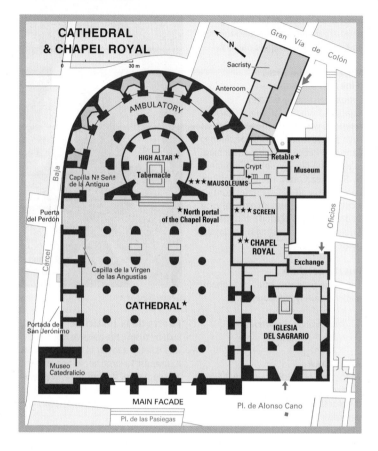

CATHEDRAL & CHAPEL ROYAL

Walking Tours

1 Cathedral Quarter ★★

Allow 2hrs.

Cathedral ★
Entrance on Gran Vía de Colón.
🕐*Open year round 10.45am–1.30pm, 4pm–8pm (Oct–Mar 7pm). Sun, afternoons only.* ⊂*€3.50.* ☎*958 22 29 59.*
Construction of the cathedral began at the centre of the Moorish city in 1518 and continued for almost two centuries. A Gothic cathedral (as at Toledo) was planned. But Diego Siloé, who replaced Enrique Egas as head of the project in 1528, introduced the Renaissance style to the building.

Interior
Enter by the ambulatory. Five lofty aisles lead to an ambulatory.

Enormous square pillars with engaged half columns support large sections of entablature, thereby considerably increasing the overall height. The vaulting above is Gothic.

The **high altar** ★ *(capilla mayor),* richly decorated, is circular and unusually high. The space above the vaulted arches, between chancel and ambulatory, was to house royal tombs; these niches were later covered by portraits of Doctors of the Church. The lower columns have ledges with statues of Apostles and saints, while the second tier contains seven paintings by Alonso Cano of scenes from the life of Mary. Note the **silver tabernacle** in the centre of the presbytery, and the pulpits at each side.

A large **main arch** linking the chapel with the aisles frames statues of the Catholic Monarchs at prayer by Pedro de Mena. Above are two medallions of Adam and Eve, by Alonso Cano. The 18C **organs** between the first two pillars are impressive.

The right transept arm opens to the **north portal of the Chapel Royal**★, dominated by a Gothic-style Virgin and Child, by Enrique Egas. Above, Fernando and Isabel's emblems, the yoke and arrow, flank their coat of arms.

To the left note the large altarpiece dedicated to St James on horseback, by Alonso de Mena.

The large marble retable in the **Capilla de la Virgen de las Angustias** (Chapel of the Virgin of Anguish) shows the Virgin with the dead Christ in her arms. The **Capilla de Nuestra Señora de la Antigua** contains a fine 15C statue of the Virgin and Child in a magnificent early-18C Baroque altarpiece by Pedro Duque Cornejo. The ambulatory contains an interesting collection of choir books from the 16C to 18C.

The small **Museo Catedralicio** (museum) exhibits silverware, tapestry, vestments, an image of the Virgin of Bethlehem, a bust of St Paul by Alonso Cano, and a bust of the Virgin and Child by Pedro de Mena.

In the **sacristy** is a delightful image of the Virgin, by Alonso Cano.

Exterior – Exit the cathedral onto calle Cárcel Baja, where there are two doorways by Siloé. On the lower section of the **Puerta del Perdón** (Pardon Doorway), Faith and Justice hold a tablet. Two magnificent royal escutcheons, of the Catholic Monarchs and Emperor Charles V, adorn the buttresses. The **Portada de San Jerónimo** (St Jerome portal) has a semicircular arch between Plateresque pilasters. The façade facing plaza de las Pasiegas was designed by Alonso Cano in 1667.

Madraza (Former University)

In calle Oficios, opposite the Chapel Royal.

The Madraza (Muslim university) was built in the 14C by Yusuf I. The Catholic Monarchs installed Granada's civil administration here. The Baroque

Cathedral
©Turespaña

façade, with adorning escutcheons, is from an 18C reconstruction. Across the inner patio, stands the Moorish **oratory**, an attractive hall of polychrome stuccowork, *mocárabe* decoration and an octagonal dome adorned with a lantern.

Capilla Real (Chapel Royal)★★

Open year-round Mon–Sat 10.30am–1pm, 4pm–7pm (Oct–Mar 3.30pm–6.30pm); Sun and public hols (all year) 11am–1pm, 3.30pm–6.30pm. Closed 2 Jan (morning), Good Fri and 12 Oct (morning). €3.50. ☎958 22 92 39.

Historic Place of Rest

The importance of the reign of the **Catholic Monarchs** cannot be underestimated, with their influence extending far beyond the Iberian Peninsula. This was particularly true of the discovery of America, to which they had given their financial and political support. Their marriage was also to have a determining effect on the history of Spain, by uniting the kingdoms of Castilla and Aragón into a political and geographical entity that would provide the basis for the future Spanish state and bring the country into the modern age. However, their reign is overshadowed by less glorious events, including the expulsion of Jews from the country and the establishment of the Spanish Inquisition.

16C screen by Master Bartolomé of Jaén in front of the chancel

akg-images/Bildarchiv Monheim

The Catholic Monarchs commissioned the Chapel Royal as their burial place. Enrique Egas began the project in 1506 and completed it 15 years later. It is a masterpiece of the Isabelline Gothic style, in its stylistic unity and ornamentation.

Outstanding **exterior** features are the fine pinnacles and elegant **cresting**. The lower section is adorned with the letters F and Y for Fernando and Ysabel. Access is via the old Lonja (Exchange).

The **Lonja** is a graceful 16C Plateresque building. Decorative columns support arches. The city's coat of arms is on the lower section. The upper floor gallery bears the emblems of the Catholic Monarchs and Charles V on the carved sills. The **interior** consists of a single nave with side chapels, and ribbed vaults. A blue fringe with a gilded inscription adorns the upper walls. Heraldic features on the walls and wrought-iron grilles are profuse. A spectacular 16C **screen**★★★ by Master Bartolomé of Jaén encloses the chancel. Note the escutcheon and yoke and arrow of Fernando and Isabel, and scenes of the life of Christ on the upper section.

The two double **mausoleums**★★★ in the chancel, one of the Catholic Monarchs, the other of their daughter, Juana la Loca (Joan the Mad), and her husband, Felipe el Hermoso (Philip the Handsome), are outstanding. The first, the work of Domenico Fancelli, was carved in Genoa in 1517 from Carrara marble, and is decorated with reliefs of Apostles and medallions. The second was carved by Bartolomé Ordóñez in 1519 on a pedestal decorated with religious scenes. The royal remains are in four simple coffins in the chapel's crypt.

The magnificent Plateresque **retable**★ with lifelike figures from the Gospels was sculpted by Felipe Vigarny between 1520 and 1522. The lower register of the predella depicts the siege of Granada. Note the statues of the Catholic Monarchs at prayer.

Museum

Access by the north arm of the transept.
Objects of priceless historical value include **Queen Isabel's sceptre and crown**, **King Fernando's sword**, plus an outstanding **collection of paintings**★★ by Flemish (Rogier van der Weyden, Memling), Italian (Perugino, Botticelli) and Spanish (Bartolomé Bermejo, Pedro Berruguete) artists. In the rear of the museum are the **Triptych of the Passion** by the Dirk Bouts and two sculptures of the Catholic Monarchs at prayer by Felipe Vigarny.

Centro de Arte José Guerrero

In calle Oficios.
This magnificent late 19C building is a centre of modern art. Its galleries show works by Spanish and foreign artists. The third floor is devoted to Granada painter José Guerrero (1914–1991), associated with the abstract movement in American art.

Curia

The doorway of this 16C Plateresque-style building is adorned with an archiepiscopal escutcheon. To the left is the simple **Palacio Arzobispal**, or Archbishop's Palace.

Iglesia del Sagrario

🕐*Open for worship only Mon–Sat 11am, 8pm; Sun and public hols 11.30am, 12.30pm, 1.30pm–7pm (8pm in summer).* ☎*958 22 85 74.*

This 18C church was built over the city's main mosque.

Plaza Bib-Rambla
This central square with its Neptune fountain is the setting for a number of colourful flower stalls.

Alcaicería
The restored area of the Moorish silk market, with winding alleyways, arches and oriental decoration, is now a centre for craft and souvenir shops.

Corral del Carbón
Open Mon–Fri 10.30am–1.30pm, 5pm–8pm; Sat 10am–2pm.
This 14C Moorish storehouse has a harmonious doorway with a horseshoe arch adorned with an *alfiz* surround and inscription. Two panels with *sebka* decoration flank the window. The doorway has *mocárabe* vaulting.

Casa de los Duques de Abrantes
In placeta Tovar, to the left of the Corral del Carbón. This 16C building has a simple Gothic-influenced doorway with heraldic decoration.

Plaza de Isabel la Católica
The Monument to the Santa Fe Agreement (1892) in this square, by Mariano Benlliure, shows Columbus presenting his plans to Queen Isabel.

Casa de los Tiros
This mid-16C palace has an unusual stone façade with five sculptures of figures in warrior dress. It houses a museum of 19C Granada. The Cuadra Dorada salon has a splendid Renaissance **artesonado ceiling**★ with famous figures in relief.

2 Carrera del Darro★
Allow 1hr.

This delightful street runs along the River Darro through an older, village-like area. Simple stone bridges providing access to Granada's legendary hills, the Alhambra and Albaicín. Start with a look at **plaza Nueva** and **plaza de Santa Ana**.

Chancillería
The former 16C chancery on plaza Nueva now houses Andalucía's High Court of Justice. The Classical façade combines elements that presage the Baroque. The balustrade is an 18C addition. The harmonious **patio**★ is attributed to Siloé.

Iglesia de Santa Ana y San Gil
Plaza de Santa Ana. This small 16C church was designed by Diego de Siloé. The bell tower has *azulejo* decoration. The nave and chancel have Mudéjar ceilings. A 16C fountain, the **Pilar del Toro**, attributed to Siloé, bears Granada's coat of arms.

▷ *Follow carrera del Darro.*

El Bañuelo★
Open Tue–Sat, 10am–2pm.
☎958 02 78 00.
The Moorish baths are opposite the ruins of 11C **Puente del Cadí** (bridge). Part of a tower and horseshoe arch remain. The 11C baths are some of the best preserved in Spain. Note star-pierced vaults with octagonal skylights. The arcades in the last two rooms have Roman, Caliphal and Visigothic capitals.

Convento de Santa Catalina de Zafra
This 16C convent has a Renaissance-type doorway with semicircular arch framed by pilasters and with medallions on the spandrels.

Casa Castril
The **archaeological museum** (*see Visit),* housed in the Casa Castril (1539), has a **Plateresque doorway**★, adorned with heraldic motifs, shells, animals, etc.

Iglesia de San Pedro
Opposite the museum. The 16C Church of St Peter is along the Darro under the Comares Tower *(torre).* The two portal sculptures are St Peter (holding the keys to Heaven), and St Paul.

Paseo de los Tristes
This avenue offers unforgettable night-time **views**★★ of the illuminated Alhambra rising above. Café terraces provide the perfect spectator seats.

③ Albaicín★★

Allow 2hrs.

This hilly district is Granada's most famous quarter and, offers magnificent views of the Alhambra at every turn. A maze of narrow alleyways wind up between the palisades of small Moorish-style villas known as *cármenes*, through delightful squares past picturesque street corners.

Palacio de los Córdova

At the foot of the Cuesta del Chapiz.
An avenue of cypress trees in the garden leads to the Municipal Archives, a palace with Renaissance doorway.

Casa del Chapiz

Entrance along camino de Sacromonte. ⏱ *Open Mon–Fri 8am–8pm (to 3pm Jun–Sept).* ☎*958 22 22 90.*
Now the School of Arabic Studies, this is a combination of two Moorish houses from the 15C and 16C, with patios and galleries. The gardens offer fine Alhambra **views**★.

▶ *Continue up along cuesta de San Agustín, between typical cármenes.*

Mirador de San Nicolás

This terrace in front of the **Iglesia de San Nicolás** enjoys magnificent **views**★★★ of the breathtaking ochre-coloured Alhambra and the outline of the Sierra Nevada.

▶ *Pass before the church; follow callejón de San Cecilio to the end, then turn right and continue through the Arco de las Pesas.*

Arco de las Pesas

This simple 11C arch alongside the pleasant plaza Larga was part of the walls of the old fortress. It has a typically Moorish structure with an angled entrance.

▶ *Return through the arch. From plaza de Minas, head along cuesta de María de la Miel, then turn right onto camino Nuevo de San Nicolás.*

Convento de Santa Isabel la Real

Enter this 16C monastery to admire the church's fine, pinnacled Gothic portal bearing the coat of arms and yoke and arrow emblems of the Catholic Monarchs.

Plaza de San Miguel Bajo

A Christ of the Lanterns stands here. Alongside is the church of San Miguel Bajo. Follow the street opposite the church. The lower town comes into view.

▶ *Turn left; left again on calle Bocanegra, then right along calle San José.*

Iglesia de San José

The 16C church incorporates a 10C minaret from a mosque as a bell tower.

▶ *Continue heading down, then look to the right immediately after some steps.*

Casa de Porras

This mansion has a simple stone doorway with heraldic decoration.
A delightful typical villa, the Carmen de los Cipreses (cypress trees), can be seen opposite. The trees that have given the house its name are visible from the street.

▶ *Descend cuesta del Granadillo and the extremely narrow cuesta Aceituneros to where you started.*

④ University to the Royal Hospital★

Allow 2hrs.

University

The Baroque seat of the university since the 18C is on plaza de la Universidad; the statue of founder Charles V is in the centre of the square. The building, with Solomonic columns, is now the Faculty of Law.

Iglesia de los Santos Justo y Pastor

The church on plaza de la Universidad once belonged to the Jesuits. Its

18C Baroque portal includes reliefs of St Francis Xavier and St Francis Borgia. The upper tier shows the conversion of St Paul. There are some fine wall paintings inside.

Colegio de San Bartolomé y Santiago

This college dates from 1621. To the left is the cupola of the Iglesia de los Santos Justo y Pastor. The elegant patio has slender Doric columns and basket-handle arches.

From the corner of calle de la Duquesa and Gran Capitán, admire the monumental **apse** in the church of the **Monasterio de San Jerónimo**★ *(entrance on López de Argueta; see Visit below)*. The **Hospital de San Juan de Dios** in calle San Juan de Dios was built between the 16C and 18C.

Iglesia de San Juan de Dios★

This is one of Granada's main Baroque churches, from the early 18C. On the **façade**★, between the bell towers, the lower niches hold images of archangels Gabriel and Raphael; the upper section features St. John of God, St. Ildefonsus, and St. Barbara. The **interior**, reached by a carved mahogany doorway, has a Latin-cross ground plan, elevated cupola, and chancel.

The massive Churrigueresque altarpiece is of gilded wood. The **camarín** (chapel) behind is accessed via a door to the right of the altar.

The middle of three lavishly ornamented rooms houses the tabernacle with the urn containing the remains of the saint – the founder of the Order of Hospitallers, who died in 1550. *(See under Visit, Casa de los Pisa).*

Monumento a la Inmaculada Concepción

This 17C monument to the Immaculate Conception stands in the **Jardines del Triunfo** (Triumph Gardens). The statue of a crowned Virgin Mary surrounded by beams of light is by Alonso de Mena.

Hospital Real

The 16C former Royal Hospital is now the university Rectorate, designed by Enrique Egas in the form of a cross in

*Detail of the façade,
Iglesia de San Juan de Dios*

a square with four patios. Plateresque windows adorn the upper storey. Note the yoke and arrows – emblems of the Catholic Monarchs – over the 17C marble doorway; above it a Virgin and Child is flanked by the statues of Fernando and Isabel. The sculptures are the work of Alonso de Mena. Stairs lead from the right-hand patio to the library *(biblioteca central)*, which has an open framework and a wooden coffered dome at its centre.

Visit

Monasterio de San Jerónimo★

Entrance on calle López Argüeta.
Open year-round 10am–1.30pm, 4pm–7.30pm; Nov–Mar 3pm–6.30pm). €3. 958 27 93 37.

Construction of the monastery, begun in 1496, involved two architects: Jacopo Fiorentino (Jacopo l'Indaco), until 1526, and Diego Siloé, afterward.

Note the **façade** of the church. The upper section shows the coats of arms of the Catholic Monarchs. A fine window is flanked by medallions and grotesque animals.

Plateresque and Renaissance doorways open onto the large **cloisters** completed in 1519 to plans principally by Diego de Siloe. The church wall has a Plateresque window and the magnificent escutcheon of El Gran Capitán.

Sacristy, La Cartuja

B. Kaufmann/MICHELIN

Church★★

Past the fine Siloé-designed **Plateresque doorway** are surprisingly rich interior elements: vaults and domes with high reliefs, a magnificent main retable and murals, an ensemble masterpiece of Spanish Renaissance architecture. Construction began during the Gothic period.

The transept and apse were completed under Siloé in Renaissance style. The widow of Gonzalo Fernández de Córdoba financed the building to create a mausoleum for her husband, El Gran Capitán.

The vault above the high altar depicts Christ accompanied by Apostles, angels and saints.

The large **retable**★★ of the Granadine School portrays God the Father above clouds on the crowning piece. Statues of El Gran Capitán and his wife at prayer are to the side; a simple stone slab marks the burial place of Don Gonzalo.

La Cartuja★

Open year-round daily 10am–1pm, 4pm–8pm (Nov–Mar 3pm–7pm). €3.50. ☎958 16 19 32.

Construction of the Carthusian monastery began early in the 16C. Enter the atrium through a Plateresque portal.

Church

The church is exuberant with Baroque stucco (1662) and paintings. The areas in the nave reserved for monks and lay brothers are separated by a gilded screen by Sánchez Cotán.

The Assumption, below the baldaquin, is by José de Mora. Behind is the overwhelmingly exuberant early 18C Baroque **sacrarium**, decorated by Francisco Hurtado.

Sacristy★★

This Baroque masterpiece (built 1727–1764) masks its structure in a sea of stucco, and cornices all arranged to create an extraordinary effect of light and shadow. Lanjarón marble is used extensively. The magnificent door and the cedarwood furnishings, inlaid with tortoiseshell, mother-of-pearl and silver, are by a Carthusian monk, José Manuel Vázquez.

Museo Arqueológico

Open Wed–Sat 9am–8.30pm, Tue 2.30pm–8.30pm, Sun 9am–2pm. €1.50 (free to EU citizens). ☎958 22 56 03.

The archaeological museum is in the Casa Castril (1539), a Renaissance palace with a fine **Plateresque doorway**★. It exhibits 9C BC Egyptian alabaster vases found in Almuñécar, numerous Roman artefacts and Moorish decorative objects.

Casa de los Pisa,
Museo de San Juan de Dios

Open Mon–Sat 10am–1pm. €2.50. ☎958 22 21 44.

In this house the La Pisa family cared for St. John of God, founder of the Order of Hospitallers, until his death in 1550. The museum displays paintings (by Alonso Cano and Flemish works), images, and silver and gold objects belonging to the order.

Fundación Rodríguez-Acosta★

Open Wed–Sun 10am–1.30pm. €4. ☎958 22 74 97.

The paintings of José María Rodríguez-Acosta (1886–1941) are shown in a Moorish-style house). The **museum**★ dedicated to archaeologist Manuel Gómez-Moreno exhibits his personal

Flamenco Caves

Many of Spain's finest flamenco singers, musicians and dancers have been of gypsy (*gitano*) stock. Consequently the cave dwellers of Sacromonte have turned their homes into flamenco nightspots for tourists but unfortunately over the years they have gained a very poor reputation for fleecing foreign visitors in particular. A reputable flamenco show in Sacromonte (on the Camino del Sacromonte) is the **Zambra Museo Flamenco** cave, also known as La Cueva de María "la Canastera" (*open Tue–Fri 4.30am–7pm; Sun and hols noon–2.30pm, 4.30pm–7pm; €1.80; 958 12 11 83, or 607 57 87 51; http://granadaocio.com/lacanastera). Flamenco show every night 10.30pm (around 1hr 15mins): €15, €21 (with transport).*

Another good place to catch authentic flamenco is **Peña Platería** (*Placeta de Toqueros, 7, Albaicín, 958 21 06 50, www.laplateria.org.es*).

---

collection: Romanesque and Gothic works, paintings by Zurbarán, Ribera, Alonso Cano and Chinese and Aztec artifacts.

Casa-Museo Manuel de Falla

Open Tue–Sun 10am–1.30pm. €3. 958 22 21 89.

Manuel de Falla (1876–1946), often called the greatest Spanish composer of the 20C, was a passionate admirer of Granada, which he only came to know after the age of 40. This 16C house, where he lived from 1919 to 1939, is unchanged.

Carmen de los Mártires

Open year-round Mon–Fri 10am–2pm, 4pm–6pm (5pm–7pm Oct–Mar); Sat–Sun and public hols 10am–6pm. Closed Aug. 958 22 79 53.

The Carmelite monastery is situated on the Alhambra hill. Terraced **gardens**★ are a beautiful setting for a stroll, with their Romantic 19C decor and views of the city.

Parque de las Ciencias★   Kids

Avda. del Mediterraneo.

Open Tue–Sat, 10am–7pm; Sun and public hols, 10am–3pm. Closed 1 Jan, 1 May, second half of Sept and 25 Dec. €5.50, child €4.50. Planetarium extra: €2.50, child €2. 958 13 19 00. www.parqueciencias.com.

This open-air complex features over 270 interactive stations spread out among two exhibition buildings, a Planetarium, Tropical Butterfly House, Observation Tower, e Astronomy Garden and more. There is a dedicated area for younger (3 to 7 year-old) explorers.

Huerta de San Vicente/ García Lorca Museum

Open Apr–Sept Tue–Sun 10am–12.30pm, 5pm–7.30pm; Jul–Aug 10am–2.30pm; Oct–Mar 10am–12.30pm, 4pm–6.30pm. Guided tours (30min), €3 (free on Wed, except in hols). 958 25 84 66.

This was the summer home of Federico García Lorca (1898–1936), one of the greatest Spanish poets and writers, conserved as it was during his life.

Sacromonte

Sacromonte hill rises alongside the Albaicín quarter, opposite the Generalife. **Flamenco shows** (*see Box*) are frequently staged in this gipsy district.

Abadía del Sacromonte

End of Camino del Sacromonte, bus no 34, then walk up the steep road.

Remains found here in the 16C were identified as those of Cecil, patron saint of Granada and an abbey was built in dedication. The museum here displays a lovely 15C Flemish panel of the **Virgin of the Rose**★ by Gerald David; a marble Calvary said to be by Alonso Cano as well as the **Libros plúmbeos** (leaden books), inscribed sheets found with St. Cecil. The **santas cuevas** (holy caves) contain a number of chapels.

Sacromonte Cave Museum

Barranco de los Negros. Buses 31 and 34. Open year-round daily 10am–2pm, 4pm–9pm (Nov–Mar 4pm–7pm). €4. 958 121 51 20.

This underground display is dedicated to the story and customs of the inhabitants of these peculiar local dwellings.

GUADIX

POPULATION: 20 322.

Guadix is perfectly framed by clay hills, with a backdrop of the **Sierra Nevada**. A forest of white chimneys poking up from an underground world gives a clue as to the secrets to be uncovered in its troglodyte dwellings.

Guadix sits at a crossroads between eastern and western Andalucía which has been settled by a succession of peoples. It reached its peak during Moorish rule; its fortress *(alcazaba)* survives from those days, though most buildings you will see today in the old quarter date from the 17C and 18C.

- **Information:** Avenida Mariana Pineda. ☎958 66 26 65. www.guadix.es. www.andalucia.org.
- ▶ **Orient Yourself:** Guadix is 57km/35mi northeast of Granada via the A 92. It is a handy starting point for visiting the Alpujarras, via Puerto de la Ragua, 30km/18mi southeast.
- **Don't Miss:** A night in a cave; the road to Purullena; the Ragua Pass; La Calahorra castle.
- **Organising Your Time:** Allow several hours, or even better a memorable cave night here.
- **Also See:** GRANADA, BAZA, SIERRA NEVADA, Las ALPUJARRAS.

Sights

Plaza de la Constitución
This pretty arcaded square dates from the 16C and 17C; along one of its sides stands the **town hall**, built at the beginning of the 17C during the reign of Felipe III.

Cathedral
Sq. de la Catedral
Open Apr–Sept Mon–Sat 10am–1.30pm and 4–6pm. Oct–Mar Mon–Fri 10.30am–1pm and 4–6pm. €3. ☎958 66 50 89.
Work began on the cathedral in 1597 to designs by **Diego de Siloé**, and continued until 1715. This is reflected inside, where the Gothic entrance aisles give way to an immense Renaissance dome adorned with a large lantern covering the false transept. The **Capilla de San Torcuato** (*second chapel to the left of the retrochoir*) was designed by Diego de Siloé. Its entrance arch is called a "bull's horn" because its width decreases as it curves. The **Fachada de la Encarnación**★ (*façade, facing the square*), exemplifies the theatricality and movement of Baroque architecture. Three horizontal registers increase in complexity as they converge.

Behind the cathedral, in calle Santa María, stand the 16C **Palacio Episcopal** (Bishop's Palace), the Hospital de la Caridad and **Palacio de Villalegre** (1592), which has an attractive Renaissance doorway flanked by two solid brick towers.

Barrio de Santiago★

This is one of the most characteristic districts with seigniorial mansions such as the **Palacio de Peñaflor** in which an unusual **balcony** decorated with wood can be seen. The mansion is built around a beautiful Renaissance patio. The seminary *(seminario menor)* next door provides access to the former Arab **alcazaba** (fortress) dating from the 11C. Although the fortress is in poor condition, a tour of it provides the best views of Guadix and the town's troglodyte district. ⚬—*Closed for restoration.* ☎958 66 93 00.

Back in calle Barradas, flights of steps lead to plazuela de Santiago. At the end of this small square is the **Iglesia de Santiago**, its lovely Plateresque **doorway**★ crowned with the shield of Charles V, recognisable by the two-headed eagle and the Golden Fleece. The Mudéjar ceiling inside is especially worthy of note. ⊙*Visits by prior arrangement.* ☎958 66 10 97/08 00.

Calle Ancha, which leads off this square, has a number of fine 19C seigniorial mansions.

Barrio de las Cuevas★

The cave district is situated in the highest part of Guadix, amid a landscape of streams, gullies and small brown hills. The caves are built on different levels,

The name Guadix

Originally known as **Acci** (hence the name *accitanos* given to modern residents of the Guadix), the name of this former Roman camp changed to the more poetic Guadh-Haix, which translates as "the river of life", during the period of Moorish occupation.

so that those dwellings hollowed into the side of hills often have their entrance on top of the roof of another cave. Solitary caves can occasionally be seen in an isolated location, occupying a single hillside.

Cueva-Museo de Costumbres Populares

⊙*Open year-round Mon–Fri 10am–2pm and 4–6pm (summer 5–7pm), Sat 10am–2pm.* ⊛€2.50. ☎958 66 55 69. www. escreativa.com/cueva.

This cave-museum of popular arts and traditions re-creates life in a cave dwelling during the 19C. Several rooms exhibit farming and shepherds' tools from the region.

Museo de Alfarería

In the Mozarabic district of San Miguel. ⊙*Open Apr–Sept Mon–Sat, 10am–1.30pm and 4–8.30pm. Oct–Apr Mon–Sat 10am–1.30pm and 5–9pm. Sun and public hols year-round 11am–2pm.* ⊛€2. ☎958 66 47 67.

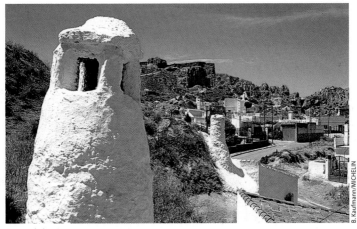

Barrio de las Cuevas

Cave dwellings

The special characteristics of the clay soil found in the **Guadix Basin** have made the construction of these unusual dwellings possible. Clay has the property of being easy to work and yet hardening upon contact with air. The end result is a cave which is impermeable, thermally insulated, and which maintains a constant temperature (18°C/64°F) all year round, making it cool during the hot summer months and warm during the cold winters.

Guadix alone has around 2 000 inhabited caves, while one of the largest groups of cave dwellings in Europe exists in the surrounding area. The origin of these dwellings is uncertain, although it would appear that most of them were built after the Christian Reconquest and the progressive segregation imposed upon the area's *morisco* population. In Guadix, these inhabitants were gradually expelled from the Santa Ana district and subsequently occupied the cave dwellings in the troglodyte district visible today.

This pottery museum is housed in a cave of Moorish origin which has retained some of its historical features, including a well dating from 1650 made from Arab bricks and a large earthenware jar from 1640 buried in the floor and possibly used to store wine. The museum clearly demonstrates the rich tradition of pottery in Granada province, including the famous **accitano pitchers**.

Barrio de Santa Ana

The town's Moorish quarter is a network of narrow alleyways, lined by whitewashed houses decked in flowers and aromatic plants. The **Iglesia de Santa Ana**, built on the site of a mosque in the 15C, can be seen at the heart of the *barrio*. Next to the façade is a Renaissance fountain dating from 1567.

Excursions

Purullena

6km/4mi on the Granada road.
The **road**★★ from Guadix crosses a beautiful landscape of tufa rock. Purullena is known for its cave dwellings and its ceramic shops which can be seen on both sides of the road running through the village. The spa of **Cortes y Graena** is reached after 6km/4mi. The road continues to **La Peza** (13km/8mi), passing through an attractive landscape of lowlying clay hills.

La Calahorra★

18.5km/11.5mi southeast on A 92.
Hidden behind the peaks of the Sierra Nevada, like an island surrounded by a sea of almond trees, La Calahorra has retained much of its historic past. One of the most spectacular approaches is the route across the Sierra Nevada via the **Ragua Pass**★★, along which the contrast between the Sierra and the Altiplano can be appreciated to the full. This isolated village, crowned by an impressive fortress, stands much as it did as the capital of the Marquisate of Zenete.

The desolate landscape of the Minas del Marquesado, mines which were abandoned in 1997, is visible 4km/2.5mi from the village.

Castillo de la Calahorra★★

Visit by guided tour only, Wed 10am–1pm and 4–6pm. ☎958 67 70 98.
Despite the castle's robust military appearance, enhanced by four cylindrical towers, one of Spain's most beautiful **Renaissance patios**★★ is hidden inside. The patio was built at the beginning of the 15C in the artistic style of the Italian *quattrocento* and is laid out in a square plan with two sections joined by a splendid **staircase**★★ comprising three flights of stairs. The decoration, particularly on the doorways and capitals, uses the full range of classical features, including mouldings, candelabra, flowers and storiated columns.

HUELVA ★
POPULATION: 150 000

This capital of the westernmost province of Andalucía lies a few kilometres inland amid marshland and channels. Associated with Columbus, Huelva cultivates its links with Latin America. The climate and nearby beaches make it a popular summer destination with Spanish holidaymakers.

- **Information:** Avenida de Alemania. ☎959 25 74 03. www.huelva.es. www.andalucia.org.
- ▶ **Orient Yourself:** Huelva is 82km/51mi west of Sevilla.
- ⏱ **Organising Your Time:** Allow several hours, or a full day with nearby sites.
- ⏱ **Also See:** AYAMONTE, MOGUER, La RÁBIDA, El ROCÍO, Parque Nacional de DONANA, SEVILLA.

A Bit of History

Mineral deposits have attracted settlers since ancient times. Phoenicians and Greeks mixed with native groups to give rise to the kingdom of Tartessus. As Muslim Guelbar, the town was known for its glazed pottery. Following the Reconquest, the Dukes of Medina came into control. Huelva was marked forever by the arrival of **Christopher Columbus**. As the Cradle of Discovery and a key port, it underwent commercial expansion; but the 1755 Lisbon earthquake and the devastating early 19C War of Independence precipitated its commercial decline. Nowadays, Huelva is the gateway to the Parque Nacional de Doñana.

Sights

Cathedral
⏱*Open for services only, Mon–Sat 7pm. Sun and public hols 11am and 7pm.* ☎959 24 30 36.
The main features of this 1605 building, are its Renaissance façade, the sculpture of Christ of Jerusalem and the carving of the Virgen de la Cinta, the patron saint of the city, by Martínez Montañés.

Iglesia de San Pedro
The **church of St Peter** is at the end of the pleasant paseo de Santa Fe.
It is painted a characteristic Huelva white. The bell tower is emblematic of the city.

Iglesia de la Concepción
Badly damaged during the 1755 earthquake, this Renaissance church is being rebuilt. It contains fine choir stalls and a number of paintings by Zurbarán.

Santuario de Nuestra Señora de la Cinta
⏱*Open for services only, Mon–Sat, 7.30pm; Sun and public hols, 1.30 and 7.30pm.* ☎959 25 11 22.
Columbus stayed in this building at the end of the elegant paseo del Conquero, on the outskirts of Huelva. The beautiful *azulejos* are by Daniel Zuloaga.

Museo Provincial
⏱*Open Wed–Sat & Mon 9am–8pm. Tue 2.30–8.30pm. Sun and public hols 9am–2pm* ☎959 25 93 00.
Exhibits relate the history of Huelva, notably of the Tartessian civilisation.

Santuario de Nuestra Señora de la Cinta
©Ismael Montero/Bigstockphoto.com

Address Book

For coin ranges, see the Legend on cover flap.

WHERE TO STAY

Los Condes – *Alameda Sundheim, 14.* 959 28 24 00. *www.hotelloscondes.com. 54 rooms.* Modern establishment on a main avenue. Short on charm, but rooms are spacious, modern and clean, and good value.

Monte Conquero – *Pablo Rada, 10.* 959 28 55 00. *www.hotelesmonte.com. 164 rooms, 2 suites.* This business-oriented hotel offers most mod cons and comforts on one of Huelva's liveliest streets.

WHERE TO EAT

Jeromo – *Plaza de la Merced, 6.* 959 26 16 18. *Closed Mon.* On a busy square, Jeromo is one of the best fish and seafood restaurants in the city. Don't be put off by its plain decor.

Taberna El Condado – *Sor Ángela de la Cruz, 3.* 959 26 11 23. *Closed Sun and Mon lunchtime.* A typical tapas bar with barrels used as tables. Good selection of sausages, grilled fish and seafood.

Barrio Reina Victoria★

The English-style houses in this district were built for the families of employees of the Río Tinto Company Limited.

Monumento a la Fe Descubridora

This large sculpture to the Spirit of Discovery is by American artist Gertrude Vanderbilt Whitney. It was erected in 1929 on Punta del Sebo, directly opposite the city.

Excursion

Paraje Natural de las Marismas del Odiel★★

2km/1.2mi SE. Leave Huelva along avenida Tomás Domínguez.
Open Fri–Sun and public hols, 10am–2pm and 4–6pm (8pm in summer). Reserve tours with reception office 959 50 90 11 or 660 41 49 20.

This marsh *(marisma)* is a World Biosphere Reserve, home to over 200 bird species, despite nearby chemical plants. Viewing is spectacular, particularly in February and March. Visit El Burro and Isla de Enmedio sections by **canoe**.

HUÉSCAR

POPULATION: 8 013

Perched on a high plateau at an altitude of 960m/3 150ft, in the southeastern corner of Andlaucia. Huéscar is a good base for exploring the east of the province of Granada, renowned for its archaeological sites and its contrasts in landscape, from the semi-desert region around Orce to the snowy winter peaks of the Sierra de la Sagra and Sierra Seca. The town was founded in 1241 by the Order of St James, fell to the Moors, and was reconquered by Fernando the Catholic in 1488.

- **Information:** www.huescar.com.
- **Orient Yourself:** Huéscar is 160km/100mi northeast of Granada.
- **Organising Your Time:** Allow half a day for Huéscar, including walks.
- **Also See:** BAZA, VÉLEZ BLANCO, the Parque Natural de las Sierras de CAZORLA, SEGURA Y LAS VILLAS.

Sights

Plaza Mayor

The town's main square is fronted by the town hall and a number of 19C houses. Note the unusual Art Nouveau-style house in one of the streets leading into the square.

Colegiata de la Encarnación

Construction of this collegiate church started in the early 16C. The dominant Renaissance style is most notable in the large polygonal ceiling above the transept.

Excursions

Galera

8km/5mi south along A 330.
Between the 13C and 15C, Galera was a border town which changed hands regularly between the Moors and Christians; this history is reflected in its layout. The lower, Christian town, is ordered and built in a square pattern in contrast to the upper town, with its Moorish maze of alleyways, and cave dwellings. Galera is the site of the 6C BC **Iberian necropolis of Tutugi**, and the Argar settlement of **Castellón Alto**, dating from 1600 BC (*Open Sat–Sun and public hols, 10.30am–1pm and 4–6pm; midweek by prior arrangement; ☎958 73 92 73*). The Iglesia de la Anunciación dates from the 15C.

Orce★

16km/10mi southeast of Huéscar. Follow the A 330 and bear left onto the SE 34 before Galera.
Orce is situated in the eastern part of the Baza Basin, in an impressively wild and desert-like landscape which undergoes surprising changes of light and colour. The elegant stone tower of the 16C **parish church** and the recently restored **Palacio de los Segura**, also dating from the 16C, stand out among whitewashed houses. The palace has a simple façade and an elegant patio supported by stone columns.

Museo Municipal de Prehistoria y Paleontología

Open Tue–Sun Jun–Sept Mon–Sat 11am–1pm and 6–8pm. Oct–May Tue–Sat 11am–2pm and 4–6pm. ☞€1.50. ☎958 74 61 01.
The museum of prehistory and palaeontology is in the **Castillo-Alcazaba de las Siete Torres**, a 16C Christian fortress with seven towers, largely restored. The museum exhibits numerous bones and stones from the region's archaeological sites, including a piece of skull which made the town famous at the beginning of the 1980s, and an infant humerus, possibly 1.5 million years old. If this date is confirmed, this would be the oldest hominid palaeontological discovery in Europe.

Fuencaliente

2km/1.2mi from Orce, on the Galera road.
Water gushes from this spring in a desert landscape at a constant 18°C/64°F. It's a pleasant spot to cool off in the summer.

Castril

22km/14mi west along A 326.
Castril is a typical mountain village at the foot of an impressive cliff, surrounded by the beautiful and little visited **Parque Natural de la Sierra de Castril**. The village is thought to have its origins in a Roman military camp; its name comes from the Arabic *qastal*, or fortress. After

---

Address Book

For coin ranges, see the Legend on cover flap.

WHERE TO STAY

Molinos de Portillo – 2.5km/1.5mi along the Santas road. ☎958 34 45 04. www.molinode portillo.com. 7 rooms. A converted early-20C flour mill, with simple rooms. Tranquillity is assured. Its restaurant specialises in grilled meats.

Casas-Cueva – calle Iglesia, 4 Galera. ☎958 73 90 68. www.casas-cueva.es. 32 caves. Unusual accommodation in pleasantly decorated caves with terrific views, and all mod cons including jacuzzi and hydro massages.

the definitive reconquest in the 15C, Castril became part of the seigniory of Hernándo de Zafra, who established the town's famous glassworks, which closed in 1878. Today, pieces of green and yellow glass are collector's items; some are in the Museo Arqueológico de Granada. The 15C **parish church** is particularly worthy of note.

Parque Natural de la Sierra de Castril★

Visitor Centre open Apr–Sept Wed–Sun and public hols 9am–2pm and 6–8pm. Oct–Mar Thu 10am–2pm, Fri 4–6pm, Sat–Sun and public hols 10am–2pm and 4–6pm. Other days of the week by prior arrangement. ☎958 72 00 59.

This natural reserve is the extension of the neighbouring **Sierra de Cazorla** (*see PARQUE NATURAL DE LAS SIERRAS DE CAZORLA*). Its most notable characteristic is its spectacular relief, mainly the result of woodcutting for local glassworks.

A walk of around two hours starting in the lower part of Castril skirts the river and continues around the outskirts of the village, which also houses an interesting ethnographical museum.

IZNÁJAR★

POPULATION: 5 200

Iznájar's site★, on top of a hill that juts out into the **Iznájar reservoir** (embalse), is worth the detour alone. Picturesque houses line steep whitewashed streets.

- **Information:** Calle Julio Burell. ☎957 53 40 33.
- **Orient Yourself:** Iznájar is at the southern tip of Córdoba province, 83km/52mi north of Málaga and 100km/61mi west of Granada.
- **Organising Your Time:** Allow two hours plus time at the lake.
- **Especially for Kids:** Playa de Valdearenas.
- **Also See:** PRIEGO DE CÓRDOBA, LUCENA, CABRA, MONTEFRÍO.

View Iznájar of with the reservoir

Walking Tour

The countryside surrounding Iznájar is never far from view. Several street corners provide stunning **views**. The panorama from the castle and around the church takes in distant landscapes carpeted in olive groves.

Castle

The origins of the castle date back to the 8C. The Moors called this strategic site Hisn Ashar. The remains of sections of wall and several towers are still visible.

Biblioteca Municipal

The municipal library is housed in the former granary, built during the reign of Carlos III.

Parroquia de Santiago

This 16C Renaissance-style parish church was built with large pieces of ashlar stone. It is topped by a truncated tower.

Mirador de la Cruz de San Pedro

This lookout point offers **views**★ of the fortress and church, lake and town. The lower part of the town is the site of the **Museo Etnográfico** (🕐 open Mon–Fri 10am–2pm; ☎957 53 40 33) displaying implements used to work the land, and the **Casa de las Columnas**, with heraldic decoration on its façade. .

Embalse de Iznájar

The 30km/18mi-long Iznájar Reservoir, also known as the Lago de Andalucía (Lake of Andalucía), dams the waters of the River Genil.

The eastern section of the lake is part of Granada province. The **Playa de Valdearenas**, on its shoreline, is a popular beach for swimmers and water sports enthusiasts.

JAÉN★

POPULATION: 107 413

Spain's olive capital rises onto Cerro de Santa Catalina (St Catherine's Hill). Jaén is a storehouse of artistic heritage, from its Moorish castle to numerous Renaissance buildings, many designed by Andrés de Vandelvira.

- **Information:** Calle Maestra, 13 bajo. ☎953 24 26 24. www.andalucia.org. www.promojaen.es.
- **Orient Yourself:** Jaén is 94km/59mi north of Granada via the A 44-E 902.
- **Don't Miss:** The Cathedral; the Chapel of the Immaculate Conception in the Chapel of San Andrés; the Moorish Baths; a drink, meal or overnight stay in the town castle, now a parador with stunning views.
- **Organising Your Time:** Allow two days.
- **Also See:** MARTOS, BAEZA, ÚBEDA, PRIEGO DE CÓRDOBA, ALCALÁ LA REAL, GRANADA.

A Bit of History

Jaén was called *Aurigi* following conquest by Roman general Publius Cornelius Scipio in 207 BC, then *Djayyân* (on the caravan route), and *Geen* under the Moors. Fernando III the Saint turned Jaén into a bastion upon its reconquest in 1246.

Jaén declined after the final Christian victory. Olive oil has brought an upturn in fortunes.

Town Centre *Allow half a day*

Cathedral★★

🕐 Open in Jul–Sept daily except Sun afternoon, 8.30am–1pm and 5–8pm. Oct–Jun 8.30am–1pm and 4.30–7pm. ⊘Cathedral free, museum €3. ☎953 23 42 33. www.catedraldejaen.org.

Towering over old Jaén, built in the 16C and 17C to plans by Andrés de Vandelvira, this is one of the most extraordinary Renaissance buildings in Andalucía.

Main façade★★

On the lower tier of the sumptuous façade, fine reliefs represent the Assumption of the Virgin, the archangel St Michael, and St Catherine. Sculptures on the full **balustrade**★ represent King Fernando, the four Evangelists and the Doctors of the Church.

Interior★★

The domed transept is a magnificent work by Pedro del Portillo and Juan de Aranda. Admire the wash of light into the huge building. The **choir stalls**★★ are by José Gallego and Oviedo del Portal, disciples of Alonso Berruguete. The altarpiece includes the Gothic **Virgin of La Antigua**★. The **Veil of the Holy Face**★, used by Veronica to wipe the face of Christ on his way to Calvary, bears His features. Note the *Annunciation* by Cellini and a *Visitation* attributed to Titian. The most outstanding side chapels are the Capilla de San Fernando *(left of the high altar,* fine statue of Our Father Jesus of Nazareth); Capilla del Santísimo Sacramento (Baroque altarpiece and image of St. Benedict by Pedro Duque Cornejo, 18C); and Capilla de la Virgen de las Angustias (sculptures by José de Mora).The chapter house *(sala capitular)* holds a fine 16C *Sagrada Familia* by Pedro Machuca.

Museum

🕐*Open daily except Sun afternoon Jul–Sept 10am–1pm and 5–8pm (Oct–Jun 4–7pm).* 👓 €3.

The Museo Catedralicio is in the **sacristy** (by Vandelvira). *Access by right transept.* Exhibits include a Flemish *Virgin and Child,* two **Ribera** canvases, choir books, gold and silverwork, and a candelabra by Maestro Bartolomé. .

Iglesia del Sagrario

In this sober, late-18C neo-Classical church designed by por Ventura Rodríguez, beside the cathedral, is an *Assumption of the Virgin*, painted by Salvador Maella.

Convento de Santa Teresa (Convento de las Descalzas)

The Convent of Poor Clares (or Discalced Nuns) has a *Spiritual Canticle* handwritten by St John of the Cross. **Pastries** produced by the nuns are on sale.

Palacio Provincial

An ex-Franciscan monastery houses the provincial administration *(Diputación Provincial)*. The internal patio is fronted by a double gallery of columns.

Partial view of the cathedral façade

B. Kaufmann/MICHELIN

Iglesia de San Bartolomé

The sober façade of this 16C–17C church belies its wonderful **Mudéjar artesonado ceiling**.

Iglesia de San Ildefonso★

Open Mon–Sat 9am–noon and 5–8pm. Sun and public hols 9am–2pm. No visits during religious services. ☎953 19 03 46.
The second-largest church in Jaén, San Ildefonso dates from the 14C. A mosaic in the main Gothic portal shows the *Descent of the Virgin of the Chapel.*
A Renaissance portal is by Vandelvira; an 18C neo-Classical portal by Ventura Rodríguez. The magnificent **main altarpiece** is by Pedro and Julio Roldán, the fine tabernacle by Pedro Duque Cornejo. An altar holds the **Virgen de la Capilla**, Jaén's patron saint.

Convento de las Bernardas

Open daily 9.30am–12.45pm and 4.30–8pm. ☎953 24 38 54.
A small church in this 16C convent houses paintings of the *Annunciation* and the *Assumption of the Virgin* by the Italian artist Angelo Nardi.

Real Monasterio de Santa Clara

The outstanding feature of this 13C monastery, the oldest in the city, is its church, with an unusual 16C bamboo image of Christ.

Iglesia de San Juan

This post-reconquest church has a noteworthy collection of Gothic carvings.

Capilla de San Andrés★

Open daily 10am–noon. ☎953 23 74 22.
This 16C Mudéjar chapel with Judaic features, on a steep street, was commissioned by Gutierre González Doncel, treasurer to Pope Leo X. The **Capilla de la Purísima Inmaculada**★★ (Chapel of the Immaculate Conception) is a Plateresque masterpiece. The gilded chapel **screen**★ is by Maestro Bartolomé (16C), a native of Jaén.

Palacio de Villardompardo

Open Tue–Fri 9am–8pm. Sat–Sun, 9.30am–2.30pm. ☎953 24 80 00 (ext 4166).

Moorish Baths

This elegant 16C palace with arcaded **patio**★ was the residence of Fernando de Torres y Portugal, Viceroy of Peru and Count of Villardompardo. It houses the **Museo de Artes y Costumbres Populares** which illuminates the lives of everyday folk through farm tools, household objects and clothing; and the **Museo Internacional de Arte Naïf**, devoted to naive art, which exhibits a fine collection of paintings and sculptures.

Moorish Baths★★

The *Baños Árabes*, situated deep below the palace, are the largest that remain in Spain. As you step into barrel-vaulted entrance hall with star-shaped skylight and alcoves at either end; note the 11C remains from its period of construction, now protected under glass. An excellent restoration allows visitors to fully appreciate this superb example of Moorish architecture. It comprises a cold room; a larger warm room, roofed with a handsome hemispherical cupola on pendentives; and a hot room next to the boilers.

Real Monasterio de Santo Domingo

Open in summer daily 9am–1pm; rest of year 8.30am–2pm. ☎953 23 85 00.
This royal monastery, founded by Juan I above a Moorish palace, became headquarters of the Inquisition. The Renaissance façade is by Vandelvira. In the 17C inner **patio**★, a delicate gallery of arches

Address Book

GETTING THERE AND GETTING AROUND

Airport – The nearest airport is in Granada (☎958 24 52 00.www.aena.es) an hour or so south along the fast N 323 highway.

Trains – From the station on paseo de las Culturas (☎953 270202) direct rains run to Madrid, Córdoba, Sevilla and Cádiz.

Inter-city buses – the central station on plaza de Coca de la Piñera (☎953 25 01 06) has routes to every provincial capital in Andalucía and to major cities around Spain.

Local buses – ☎953 21 91 00/88.

Taxis – ☎953 22 22 22.

Horse-drawn carriages – These can be hired at several central locations.

For coin ranges, see the Legend on the cover flap.

WHERE TO STAY

Hotel Husa Europa – *Plaza Belén, 1.* ☎*953 22 27 00. www.husa.es. 37 rooms.* This sleek, modern and stylish hotel lacks local charm, but rooms are functional, comfortable, and well equipped. Its central location makes it a good bet.

Parador de Jaén – *Carretera del Castillo de Santa Catalina (4.5km/2.8mi W).* ☎*953 23 00 00 . www. parador.es. 45 rooms.* Jaén's *parador* is located in the 13C Moorish fortress above town, with magnificent views of mountains and olive groves. Even if you're not staying here, stop by for dinner or drinks.

WHERE TO EAT

Mesón Río Chico – *Nueva, 12.* ☎*953 24 08 02. Closed Sun evening, Mon and in Aug.* This long-established city favourite has a tapas bar downstairs – tasty *raciones* de fish, *flamenquines* (ham and cheese rolls), mussels and more – and more formal dining upstairs.

Mesón Nuyra – *Pasaje Nuyra (close to calle Nueva).* ☎*953 24 07 63. Closed Sun evening and first two weeks of Jul.* This traditional cellar restaurant specialises in suckling pig *(cochinillo)* and sirloin steak *(solomillo)*.

Casa Vicente – *Francisco Martín Mora, 1.* ☎*953 23 22 22. Closed Sun evening, Mon and in Aug.* The dining rooms in this traditional *taberna*, very close to the cathedral, surround an attractive patio. Fine regional cuisine and traditional Jaén dishes,

TAPAS

La Manchega – *Bernardo López, 8.* ☎*953 23 21 91. Closed Tue.* This bar, est. 1886, makes no concession to current fashions and is all the better for it: excellent selection of tapas and wine.

LOCAL SPECIALITIES

Gastronomic specialities include the town's famous exquisite olive oil, *pestiños* (honeyed doughnuts) and *pipirrana*, a gazpacho-like cold soup made with garlic, green peppers, ripe tomatoes and breadcrumbs.

TAKING A BREAK

Ábaco – *Avenida Muñoz Grandes, 5.* ☎*953 27 68 71.* Modern,British-pub style bar with music, open very late.

Café-Bar del Pósito – *Plaza del Pósito, 10.* Close by the cathedral, mixes jazz and flamenco, and stages art exhibitions.

Chubby-Cheek – *San Francisco Javier, 7.* ☎*953 27 38 19.* A café which lives and breathes jazz. Concerts on Thursday evenings. A pleasant place for a coffee or quiet drink at other times.

Trujal – *Calle Hurtado, 21.* ☎*953 23 44 84.* This bar in the San Ildefonso area is for thirtysomething couples seeking cosy, rustic, candle-lit surroundings.

SHOPPING

Jaén's main shopping streets are located around **plaza de la Constitución**. Calle Virgen de la Capilla, calle San Clemente and paseo de la Estación are the main commercial arteries, along with other adjoining streets lined by small shops and the occasional large department store, such as **El Corte Inglés**, in calle Roldán y Marín.

Markets – An open-air *mercadillo* selling a wide selection of food, clothes and other goods is held on Thursday mornings at the fairground *(recinto ferial)* near Alameda de Calvo Sotelo.

ENTERTAINMENT

For an up-to-date list of cultural events in Jaén and around the province, consult *Agenda Turístico-Cultural*, published monthly by the town hall and available from tourist officesor look online at *www.promojaen.es*. The **Teatro Darymelia**, in calle Maestra (☎953 21 91 80), stages concerts.

FESTIVALS

During the **Holy Week** celebrations, religious processions and songs fill the streets.

SIGHTSEEING

Get to know Jaén's *barrios*: **La Magdalena**, at once Moorish and Christian; **San Juan**, the hub of nightlife; and **Santa María**, for heritage buildings.

rests on paired columns. Window openings are finely carved. The provincial Historical archives are kept here.

Iglesia de la Magdalena

This lovely 16C Isabelline church retains the patio of a mosque and its ritual pool. The fine *Calvary* is by Jacopo l'Indaco, the 18C relief of *La Magdalena* by Mateo Medina. The 19C fountain opposite (*Fuente del Raudal*) once provided drinking water.

Monasterio de Santa Úrsula

🕐*Open by prior arrangement.*
☎*953 19 01 15.*
The convent's church has a fine Mudéjar *artesonado* ceiling. Traditional **candied egg yolks** *(yemas)* produced by the nuns of Santa Úrsula are on sale here.

Outside the Centre

Castillo de Santa Catalina★

5km/3mi W.
🕐*Open summer Tue–Sun 10am–2pm and 5.30–9.30pm. Rest of year 10am–2pm and 3.30–7.30pm.* ⬤€3. ☎*953 12 07 33.*
This once-Moorish hilltop fortress (now a parador) became the starting point for the monumental walls of Jaén (of which only the Baroque 17C **Puerta del Ángel** and the arches of **San Lorenzo** and Consuelo remain). Remaining sections include the **Capilla de Santa Catalina** in a turret, accessed via a delicate horseshoe arch; and the graceful keep, affording stupendous **views**★★ of Sierra de Jabalcuz.

Museo Provincial

🕐 *Open Wed–Sat 9am–8.30pm. Tue 2.30–8.30pm. Sun and hols 9am–2.30pm.* ⬤€1.50 (EU citizens free). ☎953 25 06 00.
The main building from 1920 incorporates the façades of the former public granary (*pósito*) – note the reliefs of wheat and a bread basket – and of the Iglesia de San Miguel, both from the 16C. A 6C BC set of **Iberian carvings from Porcuna**★ (bulls, sphinxes, high priests and warriors) is the outstanding exhibit in the archaeological section. Roman items include the **Bruñel** mosaic, striking in its complexity and use of colour. A marble **sarcophagus from Martos**★ is a magnificent palaeo-Christian work representing seven miraculous scenes from the life of Jesus. The fine arts section displays works by Pedro Berruguete, Alonso Cano, José and Federico de Madrazo, Mariano Benlliure and Antonio López.

Excursions

La Guardia de Jaén

10km/6mi southeast along A 44–E 902.
Impressive **views** from the Moorish fortress above the village take in the Cerro de San Martos and distant fields.

Parque Natural de la Sierra Mágina

35km/22mi east. Centro de interpretación de Jodar, Castillo de Jódar. ☎*953 78 76 56. www.cerespain.com/jodar.html.*
This 20 000 ha oak forest is a refuge for the imperial eagle, peregrine falcon and mountain goat.

JAÉN

PLACES OF INTEREST

Baños Árabes	BY	Convento de Santa Teresa o de Las Descalzas	BZ B
Barrio La Magdalena	AY	Iglesia de la Magdalena	AY
Barrio San Juan	ABY	Iglesia de San Bartolomé	BZ
Barrio Santa María (Catedral y plaza)	BZ	Iglesia de San Idelfonso	CZ
Capilla de San Andrés	BY	Iglesia de San Juan	BY
Castillo de Santa Catalina	AZ	Iglesia del Sagrario (Catedral)	BZ
Catedral	BZ	Monasterio de Santa Úrsula	AY F
Convento de Las Bernadas	CZ A	Monumento a las Batallas	BY K
		Museo Provincial	BY M¹

Palacio de los Uribes	AY P¹
Palacio de los Vélez	BZ P²
Palacio de los Vilches	BZ P³
Palacio de Villardompardo	BY M²
Palacio Provincial	BZ D
Parque de la Victoria	CY
Real Monasterio de Santa Clara	BY R
Real Monasterio de Santo Domingo	AY S

JEREZ DE LA FRONTERA★★

POPULATION: 181 602

Jerez, horses and sherry go together. The aroma of sherry wafts through streets and alleyways and horses dominate the local festivals. Jerez boasts one of the finest architectural heritages of the province and with Sevilla is the birthplace of flamenco. The traditional Andalusian dance, the *bulería*, takes place in the town's humble gypsy quarters.

- **Information:** Alameda Cristina, Los Claustros de Santo Domingo. ☎956 32 47 47. www.turismojerez.com.
- ▶ **Orient Yourself:** Jerez is 35km/22mi northeast of Cádiz, 30km/19mi west of Arcos de la Frontera, and 90km/56mi south of Sevilla along the A 4-E 5.
- **Don't Miss:** The Cathedral, a visit to a Sherry Bodega, the Real Escuela Andaluza de Arte Ecuestre (Andalucían Horse School), the Palacio del Tiempo (Clock Museum), the Alcázar and views from its Camera Obscura.
- **Organising Your Time:** Allow at least two days.
- **Especially for Kids:** The zoo and perhaps the Andalucían Horse School.
- **Also See:** EL PUERTO DE SANTA MARÍA, CÁDIZ, SANLÚCAR DE BARRAMEDA, ARCOS DE LA FRONTERA and PUEBLOS BLANCOS DE ANDALUCÍA.

A Bit of History

The capture of Sevilla in 1248 by Fernando III (the Saint) led to the opening up of the Lower Guadalquivir Valley to Christian troops, who subsequently occupied cities such as Arcos, Medina and Jerez de la Frontera.

Jerez finally came under Castilian control on 9 October 1264, the feast day of St Dionysius. During this period, the city was surrounded by a rectangular wall, built by the Almohads, with a perimeter of more than 4km/2.5mi; remains of this defensive structure can still be seen in calle Porvera and calle Ancha. Three gates led into the city, which was divided into six parishes or *collaciones*

(Cádiz only had one), named after the four Evangelists, St Dionysius (the city's patron saint) and the Saviour. The suburbs of San Miguel and Santiago, as well as the Dominican and Franciscan monasteries, stood outside the walls. From the 13C onwards, the city played a key role in the defensive border system established between the Christian and Nasrid kingdom.

Sherry

Learn about sherry and other bodega tours at www.sherry.org.

The term sherry is an anglicized version of the name Jerez. The **Sherry appellation** covers the triangle between **Jerez**, **Sanlúcar** and **El Puerto de Santa María**. Wines from this area earn **Denominación de Origen Jerez-Xerez-Sherry** status and are regulated by the Consejo Regulador.

Terms you will come across:
Palomino – 95% of the grapes grown in Jerez are of the Palomino variety, introduced to the region during the time of Alfonso X.
Pedro Ximénez – This grape variety was introduced in 1680 by a Flemish soldier.

Tocino de Cielo

This delicious dessert (literally "heavenly bacon") is thought to have its origins in the Jerez wine-cellars, where local wine-producers once used beaten egg whites to clarify their wine. Not knowing what to do with the leftover egg yolks, they gave them to the neighbouring convents, where the nuns used them to make these delicious custard puddings.

Botas – Three types of barrels are used: *bocolles*, *toneles* and *botas*. The *botas* (500 litres), made from American oak, are most common.

Sobretabla – This is the youngest wine which is placed in the first *criadera*. This is the fermented must fortified to bring the alcohol level to 15%.

Flor del vino – This layer of surface yeast both ferments and prevents oxidisation.

Solera and Criaderas – The *solera* is the row of casks *(barricas)* closest to the floor, with the oldest wine. The rows above are *criaderas*. The wine descends from the top level (first *criadera*) to the *solera*, a process known as "running down the ladder".

Types of sherry

Fino – This is a very dry wine which is light and straw-like in colour, with an alcohol content of 15%. A traditional accompaniment to fish and seafood.

Amontillado – An amber sherry, medium dry and aromatic. About 17% alcohol.

Oloroso – Dark in colour with a sharp aroma. Around 18% alcohol.

Cream – A sweet, dark sherry drunk as a dessert wine.

Pedro Ximénez – The sweet ruby wine made from the Pedro Ximénez grape.

The main sherry bodegas

All bodegas are open by guided tour only and many require advance booking; enquire at the tourist office.

Pedro Domecq – *Calle San Ildefonso.* ☎956 15 15 52. www.bodegasfundador pedrodomecq.com. Guided tours Mon–Fri 9am–1pm. €4. The 18C El Molino *bodega* is impressive.

González Byass (Tío Pepe) – *Calle Manuel María González 12.* Guided tours (1hr), Mon–Sat 11am–5pm. €7. ☎956 35 70 16. www.gonzalezbyass.es. Founded in 1835, the La Concha *bodega* was designed by Gustave Eiffel in 1892; barrels in La Constancia bear famous signatures (including Margaret Thatcher, Steven Spielberg and King Juan Carlos). Original tasting room.

Williams & Humbert – *Highway 4 Km 642.* Guided tours Mon–Fri 10am, noon and 2pm. €7/8. ☎956 35 34 06.

www.williams-humbert.com. *Enquire about their equestrian show.*

Sandeman – *Calle Pizarro, 10.* Guided tours in English Mon, Wed & Fri 11.30am, 12.30pm, 1.30pm and 2.30pm; Tue, Thu and public hols 10.30am, noon, 1pm, 2pm, 3pm. (2.30 and 3pm tours only during Apr–Oct). €6. ☎956 31 29 95. www.sandeman.com.

Walking Tour

Historic Jerez★★

The itinerary below starts in the medieval quarter, with visits to several "churches of the Reconquest" *(most open during services only, from 7pm),* followed by the medieval districts of San Miguel and Santiago, now lively with outdoor cafés and shops.

Plaza del Mercado

The Moorish market once stood on this square in working-class San Mateo. The surviving façade of the Renaissance **Palacio de Riquelme** stands out like a stage set. The **Museo Arqueológico** (*see Visit*) and **Iglesia de San Mateo** are here.

Iglesia de San Mateo – One of the first churches built by Alfonso X in the 13C replaced a mosque. The present buttressed building dates from the 15C.

▶ *Follow calle Cabezas to the plaza de San Lucas.*

Iglesia de San Lucas

Baroque additions hide the medieval origin of this church.

▶ *Follow calle Ánimas de San Lucas. Turn left into calle Santa María to plaza Orbaneja. Take calle Liebre to plaza Carrizosa. Return to plaza Orbaneja and follow calle San Juan.*

Iglesia de San Juan de los Caballeros★

This 15C church has a façade added in the 17C. A magnificent nine-sided 14C **polygonal apse★**, is topped by a ten-rib cupola with jagged decoration.

Address Book

GETTING THERE AND GETTING AROUND

Airport – La Parra airport (☏956 15 00 00/1 83. www.aena.es) is located 7km/4.5mi from the city along the A 4. Take the Jerez airport public bus to the centre of town.

Trains – Plaza de la Estación (☏956 34 23 19). Services to Sevilla, Madrid, Barcelona and, most frequently, Cádiz.

RENFE (Spanish State Railways) – Ticket office at calle Tonería, 4 (☏956 33 79 75 or 902 24 02 02).

Local buses – ☏956 14 36 08/9.

Inter-city buses – The station is on calle Cartuja (☏956 34 52 07).

Taxis – ☏956 34 48 60.

Horse-drawn carriages – Horse-drawn carriages can be hired.

♿For coin ranges, see the Legend on the cover flap.

WHERE TO STAY

⊜**Nuevo Hotel** – Caballeros, 23. ☏956 33 16 00. www.nuevohotel.com. 27 rooms. This 19C mansion was one of the first hotels in Jerez. Rooms are modestly furnished but large, around a central patio; no 208 has fine plasterwork of Moorish inspiration.

⊜⊜⊜**Hotel Serit** – Higueras, 7. ☏956 34 07 00. www.hotelserit.com. 35 rooms. Central, smart, functional and modern.

⊜⊜⊜ **Hotel Doña Blanca** – Bodegas, 11. ☏956 34 87 61. www.hoteldonablanca.com. 30 rooms. This old typically Andalusian building is located in the heart of town with large, comfortable rooms.

⊜⊜⊜⊜ **Hotel Jerez** – Avenida Alcalde Álvaro Domecq, 35 (1.5km/1m from city centre). ☏956 30 06 00. www.jerezhotel.com. 126 rooms. Luxury hotel and spa with rooms overlooking the garden or the swimming pool.

WHERE TO EAT

⊜⊜**Gaitán** – Gaitán, 3–5. ☏956 16 80 21. Closed Sun. Long-established multi-award-winning restaurant serving innovative regional cuisine.

⊜⊜**San Juan** – Plaza Melgarejo. ☏956 32 64 71. Closed Mon. Reservation advised in summer. Italian restaurant arranged around a glass-covered patio. Attractive decor with enormous canvases of David by Michelangelo, and recycled theatre seats. Try fresh stuffed pasta or sirloin à la San Juan.

⊜⊜ **Tendido 6** – Circo, 10. ☏956 34 48 35 35. www.tendido6.com. Closed Sun. Next to the bullring. One of the best restaurants in Jerez, serving Andalusian meat and fish specialities on a covered patio as full meals and as tapas.

⊜⊜⊜ **La Taberna Flamenca** – Angostillo de Santiago, 3. ☏956 32 36 93. www.latabernaflamenca. com. Closed Sun–Mon. A large tavern located in a former wine storehouse. Dinner is served from 8pm; flamenco show May–Oct, Tue, Wed, Thu and Sat, starting at 2.30pm; Nov–May 10pm and Thu at 2.30pm.

TAPAS

Juanito – Pescadería Vieja, 8–10. ☏956 33 48 38. www.bar-juanito.com. Closed Feria week. On a pedestrian way teeming with outdoor cafés, the venerable Bar Juanito serves award-winning tapas. Quintessentially Andalusian: azulejos and bullfighting paintings and posters adorn the walls.

El Gallo Azul – Larga, 2. ☏956 32 61 48. Excellent choice for a break to escape the bustle. Lovely columned façade.

TAKING A BREAK

Baños Árabes Hammam Andalusí (Moorish Baths) – Salvador, 6. ☏956 34 90 66. www.hammamandalusi.com. Open 10am–10pm. ☞1hr 30min €15; plus 15min massage €27; other treatments by reservation. Return to days gone by in these beautiful candle-lit, carefully re-created baths with Moorish decor and a tea house with Cathedral views.

GOING OUT FOR THE EVENING

Jerez is famous for flamenco clubs (peñas flamencas/tablaos): for the real thing try **Peña Tío José de Paula** (calle Merced, 11. ☏956 30 32 67/01 96), or **Peña el Garbanzo** (calle Santa Clara, 9 ☏956 33 76 67).

Bereber – Cabezas, 10. ☏956 34 42 46. www.tablaodelbereber.com. The most famous dinner show and traditional-modern nightspot in Jerez, set in a 13C palace with spaces carefully decorated in Andalusian or Moorish style; includes bars and a large discoteca in adjacent cellars, and a flamenco *tablao*.

Kapote – *Avenida Álvaro Domecq, 13 (Yeguada bldg).* ☎*956 31 28 75. www. kapote.es.* Modern bar in bullfighting dress. Drinking and dancing 'til dawn.

La Carbonería – *Letrados (behind the town hall).* ☎*956 16 87 01. www.pub lacarboneria.com/* Bright modern trendy bar with DJs.

Teatro Villamarta – *plaza Romero Martínez.* ☎*956 32 73 27. www. villamarta.com.* Opera, classical concerts and occasional flamenco.

SHOPPING

The main shopping district is around pedestrianised calle Larga. At one end, in plaza Estévez, is a traditional market. You can buy sherry everywhere but few know as much about it as La Casa del Jerez *(Divina Pastora, 1.* ☎*956 33 51 84).*

Market – At the end of calle Larga in plaza Estévez, is a daily traditional market. The **mercadillo**, in the **Parque González Hontória**, offers a wide selection of goods on Monday mornings.

FESTIVALS

The **Festival de Jerez** *(www.flamenco-world.com)*, dedicated to flamenco, takes place last week February–first

©Turespaña

Feria del Caballo

week March. The famous **Feria del Caballo** (horse fair) takes place late April–early May in the Parque González Hontória. The **Fiesta de la Vendimia** (vine festival) and the **Fiesta de la Bulería**, devoted to Andalusian song, are both held in September.

SPORTS

The famous Jerez Racetrack (Circuito de Jerez) is the site of the F1 motorcycle Grand Prix. For event information, visit www.circuitodejerez.com. Nextdoor, the Montocastillo Golf club is one of the best courses in Europe, and was home to the Volvo Masters between 1997 and 2001. For information on facilities and green fees, visit www.golfdelaluz. com/montecastillogolfclub.htm. Both venues are 10km/6mi east along the A382 towards Arcos de la Frontera

---

Nearby, the **Centro Andaluz de Flamenco** is on plaza San Juan.

▸ *Take calle Francos and turn left into calle Canto. Continue to plaza Ponce de León.*

The Plateresque **Palacio de los Ponce de León** has a lovely corner **window**★★.

Convento de Santa María de Gracia

In plaza de Ponce de León. ◷*Open daily 9.30am–12.45pm and 4.45–5.30pm.* Pastries are sold from here.

▸ *Follow calle Juana de Dios Lacoste, then left onto calle Almenillas. Cross calle Francos and follow calle*

Compañía from beside the church to the Iglesia de San Marcos.

Iglesia de San Marcos

This 15C church features a beautiful 16C **star vault**. A 19C panel representing St Mark hangs above a 17C polygonal **retable**★.

Plaza de Rafael Rivero

This small square is bordered by the Palacio de los Pérez Luna, with its beautiful late-18C **doorway**, and next to it, the Casa de los Villavicencio, with an attractive patio.

▸ *Follow calle Tornería as far as plaza de Plateros.*

Cathedral

Plaza del Plateros

This was a medieval commercial centre, (see the names of nearby streets; *Sedería* denoting silk merchants...). The **Torre Atalaya** is an early 15C watchtower.

Plaza de la Asunción★

The Renaissance **Casa del Cabildo**★★ (town hall, 1575) is adorned with figures.

Iglesia de San Dionisio – The Mudéjar-influenced Church of St Dionysius honors the patron of Jerez.

▸ *Follow calle José Luis Díez down to plaza del Arroyo.*

Palacio del Marqués de Bertemati★

The façade of this palace is one of the most impressive in Jerez. The first section of the **left doorway**★ represents the secular world; the second portrays the religious world.

Cathedral★★

🕐*Open year-round Mon–Fri 11am–1pm.* ☎*956 34 84 82.*

The Colegial del Salvador was the first church built after the Reconquest. The present building was constructed in the 18C, along with new streets and squares. The tiled **cupola**★ above the transept is visible from much of the city.

Alcázar (Mosque, Arab Baths and Camera Obscura)★

Alameda Vieja.

🕐*Open year-round Mon–Sat 10am–8pm (mid-Sept–Apr 6pm). Sun 10am–3pm.* ✎*€4.50.* ☎*956 32 69 23.*

There is an excellent **view**★★ of the cathedral from here. The old Moorish fortress was part of the 4km/2.5mi 12C Almohad wall. Access is via the angled **Puerta de la Ciudad** (City Gateway), a typical Almohad structure. Along the walls are the keep and the 15C Torre de Ponce de León (📖 *see Visit for interior description*).

Plaza del Arenal

The square has been a meeting place since Moorish days. The monument, by Mariano Benlliure, honors **Miguel Primo de Rivera**, dictator of Spain in the 1920s.

▸ *Take calle San Miguel, which provides a good view of the Iglesia de San Miguel.*

Iglesia de San Miguel★★

The 1480 Hispano-Flemish **San José façade** is the oldest part of the church. St Joseph is flanked by two imposing Flamboyant pillars. The three-tiered Baroque tower is topped with a Jerez-style *azulejo* roof. The highly decorated transept and main chapel are covered by an elaborate star vault. The extraordinary late-Renaissance **retable**★ is by Martínez Montañés, with Baroque additions by Juan de Arce. Attached to the church is the Baroque-style **Capilla Sacramental** (Sacramental Chapel).

▸ *Return to plaza del Arenal and follow calle Lencería as far as the Gallo Azul building. Calle Larga leads to the Convento de Santo Domingo.*

Convento de Santo Domingo

This Dominican monastery, founded under Alfonso X, now houses exhibitions.

Casa Domecq★

This is an elegant late-18C Jerez Baroque-style palace with a highly decorative marble **doorway**★. Note the graceful iron balustrade on a curving cornice.

Visit

Palacio del Tiempo★★

Atalaya gardens.
Visit by guided tour only, Mar–Oct Tue–Sun 10am–2.15pm and 5–6.15pm, each hour and quarter past the hour). Sun and Nov, Dec and Feb mornings only. Closed 24–5 and 31 Dec and Jan. €6, combined ticket with Misterio de Jerez €9. ☎902 18 21 00. www.elmisteriodejerez.org.
This remarkable **clock museum**, in the 19C neoclassical Palacete de la Atalaya, is surrounded by gardens where peacocks roam. The collection numbers some 300 valuable antique (17C–19C) timepieces, all chiming, memorably, on the hour.

Misterio de Jerez

Atalaya gardens.
Opening days and months as Palacio del Tiempo, shows at 10am, noon and 6pm. €5, combined ticket with Palacio del Tiempo €9.
The Mystery of Jerez, housed in a 19C *bodega*, uses state-of-the-art technology to delve into Jerez wine.

Real Escuela Andaluza del Arte Ecuestre★

Opening times according to chosen tours; see website (Calendar of Events) for days and times. Horse shows: Mar–mid-Dec Tue, Thu and Fri (Fri only Aug) noon. €10 full tour, €6 half tour. Horse show €18–€24 (€24–€32 during the Jerez Feria). Tickets may be booked online. ☎956 31 80 08. www.realescuela.org.
The **Royal Andalusian School of Equestrian Art**, occupies a 19C French-style palace which is home to Museo del Arte Ecuestre (Museum of Equestrian Art) where interactive and audio-visual displays tell you in incredible detail all about the **history of the horse** and, of course, its revered role in Andalucía. You can also stroll through beautiful **Botanic gardens** The highlight of the visit however is the **equestrian show**★★ "How the Andalusian Horses Dance": an equestrian ballet with choreography taken from the school of Classical Dressage and Spanish music and costumes inspired by 18C and 19C fashions. The adjacent **Museo del Enganche** displays sumptuous coaches.

Alcázar

See Walking Tour for description.
The **mosque**★★ is in unadorned early Almohad style. Over the prayer room is a delightful **octagonal cupola**. Across the garden are 12C Roman-style baths.

Camera Obscura

This was only the second camera obscura built in Spain, and is housed high in the tower of the **Palacio de Villavicencio**, providing a unique **view**★★ of Jerez. This is an ideal first stop on a tour of the city.

Museo Arqueológico

Open Tue–Fri 10am–2pm and 4–7pm, Sat–Sun and public hols, 10am–2.30pm. €2 (no charge first Sun of every month). ☎956 14 95 60. www.museoarqueologico.webjerez.com.

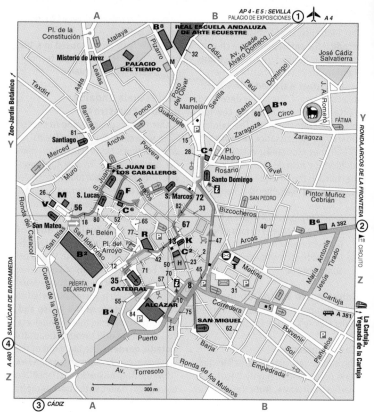

Alcázar	AZ		de Flamenco	AY	E	Misterio de Jerez	AY	
Bodega Domecq	AZ	B²	Convento de Santa María			Museo Arqueológico	
Bodega González Byass	AZ	B⁴	de Gracia	AY	F	de Jerez	AY	M
Bodega Harvey	BZ	B⁶	Convento de			Palacio de Riquelme	AY	V
Bodega Sandeman	ABY	B⁸	Santo Domingo	BY		Palacio del Marqués	
Bodega Williams			Iglesia de San Dionisio	BZ	K	de Bertemati	AZ	R
& Humbert	BY	B¹⁰	Iglesia de San Juan			Palacio del Tiempo	AY	
Cabildo	BZ	C²	de los Caballeros	AY		Real Escuela Andaluza	
Casa de los			Iglesia de San Lucas	AYˇ		de Arte Ecuestre	BY	
Ponce de León	AY	C⁶	Iglesia de San Marcos	ABY		Teatro Villamarta	BZ	T
Casa Domecq	BY	C⁴	Iglesia de San Mateo	AZ		Yeguada de la Cartuja	BZ	
Catedral	AZ		Iglesia de San Miguel	BZ		Zoo-Jardín Botánico	AY	
Centro Andaluz			La Cartuja	BZ				

The Jerez archaeological museum is housed in a restored 18C mansion. Its outstanding exhibit is a **Greek helmet**★ dating from the 7C BC, found in the River Guadalete. Simple marble Copper Age **cylindrical idols**★, discovered in Cerro de las Vacas (Lebrija) and Torrecera, portray remarkable expression.

Iglesia de Santiago

The 15C church of St James was built over a 13C chapel.Sturdy buttresses culminate in pinnacles. The Hispano-Flemish main façade is typical of this period. The portal bears the coat of arms of the Catholic Monarchs.

Zoo and Botanical Garden   Kids

🕐Open Tue–Sun and public hols: Jun–Aug 10am–8pm, Oct–Apr 10am–6pm, May 10am–7pm.👝€9, child €6.☎956 15 64 65. www.zoobotanicojerez.com/
This excellent zoo and beautiful garden in the north of the city make up one of the most pleasant parks in Jerez. More than 400 species include lions, tigers, giraffes and elephants.

Excursions

La Cartuja★

6km/3.5mi southeast along A 381 on the Medina Sidonia road.
🕐Open for Mass only, Tue–Sun 7am, Tue–Sat 8am and 5.30pm, Sun 5pm, Mon 5.30pm. ☎956 15 64 65.
Construction of the Carthusian monastery started in 1478.
The Renaissance doorway leads to a paved courtyard featuring a remarkable four-part church **façade**★★★, adorned with the saints of the Order, an Immaculate Conception and, above

the rose window, the figure of St Bruno, the founder of the Order.

Yeguada de la Cartuja (La Cartuja Stud Farm)★

Leave Jerez on the Medina Sidonia road. The Finca Fuente del Suero is at km 6.
🌬Guided tours and show (2hr), Sat 11am–1pm. €13–18. Reservations advised by phone or online. ☎956 162 809 .www. yeguadacartuja.com.
On Saturdays, the public can visit the state-run **Cartujana** stud farm and get a close-up look at the training of Andalucía's finest horses. The visit also includes a tack exhibit and an opportunity to admire a team of mares.

Lebrija

32km/20mi north along the A 4, then left at El Cuervo on the A 484.
This small city is in an area of marshland alongside the Guadalquivir Estuary. It boasts several fine historic buildings. Plaza de España is the hub of local life.

Capilla de la Vera Cruz

🕐Open Mon–Fri 8am–9.30pm.
☎955 97 54 53.
This interesting 17C neo-Classical chapel on plaza de España houses an exquisite **crucifix** carved by Martínez Montañés.

Iglesia de Santa María de la Oliva

🕐Open 10am–2pm, 6–9pm.
☎955 97 23 35.
Converted from a mosque in 1249, this church fronts the attractive plaza del Rector Merina. Its mix of styles includes Mudéjar horseshoe arches , Gothic windows, a Renaissance transept and apse, and Baroque bell tower. It boasts a fine **main altarpiece** by Alonso Cano.

JIMENA DE LA FRONTERA

POPULATION: 8 949

Amid a magnificent typically Andalucían landscape, this delightful "White Town", dominated by its Moorish castle, straddles the slopes of the Cerro de San Cristóbal above the River Hozgarganta. Only the red-brick neo-Classical bell tower of the **Iglesia de Santa María La Coronada** breaks the sea of white.

- **Information:** Iglesia de la Misericordia. ☎956 64 05 69.
- ▶ **Orient Yourself:** Jimena de la Frontera is 43km/27mi north of Gibraltar.
- **Don't Miss:** A trip to Castillo de Castellar.
- **Organising Your Time:** Allow two hours.
- **Also See:** RONDA, PUEBLOS BLANCOS DE ANDALUCÍA, ALGECIRAS (including Gibraltar).

A Bit of History

Jimena was a border outpost between Christians and Nasrids until its reconquest in 1454 by the Trastamara king, Enrique IV. Smugglers and highwaymen frequented this area of difficult access from the 19C until after the Spanish Civil War. A growing British community has settled here over the past few decades

Visit

Iglesia de la Misericordia

This simple, 15C Gothic church with a single nave has been sensitively restored to house the local tourist office and Centro de Información del Parque Natural de los Alcornocales (*see opposite*). Open 11am–1pm and 3–5pm (4–7pm in summer). Sat–Sun and public hols 10am–1pm and 3–4pm. ☎956 64 05 69.

Castle

This 13C Moorish castle-fortress is atop Cerro de San Cristóbal, where Roman Oba might have stood. Access to the main enclosure is through the double horseshoe arch of the imposing turret-watchtower. The esplanade on the hill is occupied by the town cemetery, several large water tanks and the castle enclosure, dominated by its austere **keep** (torre del homenaje).

Excursions

Laja Alta wall paintings★

Visitors must hire a local guide. Enquire at the tourist office in Jimena de la Frontera.
These wall paintings are some of the most interesting in Cádiz province as well as some of the best preserved, mainly due to their recent discovery

Cork Stripping

The extraction of cork (corcho) is a process that calls for the experience and skill of the corchero or cork-stripper. The exploitation of Andalusian cork oak began in the 1830s, since when there has been little change in working methods. The instrument used to strip the cork is a special hatchet which cuts large strips of bark known as panas. This is the most delicate phase of the whole operation as any damage to the tree might affect the regeneration of the bark, a process which normally takes ten years. Once the cork is stripped, the collectors and splitters take over; it is their job to prepare the cork ready for transport by the muleteers. Cork oaks are considered ready for exploitation once they have reached 30 years and a diameter exceeding 60cm/2ft. As the lifespan of a cork oak is about 150 years, each tree normally yields around 10 harvests. Stripping normally takes place between June and September, when the cork oak is best able to regenerate itself.

View of Jimena de la Frontera with the Moorish castle on top of the hill

©Stephen Morris/iStockphoto.com

and difficult access. The paintings on rock include six Phoenician sailing vessels of extraordinary beauty that have been dated to around 1000 BC.

Castillo de Castellar (Old Castellar de la Frontera)★

29km/18mi south along A 369 to Almoraima, then bear right.

The Nasrids built this village-fortress in the 13C to protect the recently created kingdom of Granada. For two centuries, Castellar de la Frontera (as it was known) saw frontier battles until its reconquest in 1434. In the early 1970s, following the construction of the **Embalse de Guadarranque**, a reservoir which flooded the local area, most inhabitants moved to "Nuevo Castellar", 7km/4mi to the south (confusingly marked on many maps as Castellar de la Frontera). The road to old Castellar winds up past whitewashed houses through a landscape of outstanding beauty to this half-abandoned and very atmospheric village. Entry to the village, totally enclosed in the fortress, is via the gateway to the palace of the Dukes of Arcos.

Parque Natural de los Alcornocales★

Several roads criss-cross the park, including the A 375 from Alcalá de los Gazules, the CA 503 from Arcos de la Frontera, and the A 369 from San Roque (Algeciras).Others come over the Puerto Galis. For information on the park, call ☎956 41 33 07.

The typical vegetation here includes wild olive trees and, notably, the cork oak, which covers almost half the park's area to form Europe's largest cork oak forest. Many paths and trails include old cattle tracks. Two of the best walks here are to La Sauceda (*about 5hrs*) and the more strenuous ascent of **El Picacho** (*about 3hrs*).

LINARES ★
POPULATION: 58 410

This old mining settlement, birthplace of guitar master Andrés Segovia (1893–1987) is the second largest town in Jaén province, sited amid olive groves at the foot of the Sierra Morena along a Roman road. Despite its workaday past it has several sights and monuments of interest to visitors.

- **Information:** www.linares.net.
- ▶ **Orient Yourself:** Linares is 32km/20mi northwest of Úbeda.
- ◷ **Organising Your Time:** Allow a couple of hours.
- **Also See:** ÚBEDA, BAEZA, ANDÚJAR, JAÉN.

A Bit of History

Linares originated as Roman *Linarium*. Conquered by Fernando III the Saint in the mid-13C, it became a lead and silver mining centre in the 18C during the reign of Carlos III, though In recent times, mining has been declining. Linares is associated with famed bullfighter **Manolete**, killed in the ring (1947).

Sights

Museo Arqueológico ★
◷*Open July to mid-Sept Tue–Sat 9am–2pm. Rest of year 10am–2pm, Sat–Sun, 4–7pm.* ◷*Closed Mon, pub hols (and Sun in summer).* ✆*No charge.* ☎ *953 69 24 63.*
Set in the elegant Palacio Dávalos (note the graceful watchtower) the archaeological museum exhibits pieces from the Bronze Age to the Middle Ages. One of the finest is a 1C AD bronze **Nike from** nearby Cástulo, with delicately sculpted robes. The collection of **6C BC statuettes** of Astarté is also of interest.

Iglesia de Santa María la Mayor
This magnificent 16C building is a mix of Romanesque, Gothic and Renaissance styles. Note the doors of several side chapels *(the first and second on the right)*, and the fine **main altarpiece**, depicting scenes from the Old Testament.

Hospital de los Marqueses de Linares
The exuberant neo-Classical architecture of this 20C building contrasts with the elegant simplicity of the square of the same name. The crypt of the Marquess and Marchioness of Linares inside is by Coullaut Valera.

Palacio de Justicia
The façade of this imposing 18C building is profuse with sculptures depicting religious themes and scenes of daily life.

Iglesia de San Francisco
The austere exterior, crowned by a spire and flanked by a graceful bell tower, contrasts with the beauty of the fine Baroque **retable** at the high altar.

Ayuntamiento
The monumental 18C town hall has an attractive porticoed atrium.

Casa Museo Andrés Segovia
◷*Open mid-Jun to mid-Sept Tue, Thu, Sat–Sun 10am–2pm. Mid-Sept to mid-Jun also Tue & Thu 4–7pm.* ☎ *953 65 09 36. www.segoviamuseo.com.*
Photographs, documents, memorabilia and of course guitars, relating to the life of Spain's greatest 20C classical guitarist, are housed in the 17C Orozco Palace. Segovia is buried here in the crypt.

Excursions

Ruins of Cástulo
7km/4.5mi NE along the A 312 towards Arquillos.
Cástulo was founded by the Greeks and prospered as a lead and silver mining center under Phoenicians and Romans. Imilce, wife of the Carthaginian gen-

eral Hannibal, was born here. Artefacts dating back to this time have been unearthed.

Baños de la Encina
11km/7mi NW along the A 1200.
This quiet village, set amid olive groves and the gentle hills of the **Parque** Natural de la Sierra de Andújar★ *(see ANDÚJAR)*, is overlooked by a strategic **Moorish fortress**. Vestiges of the former mosque are visible. It is well worth climbing one of the watchtowers to enjoy the superb **views**.

LOJA

POPULATION: 20 143

Loja stands on a hill overlooking the plain of the River **Genil** between Málaga and Granada. The town is dominated by its Moorish fortress, which defended the plain extending eastward towards Granada. Loja was razed on several occasions during the Reconquest, and fell definitively to the Catholic Monarchs in 1486. **General Narváez**, the authoritarian behind Queen Isabel II, was born here in 1800.

- **Information:** Calle Comedias 18300 Loja. ☎958 32 39 49. www.aytoloja.org.
- ▶ **Orient Yourself:** Loja is 55km/34m west of Granada , 77km/48mi northeast of Málaga and 44.5km/28mi east of Antequera.
- **Organising Your Time:** Take a few hours to see Loja.
- **Also See:** ALHAMA DE GRANADA, IZNÁJAR, PRIEGO DE CÓRDOBA, MONTEFRÍO, GRANADA.

Walking Tour

Old Quarter
Before you begin exploring the casco histórico you might like to gather information in advance from the **Centro De Interpretación Histórico**, located in the Antigua Casa de Cabildos on Plaza de la Constitución (*Open year-round Mon–Fri 9am–2pm, also 4.30–6.30pm in winter*).

Loja's historical centre is accessed either by the Cuesta del Señor hill, or by circling the impressive 16C–18C **Iglesia de la Encarnación**.

Above the church stands the **alcazaba** (*The fortress is currently closed for restoration; ☎958 32 39 49 – tourist office*), a fortress with an intact keep; the simple, 17C residence of the Christian Governors (*Caserón de los Alcaides Cristianos*); the Torre Ochavada (tower) and, on the parade ground, the remains of a cistern (*aljibe*).

Calle Moraima leads to the outer limits of the medieval quarter. The view from the **Mirador Arqueológico** of the **Iglesia de San Gabriel**, a fine 16C Renaissance church, is impressive. Its façade, attributed to **Diego de Siloé**, is a striking Renaissance work.

In plaza de Abajo, formerly plaza Joaquín Costa, note the 13C **Puerta de Jaufín**, the gate that provided access to the fortress. To the side stands the old granary (*pósito*); only its lower section remains.

Bell tower, Iglesia de la Encarnación

Loja Address Book

For coin ranges, see the Legend on the cover flap.

WHERE TO STAY

Barceló La Bobadilla – *18 km/11mi west by A 92, exit 175 toward Sevilla.* ☎958 32 18 61. www.la-bobadilla.com. *62 rooms.* This grand luxury hotel on an estate covering 350ha/865 acres hosts the rich, famous and powerful and has been voted one of the best hotels in the world. Its estate is a village in itself with its own spa and beautifully landscaped pool.

WHERE TO EAT

Nearby **Riofrío** has had an excellent reputation for its trout since the 17C. For dessert, try another local speciality, the cakes known as **roscos de Loja**.

SPORT

To catch your own dinner, head to the **Coto Intensivo de Pesca**, a fishing area open all year. *For permits, information and reservations, contact the Albergue de Pescadores (fishermens lodge) de Riofrío,* ☎958 32 31 77/11 56.

LUCENA

POPULATION: 35 564

Set amid olive groves just west of the Parque Natural de la Sierra Subbética, Lucena is one of the wealthiest towns in Córdoba province.

- **Information:** Calle Castillo del Moral. ☎957 51 32 82, www.turlucena.com.
- **Orient Yourself:** Lucena is 70km/44mi south of Córdoba.
- **Don't Miss:** The exuberant Capilla del Sagrario. of the Iglesia de San Mateo.
- **Organising Your Time:** Allow half a day for Lucena.
- **Also See:** CABRA, AGUILAR DE LA FRONTERA, PRIEGO DE CÓRDOBA.

A Bit of History

Roman, Moorish, Jewish – Lucena dates back to the Roman period, although it was under the Moors, in the 10C and 11C, that it enjoyed considerable development. It became an important Jewish enclave known as "The Pearl of Sefarad" and was home to a prestigious Hebrew university. In the 18C it experienced an economic and artistic revival, developing into one of the most prosperous towns in the province.

Address Book

For coin ranges, see the Legend on the cover flap.

WHERE TO STAY

Hotel Santo Domingo – *Juan Jiménez Cuenca, 16.* ☎957 51 11 00. *30 rooms.* A grand hotel with large, comfortable rooms, housed in a former 18C convent.

WHERE TO EAT

Araceli – *Avenida del Parque, 10.* ☎957 50 17 14. *Closed last two weeks of Aug.* Ordinary in appearance, this is the town's best restaurant, specialising in fish and seafood.

Visit

Iglesia de San Mateo★

Plaza Nueva. Open summer 7.30am–1.30pm and 7–9pm, rest of year 7.30am–1.30pm and 6.30–9pm. ☎957 50 07 75. Hernán Ruiz I and II were both involved in the design of this transitional Gothic-Renaissance church.

Exterior

The interplay of features gives dynamism to this large church. Buttresses frame the fine, classically inspired Ren-

©J. D. Dallet/Picture Colour Library

Olive groves near Lucena

aissance portal. A tower stands to the left; the Capilla del Sagrario (Sacrarium Chapel), with characteristic cupola, is to the right.

Interior
The interior is spacious and harmonious. The nave has wooden ceilings; the triple apse has Gothic vaulting. Polychrome reliefs on the five panels of a magnificent Renaissance **retable**★ narrate Gospel and Old Testament scenes.

Capilla del Sagrario★★
In the Epistle nave, at the foot of the church.
The walls and cupola of this early 18C Baroque jewel are covered with polychrome **stuccowork**★★ in an ensemble of unparalleled exuberance. Every type of ornamental feature is used, including geometric and plant motifs, angels, bishops, saints etc.

Castillo del Moral (Museo Municipal Arqueológico Y Etnológico)
⏱*Open summer: Tue–Fri 9am–2pm and 7–10pm, Sat 10am–1.30pm and 7–9pm, Sun and hols 10am–1.30pm. Winter: Tue–Fri 9am–2pm and 5–8pm, Sat 11am–2pm & 5–8pm, Sun and Hols 11am–2pm. ☎957 51 32 82.*
This restored medieval fortress retains two of its towers. It is said that Boabdil was imprisoned in the octagonal Torre del Mora. The castle is now home to the town's archaeological and ethnographic collections.

Iglesia de Santiago
⏱*Open 9am–1pm and 6.30–9pm.*
☎*957 50 05 45.*
The Church of St James was built over a razed synagogue. The brick façade, with late-Gothic portal, is supported by buttresses. Inside, ogival arches rest upon brick pillars that appear twisted by the weight, creating an unusual impression of fragility. The church also houses a sculpture of Christ tied to a column, by Pedro Roldán.
Other churches in Lucena are the **Iglesia de San Juan de Dios** and the **Iglesia de San Agustín**, both with handsome Baroque portals.

Excursions

Santuario de la Virgen de Araceli★
6km/4mi S, last section with a steep 20% gradient.
This sanctuary is at the highest point of the Sierra de Aras. There is an impressive **view**★ of olive groves, with the mountains acting as a backdrop.

Lucena to Iznájar
35km/22mi along the C 331.
The road crosses a charming landscape of olive orchards and mountains to **Rute** *(20km/12.5mi)* famous for its anise liqueur A donkey sanctuary is on the outskirts. The **road**★ *(15km/9.5mi)* continues with views to the right of the reservoir *(embalse)* and **Iznájar**★ *(⏱see IZNÁJAR)*, impressively positioned on top of a hill.

MÁLAGA★★
POPULATION: 534 683

The bustling gateway to the Costa del Sol is characterised by elegant promenades, impressive monuments, an active marina and port, and residential quarters with fine 19C villas. Málaga's skyline is dominated by the Gibralfaro, or Lighthouse Hill, crowned by a Moorish fortress. Despite the proximity of so many tourist-oriented seaside resorts Málaga remains a resolutely Spanish enclave.

- **Information:** The Gardener's House Avenida Cervantes, 1. ☏952 21 34 45. Plaza de la Marina, 11. ☏952 12 20 20. www.malagaturismo.com
- **Orient Yourself:** Málaga is 59km/37mi east of Marbella. Its airport, serving the Costa del Sol, is one of the busiest in Spain. To get your bearings take a hop-on, hop-off City Sightseeing bus tour (www.city-sightseeing.com).
- **Parking:** Driving in Málaga is not recommended.
- **Don't Miss:** The Picasso Museum, views from the Castillo de Gibralfaro.
- **Organising Your Time:** Allow 2–3 days.
- **Also See:** COSTA DEL SOL, ANTEQUERA.

A Bit of History

Antiquity – Phoenicians founded Malaca around the late 8C /early 7C BC. Greek and Carthaginian trading posts followed. The Romans created a colony in the 3C BC. It exported wine, oil, raisins, cereals, salted meat and fish. Christianity came in the 4C.

Moorish domination – After 716, Málaga was ruled from Córdoba, then became part of the kingdom of Granada. The fortress (*alcazaba*) was built in the

11C, when the city developed its textile industry. Following periods of Almoravid and Almohad dominion, Málaga became the chief port of the Nasrids in Granada. In the 14C, the Gibralfaro fortress was rebuilt and extended by Yusuf I. The Genoese developed the city's commerce and opened new trade routes.

The Christian city – Moorish Málaga fell in August 1487. In the 16C, under Felipe II, a new port brought renewed prosperity, heightened in the 18C by liberalised trade.

View of the city and port from the Castillo de Gibralfaro

B. Kaufmann/MICHELIN

19C – The French held Málaga from 1810 to 1812. Liberal-absolutist conflicts led to the execution of General Torrijos in 1831. The 19C was the era of the Industrial Revolution. Two wealthy families, the Heredias (iron and steel) and the Larios (textiles), developed factories. After a decline, tourism took up the slack in the 1950s.

Roman and Moorish Quarter

Alcazaba★

🕐*Open in summer, Tue–Sun, 9.30am–8pm; otherwise, Tue–Sun, 8.30am–7pm.* 🕐*Closed Mon, 1 Jan and 24, 25 and 31 Dec.* €1.95 (€3, including Castillo de Gibralfaro). ☎952 22 51 06.

Construction of the hilltop Moorish fortress started in 1040. One of the largest Muslim military installations preserved in Spain, it consists of a double enclosure with rectangular towers, all once connected to the city walls, now demolished.

Access is via a zig-zag ramp from calle Alcazabilla past sections of brick and masonry walls and through gateways, some of which re-used Roman columns. The Arco de Cristo (Christ's Arch), where Mass was celebrated after the reconquest, leads to the Moorish gardens. The **views**★ from atop of the walls take in the city and port.

In the second enclosure is the former palace, Nasrid in style.

Teatro Romano

The terraces on the slope of the hill are all that is left of this theatre at the foot of the Alcazaba (west side). Close by, the neo-Classical **Aduana** (Customs House) now houses provincial offices and an exhibit hall.

Castillo de Gibralfaro

Access: bus no 35.
Alight at paseo del Parque.
Open in summer, 9am–8pm; otherwise, 9am–6pm. €1.95. ☎952 22 51 06.

The path around the hilltop remains of the 14C Gibralfaro Castle , built to protect the *alcazaba*, provides magnificent **views**★★ of the city and the port. The

---

Málaga Wines

The city's wines were highly appreciated during Antiquity. Nowadays, the best-known Málaga wines are sweet or semi-sweet with an alcohol content of between 15% and 23%. The two grape varieties used in their production are Pedro Ximénez and Moscatel. The latter, which is also highly prized as a dessert grape, is used to produce a dessert wine known as **Málaga Dulce** (Sweet Málaga). Other wines made here include the smooth **Lágrima**, and **Pedro Ximénez**, which is created exclusively from the grape of the same name.

---

walled corridor connecting the Alcazaba with the castle was built in the 14C.

Centro de interpretación de Gibralfaro

The former powder store is now a centre retracing military life in the castle from the 15C–20C. Exhibits include collections of uniforms, weapons, maps and navigational equipment.

City Centre

Central Málaga has some delightful narrow streets and alleyways – much of the central area is pedestrianised – such as **pasaje Chinitas**, a lively shopping area near pedestrianised **calle Marqués de Larios**, the old city's main street.

Museo Picasso★★

🕐*Open Tue–Thu, 10am–8pm, Fri–Sat, 10am– 9pm, Sun and pub hols, 10am–8pm.* €6; €4.50 exhibition; €8 combined; free last Sun of month, 3–8pm. ☎ 902 44 33 77. www.museopicasso malaga.org.

The Picasso Museum opened in 2003, in the 16C Renaissance Palacio de Buenavista with its fine *artesonado* ceilings. The permanent collection comprises more than 200 works from the collections of the artist's niece and grandson, Christine and Bernard Ruiz-Picasso. Oils, sketches, engravings, sculptures and ceramics, displayed chronologi-

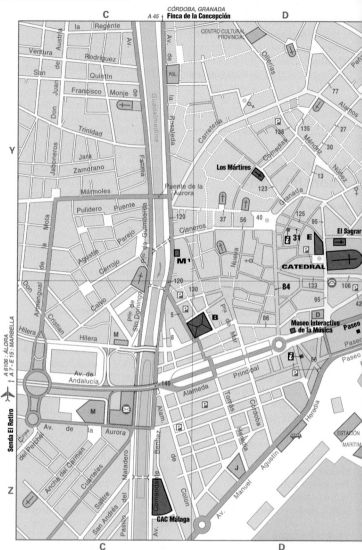

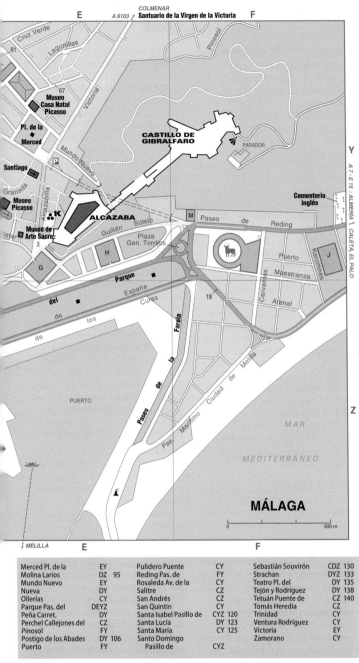

Address Book

GETTING THERE AND AROUND

Pablo Picasso International Airport – The airport is 10km/6mi SW along the coast road (☎952 04 88 04, www.aena.es).

The Portillo company operates buses between from the city centre every 25min. The local train to Fuengirola stops at the airport (every 30min). Taxis are also widely available at the airport.

Trains – The rail station (☎952 36 05 60 or 902 24 02 02) is along esplanada de la Estación and serves Spain's major cities. The Fuengirola train runs through Torremolinos, Benalmádena and other towns and resorts along its route.

RENFE (Spanish State Railways) – *The station (Information and Tickets 902 24 02 02 is on paseo de Los Tilos.* Travellers have a wide choice of departures to Spain and cities abroad.

City buses – The local bus network (SAM) provides a comprehensive service. ☎952 35 72 00 or 902 52 72 00. A private company, **Portillo**, provides periodic services to the major resorts and towns along the Costa del Sol.

Taxis – ☎952 34 56 93 or 952 33 33 33.

Ferries – Málaga's port is mainly commercial, although a passenger service operates to Morocco. Málaga is a popular port of call for cruise ships.

🕯*For coin ranges, see the Legend on the cover flap.*

WHERE TO STAY

🛏**Hotel Castilla y Guerrero** – *Córdoba, 7.* ☎95 221 86 35. www.hotel-castillaguerrero.com. *36 rooms.* Plain but good value, in a very central location.

🛏🛏**California** – *Paseo de Sancha, 17.* ☎952 21 51 64. www.hotelcalifornianet. com. *24 rooms.* A stone's throw from the sea, ten minutes from the old city. Old-fashioned, but with cosy rooms.

🛏🛏🛏**Hotel Monte Victoria** – *Conde de Ureña, 58.* ☎952 65 65 25. www.hotel-montevictoria.com. *8 rooms.* *Reservation advised.* Family villa hotel, with a garden-terrace which enjoys fine city views. Impeccable rooms. On a narrow, inclined street (hard to park), 15min on foot from the historic centre.

🛏🛏🛏**Hotel Don Curro** – *Sancha de Lara, 7.* ☎95 222 72 00. www. hoteldoncurro.com. *118 rooms.* The Don Curro occupies a seventies tower in the city centre. All rooms have recently been refurbished to 21C standards.

🛏🛏🛏🛏 **Parador de Málaga-Gibralfaro** – *Castillo de Gibralfaro.* ☎952 22 19 02. www.paradores-spain. com. *38 rooms.* Málaga's charming *parador* looks down onto the city. Have a drink on the bar terrace and enjoy delightful views of city and coast.

WHERE TO EAT

🍴**El Chinitas** – *Moreno Monroy, 4–6.* ☎952 21 09 72. www.chinitas.arrakis. es. A restaurant emblematic of Málaga with old-time photos, ceramics, and paintings. Lovely terrace on a pedestrian street, three floors of dining.

🍴🍴**El Campanario Ignacio** – *Paseo de la Sierra, 36.* ☎952 20 24 48. *Closed Sun eve and Mon.* Ignacio, the owner, is often at the stove. Great bay views, and a mix of updated classic dishes and the chef's creations.

🍴🍴🍴 **Restaurante-Museo La Casa del Ángel** – *Madre de Dios, 29 (facing Teatro Cervantes).* ☎95 260 87 50. *Closed Mon and 2 weeks in Jun.* Angel Garó combines art and tradition in an ambience that captivates the senses. Enjoy delicious cuisine surrounded by originals by Picasso, Dalí, and Miró.

TAPAS

Orellana – *Moreno Monroy, 5.* ☎952 22 30 12. *Closed Sun.* Short on decor, but the Orellana is one of the city's best-known and liveliest tapas bars.

La Posada de Antonio – *Granada, 33* ☎952 21 70 69. This bar decorated with barrels is at the heart of Málaga's nightlife area. Regional dishes and meats grilled in an open kitchen. A favourite meeting point for young *malagueños*.

Bar La Mesonera – *Gómez Pallete, 11.* This small bar fills up with stars and the rich and famous before and after flamenco performances at the Teatro Cervantes opposite. Delicious tapas and a colourful Andalusian atmosphere.

TAKING A BREAK

Café Central – *Plaza de la Constitución, 11.* A century-old coffee house frequented by faithful regulars. Pleasant terrace on the square, but don't miss the large tea room.

Casa Aranda – *Herrería del Rey, 2.* ☎*952 22 12 84. Open 9am–9pm.* This lively, atmospheric café has taken over every building on its street. Great place for chat over *chocolate con churros.*

GOING OUT

The central area around the cathedral and calle Larios has numerous lively old bars, mainly frequented by Málaga's younger generations and foreign visitors, and quieter cafés and tea shops (*teterías*). In summer, locals tend to spend more of their time along the paseo Marítimo. The more exclusive bars and clubs are in the upscale El Limonar district at the foot of the mountains.

Parador Málaga Gibralfaro

Paradores

El Pimpi – *Calle Granada, 62.* A Málaga tradition, on a pedestrian way in the old town. This old-time tavern is good for a quiet beer, coffee or tapas in the afternoon and early evening; and for lively nights, when more boisterous parties turn up the volume.

La Tetería and **Tetería Alcazaba** – *Calle San Agustín, 9 and 21.* Two small bars, popular with a younger set, in a pedestrianised street. The Moorish feel and aroma of the many teas on offer add to the atmosphere.

Siempre Así – *Calle Convaleciente, 5.* ☎*952 21 54 12. Open Thu–Sat.* This central bar is a favourite of the city's jet set. From midnight onwards the dance floor fills with people dancing to rumbas, *sevillanas* and the latest latino hits.

BEACHES

Málaga is blessed with a series of beaches, from La Malagueta and Las Acacias to Playa del Palo, 5km/3mi to the east. All have excellent facilities and a wide choice of bars and restaurants.

SHOPPING

The main shopping streets are concentrated between calle Puerta del Mar (which runs into plaza de Félix Sáez and becomes calle Nueva) and **calle Marqués de Larios**. Many street vendors also have their pitch here. Look for shops selling the typical puff pastry cakes (*hojaldres*), a local speciality. A good selection of more modern stores, as well as two large department stores of the El Corte Inglés chain, are just outside the historical centre in calle Armengual de la Mota. Large hypermarkets such as Pryca and Continente are on the city's outskirts.

MARKETS

A colourful market with everything from second-hand clothes to antiques is held on Sunday mornings near the La Rosaleda football stadium.

LOCAL SPECIALITIES

If you are in Málaga in summer, make sure you try fried fish (*pescaíto frito*), as well as the city's traditional dishes, *ajoblanco*, a refreshing chilled soup imade from almonds, garlic, breadcrumbs, salt and olive oil. It is normally served with Moscatel grapes.

ENTERTAINMENT

Teatro Cervantes – *calle Ramos María.* ☎*952 22 41 00/09*, which opened in 1870, offers an extensive programme of theatre and concerts.

FILM FESTIVAL

Málaga is home to the Festival of Spanish Film, the most important of its kind.

LOCAL FIESTAS

Semana Santa – Málaga, like all Andalucía, celebrates Holy Week to the full, with processions rooted in the 16C. Huge floats, known as *tronos* (thrones), are erected in the open. The moment at which these floats are lifted and subsequently "rocked" is one of the most spectacular of the entire week.

The most important **processions** during Holy Week are: Señor de los Gitanos (Easter Monday), El Cautivo (Wednesday), Cristo de la Buena Muerte and Esperanza Perchelera (Maundy

Thursday). For more detials visit www.semana-santa-malaga.com.

The Feria – The annual fair, commemorating Málaga's reconquest, is held the middle week of August. It includes entertainment booths, copious eating and drinking, dancing, and general merriment by both locals and visitors.

TOURS

Horse-drawn carriages – These can be hired at a number of places around the city for tours of the main sites.

The hop-on, hop-off city **sightseeing bus,** departing from the bus station, is good value, www.city-sightseeing.com.

cally, illuminate the artist's journey. Early works show his technical mastery, notably *Olga Kokholva with Mantilla* (1917, note the penetrating gaze). Among other significant canvases are *Mother and Child* (1921–1922); the *Portrait of Pau with White Cap* (1923); *Bust of Woman with Arms Crossed Behind Head* (1939), an expressive work with surrealist influences; and *Woman in Armchair* (1946).

Cathedral★

🕐*Open Mon–Fri 10am–6pm. Sat 10am–5pm. Sun and public hols for worship only.* ⊜*€3.50.* ☎*952 21 59 17.*

Construction took place between the 16C and 18C, hence the mix of styles: Renaissance predominates, the ground plan is Gothic, the ceilings and façade Baroque. The design is believed to be the work of Diego de Siloé, who was also responsible for Granada Cathedral, with the assistance of Andrés de Vandelvira.

Exterior

The Baroque main façade, fronts plaza del Obispo. The tower on the right is unfinished, hence the nickname "La Manquita" (Missing One). Note the relief of the Incarnation (the Cathedral's name) on the middle portal.

Interior

Enter through the garden, left side of the cathedral.

The proportions are monumental: a hall-church ground plan with three aisles, side chapels and an ambulatory.

The lofty naves rest on layers of columns, and are crowned by fine **oven vaulting**★ bearing attractive decoration. Handsome 17C choir **stalls**★, were partly carved by Pedro de Mena. Note the two magnificent 18C Baroque organs, large choral stands, and the 17C marble pulpits with ecclesiastical escutcheons. The tabernacle at the high altar dates from the 19C.

Behind the choir is a lovely *Pietà* (1802) in Carrara marble by the Pisan brothers. The **side chapels** hold notable works: in the Capilla de los Caídos, a *Dolorosa* by Pedro de Mena below a *Christ Crucified* by Alonso de Mena, both 17C; a huge canvas of the *Virgin of the Rosary* by Alonso Cano in the Capilla del Rosario; and a 17C *Immaculate Conception* by Claudio Coello in the Capilla de la Inmaculada Concepción.

In the **ambulatory**, the Capilla de Nuestra Señora de los Reyes boasts a *Virgin and Child*, and a sculpture of the Catholic Monarchs, by Pedro de Mena; the Capilla de Santa Bárbara has an impressive early-15C **Gothic retable**★★. The 18C Capilla de la Encarnación or Capilla del Sagrario (Sacrarium Chapel) is entirely of marble.

G. Bludzin/MICHELIN

Towers and ramparts of the Alcazaba

Museo

Enter from the ticket window, downstairs.
This small museum exhibits religious paintings, anonymous 16C and 17C sculpture, and silver and gold objects.

El Sagrario

🕐*Open 9.30am–12.30pm and 6.30–9.30pm.* ☎*952 21 19 35.*
This unusual 16C rectangular church in the cathedral gardens has a superbly sculptured Isabelline Gothic **side portal**★ *(giving onto calle Santa María).* The single-nave Baroque interior dates from an 18C renovation. The superb sculpted **altarpiece**★★ in the apse is Mannerist in style and crowned by an impressive Calvary.

Palacio Episcopal

The 18C Baroque Bishop's Palace, on plaza del Obispo, has a beautiful pink and grey marble doorway adorned with Corinthian columns and broken entablatures. The upper niche houses a *pietà*. There is also an exhibit hall for the Andalusian council.

Museo de Arte Sacro

The Abbey of Santa Ana hosts this collection of sacred art, including 17C–18C carvings with outstanding works by Pedro de Mena *(Ecce Homo, Child Jesus).*

Iglesia de Santiago

🕐*Open 9am–1pm and 6–9pm.* ☎*952 21 03 99.*
The Church of St James, founded after the Reconquest, is on calle Granada, near plaza de la Merced. A brick tower is in primitive Mudéjar style with *sebka* decoration on its second section, and a portal (now sealed) with geometric *lacería* motifs. The 18C Baroque interior houses the venerated statue of **Jesus the Rich** in a chapel off the Evangelist nave. Pablo Picasso was baptised in this church.

Plaza de la Merced

An obelisk recalls General Torrijos, executed in 1831 for defending liberal ideas. One of two identical buildings on the northeast side was the birthplace of Picasso.

Museo-Casa Natal Picasso

🕐*Open Mon–Sat 10am–8pm.* 🎫*€1.* ☎*952 26 02 15. www.fundacionpicasso.es.*
Picasso was born in the mid-19C building at no 15. The first floor displays a number of his drawings and ceramics well as photos and memorabilia.

Museo de Artes y Costumbres Populares

🕐*Open Mon–Fri 10am–1.30pm, 4–7pm (mid-Jun to late Sept 5–8pm), Sat, 10am–1.30pm all year.* 🎫*€2.* ☎*952 21 71 37. www.museoartespopulares.com.*
The charming and very informative Museum of Popular Arts and Traditions is set in an attractive 17C inn, the Mesón de la Victoria. It provides an insight into traditional rural and urban life a century or more ago.

Mercado Central

The main market is a 19C iron structure on the site of the old Moorish dockyards.

CAC Málaga

🕐*Open late Jun to late Sept Tue–Sun 10am–8pm. Rest of year Tue–Sun 10am–2pm and 5–9pm.* ☎*952 12 00 55.*
The former wholsale market is now the **Centro de Arte Contemporáneo de Málaga** (modern art centre). It holds 400 works donated from private collections, shown on a rotating basis. Notable are 20C Spanish paintings (by Sicilia, Broto, Barceló, etc.).

Museo Interactivo de la Música

🕐*Open Mon–Fri 10am–2pm, 4–8pm, Sat–Sun 11am–3pm, 4.30–8.30pm.* ☎*952 21 04 40. www.musicaenaccion.com.*
This lively new museum has an entertaining and well-presented collection of over 300 musical instruments from different eras and regions and musical styles from Eminem to Mozart. Some can be played and the emphasis throughout "se ruega tocar" ("please play") is on being involved.

Museo Municipal Málaga

Paseo Reding, 1. 🕐*Call for opening times.* ☎*952 22 51 06. www.museomunicipal malaga.es*

Finca de la Concepción

The Municipal Museum explores the history of Málaga thematically on an exhibition by exhibition basis.

Paseo del Parque

This stretch of greenery is a botanical garden, a haven amid the urban bustle. In **paseo de la Farola**, to the east, is the **statue of the Cenachero**, a fish peddler and Málaga character. The La **Malagueta** quarter, beyond, marks the beach area.

Outside the City Centre

Santuario de la Virgen de la Victoria★

Calle Compás de la Victoria.
Open 9am–12.30pm and 5–6.30pm, no visit during services; camarín and crypt by appointment. €1.50. 952 25 26 47.
The church of this 15C sanctuary has a simple brick exterior and restrained Andalusian Baroque interior. The 17C carved altarpiece narrates scenes from the life of St Francis of Paola; in the Evangelist nave is a highly expressive *Dolorosa* by Pedro de Mena.

The **camarín**★★, at the centre of the main altarpiece, a masterpiece of exuberant Baroque architecture, is engulfed by stuccoed cherubs, acanthus leaves, etc. The **crypt**★ for the Counts of Buenavista could not be more sombre, with its black background festooned with skeletons and skulls.

Cementerio Inglés

Avenida Pries, 1.
The **English cemetery**, the first Protestant burial ground in Spain, was ceded to the British consul in 1829. Poet Gerald Brennan is buried here.

Excursions

Finca de la Concepción★

7km/4.5mi north. Open year-round Tue–Sun 9.30am–8.30pm (Oct–Mar 5.30pm). Last admission 90mins before closing. €3.15 952 25 21 48. http://laconcep cion.ayto-malaga.es.
This magnificent botanical garden was created in the middle of the 19C by Jorge Loring and his wife, Amalia Heredia, who brought tropical and subtropical species to Málaga on ships owned by her father. The delightful estate is a forest of greenery dissected by small streams and embellished with lakes, waterfalls and Roman remains.

Senda El Retiro★

Near Churriana, 5km/9.5mi SW.
Call for prices and times.
952 62 35 40.
The 17C estate of the bishop of Málaga, is now a botanic and ornitholgical garden, featuring **aviaries** with 150 species of birds, an aquarium, reptile house, and Andalusian village. The **historical garden**★ is made up of 17C and 18C gardens.
The most spectacular sections are the French-influenced garden-court, with lion fountain and impressive **water staircase**; and the patio-garden.

MARBELLA★★

POPULATION: 98 377

Marbella is the most exclusive resort along the Costa del Sol. A magnificent climate, superb beaches and leisure facilities have transformed a simple fishing port into a playground of seafront apartment blocks and inland holiday complexes. It is a shoppers' paradise, particularly for luxury goods, and has developed a reputation for its exclusive nightlife, health clubs and spas. Superb sporting facilities include famous golf courses and its cosmopolitan appeal – there has been a huge investment in Arab funds recently – means there are mosques and even a synagogue

Traditional Andalucía still survives however, in the old quarter, where white-washed houses are adorned with wrought-iron grilles and displays of flowers.

- 🖪 **Information:** Glorieta de la Fontanilla, Paseo Marítimo. ☎952 77 14 42. www.marbella.es.
- ▶ **Orient Yourself:** Marbella is 32km/20mi northwest of Málaga.
- 🐎 **Don't Miss:** People-watching at Puerto Banús.
- 🕐 **Organising Your Time:** Allow two days.
- 🄺🄸🄳🄂 **Especially for Kids:** Beaches here and along the coast.
- 🕭 **Also See:** COSTA DEL SOL, MÁLAGA, RONDA, MIJAS (29km/18mi E).

Old Town Tour★
Allow 2hr

Marbella's old Moorish quarter is a delightful maze of narrow, twisting alleyways lined by whitewashed old buildings, and shops, bars and restaurants.

Plaza de los Naranjos★
This enchanting centre of the old quarter is perfect for unwinding at an out-door café facing the 16C stone fountain, delightful floral displays and orange trees *(naranjos)*. Buildings around the square include the 16C **town hall**, with its wrought-iron balconies and handsome Mudéjar doorway, the 17C **Casa del Corregidor** (Magistrate's Mansion), with monumental stone **façade**★ and elegant balcony, and the 15C **Ermita de Nuestro Señor Santiago**, the first Christian church erected in Marbella.

Plaza de los Naranjos

©Turespaña

The Price of Paradise

While the very name Marbella still oozes quality, glamour and luxury, in latter decades it has also come to have connotations of a rather brash and ostentatious style with dubious links. The resort's original rich and famous 1960s entrepreneurs retreated back in to the hills or moved on to the "next big thing" long ago. In the 1970s Marbella's reputation was tarnished, as it became a refuge for British criminals, hiding here under Spain's non-extradition treaty with Britain (since Spain has joined the EU this loophole has been closed). In the 1980s and 1990s Russian mafia money is reputed to have moved in and one of Europe's largest ever money laundering rings was uncovered here in 2005.

Iglesia de Santa María de la Encarnación

The church, in the square of the same name, is at the end of the busy calle Nueva, where a Moorish tower still stands. This Baroque building has a splendid stone **portal** and large bell tower. It holds a carving of St Barnabas, the patron of Marbella, and a sumptuous organ, the **Órgano del Sol Mayor**.

Museo del Grabado Español Contemporáneo★

🕐*Open mid-Jun to Sept Tue–Sat 10am– 2pm and 7–9pm. Oct to mid-Jun Mon 10am–2pm, Tue–Fri 9am–9pm, Sat 9am–2pm.* ✺*€3.* ☎*952 76 57 41. www. museodelgrabado.com.*
The Contemporary Spanish Print Museum, unique in Spain, is located in the 16C former Hospital de Bazán. Works by Tàpies, Alberti, Chillida and Maruja Mallo are on display.

Museo del Bonsai

🕐*Open daily year-round 10.30am– 1.30pm and 4–6.30pm (Jul–Aug 5–8pm).* ✺*€4.* ☎*952 86 29 26*
Set in the Parque Arroyo la Represa this museum of miniature Japanese bonsai trees is an unlikely but popular visitor attraction.

Hospital de San Juan de Dios

This hospital in calle Misericordia dates from the Reconquest. Its outstanding features are the pleasant cloisters and the Mudéjar *artesonado* work in the chapel.

Seigniorial mansions

Mansions in plaza Ancha and plaza de Altamirano include the 16C Casa de los Cano Saldaña, and the house of Ferdinand de Lesseps, of Suez Canal fame.

Excursions

Villa Romana de Río Verde

2km/1.2mi west along A 7.
This 1C–2C Roman villa has attractive mosaic paving.

Puerto Banús★★

5km/3mi west along the A 7.
This superb marina shelters some of the world's most expensive sailing vessels. Alongside the moorings (and an impressive collection of fast cars), are some of the region's most fashionable bars, restaurants, and luxury boutiques. The marina attracts all kinds of visitors on summer evenings for a drink or meal and shopping in late-hours boutiques. By day, Puerto Banús is a more relaxed and very pleasant place for a stroll and views down the coast.

Istán

15km/9.5mi northwest along the A 6206. Follow signposts west from Marbella. This former Moorish village is set along the River Verde among terraced fields of fruits and vegetables. The Iglesia de San Miguel, a 16C church, has an impressive belfry.

Driving Tour

Inland

51km/32mi (one way).

▶ *Head north out of Marbella along the A 355; turn where signposted.*

Ojén

This whitewashed village with its old Moorish quarter is set amid orange and pine groves. The **Iglesia de Nuestra Señora de la Encarnación** is a 15C church with a single nave and a fine *artesonado* ceiling. Ojén is famous for its brandy *(aguardiente)*.

▶ *Return to the A 355, then bear left.*

Refugio de Juanar

This refuge in a lovely setting offers stunning **views**★ over the Sierra Blanca.

▶ *Take the A 355 north to Monda.*

Monda

This village shelters below the remains of a Moorish fortress. The 16C **Iglesia de Santiago**, modified in the 18C, has profusely decorated vaulting in its triple nave.

▶ *Exit Monda on the A 6207, bear left onto the A 366, continue on MA 412.*

Tolox

Tolox lies in the **Parque Natural de Sierra de las Nieves**. The 16C church, **Iglesia de San Miguel** (○*open daily, 11am–2pm and 6–9pm.* ☎*952 48 73 33)* has three aisles separated by semicircular arches and topped by an attractive *artesonado* ceiling. The ceiling is elliptical, decorated with paintings.

MARCHENA

POPULATION: 18 018

This Sevillian country town prospered in the 15C and 16C under the Dukes of Arcos and retains many fine buildings from that period, while its imposing towers recall Moorish times. Remains of earlier settlements have been dated back to the Bronze Age.

▯ **Information:** Calle Las Torres 48. ☎955 84 61 67. www.turismodemarchena.org.

▶ **Orient Yourself:** Marchena is 68km/42mi, southeast of Sevilla and 27km/17m southeast of Carmona.

☺ **Don't Miss:** The Iglesia de San Juan Bautista.

○ **Organising Your Time:** Take a day to see Marchena and towns nearby.

ₑ **Also See:** UTRERA, CARMONA, ÉCIJA, OSUNA, SEVILLA.

Walking Tour

Arco de la Rosa

This 15C gateway in a remaining section of the town wall is a horseshoe arch framed by bastions.

Iglesia de San Juan Bautista★★

The 15C Gothic-Mudéjar Church of John the Baptist fronts a pleasant square with several seigniorial doorways. The spire on the bell tower bears *azulejo* decoration. The **interior** comprises three central aisles with *artesonado* ceilings, and two side aisles – in 16C extensions – covered by arris vaults. Numerous **works of art** adorn the walls. In the presbytery is a sumptuously carved and painted early 16C **retable**★★★ narrating scenes from the life of Christ (paintings by Alejo Fern-

Iglesia de San Juan Bautista

ández, sculptural groups by his brother, Jorge). The 16C **grille** was made locally. The wrought-iron pulpits are 18C, as is the impressive choir **grille**. The 18C mahogany and cedar **choir stalls**★ were carved by Jerónimo de Balbás. The two organs are Rococo and neo-Classical.

The Capilla del Sagrario, a chapel to the left of the presbytery, has a magnificent 16C **carved retable**★★ by Roque Balduque and Jerónimo Hernández. Note the unusual Last Supper arrangement.

Noteworthy statues include an *Immaculate Conception* by Pedro de Mena *(first chapel in the Epistle nave)* and a *St Joseph and Child (chapel to the right of the apse)*. The St Joseph figure is by Pedro Roldán.

Museo Zurbarán, Orfebrería y Bordados★★

Entrance from church.

⟳Open by prior arrangement, 10.30am–1.30pm. ⟳€1.50. ☏955 84 51 21 (tourist office).

The centrepiece of this museum are the nine paintings by Francisco de Zurbarán (1598–1664) the Baroque master, based in nearby Seville, famous for his religious scenes. The examples here include *Christ, The Immaculate Conception, St Peter, St James, John the Evangelist, John the Baptist, St Paul, St Andrew* and *St Bartholomew*. These were com-

missioned for the sacristy and date from the same period as those in the Monasterio de Guadalupe, in Cáceres province. Other valuable items on dislpay are a huge (1.62m/4.9ft high), 16C silver monstrance, 15C–16C books, and 16C–17C embroidery and silverware.

▷ *Head up to the highest part of the town.*

Plaza Ducal

The 18C former town hall with a sober stone doorway faces the square, itself a former castle parade ground. Parts of the nearby castle are well preserved.

▷ *Pass through the 11C Arco de la Alcazaba.*

Iglesia de Santa María la Mayor (de la Mota)

This sombre Gothic-Mudéjar church lies within the ducal palace. Modifications are evident on the tower. The façade has a single trumpet-shaped doorway.

Nearby are the **Iglesia de San Agustín**, a church built during the transition from Baroque to neo-Classical, and the **Puerta de Morón**, a fortified tower that houses the tourist office and a museum dedicated to sculptor Lorenzo Coullault Valera.

Excursions

Paradas

8km/5mi SW along the SE 217.

Paradas was a stopping-point *(parada)* for caravans to Sevilla in the Middle Ages.

The **museum** (⟳*Open by prior arrangement;* ☏*954 84 90 39)* in the 16C Baroque **Iglesia de San Eutropio** displays religious gold and silverware, illuminated books, and an outstanding *Magdalena* by El Greco.

El Arahal

15km/9.5mi SW along the SE 217.

In the old quarter of this tranquil town, small whitewashed houses stand alongside elegant Baroque and neo-Classical buildings. Among them are the 18C Capilla de la Vera Cruz, in colonial style;

the Mudéjar Iglesia de Nuestra Señora de la Victoria; the 17C **Iglesia de Santa María Magdalena**; and the **Iglesia de San Roque**, containing several 18C altarpieces.

Morón de la Frontera

27km/17mi S. Follow the A 364 to Montepalacio, then take the A 361.
Morón de la Frontera surrounds the ruins of a Moorish castle. The Gothic **Iglesia de San Miguel** with neo-Classical portal features 18C Baroque details inside. The **Iglesia de San Ignacio** (or Iglesia de la Compañía, as it was built by Jesuits) houses outstanding Flemish canvases. The 16C Renaissance **Iglesia de San Francisco** contains paintings by **José Ribera.**

MARTOS

POPULATION: 22 391

Martos, set amid a seas of olive groves, has a picturesque old quarter. Numerous 15C and 17C ancestral homes lend an elegant and seigniorial air.

- ▌ **Information:** www.martos.es
- ▶ **Orient Yourself:** Martos is 26km/16mi southwest of Jaén along the A 316.
- ⏱ **Organising Your Time:** Allow an hour or two.
- ⚲ **Also See:** JAÉN, BAENA, ALCALÁ LA REAL, CÓRDOBA.

Visit

Plaza de la Constitución

This graceful square is the heart of the old quarter.

Iglesia de Santa Marta

⏱*Open 9.30am–1pm and 6–8pm(9pm in summer). No visits during services.* ☎*953 55 02 68.*
Originally Gothic-Mudéjar, the church was remodelled in the 16C by Francisco del Castillo. The handsome **portal** is Isabelline. The sober interior has monumental pillars linked by arches with decorative plasterwork.

Ayuntamiento

The late-16C Renaissance town hall, once a prison, is adorned with an elegant portico of semicircular arches and a balcony with reliefs.

Fortaleza de la Virgen de la Villa

This fortress rises on the outskirts. Only two towers – the keep and the Torre de Almedina – remain but they give a very good idea of the immensity of the fortress in its prime.

Fuente Nueva★

This large 16C Renaissance fountain by Francisco del Castillo, near the bullring, bears the town's coat of arms.

Calle Real

Modernist buildings contrast with an old fortified tower, originally part of the defensive walls, and the Iglesia de las Madres Trinitarias, a Baroque church built in the 18C, damaged during the Spanish Civil War.

An eventful past

The former Iberian settlement of *Tucci* was used by the Lusitanians and their leader, Viriatus, as a winter camp in 142 BC.

A little over a century later, in 27 BC, Augustus transformed it into a colony for veteran legionaries. In the early days of Christianity, the town was the seat of a bishopric. Following five centuries of Arab domination, Martos was finally reconquered in 1225 by Fernando III (the Saint), and was later ceded to the Order of Calatrava.

Treasure

In 1931, local farmworkers discovered a chest full of valuable objects from the Visigothic period. The "Treasure of Torredonjimeno", as it has come to be known, is now on display in the archaeological museums of Madrid and Barcelona.

Iglesia de San Francisco

The elegant colonial-style portal is the oldest feature of the Church of St Francis.

Iglesia de Santa María de la Villa

Only the monumental four-storey tower remains from the original 13C church.

Excursion

Torredonjimeno

7km/4.5mi N.

Torredonjimeno is renowned for its wrought-iron work – it has the only bell foundry remaining in Andalucía – as well as for *encebollado*, a stew of cod, tomatoes, onions, garlic and herbs.

Old quarter

The historical quarter is to the right as you enter the town. The 16C Renaissance **town hall** fronts the plaza. The 16C **Iglesia de San Pedro** is Renaissance-style with an occasional Mudéjar feature. The 13C **castle** covers a Roman and Visigothic fortress. The slender, Gothic 16C **Iglesia de Santa María** is dedicated to the Immaculate Conception.

MEDINA SIDONIA★

POPULATION: 10 872

Medina Sidonia is at the centre of Cádiz province close to the **Parque Natural de los Alcornocales**. From its elevated site, it is possible to make out **El Puerto de Santa María** and **Vejer de la Frontera** on a clear day. Steep, narrow alleyways lend a Moorish feel, though Roman remains are the main interest for most visitors.

- **Information:** Plazuela de la Iglesia Mayor. ☎956 41 24 04.
- **Orient Yourself:** Medina Sidonia is 35km/22mi southeast of Jerez.
- **Organising Your Time:** Allow a day.
- **Also See:** CÁDIZ, El PUERTO DE SANTA MARÍA, JEREZ DE LA FRONTERA, ARCOS DE LA FRONTERA, VEJER DE LA FRONTERA.

A Bit of History

A Phoenician, Roman, Visigothic, Moorish and Christian town – The name Medina Sidonia reflect the key periods in the town's history: under the Phoenicians, the Moors and the Romans. The Phoenicians referred to their settlement here as Assido, while the Moors, who conquered the town in 712, named it Medina (city).

Medina Sidonia was an important Roman town and the seat of one of the first Visigothic councils, the Assidonensis, in the 6C.

Alfonso X the Wise reconquered it in the 13C, and in 1430 Juan II handed the town over as a dukedom to the Guzmán family.

The seventh Duke of Medina Sidonia has gone down in history as the commander of the ill-fated Spanish Armada.

Medieval Town

- *Climb calle Espíritu Santo as far as the Arco de la Pastora.*

Arco de la Pastora

Built in the 10C, this is one of three surviving medieval gateways (with Arco del Sol and the **Arco de Belén**).

The double, pointed horseshoe arch supported by two sturdy marble columns is probably Phoenician in origin.

Iglesia Santa María la Mayor, la Coronada

Iglesia Santa María la Mayor, la Coronada★

🕐*Open 10am–2pm and 4–6pm; summer, 9.30am–2pm and 4–9.30pm.* 🎫€2.50. ☎956 41 03 29.

This 15C "aristocratic Gothic" church has a tower finished in 1623 in Baroque style. Access is via a patio from an earlier church, with strong Mudéjar influence. Note the fine **Plateresque retable**★ at the high altar by Roque Boldaque, Juan Bautista Vázquez and Melchor de Turín. It shows the life of Jesus, and the Virgin Mary, with the mystery of the coronation as its central theme. To the left of the high altar is the 17C statue of Nuestra Señora de la Paz (Our Lady of Peace), the town's patron saint.

A monstrance of Mexican silver, by Martínez Montañés, is in the chapel to the right of the transept. A Plateresque doorway leads to the patio.

Alcázar and old town

🔍*visit by guided tour only (20min), Tue–Sun 10am–2pm and 4–6pm (5–7pm in summer).* 🎫 €2. ☎956 41 24 04.

The Moorish fortress *(alcazaba)* became a fortified Christian palace *(alcázar)* in 1264 with a triple walled enclosure and angled access gateway. The surrounding medieval district was abandoned in the 16C and used as a quarry. Some 16C houses and silos survive. The enclosure is guarded by the **Torre de Doña Blanca**, a watchtower which offers excellent views.

New Town

Go through the 15C **Arco de Belén** (Bethlehem Arch), and cross to the "newer" part of Medina Sidonia, built between the 16C and 19C.

Address Book

WHERE TO EAT

🍽🍽**Mesón Rústico Machín** – 2.5km/1.5mi on Medina–Chiclana road. ☎956 41 13 47. *Closed Wed.* A regional restaurant with fine views. Specialities include grilled asparagus, braised oxtail, *(rabo de toro)* and game in season.

LOCAL SPECIALITIES

Pastries – Since Moorish times, Medina Sidonia has been famous for its delicious cakes and biscuits, including the ever-popular **alfajor** – a type of macaroon made with almonds, eggs and honey. You can buy them direct from:

Convento de Jesús, María y José – in the old quarter behind the Iglesia de Santa María Mayor. 🕐*Open 9.30am–12.15pm and 4.30–6.15pm.*

Convento de San Cristóbal – *Calle Hércules, 1.* In the **New Town**, behind the municipal market. 🕐*Open 10am–2pm and 4–6pm.*

Plaza de España

A neo-Classical 18C **town hall** fronts this triangular *plaza* .

Beside the **market,** dating from 1871, on plaza de la Cruz, is a late-17C Baroque church, the Iglesia de la Victoria.

Calle de Fray Félix★ (calle de la Loba), is lined by 18C and 19C houses adorned with charming balconies. Outside of the walls is the 16C Iglesia de Santiago, with a fine *artesonado* ceiling.

Archaeological site★

🕐*Open daily 10am–2pm and 4–6.30pm (8pm Apr–Jun).* €3.10. ☎956 41 24 04.

This Roman drainage system dates from the 1C AD. Excavations offer a look at a a barrel-vaulted channel with tile flooring, which collected waters from smaller galleries.

Cryptoporticoes, used to terrace the terrain, have been unearthed. The *cardo maximus* was the main Roman street.

Excursions

Ermita de los Santos Mártires Justo y Pastor

On the ring road. 🕐*Open daily 10.30am–1.30pm and 5–8pm.* ☎956 41 24 04.

Founded by bishop Pimenio in 630, this hermitage is one of the oldest churches in Andalucía, with a large medieval tower possibly of Roman origin. The interior reuses Roman stelae and capitals.

Alcalá de los Gazules

25km/15.5mi east along the A 381.

This white hilltop town is the gateway to the **Parque Natural de los Alcornocales** (🕮 *see JIMENA DE LA FRONTERA*).In the upper section is the **Iglesia de San Jorge**, with its 18C Baroque tower and Gothic façade showing San Jorge on horseback.

The 16C former **town hall** houses the park visitor centre, the **Centro de Interpretación del Parque Natural de los Alcornocales**. (🕐*open Tue–Sun 10am–2pm and 4–6pm (summer, 5–7pm); ☎956 41 24 04).* The climb up to **El Picacho** and the Ruta de los Molinos (Route of the Windmills) are popular excursions. .

Benalup

20km/12.5mi SE of Medina Sidonia on the A 393.

This was the site of the **Casas Viejas** (the former name of Benalup) incident. In 1933, anarchists disenchanted with agrarian reforms were brutally repressed by the government under **Azaña**.

Cueva del Tajo de las Figuras – *8km/5mi SE on the A 5203 towards Algeciras, lefthand side.* 🕐*Open Wed–Sat and public hols exc. Sun 9am–3pm.* ☎956 42 41 29. These caves contain wall paintings from the post-Palaeolithic period.

MIJAS★

POPULATION: 37 490

Picturesque Mijas (also known as Mijas Pueblo), high on a hill amid pines in the foothills of the sierra, offers stunning **views**★ of the Costa del Sol.

Its winding streets, charming nooks and crannies, flower-decked houses and numerous tiny squares draw thousands of annual visitors.

🛈 **Information:** Avenida Virgen de la Peña. ☎952 58 90 34. www.mijas.es.

▶ **Orient Yourself:** The A 7–N 340, between Mijas Pueblo and Mijas–Costa (12km/7mi south on the Mediterranean), provides a fast road link to Málaga, 24km/15mi northeast, and Marbella, 33km/21mi southwest.

🅿 **Parking:** Park on the edge of town and then walk, or use the donkey taxi.

🕐 **Organising Your Time:** Allow half a day.

Kids Especially for Kids: A ride on a donkey taxi, the Miniatures Museum.

👣 **Also See:** MÁLAGA, COSTA DEL SOL.

Address Book

🎨 For coin ranges, see the Legend
on the cover flap.

WHERE TO STAY

🍷🍷🍷 **Hotel Mijas** – Urbanización
Tamisa, 2. ☎952 48 58 00. 197 rooms,
4 suites. Inspired by typical Andalusian
architecture, dazzling white façade
below the pines. Rooms are elegant
with country wood decor. Good value.

WHERE TO EAT

🍷🍷 **El Olivar** – Av. Virgen de la Peña,
6. ☎952 48 61 96. Closed Sat and in Feb.
Andalusian country restaurant with
great views from its terrace.
🍷🍷🍷 **El Padrastro** – Paseo del
Compás, 22. ☎952 48 50 00. Reservation advised. El Padrastro is unbeatable
for panoramas of the town, coast and
mountains. Original menu, romantic
and candlelit at night.

Visit

Old Quarter★

This photographer's paradise is a network of bright streets lined by low-
roofed houses decorated with wrought-
iron balconies and grilles. Boutiques and
souvenir shops can be found in calle de
Charcones, calle de San Sebastián and
calle de Málaga. Sections of the old
Moorish walls remain.

Iglesia de la Inma
culada Concepción

The 16C Church of the Immaculate
Conception retains an imposing Mudéjar tower. One of the side chapels has
attractive polychrome stuccowork
adorned with plant motifs.

Museo de Miniaturas

🕐 Open year-round daily 10am–7pm
(summer 10pm). 🎫€3. ☎952 58 90 34.
The Miniatures Museum displays a
shrunken head and a *Last Supper* by
Leonardo painted on a grain of rice,
among several other curiosities.

Museo Histórico-Etnológico

🕐 Open daily year-round 10am–2pm
and 4–7pm (5–8pm in summer).
☎952 59 03 80.
The old town hall houses a **museum**
relating to old ways of life at home, on
land and at sea.

Plaza de Toros

This small picturesque bullring has
an unusual rectangular design and a
bullfighting museum (museo taurino

🕐 open daily year round 10am–7pm (summer, 10pm); 🎫 €3; ☎952 48 52 48).

Santuario de la Virgen
de la Peña

🕐 Open daily 9am–9pm. ☎952 48 50 22.
This sanctuary was excavated out of the
rock in the 16C. Its attractive **mirador**
(lookout) provides great views.

R. Mattes/MICHELIN

The Donkey Taxi

This unusual form of transport is the
most frequently used by visitors to
the town. Although these colour-
fully decked-out animals travel at a
less than breakneck pace, they are a
popular aspect of local life.

MINAS DE RIOTINTO ★★

POPULATION: 5 500

This small community is set in a landscape of breathtaking colours, oak forests, and reservoirs and lakes, such as the Cobre-Gossan, Campofrío and Agua. The scars of excavated mountain slopes, deep-red in colour, bear witness to a mining tradition dating back some 5 000 years. Mining has ceased but the town's industrial heritage and the British-influenced district of Bellavista draws visitors and ensures a degree of prosperity.

- **Information:** www.parquemineroderiotinto.com
- ▶ **Orient Yourself:** Minas de Riotinto is in the Sierra de Aracena, near Parque Natural Sierra de Aracena y Picos de Aroche, 73km/45mi northeast of Huelva by the N 435, and 85km/53mi northwest of Sevilla.
- **Don't Miss:** The Maharajah's carriage in the Mining Museum, the Corta Atalaya.
- **Organising Your Time:** Allow at least half a day.
- **Especially for Kids:** The tourist train.
- **Also See:** ARACENA, Parque Natural Sierra de ARACENA Y PICOS DE AROCHE.

Visit

Parque Minero de Riotinto ★★

This mining-themed park lies within the town and in the surrounding area.

Museo Minero y Ferroviario ★

Open daily year-round 10.30am–3pm, 4–7pm (mid Jul–Sept 8pm). €4. 959 59 00 25. www.parquemineroderiotinto.com. The mining and railway museum is set in the former British hospital. Exhibits include early-20C locomotives and the popular **Maharajah's carriage** ★★★, built in England, for a planned journey to India by Queen Victoria. This work of art is a mass of carved wood and leather. The museum also displays artefacts of mining as far back as the Bronze Age, and a reconstruction of a **Roman mine**.

Casa 21 is a restored grand dwelling which depicts how the English mine owners and their families lived, around the turn of the 20C.

Enquire at the mine about the following excursions:

Corta Atalaya ★★★

2km/1.2mi northwest.

This huge open-cast mine is over 1 000m/3 280ft in length, 900m/2 950ft wide and 350m/1 150ft deep.

The **views** ★★★ of the striated crater from the lookout point are exceptional. Horizontal seams are cut in perfect straight lines by huge machines.

Other facilities can be visited nearby, showing how gossan (mineralised iron) is extracted and transported in enormous vehicles capable of carrying up to 200 tons.

Cerro Colorado ★★

2.5km/1.5mi northwest.

The pit of the second largest mine in Riotinto is an unusual red colour. Unexpectedly beautiful, it appears to twinkle in the late afternoon sun.

The British in Riotinto

It is odd to discover the vestiges of Anglo-Saxon culture, so out of keeping with the character of the local population and landscape, in an isolated backwater such as Riotinto.

It should be remembered, however, that at the beginning of the 20C, Britain had developed into a huge economic power, partly due to its colonial possessions and to the role played in this economic development by mining operations in outposts such as Riotinto.

Address Book

WHERE TO STAY

🛏🛏**Santa Bárbara** – *Cerro de Los Embusteros.* ☎959 59 11 88. *19 rooms, 1 suite.* This recently opened hotel, with its modern, spacious rooms, pool and restaurant, is situated in the upper section of the town, from where it enjoys impressive views of the mountains and local open-cast coal-mines.

LOCAL SPECIALITIES

Typical products from the area include *migas* (breadcrumbs fried in olive oil and garlic, and traditionally served with grilled sardines), *gurumelos* (a local cep mushroom), *pestiños* (honeyed doughnuts), and a whole variety of pork-based products.

SPORT

Wherever the British went around the world, they took their sporting activities with them. So, when the Rio Tinto mining operation opened here the mine managers decided to build an on-site golf course. In 1990 the course was rebuilt on a new site, also part of the mine. Fairways are bare earth so the Club provides carpets of artificial grass to allow play. If you are interested in playing a round on this very unusual course call ☎959 59 04 75.

Tourist train★★

The train runs from an old station to Cerro Colorado. Trips (10km/6mi or 23km/14.5mi) along the river on a line built at the end of the 19C to carry ore to Huelva for export to Great Britain. This journey in old-fashioned carriages offers surprises at every turn, including stunning glimpses of the reddish-coloured River Tinto as it winds through dense woods, views of the very first stations, and an impressive bridge, the Puente de Salomé, from which views of the river and surroundings are spectacular.

Bellavista district

This district of Victorian-style houses, was built at the beginning of the 20C to accommodate the huge numbers of British workers. It is now uninhabited, A Presbyterian church, social club and British cemetery remain.

Necrópolis de la Dehesa

3km/2mi N along the A 461.
This large Roman cemetery dating from the 2C AD was part of the Corta de Lago settlement. Tombs bearing inscriptions and personal effects have enabled

Impressive Corta Atalaya mine

B. Kaufmann/MICHELIN

archaeologists to ascertain the social class of those buried here.

Pozo Alfredo
1km/0.6mi NW.
This underground mine, linked to Corta Atalaya, will be extended to a length of 600m/1 968ft. Only parts of this sizeable project can be visited.

Excursions

Nerva
4km/2.5mi east along the A 476.
A Roman tablet found here is dedicated to Emperor Nerva. The village is in a lunar landscape, where mining debris, piled to the edges of reddish water, produces an acrid odour.

Zalamea la Real
12km/8mi west. Follow the A 461, then the N 435 after El Campillo.
The **road**★★ winds across mountain spurs past the Cobre-Gossan Reservoir *(embalse)* to the village of Zalamea, renowned for its anise-flavoured liqueurs. Visit the Iglesia de Nuestra Señora de la Asunción and the El Pozuelo dolmen.

Valverde del Camino
45km/28mi southwest.
Follow the A 461, then bear onto the N 435 after El Campillo.
This community is so famous for its shoes that many Andalusians make a special trip to Valverde to buy walking shoes, boots and dancing footwear made to exacting standards.

MOGUER★

POPULATION: 11 000

Elegant Gothic and Baroque houses line the quiet avenues of noble Moguer. This town is associated with Columbus, who sailed from nearby Palos de la Frontera. Fishing and agriculture are mainstays. Moguer is the birthplace of the writer and poet, **Juan Ramón Jiménez**, whose verses adorn *azulejo* panels. The town is also famed for its *pastelillos* of almond paste and candied fruit.

- **Information:** Calle Castillo. ☎959 3718 98. www.aytomoguer.es.
- ▶ **Orient Yourself:** Moguer, along the River Tinto, is 20km/12mi east of Huelva.
- **Don't Miss:** Monasterio de Santa Clara.
- **Organising Your Time:** Allow half a day.
- **Also See:** LA RÁBIDA, HUELVA, COSTA DE HUELVA.

Juan Ramón Jiménez

1881–1958
A contemporary of Lorca, Jiménez was not only a cultured man of letters, but also a passionate popular writer.
The bitterness and anger of his literary assaults contrast with his gentle portrayals of his beloved Moguer. In 1956 he was awarded the Nobel Prize for Literature.

Casa-Museo "Zenobia y Juan Ramón"★
*Visit by guided tours (45min) Tue–Sat, 10.15am–1.15pm and 5.15–7.15pm. Sun,*

10.15am–1.15pm. €2.50. ☎959 37 21 48. www.fundacion-jrj.es/casamuseo.htm.
The traditional Andalusian home of Juan Ramón Jiménez and his wife Zenobia is now a museum displaying photographs, books and other memorabilia.

Casa Natal de Juan Ramón Jiménez
Visit by appointment.
☎959 37 18 98 (Turismo).
The poet's birthplace *(casa natal)* is in calle Ribera. Today, it is used as the setting for important literary contests.

Sights

Monasterio de Santa Clara★

🔊Visit by guided tour (40min), Tue–Sun, 11am–12.30pm and 5–7pm. €2. ☎959 37 01 07.

Columbus prayed at this 14C Gothic-Mudéjar monastery on the morning of 16 March 1493, in fulfilment of a promise made during a storm on the high seas. The interior, now occupied by an order of Conceptionist nuns, is made up of monastic rooms and porticoed patios with elegant balconies.

Orange trees and banana trees are reminders of the lands touched by Columbus. The buttressed façade of the convent fronts the attractive square, **plaza de Portocarrero**.

Church

The **tombs of the Portocarreros**★, lords of Moguer, are an outstanding example of the Andalusian Renaissance style, carved in Carrara marble by Giacomo, Michelangelo's master. Note also the 16C main altarpiece, a fine 17C carved depiction of the Immaculate Conception, and the set of **tombs**★ at the high altar, including that of Beatriz de Henríquez, who partly financed the Voyages of Discovery.

Cloisters

This tranquil area is enclosed by galleries of pointed arches and includes the former infirmary – now a display of 16C–18C vestments – and the storeroom, which houses a 16C Gothic carving and a skullcup worn by Pope John Paul II.

Choir and antechoir

The choir has exceptional 14C **Nasrid-Mudéjar stalls**★★. The arms of these magnificently carved stalls depict the lions of the Alhambra; the heraldic coat of arms of each nun adorns the seat backs. The antechoir has a fine Mudéjar-style artesonado ceiling and contains several 15C books of Gregorian chants.

Calle Andalucía★

This attractive pedestrianised street runs from plaza del Cabildo to the **Archivo Histórico Municipal y Biblioteca Iberoamericana** (Historical Archives and Ibero-American Library), containing many precious old documents. 🔊Visit by guided tours only (15min), Mon–Fri 11am–2pm. ☎959 37 27 13.

Along this street are the modern **Teatro Felipe Godínez**, a theatre with façade of azulejos; the chapel of the Hospital del Corpus Christi; the heritage houses along the **pasaje de Nuestra Señora de la Esperanza**; and the Convento de San Francisco.

Convento de San Francisco

This 15C convent, built under the initiative of Pedro Portocarrero, was important in spreading Christianity to the New World. It has Mannerist cloisters, a 17C belfry and an interesting 18C Baroque main altarpiece.

Ayuntamiento

The Renaissance town hall on plaza del Cabildo has a handsome porticoed **façade**★, with fine wood artesonado work and galleries comprising five semi-circular arches.

Iglesia de Nuestra Señora de la Granada

This 18C church, opposite the plaza del Marqués, holds a carving of Nuestra Señora de la Granada, protected by a baldaquin in the middle of the presbytery. The **bell tower**★, Moguer's principal landmark, remains from an earlier church.

Monasterio de Santa Clara

MONTEFRÍO★

POPULATION: 7 030

Montefrío is one of the prettiest towns in western Granada province. Standing at the foot of the Sierra de la Paparanda, it enjoys an impressive **setting**★★ on two hills which resemble islands in a sea of olive groves. Several Castilian kings tried and failed to conquer Montefrío until the triumph of the Catholic Monarchs in 1486.

- **Information:** Plaza de España, 1. ☎958 33 60 04. www.montefrio.es.
- ▶ **Orient Yourself:** Montefrío is 58.5km/36mi northwest of Granada via the A 92 and A 335.
- **Don't Miss:** The views from calle Cruz de Calvario.
- **Organising Your Time:** Allow several hours to stroll.
- **Also See:** PRIEGO DE CÓRDOBA, ALCALÁ LA REAL, IZNÁJAR, LOJA, GRANADA.

Walking Tour

Approximately 2hr.

Iglesia de la Encarnación
On the main square of **plaza de España,** this circular neo-Classical church has an orange cupola visible from all over Montefrío.

▶ *Climb up to the Villa section of town along calle del Arco Gracia.*

Iglesia de la Villa★
🕙*Open 10am–2pm and 4–6pm.* ☎*958 33 60 04 (tourist office).*
This hilltop church stands above the remains of a **Nasrid fortress**, of which the original cistern survives. The ubiquitous **Diego de Siloé** was responsible for its design.

▶ *Walk down to plaza de España; follow calle Enrique Amat to placeta del Pósito.*

Placeta del Pósito
This simply designed former **granary** *(pósito)*, dating from the 18C, dominates the small square.

▶ *From here, head up Monte del Calvario to the Iglesia de San Antonio.*

Iglesia de San Antonio
The **Iglesia de San Antonio de Padua** is a Baroque church with a handsome façade, and a three-sectioned retable with a statue of St Anthony. The church was part of a convent, which became a flour mill after the 19C confiscation of church property.

Montefrío

B. Kaufmann/MICHELIN

▶ *From here, it is well worth walking along calle Cruz del Calvario for one of the best* **views**★★ *of the town.*

Excursions

Peña de los Gitanos★
5km/3mi easr of Montefrío along the Illora road. Pass the Mesón Curro on your right, continue to a sign for Peña de los Gitanos. Park, and continue on foot (15min).

The track to Gipsys' Rock climbs gently through olive groves. Take the right fork past an abandoned mine. Cross a meadow, passing a dolmen to the right, to a second meadow with oaks.

Here you will find some very well preserved megalithic tombs. The most spectacular is to the right, behind some oaks. This **dolmen**★ has a corridor and burial chamber.

Moclín
33.5km/21mi east. Follow the no 26 to Illora, the no 19 to N 432, then left towards Alcalá la Real to Puerto López.
Illora is dominated by the 16C Iglesia de la Encarnación. Beyond, on a hilltop **Castillo de la Mota**★ suddenly appears over Moclín. This Nasrid fortress holds a 16C granary *(pósito)*, the Iglesia de la Encarnación, and the remains of the keep and a cistern.

MONTILLA
POPULATION: 22 792

Set amid gently undulating hills in the province of Córdoba, Montilla is at the centre of a large wine-producing region, of the Montilla-Moriles appellation.

Montilla enjoyed its period of greatest splendour in the 16C, when influential personalities such as the writer Inca Garcilaso de la Vega and St John of Ávila took up residence. Montilla's most important buildings date from this time.

- 🏢 **Information:** Capitán Alonso Vargas, 3. ☎957 65 24 62. www.montilla.es.
- ▶ **Orient Yourself:** Montilla is 48km/30mi south of Córdoba via the A 4–E 5, N 331 and A 309.
- 🏛 **Don't Miss:** A bodega tour.
- 🕐 **Organising Your Time:** Allow at least a day.
- 🪙 **Also See:** AGUILAR DE LA FRONTERA, LUCENA, CABRA, BAENA, CÓRDOBA.

A Bit of History

Fiefdom of the Fernández de Córdobas – Historians identify the town as the site of a battle between troops of Caesar and Pompey in AD 45.
From 1375, Montilla is intimately linked to the **Fernández de Córdoba** family, who moved the family seat here from

Aguilar. An illustrious family member was Gonzalo Fernández de Córdoba, known as **El Gran Capitán** (1453–1515), who took part in the capture of Granada. In 1508, King Fernando the Catholic ordered the razing of the castle to punish the disloyalty of Don Pedro Fernández de Córdoba.

Address Book

⌚*For coin ranges, see the Legend on the cover flap.*

WHERE TO STAY

⊜⊜**Hostal Bellido** – *Enfermería, 57.* ☎*957 65 57 87. www.hostalbellido.com. 29 rooms.* Historic building, centrally located, with modest, comfortable rooms.

⊜⊜⊜**Hotel Don Gonzalo** – *Córdoba-Málaga road, km 47 (3km/ 1.9mi SW of Montilla).* ☎*957 65 06 58. www.hoteldongonzalo.com. 35 rooms.* Smart modern hotel in old building with comfortable rooms, gardens, pool, tennis court, cafe and bar.

WHERE TO EAT

⊜ **Las Camachas** – *Av. Europa, 3 .* ☎*957 65 00 04. www.restaurantelas camachas.com.* One of the best-known restaurants in the area, in a traditional house. Here you can dine well on Montilla artichokes, bull's tail, or partridge.

LOCAL SPECIALITIES

Visit the 100-year old **pastelería Manuel Aguilar** (*Corredera,29*) for a range of local specialties: *alfajores, roscos de Pedro Ximénez* and *pastelones de cabello de ángel* (angel hair tarts).

Sights

Follow signs to the centre (centro). Leave your car in the signposted car park.

Iglesia Parroquial de Santiago

Calle Iglesia. ⌚*Open only during services.* This 16C parish church, dedicated to St James, was restored in the 18C, when the façade was much altered. It re-used materials from the nearby castle razed by Fernando the Catholic. The handsome brick tower is decorated with attractive blue *azulejos* around the bays, and the cupola is also covered with glazed ceramics.

Explore the, narrow, cobbled streets around the church.

At no 2 calle Miguel Molina, the **Museo Histórico Local** (⌚*open Tue–Sun and public hols 10.30am–1.30pm and 5–7pm;* ☎*957 65 59 81; www.montilla.es/museo_ historico.htm*) exhibits local artefacts from prehistory to the modern era.

Iglesia de San Francisco Solano

Calle San Francisco Solano. ⌚*Open Mon– Fri 10am–noon and during Masses.* This 17C–18C church stands where St Francis Solano was born in 1549. The peculiar **façade**★ has a porticoed atrium, with semicircular arches on Doric columns. A statue of the town's patron is above the entrance. The bell tower and the spire above are totally covered by *azulejos*.

Ayuntamiento

Calle Corredera. The town hall was built on the site of the former Convento-Hospital de San Juan de Dios. Only the 18C church (now an exhibition hall), with its simple portal, remains.

Convento de Santa Clara

calle Santa Clara. ⌚*Open Wed all day, Thu–Tue 5.30–8pm and during Masses.* Don Pedro Fernández de Córdoba (⌚*see A Bit of History*), commissioned Hernán Ruiz the Elder to build this convent, completed in 1524 and later extended.

The façade of the **church** has a fine Flamboyant-Gothic **portal**★. The family escutcheon is above the door, alongside the niche housing an image of St Clare. The *artesonado* ceilings above the nave and main altarpiece are the highlights inside the church.

Upon leaving the convent, pass through an arch to the Llano de Palacio, the setting for the **Palacio de los Duques de Medinaceli** which was built by the Marquess and Marchioness of Priego as a residence following the destruction of their castle.

Convento de Santa Ana

⌚*Open only during services.* Only the 17C church with its simple doorway remains from the original 16C convent. The main altarpiece includes an Immaculate Conception by renowned

Wines of Montilla-Moriles

As a result of the region's continental climate, Montilla-Moriles wines have developed their own personality.

The main grape variety grown here is Pedro Ximénez.

Four different sherry-style wines are produced: fino, amontillado; oloroso and Pedro Ximénez.

A visit to one of the bodegas such as **Alvear** *(guided tour Mon–Fri 12.30pm, www.alvear.eu* founded in 1729 and one of the region's oldest producers, is highly recommended.

Vineyards of Montilla-Moriles

B. Kaufmann/MICHELIN

sculptor Pedro Roldán. The belfry is decorated with *azulejos*.

Casa-Museo del Inca Garcilaso

🕐*Open Mon–Fri 10am–2pm and 5–7pm (Dec–Mar, 4.30–6.30pm and closed afternoons in Jul–Aug). Sat–Sun and public hols, 11am–2pm.* ☏*957 65 23 54.*
Inca Garcilaso de la Vega lived in this house between 1561 and 1591 and wrote several important works such as *La Florida* and *Los Comentarios Reales*. It is an interesting example of civil architecture from the period, with a sober façade of golden-hued stone. Furniture inside is both original and reproduction.
Other fine buildings in the centre include **La Tercia**, in plaza de la Rosa, the **Teatro Garnelo** (1921), the **Colegio de las Monjas Asuncionistas** (School of Assumptionist Nuns, the former residence of the Count of La Cortina), and the **Iglesia de San Agustín**.

Excursions

Espejo

13.5km/8.5mi northeast along the A 309.
Espejo's whitewashed houses, cobbled lanes and flights of steps stand on a hill beneath a castle amid a landscape of olive groves.

▶ *Leave your car in paseo de Andalucía and walk up to the castle.*

Castle

☞*Private property; closed to visitors.*
The 15C castle with lofty keep belongs to the ducal house of Osuna. It is in the upper town, from where there are magnificent **views**★.
The nearby **Iglesia Parroquial de San Bartolomé**, a Gothic parish church modified over time, contains works by Pedro Romaña (including the retable of St Andrés), an 18C Corpus Christi monstrance, and fine gold and silverwork.

Montemayor

14km/9mi northwest along the N 331.
A well-preserved 14C Mudéjar **castle** with an impressive keep rises among the houses of Montemayor.

Iglesia de la Asunción

This impressive 16C–17C church with Renaissance bell tower sits on the **plaza de la Constitución**, together with the town hall The remains of a Roman mill are embedded in one of the church walls. It has a richly decorated triple apse and three Baroque cupolas, a large 17C carved Renaissance altarpiece in the presbytery, and Baroque side chapels with rich stuccowork. The Capilla del Rosario (Rosary Chapel) contains interesting gold and silverwork, including a superb 18C altar frontal.
The **Museo de Ulía**, (🕐*visits are possible only when the church is open),* housed in

the former the ossuary and cistern, displays objects from the 5C BC to the 15C. The delightful streets around the square boast fine architecture, with picturesque corners and whitewashed houses, some with impressive doorways.

Fernán Núñez
18km/11mi northwest along the N 331. This town, on the site of Roman Ulía, is named for its 13C founding noble.

Palacio Ducal
This impressive ducal palace was built around a square in the 18C. The vermilion of its plasterwork, and white mouldings on the windows inject life into the decoration.

Iglesia de Santa Marina de Aguas Santas
The interior of this 18C church retains original Baroque frescoes and stuccowork on the vaulting and cupolas.

La Rambla
16km/10mi NW along the N 331 and A 386. The town of La Rambla has a long pottery tradition. Miguel de Cervantes worked here as tax collector and treasurer for the royal storehouses.

Iglesia Parroquial de la Asunción
Built during the Reconquest and rebuilt in the 18C, this parish church has a superb **Plateresque portal**★, the work of Hernán Ruiz I. Note the Baroque Capilla del Sagrario to the left of the chancel, with imitation marble retable and cupola. Some of the statues in the church are attributed to Martínez Montañés: St Joseph with the Infant Jesus, St Ann with the Virgin Mary, John the Baptist, and St Rose.
On the same street are the remains of a massive tower of the old **fortress**.

Torre del ex-Convento de la Consolación
This fine Baroque brick tower is abundantly decorated, particularly on its west side around the windows and bays.

Colegio del Espiritú Santo
The church belonging to this school houses a sculptural jewel which is the pride and joy of La Rambla's inhabitants: the wooden carving of **Jesus of Nazareth**★ bearing a cross on his shoulders, by Juan de Mesa. This impressive sculpture shows exceptional skill in its portrayal of the subject's emotion.

Santaella
32km/20mi west along the N 331 and A 386.
There are fine views of this small town from the main road. In the main square *(plaza Mayor)* to the right of the town hall, the vestiges of a Moorish fortress are visible. The 18C Casa de las Columnas is set to house the **Museo de Arqueología Local** (🕐open Sat 5–7.30pm (6.30–9pm in summer); Sun and public hols, 11am–1pm; ☎957 31 32 44), currently in the former granary. The museum contains a fine collection of exhibits, including the *Leona de Santaella* (The Santaella Lioness), Iberian votive offerings, an Ibero-Roman lion and a set of Visigothic monograms. .

▶ *Climb the ramp in front of the castle.*

Views from the top of the ramp take in the church and countryside.

Iglesia de la Asunción
Walk around the 16C–17C Church of the Assumption to appreciate its monumental stature. The Baroque **façade** is preceded by a wall, a windbreak which obstructs a full view. To the left, a **Renaissance tower** bears heraldic decoration. The wall on the northwest side retains its original decoration. Note the Mudéjar *artesonado* in the Capilla de las Ánimas, and several retables.
The 18C Baroque sanctuary of **Nuestra Señora del Valle**, housing the image of Our Lady of the Valley, the town's patron saint, can be visited on the outskirts.

MONTORO ⭐
POPULATION: 9 489

Montoro's impressive site, on a loop of the Guadalquivir, is best viewed from a bend on the main road, from where the full contrast between the reddish tones of its soil and the ochre and whitewash of its houses can be admired. The Baroque tower of the Iglesia de San Bartolomé rises majestically above the rooftops of this attractive town, which descend gently to the river, spanned by a graceful 15C bridge.

- **Information:** Plaza de España, 8. ☎957 16 00 89. www.montoro.es.
- ▶ **Orient Yourself:** Montoro is 44km/27mi east of Córdoba along the N IV-E 5.
- P **Parking:** Leave your vehicle at the entrance to the town, as driving and parking in Montoro is particularly difficult.
- ◉ **Organising Your Time:** Allow half a day.
- ⛷ **Also See:** ANDÚJAR, CÓRDOBA.

Walking Tour

Plaza de Españaa
This charming square at the heart of the old town is lined by three interesting buildings: the Iglesia de San Bartolomé, the town hall and a fine seigniorial mansion. All three are built in the characteristic stone of the area and add a sense of harmony to the square's appearance.

Iglesia de San Bartolomé
◉*Open 11am–2pm.* ☎*957 16 00 89.*
This handsome 15C church is the dominant feature of the square with its monumental Baroque bell tower standing proudly at the east end. Note the finely carved elegant Gothic-Mudéjar **portal**⭐, in the upper section of which the arch and a statue of the Virgin Child are framed by an *alfiz* surround. To the left of the doorway, embedded in the wall, a Visigothic slab can also be seen. Two coats of arms appear on the portal, while another adorns the Baroque window to the right of the façade. The triple-aisled interior contains some interesting marquetry, in addition to a delicately carved statue of the Virgin of the Rosary in a side chapel on the left-hand side.

Montoro, nestling in a meander of the Guadalquivir river

B. Kaufmann/MICHELIN

Handicrafts: The town is renowned for its traditional handicrafts and leather and wrought-iron workshops can be found in calle Corredera.

The headless statue of the archangel Raphael stands alongside the church.

Ayuntamiento
The Renaissance-style town hall is fronted by a harmonious two-storey façade bearing the coat of arms of the ducal house of Alba-Montoro. Between the façade and the vaulted arch on its left, note the stone commemorating the order given by Felipe III to build the old prison next door. The interior is crowned by some fine Mudéjar *artesonado* ceilings.

Seigniorial mansion
To the right of the church.
It was in this building that justice was formerly administered in Montoro. Four escutcheons can be seen on the second floor, while the heads of a man and woman above the doors denote the entrances through which the accused of each sex would have entered the building.
The area surrounding the square is a maze of narrow cobbled streets, picturesque nooks and crannies, and typical examples of local architecture, with whitewashed houses framed by the traditional stone of the area.
The **Casa de las Conchas** (House of the Shells) is an unusual modern building built in 1960 and, as the name would suggest, is completely covered by shells. Walk along calle Bartolomé Camacho, next to the church in plaza de España, to the **Ermita de Santa María**, a 13C chapel, now home to the town's **Museo Arqueológico** (🕐 *open Sat–Sun and public hols 11am–1pm;* ☎957 16 00 89). Return to the square; there is an impressive view of the church tower. .

Sights

Iglesia del Carmen
Calle El Santo.
The façade of this church, built out of local stone, is dominated by the image of St John of the Cross. Inside, the three naves are overshadowed by an 18C Baroque **retable** in the chancel, with a Virgin and Child enthroned at its centre.

Hospital de Jesús Nazareno
This hospital was built in the 17C and 18C, although it has undergone subsequent restoration on a number of occasions. It is now used as a rest home. The cupola of the church is brightly decorated in tones of blue and gold.

Excursions

Adamuz
24km/15mi west. Take the E 5 motorway towards Córdoba. Exit at Km 367 and follow signs to Adamuz.
The road passes through an area of abundant vegetation, following the wide course of the Guadalquivir until it crosses the river at El Salto. Continue along the opposite bank, before leaving the river behind and ascending a winding route towards Adamuz, set amid a landscape of olive groves.
The town's whitewashed streets are overlooked by the Gothic **Iglesia de San Andrés**, built in red sandstone in the late 14C and early 15C. The sober appearance of the church, enhanced by the absence of decoration, is counteracted only by its impressive bulk. The main civil building is the **Torre del Reloj**, a clock tower built by the Marquess of El Carpio in 1566, but subsequently restored.

El Carpio
19km/12mi southwest along the E 5. Exit at Km 374.
The houses of El Carpio rise up a hill dominated by a 14C tower, the Mudéjar-style **Torre de Garci Méndez**. The best view of this imposing brick tower can be

enjoyed from plaza de la Constitución, a pleasant square fronted by a 17C parish church and adorned with orange trees and arrangements of flowers.

Parque Natural de la Sierra de Cardeña y Montoro

15km/9.5mi north along the N 420.
The gentle features of this protected area to the south of the Sierra Morena give way to steeper landscapes and numerous ravines further to the west. The predominant tree species found here are holm oak, arbutus, the occasional downy oak, and areas replanted with pines. Local wildlife includes wolves, otters, lynx, wild boar, genet and deer. The numerous marked paths criss-crossing the area make the park very popular with hikers.

Bujalance

14km/9mi south along the A 309.
This pleasant town in the Córdoban countryside is set in a landscape dominated by the ubiquitous olive. It has preserved much of its popular Andalusian architecture, characterised by a number of noble mansions, most of which were built in the 17C.

▷ *Follow signs to the town centre (centro ciudad) and park next to the plaza Mayor.*

Plaza Mayor

This sloping, triangular square, with its attractive orange trees, is overlooked by the tower of the Iglesia de la Asunción. The 17C **town hall**, with its heraldic decoration, encloses the upper part of the square, alongside a vaulted arch which leads to the Iglesia de la Asunción.

Iglesia de la Asunción

Entrance through the sacristy (the first house on the left upon leaving the square through the arch).
The Church of the Assumption dates from the 16C, although an earlier church occupied this site. The ground plan is in keeping with the majority of Córdoban churches of the period: three aisles, no transept and a rectilinear apse with three rectangular chapels. The side aisles have retained their original wooden ceiling, unlike the nave which is topped by an 18C vault. The apsidal end has Gothic vaulting, with a star vault in the chancel with tierceron features to the sides.
Works of art in the church include the 16C carved and painted Renaissance altarpiece in the presbytery and the Baroque retable in the chapel on the right side of the apsidal end.
The outstanding feature of the exterior is the fine 18C Baroque **tower** which at 55m/180ft in height is the tallest in the province.

Alcazaba

Entrance to the left of the main façade of the church.
Despite the fact that this former Moorish fortress is now in ruins, the towers and curtain wall which were part of the external defences are still visible. Built during the reign of Abd ar-Rahman III, it was modified after the Reconquest. The castle's seven towers form the basis for the town's coat of arms.

Iglesia de San Francisco

From the plaza Mayor, head down calle E Sotomayor to calle Ancha de Palomino.
The church is of new construction, with the exception of the portal and the fine Baroque tower. The earlier building, which was considered a jewel of Córdoban Baroque, was destroyed during the Spanish Civil War.

Ermita de Jesús

On the outskirts of the town. Follow calle San Antonio to the left of the façade of the Iglesia de San Francisco.
The chapel is situated in the Parque de Jesús, on top of a promontory affording a pleasant view of the olive groves that extend to the horizon. The style is 18C, although the chapel's origins are earlier. The Baroque portal is adorned with *estípites* and an abundance of minute decoration.

OSUNA ★★

POPULATION: 17 306

This elegant Andalusian town, built on a hill at the heart of the Sevillian country-side, has preserved a beautiful **monumental centre**★ inherited from its former status as a ducal seat. The dukedom was created in 1562 and the House of Osuna was to become one of the most powerful on the Iberian Peninsula. The prosperity that Osuna enjoyed in subsequent centuries is reflected in the fine examples of civil and religious architecture embellishing the town.

- 🛈 **Information:** Calle Sevilla, 22, 41013 Osuna. ☎954 81 22 11. www.ayto-osuna.es.
- ▶ **Orient Yourself:** Osuna is 85km/53mi southwest of Granada and 92km/58mi east of Sevilla.
- ⚐ **Don't Miss:** La Colegiata church. The town's Baroque palaces and seigniorial residences.
- 🕐 **Organising Your Time:** Allow at least a day
- 🖐 **Also See:** MARCHENA, ÉCIJA, ESTEPA, ANTEQUERA, CÓRDOBA, SEVILLA.

A Bit of History

Initially inhabited by the Iberians, who named it Urso, this elegant town was subsequently conquered by the Romans, under Caesar. Following the period of Moorish occupation, it was reconquered by Fernando III the Saint in 1239, and then ceded to the Order of Calatrava by Alfonso X the Wise in 1264. However, its period of greatest splendour is inextricably linked with the House of Osuna, under whose control it passed in 1562, when Felipe II granted the title of Duke of Osuna to the fifth Count of Ureña. The dukedom was responsible for the embellishment of Osuna, as well as its artistic and cultural development.

Walking Tours

Monumental Centre★

▶ *Follow signs to the town centre (centro ciudad) and Zona Monumental.*

La Colegiata★

🎧*Guided tours (45min), May–Sept Tue–Sun 10am–1.30pm and 4–7pm (closed Sun afternoon Jul–Aug). Oct–Apr Tue–Sun, 10am–1.30pm and 3.30–6.30pm. ⊛€2. ☎954 81 04 44.*

This imposing 16C Renaissance-style collegiate church stands impressively above the town. The façade is adorned with a handsome, finely sculpted Plateresque doorway.

Interior

The **church** is composed of three elegant Renaissance aisles opening out onto several chapels and a Baroque apse with an interesting retable in the same style, bearing the coat of arms of the House of Osuna. The organ dates from the 18C.

The church contains several important works of art within its walls: *Jesus of Nazareth* by the "divine" Morales, a *Christ of Mercy* by Juan de Mesa, the superb tenebrist canvas, **The Expiration of Christ**★★, by **José Ribera**, "lo Spagnoletto".

The **sacristy** is adorned with 16C **azulejos** and some original **artesonado** work. Exhibits include several books of Gregorian chants dating from the 16C, and four more **paintings by Ribera**★★, dating between 1616 and 1618.

Additional works of art on view in other rooms include an *Immaculate Conception* by Alonso Cano, a silver processional cross (1534), Flemish paintings, and 16C gold and silver and vestments. .

Panteón Ducal★★

The ducal pantheon was built in Plateresque style in 1545 as the burial place for the Dukes of Osuna. It is approached by a delightful patio, designed in the same style. The chapel stands just below the Colegiata's main altar, and despite its tiny dimensions (8m/26ft long, 4.5m/15ft wide and 2.5m/8ft high), it comprises three aisles and a choir. It is crowned by a blue and gold polychrome coffered ceiling.

The **crypt** beneath the chapel contains the tombs of the most notable Dukes of Osuna and the founders of the Colegiata (the parents of the first duke).

Former university

The old university *(antigua universidad)*, created in 1548 and in existence until 1824, was founded by Juan Téllez, the Count of Ureña and father of the first Duke of Osuna. It is a large square building made of stone; the circular towers on its corners are crowned by spires decorated with blue and white *azulejos*. Note also the attractive inner patio.

Monasterio de la Encarnación★

🕐 *Open May–Sept Tue–Sun 10am–1.30pm and 4–7pm (closed Sun afternoon Jul–Aug). Oct–Apr Tue–Sun, 10am–1.30pm and 3.30–6.30pm.* ✎€2. ☎954 81 11 21.

This convent of discalced nuns was founded by the fourth Duke of Osuna in the 17C. Its outstanding feature is the magnificent **dado**★ of 17C Sevillian *azulejos* in the patio, dedicated to the five senses. This decoration continues up the stairs and on the patio's upper floor. It holds a large collection of paintings, statuary and other objects of artistic interest. The church is also Baroque in style. Like many convents in Andalucía, the nuns here produce and sell several types of delicious biscuits and pastries.

Torre del Agua

On the way down to the plaza Mayor.
🕐*Open May–Sept 11.30am–1.30pm and 5–7pm (10am–2pm, Jul–Aug). Oct–Apr, 11.30am–1.30pm and 4.30–6.30pm.* ✎€1.60. ☎954 81 12 07.

This medieval defensive tower dates from the 12C–13C, although its origins can be traced to the Carthaginians. Nowadays, it is home to the town's **Museo Arqueológico**, displaying a range of

Cilla del Cabildo

Iberian and Roman objects discovered in Osuna, as well as reproductions of Iberian bulls and Roman bronzes (the originals can be seen in the Museo Arqueológico Nacional, Madrid).

The Town

The centre of Osuna has some fine examples of civil architecture, including an impressive array of Baroque **palaces and seigniorial residences**★★.

Calle San Pedro★

In addition to several interesting town houses and churches, this street contains two magnificent palaces:

Cilla del Cabildo

This original 18C Baroque edifice was designed by Alonso Ruiz Florindo, who was also responsible for the tower of the Iglesia de la Merced (👁*see Torre de la Iglesia de la Merceda*). In both buildings he incorporated unusual pilasters with individual decoration. Above the doorway, a curious copy of the Giralda (Sevilla) dominates the façade.

Palacio de los Marqueses de la Gomera

This 18C Baroque palace (now a hotel 👁*see Address Book*) has a striking cornice and a beautiful stone doorway crowned by a large escutcheon.

Antiguo Palacio de Puente Hermoso

Calle Sevilla, 44.

The handsome 18C Baroque **portal**★ adorning the façade of this former palace is embellished by Solomonic columns. The street has several other notable civil and religious buildings.

Palacio de los Cepeda

Calle de la Huerta. This palace is now the home of the town's law courts. It is a handsome 18C construction with an impressive main doorway and a fine cornice crowning the building. However, its most outstanding features are the *estípites* on the doorway and, in particular, the large coat of arms with the two halberdiers flanking it.

Torre de la Iglesia de la Merceda

The church tower, designed by the same architect as the Cilla del Cabildo, is an impressive monument with a number of decorative elements.

Osuna's religious architecture is represented by numerous convents and churches (Santo Domingo, la Compañía, la Concepción etc), predominantly dating from the 17C and 18C.

PALMA DEL RÍO

POPULATION: 18 948

Palma del Río, a tranquil town which has preserved substantial sections of its Arab walls, is situated on a plain, close to the confluence of the River Guadalquivir and River Genil. Approaching from Córdoba along C 431, the whitewashed Ermita de la Virgen de Belén can be seen on top of a small hill to the right. The views of the town from here are particularly impressive.

🛈 **Information:** Calle Cardenal Portocarrero. ☎957 64 43 70. www.palmadelrio.es.

▶ **Orient Yourself:** Palma del Río is 58km/36mi southwest of Córdoba.

🅿 **Parking:** Park near plaza de Andalucía.

🕐 **Organising Your Time:** Allow half a day.

♿ **Also See:** ÉCIJA, CÓRDOBA, CARMONA.

The Town

Plaza de Andalucía

The town's main square is lined by three major buildings: the town hall, post office *(correos)* and law courts *(juzgados)*. The most interesting constructions in the square are the **Puerta del Sol** (Sun Gateway) and the 16C **Renaissance balcony**, which was part of the Palacio de los Portacarrero, above which rises the tower of the Iglesia de la Asunción. The palace originally stood through the arch on the right-hand side.

Town walls★

These date from the 12C and formed part of an extensive walled enclosure built during the Almohad period to provide protection for the town. Substantial parts of the walls still remain intact, including several solid sections, in addition to several square towers and one octagonal one.

Museo Municipal

Calle Cardenal Portocarrero.
🕐*Open mid-Jun to mid-Sept Tue–Sat 10am–2pm, Mid-Sept to mid-Jun Tue–Sat 5–8pm. Sun and public hols year-round 11am–2pm.* ☎957 64 43 70.

The municipal museum is housed in the former royal stables. It is divided into three sections, devoted to archaeology, ethnography and fine arts.

Iglesia de la Asunción

🕐*Open Fri–Wed 11am–1pm.* ☎957 64 56 76 (Cultural Office).

The Church of the Assumption was built in the 18C. The exterior is dominated by an elegant **tower**★, above a red-brick Baroque portal. The rich decoration on the belfry (*estípites*, frets and Solomonic columns) is enhanced by the blue-tinged tones of its *azulejos*.

The **interior**★ is particularly harmonious with its wide nave and transept, above which rises a cupola, with pendentives decorated with stuccowork bearing plant motifs. The nave is supported by enormous pilasters, above which runs a cornice adorned with further stucco features. The wrought-iron balconies add an element of dynamism to the overall effect. The church is presided over by a Baroque altarpiece.

Iglesia y Convento de San Francisco

The church and convent were founded in the 16C, and modified in the 17C and 18C. Noteworthy external features include the cupolas above the side chapels and the transept.

Other sights of interest in Palma del Río include the 18C Baroque **Capilla del Virgen del Rosario**, a chapel dedicated to the Virgin of the Rosary, in the Iglesia de Santo Domingo, and the **Hospital de San Sebastián** (now a retirement home), with its attractive patio and a church with a Mudéjar-influenced façade. Inside, note the unusual retable of the Virgin of Sorrow and a chapel with a fine dado of old *azulejos* and a Mudéjar *artesonado* ceiling.

Excursions

Hornachuelos

18km/11mi northeast.
Head along the A 431 for 10km/6mi, then bear left onto the CO 141.

This small whitewashed town in the sierra of the same name has preserved vestiges of its castle and walls, built during the period of the Córdoban Caliphate.

Several vantage points, including one in plaza de la Iglesia, offer impressive views of the mountains.

Hornachuelos is renowned for its local gastronomy, which is based on venison and wild boar.

Walk along calle Palmera, so named after the palm tree *(palmera)* engraved on its pavement, to the 16C **Iglesia de Santa María de las Flores**, a church embellished with a handsome late-Gothic **portal** attributed to Hernán Ruiz I, and an 18C tower.

Las Erillas can be seen on the outskirts of Hornachuelos, heading east. This area of limestone has been eroded by water to produce some extraordinary rock formations such as the so-called *casas colgantes* or "hanging houses".

Parque Natural de la Sierra de Hornachuelos

This park covers an area of 67 000ha/ 165 557 acres in the west of the province. Despite its relatively low altitude – its highest peak is the Sierra Alta (722m/2 368ft) – the scenery is grand: rivers running through the park have sculpted a landscape of gorges and lakes, one of which (El Retortillo) is popular with local swimmers.

The vegetation here is mainly holm, cork and gall oak and wild olives, with poplar, alder and ash closer to water. The park is

Address Book

For coin ranges, see the Legend on the cover flap.

WHERE TO STAY

Castillo – *Portada, 47. ☎957 64 57 10. 48 rooms.* A modern, comfortable hotel in traditional style in the centre of town.

Hospedería de San Francisco – *Avenida Pio XII, 35. ☎957 71 01 83. 21 rooms, 1 apartment.* This luxury hotel and restaurant is housed in a former 15C Franciscan monastery. The impressive guest bedrooms are all furnished with antiques. The restaurant, in the monks' refectory, serves Basque specialities. ( ). Swimming pool.

LOCAL SPECIALITIES

A tradition of pottery – The town's inhabitants claim that it is the quality of the clay used in the production of the local earthenware pots that keeps the water stored in them so cool. Other typical items of pottery from Palma del Río include wine pitchers, gazpacho bowls and flowerpots.

FESTIVALS

On the first Sunday in September is the Romería de la Virgen de Belén (Virgin of Bethlehem Open-Air Festival). A Sunday morning dawn rosary takes place at the chapel, followed by a flamenco-style Mass. Then in the afternoon the statue of the Virgin is carried to Our Lady's Parish Church (Parroquia de la Asunción) accompanied by horsemen in traditional dress and by the people of the town praying and cheering them on.

---

a popular area for hunting, particularly for deer and wild boar; other species found here include the black vulture and the golden eagle, as well as otters, wolves and the rare Iberian lynx.

Centro de Visitantes Huerta del Rey

1.5km/1mi from Hornachuelos along the CO 142.

Open in summer Tue–Sun, 10.30am–2.30pm and 4–7pm. Rest of year Tue–Sun 10am–2pm and 4–7pm. ☎957 64 11 40 or 957 45 32 11.

The Huerta del Rey visitor centre is devoted to interactive exhibitions on the park.

Information is available on the extensive network of footpaths on offer to visitors, as well as details on camping permits. You can organise tours of the park by donkey and jeep *(advance booking required)*.

San Calixto

16km/10mi from the visitor centre along the CO 142.

San Calixto was developed as part of Carlos III's land colonisation policy in the 18C. Its major buildings are the Palacio del Marqués de Salinas and its gardens; the Iglesia de Nuestra Señora de la Sierra, a church rebuilt in the 18C' and a 16C convent for discalced Carmelite nuns. The nuns have developed a reputation for their handicrafts, in particular, embroidered table linen, trays decorated by hand, and receptacles made from deerskin.

El Córdobés

It was in Palma del Río that one of Spain's greatest bullfighters, Manuel Benítez Pérez, known as El Córdobés, was born. Between 1964 and 1971, he established himself as probably the best known matador in the history of bullfighting with his endeavours both in and out of the ring, The awarding of the honorary title of "Caliph of bullfighting" by the city authorities in Córdoba in the presence of the province's highest dignitaries in November 2002 was a noteworthy achievement for this former outcast who in his younger years earned his living from theft and on more than one occasion was arrested by the Guardia Civil.

PRIEGO DE CÓRDOBA★★
POPULATION: 22 196

Situated at the heart of the Subbética Córdobesa mountain range, nestled at the foot of the **Pico de la Tiñosa** (1 570m/5 150ft), in an isolated area away from the region's major roads, the delightful town of Priego de Córdoba is the capital of Córdoban Baroque. It reached its economic zenith in the 18C thanks to the silk industry and the wealth generated led to the construction of the numerous fine buildings and an artistic and cultural legacy that can still be traced today.

- **Information:** Calle Carrera de las Monjas. ☎957 70 06 25. www.turismodepriego.com.
- **Orient Yourself:** Priego de Córdoba is 79km/49mi northwest of Granada.
- **Parking:** Park near plaza de la Constitución.
- **Don't Miss:** The El Sagrario chapel in the Church of the Assumption, the Barrio de la Villa quarter, the city's monumental fountains.
- **Organising Your Time:** Allow at least a day.
- **Also See:** CABRA, LUCENA, ALCALÁ LA REAL, BAENA, JAÉN , GRANADA, ANTEQUERA.

Walking Tour

> *Follow signs to the town centre (centro ciudad).and begin in the plaza de la Constitución .*

Hospital-Iglesia de San Juan de Dios

This hospital was founded in 1637 by Juan de Herrera and completed in 1717. The first feature of interest inside the building is the attractive cloistered patio. The handsome Baroque church, with its single nave and fine cupola above the transept, stands to the rear, on the right-hand side. Several broken cornices run along the upper sections of the side walls, providing the church with a certain dynamism. The building is completely whitewashed, with vegetal decoration arranged in bands or garlands. The Virgin of Mercy (Virgen de las Mercedes) presides over the main altarpiece, which is also Baroque.

> *Exit calle Ribera and head along paseo del Abad Palomino.*

Castle

Open Tue–Sun 11.30am–1.30pm. Sat also 6–8pm.

The significant remains of this sober and imposing fortress, of Moorish origin but modified in the 13C and 14C,

can be seen from the **paseo del Abad Palomino**. The wall is punctuated with square towers, including the **keep**, with its paired windows. It is possible to walk around most of the outside of the castle, where houses can be seen built against the wall.

Parroquia de la Asunción★

Visits by prior arrangement.

Open summer Tue–Sat 11am–2pm and 5.30–8pm. Sun 11am–2pm. Rest of year Tue–Sat, 10.30am–1.30pm and 4–7pm. ☎606 17 16 53.

This 16C late-Gothic Church of the Assumption was remodelled in the 18C in Baroque style. Note also the fine Renaissance portal on the right-hand side. The bright, spacious interior comprises three aisles crowned with arris vaults and decorated keystones, and an adorned cupola. The presbytery is dominated by an impressive carved and painted 16C Mannerist-style **retable**. In the chapels, several altarpieces and a Christ attributed to Alonso de Mena are also worthy of note.

El Sagrario★★

This chapel, which opens onto the Evangelist nave, is a masterpiece of Priego and Spanish Baroque. Its ground plan consists of a rectangular antechamber leading into an octagonal space surrounded by an ambulatory, in the centre of which stands the chapel. Light plays an important part in the overall scene, and is intensified by the whiteness of the walls and ceiling, inundating the central area with a dazzling brightness and creating a magical atmosphere. The interior is enhanced by sublime **plasterwork**★★★ by the local artist Francisco Javier Pedrajas (1736–1817), which covers the entire chapel. Pay particular attention to the keystone of the large cupola which is adorned with numerous small heads. Lower down, a sculpture of an Apostle can be seen against each pillar. The decoration combines plant motifs, rocaille work and scenes with characters illustrating themes found in both the Old and New Testaments. Despite the profuse decoration, the overall effect is one of lightness and delicacy.

Barrio de la Villa★★

Tucked away behind the church, this charming quarter, dating back to medieval and Moorish times, is characterised by narrow, winding streets and flower-decked whitewashed houses. The combination of its myriad colours and scents has made the Barrio de la Villa one of Andalucía's archetypal sights. A leisurely stroll along calle Jazmines, calle Bajondillo, calle Reales and through plaza de San Antonio is highly recommended.

El Adarve★

To the north of the Barrio de la Villa, this delightful balcony looks onto the Subbética mountain range. The impressive **views**, attractive lamp posts, iron benches and contemplative atmosphere transport visitors back to bygone days.

▶ *Return to the beginning of paseo del Abad Palomino and follow carrera Álvarez.*

Iglesia de la Aurora

🕐*Open daily 10am (Sun 11am)–1pm.*
The former 15C church was remodelled in the 18C by Juan de Dios Santaella in Baroque style, although it has preserved its 16C tower and belfry. It has a fine polychrome marble Baroque portal on two levels, presided over by the Virgin

of the Aurora between two Solomonic columns. The single-nave interior has profuse Baroque decoration.

▶ *Retrace your steps as far as plaza de San Pedro.*

Iglesia de San Pedro

🕐*Open Mon–Sat 10am–1.30pm.*
The Baroque additions to this church were completed in 1690. The interior contains some interesting statuary, including an outstanding **Immaculate Conception**★ in the *camarín* behind the main altarpiece; this statue is attributed by some to Diego de Mora, and by others to Alonso Cano. The first chapel to the side of the Evangelist nave houses an image of the **Virgin of Solitude**, while the last chapel on the Epistle nave contains a delightful wooden **recumbent Christ** (1594) attributed to Pablo de Rojas, on display inside a glass urn.

▶ *Head along calle Pedrajas.*

Carnicerías Reales

🕐*Open Tue–Sun 11.30am–1.30pm. Sat also 6.30–8.30pm.*
The former royal abattoir and market was built in the 16C along Classical lines, and is a somewhat surprising addition to a town dominated by Baroque architecture. The simple stone doorway, presided over by the coat of arms of the Fernández de Córdoba family, is adorned with two unusual engaged columns. The square-shaped interior has a central patio and towers on its corners. To the rear, to the right of the window with views of the local countryside, a spiral staircase descends to the room where animals were slaughtered. Nowadays it is used as an exhibition hall.

▶ *Return to plaza de la Constitución, at the start of calle del Río.*

Las Angustias

No formal opening hours; knock on the door of the adjacent building; if possible the nuns from the school will show visitors around.
Built in 1772 by Juan de Dios Santaella, the church's outstanding feature is the twin-sectioned polychrome doorway

with its abundant broken lines. Note also the unusual Virgin and Child in the vaulted niche and the finely worked *estípites* on the lower section. The church belfry can be seen to the left side.

The inside of the church, which is surprisingly small in size, is Rococo. The area above the altar is covered by an attractive moulded dome above pendentives. On the gilded retable, the 18C middle sculptural group is from the Granada School and depicts the Virgin with the dead Christ in her arms. Also worthy of note are two terracotta sculptures by José Risueño beneath this work.

Follow **calle del Río**, which is lined by several seigniorial houses. The **birthplace of Niceto Alcalá-Zamora** (1877–1949), President of the Second Republic, is now home to the town's tourist office.

Iglesia del Carmen

🕐 *Open Thu–Tue 7.30–8pm.*

This 18C church was built in the transitional style between Baroque and neo-Classical. The façade combines elements of both styles, with a tower directly incorporated onto it. Last to be built, the portal is pure neo-Classical.

Fuentes del Rey y de la Salud★★

Calle del Río.

The Fountains of the King *(Rey)* and the Fountain of Health *(Salud)* are the best-known sight in Priego de Córdoba.

The older of the two, the **Fuente de la Salud**★, was sculpted in the 16C by Francisco del Castillo. It is a stone frontispiece built in Mannerist style with, at its centre, a small niche containing the Virgin of Health, hence its name. The green of the vegetation contrasts with the golden stone, helping to create a charming scene enhanced by the proximity of the lavish **Fuente del Rey**★★, which was completed at the beginning of the 19C. Both its dimensions and the richness of its design, characterised by curves and counter-curves, evoke the gardens of a Baroque palace. It is arranged on three levels with 139 jets spouting water from the mouths of masks. The sculptural groups are the work of Remigio del Mármol: the central work represents Neptune's chariot

Brothers of the Aurora

The brotherhood of the Iglesia de la Aurora keeps alive a time-honoured tradition every Saturday night, when it takes to the streets of Priego de Córdoba singing songs in honour of the Virgin.

and Amphitrite. The lion fighting the snake on the top section is attributed to the neo-Classical sculptor J Alvarez Cubero.

▶ *Head along calle Obispo Pérez Muñoz as far as carrera de las Monjas.*

Museo Histórico Municipal

🕐 *Open Tue–Fri 10am–1.30pm and 6–8.30pm. Sat 10am–1.30pm and 5–7.30pm, Sun and public hols 10am–1.30pm.* ☎957 54 09 47.

This local museum, housed in the birthplace of the painter and illustrator Adolfo Lozano Sidro (1872–1935), displays a number of archaeological exhibits discovered in and around Priego de Córdoba.

Two other Baroque monuments of interest are the **Iglesia de las Mercedes** and the **Iglesia de San Francisco**, the latter fronted by a neo-Classical portal (the former is only open for a limited number of hours Wed, Fri, Sat).

Fuente del Rey

Excursion

Carcabuey
8km/5mi west.

Sitting at the foot of a hill crowned by the ruins of a castle and chapel, amid a landscape of olive groves, behind which stands the impressive backdrop of the Subbética mountain range.

▶ *Follow the street with flights of steps, which comes out opposite the town hall, then continue along a cobbled ramp.*

It is well worth climbing up to the castle precinct, inside which a chapel, the **Ermita de la Virgen del Castillo**, can be seen. The views of the town and the surrounding countryside from this elevated spot are delightful. Walk around the right-hand side of the hermitage to see the remains of the castle, including its walls and turrets.

The **Iglesia de la Asunción**, a solid stone construction, dominates the upper part of the town. The most impressive feature of the 16C–17C church are the two imposing buttresses connected via an arch, and its brick tower.

A track leads from Carcabuey towards Luque across the **Parque Natural de las Sierras Subbéticas** (*see CABRA, Excursions*).

PUEBLOS BLANCOS DE ANDALUCÍA★★
WHITE VILLAGES OF ANDALUCÍA

The route through the White Villages of Andalucía crosses one of the most beautiful parts of the Iberian Peninsula. Delightful whitewashed towns and villages with a maze of lanes, once Moorish, are often crowned by the ruins of a castle, and dominated by the silhouette of a bell tower.

🛈 **Information:** Plaza de España, Grazalema ☎956 13 20 73. Avenida Moreno de Mora 19, Ubrique ☎956 46 49 00, www.sierradeubrique.com. Calle Villa 2, Setenil ☎956 13 42 61, www.setenil.com. Plaza de la Iglesia (Edificio La Cilla), Olvera ☎956 12 08 16, www.olvera.es. Plaza Alcalde José González (Palacio de los Ribera). Bornos ☎956 72 82 64, www.bornosweb.org. Ronda (*see RONDA*). Arcos de la Frontera (*see ARCOS de la FRONTERA*).

▶ **Orient Yourself:** This area stretches between Ronda and Arcos in a region formed by four sierras (Grazalema, Ubrique, Margarita and Ronda). Málaga is 98km/61mi east of Ronda, Jerez De La Frontera is 24km/15mi west of Arcos de la Frontera.

🚫 **Don't Miss:** The respective hilltop settings of Zahara de la Sierra and Olvera.

🕐 **Organising Your Time:** Allow at least three days to tour the Pueblos Blancos.

👓 **Also See:** COSTA DEL SOL, ALGECIRAS (including Gibraltar), MÁLAGA, JEREZ DE LA FRONTERA.

Driving Tour

Round trip from Arcos de la Frontera

217km/135mi – allow half a day

This itinerary departs from **Arcos de la Frontera** and continues through the delightful **Sierra de Grazalema**, to

Ronda, then skirts mountain folds on a road back to Arcos.

Arcos de la Frontera★★ – *see ARCOS DE LA FRONTERA*

▶ *Leave Arcos de la Frontera along the A 372 heading east towards El Bosque.*

Enjoy one of the best **views**★ of Arcos de la Frontera is from this road.

Prado del Rey *(7km/4.5mi N of El Bosque, turn before town)* was founded in the 18C by **Carlos III**.

El Bosque
30km/19mi east of Arcos.
If you wish to organise an excursion into the **Parque Natural Sierra de Grazalema** then call at the **Centro de Visitantes** (🕐*open year-round 10am–2pm and 4–6pm; Apr–Sept 10am–2pm and 6–8pm; Sat–Sun 9am–2pm; ☎956 71 60 63)*. A small botanical garden includes native species (Spanish fir, gall oak and cork oak).
From El Bosque, the direct road to Grazalema *(description below)* passes through **Benamahoma**, with a small **water museum** *(museo del agua)* in its old mill. The River Bosque originates here. An alternative route is via Ubrique.

Ubrique
12km/7.5mi southeast of El Bosque along the A 373.
The **road**★ enters the heart of the Sierra de Grazalema in the most beautiful part of the tour.
Ubrique extends across the hill of Cruz del Tajo, its **setting** one of the most attractive in the sierra. Ubrique specialises in leather goods. The 18C parish church of **Nuestra Señora de la O** dominates the upper section of the town beyond the **plaza del Ayuntamiento**.

▶ *Leave Ubrique on the A 374 towards Benaocaz.*

The 2C **Roman settlement of Ocurri** is 2km/1.2mi outside of Ubrique, at Salto de la Mora (👣*visit by guided tours (2hr), Sat–Sun and public hols at noon; 🎫€4.50; ☎956 46 49 00 tourist office)*. The road continues through mountains to Benaocaz *(6km/4mi)* and Villaluenga del Rosario *(11km/7mi)*.

Benaocaz
Benaocaz has an attractive 18C town hall built under Carlos III and a small museum, the **Museo Municipal** (🕐*open*

Lime
A particular feature of Andalusian architecture is the use of white-washed lime. A number of theories have been put forward to explain the use of lime, the origins of which can be found in the Middle Ages. When used on walls, lime acts as a consolidating agent and an insulator against fierce heat; in times past it was also used as a disinfectant against disease.

Sat–Sun and public hols, 11.30am–1.30pm and 5–7pm; ☎956 12 55 00)

▶ *Continue on the A 374.*

Villaluenga del Rosario
This unspoilt village is the highest in Cádiz province, its cobbled streets lined by whitewashed houses. Oddities are a falling-down brick tower in the upper town, the neo-Classical façade of the cemetery entrance, and a **bullring** *(plaza de toros)* perched on an outcrop.

▶ *The road continues along the La Manga defile (desfiladero).*

Grazalema
The approach to the beautiful village of Grazalema (Moorish *Ben-Zalema*) is through the Los Alamillos Pass, revealing **Peñón Grande**, a peak rising to

H. Champollion/MICHELIN

Grazalema

Setenil

1 000m/3 328ft behind the village. It is perhaps surprising to note that Spain's wettest village is not in the region of Galicia, in the northwest of the country, but here in the heart of Andalucía. This quirk of nature is due to the **föhn effect**, whereby warm clouds full of moisture from the Atlantic penetrate inland areas.

The tower of the **Iglesia de San Juan** is of Moorish origin. The tower of the 16C **Iglesia de la Encarnación** is Mudéjar in style. The 18C **Iglesia de la Aurora** on **plaza de España** is also worth a visit.

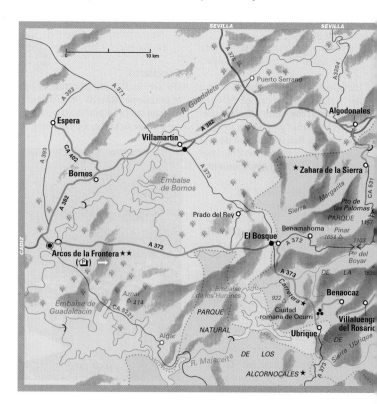

Grazalema is known for its basketwork and woollen blankets. Visit the **La Antigua Fábrica de Mantas** (The Old Blanket Factory) at the entrance to the town (🕐 open Sept–Jul Mon–Thu, 8am–2pm and 3–6.30pm, Fri 8am–2pm (shop open Fri afternoon); Jul, Mon–Fri, 7am–3pm. ☎956 13 20 08).

To bypass Ronda, take the CA531 over the **Las Palomas Pass**, with its dramatic **views★**, to **Zahara de la Sierra**

Ronda★★ – *see RONDA*

▷ *Leave Ronda along the MA 428 towards Arriate.*

Setenil★

This is the only village in this region with troglodyte dwellings built into the rock. Unlike at Guadix (*see GUADIX*), no chimneys are visible, just rows of houses which appear to support the weight of the rock above. Fine examples are the **Cuevas del Sol** (Caves of the Sun) and **Cuevas de la Sombra** (Caves of the Shade). The **tourist office** is in an impressive building with a 16C *artesonado* ceiling (🕐Open 10.30am (noon Sat–Sun and public hols)–2pm and 4–7pm (5–8pm Jun–Sept); ☎956 13 42 61).

Neighbouring Olvera is visible from a keep in the upper town. The **Iglesia de la Encarnación**, higher still, is Gothic in style, with neo-Gothic frescoes.

Olvera

13km/8mi NW from Setenil along the CA 422.

The triangular-shaped 12C **castle** (🕐open Tue–Sun 10.30am–2pm and 4–6.30pm; 7pm Mar–Oct. ☎€2. ☎956 12 08 16) overlooking Olvera's hilltop **site★★** defended the Nasrid kingdom until its conquest by Alfonso XI in 1327. Olvera's **olive oil** is considered some of Spain's finest.

Algodonales

22km/14mi from Olvera along the CA 342.
Keep your eyes peeled for activity overhead, this is one of Spain's top hang-gliding spots.

Zahara de la Sierra★

6km/4mi south of Algodonales along the CA 531.
Even by Pueblo Blanco standards Zahara de la Sierra enjoys a splendid hilltop **setting★★**. The view from the castle encompasses the **Zahara Dam**, neighbouring Algodonales and as far as Olvera. The clock tower is from the 16C, the Baroque **Iglesia de Santa María de Mesa** dates from the 18C.

Villamartín

The flat streets here are decidedly uncharacteristic of the Pueblos Blancos. The **plaza del Ayuntamiento** is the hub of Villamartín; the **calle de El Santo** leads past mansions such as the 19C **Casa-Palacio de Los Ríos**, and the 16C Casa-Palacio de los Topete.

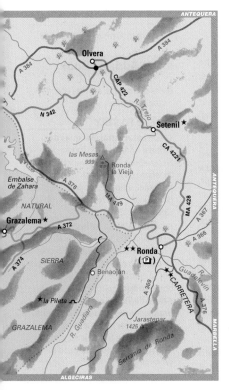

The Spanish fir

This species, a relic of the Tertiary Era, is the most common tree to be found in the local sierra. Known popularly as the Spanish pine, the Spanish fir *(pinsapo)* is a tree which is more commonly found in Mediterranean areas. Today, it is only found in the Sierra de Grazalema and the Serranía de Ronda in Spain, and the Rif mountains in Morocco. The Spanish

Foliage of Spanish fir with its pollen cones

©www.tree-species.blogspot.com

fir was officially classified as an arboreal species in 1837 by the Swiss botanist Edmond Bossier. It can grow to a height of some 30m/100ft and attain a diameter of around 1m/3ft. Its branches, which grow horizontally, and its leaves, with their helicoidal shape, give the tree an unusual appearance which is quite unique in Spain.

Calle de la Feria leads to the **Museo Histórico Municipal** (Ⓒ*open summer, Tue–Sat 10am–2pm and 4–6pm; 6–9pm rest of year;* ✆€1.50; ☎956 73 33 96).
The **Alberite dolmen**, dating from around 4000 BC, is 4km/2.5mi to the south of Villamartín. It consists of a gallery 20m/65ft long formed by large stone slabs, and a funerary chamber.

Bornos

13km/8mi east of Villamartín along the A 382.

Bornos extends gracefully along the reservoir *(embalse)* of the same name. Unlike neighbouring villages, it is not surrounded by mountains, nor is it completely white. It does, however, have some of the best architecture in the whole area.

The plaza del Ayuntamiento is fronted by the **Castillo-Palacio de los Ribera**★ (Ⓒ*open 9am–2pm, 3–6pm; Apr–Sept, 11am–2pm and 3–10pm;* ✆*no charge;* ☎*956 72 82 74)*, a castle-cum-palace which is now home to the **tourist office** and a workshop-school.
The attractive Renaissance-style **patio**★ has an ogival balustrade running along the upper gallery, from where there is access to one of the village's hidden treasures: a garden laid out in the 16C, one of the first of its kind designed in pure Renaissance style. At one end, note the loggia-type gallery.
Also on the plaza del Ayuntamiento is the **Iglesia de Santo Domingo**, a Gothic church built in the late 15C.

Espera

10km/6mi northwest along the CA 402.
The village of Espera stands on a small outcrop in the middle of a fertile landscape. The Moorish **Castillo de Fatetar**, looks down from on high. Note the Baroque façade of the adjacent Ermita del Cristo de la Antigua. If you have time, the **Iglesia de Santa María de Gracia**, is also worth a visit

▶ *Return to Arcos along the A 393.*

EL PUERTO DE SANTA MARÍA ★

POPULATION: 73 728

The mansions of El Puerto de Santa María were erected when the town prospered following the discovery and exploitation of the Americas. The ordered old quarter, predominantly built in the 18C and 19C, is best discovered on foot.

Modern El Puerto has the *joie de vivre* typical of Andalucía, Streets are thronged in summer with visitors from around Spain who come to enjoy superb gastronomy and a lively nightlife. El Puerto de Santa Maria is also famous for its sherry bodegas.

- **Information:** Calle Luna, 22. ☎956 54 24 13. www.elpuertosm.es.
- **Orient Yourself:** Puerto de Santa María is directly opposite Cádiz, 10 km/6mi by road, on the other side of the Bay of Cádiz. Jerez de la Frontera is 12km/7.5mi north.
- **Organising Your Time:** Allow a day for lingering in El Puerto de Santa María.
- **Parking:** The cobbled streets are fairly free from traffic, so park your car on the outskirts, and explore on foot.
- **Don't Miss:** Try some of the locally produced '*fino*' sherry at one of the towns.
- **Especially for Kids:** The Castillo (castle) of San Marcos.
- **Also See:** JEREZ DE LA FRONTERA, CÁDIZ, ARCOS DE LA FRONTERA, SANLÚCAR DE BARRAMEDA, MEDINA SIDONIA.

Visit

Iglesia Mayor Prioral

⊙*Open Mon–Fri 8.30am–12.45pm (Sat, to noon; Sun, to 1.45pm) and 6.30–8.30pm.* ☎956 85 17 16.

This priory church was founded in the 13C though the late-Gothic style building you see today is from the 15C. The **Portada del Sol**★ (Sun Gateway), with its profuse Plateresque and Baroque decoration, opens onto plaza de España. The interior is in many styles as a result of many renovations at different times. Follow calle Pagador, by the **Museo Municipal** (⊙*open Tue–Fri 10am–2pm, Sat–Sun 10.30am–2pm.* ☎956 54 27 05), as far as calle Santo Domingo.

Fundación Rafael Alberti

⊙*Open mid-Jun to mid-Sept Tue–Sun 11am–2.30pm. Rest of year Mon–Fri, 11am–2.30pm.* ☜€3. ☎956 85 07 11. www.rafaelalberti.es.

The Rafael Alberti Foundation honours the town's famous poet. Photos, letters and copies of his works trace Alberti's long life (1902–99), and reflect Spain over the past 100 years.

Casa-Museo Pedro Muñoz-Seca

C/ Neveria, 48.
⊙*Call for opening times.* ☎956 85 17 31. www.fundacionpedromunozseca.org.

This acclaimed son of El Puerto, Pedro Muñoz-Seca (1879–1936), is most famous as the author of *La venganza de don Mendo*. The exhibit recalls his life and work.

Castillo de San Marcos

☜*Visit by guided tours only (30min), Jul–Sept Tue–Sat 10am–1.30pm. Jan–Jun Tue 12.30–1.30pm, Thu and Sat 11.30am–1.30pm.* ☜€5. ☎956 85 17 51.

Alfonso X had the first castle-church built over the main mosque of Moorish **Alcanatif** in the 13C. It was modified

---

The voyages of Columbus

It was from El Puerto de Santa María that **Columbus** departed on two occasions on his journeys of discovery to the Americas; **Juan de la Cosa** also created his **Mapamundi** in the town in 1500, the first map to show the recently discovered New World.

Address Book

GETTING THERE AND GETTING AROUND

Airport – The nearest airport is in Jerez de la Frontera, 20km/12mi along the main A 4 Cádiz-Madrid road. (☎956 15 00 00/01 83. www.aena.es).

Trains – The station (☎956 54 25 85) is on plaza de la Estación. Trains between Cádiz and Sevilla stop in El Puerto de Santa María. Trains operate from Cádiz and Sevilla to every corner of Spain.

Inter-city-buses – The stop for all services is at the bullring (plaza de toros).

Transportes Comes (☎956 80 70 59) operates in the province and to Sevilla.

Transportes Los Amarillos (☎956 29 08 00) mainly operates to the provinces of Sevilla and Málaga.

City buses – Six lines serve El Puerto de Santa María (☎900 70 07 71).

For coin ranges, see the Legend on the cover flap.

WHERE TO STAY

⊜⊜**Hostal Chaikana** – *Javier de Burgos, 17.* ☎956 54 29 02. www.hostal chaikana.com. 35 rooms. Small, modern and spotless hotel in the centre.

⊜⊜⊜**Hotel Dunas Puerto** – *Camino de Los Enamorados.* ☎956 85 03 11. www.jale.com/dunas. 62 rooms. Bungalows in an area of greenery by the sea. Very smart bedrooms and swimming pool.

⊜⊜⊜**Hotel Los Cántaros** – *Curva, 6.* ☎956 54 02 40. www.hotelloscantaros. com. 39 rooms. Very smart well-maintained hotel, on a small square in the town centre.

⊜⊜⊜⊜**Monasterio de San Miguel** – *Virgen de los Milagros, 27.* ☎956 54 04 40. www.hotelesjale.com. 165 rooms. This former Capuchin monastery dates from the 18C. Rooms are tastefully decorated and crowned by impressive vaulted ceilings. Swimming pool and garden.

WHERE TO EAT

Ribera del Marisco – The attractive **plaza de la Herrería** and Ribera del Marisco are the liveliest parts of El Puerto. Two well-known bars are **Romerijo 1** and **Romerijo 2** (www. romerijo.com), where fish and seafood can be bought by weight and eaten on the terrace. Arrive early to get a table.

⊜⊜⊜**Los Portales** – *Ribera del Río, 13.* ☎956 54 18 12. www.losportales.com. Excellent seafood fresh from the bay, in beautiful traditional surroundings

⊜⊜⊜ **Casa Flores** – *Ribera del Río, 9.* ☎956 54 35 12. You can't go wrong with "pescaito" (fried fish), crayfish or prawns. The decor mixes sea and bullring.

⊜⊜⊜ **El Faro del Puerto** – *Avenida de Fuentebravía.* ☎956 87 09 52. www. elfarodelpuerto.com. Closed Sun evening excluding Aug. This exclusive restaurant away from the noise of the town centre is one of El Puerto's most elegant establishments. Creative international and Andalusian cuisine.

GOING OUT

Café-Pub Blanco y Negro – *Ricardo Alcón, 10.* ☎956 54 15 59. This former wine storehouse, tucked in an alleyway, is renowned for its locally roasted coffee and occasionally hosts art and photography exhibitions; by night it is a late and lively drinking den popular with 25-and-overs.

El Resbaladero – *Micaela Aramburu (Castillo de San Marcos).* www. elresbaladero.com. One of the nocturnal hotspots in El Puerto with dancing to the latest DJs and theme parties.

La Pontona – *Parque Calderón (next to Vaporcito ferry).* ☎956 851 335. www. puertodenoche.com/Pontona. Party Bar on the river, good for a coffee or a cocktail; splendid views.

WINE CELLARS

No visit to El Puerto de Santa María is complete without a bodega tour and tasting.

Bodegas Osborne: Osborne have two bodegas in town. In the centre is the **Bodega Mora** (*Calle Las Moros;* ⏱*guided tours in English, Mon–Fri 10.30am, Sat 11am;* ☎956 86 91 00; *www.osborne.es; Booking required*).

The **Bodega El Tiro** *is on the western fringe of town.* (Ctra Nacional 4, km 651; ⏱*guided tours in English, Mon–Fri 11.30am;* ☎956 85 42 28; www.osborne. es; booking required).

At **Bodegas Terry** (Calle Toneleros; ⏱call for times; ☎956 54 36 90 or 956 857 700) the visit includes a tour of the **Carriage Museum**.

SHOPPING

The main shopping district in the town centre is concentrated around three streets: **calle Luna**, **calle Palacios** and **calle Larga**. The first two head off from the **Iglesia Mayor Prioral** and are predominantly pedestrianised. This part of El Puerto is also pleasant for a stroll.
Arte Sano (calle Santo Domingo) selling high-quality original ceramics and basketwork, is recommended.
A small **market** selling a whole range of goods is held every Tuesday on rotonda de la Puntilla.

SIGHTSEEING

El Vaporcito del Puerto

(Little Steamer) is the affectionate name for the Adriano III which plies the route between Puerto de Santa María (from plaza de las Galeras Reales) and Cádiz (⏱see website for schedule; €3, €4 return, €10 night cruise; ☎629 46 80 14; www.vapordeelpuerto.com). Juan Fernández has operated the service since 1927. The 45min crossing offers visitors a different perspective of Cádiz. An evening bay cruise (2hr) operates in summer.

SPORT AND LEISURE

There are several internationally renowned golf courses in the area.

---

during the 14C and 15C, and restored in the 20C.
The former fish exchange (lonja de pescado) can be seen behind the castle.

Plaza del Polvorista

The **Palacio de Imblusqueta** on the square, a 17C mansion, is the town hall.

Plaza de Toros

⏱Open Tue–Sun 11am–1.30pm and 5.30–7pm (May–Sept 6–7.30pm). ⏱Closed on days preceding and following bullfights. ☎956 54 15 78.
The 1880 bullring, one of the largest in Spain, seats over 12 000. It is arcaded and solid on the outside, graceful inside.

Monasterio de Nuestra Señora de la Victoria

This monastery on the western outskirts of town is austere but for its exuberant **portal**★, framed by two buttresses ending in pinnacles.
A gable bears the Cerda family coat of arms. Once a prison, the monastery now hosts official ceremonies.

Excursions

Rota

27km/17mi west.
Past an American military base, the 16km/10mi of beaches of Rota at the northern tip of the Bay of Cádiz are sheltered from strong coastal winds.

Old town★

Rota's old fishing village is between two beaches, **Playa de la Costilla**★ and Playa del Rompidillo.
The **Parroquia de Nuestra Señora de la O** is a church with a fine late-Gothic **interior**★. The **Castillo de Luna** now functions as the town hall.

Cádiz

45min by boat
There is a ferry service from El Puerto de Santa María to Cadiz ⏱see Address Book, Sightseeing.

Local specialities

Rota's speciality is *urta a la roteña*, sea bream cooked with peppers, tomatoes, white wine and thyme. It is a traditional feature of one of the region's most unusual festivals, the **Fiesta de la Urta**, when locals compete to produce the best recipe for this dish. The festival has been held for the past 30 years and takes place in mid-August.

LA RÁBIDA★

Whitewashed houses cluster around the La Rábida monastery just a few kilometres from Palos de la Frontera. Originally constructed in 1412, La Rábida (an Arabic word meaning fortress) is a vital and interesting stepping stone along the "Columbus Route".

- **Information:** La Casita de Zenobia. ☎959 53 05 97.
- **Orient Yourself:** La Rábida is 10km/6mi south of Huelva.
- **Organising Your Time:** Allow half a day
- **Especially for Kids:** The life-size replica boats at Muelle de las Carabelas.
- **Also See:** HUELVA, MOGUER, EL ROCÍO.

Visit

Monasterio de Santa María de la Rábida

Open Jun–Sept Tue–Sun 10am–1pm and 4–6.15pm (Aug 4.45–8pm, rest of year 4–7pm). €3. Visit by guided tour only. ☎959 35 04 11. www.monasteriodelarabida.com (in Spanish only).

Monks still live at this 14C Mudéjar-Gothic Franciscan monastery, famous for its associations with Christopher Columbus. It was here that he stayed and, with the help of the Pinzón brothers and two monks, Antonio de Marchena and Juan Pérez, that he planned his voyage of discovery – as depicted in the magnificent frescoes by **Daniel Vázquez Díaz** (1930) in the rooms on the ground floor.

Before entering, note the large white stone monument, the **Columna de los Descubridores** (Discoverers' Column), in a large rotunda, depicting scenes from the Discoveries. It was erected on the 400th anniversary of landing in the New World.

B. Kaufmann/MICHELIN

Monasterio de Santa María de La Rábida

Church★

The small church contains many items of great artistic value including old frescoes, polychrome wood *artesonados* (whose delicate filigree work contrasts with the austere appearance of the building) several 18C paintings by Juan de Dios. The greatest treasure however is the **Virgin of the Miracles**★, an exceptional 14C alabaster figure, sculpted by an Andalusian workshop. It is the monastery's patron and stands in a chapel to the left of the altar.

Legend has it that Columbus and the crew of his three caravels prayed before the figure on the two days before departure.

Cloisters

The Mudéjar-style cloisters comprise two galleries of columns: the lower tier was built in the 15C, while the upper section, added in the 18C, contains models of the *Pinta*, the *Niña* and the *Santa María*. The cloisters have all the charm of typical Andalusian patios, with abundant vegetation and the gentle bubbling of water.

Dining room

A whitewashed pulpit which was formerly used for readings during meals can be seen to the side of this austere rectangular room.

Chapter house

Tradition has it that the large table in this bright, spacious room was used by Columbus to plan his voyage with his advisors. Note the 18C Mudéjar *artesonado* ceiling.

Sala de las Banderas

This "Room of Flags" exhibits the flag of every country on the American continent as well as a small chest with earth from each.

In a small room to the right is a historic **mapamundi**★, a work by Juan de la Cosa (&see Box below), which outlined the coast of America for the first time.

Sights

Muelle de las Carabelas★

Open Jun–Sept Tue–Fri 10am–2pm and 5–9pm. Sat–Sun 11am–8pm. Rest of year Tue–Sun 10am–7pm. €3.20. 959 53 05 97. www.diphuelva.es.

Life-size replicas of the three caravels of Columbus are moored at this modern dock on the Tinto Estuary. A tour of the berths, storerooms and decks of these old vessels enables visitors to observe the detailed decoration and the firearms, anchors, and sails used by the crew. Audiovisual presentations are given in the building at the entrance to the dock. A small **museum** displays 15C navigational tools and there is also a small **cafe** where you can take a break.

Muelle de la Reina

The small Queen's Dock, alongside the three caravels, is dominated by the monument to Icarus of the Triumph (*Ícaro del Triunfo*), commemorating the first transatlantic flight by the Plus Ultra seaplane from Palos de la Frontera to Buenos Aires in 1926.

Avenida de los Descubridores

This wide avenue, named in honour of the Great Discoverers, links Palos de la Frontera with La Rábida and is decorated with the coats of arms of every Ibero-American country. The Glorieta del Pueblo Argentino, a square named in honour of the Argentinian people, stands at the end of the avenue, with a glazed ceramic Aztec calendar as its centrepiece.

Parque Botánico José Celestino Mutis

The botanical garden, dedicated to this Andalusian scientist, is a maze of leafy avenues, canals and bridges displaying the most typical plant species to be found on the five continents.

Foro Iberoamericano de la Rábida

The Ibero-American forum is a building with a large open-air auditorium used as a venue for congresses, concerts and theatrical performances.

Universidad Internacional de Andalucía

This prestigious university is devoted to the study of American cultures.

Plaza de Macuro

A modern sculpture in the square recalls a crossing of the Atlantic by helicopter from Macuro, Venezuela, to La Rábida.

Mapping America

Juan de la Cosa (c. 1460 –1510), was born in El Puerto de Santa María. He was the owner and captain of the Santa María and sailed on the first three Voyages of Discovery with Christopher Columbus, He was also a gifted cartographer, producing the earliest known European world map to incorporate the territories of the Americas that were discovered in the 15C. He continued to explore the New World visiting the countries that would become known as Colombia and Panama but was killed by Indians in Haiti.

EL ROCÍO

This small village of whitewashed houses and sandy streets is the site of the Iglesia de la Virgen del Rocío, the most venerated pilgrimage site in Spain. For all but one weekend of the year it is peaceful, inhabited by a few locals (many of whom use horses as their main mode of transport), second-homers (particularly from Almonte), and brothers of religious orders. During Whitsun weekend, however, the village's tranquillity is broken when around a million pilgrims make their way here to show their devotion to the Virgin of the Dew (Virgen del Rocío).

- ▣ **Information:** Avenida de la Canaliega.☎959 44 38 08.
- ▶ **Orient Yourself:** El Rocío is 80km/50mi southwest of Sevilla, on the border of Parque Nacional de Doñana.
- ◷ **Organising Your Time:** El Rocío will take up from a few hours to a day, depending on your religious interest.
- ◔ **Also See:** COSTA DE HUELVA, Parque Nacional de DOÑANA.

El Rocío Pilgrimage

For those born outside Andalucía, the deep significance of the Romería (pilgrimage) to El Rocío – the largest and most famous in Spain – is difficult to comprehend. But for hundreds of thousands, including an increasing number of pilgrims from outside Spain attracted by its beauty and significance, the journey here is an important annual event. According to tradition, the Church of the Virgin of the Dew was erected at the beginning of the 15C to house a statue found by a hunter in the hollow of an oak. In the mid-17C, during an epidemic, the church developed into a place of pilgrimage which attracted the devout from far and wide to implore the Virgin for good health.

Almonte, the nearest town to El Rocío, and Villamanrique, became the first two towns to establish brotherhoods or religious associations, which now number around 100.

"The Route"

During the course of the week preceding Pentecost, members of each brotherhood make their way towards the shrine. These pilgrims follow long-established routes on foot, in carts adorned with colourful decoration and paper flowers, on horseback and even nowadays by jeep. Women wear the traditional *rociero* skirt, decorated with one or two pleated ruffles, and hats to offer protection against the hot sun; men tend to wear a white shirt, tight-fitting trousers and a Córdoban sombrero or cap. Almost everyone wears leather boots. A sprig of rosemary and the medallion of the brotherhood complete the attire. Each brotherhood follows its own *simpecado*, a silver cart pulled by oxen carrying a standard bearing the image of the Virgin of the Dew. At night the scene transforms into one of dancing and singing around open fires. The rosary is always recited at nightfall and Mass is celebrated at dawn.

The village of El Rocío

Pilgrims arrive at El Rocío throughout **Saturday**, where they pay homage to the White Dove (*Blanca Paloma*) or to Our Lady of the Marshes (*La Señora de las Marismas*), two of the many names given to the Virgin Mary. **Sunday** is given over to masses, recitals of the rosary and socialising, culminating in the most eagerly awaited moment in the **early morning on the Monday of Pentecost**. Just before daybreak, youngsters from the nearby town of Almonte climb over the gate of the church and remove the statue of the Virgin, which they carry in procession through the streets, surrounded by a security cordon to prevent pilgrims from approaching. The night is long, full of emotion, fatigue and happiness, the culmination of a week of physical effort and devotion for which

Simpecado with pilgrims on their way to the Ermita

R. Mattes/MICHELIN

pilgrims have been preparing throughout the year.

If you intend staying the night locally make your arrangements well in advance.

Driving Tour

The Wine Route from El Rocío to Niebla

36km/22mi. Allow half a day.

The highlight of this itinerary is the tasting of excellent local white and sweet wines which fall under the Condado de Huelva appellation. It is well worth visiting the local *bodegas* to try specialities such as old *oloroso*, fruity whites, *mistela* (a flavoured brandy), *moscatel* and sweet orange wine *(vino dulce de naranja)*.

Almonte

15km/9.5mi north of El Rocío along the A 483.

Because Almonte is within the Parque Nacional de Doñana, close to the popular beach of Playa de Matalascaña, and near the village of El Rocío, it welcomes many visitors. However, much of the town's prestige stems from wine, the aroma of which is ever-present. Whitewashed houses adorned with wrought-iron grilles and resplendent doorways are a typical feature of Almonte, as are the carts used to transport grapes at harvest time. The **plaza Virgen del Rocío**, the hub of town life, is a delightful haven of peace and tranquillity fronted by two of Almonte's main buildings: the parish church, an attractive example of colonial-style architecture, and the town hall, with its elegant gallery of arches on the upper floor.

Bollullos del Condado

9km/5.5mi north.

Every corner of this town appears to be devoted to wine production, with numerous old *bodegas* lining its well-maintained streets with their seigniorial air.

Behind the impressive façades of these imposing buildings, visitors can learn more about ancestral wine-making techniques, and taste and purchase some of the excellent sweet and white wines produced in large vats and served in attractive earthenware cups.

Bollulos is also home to several craft workshops producing iron utensils, carriages, gold embroidery and barrels, and boasts a number of bars and restaurants specialising in seafood.

The **plaza del Sagrado Corazón de Jesús**, a picturesque square fronted by the **Iglesia de Santiago Apóstol**, with its Andalusian Baroque façade and tower, and the town hall, its attractive façade composed of two storeys of stilted arches, are worthy of note.

La Palma del Condado
4km/2.5mi north of Bollulos.
Renowned for its excellent wines, this bright town is embellished with a number of seigniorial squares, elegant whitewashed houses and notable monumental buildings.

The main event in the local calendar is the *Fiesta de la Vendimia*, the wine harvest festival held at the end of September, the origins of which date back to the 14C.

Ayuntamiento
The former 16C Hospital of the Immaculate Conception was restored in 1929 in the Regionalist style employed for the Ibero-American Exhibition of the same year. It is now the town hall.

Plaza del Corazón de Jesús
This attractive square is dominated by the statue of the Sacred Heart of Jesus (Corazón de Jesús), a work created in 1927 by local sculptor Antonio Pinto Soldán The plaza is surrounded by elegant, colonial-inspired buildings.

Plaza de España
This well-proportioned square is the centre of local life. One side of the *plaza* is bordered by the former Palacio del Señorío, the theatre and the Casa de los Arcos, while the opposite side is fronted by the Casa de Tirado, with an exquisite **grille** and *azulejos* which reproduce *Las Meninas* and *Las Hilanderas* by Velázquez. However, the most interesting construction on the square is the **Iglesia de San Juan Bautista**, a sober Baroque church, its impressive whitewashed façade crowned by a graceful tower used by storks as a nesting place.

Iglesia del Valle
The *camarín* behind the main altar of this 15C Mudéjar-style church houses a statue of the Virgin of the Valley, the patron saint of La Palma del Condado.

Niebla★
8km/5mi southwest of La Palma del Condado along A 472.

The historical centre of Niebla is graced with several old monuments of significant interest, in particular the series of **walls**★, one of the most complete of any in Spain. Erected during the period of Almohad domination in the 12C using clay from the banks of the River Tinto – hence their reddish colour – they run for a length of 2km/1.2mi and are punctuated by a total of 50 towers and five entrance gateways.

Several cultural itineraries depart from the tourist office, Calle Campo del Castillo (◷*open 9.30am–2pm and 4–6pm;* ☎*959 36 22 70*).

The **Iglesia de Santa María de la Granada**, built on the site of the former mosque, combines features from the earlier construction, such as the peaceful patio of orange trees which opens onto the entrance of the church, with additional Gothic elements. The **alcázar** or **Castillo de los Guzmanes**, dating from the 15C, has retained several interesting vestiges of Moorish architecture. The **Iglesia de San Martín**, divided into two by a street, is a building formerly used both as a mosque and synagogue.

On the outskirts of Niebla, the River Tinto is spanned by a large Roman bridge.

RONDA ★★

POPULATION: 35 788

Ronda stands at the heart of the Serranía de Ronda, split by the famous ravine (**tajo**★) of the River Guadalevín. Its isolation and legends of highwaymen made it an obligatory destination for 19C Romantic writers. Nowadays it is much less isolated and visitors flock here all year round.

- **Information:** Plaza de España, 9. ☎952 87 12 72. Paseo Blas Infante. ☎952 18 71 19. www.turismoderonda.es.
- ▶ **Orient Yourself:** Ronda is 113km/68mi north of Málaga
- **Don't Miss:** The Palacio Mondragón; the view of the ravine and bridge from the Arco de Cristo; the vew of Ronda from the Iglesia Rupestre de la Virgen de la Cabeza; the drive to San Pedro de Alcántara.
- ○ **Organising Your Time:** Allow at least a full day.
- **Also See:** COSTA DEL SOL, MÁLAGA, ANTEQUERA, ARCOS DE LA FRONTERA.

A Bit of History

Ronda under the Moors –Invaders under **Tarik-ibn-Zeyad** followed the Roman way from Gibraltar. They founded *Izna-Rand-Onda*, some 20km/12mi from old Roman **Acinipo**. Under the Umayyads, Ronda was the capital of a Moorish region *(cora)*, then became a taifa capital after the fall of the Caliphate. Ronda prospered under the Almohads and into the Nasrid era, and fell to the Christians in 1485.

Walking Tour

La Ciudad ★★

The Moorish quarter of narrow alleys, lined by mansions and whitewashed houses with iron balconies offers fine views of the countryside, and impressive churches.

Puente Nuevo★

The New Bridge, a manificent 18C engineering feets, is the best place to start your visit. Take the path to the coffee

Puente Nuevo

Detail of the façade of the Palacio del Marqués de Salvatierra

shop of the *parador* for a superb view of the bridge, the Guadiaro valley, and the Sierra de Grazalema. A chamber under an arch, once a jail, now houses the **Centro de Interpretación del Puente Nuevo** (◷open Mon–Fri 10am–9pm, Sat 10am–1.45pm and 4–8pm, Sun 10am–3pm; ⊜€2; ☎649 96 53 38)

▶ *Cross the bridge and follow calle Santo Domingo.*

The Convento de Santo Domingo (left hand side) was the first construction by victorious Christians after 1485.

▶ *Head down calle Santo Domingo.*

Casa del Rey Moro

According to legend, this was the mansion of Almonated, king of Ronda, who drank wine from the skulls of vanquished enemies. The current 18C building has Mudéjar-style brick towers and wooden balconies.
A 200-step Moorish staircase, **La Mina**, descends to the river.

La Mina and Jardines de Forestier★

◷*Open year-round daily 10am–7pm.* ⊜€4. ☎952 18 72 00.
In 1912 the French landscaper **Forestier** (who later designed María Luisa

Park in Sevilla) was commissioned to design these lovely gardens. Despite narrow terrain, he managed to create a jewel. Three terraces combine Moorish features (fountains, water and *azulejos*) with the pergolas and parterres of European tradition.

Palacio del Marqués de Salvatierra

☯ *Interior closed to visitors.*
This small mansion is typical of noble 18C architecture, The **portal**★★ is exceptional. The door is flanked by pairs of Corinthian columns topped by an architrave decorated with medallions. Above, human figures with strong pre-Columbian influence substitute for columns.

▶ *Walk towards the old bridge. Beyond the Puerta de Felipe V, follow a stone path to the Moorish Baths.*

Moorish/Arab Baths★

◷ *Open Mon–Fri 10am–9pm. Sat 10am–1.45pm and 4–8pm. Sun and hols 10am–3pm.* ⊜€3. ☎952 18 71 19 or 656 95 09.
These 13C baths are some of the best preserved on the Iberian Peninsula. They were built close to the river along the Las Culebras stream in the Arrabal Viejo, a district then popular with artisans and tanners. The first part of the building, unroofed, leads to the baths themselves, comprising three transversal rooms topped with barrel vaults and illuminated by star-shaped lunettes. The middle room, divided by horseshoe arches and brick columns, is the most impressive. The cauldron which was used to heat water for the baths is to sited to the rear.

▶ *Climb a stone staircase parallel to the walls, then pass through the 13C Puerta de la Acijara gateway.*

Minarete de San Sebastián★

Iplaza del Poeta Abul-Beca.
This graceful minaret is the only remnant of a 14C Nasrid mosque, which victorious Christians converted to a church. The lower stone section is Moorish; the

upper brick section is Mudéjar in style. The horseshoe arch doorway is particularly noteworthy. This is the smallest minaret still standing in Andalucía.

Museo del Bandolero

🕐 *Open daily 10.30am–8pm (autumn and winter 7pm).* €3. ☎952 87 77 85. www.museobandolero.com.
Bandits, brigands and outlaws of Andalucía ride again in this museum, including legendary Diego Corrientes and José María el Tempranillo, who were variously perceived as either romantic travellers or bloodthirsty murderers. A video *(in Spanish)* and documents sheds some light on these enigmatic figures.

▸ *Go down calle Arminán to Espíritú Santo church.*

Iglesia del Espíritu Santo

The fortress character of the late 15C Church of the Holy Spirit derives from its position by the town walls. The façade is elegant; the interior, remodelled several times, has a single nave crowned by a stellar vault with tiercerons.

Puerta de Almocabar

This gateway of three horseshoe arches, now flanked by 18C towers, led to a cemetery (*al-maqabir* in Arabic). To one side note the **Puerta de Carlos V** (Charles V's Gateway) and opposite, beyond the walls, the **San Francisco district**, site of a 17C Franciscan convent.

▸ *Return and go left into plaza de la Duquesa de Parcent.*

Santa María la Mayor★

🚻 🕐 *Open Mon–Sat 10am–8pm, Sun 10am–1pm.* €3. ☎952 87 22 46. www.colegiata.com.
The Collegiate Church of St Mary is, like many Andalusian churches from the period, dedicated to the Incarnation. It replaced the main mosque of which the original Mihrab Arch *(in the entrance*

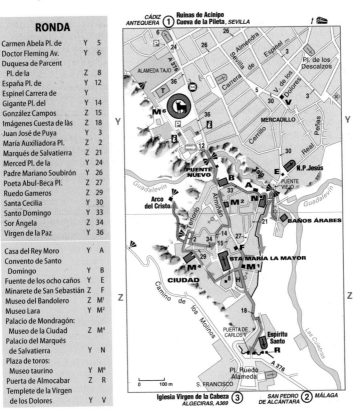

Address Book

For coin ranges, see the Legend on the cover flap.

WHERE TO STAY

Hotel Virgen de los Reyes – *Lorenzo Borrego, 13.* ☎*952 87 11 40. 52 rooms.* An inexpensive hotel with clean, simple rooms.

Alavera de los Baños – *Hoyo San Miguel.* ☎*952 87 91 43. www.alaveradelosbanos.com. 9 rooms.* This charming hotel next to the Moorish Baths incorporates tasteful interior designs, atmospheric colours, Moroccan rugs and lamps to create a very Moorish ambiance. Ask for a room with a terrace. Restaurant and tapas options.

Hotel San Gabriel – *Marqués de Moctezuma, 19.* ☎*952 19 03 92. www.hotelsangabriel.com. 21 rooms.* Magnificently decorated if somewhat formal mansion dating from 1736. Ask for a room with a view to the charming patio.

Parador de Ronda *78 rooms. Plaza de España.* ☎*952 87 75 00. www. parador.es.* Luxury modern parador hotel set in the old town hall on the edge of the gorge. From the swimming pool and many bedrooms there are magnificent views. Excellent restaurant (☺☺☺).

La Fuente de la Higuera, (Los Frontones) – *5.5km/3.4mi along A 376 towards Sevilla, then bear right for 3.2km/2mi.* ☎*952 11 43 55. www. hotellafuente.com. 11 rooms.* This luxury small country hotel in a beautifully renovated rural olive mill manor combines Mediterranean style with all mod cons.

BENAOJÀN

Molino del Santo – *(10km/6mi SW of Ronda).* ☎*952 16 71 51. www.molinodelsanto.com. 18 rooms.* This former 16C flour and oil mill by the river source, completely restored by a British couple, offers charming rooms, and a lovely restaurant with vegetarian options.

WHERE TO EAT

Doña Pepa – *Plaza del Socorro, 10.* ☎*952 87 47 77. www.dpepa.com .* Enjoy Ronda's signature plates, such as *rabo de toro* (braised bull's tail) in an enchanting Andalusian ambience.

Don Miguel – *Plaza de España, 5.* ☎*952 87 10 90. www.dmiguel.com. Closed Sun lunch Jun–Aug.* A pleasant terrace with wonderful views of the Puente Nuevo, the ravine and the River Guadalevín. Quality cuisine includes specialities such as *rabo de toro* (braised bull's tail), *solomillo de venado* (venison loin) and *cordero a la menta* (lamb with mint sauce). Rooms are available (☺☺☺).

Casa Santa Pola – *Santo Domingo, 3.* ☎*952 87 92 08. www.casasantapola.com. Closed Sun in summer and Wed in winter.* Charming restaurant with several Moorish-style rooms overlooking the ravine, offering gourmet regional cuisine.

Tragabuches – *José Aparicio, 1.* ☎*952 19 02 91. www.tragabuches.com. Closed Sun evening and Mon.* Considered by many locals to be the best in Ronda, Tragabuches is just a stone's throw from the Parador and the bullring. It offers modern cuisine in an avant-garde setting.

SIGHTSEEING

Buy a tourist pass (*bono turistico*, €7) valid for four of Ronda's attractions, available from participating attractions and the tourist office.

---

room), decorated with *atauriques* and calligraphic motifs, remains. The church interior is Gothic and Renaissance.

▸ *Take calle Manuel Montero.*

Palacio de Mondragón (Museo de la Ciudad)★★

🕐*Open Mon–Fri 10am–9pm. Sat 10am –1.45pm and 4–8pm. Sun and hols 10am– 3pm.* ☞€3. ☎*952 87 84 50.*

The palace foundations are from a 14C Moorish residence. The present building

The legend of Tragabuches

In the early 19C, a Ronda gypsy by the name of José Ulloa (nicknamed Tragabuches) developed a certain renown as a bullfighter. Alas, having returned home on the evening of a bullfight, he caught sight of the silhouette of a man sneaking out of the window of his house.

Mad with rage, Tragabuches murdered his rival before throwing his wife out of the window and disappearing to join the band of brigands known as the "seven sons of Écija", of which he was to become one of the most merciless. Learn more about him at the Museo del Bandolero.

mixes Mudéjar (towers and patios) and Renaissance styles, the latter best seen on the doorway.

The charming **Mudéjar patio**★★ retains traces of *azulejos* and stuccowork between its arches. The palace houses the town **museum**, with exhibits on history, ethnography, and the environment, including the Serranía de Ronda.

▶ *Continue to plaza del Campillo.*

Follow the path heading down to the 18C **Arco de Cristo** (Christ's Arch), from where there is a magnificent **view**★★ of the **ravine** *(tajo)* and bridge. During the Spanish Civil War Franco's forces threw prisoners to their deaths from here (as recorded in Hemingway's *For Who the Bell Tolls*).(

▶ *Follow calle Sor Ángela to plaza del Gigante.*

The square is named for a barely discernible relief of Hercules on one of its 14C houses.

▶ *Return to calle Armiñán.*

Museo Lara

🕐 *Open year-round daily 11am–8pm.* €4. ☎952 87 12 63. *www.museolara.org.* The owner, Juan Antonio Lara, has assembled an extraordinary eclectic **collection**★ of superb 18C enamel clocks, fans, and an armoury. The museum is in the Casa-palacio de los Condes de las Islas Batanes, fronted by an attractive façade.

▶ *Follow calle Armiñán to return to plaza de España.*

El Mercadillo

This district, which grew in the 16C, connects to **La Ciudad** by the **Puente Nuevo** (New Bridge) and the Puente Viejo (Old Bridge). El Mercadillo is the commercial area, with pedestrianised streets such as calle Nueva, **calle Remedios**, calle Ermita and the **plaza del Socorro**, a square fronted by attractive 19C and 20C buildings.

Bullring (Museo Taurino)★

🕐 *Open daily: Apr–Sept 10am–8pm. Mar & Oct 10am–7pm. Nov–Feb 10am–6pm.* €6. ☎952 87 15 39. *www.rmcr.org.* The bullring, built in 1785 by the Real Maestranza de Caballería (Royal Institute of Knights), is one of Spain's most beautiful, with a tradition to match. At 66m/216ft, it is the widest bullring anywhere. The twin-tier interior is neo-Classical with Tuscan columns and a stone barrier, but the overall effect is one of great simplicity. Note the statues immortalising Ronda's most honored bullfighting dynasties, the Romero and Ordóñez families. The bullring also houses a colourful **museum** which displays old bullfighting posters and photogrpahs of Orson Welles and Ernest Hemingway, both of who were regular visitors.

Templete de la Virgen de los Dolores★

Built in 1734, this small temple is crowned by a plain vault resting on two columns and two pilasters. Each column is adorned with four half-human, half-fantasy **figures**★ with arms interlinked and attached by the neck, all showing great expression.

Iglesia de Nuestro Padre Jesús

The oldest part of this heavily restored church is the 15C Gothic tower-façade; the roof dates from 1735. Opposite stands the **Fuente de los Ocho Caños** (Fountain of the Eight Spouts), created during the reign of Carlos III in the 18C.

Excursions

Iglesia Rupestre de la Virgen de la Cabeza★

2.7km/1.7mi south via the A 369.
Upon leaving the town, take a sign-posted road to the right (after approx 700m/770yd) leading to the chapel.
🕐*Open Tue–Sun 10.30am–2pm.* €*2.*
☎*952 18 71 19 or 649 36 57 72.*

This small Mozarabic cave chapel probably founded by Hispano-Visigoths in the 9C, is sited on the opposite bank of the River Guadalevín, affording one of the best **views**★★ of Ronda. Is interior occupies almost 280m2/3 013sq ft. and is split into three parts: the store, the monastic quarters and the church. The frescoes here were painted in the 18C. In the middle of August every year the Virgen de la Cabeza (Virgin of the Head) is ceremoniously taken from the collegiate church to the chapel next to the monastery.

Ruinas de Acinipo

22km/13mi northwest.
Leave Ronda via the A 376, then head along the MA 449 towards Ronda la Vieja.
🕐*Open Wed–Sun 9am–3pm; Sun and public hols, 9am–2pm.* 🕐 *Hours subject to change; call to confirm.* ☎*952 18 71 19.*
Known popularly as **Ronda la Vieja**, this ruined settlement retains a large 1C AD **theatre**, including part of the stage.

Cueva de La Pileta★

20km/12mi southwest.
Leave Ronda via the A 376, then take the MA 555 towards Benaoján. From here, bear onto the MA 501.
👉*Visit by guided tours only (1hr) daily 10am–1pm and 4–5pm (6pm in summer).*
🕐€*8.* ☎*952 16 73 43.*

This cave was discovered in 1905 by Don José Bullón Lobato when he was search-ing for bat droppings for use as fertiliser. The importance of the discovery was such that in 1912 studies were carried out here by the eminent prehistorians **Hugo Obermaier** and **Abbé Breuil**. The Pileta Cave is a limestone formation with over 2km/1.2mi of galleries of which some 500m/550yd are open to the public.

The red and black wall paintings down here span an extensive period of prehistory, with figurative motifs dating from the Palaeolithic era (20000 BC) and symbolic art from the Neolithic period (4000 BC).

Driving Tour

From Ronda to San Pedro de Alcántara★★

49km/30.5mi – allow 1hr.

The A 376 was built in the 1970s to connect the Serranía de Ronda with the Costa del Sol. Although it does not pass through any towns or villages, it runs between two of the most spectacular mountain ranges in Málaga province: to the left the **Parque Natural de la Sierra de las Nieves** and to the right, the **Sierra Bermeja**.

The road climbs gradually though a landscape of pines and Spanish fir to the Alijar Pass (410m/1 345ft), then descends steeply towards the coast.

Parque Natural de la Sierra de las Nieves

This small nature park (18 500ha/ 45 713 acres), a UNESCO **Biosphere Reserve**, is home to the **Spanish fir** *(pinsapo)*, as well as one of the largest **mountain goat** colonies on the Iberian Peninsula. The relief here is characterised by steep escarpments and a limestone landscape. One of the world's deepest chasms, known as **GESM** (named after the Grupo de Exploraciones Subterráneas de Málaga who attempted to explore it in 1978), is located within the confines of the park.

SANLÚCAR DE BARRAMEDA★

POPULATION: 61 382

The soil and climatic conditions around Sanlúcar has given birth to one of Andalucía's best dry sherries, *manzanilla*. The old monumental quarter of Sanlúcar is occupied by numerous sherry *bodegas*; the waterfront is lined with some superb seafood restaurants.

- **Information:** Calzada del Ejército. ☎956 36 61 10. www.aytosanlucar.org.
- ▶ **Orient Yourself:** Sanlúcar is at the mouth of the River Guadalquivir, near the southern end of Parque Nacional de Doñana, 22km/14mi southeast of Jerez de la Frontera.
- **Don't Miss:** Visiting a bodega.
- **Organising Your Time:** Allow a half to a full day, more for a beach vacation.
- **Especially for Kids:** Beach time at the Playa de Regla.
- **Also See:** JEREZ DE LA FRONTERA, El PUERTO DE SANTA MARÍA, CÁDIZ, MEDINA SIDONIA, VEJER DE LA FRONTERA.

A Bit of History

Looking seaward – Sanlúcar's position ensured its rise in the 15C as a stopping point for galleys returning to Sevilla from the Americas.

In 1519, **Magellan**'s expedition left to circumnavigate the globe, and here it returned three years later under **Juan Sebastián Elcano**.

The fall from grace of the Duke of Medina Sidonia and the transition to larger ships unable to negotiate the sandbanks, heralded the town's decline. At the end of the 19C the sherry industry developed.

Horseracing on sand – The horse race that has taken place on the beaches of Sanlúcar for the past 150 years is one of Spain's most picturesque events, in a spectacular setting, combining water, light and superb horsemanship. Its origins date to the 19C, a time when horse races were a novelty. It is the oldest official set of horse races in the country, held every August at low tide, around 6pm, on the 2nd and 4th weekends of the month from Thursday to Saturday.

Walking Tours

From Plaza del Cabildo to the Barrio Alto
1hr

This itinerary includes the main sights of interest in the Barrio Alto (Upper Town).

Plaza del Cabildo

This large square with a 19C appearance, embellished with orange and palm trees, is the focal point of Sanlúcar. To one side is the 18C former **town hall** (*cabildo*).

Plaza de San Roque

This small square in one of the liveliest areas is the setting for a morning market.

Manzanilla

This superb wine has a taste both penetrating and dry on the palate. From May onwards, the triangle between Sanlúcar de Barrameda, El Puerto de Santa María and Jerez is a swathe of leafy **Palomino** vines. The harvest is in September. This dry sherry is fortified to 15% and then transferred to American oak barrels, where the *solera* and *criadera* system applies (*see Sherry under JEREZ*). The difference between *manzanilla* and *fino* sherry is due to Sanlúcar's climate: a layer of yeast (*flor*) remains in place during ageing– a minimum of three years for *manzanilla*.

Address Book

For coin ranges, see the Legend on the cover flap.

WHERE TO STAY

Cruz del Mar – *Avenida de Sanlúcar, 1, Chipiona.* ☎956 37 11 00. *93 rooms.* A modern hotel on the seafront with views across to the Parque de Doñana. Its wide range of facilities include a pool and fitness room. The local golf course is 6km/3.5mi away.

Posada de Palacio – *Caballeros, 11 (Barrio Alto).* ☎956 36 48 40. *www.posadadepalacio.com. 34 rooms .* This family-run hotel is in an 18C mansion in the upper section of Sanlúcar. The rooms, set around an splendid patio, are beautifully decorated with antiques.

Tartaneros – *Tartaneros, 8.* ☎956 38 53 93. *22 rooms, 2 suites.* This attractive early-20C mansion is decorated with columns and balconies.

WHERE TO EAT

Casa Bigote – *Bajo de Guía, 10.* ☎956 36 26 96. www.restaurantecasa bigote.com. Closed Sun and in Nov. This venerable tavern and restaurant in the Bajo Guía river district is a gastronomic landmark. Run by the same family for 50 years, it is decorated with old photos, fishing mementoes and antiques. Pride of place on the extensive menu is given to the excellent local fish and prawns.

LOCAL FESTIVALS

Carnival *(February)*, Feria de la Manzanilla *(late May)*, horse race *(August, see A Bit of History).*

TOURS

Bodega visits – Guided visits are offered by several companies, including **Barbadillo** *(next to the castle; tours in English, Tue–Sat 11am; €3)*, a local institution since the 18C, **Pedro Romero** *(calle Trasbola 84; tours in English Tue–Sat noon and Tue–Fri 6pm; €6; ☎956 36 07 36 www.pedroromero.es/ingles/visita. asp)* and **La Cigarrera** *(plaza Madre de Dios. Mon–Sat 10am–2pm; €2.80; ☎956 38 12 85).*

Iglesia de la Trinidad

Open Mon–Sat 9.30am–1.30pm.
The Church of the Trinity is half-hidden on the side of the plaza de San Roque. It contains a magnificent 15C Mudéjar **artesonado**★★ ceiling. The 17C Baroque retable includes a fine statue of Our Lady of the Sorrows.

▸ *Continue along calle Regina.*

Convento de Regina Coeli

This early 16C convent housed an order of Poor Clares. It has a handsome Pompeii-red façade. In the two elegant portals are statues of St Clare and the Virgin and Child.

▸ *Return to plaza de San Roque and follow calle Bretones.*
Head up cuesta de Belén, passing the municipal market along the way.

Covachas★

These are five recently restored ogee stone arches decorated with Gothic tracery and winged dragons. They were probably part of the 15C palace of the Dukes of Medina Sidonia.

Palacio de Orleans y Borbón

Entrance on calle Caballeros.
Open 11am–1pm and 4–6pm. Sun and public hols 11am–1pm. €3. ☎958 66 51 08.
This magnificent Moorish-style palace was built in the 19C as a summer residence for the Duke of Montpensier, with delightful **gardens**. It is now Sanlúcar's town hall.

Parroquia de Nuestra Señora de la O

Open for services only, Mon–Sat, at 7.30pm; Sun at 9am, noon and 7.30pm.

The west façade has a majestic 14C **Mudéjar portal**★★ and the church's superb 16C **artesonado**★ ceiling is from the same period.

Alongside the church is the **Palacio de los Condes de Niebla**, (☞visit by guided tours only, Sun 10am–1.30pm. ☎956 36 01 61) the former residence of the Duchess of Medina Sidonia.

▶ *Walk along calle Luis de Eguilaz.*

At no 21 note the **Casa de la Cilla**, an attractive small 18C Baroque palace now owned by the Barbadillo *manzanilla* company. Enjoy strolling along callejón de las Comedias and calle Eguilaz, with their whitewashed façades and scent of *manzanilla*.

Castillo de Santiago
The oldest section is the 13C keep, built by Guzmán the Good. The remainder is from the 15C. Isabel the Catholic, among other notables, stayed here.

The Modern Town and Bajo de Guía

The Barrio Bajo (Lower Town) is Sanlúcar's 16C expansion and the commercial hub of town.

Iglesia de Santo Domingo
Open 10am–noon and 3.30–8pm. No visits during religious services. ☎956 36 04 91.
The former Convento de Santo Domingo, built 1548, once sheltered Dominicans returning from afar. A portal attributed to Cristóbal de Rojas leads to a cloistered atrium.

▶ *Continue along calle de Santo Domingo to plaza de San Francisco.*

The square is fronted by the imposing 17C **Iglesia de San Francisco**.

▶ *Follow calle de San Nicolás and avenida del Cabo Nobal to avenida Bajo de Guía where you will find, not one but two visitor centres devoted to the Parque Nacional de Doñana*

Local pastries

Convento de la Madre de Dios: The nuns from this handsome 17C convent are famed for their *tocino de cielo* (custard puddings), said to be the best in the province. You can buy them at the entrance on calle del Torno (open Mon–Sat 10am–1pm and 5–7pm). The convent looks onto a pleasant colonial-style square.

Parque a (☞see Parque Nacional de DOÑANA) on the opposite bank of the Guadalquivir.

Centro de Visitantes Bajo de Guía
Open Tue–Sun 10am–2pm and 6–8pm. ☎956 38 09 22.

Centro de Visitantes Fábrica de Hielo
Open in summer 9am–8pm; otherwise, 9am–7pm. ☎956 38 65 77 or 956 38 16 35. www.visitasdonana.com.
Buy your tickets here for a half-day trip on the *Real Fernando* boat. This includes full commentary on the wildlife and habitat of the park and two short guided walks. Visit for full details. Another option is a guided tour by Landrover which can also be booked here.

Excursions

Parque Nacional de Doñana★★★ – ☞see Parque Nacional de DOÑANA

Chipiona   Kids
9km/5.5mi southwest along the A 480.
The Playa de la Regla★ and other beaches at this resort are well worth the trip.
In the town the 16C **Parroquia de Nuestra Señora de la O** has an Isabelline north façade, and the **Santuario de Nuestra Señora de la Regla** (open summer 8am–1.30pm, 5–7.30pm. ☎956 37 01 89) boasts some fine *azulejos*.

SEVILLA

POPULATION: 701,927

A city of great art and prodigious history, Andalucía's capital has managed to maintain its magnificent traditions without turning its back on modernity. It's said that Sevilla is a feminine city, secure in its charms and happy to display them to visitors. *Sevillanos* are passionate about where they live and take every opportunity to extol their city's virtues. Sevilla is more than a city: it is a way of embracing life to the full that is exuberant, festive and, above all, passionate. It is Velázquez, Murillo, Don Juan and Carmen; the scent of orange blossom; a lively gatherings of friends; the world famous celebrations of Semana Santa (Holy Week) the Feria de Abril (April Fair); the dancing of *sevillanas* in the street and, like it or not, the blood and drama of the *corrida* (bullfight). Sevilla is bright, colourful, and, in summer, extremely hot!

- **Information:** Avenida de la Constitución, 21B, ☎954 78 75 78; Plaza del Triunfo, ☎954 21 00 05 or 902 07 63 36; Plaza de San Francisco, ☎954 59 01 88; Calle Arjona, 28; Naves del Barranco, ☎902 194 897; Santa Justa train station, ☎954 53 76 26; Aeropuerto de San Pablo, ☎954 44 91 28. www.turismosevilla.org. www.andalucia.org.
- **Orient Yourself:** Sevilla lies in west-central Andalucía, an inland port on the Guadalquivir. The A 4-E5 motorway connects with Cádiz to the south and Córdoba to the northeast. The E-1 runs towards Huelva to the west, and Portugal.
- **Parking:** Leave your car and get around by bus, taxi, or on foot.
- **Don't Miss:** The Giralda, the Real Alcázar, Parque María Luisa, a stroll in the Santa Cruz quarter and, if you can make it, Holy Week.
- **Organising Your Time:** Two days are the minimum to see the Giralda, Cathedral, the Santa Cruz quarter, and your choice of shops, markets and streets. It's best to allow at least three days here.
- **Especially for Kids:** Isla Mágica theme park.
- **Also See:** CARMONA, ÉCIJA, UTRERA, MARCHENA, HUELVA.

A Bit of History

"Hércules me construyó, Julio César me rodeó de murallas y altas torres y el Rey Santo me conquistó"

(Hercules built me; Caesar surrounded me with walls and towers; and the King Saint conquered me), said the inscription on the former Jerez Gate (Puerta de Jérez), destroyed in the 19C. From its earliest days Sevilla's fate has been determined by its role as a river port. Although its origins are less than clear, the city was probably founded by Iberians. It became a Greek, Phoenician and Carthaginian colony, which was subsequently overrun by the Romans in 205 BC following a long siege.

Romans and Visigoths – Roman occupation was at first marked by factional disputes. Julius Caesar seized the city in 42 BC, fortified it, and transformed

No me ha dejado

The emblem on the city's coat of arms was given to Sevilla by Alfonso X (the Wise, 1221–84) to commemorate the loyalty and support he had received from the city. The figure of eight in the emblem, representing a skein of wool (madeja), creates the motto "No madeja do" or "No me ha dejado", which translates as "It has not forsaken me".

Sevilla into one of the main cities in Baetica.

In the 5C the Vandals invaded the region; they were expelled by the Visigoths who made the city their capital until the court was transferred to Toledo.

The 6C saw the rise of the bishop St Isidore, author of *Etymologies*, who was to have great influence on medieval European culture.

The Moors – The Moorish conquest in 712 heralded a long period of Arab domination. During the Caliphate, the city came under the control of Córdoba; upon its fall in 1031 it became a taifa kingdom. During the reign of Al Mutamid, Sevilla experienced great cultural development. However, difficult relations with the Christian king, Alfonso VI, obliged Al Mutamid to seek aid from the Almoravids who subsequently seized the kingdom in 1091. In the 12C, the Almohads took control from the Almoravids and began a period of urban transformation that included construction of both the Giralda and the *mezquita* (mosque), on the site now occupied by the cathedral.

The Reconquest – On 23 November 1248, Fernando III (the Saint) reconquered Sevilla and established his court in the city. He was followed by Alfonso X the Wise and then Pedro I, who restored the Alcázar, and took up residence there.

16C: The Golden Age – Following the discovery of America in 1492, Sevilla held a monopoly on trade with the New World and became the departure and arrival point for every expedition. Among those who sailed from Sevilla were Amerigo Vespucci, and Magellan, who set out in 1519 and whose expedition was the first to circumnavigate the globe. 1503 saw the founding of the **Casa de Contratación**, a body established to encourage, inspect and control trade with the Americas.

Sevilla began to amass great wealth, foreign merchants and bankers heeded the call of American gold. Palaces were built, new industries were created and the smell of money and frenetic activity attracted hustlers, villains and people from every sector. The population of Sevilla almost doubled during the 16C, rising to some 200 000 inhabitants.

Decline – Following the plague of 1649, the city entered a period of decline, exacerbated by the transfer of the Casa de Contratación to Cádiz in 1717.

20C – During the 20C Sevilla hosted two major international exhibitions: the 1929 Ibero-American Exhibition and Expo'92, both of which had a significant effect on the layout of the city.

Expo'92 saw the realisation of a number of large projects, in particular the Isla de la Cartuja, where the fair was held. The Isla Mágica theme park and the Centro Andaluz de Arte Contemporáneo are now on the site.

Sights

Sevilla's two most important monuments, the cathedral and the Alcázar, as well as its famous Santa Cruz quarter, are near each other in the centre of the city.

The Giralda and Cathedral★★★

🕐 *Open Mon–Sat, 11am–5pm; Sun, 2.30–6pm. Restricted opening times on Tue of Holy Week, Maundy Thu and Good*

©Turespaña

Giralda at night

Cathedral

Fri. ⊗Closed 1 and 6 Jan, 30 May, Corpus Christi, 15 Aug, and 8 and 25 Dec. ⊜€7.50, no charge Sun. ☎954 21 49 71.

Giralda★★★

Elegant and lofty, the Giralda is the symbol of Sevilla. Built at the end of the 12C, this brick minaret (96m/315ft), part of the mosque (*mezquita*) was once surmounted by three gilded spheres, which sadly fell off in a 14C earthquake. The belfry, three superimposed stages and balconies are 16C additions by Córdoban architect Hernán Ruiz. These were crowned with an enormous weather vane, the statue of Faith, known as the Giraldillo (from *girar*: to turn), from which the tower's name evolved.

The tower is a masterpiece of Almohad art, delicate yet restrained. This purist dynasty shunned ostentation, yet managed to create a harmonious style of beauty and simplicity. The decoration on each side is organised into three vertical registers with *sebka* panels. *Access to the Giralda is from inside the cathedral (see below).*

Cathedral★★★

"Let us build a cathedral that will make them think us mad", the chapter is said to have declared in 1401 when it ordered the demolition of the mosque. The cathedral is impressive in its dimensions, and is considered to be the third largest in floor space in the Christian world after St Peter's in the Vatican and St Paul's in London. One of the last Gothic cathedrals built in Spain, it shows obvious Renaissance influence.

View the massive **exterior** to appreciate its size. The Cristóbal (or Príncipe), Asunción and Concepción (in the Patio de los Naranjos) doorways are modern (19C and 20C), yet respect the style as a whole. The Puerta del Nacimiento and Puerta del Bautismo, which open out onto the Avenida de la Constitución, include beautiful sculptures by Mercadante de Bretaña (1460). At the east end, admire the rounded Chapel Royal (*Capilla Real* – 1575), decorated with coats of arms and, on either side, the Gothic Puerta de Palos and Puerta de las Campanillas with Renaissance-style tympana in which Miguel Perrin has made full play of perspective.

Interior

This universe of stone, stained glass and grilles is striking in its size and richness, while its extraordinary height is the result of tall, slender pillars. The ground plan consists of five aisles – the central nave being wider and higher – with chapels in the side aisles. The column shafts support simple Flamboyant Gothic pointed vaults, except in the central section. The vault of the transept, also Flamboyant, reaches to 56m/184ft. A **mirror (1)** on the floor enables a striking view.

Address Book

♿For coin ranges, see the Legend on the cover flap.

GETTING THERE AND GETTING AROUND

Airport – San Pablo international airport, 8km/5mi along the A 4 towards Madrid (☎954 44 90 00, www.aena.es). A direct bus service operates to the city centre and Santa Justa rail station.

Trains – Estación de Santa Justa, Avenida Kansas City, ☎954 41 41 11. Trains run to destinations in the province and throughout Spain, The AVE high-speed train connects Sevilla with Madrid in just 2hr 25min; Córdoba in 45min. Information and reservations, ☎902 24 02 02.

Inter-city buses run from **Estación Plaza de Armas** (☎954 90 77 37/80 40) run to Sevilla province, Huelva, elsewhere in Spain, and Europe.

The **Estación del Prado de San Sebastián** (☎954 41 71 11) services other localities in Andalucía.

City buses (☎954 22 81 77/53 60). Buy a strip of tickets to save money.

Taxis – ☎954 58 00 00 and 954 62 22 22.

WHERE TO STAY

If you're planning to stay for Holy Week or the Feria, book months ahead and beware the room rate, as prices can double (or even more) at these times.

⊜**Hotel Sevilla** – Daóiz, 5. ☎954 38 41 61. 35 rooms. Excellent location in a pleasant small square near the Palacio de la Condesa de Lebrija, basic comfort at budget prices. The faded decor adds to the overall charm.

⊜⊜**Hostal Sierpes** – Corral del Rey, 22 (Santa Cruz). ☎954 22 49 48. www.hsierpes.com. 35 rooms. This 17C mansion on an alley in the Santa Cruz barrio has rooms around a patio and is good value. Its tavern, Melquiades, serves inexpensive tapas.

⊜⊜**Hotel Londres** – San Pedro Mártir, 1. ☎954 50 27 45. www.londreshotel.com. 25 rooms. This charming Sevillian house has basic, clean rooms. Those with balcony are generally more pleasant and, despite the central location, are relatively quiet.

⊜⊜**Hotel Doña Blanca** – Plaza P Jerónimo de Córdoba, 14. ☎954 50 13 73. www.donablanca.com. 19 rooms. A newly built mansion with distinctive red façade, very reasonably priced given the decor and comfort. In the bustling area by the church of Santa Catalina.

⊜⊜**Hostería del Laurel** – plaza de los Venerables, 5 (Santa Cruz). ☎954 22 02 95. www.hosteriadellaurel.com. 20 rooms. Unbeatable location on one of Sevilla's most charming plazas. Comfortable rooms, Provençal furniture, and restaurant with regional dishes.

⊜⊜**Hostal Van Gogh** – Miguel de Mañara, 4. ☎95 456 37 27. www.grupopiramide.com. 14 rooms. Entirely Sevillian, despite the name: bull's head over the door, bright colours and geraniums on the balconies. Modest rooms, near the barrio of Santa Cruz.

⊜⊜⊜**Hotel Simón** – García Vinuesa, 19. ☎954 22 66 60. www.hotelsimonsevilla.com. 29 rooms. This historic white mansion by the cathedral, arranged around a cool patio, seems to be from another era, with antiques and large mirrors. Rooms are comfortable, the best are decorated with colourful azulejos

⊜⊜⊜**Hotel Amadeus Sevilla/ La Música** – Farnesio, 6. ☎954 501 443. www.hotelamadeussevilla.com. 20 rooms. A family of musicians transformed this magnificent 18C house in Santa Cruz. Musical instruments are available for guests' use including a grand piano on the patio!

⊜⊜⊜**Hotel Las Casas de la Judería** – Callejón Dos Hermanas, 7. ☎954 41 51 50. www.casasypalacios.com. 119 rooms. Modern luxury meets old-world charming, in the former mansion of the Duke of Béjar, in the old Jewish quarter. Swimming pool.

⊜⊜⊜**Hotel Doña María** – Don Remondo, 19. ☎954 22 49 90. www.hdmaria.com. 64 rooms. Tastefully renovated and arguably the finest location in town right below the Giralda with views to it from its delightful roof terrace bar (open to non-residents), with small swimming pool (residents only). Rather formal and bland bedrooms.

H. Champollion / MICHELIN

El Rinconcillo

☺☺☺☺**Casa Imperial** – *Imperial, 29.* ☎*954 50 03 00 . www.casaimperial. com. 18 rooms, 8 suites.* This luxuriously decorated 16C palace with an attractive main patio sits in a quiet street behind the Casa de Pilatos.

☺☺☺☺**Hotel Alfonso XIII** – *San Fernando, 2.* ☎*954 91 70 00. www. alfonsoxiii.com. 147 rooms.* Built in 1928 in neo-Mudéjar style, opposite the Alcázar gardens, Sevilla's most luxurious and famous hotel is where royalty and the stars stay in style when in Seville.

WHERE TO EAT

☺☺**Bodegón La Universal** – *Betis, 2 (Triana).* ☎*954 33 47 46. Closed Wed.* Lovely view of Seville and bullring from riverside terrace. Try a regional speciality before or after a stroll in Triana. Nicely decorated.

☺☺ **Corral del Agua** – *Callejón del Agua, 6.* ☎*954 22 07 14. Closed Sun.* Pleasant place serving Andalusian cuisine, on a quiet alley. The terrace, with its abundant vegetation, is delightful in the heat of summer. .

☺☺☺**La Albahaca** – *Plaza de Santa Cruz, 12.* ☎*954 22 07 14 . Closed Sun.* Choose from three dining rooms in this elegant 1920s mansion with a lovely terrace. Local, Basque and French cuisine available.

☺☺☺☺ **Taberna del Alabardero** – *Zaragoza, 20.* ☎*954 50 27 21. Closed Aug.* This 19C mansion houses one of the best restaurants in town, a seven-room hotel (☺☺☺☺), tea room and a hotel school. Worth a visit just to look.

TAPAS

SANTA CRUZ DISTRICT

Calle Mateos Gago – This street by the Giralda is full of bars and restaurants.

Bodega de Santa Cruz attracts a young crowd who spill onto the street. The **La Giralda** *cervecería* (*no 1*) is a very traditional bar with tasty *raciones*. **Bodega Belmonte** (*no 24*) is known for its *lomo a la pimienta* (spicy pork loin). **Las Teresas** – *Santa Teresa, 2.* ☎*954 21 30 69.* A small, typically Sevillian tavern – one of the oldest in the Barrio Santa Cruz – with attractive early-19C decor, set on a picturesque alley. **Casa Plácido,** opposite, is also recommended.

CENTRO

El Patio de San Eloy – *San Eloy, 9.* ☎*954 22 11 48.* This small wine bar has a counter with all kinds of sandwiches (*bocadillos*) and *azulejo*-clad benches at the back. Packed at lunchtime.

SANTA CATALINA

El Rinconcillo – *Gerona, 40.* ☎*95 422 31 83. www.elrinconcillo1670.com. Closed mid-Jul–first week Aug.* Charming old-world taverna dating to 1670, with 18C and 19C *azulejo* panelling and fine wooden ceiling. Menu del día from around €12.

ARENAL AND PLAZA NUEVA

Bodega San José – *Adriano, 10.* ☎*954 22 41 05.* A no-nonsense *bodega* with dirt floor and fumes from the immense wine casks; meeting point for bullfight fans.

Casablanca – *Zaragoza, 50.* ☎*954 224 698. Closed Sun.* This famous small bar is always full of locals.

Bodeguita Romero – *Harinas, 10.* ☎*954 22 95 56. Closed Mon and in Aug.* Next to the Maestranza bullring. Famous for its exquisite *pringá* (roast or stewed meat eaten with bread). Regional decor.

TRIANA

Casa Cuesta – *Castilla, 3.* ☎*954 33 33 35. www.casacuesta.net. Closed Tue.* Founded in 1880, this tapas bar has a rustic dining room and, in good weather, tables in the small square nearby.

Kiosco de Las Flores – *Betis.* ☎*954 27 45 76. www.kioscodelasflores.com. Closed Sun lunch and Mon.* This family-run riverside tapas bar, founded in 1930, specialises in fried fish and seafood.

Sol y Sombra – *Castilla, 149–151.* ☎*954 33 39 35. www.tabernasolysombra.com. Closed all day Mon and Tue lunchtime.*

This bustling bar, opened in 1961, with walls covered in bullfighting posters, is rich with the odours of ham and cheese.

TAKING A BREAK

Horno San Buenaventura – *Avenida de la Constitución, 16.* ☎*954 45 87 11.* Near the cathedral with a spacious and popular ground floor tea-room. Its cakes, based in its own *horno* (oven) are justifiably famous.

La Campana – *Sierpes, 1.* ☎*954 22 35 70. www.confiterialacampana.com.* One of Sevilla's classic coffee houses, dating from 1865. Everyone from local seniors to tourists enjoys pastries served in a pleasant Rococo atmosphere.

GOING OUT

The most popular areas for a drink are the city centre and the attractive Santa Cruz and Arenal districts, all of which provide a magnificent historical backdrop. Working-class Triana, in particular calle Betis, across the Guadalquivir, is also lively, with bars and clubs with a local flavour. Sevilla's younger crowd prefers the Nervión district where many nightclubs stay open until dawn. The alternative crowd heads for Alameda de Hércules, a borderline neighbourhood at night, where interesting haunts include **Fun Club**, a popular concert venue, and the La **Habanilla** café/bar with its large and unusual collection of old coffee pots.

In summer, the action moves down to the river, where several kilometres of bars and outdoor terraces are popular with people of all ages and tastes.

Antigüedades – *Calle Argote de Molina, 40.* One of Sevilla's most colourful spots, this club changes decor according to what's on. Particularly popular with thirty-somethings. Very lively around midnight.

Café de la Prensa – *Betis, 8.* This riverside café, with modern decor and outside tables with priceless views of the Guadalquivir and old city attracts the young and intellectuals. Perfect for drinks at any time.

La Sonanta – *Calle San Jacinto, 31 .* This small bar across the river in Triana serves tapas by day and fills up with flamenco lovers by night. Live shows Thursdays and Fridays, flamenco festival twice yearly.

El Tamboril – *Plaza de Santa Cruz, 12. Open 10pm–5am.* Tucked in a corner of the Santa Cruz district, this *taberna* hums into the early hours with a faithful clientele who might burst into an impromptu *sevillana* or *rumba* or flamenco performance at any minute. The *Salve Rociera,* a prayer to Our Lady of El Rocío, is traditionally sung at midnight.

La Carbonería – *Levíes, 18.* A Sevilla institution, home to the alternative crowd. In various parts of this former coal warehouse in the Jewish Quarter (Judería), you can listen to an intimate recital around a fireplace, watch live flamenco, or view an art or photography exhibition. A must!

Paseo de las Delicias – Four venues on this avenue (Chile, Líbano, Alfonso and Bilindo) shine for summer bar-hopping and outdoor dancing, all popular with the 25–40 crowd. In winter they are ideal for a quiet drink in María Luisa park, surrounded by the buildings of the 1929 Ibero-American Exhibition.

Sopa de Ganso – *Calle Pérez Galdós, 8.* The playlist and rustic decor attract a fashionable crowd at night, including many tourists. By day its pastries are the big draw.

Voulez-Bar/Wall Street – *Calle Ramón y Cajal, 1-A (Viapol building). Open Wed–Sat, midnight–6am.* Two fashionable adjoining bars in the city's favourite clubbing district, Nervión, where you can catch salsa and flamenco sessions and occasionally leading bands. At Wall Street, fluctuating drink prices are shown on screens all along the bar. Huge numbers of 25–35 year olds move back and forth throughout the night.

Terrace of La Campana

ENTERTAINMENT

Sevilla is a lively and festive capital offering varied cultural activities all year.

El Patio Sevillano – *Paseo Cristóbal Colón, 11-A.* ☎*954 21 41 20. www. elpatiosevillano.com. Shows: 7.30–9pm and 10–11.30pm by reservation; drink and show: €35; dinner/tapas and show: €68/57.* An institution since 1952, offering a flamenco retrospective. Near the bullring.

Tablao El Arenal – *Rodó, 7 (El Arenal).* ☎*954 21 64 92. www.tablaoelarenal. com. Open from 7.30pm. Shows 8.30pm and 10.30pm by reservation: one drink and show €36; dinner/tapas and show €55/70.* One of Sevilla's most important *tablaos*, said by those in the know to feature flamenco at its purest.

Teatro Central – *Avenida José de Gálvez.* ☎*955 037 200. www.teatro central.com.* This modern theatre, built on Isla de la Cartuja for Expo'92, offers theatre, dance and music including flamenco, jazz, folk, rock and pop,

Teatro de la Maestranza – *Paseo de Cristóbal Colón, 22.* ☎*954 22 33 44 73. www.teatromaestranza.com.* Full season of theatre, dance opera and flamenco with performances by international stars.

Teatro Lope de Vega – *Avenida María Luisa.* ☎*954 59 08 53. www.teatro lopedevega.org.* This theatre concentrates on drama and flamenco.

SPA

Baños Árabes-Tetería Aire de Sevilla – *Aire, 15 (Santa Cruz).* ☎*955 01 00 24. www.airedesevilla.com. Arab bath: 10am–2am in 2hr sessions. Tea house: Thu–Sun 4pm until late.* This late 16C palace houses magnificent baths in the best of Andalusian-Moorish style, as well as an upstairs patio-tea room. Excellent for a break during your tour of the Santa Cruz neighbourhood. Reserve for steam baths.

SHOPPING

Traditional shops are to be found in the historic centre, particularly along calle Tetuán, in the plaza del Duque de la Victoria, calle de San Eloy and other pedestrian areas. Historic **calle Sierpes** has traditional and more unusual shops and boutiques, including several **Foronda** boutiques selling the hand-embroidered shawls created by this famous local artisan. The **Ochoa** pastry shop is perfect for breakfast or an afternoon snack, and has take-away pastries. The streets at right angles to Sierpes and those around the El Salvador church are popular with jewellery hunters, who are spoilt for choice in the plaza del Pan and the calle Alcaicería.

In the **Los Remedios** district across the river, calle Asunción has a number of leading brand-name stores.

In the modern Nervión district are two large shopping centres (**El Corte Inglés** and Nervión Plaza), and clothing chains.

Another leading shopping centre is the former **Plaza de Armas railway station**, an early 20C regionalist building that even includes its own brewery, La Fábrica de Cerveza.

Markets – The "jueves" (Thursday) market in calle Feria is popular for antiques and second-hand goods. Sunday morning markets are held in plaza de la Alfalfa (a much-frequented livestock market); plaza del Cabildo (stamps and old coins); and along Alameda de Hércules (second-hand goods early in the day).

SIGHTSEEING

Publications – **Welcome Olé** and **The Tourist** are free from hotels and tourist sites. Sevilla's culture department publishes a monthly cultural brochure. The monthly **El Giraldillo** (in Spanish only) covers Andalucía's fairs, exhibitions and diversions. *www.elgiraldillo.es.*

Horse-drawn carriages for visiting major sites can be hired (haggle on the price) in plaza de la Virgen de los Reyes, plaza de España, avenida de la Constitución and at the Torre del Oro.

Boat trips on the Guadalquivir run every 30min from the Torre del Oro (*1hr during by day, 1hr 30min at night*). A trip to the mouth of the river at Sanlúcar de Barrameda passes the Parque Nacional de Doñana. ☎*954 56 16 92.*

City Sightseeing Bus – The open-top hop-on, hop-off *bus turístico* itinerary begins at the Torre del Oro, thogh you can board at any stop (*www.city-sightseeing.com*).

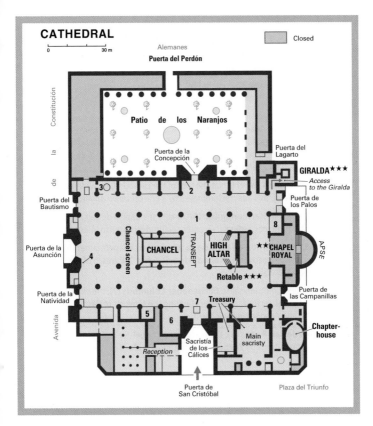

CATHEDRAL

0 — 30 m

Closed

Alemanes

Puerta del Perdón

Constitución

Patio   de   los   Naranjos

Puerta de la Concepción

Puerta del Bautismo

Puerta del Lagarto

GIRALDA★★★

Access to the Giralda

Puerta de los Palos

3○

2

la

1

8

Chancel screen

de

CHANCEL

TRANSEPT

HIGH ALTAR

★★CHAPEL ROYAL

APSE

Puerta de la Asunción

4

Retable ★★★

Puerta de las Campanillas

Puerta de la Natividad

7   Treasury

5   6

Chapter-house

Avenida

Main sacristy

Sacristía de los Cálices

Reception

Puerta de San Cristóbal

Plaza del Triunfo

Climbing the Giralda

It is possible to climb up to the tower's belfry (70m/230ft) on a ramp with 34 sections. The ascent is not particularly difficult; take your time to admire views of the Patio de los Naranjos, the gargoyles and pinnacles of the cathedral and the Alcázar from the balconies on the way up. Your efforts will be well rewarded at the top with a magnificent **panorama**★★★ over the city.

High Altar

The high altar (*capilla mayor*), rich in surprising decoration, is enclosed by a splendid 16C Plateresque **grille**★★, by Fray Francisco de Salamanca. The immense Flemish **altarpiece**★★★ (1482–1525), the largest in Spain, is profusely and delicately carved with colourful scenes from the lives of Christ and the Virgin Mary (except the predella, decorated with saints). The altarpiece has seven vertical panels, the widest is in the centre. Unfortunately, it is impossible

The "Seises" – A Fine Tradition

The Seises are a group of 12 brightly dressed choir boys who perpetuate a tradition dating back to the 16C, by which they sing and dance in front of the cathedral's high altar during the eight days following Corpus Christi and the Feast of the Immaculate Conception.

Initially the group consisted of 6 (*seis*) boys, hence the name. They also accompany the **Corpus Christi** procession when this stops in the plaza del Ayuntamiento and the plaza del Salvador.

Chapels and Altars

Once you have seen the cathedral's major works, take time to admire its chapels, which themselves contain numerous works of art.

◆ **Altar de Nuestra Señora de Belén (2)** (Our Lady of Bethlehem): north side, to the left of the Puerta de la Concepción. Fine portrayal of the Virgin Mary by Alonso Cano.

◆ **Capilla de San Antonio (3):** this chapel contains several interesting canvases dominated by Murillo's Vision of St Anthony of Padua, on the right-hand wall. Also worthy of note are *The Baptism of Christ*, also by Murillo, and two paintings of St Peter by Valdés Leal.

◆ **Altar del Santo Ángel (4)** (at the foot of the cathedral, to the left of the Puerta Mayor): this altar is dominated by a fine *Guardian Angel* by Murillo.

◆ **Capilla de San Hermenegildo (5)** (next to the Capilla de San José): the 15C alabaster tomb of Cardinal Cervantes sculpted by Lorenzo Mercadante.

◆ **Capilla de la Virgen de la Antigua (6)** (the next chapel): larger than the others and covered with an elevated vault. A fine 14C fresco of the Virgin adorns the altar.

◆ 19C funerary monument to **Christopher Columbus (7)**: the explorer's coffin is borne by four pallbearers bearing the symbols of Castilla, León, Navarra and Aragón on their chest.

◆ **Capilla de San Pedro (8):** the walls of this chapel are hung with a superb series of paintings by **Zurbarán** illustrating the life of St Peter.

to get close enough to admire one of the world's most impressive altarpieces.

Chancel

In the main nave, partly hidden by a 16C grille is the *coro*, with fine 15C–16C choir stalls. The majestic organs are from the 18C. The **trascoro** (chancel screen) of multi-coloured marble, jasper and bronze, is 17C.

Treasury

The treasury in the 16C **Sacristía de los Cálices** (Chalice Sacristy) is surmounted by a fine vault. Interesting paintings exhibited are: *Santa Justa* and *Santa Rufina* by Goya, a Zurbarán, a triptych by Alejo Fernández and several canvases by Valdés Leal. The anteroom of the sacristy houses the **Tenebrario**, a 7.80m/25ft, fifteen-branch Plateresque candelabrum, used during Holy Week processions.

The main **sacristy** (*sacristía mayor*), a fine 16C room with a Greek cross plan, contains the impressive Renaissance silver **monstrance** (*custodia*) by Juan de Arfe, measuring 3.90m/13ft and

weighing 475kg/1 045lb; a *Santa Teresa* by Zurbarán and *The Martyrdom of San Lorenzo* by Lucas Jordán can be seen on the rear wall.

Chapter house

The fine 16C Renaissance chapter house (*sala capitular*) has an elliptical dome and a characteristic *Immaculate Conception* by Murillo.

Capilla Real★★

⊶ *Closed to visitors.*

The Plateresque Chapel Royal, built during the reign of Charles V over an earlier chapel, is of monumental size.

Square in shape, it is covered by an elegant, richly ornamented coffered dome with carved busts and contains a small apse, itself covered by a scallop shell decorated with figures.

A wooden carving of the **Virgen de los Reyes**, patron saint of Sevilla, decorates the altar.

Behind it, in a silver urn of great value, are the remains of Fernando III the Saint. On either side are the tombs of Alfonso X and of his mother, Beatrice of Swabia.

The Capilla Real is enclosed by a majestic grille dating from 1771.

Patio de los Naranjos
This exceptional rectangular patio is planted with orange trees (*naranjos*) and was used for ritual ablutions in the former mosque.

Puerta del Perdón
The Almohad arch and the door leaves survive from the original mosque on this majestic portal. The impressive sculptures and the relief, representing the Expulsion of the Money Changers from the Temple, are from the 16C.

Palacio Arzobispal
The residence of the Archbishop of Sevilla is in the attractive plaza de la Virgen de los Reyes, with its monumental lantern (and numerous horse-drawn carriages). The edifice has an elegant, late-Baroque façade from the beginning of the 18C.

Plaza de Santa Marta
Take the narrow callejón de Santa Marta, opposite the Palacio Arzobispal.
The alleyway offers the only access to this delightful small square of white-washed façades, simple wrought-iron grilles and a small stone cross shaded by orange trees. The charming, hushed atmosphere is typical of so many of the city's squares.

Archivo General de Indias
Open Mon–Fri 8am–3pm. ☎954 50 05 28. www.mcu.es/archivos/MC/AGI/index.html.
The historical archives relating to the Spanish conquest of the Americas are housed in the former Exchange (*lonja*), built at the end of the 16C to plans by Juan de Herrera, architect of El Escorial. The archives were established here by Carlos III in 1785. This sober, Renaissance-style building has two floors with architrave bays. Note the sumptuous 18C pink and black marble staircase. Only the upper floor, with large rooms topped with elegant vaults, can be visited. It houses priceless documents on the conquest and colonisation of the Americas, as well as the signatures of Columbus, Magellan, Hernán Cortés, Juan Sebastián Elcano and others.

Plaza del Triunfo
Some of Sevilla's most impressive buildings surround this square. In the centre stands a "triumph" (*triunfo*) to the Immaculate Conception. Along the sides are the Archivo General de Indias; the cathedral (south side); the Alcázar; and the former Hospital del Rey, now the Casa de la Provincia.

Real Alcázar★★★

Entrance through the Puerta del León.
Open Apr–Sept Tue–Sun 9.30am–7pm (Sun and pub hols, to 5pm). Oct–Mar Tue–Sat 9.30am–5pm (Sun and public hols, to 1.30pm). Last admission 1hr before closing. Closed 1 and 6 Jan, Good Fri, 25 Dec and for official ceremonies. €7, Cuarto Alto: €4. ☎954 50 23 24. www.patronato-alcazarsevilla.es.

This magnificent palace is the result of several phases of construction from the 10C onwards, in a variety of architectural styles. All that remains of the 12C Alcázar of the Almohads are the Patio del Yeso and the fortified arches separating the Patio de la Montería from the Patio del León. In the 13C Alfonso X (the Wise) built the Gothic-style apartments known as the Salones de Carlos V. The nucleus of the palace was built by Pedro I (the Cruel) in 1362. This Mudéjar masterpiece was built by masons from Granada, as can be seen in the decoration, highly influenced by the Alhambra (*see

---

The Cuarto Real Alto

An optional 30min guided tour (booking advisable ☎954 56 00 40) enables visitors to view the King and Queen of Spain's official residence in Sevilla. The various rooms contain an impressive display of 19C furniture and clocks, 18C tapestries and French lamps. Of particular note are the **Capilla de los Reyes Católicos** (Chapel of the Catholic Monarchs) – an exquisite oratory with a ceramic font, by Nicola Pisano – and the Mudéjar **Sala de Audiencias**.

SEVILLA

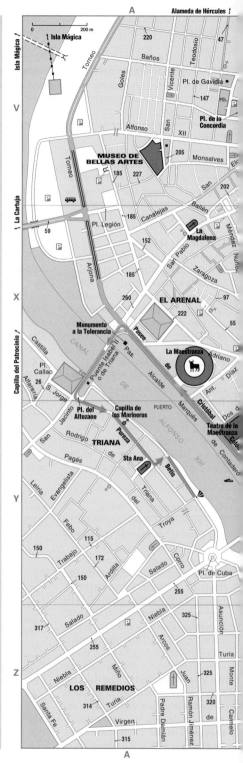

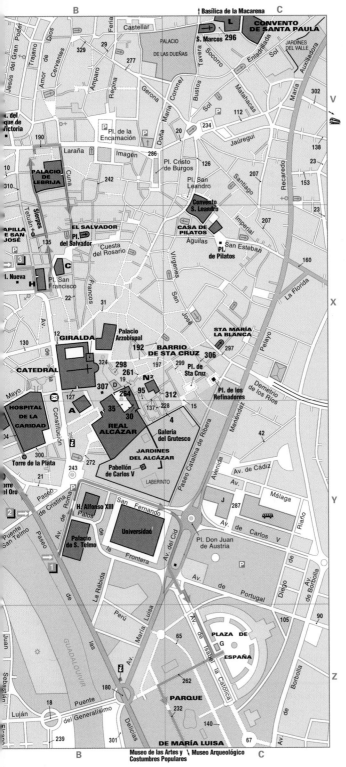

† Basílica de la Macarena

SEVILLA

GRANADA), which dates from the same period. Modifications were made by Juan II, the Catholic Monarchs, Charles V and Felipe II.

Cuarto del Almirante

To the right of the Patio de la Montería. Isabel the Catholic founded the Casa de Contratación in the Admiral's Apartments in 1503. The Sala de Audiencias (Audience Hall) has an altarpiece, the **Virgin of the Navigators**★ (1531–36), by Alejo Fernández.

Sala de la Justicia and Patio del Yeso

To the left of the Patio de la Montería. The Sala de la Justicia (Justice Chamber) was built in the 14C over the remains

of the Almohad palace. Note the finely sculpted plasterwork *(yesería)* and the magnificent cupola.

Palacio de Pedro el Cruel★★★

The façade of Pedro the Cruel's Palace is reminiscent of the Patio del Cuarto Dorado in Granada's Alhambra, with its *sebka* decoration, fragile multifoiled arches and a large epigraphic frieze beneath its carved wood overhang.

A small hallway leads left from the entry to the **Patio de las Doncellas**, around which are rooms for official functions. Note the exquisite *yesería* decoration over a gallery of foliated arches above paired columns; and magnificent 14C *azulejo* panels. The Italian upper storey was added under Charles V.

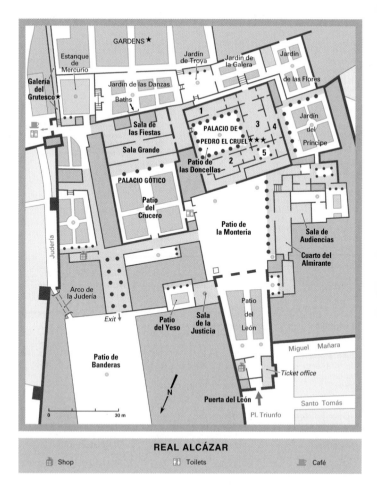

REAL ALCÁZAR

🏛 Shop   🚻 Toilets   ☕ Café

A number of Mudéjar rooms open onto this patio: **the Salón del techo del Carlos V (1)** (Carlos V's Room), the palace's former chapel, with splendid Renaissance ceiling with polygon caissons; the **Dormitorio de los Reyes Moros (2)** (Bedroom of the Moorish Kings), two rooms with blue-toned stucco and magnificent artesonado ceilings; and the **Salón de Embajadores (3)** (Ambassadors' Hall), the most sumptuous room in the Alcázar, with remarkable 15C half-orange cedarwood **cupola**★★★ with stucco decoration and exceptional azulejo panelling.

The pendentives have decorative Moorish motifs (*mocárabes*). This room connects with the **Salón del techo de Felipe II (4)**, with its magnificent Renaissance coffered cedarwood ceiling.

The Salón de Embajadores leads to the smaller **Patio de las Muñecas (5)**, in the family area. Foiled arches with *alfiz* surround are clearly Granadan. The upper floors are from a 19C restoration. This patio opens to the Cuarto del Príncipe (Prince's Room).

▷ *From the Patio de la Montería follow Corredor de Carlos V, a low-vaulted gallery.*

Palacio Gótico (Salones de Carlos V)

The Baroque doorway to the Gothic Palace is to the rear of the **Patio del Crucero**. Built by Alfonso X, it was restored in the 18C after the Lisbon earthquake. In the Sala Grande is part of a collection of 17C **tapestries**★★ from the Real Fábrica de Tapices in Madrid relating the Conquest of Tunis in 1535. The 13C **Sala de las Fiestas**, or **Sala de las Bóvedas**, the oldest section, retains its original structure and groin vaults (*bóvedas*). It was here that Carlos V married Isabel of Portugal. The walls, with 16C *azulejo* panelling, are hung with the remainder of the tapestry collection. Large windows look onto enchanting gardens.

Gardens★

The extensive gardens are a Paradise of sensations. Like the palace, they were created over different periods; Moor-

Patio de las Doncellas, Real Alcázar

©Thomas Snaaijer/Dreamstime.com

ish, Renaissance and Baroque styles are all represented. Their terraces and ornamental basins occupy 80% of the Alcázar's total area.

Leave Carlos V's Rooms and pass the Mercurio Pool to reach the 17C **Galería del Grutesco**★, which masks the front of an old wall and affords the best views.

Lower down is the Jardín de las Danzas (Dancing Garden). From here, head to the baths (*baños*) of Doña María de Padilla, a large vaulted pool.

Beyond the 15C **Pabellón de Carlos V** (pavilion) is the labyrinth, with clipped hedges. A modern, English-style garden is to the right. A quiet wander with just the gentle bubbling of water in the background is unforgettable.

The Baroque *apeadero* (to alight from horses) leads to the Patio de Banderas.

Patio de Banderas

The Flag Court was the parade ground (*patio de armas*) of the original Alcázar. This enclosed rectangle, with characteristic orange trees and a single fountain, is bordered by elegant façades, notably the silhouette of the Giralda.

Barrio de Santa Cruz★★★

These delightful twisting streets, white-washed houses, flower-filled patios and shady squares are the quintessential *barrio* of Sevilla. In the Middle Ages it was the Jewish quarter (*Judería*). It had

The Barber of Seville

The city was to provide the inspiration for this comic opera, created in 1816 by the Italian composer Gioacchino Rossini (1792–1868). Written in two acts, this masterpiece tells of the attempts of Bartolo, an elderly doctor, to marry his pretty ward, Rosina. His plans are foiled by another admirer, Count Almaviva, through the help of his acquaintance, Figaro, who also happens to be Bartolo's barber.

royal protection until the end of the 14C, when it was seized by Christians, who converted the synagogues into churches.

Today, it is a haven of peace and quiet in the heart of Sevilla, where time has stood still. Visitors will want to meander through its alleyways – resplendent in the bright sunshine, and equally delightful at night – to discover its many facets and its hospitality, particularly during the *paseo*. Many of the barrio's street name are evocative of past times: Mesón del Moro (Moor's Inn), Pimienta (Pepper) and Susona, from the legendary love affair between a Jewess and Christian man.

One of the best entrances to the quarter is through the **Arco de la Judería**, a covered alleyway leading centuries back in time to the Patio de Banderas. Continue to the **callejón del Agua**, which runs

Street in the Barrio de Santa Cruz

©Turespaña

alongside the district's outer wall. A less theatrical, yet equally interesting route upon leaving the Patio de Banderas, is through the **calle Romero Murube**, continuing along the wall of the Alcázar to the plaza de la Alianza. Cross the square and follow the street ,which becomes the twisting yet delightful **callejón de Rodrigo Caro**, ending up at the **plaza de Doña Elvira**, one of Santa Cruz's most typical squares with *azulejo*-adorned benches shaded by orange trees, a small stone fountain at its centre. The calle Gloria leads to the lively **plaza de los Venerables**.

Hospital de los Venerables★

🕐*Open daily year-round 10am–2pm and 4–8pm.* 🕐*Closed 1 Jan, Good Fri and 25 Dec.* ⊛€4.75. ☎954 56 26 96. http://focus.abengoa.es.

Founded in 1675, this priests' hospital (now the seat of the Focus-Abengoa cultural foundation), by Leonardo de Figueroa, is one of the finest examples of the 17C Sevillian Baroque. Its attractive patio is decorated with 19C *azulejos*.

The **church**★, with its single nave and barrel vault with lunettes, is covered with **frescoes**★★ painted by Valdés Leal and his son Lucas Valdés. *The Last Supper* by Valdés the Younger and, above it, *The Apotheosis of San Fernando*, by Valdés the Elder, are at the apsidal end. The nave contains four Flemish works on copper and two smaller works painted on marble. Two fine statues by Pedro Roldán, *San Fernando* and *San Pedro*, are at the foot of the church. Organ concerts are held frequently.

In the **sacristy** is a fresco by Valdés Leal on the theme of the triumph of the Cross. The balustrade appears to change position if you watch it as you move around the room. Admire also the anonymous 18C figures of Christ in ivory.

Above the attractive **main staircase**★ is an elliptical Baroque dome adorned with stuccoes bearing the papal arms. *The Presentation of the Infant Jesus in the Temple*, by Lucas Valdés, hangs on the wall.

Streets and squares

Follow calle Santa Teresa – at no 7 is where the artist Murillo lived (now

Don Juan

This legendary character, the archetypal seducer who shows no respect for anyone or anything, appears for the first time in Tirso de Molina's *The Trickster of Seville and His Guest of Stone* (1630). It is said that he may have found his inspiration for the character in Don Miguel de Mañara, the founder of the Hospital de la Caridad (👉 *see Walking Tours, The River Bank*).

Although the character is known to the world of opera as Mozart's *Don Giovanni* and has been re-created time and time again over the centuries by writers of the stature of Molière, Dumas and Byron, none of whom could resist his attraction, the best-known version in Spain is that of *Don Juan Tenorio* (1844) by Zorrilla, in whose memory the statue in the plaza de los Refinadores has been erected.

an exhibition room) – or exit plaza de Alfaro to **plaza de Santa Cruz**. Amid the orange trees of the square stands an impressive iron cross, the 17C Cruz de la Cerrajería, where one of the city's favourite sons, Murillo, is buried. Gardens nearby carry his name.

Calle Mezquita leads to the majestic **plaza de los Refinadores**. Continue to the **plaza de las Tres Cruces**, a triangle with three columns upon which stand three wrought-iron crosses, via a narrow alleyway.

Calle Mateos Gago, which runs into plaza de la Virgen de los Reyes, has a number of popular tapas bars as well as several early-20C houses.

Walking Tours

1 Palacio de San Telmo and Parque de María Luisa★

Palacio de San Telmo

This impressively wide late 17C palace is the seat of the Presidencia de la Junta de Andalucía (Regional Council). It was once a naval academy, then the residence of the Dukes of Montpensier, and a seminary. Its **main portal**★, one of the finest works of Sevillian Baroque, is by Leonardo de Figueroa. It is completely covered with reliefs and sculptures. Above, a statue of San Telmo is silhouetted against the sky.

Hotel Alfonso XIII

(👉 *See Where to Stay in the Address Book.*) The most famous of all Sevilla's hotels

was built for the 1929 Ibero-American Exhibition in regionalist style with neo-Mudéjar features.

University

The city's university is a fine building with classical, harmonious lines and impressive dimensions, built in the 18C as a tobacco factory (and entrenched in the Sevilla myth by Bizet's *Carmen*). The **portal** fronting calle San Fernando has paired columns, and is crowned by a pediment bearing a large coat of arms, and a statue of an angel of the apocalypse representing Fame. In the doorway arch are medallions of Columbus and Hernán Cortés. Inside are attractive patios and a monumental staircase.

Parque de María Luisa★★

The popular park was a gift from the Infanta María Luisa Fernanda, Duchess of Montpensier. Once part of the gardens of the Palacio de San Telmo, it was landscaped for the 1929 Ibero-American Exhibition by Jean-Claude Nicolas Forestier, and enhanced with gazebos,

R. Mattes/ MICHELIN

Horse-drawn carriage in Parque de María Luisa

Gazebos, Statues and Fountains

The Parque de María Luisa is much more than just a collection of attractive buildings and long, tree-lined avenues. Its fountains, with their gentle murmuring of water, its gazebos and its statues of famous characters add an intimate, romantic air to this delightful park. The memorials to Gustavo Adolfo Bécquer and Cervantes, with its *azulejos* illustrating scenes from *Don Quixote* (at one end of plaza de América), are just two examples of the surprises awaiting visitors as they stroll around the gardens.

pools and exhibition buildings, some of which remain.

Plaza de España★

This magnificent creation of Sevillian architect Aníbal González is semicircular, fronted by a canal where rowboats can be hired. The enormity of the plaza is striking, and the ceramics exquisite. Before the brick building with towers at either end are *azulejo* scenes, illustrating an episode from the history of each province of Spain.

Plaza de América

Here are three buildings from the 1929 Exhibition by the same architect: the Isabelline Pabellón Real (Royal Pavilion); the Renaissance pavilion, now the **archaeological museum**★ (*see Visit: Museo Arqueológico de Sevilla*), and the Mudéjar pavilion, now a museum of popular arts (*see Visit: Museo de las Artes y Costumbres Populares*).

2 The River Bank★

The **paseo de Cristóbal Colón** runs parallel to the river between the San Telmo and Triana bridges. Along it are the Torre del Oro and the Real Maestranza bullring and other impressive sights. From the paseo are fine views across to the Triana district.

Torre del Oro

The splendid Gold Tower was built by the Almohads in the 13C, along with the Torre de la Plata or Silver Tower, as part of a defensive system. The main part of the tower is a dodecagonal stone structure crowned with merlons, topped by two levels in brick, the second added in the 18C. The interior houses the **Museo de la Marina** (*open Tue–Fri, 10am–2pm; Sat–Sun and public hols, 11am–2pm; Closed public hols and in Aug; €1; 954 22 24 19*) with documents, engravings, boat models and other items of maritime life.

Cruises along the Guadalquivir depart from just below the tower.

Opposite the Torre del Oro is the **Teatro de la Maestranza**, with an unusual false façade. The Hospital de la Caridad, with an important art collection, is behind.

Hospital de la Caridad★

The Hospital of Charity was founded in 1667 by Don Miguel de Mañara (1627–79). The white façade of the church, dazzling in sunlight, has five murals of blue and white ceramics apparently based on drawings by Murillo: theological virtues predominate (Faith, Hope and Charity); the two below show St George slaying the dragon and St James (Santiago), the Moorslayer (*see tour description under Visit*).

As you leave, the founder's statue is opposite; to the left is the **Torre de la Plata**.

▶ *Return to the paseo de Cristóbal Colón and continue towards the Puente de Triana.*

La Maestranza

Visit by guided tours, daily 9.30am–7pm. €4. 954 22 45 77. www.real maestranza.com.

Sevilla's famed *plaza de toros*, with attractive red and white façade, was built between 1758 and 1881. Unusually, the bullring itself is not quite circular. Triumphant bullfighters are carried on the shoulders of fans through the Puerta del Príncipe (Prince's Gate). The **museum** has an interesting assortment of posters, paintings, and costumes.

Carmen

This legendary character created by the French writer Prosper Merimée in 1845 was subsequently used by Bizet as the subject of his famous opera (1874), in which he narrates the story of a triangle of love and jealousy involving Carmen the gypsy, a soldier and a bullfighter.

In front of La Maestranza, where the tragic finale of the opera played out, is a bronze statue to Carmen, the personification of passionate female love.

Before the Puente de Triana is the **Monumento a la Tolerancia**, a large sculpture with the stamp of the acclaimed contemporary Spanish sculptor, Eduardo Chillida, who spent time here in April 1992.

Triana★

Triana, one of the city's most colourful areas, is across the Puente de Triana (or Puente de Isabel II), a bridge built in 1845. It offers fine **views** of the Guadalquivir and the east bank. Triana is a fishermen's and merchants' quarter, which has also produced famous singers and bullfighters.

To the left of the bridge, the **plaza del Altozano** has a monument to bullfighter Juan Belmonte (1892–1962) a *trianero* (though born across the river).

Enter the district by the **calle Pureza**. At no 55, between simple, well-maintained houses, stands the **Capilla de los Marineros**, a chapel dedicated to sailors, with a statue of the **Esperanza de Triana** (Hope of Triana), one of the

The Ceramics Quarter

A number of ceramics workshops and boutiques can still be seen in the area near the plaza del Altozano occupied by the calle de Callao, calle Antillano and calle de Alfarería, perpetuating an artistic tradition which has always existed in this quarter. The façades of some of these shops and workshops are decorated with *azulejos* advertising the wares inside.

most venerated statues of the Virgin Mary, whose procession rivals that of La Macarena. A late 16C Christ of the Three Falls is to the right of the high altar.

Parroquia de Santa Ana

Calle Pureza. A little farther on, the Iglesia de Santa Ana in the parish (*parroquia*) of the same name is the oldest in Sevilla. The original church, founded by Alfonso X the Wise in the 13C, was restored and altered in the 18C.

Exterior

The most striking feature is the tower, with multifoiled arches in the lower sections showing clear Mudéjar influence, and *azulejo* decoration in the upper part.

Interior

Entrance at the side, in calle Vázquez de Leca.

A **Renaissance altarpiece** in the chancel comprises a fine ensemble of sculptures and paintings dedicated to the Virgin Mary; several of the canvases are by Pedro de Campaña. A sculpture of St Anne and the Virgin and Child is in the central vaulted niche. The Child is modern; the other figures are from the 13C, but have been altered.

The retro-choir contains a delicate early 16C **Virgin of the Rose**, by Alejo Fernández. Admire the panelling and altar, decorated with *azulejos*, in the Evangelist nave.

"El Cachorro"

The **Capilla del Patrocinio**, a chapel situated at the end of the calle Castilla in the most northerly section of the Triana district, is where the **Christ of the Expiration**, commonly known as "El Cachorro", is venerated. It is said that the artist, Francisco Antonio Gijón, used a sketch of a murdered gypsy known as "El Cachorro" for the face of Christ in this late-17C masterpiece. Once he had finished carving Christ, the sculpture was so realistic that when people saw it they immediately recognised the dead gypsy, hence its name.

Calle Betis

Stroll this riverside street and enjoy a completely different perspective of Sevilla: the Torre del Oro and La Maestranza in the foreground, dominated by the majestic Giralda. Calle Betis is known for its traditional houses, bars and open-air kiosks. At night, with the moon reflected on the river, the street makes a romantic setting.

③ Centro★

Plaza Nueva

This spacious square is on land previously occupied by the Convento de San Francisco. The equestrian statue is of Fernando III the Saint, the city's Christian conqueror. Tall palms, benches and street lamps attract locals and tourists.

Ayuntamiento

The west front of the neo-Classical 19C town hall faces the square. The more interesting east side, on plaza de San Francisco, has an attractive Plateresque 16C **façade★**, the work of Diego de Riaño, adorned everywhere with delicate classical motifs (fantastic and grotesque animals, medallions with faces, escutcheons etc).

The palace opposite the town hall in plaza de San Francisco is the Caja de Ahorros San Fernando (savings bank). It was formerly the seat of the Royal Court of Justice (Audiencia). Its classical late-16C façade is attributed to Alonso de Vandelvira.

Calle Sierpes

Sevilla's most famous street, now pedestrianised, is lined with traditional and modern shops. Calle Sierpes is liveliest in the late afternoon and early evening when locals window-shop or enjoy pastries in its renowned *pastelerías*.

The famous **La Campana** coffee and pastry shop, founded in 1885, is at the very end of Sierpes on the corner with Martín Villa).

Capilla de San José★

🕐 *Open year-round Mon–Fri 8am–12.30pm and 7–8.30pm. Sat, Sun and public hols 9am–1pm and 6.30–8.30pm. No visits during services.* ☎954 22 31 42 or 954 22 32 42.

This chapel, a masterpiece of Sevillian Baroque, dates from the end of the 17C. Its 18C façade and belfry with bright blue azulejos can be seen from the corner of calle Sierpes and calle Jovellanos. St Joseph with the Infant Christ in his arms is on the portal. The exuberance of the Baroque decoration in the small interior is a surprise, particularly at the apsidal end. The large wooden **altarpiece** in the presbytery depicting angels, saints and God the Father, is an ornamental outcry. The image of St Joseph in the centre is venerated here.

▷ *At the end of calle Sierpes, take calle Cuna, which runs parallel to it.*

The most impressive building along this street is the magnificent **Palacio de la Condesa de Lebrija**★ (ⓒ*see Visit*).

▷ *Continue along calle Cuna to plaza del Salvador.*

Plaza del Salvador

The huge parish church of El Salvador looks over this large square, one of the most popular places for an afternoon drink and lively socialising, especially on Sundays.

Iglesia del Salvador★

🕐 *Open year-round daily 9–10am and 6.30–9pm.* ☎954 21 16 79.

Calle Sierpes

G. Bludzin / MICHELIN

This church, rising majestically on one side of the square, replaced the former main mosque, demolished in 1671. Construction lasted until 1712, to plans by José Granados; the cupolas were designed by Leonardo de Figueroa. The elegant façade of attractive pink brick and stone, is a fine example of the ornamental Baroque style.

A sensation of vastness pervades the interior. There are three short aisles. Note the high lanterned cupola above the transept.

Some of the city's most notable **Baroque retables**★★ (all from the 18C) are inside. The one in the chancel, dedicated to the Transfiguration of the Lord, is the work of Cayetano Acosta. It covers the entire wall with unrestrained decoration.

The frontispiece of the **Capilla del Sagrario**, the sacrarium chapel which opens onto the left transept, takes the form of a gigantic retable. This is also the work of Cayetano Acosta, dedicated to the exaltation of the Sacred Host; it displays the same exuberance as the main altarpiece. Inside, the most interesting object is the 17C **Christ of the Passion**, by Martínez Montañés. Part of an opulent silver altarpiece, it conveys an image of serene suffering on the face of Christ. Another fine retable, by José Maestre, with a shrine dedicated to the Virgin Mary, is in the right transept.

The chapel to the right displays the 17C **Crucificado del Amor**, by Juan de Mesa, a moving interpretation of the suffering and solitude of Jesus on the Cross.

4 La Macarena and Calle San Luis★

Basílica de la Macarena

🕐 *Open daily year-round 9.30am–2pm and 5–8pm.* 🕐 *Closed during Holy Week and one week before and after in preparation for religious processions.* 👓 *Museum €3.* ☎ *954 90 18 00.*

The Iglesia de Nuestra Señora de la Esperanza (Church of Our Lady of Hope), built in the middle of the 20C, contains one of Sevilla's most famous statues: **La Macarena**★. This carving of the Virgin Mary, the work of an anonymous 17C artist, looks down from the high altar.

Sevillians say that only angels could have created such a work. The beauty of her tearful face unleashes fervour during her procession, in the early morning of Good Friday. A Christ under Sentence in a chapel on the Evangelist side of the church is also venerated, and carried alongside the Virgin.

The **museum** displays cloaks and skirts, as well as the impressive floats which bear La Macarena and Christ, conveying the splendour of these occasions.

The **Arco de la Macarena** stands opposite the church. This arch was part of the Arab walls. The remaining section continues as far as the Puerta de Córdoba (Córdoba Gate). The walls have barbicans and are punctuated with large, square fortified towers.

Hospital de las Cinco Llagas or Hospital de la Sangre

Opposite the Arco de la Macarena.

The former Hospital of the Five Wounds (*llagas*) or Blood (*sangre*), is the seat of the Andalusian Parliament. Until the mid-20C, this Renaissance-style building was Sevilla's main hospital. It is sober and harmonious, with a tower on each end. Two floors open onto a green square. The white marble doorway is crowned by the escutcheon of the Five Wounds.

Return to La Macarena. Behind it is the 13C parish church of **San Gil**, which has undergone significant restoration over the centuries. Follow calle de San Luis.

Iglesia de Santa Marina

This 14C brick church has a simple stone ogival portal with minor sculpted decoration and a sober Mudéjar tower with staggered merlons. A tour of the exterior reveals the church's sturdy buttresses and the large Gothic windows at the apsidal end.

Iglesia de San Luis de los Francesesa

🕐 *Open Tue–Thu 9am–2pm. Fri–Sat 9am –2pm and 5–8pm.* 🕐 *Closed public hols and in Aug.* ☎ *954 55 02 07.*

This church, the work of Leonardo de Figueroa, is one of the best examples of Sevillian Baroque architecture. The **façade** is clearly compartmentalised:

SEVILLA

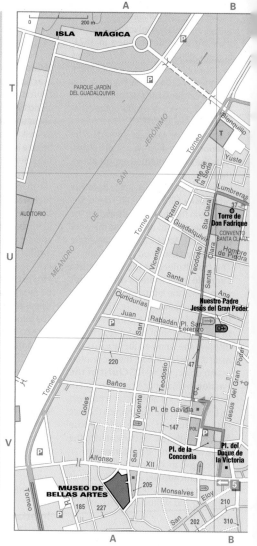

two storeys, with octagonal tower on each side, and central cupola with ceramic decoration.

The **interior**★★ is surprisingly exuberant, with murals on the magnificent cupola by Lucas Valdés and outstanding retables by Pedro Duque Cornejo. The fine *azulejos* complete this superb ensemble, which manages to combine a richness of decoration with harmony. Note also the unusual reliquary on the frontal of the chancel.

Iglesia de San Marcos

The impressive 14C façade blends Gothic and Mudéjar features. The attractive **Mudéjar tower**★ stands out, clearly Giralda-influenced (multifoiled arches and *sebka* work on the upper frieze). The tower is brick, with the exception of the Gothic stone portal which has three 18C sculptures (God the Father, the Virgin Mary and an angel), which replaced the original works, and an elegant and unusual *sebka*-style frieze.

The whitewashed interior contains a handsome 17C sculpture of **St Mark**

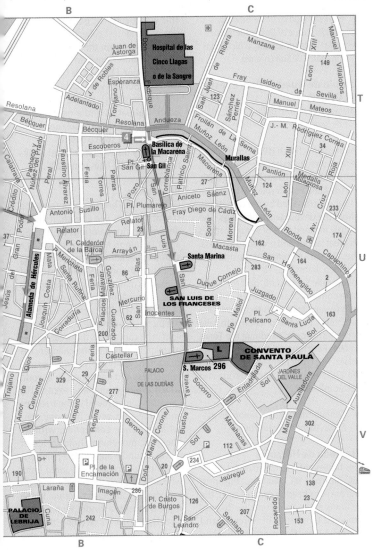

(*Evangelist nave*) and an 18C **Recumbent Christ** (*Epistle nave*).

In the **plaza de Santa Isabel** behind the church, admire the doorway of the **church of the convent of Santa Isabel** (🕐*open only for morning Mass*). A relief depicts the Visitation of the Virgin to her cousin Elizabeth. The work, from the early 17C, is by Andrés Ocampo.

A little farther along stands the **Convento de Santa Paula**⋆, one of the most ornate convents in the city (🕐 *see description under Visit*).

5 From Plaza del Duque de la Victoria to Alameda de Hercules

Plaza del Duque de la Victoria is the commercial heart of this part of the city with several department stores and numerous smaller shops.

The church of the former Colegio de San Hermenegildo (1616–20) in nearby **plaza de la Concordia**, with a fine oval cupola, is a municipal exhibition centre.

▸ *Walk through plaza de Gavidia, with its statue of Daoíz, then take calle Cardenal Spínola, which leads into plaza de San Lorenzo.*

Templo de Nuestro Padre Jesús del Gran Poder

🕐*Open year-round daily 8am–1.30pm and 6–9pm (Fri 7.30am–10pm).* ☎954 91 56 72.

This modern church (1965) in the Plaza de San Lorenzo houses the magnificent statue of **Jesus of Great Power**★ (1620). Juan de Mesa's masterpiece is housed in a shrine surrounded by red carnations, where the devout leave offerings. The slightly inclined face of Jesus portrays his great fatigue and profound sadness. The 13C parish church alongside was modified in the 17C.

Follow calle Santa Clara, past the Santa Clara convent of an enclosed order of nuns *(○━not open to visitors).* Take calle Lumbreras. Past the junction with calle Becas, turn around to admire the **Torre de Don Fadrique**, all that remains of a palace. This battlemented tower, built in the 13C, shows both Romanesque and Gothic influence.

▸ *Continue along calle Lumbreras as far as Alameda de Hércules.*

Alameda de Hércules

This boulevard was constructed in the 16C. Atop two 18C columns at the north end are lions bearing coats of arms; the columns at the south end are Roman, crowned by statues of Hercules and Caesar. A lively **flea market** is held on Sunday mornings.

Visit

North of the Cathedral

Museo de Bellas Artes★★★

Entrance via the plaza del Museo. 🕐*Open year-round Wed–Sat 9am–8.30pm. Tue 2.30–8.30pm. Sun and public hol, 9am–2.30pm.* 🕐*Closed 2 and 6 Jan, 28 Feb, 13–14 Apr, 1 and 30 May, 15 Jun, 15 Aug, 12 Oct, 1 Nov, and 6, 8 and 25 Dec.* ☞ *€1.50 (free to EU citizens).* ☎954 78 65 00. *www.juntadeandalucia.es/cultura/museos.*

This world-class art gallery contains one of the largest collections of Spanish paintings from the Golden Age. It is in the former Convento de la Merced (17C), designed by Juan de Oviedo ; the Baroque doorway was added in the 18C. The museum is built around three delightful patios and a magnificent staircase, covered by a cupola decorated with Mannerist stucco designs.

The gallery displays significant works from the Middle Ages to the 20C.

Room V★★★

Ground floor. This is undoubtedly the star attraction. The church, its walls decorated with paintings by the 18C artist Domingo Martínez, provides a stunning backdrop to an outstanding collection of work by Murillo and one of Zurbarán's masterpieces, *The Apotheosis of St Thomas Aquinas* (*in the nave*).

Murillo (1617–82), a master of both the pictorial technique and the use of light in his canvases, is the great painter of religious subjects and children. His characters, always very human, exude tenderness and gentleness in a world which avoids drama and excess. His canvases can be found in the transept and in the apse, where his monumental *Immaculate Conception*, with its energetic movement, holds pride of place. Around it are notable paintings of saints: *Santa Rufina* and *Santa Justa*, who are clutching the Giralda, and *San Leandro* and *San Buenaventura*. In the right transept, a kindly *Virgin of the Cloth* is particularly interesting (the child seems to move towards you). Note also *St Francis Embracing Christ on the Cross* and another Immaculate Conception, also known as *La Niña* (*The Child*). On the left-hand side, *St Anthony and Child*, *Dolorosa* and *St Felix of Cantalicio and Child* are all worth a closer look.

Room X★★

Upper floor. This room is dedicated to works by **Francisco de Zurbarán** (1598–1664). This artist had a particular skill for painting the shades of white of monks' habits and the pure cloth of Christ, as in the fine *Christ on the Cross*, in which the body of Christ, painted against a dark background, appears as if sculpted in

B. Kaufmann / MICHELIN

Former church, dominated by Murillo's Immaculate Conception

relief. Zurbarán's compositions are simple and peaceful. A lack of correct perspective is seen in *St Hugh and Carthusian Monks at Table* which is otherwise quite outstanding. His preoccupation with the treatment of cloth, seen in his depiction of the Fathers of the Church in *The Apotheosis of St Thomas Aquinas*, is also evident in the splendid velvet brocade in *San Ambrosio*. Apart from his saints, his *Virgin of the Caves* and *San Bruno's Visit to Urbano II* are interesting. Sculptures in the same room include *St Dominic* by Martínez Montañés. Note the splendid *artesonado* ceiling in the inner room.

Other rooms

Room I displays interesting medieval works. **Room II**, once the refectory, is dedicated to Renaissance art, in particular a fine sculpture of *St Jerome* by Pietro Torrigiani, a contemporary of Michelangelo. Other works of note include Alejo Fernández's *Annunciation*, with Flemish and Italian influence clearly evident, a painting by El Greco of his son *Jorge Manuel*, and a diptych of *The Annunciation and Visitation* by Coffermans. Two magnificent portraits of *A Lady and a Gentleman* by Pedro Pacheco are the highlights in **Room III**.

Upper floor: Room VI displays a fine collection of richly decorated female saints (anonymous, some by followers

of Zurbarán) and two male saints. **Room VII** contains more works by Murillo and his disciples while **Room VIII** is devoted to the other great Baroque artist Valdés Leal, a more expressive and dramatic painter than Murillo. European Baroque is represented in **Room IX** by, among others, Ribera's powerful *St James the Apostle*, canvases by Brueghel and the supreme *Portrait of a Lady* by Cornelis de Vos. **Room XI**, devoted to 18C art, is enlivened by Goya's *Portrait of Canon José Duato*, and several works by Lucas Valdés. The following two rooms (**XII** and **XIII**) display 19C art, in particular superb portraits by Esquivel, while the final room (**XIV**) shows 20C canvases by Vázquez Díaz and Zuloaga, among others.

Casa de Pilatos★★

🕐 *Open year-round daily 9am–6pm (Apr–Oct 7pm).* 🚶 *€8, ground floor and gardens only: €5.* ☎*954 22 52 98. www. fundacionmedinaceli.org.*

This palace is one of Sevilla's most famous and beautiful monuments. It is on the pleasant plaza de Pilatos to which it has lent its name. The statue in the square is of Zurbarán.

Construction began at the end of the 15C. However, it was Don Fadrique, the first Marquess of Tarifa, who was responsible for most of the palace that we see today. It is said, quite fancifully, that he took his inspiration from Pontius Pilate's house in Jerusalem, hence the name of the palace. It is a mixture of Mudéjar, Renaissance and Flamboyant Gothic styles, although the Mudéjar style predominates.

The delightful **patio** recalls an elegant Moorish palace with its finely moulded stuccowork and magnificent 16C lustre **azulejos**★★. Note the unequal arches and the different motifs of the *azulejo* panels. The fountain was carved in Genoa in the 16C. Statues in the palace include **Athena**, a 5C BC Greek original; the others are of Roman origin. Rounded niches in the walls hold superb busts of Roman emperors. The rooms around the patio have fine *artesonado* ceilings, panels of *azulejos*, sculpted plasterwork, groined vaulting and the palaeo-Christian sculpture of the Good Shepherd in

Detail of azulejos, Casa de Pilatos

the chapel, the oldest part of the house. The gardens can also be visited.

The sumptuous *azulejo*-adorned **staircase**★★ leading up from a corner of the patio has a remarkable half-orange **wooden dome**★.

On the upper floor, frescoes from the 16C represent characters from Antiquity. Several rooms have interesting ceilings, particularly one painted by Francisco Pacheco in 1603 illustrating the Apotheosis of Hercules.

A visit to the nearby **Convento de San Leandro** is particularly recommended. Although access to the church is difficult, it is still worth a visit to buy the convent's famous *yemas*, delicious sweets made with egg yolk and sugar.

Convento de Santa Paula★

⏱*Open year-round Tue–Sun 10am–1pm and 3.30–6.30pm.* ⏱*Closed public hols and for certain religious ceremonies.* ◎€2. ☎954 53 63 30.

This historic convent of an order of enclosed (Hieronymite) nuns was founded at the end of the 15C. Its elegant and lofty 17C belfry is one of the finest in Sevilla. The nuns prepare tasty cakes and jams, which are on sale here.

Church★

Entrance through the left-hand door with the azulejo depicting St Paula. Note the interesting atrium and the fine **portal**★, worked on by Nicola Pisano and completed in 1504. The portal is made of brick with alternating twin-coloured rows and is profusely adorned with ceramics. In spite of the evident mixture of styles – Mudéjar in the use of brick, Gothic in the arches, and Renaissance in the medallions and cresting – the effect is of perfect cohesion and harmony. The escutcheon on the tympanum is of the Catholic Monarchs. The central medallion, attributed to Luca della Robbia, represents the Birth of Jesus.

The **interior**★, a single nave topped by a 17C *artesonado* ceiling, comprises a presbytery with Gothic vaults, totally covered with delightful polychrome frescoes. Two niches on either side of the high altar contain the tombs of the Marquess and Marchioness of Montemayor, the benefactors of this church. The brother of the Marchioness is laid to rest in a separate niche.

The main altarpiece dates from the beginning of the 18C, though it retains the image of St Paula, in the centre, from an earlier retable. Note the movement of the two lamp-bearing angels. Two altars in the nave, opposite each other, are dedicated to John the Evangelist and John the Baptist.

Two finely carved sculptures are the work of Martínez Montañés. A Gothic Christ can also be seen in a large window in the Epistle nave. The enclosed choir is separated from the rest of the church by an iron grille.

Museum★
(Entrance at no 11 on the plaza).

The museum is in several tall outbuildings. Two have fine *artesonado* ceilings. The museum contains objects of great value, including canvases by **Ribera** (*St Jerome* and *The Adoration of the Shepherds*), two works by Pedro de Mena (*Our Lady of Sorrows* and *Ecce Homo*), an Immaculate Conception by Alonso Cano, and a charming 17C crib with many figurines.

Palacio de la Condesa de Lebrija★

Open year-round Mon–Fri 10.30am– 1.30pm and 4.30–7.30pm (5–8pm late Apr–Sept). Sat, 10am–1pm. €4 (€7 for both floors). 954 22 78 02. www. palaciodelebrija.com.

This private residence provides an opportunity to visit a palace with a typically Sevillian layout, comprising a hallway, central patio and interior garden. Inside, a pleasant surprise awaits: a floor that appears to be completely covered with Roman **mosaics**★ from nearby Itálica (*see Excursions*). The patio floor depicting mythological scenes is particularly fine, as is the octagonal room with its volutes and large vases. The attractive patio also has elegant foiled arches, Moorish-influenced panelling and *alfiz* rectangular moulding, a colourful plinth of Sevillian *azulejos* and showcases displaying archaeological remains. The **staircase**★, rich in ceramic tiles, has a mahogany bannister, marble steps and an outstanding Mudéjar marquetry ceiling, which originally graced a palace in Marchena.

The rooms and galleries on the upper floor are embellished with a mix of Renaissance, Baroque and romantic decorative features.

Iglesia de la Magdalena

The church was built in the late 17C and early 18C according to designs by Leonardo de Figueroa. It is possible to discern the layout of the church from the exterior: aisles, transept and elegant dome ornamented with *azulejos*.

The **interior**★ contains a number of treasures. The ceiling paintings are the work of Lucas Valdés. A lanterned

cupola rises majestically above the transept, while the exuberant Baroque altarpiece in the chancel dates from the early 18C; the paintings on the vaults illustrate allegories of saints. The **Capilla del Cristo del Calvario** (*to the right of the presbytery*) takes its name from *The Exposed Christ*, an 18C work by Francisco Ocampo. In the Epistle nave are the fine **high-relief of the Assumption** supported by four small angels, by Juan de Mesa (1619), and the Sacramental and Quinta Angustia chapels. The former contains two canvases by **Zurbarán**: *St Dominic in Soria* and *The Miraculous Healing of the Beatified Reginald of Orleans*. The **Capilla de la Quinta Angustia**★ is situated in the vestibule of the main entrance doorway. The magnificent sculpture at the altar, depicting a highly moving Deposition, is attributed to the followers of Pedro Roldán. Look up to admire the three Moorish-influenced cupolas. Ten canvases of saints by Valdés Leal hang on the walls of the chapel.

In the left transept, next to the door, stands a 16C sculpture of the **Virgin of the Fever**, an elegant and maternal Virgin with the Infant Christ in her arms.

Around the Cathedral

Hospital de la Caridad

Open year-round Mon–Sat 9am– 1.30pm and 3.30–7.30pm. Sun and public hols 9am–1pm. Closed on certain public hols. €5. 954 22 32 32.

Enter the church via the hospital, with its harmonious double patio adorned with panels of *azulejos* representing scenes from the Old and New Testaments.

Church★★

The single-nave Baroque church contains artistic gems commissioned by Mañara from Sevilla's leading artists of the period. The pictorial representations of Death and Charity would have created an example of the path that the brothers of Charity were expected to follow.

Two **paintings**★★ by **Valdés Leal** beneath the chancel tribune are quite staggering in their severity. In **Finis Gloriae Mundi**, Valdés Leal depicts with macabre realism a dead and half decomposed bishop and knight; the scales held in the hand of Christ refer to the moment of judgement. **In Ictu Oculi** (In the Blink of an Eye) is an allegory of death in which the skeleton has earthly symbols at its feet (a globe, a crown, books etc). An *Exaltation of the Cross*, by the same artist, can be seen above the choir.

In the nave, **Murillo** has illustrated the theme of Charity through several **works**★. The sense of submission to one's fellow man is exalted in the fine **St Isabel of Hungary Curing the Lepers**, and in **St John of God Carrying a Sick Man On His Shoulder**, in which the artist demonstrates his mastery of *chiaroscuro*. Two paintings of children on the side altars are also by Murillo. Another side altar has a 17C bleeding Christ casting a distressed gaze toward the sky, by Pedro Roldán. The two horizontal paintings facing each other in the transept are *The Miracle of the Loaves and Fishes* (representing the gift of food) and **Moses Smiting Water from the Rock** (representing the gift of water). The canvases in the dome of the transept are by Valdés Leal: in each echinus is an angel bearing the instruments of the Passion; the Evangelists are depicted in the pendentives. Note also the fine lamp-bearing angels.

At the main altar, a splendid Baroque altarpiece by Pedro Roldán has at its centre a fine sculptural group representing the **Holy Burial of Christ**★★ in which the artist has interpreted with great beauty the pain in the contained emotion of the faces.

Iglesia de Santa María la Blanca★

This former synagogue was transformed into a church in the 14C; the simple Gothic portal is from this period, but the façade and the **interior**★ are 17C reconstructions. Three aisles are separated by semicircular arches resting on pink marble columns. The barrel vaults adorned with lunettes and the dome over the transept are completely covered with delightful plasterwork decoration. Baroque exuberance is balanced by the lightness of the columns, creating an effect which is both attractive and harmonious. The Evangelist nave contains a *Last Supper*, attributed to Murillo, which is surprising in its dramatic use of light, in keeping with the pure tenebrist style.

South of the Cathedral

Museo Arqueológico de Sevilla★

🕐*Open year-round Wed–Sat 9am–8.30pm. Tue 2.30–8.30pm. Sun and public hol, 9am–2.30pm.* €1.50 *(free to EU citizens).* ☎954 78 64 74. *www.juntade andalucia.es/cultura/museos/MASE.*

Housed in a Renaissance pavilion in the Parque María Luisa, Seville's archaeo-

Presbytery vault, Iglesia del Convento de Santa Paula

logical museum contains an interesting collection of prehistoric and Roman objects.

The prehistoric collection, on the ground floor, includes items discovered at archaeological excavations in the province. The exhibits in **Room VI** are particularly exciting, comprising the 7C–6C BC **El Carambolo treasure**★, a superb collection of gold jewellery of Phoenician inspiration with a surprisingly modern design, and the Goddess Astarte (8C BC), a small bronze statue bearing an inscription said to be the oldest script found on the Iberian peninsula.

The first floor is dedicated exclusively to the **Roman collection**★ (Rooms XII to XXV), largely discovered at Itálica (see Excursions). Exhibits include magnificent sculptures and mosaics which provide an insight into the artistic development of the Romans in the region. Other displays show objects which re-create aspects of Roman civilisation.

Other items of interest include a Mercury with a large mosaic at his feet (Room XIV); an unusual collection of marble plaques with footprint markings offered at games ceremonies (Room XVI); a Venus in Room XVII; fine sculptures of Diana in Room XIX; and bronze plaques from the Roman Lex Irnitana in the annexe. The oval room (Room XX) contains an impressive statue of Trajan, while Room XXV, dedicated to funerary art, has a variety of sarcophagi, columbaria and household objects.

Museo de las Artes y Costumbres Populares

Open year-round Wed–Sat 9am–8.30pm. Tue 2.30–8.30pm. Sun and public hols, 9am–2.30pm. €1.50 (free to EU citizens). 954 71 23 90. www.juntade andalucia.es/cultura/museos/MACSE

The Museum of Popular Art and Traditions, in the Mudéjar pavilion of María Luisa park, displays costumes worn for romerías and fiestas, models of workshops, musical instruments, farming tools, and a collection of posters for the April Fair.

Hispano-Roman Ceramics

The export of agricultural products to the Italian peninsula encouraged the development of the ceramics in Baetica, especially amphorae, of a type now known as Dressel 20. Over 70 kilns have been discovered in the lower Guadalquivir Valley.

Other workshops, sited outside of towns to reduce the risk of fire, produced a widely used domestic pottery known as sigillata hispanica.

Typical pieces were bright red in colour and decorated with plant or animal motifs.

Isla de la Cartuja

Isla Mágica★   Kids

Open daily Apr through Sept, certain days Oct–Dec and Jan following Christmas hols. Consult the website for opening times. Prices vary according to season (half-day tickets available) check the website to confirm. Full day ticket prices: Adults €23.50–27; child €17–19. 02 16 17 16. www.islamagica.es.

Isla Mágica (Magic Isle) amusement park, spread over 40ha/99 acres on the island of La Cartuja, is themed to take visitors on a journey back to the century of the Discoveries. The park's eight areas are: Sevilla, the Gateway to the Indies; Quetzal, the Fury of the Gods; The Balcony of Andalucía; The Gateway to America; Amazonia; The Pirates' Den; The Fountain of Youth; and El Dorado. Facilities and attractions include all manner of rides (from terrifying white-knuckle rides for teens to gentle traditional funfair rides for little ones), live shows, spectacular audio-visual shows, street entertainers, souvenir shops, and a good selection of bars and restaurants.

The following are some of the park's main attractions:

◆ **Quetzal, the Fury of the Gods** – An exciting journey to the Mayan world. Ride a plumed serpent across Central America to escape the fury of the gods.

- **The Balcony of Andalucía** – An enjoyable stroll through this miniature world highlighting important monuments and geographical features of the region.
- **Anaconda** – A breathtaking water ride to satisfy the most intrepid of sailors.
- **Iguaçu** – These impressive waterfalls are bound to get your nerves tingling as you are propelled into a lagoon at speeds of over 50kph/32mph.
- **The Jaguar** – For an extra rush of adrenaline try this huge roller coaster with its vertigo-inducing descents that reach speeds of up to 85kph/53mph.
- **The Fountain of Youth** – This enchanting world of ponds and streams delights young children with the Tell-Tale Toad and the story-telling Tadpoles.
- **The Rapids of the Orinoco** – Challenge the river on an inflatable raft.
- **The House of Superstition** – A state-of-the-art film projected onto a gigantic spherical screen. Experience a whole new world of sensations.
- **El Arte Ecuestre de Andalucía** – An equestrian ballet.
- **Dimension 4** – an entertaining "4-D" audio-visual with special effects.
- **El Desafío** – a heart-in-mouth free fall from 68 metres!

La Cartuja: Centro Andaluz de Arte Contemporáneo

Open Apr–Sept Tue–Fri 10am–8pm. Sat 11am–8pm. Sun, 10am–3pm. Oct–Mar Tue–Fri 10am–9pm. Sat 11am–9pm Sun, 10am–3pm. €3 (free Tue to EU citizens. 955 03 70 70. www.juntadeandalucia. es/cultura/caac.

The Andalusian Centre for Contemporary Art, housed in the former monastery of La Cartuja, is part of an unusual complex with a colourful and varied history. The monastery was founded at the end of the 14C in honour of an apparition of the Virgin Mary in this district.

It was visited by royalty and such notable figures as Columbus, who prepared his second journey of discovery here. The French converted it into a barracks during the Napoleonic invasion and it was later acquired by Charles Pickman, who set up a ceramics factory, which closed in 1982. The chimneys and kilns are still visible.

Monastic buildings★

These mainly date from the 15C, 16C and 17C. Some have managed to preserve their original *azulejos*. The church is of particular interest with its delightful *azulejo* rosette, a sacristy with Baroque plasterwork and charming Mudéjar brick cloisters supported by slender marble columns.

The monks' chapter house, containing a number of interesting tombs, and the long refectory with a superb 17C *artesonado* ceiling, are also well worth a visit.

Museum

The museum's collection mainly comprises early-20C works by major names such as Miró and Chillida, and by young Andalusian contemporary artists.

Excursions

Itálica★

9km/5.5mi NW along the A 66–E 803. Bear left after Santiponce.
Open Apr–Sept Tue–Sat 8.30am–8.30pm, Sun and hols 9am–3pm. Oct–Mar Tue–Sat 9am–5.30pm, Sun 10am–4pm. €1.50 (free to European Union citizens). 955 62 22 66. www.juntadeandalucia. es/cultura/museos/CAI.

The remains of Roman Itálica, founded by Scipio Africanus in 206 BC, stand on a cypress-shaded hill above the Guadalquivir Plain. Its golden age was in the 2C AD. Emperors **Trajan** (AD 53–117) and **Hadrian** (AD 76–138) were born here. Hadrian granted Itálica the title of Colony, transforming it into a monumental city. Its decline began in the Late Empire period.

The excavated area is a district created under Hadrian, with streets laid out according to an orthogonal plan and lined by public buildings and luxurious private houses. Original **mosaics** of

Neptune, birds, and planetary divinities have been preserved.

Amphitheatre

This elliptical amphitheatre, one of the largest in the Roman Empire with a capacity for 25 000, is relatively well preserved. Sections of tiered seating and the pits beneath the arena remain.
The town of **Santiponce** stands on the oldest part of Itálica. The former Roman theatre can be seen at its centre.

Bollullos de la Mitación

18km/11mi west along the A 49 towards Huelva to exit 11.

Iglesia de San Martín

⏱*Open year-round Mon–Sat 7–9pm, Sun and public hols 11am–noon and 5–7pm (for religious services).*
Plaza de Cuatrovitas is fronted by the town hall and the Church of St Martin, an 18C Baroque construction. The brick tower has detailed *azulejo* decoration. Inside, note the **retable** with four paintings by Zurbarán.

Santuario de Cuatrovitas

Head toward Aznalcázar. After 4km/2.5mi, bear left just after a pine grove, then go 2km/1.2mi along an unmetalled road.
⏱*Open Sat–Sun and public hols 10am–1pm and 5–7pm (otherwise, contact the church warden in the house opposite).*
The drive to this simple sanctuary, one of the few rural mosques still standing in Andalucía, is particularly pleasant. Built during the Almohad period, its most striking features are a brick **tower** and foliated horseshoe arch decoration. The interior contains a 16C ceramic altar frontispiece representing the Virgin and Child and the Four Evangelists.

Alcalá de Guadaira

20km/12mi SE along the A 92.

Iglesia de Santiago

The Church of St James was built in the 15C and 16C. Elegant ceramic decoration covers the upper sections and the spire of the lofty bell tower. The presbytery is crowned with an unusual trumpet-shaped and coffered vault.

Castle

Climb the stepped ramps next to the church. The remains of this important Almohad fortress stand atop a hill, dominating the town and rolling landscape. The walls and towers of the original outer enclosure can still be seen. This pleasant site is now a leisure area with a children's park. The 14C–16C **Ermita de Nuestra Señora del Aguila**, a chapel with a solid brick tower topped by merlons, stands at its centre. Note the remains of a medieval fresco inside the chapel (*to the right of the presbytery*).

Fiestas

In spring, Sevilla lives for two fiestas that have brought it international fame: Holy Week (Semana Santa) and the April Fair (Feria de Abril). For those yet to experience either, it is difficult to imagine their splendour or how *Sevillanos* embrace these two authentic, yet totally distinct expressions of the Sevillian soul.

Semana Santa – Holy Week is celebrated between Palm Sunday and Easter Sunday, in March or April, depending on the dates. The origins of Sevilla's Semana Santa date back to the 16C, when the first brotherhoods or fraternities were formed to assist guild associations. Over 50 brotherhoods participate in the Holy Week processions, each carrying its own statue of Christ or the Virgin Mary.
The whole city comes onto the street to relive the Passion of Christ and the pain of his mother. The spectacle is impressive, with the streets and street corners of the city providing a magnificent backdrop to processions. In an extravagant religious ritual, breathtakingly beautiful statues are borne aloft on floats, each exquisitely adorned with gold and silver, as popular religious fervour erupts in an atmosphere bordering on ecstasy.

The processions – These take place throughout the week. Every brotherhood departs from its own church or chapel and usually carries two floats *(pasos)*: one bearing Christ, the other the Virgin Mary. They make one journey to the cathedral and then return to their

A Bit of Advice

The Feria is created by *sevillanos* for *sevillanos;* many of the entertainment booths *(casetas)* are private and if you don't know anyone who can provide you with an introduction or ticket you may feel somewhat left out of proceedings.

headquarters, always by way of calle Sierpes and the town hall. More than 100 floats wind through the city's streets; each carried by *costaleros* – young men who take immense pride in transporting these holy figures and demonstrate great skill and physical prowess in this feat of endurance. They are accompanied by a band of musicians.

Some of the statues borne aloft in procession are priceless works by leading 17C sculptors, including *Jesus of Great Power* and *Christ of Love*, by Juan de Mesa; the *Christ of the Passion*, by Martínez Montañés; *La Macarena*, by an unknown artist; the *Holy Christ of the Expiration* ("El Cachorro"), by Francisco Antonio Gijón; and *Our Father Jesus of Nazareth*, by Francisco Ocampo.

A number of these famous processions take place on the **madrugá,** the early morning of Good Friday, including those of El Silencio (the oldest brotherhood, who, as their name suggests, march in complete silence), La Macarena, La Esperanza de Triana, Los Gitanos and, on Friday afternoon, El Cachorro. Pick up an official programme or look in the local paper for the full schedule.

Tapas

Seville claims to have invented the tradition of tapas and the local saying goes "En Sevilla no se come que se tapea" which means "When in Seville don't dine, eat tapas instead". You'll quickly note that the locals tend to stand while eating or even eat on the hoof. Sitting down for tapas is for tourists!

Feria de Abril – This started from humble beginnings in the mid-19C as a purely commercial animal exchange, but soon developed into a very colourful and boisterous celebration. It is now the major annual fiesta held in Sevilla, which for a city with a huge reputation for partying, says something!

The April Fair takes place two or three weeks after Holy Week in the Los Remedios district, where a veritable city of light is created by thousands of electric bulbs and fairy lights. The streets are also full of traditional *casetas* – stands or marquees, which hold their own little parties. Festivities commence late Monday evening and in the early hours of Tuesday, and continue until the closing fireworks display the following Sunday.

During the *feria* a high-spirited, good-humoured crowd throngs the streets. Sherry from Jerez and *manzanilla* from Sanlúcar flow in the *casetas*, tapas are munched, and *sevillanas* are danced with great passion until the early hours.

During the day, the women of Sevilla do their best to upstage each other with the beauty and grace of their flamenco costumes as they dance, stroll the streets with friends and family, or wander around the *feria* area itself.

In the Feria parade, horsemen dress in tight-fitting costumes and wide-brimmed *sombreros cordobeses*. Carriages are drawn by horses with their colourful harnesses.

The calle del Infierno funfair has attractions to delight young and old alike.

El Rocío – Any mention of local fiestas would not be incomplete without El Rocío (*see EL ROCÍO*). This religious pilgrimage, a combination of devotion to the Virgin and devotion to the festive spirit, converges on a chapel in the village of El Rocío, south of Almonte in the province of Huelva.

SIERRA NEVADA★★

Many visitors are surprised to find Europe's second-highest mountain range so far south. Rising above Granada, the Sierra Nevada's highest peaks are perpetually snow-capped. The area's many attractions include a superb ski resort and magnificent mountain landscapes, characterised by steep valleys and breathtaking ravines. The range covers 170 000ha/420 070 acres , and just over half of this is protected as the Parque Nacional de Sierra Nevada. Snow and ice have sculpted this young mountain chain into a twisted profile. Fourteen of the Sierra Nevada's 70 or so peaks are over 3 000m/9 840ft high The very highest peaks, Mulhacén (3 482m/11 424ft), Veleta (3 394m/11 132ft) and Alcazaba (3 371m/11 057ft) are all in the western part of the range.

- 🖹 **Information**: Centro de Visitantes "El Dornajo" Ctra. de Sierra Nevada, Km. 23, Güéjar Sierra. ☎958.34.06.25. www.nevasport.com/sierranevada/montana/ dornajo. http://reddeparquesnacionales.mma.es. *See also Address Book*.
- ▶ **Orient Yourself:** The Sierra Nevada lie immediately southeast of Granada.
- 👁 **Don't Miss:** The scenic drive(s) from Granada to the Borreguiles crossroads via El Dornajo; Solynieve if you're a skier.
- 🕐 **Organising Your Time:** Allow several days if you are a keen hiker or skier.
- 🖐 **Also See:** GRANADA, GUADIX, Las ALPUJARRAS.

The Great Outdoors

Winter options include downhill skiing, various excursions, and treks to some of the highest snow-capped peaks. In summer, hiking and horse riding are popular. Snow can start to fall in October and even into June; despite this, the Sierra Nevada is renowned for glorious sunny days for two-thirds of the year, when sun, snow and the blue sky combine to create a scene of almost unparalleled beauty

Head for the visitor centre to obtain information on marked walks and the length of time needed. The most popular departure points are: from the El Dornajo visitor centre in Güéjar Sierra, and the **Albergue Universitario**. The most interesting routes are the climb to the Laguna de las Yeguas lagoon and the ascents of Pico Veleta and Mulhacén.

Solynieve★★

The Sierra Nevada's ski resort was built in 1964 and held a World Cup downhill race in 1977, but struggled financially thereafter. The situation improved as protective measures for the Sierra Nevada were put into place. Investments made for the 1996 World Skiing Championships transformed Solynieve. It has 84km/43.7mi of skiable trails, 80 runs and over 20 lifts, and offers weekend night skiing. And, if nature fails to deliver, there are 428 snow canons to provide its 32km of slopes with artificial snow A full range of apartment and hotel accommodation is available in Pradollano.

Driving Tours

From Granada to El Dornajo★★

Road open only in summer – 1hr
Leave Granada on the old mountain road (*carretera de la Sierra*). After 8km/5mi

Mulhacén

According to legend, the name of the highest peak on mainland Spain originates from a story which recounts that the king of Granada, Muley-Hacén, the father of Boabdil, is buried here. The king fell in love with a beautiful Christian maiden by the name of Zoraida, who, after the king's death in Mondújar Castle, had him buried on the highest peak of the Sierra Nevada to hide him from his enemies.

Address Book

For coin ranges, see the Legend on the cover flap.

GETTING THERE AND AROUND

By car – The fastest route from Granada is along the A 395. In Pradollano visitors must leave their vehicles in the underground car park. A more attractive alternative is to combine the two suggested driving itineraries (*see Driving Tours*).

By bus – The BONAL company (☎958 27 31 00) operates several daily services from Granada to Pradollano, from the stop next to the Palacio de Congresos.

TOURIST INFORMATION

Centro de Visitantes del Dornajo – *Km 23, Sierra Nevada road. Open summer 9am–2.30pm and 4.30–7pm; rest of year 9am–2pm and 4.30–6pm. ☎958 34 06 25. www.nevasport.com/sierra nevada/montana/dornajo/informacion. htm.* An ideal starting-point, with a wide range of information on the park, including a Museum of the Mountain, exhibition on local crafts and foods, cafe and excellent bookshop. The centre also organises many activities.

Punto de información del Puerto de la Ragua – *Puerto de la Ragua road.* ☎958 76 02 31. www.laragua.net.

Punto de Información del Parque Nacional de Sierra Nevada – *Pampaneira (plaza de la Libertad).* From here the **Nevadensis** agency (☎958 76 31 27. www.nevadensis.com) organises activities in the Sierra Nevada and Alpujarras.

Mountaineering – *Federación Andaluza de Montañismo. Camino de Ronda, 101 (edificio Atalaya), Granada.* ☎958 29 13 40. www.fedamon.com.

WHERE TO STAY

Hotel Kenia Nevada – *Virgen de las Nieves, 6. ☎958 48 09 11. www.kenianevada.com. 67 rooms.* A classic Alpine-style hotel with plenty of exposed stone and wood, and cosy rooms, as well as a pool. They organise skiing, hiking, hang-gliding, canyoning, and more.

---

turn towards Pinos Genil. The road skirts the Canales Reservoir (*embalse*) to reach **Güejar-Sierra**. After Maitena, the road crosses and then follows the Genil, twisting sharply up to the Hotel del Duque, now a seminary, and the El Dornajo visitor centre.

From El Dornajo to the Borreguiles crossroads★★

From the El Dornajo Visitor Centre take the left fork to climb to the Collado de las Sabinas pass, a steep ascent punctuated with sharp bends. The view is of native pines, and of the Genil Valley. Continue to Pradollano, and the Borreguiles crossroads.

Excursions

Valle del Lecrín★
Head south from Granada along the A 44-E 902, then turn off the main road in Dúrcal.

The little-known Lecrín Valley is a delight of orange groves and hillside villages.

Dúrcal
This village of Moorish origin has a charming main square.

Nigüelas
Nigüelas is one of the prettiest settlements in the Sierra Nevada. The town hall is in the 16C Palacio de los Zayas. The 14C **Las Laerillas oil mill**★ contains presses, instruments, olive bins and,two large mills. *Visits by prior arrangement.* ☎958 77 76 07 (town hall).

Mondújar
The Mudéjar-style church has an impressive tower. The road continues along the Torrente river valley, skirting Murchas, Restábal, **Melegís** and **Saleres**. The churches in Melegís and Saleres have retained Mudéjar *azulejos* on their towers.

PARQUE NATURAL DE LA SIERRA NORTE DE SEVILLA

This park covers 164 840ha/407 320 acres of outstanding natural beauty in the Sierra Morena north of Sevilla. Along its rivers – the Viar, Huéznar and Retortillo – lush vegetation includes cork oak, horse chestnut, elm, holm oak and hazel. Fauna include wild boar, harrier eagles and tawny vultures.

- **Information:** Constantina (*see Address Book*). ☎955 88 15 97. www.sierranortedesevilla.com.
- **Orient Yourself:** The park is in the north of Sevilla province.
- **Don't Miss:** Visiting the Centro de Información del Parque in Constantina. Here you will find information about trails and activities in the park.
- **Organising Your Time:** Allow a day for the driving tour through the park.
- **Especially for Kids:** The many watersports available – ask at the information centre.
- **Also See:** SEVILLA, CARMON, Parque Natural SIERRA DE ARACENA Y PICOS DE AROCHE.

Driving Tour

From Lora del Río to Guadalcanal

90km/56mi – allow one day

Lora del Río

Situated on the Guadalquivir, at the base of the Sierra Morena foothills (just outside the park, in fact) Lora is peaceful and steeped in tradition. Its neatly maintained streets and buildings lend it a slightly solemn air.

Local delicacies include snails (*caracoles*), *sopeaos* (a variant of gazpacho), and *gachas con coscurros*, a flour-based pureé sprinkled with breadcrumbs fried in olive oil.

Iglesia de la Asunción

This 15C Mudéjar-Gothic church has undergone considerable restoration. Its 19C bell tower is one of the tallest in Sevilla province.

Ayuntamiento

The 18C Baroque town hall has a magnificent floral **façade**.

Casa de los Leones

This fine example of Baroque civil architecture has an impressive façade and an elegant patio.

Casa de la Virgen

The doorway of this unusual late-18C palace is embellished with elegant marble columns.

Santuario de Nuestra Señora de Setefilla

This handsome isolated Mudéjar sanctuary, in the mountains outside Lora del Río, was rebuilt in the 17C. Its statue of the Virgin of Setefilla is venerated in a lively pilgrimage every 8 September.

Constantina

29km/18mi north along the A 455.

The town, surrounded by delightful forests and streams of crystal-clear water, is named for Roman emperor Constantine. Its centre is a mix of Moorish and distinctive 15C–17C noble edifices.

Barrio de la Morería★

The Moorish quarter sits at the foot of the old fortress above Constantina.

Cep Mushrooms

The area around Constantina is a paradise for mushroom-lovers. During the autumn, the town is inundated by visitors who come here to pick them or simply to enjoy them in one of Constantina's many bars and restaurants.

Address Book

For coin ranges, see the Legend on the cover flap.

WHERE TO STAY

San Blas – *Miraflores, 4. Constantina.* ☎955 88 00 77. *www.fp-hoteles.com. 15 rooms.* Featureless from the exterior, but with large, smart, modern rooms, and a small swimming pool on the terrace.

Posada del Moro – *Paseo del Moro. Cazalla de la Sierra.* ☎954 88 48 58. *www.laposadadelmoro. com. 31 rooms.* A beautiful very atmospheric Moorish-style family-run hotel with fountains, a high-quality restaurant and a garden with swimming pool. Excellent value.

Las Navezuelas – *Cazalla de la Sierra. 2km/1.2mi from the centre of Cazalla towards El Pedroso* ☎954 88 47 64. www.lasnavezuelas.com. *6 rooms, 2 suites, 3 apartments.* An attractive old olive oil mill from the 18C. The guest rooms are tastefully decorated, while the swimming pool offers a magnificent view of the Sierra Morena. A secluded and bucolic setting. A set dinner menu is available to guests.

SIGHTSEEING

The **Centro de Información del Parque** in Constantina has plans, maps and other documentation on activities in the park. *Open Jan–Mar and Oct–Dec Fri–Sun and public hols 10am–2pm and 6–8pm. Apr–Sept Fri–Sun and public hols 10am–2pm and 4–6pm. Also open Thu 10am–2pm, Jan–15 Jun and 15 Oct–Dec.* ☎955 88 15 97.

Steep, winding alleyways lined by whitewashed houses and connected by flights of steps preserve the enchantment and flavour of an Arab district.

Two churches are worthy of note. The impressive **Iglesia de la Encarnación** is an elegant Mudéjar construction with handsome Plateresque façade. Outstanding stone decorative motifs on its portal (Puerta del Pardón) incude a delicate sculpture of the archangel Gabriel. The **Iglesia de Nuestra Señora de los Dolores** preserves notable Renaissance cloisters and an interesting Baroque retable at the high altar.

Ermita de El Robledo

5km/3mi NE of Constantina along the SE 156.
Open Mar–Sept daily 9am–9pm. Oct–Feb daily 10am–7pm. ☎955 95 41 14. This isolated white Mudéjar chapel houses a statue of the Virgin of the Oak Wood.

El Pedroso

18km/11mi west of Constantina along the A 452.
Sited in a landscape of outstanding beauty, El Pedrosos has two impressive religious buildings: the church of Nuestra Señora de la Consolación and the Ermita de La Virgen del Espino. The nearby hills of Monteagudo and La Lima offer **views** of the sierra.

Cazalla de la Sierra

17km/10.5mi north along the A 455.
This delightful town is hidden in the heart of the Sierra Morena amid holm and cork oak forests. The centre is characterised by picturesque streets fronted by attractive seigniorial houses with elegant stone façades. The town is renowned for its brandies.

Plaza Mayor

This large square, the hub of Cazalla, is bordered by a singular array of 16C popular Andalusian architecture. Also note the fine Baroque façade of the courts (*Juzgado*) and the 14C **Iglesia de Nuestra Señora de la Consolación**, its red-brick Mudéjar tower adorned with pointed and trefoil arch windows. The church interior is a mass of pillars, topped by coffered Renaissance vaults.

Convento de San Francisco

The notable Baroque cloisters have slender columns supporting semicircular arches.

Ruinas de la Cartuja
3km/1.82mi north of Cazalla.
🕐 *Open daily 10am–2pm and 4–8pm.*
€3. ☎954 88 45 16.
The monumental ruins of this former 15C Carthusian monastery are in an attractive leafy woodland. The Mudéjar paintings in the cloisters are of particular note. The former monk-gatekeeper's lodge is now a small hotel.

Alanís
17km/10.5mi north of Cazalla along the A 432.
Alanís stands in a near-impregnable mountain area, at the foot of a medieval castle.

The Casa de Doña Matilde Guitart has an elegant two-storey patio. The **Iglesia de Nuestra Señora de las Nieves**, originally a Gothic church, was rebuilt in neo-Classical style. The vault above the high altar is decorated with attractive frescoes. Exceptional Mudéjar **azulejos** are on view in the 16C Capilla de los Melgarejo.

Guadalcanal
11km/7mi northwest along the A 432.
This old fortified settlement retains interesting vestiges of its medieval walls. Its outstanding architectural features are the Iglesia de la Asunción, built above a mosque, and the Ermita de Guaditoca.

TABERNAS
POPULATION 3 241

Tabernas stands in the Almerían desert, in a near-lunar landscape of eroded hills, not unlike the American West. In the 1960s and 1970s, it provided the backdrop for a number of spaghetti westerns.

- **Information:** Highway N-340, Km 364. ☎950 52 50 30. www.porlibre.com/ANDALUCIA/tabernas.htm.
- ▶ **Orient Yourself:** Tabernas is 29km/18mi north of Almería.
- 🕐 **Organising Your Time:** Allow half a day to include the theme park.
- **Especially for Kids:** Oasys Theme Park. Going underground at Cuevas de Sorbas.
- **Also See:** ALMERÍA, Sierra de los FILABRES, COSTA DE ALMERÍA.

Visit

Tabernas is crowned by the partially restored ruins of its fortress (*access via a track next to the sports centre*), best viewed from the A 340a to the east. Like many of the religious buildings in the area, the parish church, on a pleasant shady square, is built of brick. It has two simple Renaissance portals.

Oasys Parque Tématico (Mini Hollywood)
5km/3mi SW on the A 370-N340A.
🕐 *Open 10am–9pm. €17 child €9.*
☎950 36 52 36. www.minihollywood.es.
This unusual complex is part zoo and also touches on bio-biodiversity themes, but almost everyone visits to see Spain's very own Wild West, which includes the old "Mini-Hollywood" set where *A Fist-*

The Tabernas Desert

The town's location between two ranges of mountains produces the so-called "orographic shadow" phenomenon, which explains the sparse rainfall in the area. As a result, the vegetation and fauna found in this part of Andalucía are adapted to conditions of extreme aridity. In general, flora, such as the hardy everlasting or curry plant, is small in size, while the local fauna mainly consists of insects, toads, scorpions and hedgehogs.

B. Kaufmann / MICHELIN

Spain's American West

ful of Dollars was filmed. As you walk the dusty streets past the saloon and bank you'll be transported to another era (and continent) against a backdrop of bare rocky mountains. Brawls and shoot-outs in the best traditions of the Wild West are staged and there is a film museum. Almost as an incongruous add-on the zoo includes 150 species of animals including giraffes, bears, hippo, elephants and kangaroos

Other old Western film sets can also be seen along the A 370.

Driving Tour

From Tabernas to Los Molinos del Río Aguas

41km/25.5mi.

▶ *Head east along the A 370-N340A. Bear right after 17km/10.5mi.*

Lucainrena de las Torres

This former mining town is on the eastern edge of the Sierra de la Alhamilla. Its main attractions are its white streets, 18C parish church, a square with a centenary tree, and, on the outskirts, old iron-smelting furnaces. The **Mesón Museo**, displays works by local artists and traditional farming implements, and offers regional cuisine.

▶ *Return to the A 370 and continue 9km/5.5mi farther.*

Sorbas

Sorbas is an attractive town on a clay escarpment encircled by a meander in the River Aguas. The best view of its picturesque **setting**★ is from Los Molinos del Río Aguas. Its cliff-clinging houses have made Sorbas known as "Little Cuenca", after the town of Cuenca in the region of Castilla-La Mancha.

Plaza de la Constitución

The hub of Sorbas, the plaza de la Constitución is fronted by the 16C Iglesia de Santa María, the town hall, the house of Francisco García Roca (both buildings are from the 19C), and the 18C Palace of the Duke of Alba The town has several **miradors** overlooking the river and plain beyond. The houses built above the ravine are particularly impressive.

Local Arts and Crafts

Sorbas still maintains its tradition of pottery-making. It is particularly famous for its red ceramic earthenware, which is mainly used for cooking, due to its resistance to heat. Workshops producing this pottery can still be visited in the lower section of the town.

Paraje Natural de Karst en Yesos

On the AL 8203 towards Los Molinos del Río Aguas. Visit www.porlibre.com/ANDALUCIA/sorbas.htm.

This reserve of thousands of limestone caves, formed by erosion of gypsum, is a must for adventure-seekers. Torch, helmet, outer clothing and boots are all available on site. A tour of the **Cuevas de Sorbas** (Kids ○ *call for opening times and days;* ☎ *€12, child €8;* ☎ *950 364 704, www.cuevasdesorbas.com)* led by specialist guides, involving climbs, descents and sometimes even crawling on all fours, enables visitors to see how gypsum crystallises into spectacular formations.

Molinos del Río Aguas

5km/3mi southeast of Sorbas along the A 8203.

Past the village, the road climbs to offer attractive views of the valley.

Several foreign families settled here in the 1960s and 1970s to develop solar cooking, water purification, and organic farming for desertic areas.

🚶 Pleasant walks along marked paths *(max 2hr)* provide an opportunity to see Roman irrigation ditches, the remains of flour mills and local gypsum furnaces.

TARIFA

POPULATION 15 118

Tarifa is the most southerly town on the Iberian Peninsula, on the **Straits of Gibraltar** just 13km/8mi from the North African coast. Converging Atlantic and Mediterranean air masses and unspoilt beaches nearby have made it one of Europe's most important windsurfing and kitesurfing centres. Its charming little old town, popular with an alternative crowd, exudes tranquillity and well-being with its small squares and enchanting nooks and crannies.

- 🛈 **Information:** Paseo de la Alameda. ☎956 68 09 93. www.aytotarifa.com.
- ▶ **Orient Yourself:** Tarifa is 21km/13mi southwest of Gibraltar.
- 👁 **Don't Miss:** The old quarter. The views of Africa from the Mirador del Estrecho. Whale and dolphin watching.
- ○ **Organising Your Time:** Allow a day for Tarifa.
- Kids **Especially for Kids:** Whale and dolphin watching and the beaches (but beware the wind!)
- ⌚ **Also See:** ALGECIRAS, GIBRALTAR, VEJER DE LA FRONTERA.

Walking Tour

Enter the old quarter by the particularly impressive **Puerta de Jerez**.

Castillo de Guzmán el Bueno

⊶ *Closed for restoration.*
☎956 68 46 89.

Abd ar-Rahman III, first Moorish governor to adopt the title of Caliph, realised the strategic importance of the Straits of Gibraltar, which led him to capture the African strongholds of Ceuta and Melilla across the water. He started construction of Tarifa's fortress in 960. The castle visible today is the result of later modifications by both Moors and Christians. Access is via the 13C **Almohad wall** (*coracha*); to the right, note the **Torre de Guzmán el Bueno**, a 13C turret, from which the Christian commander Don Enrique de Guzmán is said to have thrown down his dagger to besieging Moorish troops to execute his captured son rather than hand over the castle. Access is through a 14C angled doorway. A 14C church, the Iglesia de Santa María, stands within the walls.

- ▶ *Leave the castle and walk along calle Guzmán el Bueno to Plaza Santa María.*

Windsurfing in Tarifa

Plaza Santa María

Alongside this small square are the **town hall** and the Museo Municipal. An attractive *azulejo*-decorated fountain stands in the centre.

▶ *Follow calle de la Amargura to plaza del Viento.*

The **views**★★ of Africa across the Straits from the Mirador del Estrecho are superb.

Iglesia Mayor Parroquial de San Mateo Apóstol

The parish church of St Matthew the Apostle was built in the early 16C in Flamboyant Gothic style. The main façade was completed in the 18C. In the surprisingly spacious interior, the central nave is crowned by a star vault, the side aisles by groin vaulting.

In plaza de Oviedo, opposite the church, are numerous cafés and bars.

Iglesia de San Francisco

The Church of St Francis is on the plaza del Ángel. The Baroque **tower-façade**★ consists of a large Franciscan cordon on two columns with Corinthian capitals. The small cove next to Tarifa's port is known as **Playa Chica** (small beach). On the other side of Isla de las Palomas is a spectacular beach, Kids **Playa de los Lances**★. Opposite, atop Santa Catalina Hill, note the unusual building dating from the early 20C.

Excursions

The road from Tarifa to Punta Paloma

Follow the N 340 towards Cádiz.

This short stretch parallels the sea (**Playa de los Lances**), separated by a copse of pines. Campsites and hotels line the road, and it is possible to pull over for a swim.

Enter the Moors

The origins of the name Tarifa date from the time of the Moorish invasions when the Berber general **Tarif ibn Malluk** is said to have landed here in July 710 with 400 men. This incursion, the first Moorish expedition to set foot on the Iberian Peninsula, has spawned a number of legends. The reasons behind the invasion would appear to lie in a dispute between the Visigothic king, **Roderick**, and the descendants of the former king **Witiza**. Seeing the weakness of the Visigoths, the Moors, "invited" by the Witiza faction, disregarded the pacts they had made with them and embarked upon the conquest of the whole peninsula.

Address Book

For coin ranges, see the Legend on the cover flap.

WHERE TO STAY

Aparthotel La Casa Amarilla – Sancho IV el Bravo, 9. ☎956 68 19 93. www.lacasaamarilla.net. 8 apartments, 3 studios. This old house in the centre is next to the Iglesia Mayor de San Mateo. Apartments are all different and tastefully decorated. The proprietors also own the nearby **Café Central**, which is particularly lively in the evening.

Hotel La Codorniz – 6.5km/4mi NW along the Cádiz road. ☎956 68 47 44. www.lacodorniz.com. 35 rooms. An attractive bungalow complex with a swimming pool and a restaurant which specialises in seafood and boasts an ample wine cellar.

WHERE TO EAT

Mesón Juan Luis – San Francisco, 15. ☎956 68 12 65. Closed Sun. A small restaurant in an old building on a pedestrianised street with an almost exclusive and surprisingly large pork-based menu. The Rincón de Juan on the same street is also worth considering.

SIGHTSEEING

IN THE STRAITS OF GIBRALTAR

Whale- and dolphin-watching boat tours★★ are very popular. Reservations are necessary for both companies:

Turmares Tarifa – Av. Alcalde Juan Nuñez, 3. ☎956 68 07 41. www.turmares.com. €25/40. A boat for larger groups provides underwater viewing; a smaller, faster boat provides more thrills.

Whale Watch – Av. de la Constitución. ☎956 627 013. www.whalewatchtarifa.net. Closed Nov–Mar. €25/42, child €18/30. This whale-protection group organises sightings of whales, dolphins and orcas, according to the season.

After 4km/2.5mi, a road to the right leads to the **Santuario de Nuestra Señora de la Luz**, named for Tarifa's patron saint. Two beaches, **Playa de Valdevaqueros**★ and the **Playa de Punta Paloma**, an impressive series of sand dunes, are a little farther along.

Ruinas Romanas de Baelo Claudia★

22.5km/14mi NW. Open Tue–Sat 10am–8pm (6pm Nov–Feb; 7pm Mar–May). Sun and public hols 10am–2pm €1.50 (free to EU citizens). ☎956 68 85 30.

The Roman city of Baelo Claudia was founded in the 2C BC as a salting factory (see Box below).

Emperor Claudius granted it the title of municipality in the 1C AD and the remains visible today date mostly from this period.

Baelo was a walled city, accessed through large gateway and sections of the wall remain.

Garum

Since time immemorial, the Cádiz coast has been one of the main areas for tuna fishing in the whole of Spain. Phoenicians and Romans alike took advantage of the movements of shoals of tuna to the Mediterranean during the spawning months of May and June. The technique used by the Romans, and still used in Cádiz province today, is known as the **almadraba**. Many of the Roman cities along the Andalusian coast, such as Baelo, were originally outposts whose primary function was the salting of fish. Once the tuna had been cut into sections, they were placed in large silos and covered with a layer of salt, where they would remain for several months before being transported throughout the Empire in a special type of amphora. The best-known and most expensive product from this industry was without doubt **garum**, a sauce produced from the head, entrails, blood and other remains of fish, and used as a condiment or even a main dish to which oil or vinegar would then be added.

ÚBEDA★★

POPULATION 32 524

Úbeda is a town of gracious monuments, widely renowned as one of Andalucía's architectural treasure houses, celebrated by illustrious travellers and recently designated as a World Heritage Site. Úbeda has a great cultural tradition as well – visitors come to see its austere palaces, its elegant squares, and the fine detail where Andalusian art reached its zenith. The Moorish quarter, the barrio de San Millán, delightfully contrasts the town's 16C masterpieces with its maze of narrow streets.

It was home to writer Antonio Muñoz Molina and singer Joaquín Sabina. Antonio Machado called it "a queen and gypsy"; Eugenio d'Ors compared Úbeda to the most beautiful cities in northern Italy.

- **Information:** Plaza Baja del Marqués, 4 (Palacio del Marqués de Contadero), ☏953 75 08 97. www.andalucia.org. www.ubedainteresa.com.
- **Orient Yourself:** Úbeda stands in a plain set with olive groves at the centre of the province of Jaén between the Guadalquivir and Guadalimar Valleys. The town is linked with Jaén, 57km/36mi southwest via the A 316, and Córdoba, 146km/91mi west, via the N 322 and A 4–E 5.
- **Don't Miss:** Plaza Vázquez de Molina.
- **Organising Your Time:** Allow at least a day.
- **Also See:** BAEZA, JAÉN, LINARES, CAZORLA, SEGURA Y LAS VILLA, Parque Natural de las SIERRAS DE CAZORLA.

A Bit of History

Although its origins are Roman, it was the Moors who founded Ubbadat Al Arab, one of the major cities in Al-Andalus. In 1234, Fernando III (the Saint) reconquered the city. In the 16C, during the reigns of Charles V and Felipe II, Úbeda enjoyed its greatest splendour. Its citizens held important positions in the Empire, magnificent Renaissance buildings were erected, and members of the nobility took up residence.

Walking Tours

Old Town★★

Allow one day

Plaza Vázquez de Molina★★

This magnificent square, the monumental centre of Úbeda, is at the heart of the old quarter whose sumptuous buildings and delightful streets transport visitors to another era. It is lined by impressive buildings, including the Capilla del Salvador, Palacio de las Cadenas, Iglesia de Santa María de los Alcázares and the Casa del Deán Ortega, now a *parador* (*see Address Book*). Other buildings worthy of note include: the former granary (*pósito*); the **Cárcel del Obispo** (Bishop's Prison), so called as it was here that nuns were obliged to suffer the canonical punishments imposed by the bishop; the **Palacio del Marqués de Mancera**, the Renaissance façade of which is crowned by a quadrangular tower; and the **Casa del Regidor**.

Palacio de las Cadenas★

Open daily 8am–1pm and 3–9pm. ☏953 75 04 40.

This palace was built by Vandelvira in the middle of the 16C at the command of Don Juan Vázquez de Molina, nephew of Don Francisco de los Cobos, a leading political and cultural figure during the reigns of Carlos I and Felipe II. In 1566 it was adapted for use as a convent. It was subsequently a jail and became the town hall in 1868.

The name, Palace of the Chains, derives from the iron chains that once stretched across the entry. The **façade**★★, which

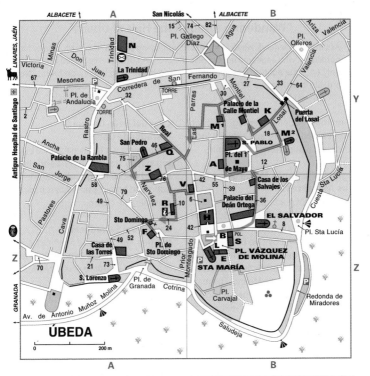

ÚBEDA

bears the family coat of arms, unusually combines decorative Andalusian features with the harmony of classical architectural orders. Note the alternating bays and pilasters which are replaced on the upper tier by caryatids and atlantes in which the influence of the French sculptor Jamete is clear. Two elegant lanterns on the ends add a lighter touch.

Inside is a delightful Renaissance patio with refined arcades and a central fountain. On the upper floor, embellished with a colourful *artesonado* ceiling, is the **Archivo Histórico Municipal** (municipal archive), whose windows afford lovely views of the plaza area. The basement holds the **Centro Municipal de Interpretación Turística**, (☎953 75 62 34, www.renacentalia.net) which

"Wandering through the Hills of Úbeda"

According to legend, when Fernando III was laying siege to the town, one of his noblemen, who appeared not to relish the prospect of battle, appeared at his side only once the fighting was over. When asked by the king the reason for his late arrival, he replied that he had got lost in the many hills around Úbeda.

illuminates Úbeda's heritage through models and panels, and exhibits local crafts such as pottery and ceramics.

Iglesia de Santa María de los Alcázares★
○━*Closed for restoration.*
This church was built in the 13C above the remains of a mosque. Its harmonious façade, crowned by two belfries, each with three large bells and a smaller one, is one of the most attractive features on the plaza Vázquez de Molina. The main doorway is the work of López de Alcaraz and Pedro del Cabo (17C). The Puerta de la Consolada, on the left-hand side (late 16C) is also outstanding.

The interior, badly damaged during the Spanish Civil War, contains several beautiful **chapels**★ adorned with sculptures and profuse decoration, in particular the Capilla de La Yedra and Capilla de los Becerra, both enclosed by impressive **grilles**★ designed by Master Bartolomé. Sculptures in the church include a *Fallen Christ* by Mariano Benlliure and *Christ of the Bullfighters*, from a nearby convent. The patio of the mosque was replaced in the 16C by handsome Renaissance **cloisters** of irregular shape with elegant pointed arches and groin vaulting.

Casa del Deán Ortega (Parador de Úbeda)
The *parador* is a 16C Renaissance building partly designed by Vandelvira. Behind the building's sober façade is a patio, and hotel (⑥ *see Address Book*), of considerable charm.

Capilla del Salvador★★
🕐*Open Apr–May and Sept–Oct 4.30–7pm. Jun–Aug 10am–2pm and 5–7.30pm. Nov–Mar 4–6.30pm.* ✆€3. ☎953 75 81 50.
Designed by Diego de Siloé in 1536 and built by Andrés de Vandelvira between 1540 and 1556, this chapel is one of the finest religious buildings of the Andalusian Renaissance. It was commissioned as a family pantheon by Don Francisco de los Cobos, secretary to Charles V, who, as a result of his vast fortune and artistic leanings, became a leading figure in 16C imperial Spain.

The main **façade** combines several ornamental motifs popular in Renaissance art: Christ's ascent to Mount Tabor appears above the door, while representations of St Peter and St Paul can be seen on both sides. The intrados of the inner arch bears reliefs depicting figures from Greek mythology, and the Cobos and Molina escutcheons.

Casa del Deán Ortega - Parador de Úbeda (left) and Capilla del Salvador (right)

Address Book

&For coin ranges, see the Legend on the cover flap.

WHERE TO STAY

◄Hostal Victoria – *Alaminos, 5.* ☎*953 75 29 52. 15 rooms*. Clean and reasonably priced are the words to describe this small, family-run hotel. Despite being on the basic side, the bedrooms are comfortable and well maintained.

◄◄◄Palacio de la Rambla – *Plaza del Marqués, 1.* ☎*953 75 01 96. www.palaciodelarambla.com. 8 rooms. Closed mid-Jul–mid-Aug.* This glorious 16C palace is now a splendid hotel where guests are treated like family friends in an atmosphere that is very refined yet relaxed. Its most impressive features are the magnificent Renaissance patio and life-size warrior figures.

◄◄◄Parador de Úbeda – *Plaza Vázquez Molina.* ☎*953 75 03 45. www.parador.es. 36 rooms*. The town's parador fronts one of Andalucía's finest Renaissance squares. The coat of arms of this 16C palace's first owner, Fernando Ortega Salido, is engraved on the façade. Lovely patio; impeccable rooms.

WHERE TO EAT

◄◄Mesón Gabino – *Fuente Seca.* ☎*953 75 75 53. www.mesongabino.com.* This attractive restaurant with a stone roof and ceiling is located within the walls of the fortress. Specialities here include grilled meats and regional dishes including *andrajos* (a stew) and partridge.

SHOPPING

In the **barrio de San Millán** local products such as hand-embroidered esparto matting, rugs, pottery, and lanterns made of tin and glass can be purchased.

LOCAL SPECIALITIES

Úbeda's artisan work is one of the highlights of a visit. Local ceramics, earthenware and wrought-iron are characteristic crafts

FESTIVALS

The nocturnal Semana Santa procession on Good Friday is known for its great solemnity.

The lavish **interior**★★ has a single nave, its vaulting outlined in blue and gold. The central part, intended for the tombs of Don Francisco de los Cobos and his wife, is separated from the remainder of the chapel by a monumental grille attributed to Villalpando. The presbytery, by Vandelvira, is a rotunda in which an immense 16C altarpiece includes a baldaquin with a sculpture of the Transfiguration by Alonso Berruguete; only the carving of Christ remains.

The **sacristy**★★, also by Vandelvira, is an architectural jewel, containing interesting decoration based on caissons, caryatids, atlantes and medallions, in which the stylistic influence of the Italian Renaissance is clear.

Note the harmonious south doorway and the impressive grille enclosing the nave, a work by two local artists.

Casa de los Salvajes

The 17C Renaissance House of the Savages – or Casa de Camarero Vago, for the steward (*camarero*) of Bishop Francisco de Yago who lived here – owes its unusual name to two figures in animal skins on the façade, supporting the bishop's coat of arms.

Plaza del Primero de Mayo

Popularly known as the plaza del Mercado (Market Square), this square was the setting for bullfights, autos-da-fés, outdoor fairs, executions and theatre

Calle Real

This attractive thoroughfare, one of the most elegant in Úbeda, provides visitors with an insight into the town's architectural splendour during the 16C, when Úbeda was at its economic and artistic peak. It is lined by monumental buildings, typical local shops and refined decorative detail. The residents of Úbeda are particularly proud of this street.

performances in days gone by. It is bordered by the former town hall and the Iglesia de San Pablo.

Antiguo Ayuntamiento

The 17C former town hall shows clear Palladian influence. A lower tier comprises an elegant porch with three semi-circular arches and paired columns. An upper register is in the style of a double loggia or porticoed gallery, from where the town's council presided over events in the square below.

Iglesia de San Pablo★

Open for worship only. Mon–Fri noon–1.30pm and 5–7pm. Sat, 12–1.30pm and 7–7.30pm.

The harmony of the main Gothic portal with Plateresque bell tower, contrasts with the south doorway (1511), featuring attractive Isabelline-style reliefs. On the southwest corner, to the left of the main façade, admire the Renaissance gallery. Two chapels stand out: the **Capilla de las Calaveras** (third on the right), with an impressive arch by Vandelvira, and the Isabelline **Capilla de las Mercedes**, enclosed by extraordinary **grilles★★** created in Úbeda. Note the highly imaginative scene of Adam and Eve.

Museo de San Juan de la Cruz

Open Tue–Sun 11am–12.45pm and 5–6.45pm. €1.20. 953 75 06 15.

The Museum of St John of the Cross is in the oratory of the same name – a Baroque room containing a sculpture of the saint. A guided visit through the monastery retraces the final days of this mystical poet who died in Úbeda.

Casa del Obispo Canastero

This former residence stands close to the **Puerta del Losal**, a 15C Mudéjar gateway that formed part of the town walls and provided access to the San Mil-

lán district. The Plateresque mansion is named after one of the numerous reliefs which decorate the façade, representing a bishop (*obispo*) holding a basket (*canasta*).

Palacio de la calle Montiel

This palace is a fine example of early Plateresque in Úbeda. The handsome façade is emblasoned with the poorly preserved coat of arms of its former owners, indicating that the residents supported the *comuneros* who rose against Carlos V in the early 16C.

Casa Mudéjar

The **Museo Arqueológico** (*open Wed–Sat 9am–8.30pm, Tue 2.30–8.30pm, Sun, 9am–2.30pm; €1.50 (free to citizens of the European Union); 953 77 94 32; www.juntadeandalucia.es/cultura/museos), housed in this restored 14C Mudéjar house, displays artifacts ranging from the Neolithic era to Moorish occupation, all from Úbeda and the surrounding area.

Palacio del Conde de Guadiana

Built in the early 17C, the Palace of the Count of Guadiana is crowned by a fine **tower★** with angular balconies divided by small columns and galleries on the third floor.

Iglesia de San Pedro

This church, sited on the tranquil square of San Pedro, retains its original Romanesque apse. Note the harmonious Renaissance façade and several Gothic chapels.

Real Monasterio de Santa Clara

This monastery is the oldest Christian church in Úbeda (1290), although it also includes later Renaissance and Gothic-Mudéjar features.

Convent Pastries

Delicious cakes and pastries such as *magdalenas* (madeleines), *tortas de aceite* (olive oil tarts), *pastas de té* biscuits and *roscos de ajonjolí* (sesame seed cakes), can be purchased from the Convento de las Carmelitas Descalzas and the Convento de Santa Clara respectively. They come with a seal of quality that has been developed with patience and care over the past 300 years.

Palacio de Vela de los Cobos

This palace was commissioned from Vandelvira by Don Francisco Vela de los Cobos, governor of Úbeda, in the mid-16C. Its Renaissance façade has an elegant arcaded gallery extending to the corners, where there are two unusual white columns.

Palacio del Marqués del Contadero

Although the façade of this palace dates from the late 18C, its Renaissance features bear witness to the enduring popularity of this style in Úbeda. The upper floor has a blunt-arched gallery.

Plaza de Santo Domingo

This pleasant square is bordered by two buildings of interest: the **Iglesia de Santo Domingo**, with its Plateresque façade, and the **Casa de los Morales**, (a replica of which has been built in the Poble Espanyol (Spanish Village) in Barcelona).

Outside the Old Town

Casa de las Torres

The mansion of High Constable Dávalos has a Plateresque façade flanked by monumental square towers, with finely sculpted reliefs and gargoyles on the cornice.

Iglesia de San Lorenzo

The main attraction of this church is the placement of its façade on the parapet of the old city walls, where it is supported by the barbican of the Puerta de Granada.

Palacio de la Rambla

This palace on one side of the elegant plaza del Marqués (now a hotel – *see Address Book*) includes two impressive life-size warrior figures supporting a coat of arms.

Iglesia de la Santísima Trinidad

The portal of this church, above which a sober, three-storey bell tower has been added, is one of the finest examples of Baroque decoration in Úbeda.

Palacio de los Bussianos

This late-16C Renaissance palace has an attractive staircase leading to a delightful gallery of pointed arches on the first floor.

Iglesia de San Nicolás

Although Gothic in style, the trumpet-shaped vault over the entrance was built by Vandelvira during the Renaissance period.

Antiguo Hospital de Santiago

Head out of town along calle Obispo Cobos.

Construction of this hospital was ordered by Don Diego de los Cobos, bishop of Jaén and a native of Úbeda. The façade, which is preceded by a large portico flanked by two towers, is a work of restrained size by Vandelvira. The only decorative features are the relief of St James the Moorslayer(*Santiago Matamoros*), above the doorway, and the glazed ceramic medallions on the cornice. A chapel houses an impressive wooden altarpiece. Note the double-arcaded **patio** and the elegant staircase under a coffered vault, the columns of which were carved from marble brought from Italy.

The hospital houses the **Museo de la Semana Santa**, dedicated to Holy Week celebrations. ◷*Open Mon–Fri 8am–10pm. Sat–Sun and public hols, 11am–2.30pm and 6–9.30pm.* ☏*953 75 08 42.*

Patio, Hospital de Santiago

G. Bludzin / MICHELIN

Excursions

Sabiote
9km/5.5mi northeast along the A 1202.
This peaceful old town has elegant houses and ancient narrow alleyways. Sabiote was the place of residence of Alonso de Vandelvira, who built mansions here for the Mendoza, Melgarejo and Higuera Sabater families.

Buildings of interest include the 15C **Iglesia de San Pedro Apóstol**, a monumental Gothic church, and the **castle** outside the walls, once a Moorish fortress, restored by Vandelvira.

Torreperogil
10km/6mi east along the N 322.
Torreperogil is a charming small town with a maze of medieval streets. Its church, the Iglesia de la Asunción, has a handsome double-entrance portal with central column. A stone retable depicts the Deposition.

Villacarrillo
32km/20mi northeast along the N 322.
This agricultural and industrial centre is one of the oldest settlements in the province, dating to the Bronze Age.

Iglesia de la Asunción
🕑*Open daily 7.30–9pm.*
If closed, ask next door for the key.
Another 16C work by Vandelvira, the church was erected on the foundation of an earlier castle, from which three monumental towers have survived. The ground plan consists of three aisles and side chapels covered with sober groined vaulting.

Casa de la Inquisición
Associated with the feared Spanish Inquisition during the Middle Ages, this monumental three-storey building has a number of fine features, including several attractive wrought-iron balconies on the façade

UTRERA ★
POPULATION: 45 947.

Utrera sits on a rise at the heart of the Sevillian countryside, amid eucalyptus groves and cultivated land. Although of Roman origin, it developed only in the 16C, then ground to a halt with an epidemic in the middle of the 17C, as a result of which is an intact historical centre with many outstanding monuments.

- **Information:** Rodrigo Caro, 3. ☎955 86 09 31.
- ▶ **Orient Yourself:** Utrera is 33km/21mi southeast of Sevilla.
- 🕑 **Organising Your Time:** Allow a couple of hours.
- ♿ **Also See:** SEVILLA, MARCHENA, OSUNA.

Sights

Castle
This fortress of Almohad origin was part of the defensive walls. Today, only a few sections and an arch, the Arco de la Villa – to which an upper, chapel-like section was added in the 18C – remain. An impressive keep and parade ground lie within.

Iglesia de Santa María de la Asunción (de la Mesa)★
This Gothic church with additional Renaissance and Baroque features dominates a charming square. The handsome façade centres on a large splayed arch, above which rises a graceful Baroque tower.

Outstanding features include **choir stalls** by Duque Cornejo (1744), the main altarpiece and the sepulchre of the Count of Arcos.

Iglesia de Santiago
This triple-nave Gothic church dates from the 15C. Its severe, defensive look contrasts with the ostentatious Isabelline-Gothic decor of the **Puerta del Perdón** gateway.

Plaza del Altozano★

This elegant square at the heart of Utrera is framed by an attractive three-storey 17C and 18C mansions with pitched roofs and delicate unbroken balconies.

Ayuntamiento

The town hall, an 18C mansion on elegant plaza de Gibaxa, has a magnificent Rococo façade and period rooms. Note the furniture in the Salón Azul (Blue Room).

Casa Surga

This late-18C mansion has a charming Baroque façade and rooms in period decor.

Iglesia de San Francisco

🕐Open Mon–Sat 7–8.30pm.
☎955 86 09 31.

This 17C late-Renaissance church has a large cupola adorned with paintings.

Santuario de Nuestra Señora de la Consolación★

Avenida de Juan XXIII. 🕐Open 9am–2pm and 4–6.30pm. ☎954 86 03 30.

This outstanding 17C and 18C Mudéjar-style sanctuary occupies a former Franciscan monastery. The impressive Baroque façade and the delicate *artesonado* work in the sanctuary are particularly noteworthy. On 8 September a popular pilgrimage (*romería*) is held in honour of the Virgin of Solace (*Consolación*).

Excursion

El Palmar de Troya

13km/8mi south along the A 394.
The heretical Order of the Carmelites of the Holy Face, founded by the controversial priest Clemente Rodríguez (1946–2005), who proclaimed himself Pope in 1978, is headquartered here. The enormous church holds statues of venerated saints, presided over by a sculpture of Our Crowned Lady of El Palmar. In the afternoon, Mass is held in Latin in accordance with the liturgy in use before the Second Vatican Council.

Women must cover their heads, wrists and necks and wear skirts that come "at least four fingers below the knee." Trousers for women are forbidden. A female follower of the church stands at the entrance to checks women's skirts for transparency.

VEJER DE LA FRONTERA★

POPULATION: 12 731

Vejer de la Frontera perches prettily on a rocky crag dominating the valley of the River Barbate, just a few kilometres from the Atlantic coast. One of Andalucía's most picturesque *pueblos blancos*, it has very strong Moorish roots, reflected in its maze of narrow, cobbled streets and whitewashed houses, enclosing verdant patios and crowned by flat terraced roofs.

- **Information:** Avenida de los Remedios, 2, Vejer de la Frontera. ☎956 45 17 36. Plaza de la Constitución, 1.Conil de la Frontera. ☎956 44 03 06. www.turismovejer.com. www.infovejer.com.
- **Orient Yourself:** Vejer de la Frontera is 51km/32mi southeast of Cádiz and 50km/31mi northwest of Tarifa. It is linked to both towns via N 340-E 5 coastal route. Guided tours (1hr 30min) of the town's major sights depart from the tourist office: ☞€3.
- **Don't Miss:** Playa de los Caños de Meca.
- **Organising Your Time:** Allow two hours for Vejer, more for the beach.
- **Especially for Kids:** Cove beaches and La Breña park are great for small swimmers.
- **Also See:** TARIFA, MEDINA SIDONIA, CÁDIZ.

Village of Vejer de la Frontera

H. Champollion/MICHELIN

Visit

Walls

Four 15C gateways in walls built to protect against Nasrid attacks survive to this day. The **Arco de la Segur**, a basket-handle arch, is the entrance to Vejer's old quarter.

Iglesia Parroquial del Divino Salvador

Open daily 11am–1.30pm and 7.30–9pm (15 Apr–Oct, 8.30–10pm). ☎956 45 17 36.

Vejer's parish church retains the minaret from the mosque that preceded it. The three-aisle **interior**★ manifests an odd mixture of styles. The oldest part of the church is the apsidal end, which combines Romanesque and Gothic features.

Convento de las Concepcionistas

This 17C convent with a sober Classical façade, sits in one of Vejer's most charming corners, beside the **Arco de las Monjas**. It is used for cultural programmes.

Castle

The castle may be in a poor state of repair, but it is worth the trip for its views. Access is via what looks like an ordinary neighbourhood patio .

Casa del Mayorazgo

Private house. This 17C Baroque residence with a simple façade backs onto the town walls. It is possible to climb one of the defensive towers from inside the building.

▶ *Arco de la Villa leads to plaza de España.*

Plaza de España

Also known as plaza de los Pescaítos, after the fish decorating its fountain, this square is of the liveliest and most attractive in town. It is surrounded by palm trees, several whitewashed houses and the town hall, and has colonial air to it.

Excursions

The coastal towns between **Chiclana** and **Zahara de los Atunes** are not Andalucía's most attractive, but the beaches are some of the area's best.

Conil de la Frontera

15.5km/9.5mi northwest.

Like its neighbours along the Cádiz coast, Conil is a tranquil town where life almost comes to a standstill in winter. But in summer it is transformed into a lively resort, whose main attractions are 14km/8.5mi of beach and low-key tourism. In the oldest section, between the sea and the **Puerta de Conil,** is an 18C colonial-style former church, the **Iglesia de la Misericordia**, now a school. A heavily restored tower, the **Torre de los Guzmanes**, is all that remains from the castle (*open mid-Jun to mid-Sept*

The "Cobijado"

This name was given to the traditional garment worn by the women of Vejer up until the Spanish Civil War. Although its origins are uncertain, this simple black headdress is also worn in a number of towns and villages in North Africa.

It is traditionally worn during the **Velada de Agosto**, a festival held in honour of the **Virgin of the Olive**, the town's patron saint, between 10 and 24 August every year.

The Battle of Trafalgar

On 21 October 1805, Admiral de Villeneuve's Franco-Spanish fleet confronted the British, commanded by Nelson, off Cape Trafalgar, 14km/9mi from Vejer de la Frontera. After an heroic combat, in which Nelson and the Spanish admirals Gravina and Churruca were all mortally wounded, Villeneuve's fleet was destroyed. The battle sounded the death-knell for Napoleon's hopes of defeating the British, who emerged as the dominant naval superpower.

10.30am–2pm and 6–9pm; rest of the year 9am–2pm; ☎956 44 05 00) in plaza de Santa Catalina.

Also bordering the square are a chapel, the Capilla de Jesús, and the **Museo de Raíces Conileñas** (☼open Jul–Sept Tue–Sat 11am–2pm and 8.30–11.30pm; Sun and public hols, 11am–2pm; ⊚ €1, no charge Sun; ☎956 44 05 01) with displays on local life and traditions.

Beaches
Kids
The beaches north, towards the port, tend be of the cove variety, such as the **Cala del Aceite**, while long, windy beaches—**Playa de la Fontanilla** and **Playa de los Bateles**—are to the south. **El Palmar**, considered to be the best-beach in the area, is a few kilometres farther.

Barbate
10km/6mi south.
Barbate is a fishing port with a tuna industry, and bars and restaurants renowned for fish and seafood.

Parque Natural La Breña and Marismas de Barbate★
Access from Vejer along the A 5206 or from Barbate.
The main attractions of this nature reserve are its lovely coves, nestled between rocky cliffs, and beaches, bordered by umbrella pines. The best-known beach is the **Playa de los Caños de Meca★★**.

Tuna Fishing

The technique used locally to catch tuna, known as almadraba, derives from the Arabic word al-madraba. It involves a complex labyrinth of vertical nets, some of which reach lengths of several kilometres, which lead the tuna to a circular area of permanent or temporary netting. Tuna migrate through this part of the coast twice a year: on their way to the spawning grounds in the Mediterranean in spring, and upon their return to the Atlantic in the autumn.

Address Book

ⓒFor coin ranges, see the Legend on the cover flap.

WHERE TO STAY
⊝ **Hostal La Posada** – Los Remedios, 21. ☎956 45 02 58. 6 rooms, 6 apartments. A family-run hotel with pleasant rooms, three with wonderful views of the valley. La Posada also has a number of apartments for rent (⊝⊝), some with a terrace.

⊝⊝ **Hotel Convento de San Francisco** – La Plazuela. ☎956 45 10 01. 25 rooms. Restaurant (⊝⊝⊜). This former Poor Clares convent dating from the 17C is in Vejer's old quarter.

Rooms are soberly decorated and cosy, with high ceilings and exposed beams. The restaurant, El Refectorio, has good food.

WHERE TO EAT
⊝⊝ **Trafalgar** – Plaza de España, 31. ☎956 44 76 38. Closed Jan–mid-Feb, Sun eve and Mon (except Jun–Sept). This welcome culinary surprise specialises in delicious fresh fish in minimalist and rustic dining rooms. Tapas are also served at the entrance. Guests can dine on the terrace in summer.

Zahara de los Atunes

20km/12mi southeast.

This small fishing community (de los Atunes translates as "of the tunas") has some of the longest and most unspoilt beaches on the Costa de la Luz. The town was controlled from the 15C on by the Dukes of Medina Sidonia, who exploited the tuna industry. The dukes lost their domain in the 19C, by which time Zahara had been reduced to a village. A few ruins remain from its 15C castle. Today, the town lives mainly off fishing and tourism.

VÉLEZ BLANCO

POPULATION: 2 190

In the foothills of the Sierra de María, Vélez Blanco's whitewashed houses extend across a hillside below a majestic Renaissance castle. It and nearby Vélez Rubio are linked with the Marquess of Vélez, a title bestowed upon Don Pedro Fajardo y Chacón by the Catholic Monarchs in 1506. Numerous archaeological remains include such significant sites as the Cueva de los Letreros, a cave containing rock paintings.

- **Information:** Visitor Centre Almacén del Trigo/Centro de Visitantes del Parque Natural de Santa María, Avda Marqués de los Vèlez. ☏ 950 41 56 51.
- ▶ **Orient Yourself:** Vélez Blanco is 172km/107mi northeast of Almería and 121km/75mi southwest of Murcía.
- **Don't Miss:** The Cueva de los Letreros.
- **Organising Your Time:** Spend hours in town, or days in the nature park.
- **Also See:** BAZA, Sierra de los FILABRES.

Visit

Castle★

Open daily 11am–1.30pm and 4–6pm. ☏ 950 41 50 01 (town hall).

Construction of this impressive 16C fortress was ordered by the first Marquess of Vélez, who commissioned Italian artists for the project. Sadly, its charming Renaissance marble patio was sold to a French antique dealer, and ended up at the Metropolitan Museum in New York, where it is now displayed.

The castle is no traditional fortress, as shown by its large miradors which offer superb views, and the numerous wall openings in its lofty walls. The Salón del Triunfo and the Salón de la Mitología originally contained wooden friezes depicting Caesar's triumph and the labours of Hercules. These are now in the Musée des Arts Décoratifs in Paris.

Centro de visitantes del Parque Natural de la Sierra de María

Housed in a converted grain storehouse, (see Information) the visitor centre is a sight in itself.

Churches

The town has two churches of interest. The 16C Iglesia de Santiago has fine Mudéjar *artesonado* work.

The church of the Convento de San Luis bears the coat of arms of the Marquisate of Vélez, and has a large number of fountains.

Excursions

Vélez Rubio

6km/3.5mi south.

Vélez Rubio extends across a small plain below the towers and dome of its parish church. Its two main streets, carrera del Carmen and carrera del Mercado, are lined with mansions, the Baroque church of the Convento de la Inmaculada, and the 17C Iglesia del Carmen.

Vélez Blanco

Parroquia de la Encarnación★

🕐*Open Tue–Sun 5–8pm.*

Construction of this magnificent parish church was ordered by the 10th Marquess of Vélez in the 18C. In such a small settlement, its monumental proportions come as something of a surprise. Two bell towers flank the richly decorated Baroque stone **portal**★, sectioned by pilasters and architraves. Note the coat of arms and a fine relief of the Annunciation. The main altarpiece and organ, both made of wood, stand out. A St Antony of Padua, by Salzillo, dominates the altarpiece in the Capilla de la Encarnación.

The town hall, built as an 18C seigniorial residence, fronts the same square.

Museo Comarcal Velezano

🕐*Open Tue–Sun 10.30am–2pm and 5–8pm.* ☎950 41 25 60.

This museum, devoted to local traditions, is housed in the former 18C Royal Hospital. It displays archaeological items from nearby, southeast Andalucía and even the Sahara.

Cueva de los Letreros★

3km/1.8mi north via the A 317, kiosk opposite petrol station.

Visit by guided tour only, Jul–Sept daily noon and 6pm, Oct–Jun daily noon and 4pm. €3.

The cave boasts vibrant red and brown sketches of human figures, birds, animals, astronomical signs and "indalos" (see Box) which have been dated to around 4000 BC. They are amongst the oldest representations of people and animals in the world.

María

9km/5.5mi northwest.

Nestled in the Sierra de María hills, this whitewashed village is worth a visit for its 16C Mudéjar-style parish church and its 18C Edificio de la Tercia. Note too the unusual public wash house.

A 16C chapel, the Ermita de la Virgen de la Cabeza, lies 3km/1.8mi outside María.

Parque Natural de la Sierra de María★

Centro de Visitantes Umbría de María, 2km/1.2mi from María along the A 317.

🕐*Open Fri–Sun 9am–1pm and 3–5pm.* ☎950 72 50 05.

This reserve extends over 22 500ha / 55 600 acres. The landscape here is steep – several sections are above 2 000m/6 560ft – and varied, with cereal crops, fields of thyme, forests of oak and pine, and even Spanish broom in the higher mountain areas. A number of recreational areas and shelters are dotted throughout the park.

The Indalo

The origins of this figure, the symbol of Almería, can be found in the Cueva de los Letreros, for it was here, in the 19C, that wall paintings of human figures and animals dating from about 4 000 BC were discovered.

INDEX

INDEX

WHERE TO STAY

INDEX

WHERE TO EAT

INDEX

MAPS AND PLANS

LIST OF MAPS

COMPANION PUBLICATIONS

MICHELIN MAP 578 ANDALUCÍA, COVERING THE WHOLE REGION

- a 1:400 000 scale map detailing sights and monuments described within this guide, street plans of Sevilla, Málaga and Granada, and a full index of place names

MICHELIN ESPAÑA/ PORTUGAL ROAD ATLAS

- similar in scale to Michelin map 578, but covering the whole Iberian Peninsula

MICHELIN MAP 734 ESPAÑA/ PORTUGAL

- a 1:1 000 000 scale map of the Iberian Peninsula

MICHELIN EUROPE ATLAS

- a 1:1 000 000 scale atlas of Western Europe in a single volume
- all major roads and 70 town/ city maps
- driving regulations in force in each country

LEGEND

	Sight	Seaside resort	Winter sports resort	Spa
Highly recommended ★★★	☆☆☆	❄❄❄	♉♉♉
Recommended ★★	☆☆	❄❄	♉♉
Interesting ★	☆	❄	♉

Additional symbols

🛈	Tourist information
═══ ═══	Motorway or other primary route
❶ ❶	Junction: complete, limited
▭▭▭ ▭▭▭	Pedestrian street
⌶═══⌶	Unsuitable for traffic, street subject to restrictions
▭▭▭ - - - -	Steps – Footpath
🚆 🚉	Train station – Auto-train station
🚌 S.N.C.F.	Coach (bus) station
╼╾	Tram
⊛	Metro, underground
P R	Park-and-Ride
♿	Access for the disabled
✉	Post office
☎	Telephone
✉	Covered market
⋄⤫⋄	Barracks
△	Drawbridge
⋃	Quarry
✗	Mine
B F	Car ferry (river or lake)
⛴	Ferry service: cars and passengers
⛵	Foot passengers only
③	Access route number common to Michelin maps and town plans
Bert (R.)...	Main shopping street
AZ B	Map co-ordinates

Sports and recreation

🏇	Racecourse
⛸	Skating rink
♨ ♨	Outdoor, indoor swimming pool
🎥	Multiplex Cinema
⛵	Marina, sailing centre
⛺	Trail refuge hut
▭■▭■▭	Cable cars, gondolas
▭+++++▭	Funicular, rack railway
🚂	Tourist train
◈	Recreation area, park
⛹	Theme, amusement park
♈	Wildlife park, zoo
❀	Gardens, park, arboretum
◎	Bird sanctuary, aviary
🚶	Walking tour, footpath
☻	Of special interest to children

Selected monuments and sights

Tour - Departure point

Catholic church

Protestant church, other temple

Synagogue - Mosque

Building

Statue, small building

Calvary, wayside cross

Fountain

Rampart - Tower - Gate

Château, castle, historic house

Ruins

Dam

Factory, power plant

Fort

Cave

Troglodyte dwelling

Prehistoric site

Viewing table

Viewpoint

Other place of interest

Abbreviations

D	Provincial Council (Diputación)
G	Central government representation (Delegación del Gobierno)
H	Town hall (Ayuntamiento)
J	Law courts/Courthouse (Palacio de Justicia)
M	Museum (Museo)
POL.	Police station (Policía)
T	Theatre (Teatro)
U	University (Universidad)

Special symbols

Civil Guard (Guardia Civil)

Parador (hotel run by the State)

Bullring

Olive grove

Orange grove

Michelin Apa Publications Ltd

A joint venture between Michelin and Langenscheidt

Suite 6, Tulip House, 70 Borough High Street, London SE1 1XF, United Kingdom

No part of this publication may be reproduced in any form
without the prior permission of the publisher.

© 2009 Michelin Apa Publications Ltd
ISBN 978-1-906261-39-9
Printed: September 2008
Printed and bound: Himmer, Germany

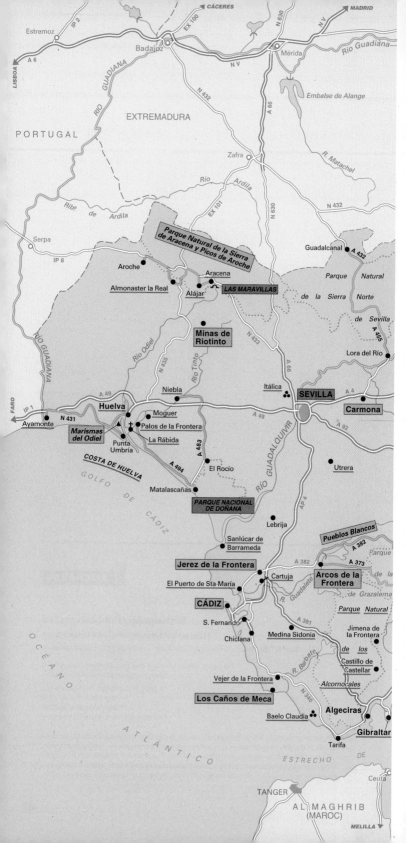